R. Gupta's®

POPULAR MASTER GUIDE

DSSSB–TEACHERS

PGT

HISTORY

Recruitment Exam

by

RPH Editorial Board

RAMESH PUBLISHING HOUSE, NEW DELHI

Published by

O.P. Gupta *for* Ramesh Publishing House

Admin. Office

12-H, New Daryaganj Road, Opp. Officers' Mess,
New Delhi-110002 ✆ 23275224, 23245124

E-mail: info@rameshpublishinghouse.com

For Online Shopping: www.rameshpublishinghouse.com

Showroom

- Balaji Market, Nai Sarak, Delhi-110006 ✆ 23282525 📱 9354373464
- 4457, Nai Sarak, Delhi-110006

Book Code: R-1307

ISBN: 978-93-5012-006-4

Price: ₹ 330

Printed at: Deepak Offset, Delhi

Contents

Scheme of Examination

DSSSB will conduct **One Tier Exam** for PGT posts having two section:

Section-I

S.No.	Subject	Questions	Marks
1.	Mental Ability and Reasoning Ability	20	20
2.	General Awareness	20	20
3.	English Language & Comprehension	20	20
4.	Hindi Language & Comprehension	20	20
5.	Numerical Aptitude & Data Interpretation	20	20
	Total	**100**	**100**

Section-II

S.No.	Subject	Questions	Marks
1.	MCQs pertaining to Post-Graduation qualification and teaching methodology required for the post.	**200**	**200**

Previous Years' Paper

Delhi Subordinate Services Selection Board (DSSSB)

PGT–HISTORY, Recruitment Exam, 2025

(Exam held on 01-08-2025)

Subject Knowledge – History & Teaching Methodology

1. In the Jambudvipaprajnath, a twelfth-century text derived from an earlier Prakrit source, which of the following social groups is notably listed among the 18 recognised guilds?

1. Kiratas
2. Shabaras (Sabaras)
3. Nishadas
4. Bhillas (Bhils)

2. Which feminist scholar developed the theory of "public/private dichotomy" in gender relations?

1. Carole Pateman
2. Shulamith Firestone
3. Sylvia Walby
4. Judith Butler

3. Who among the following suggested that the Harappan civilisation flourished between c. 3250 and 2750 BCE?

1. Daya Ram Sahni
2. John Marshall
3. Mortimer Wheeler
4. Ernest Mackay

4. During the Russian Revolution the 'Bloody Sunday' incident occurred in:

1. 1913 2. 1912
3. 1905 4. 1901

5. Who authored 'The Civilization of the Renaissance in Italy'?

1. Giovanni Boccaccio
2. Giotto di Bondone
3. Jakob Burckhardt
4. Francis Bacon

6. Which of the following auxiliary sciences of history studies the physical remains of human civilisation?

1. Anthropology
2. Sociology
3. Astronomy
4. Archaeology

7. Which of the following historians is most associated with the phrase 'wie es eigentlich gewesen' (to show how it actually happened)?

1. Keith Jenkins
2. Leopold von Ranke
3. EH Carr
4. RG Collingwood

8. Which of the following is the oldest inscription of India?

1. Samudragupta's Prayag Prashasti
2. Harshavardhana's copper plates
3. Ashoka's Rock Edicts
4. Ramagupta's Vidisha pillar

9. Which of the following statements most accurately encapsulates the core political doctrine underlying nationalism?
   1. Nationalism asserts that the interests of the global community should take precedence over national priorities.
   2. Nationalism seeks to dissolve national identities in favour of transnational alliances for economic cooperation.
   3. Nationalism promotes multicultural integration within existing political institutions without emphasising sovereignty.
   4. Nationalism is founded on the belief that a distinct nation should pursue maximum self-governance and prioritise its values above others.

10. Which culture is associated with a distinctive ceramic assemblage discovered at the beginning of the fourth millennium BCE?
    1. Hakra ware culture
    2. Mehrgarh culture
    3. Amri-Nal culture
    4. Kot Diji culture

11. Which of the following works, authored by Bayazid Bayat, provides a narrative of events spanning from the reign of Humayun to that of Akbar between 1542–43 and 1590–91?
    1. Ain-i-Akbari
    2. Tabaqat-i-Akbari
    3. Tadhkira-i Humayun o Akbar
    4. Akbarnama

12. Who invented the cotton gin in 1793, making American cotton production more cost-effective?
    1. James Hargreaves
    2. Samuel Slater
    3. Eli Whitney
    4. Richard Arkwright

13. Who among the following is known as the 'Father of Humanism'?
    1. Francesco Petrarch
    2. Dante Alighieri
    3. Giotto
    4. Pico della Mirandola

14. Who among the following thinkers is NOT associated with the Social Contract Theory of the origin of the state?
    1. Aristotle
    2. Rousseau
    3. Thomas Hobbes
    4. John Locke

15. Approximately how many wells are estimated to have existed in the city of Mohenjodaro, as noted by Jansen (1989)?
    1. 100 wells
    2. 500 wells
    3. 700 wells
    4. 300 wells

16. Which ruler is known for patronising the observatory at Jaipur?
    1. Tipu Sultan
    2. Sawai Jai Singh II
    3. Aurangzeb
    4. Akbar

17. Which of the following best defines the term 'Decolonise'?
    1. To administer governance over newly acquired colonies
    2. To release from being a colony and grant independence
    3. To strengthen the economic dependence of a colony on its coloniser
    4. To establish new colonial territories in foreign regions

18. What was the standard proportion of baked bricks used in the construction of Mohenjo-daro?
    1. 4 : 2 : 1
    2. 3 : 2 : 1
    3. 5 : 3 : 2
    4. 2 : 2 : 1

19. Which metal was most commonly used by the Harappans for crafting artefacts, including vessels, tools and ornaments?
    1. Iron
    2. Bronze
    3. Lead
    4. Copper

20. In which ancient text does every verse end with the refrain "Charaiveti Charaiveti"?
    1. Brihadaranyaka Upanishad
    2. Bhagavad Gita
    3. Aitareya Brahmana
    4. Yajurveda

21. According to Buddhist tradition, after how many days of continuous meditation did the Buddha attain enlightenment under the Bodhi tree at Uruvela?

1. 49 days 2. 7 days
3. 21 days 4. 35 days

22. Who among the following has been described as an exterminator of all Kshatriyas in Puranic tradition?

1. Mahapadma Nanda
2. Dhana Nanda
3. Kharavela
4. Mahanandin

23. Which of the following trade routes contributed to the economic expansion of Magadha during the early historic period, apart from Uttarapatha and Dakshinapatha?

1. Chandrapatha 2. Rajapatha
3. Kambojapatha 4. Pragjyotishapatha

24. Which ruler of Magadha strategically reinforced his kingdom's power through multiple matrimonial alliances, including marriages with princesses from Kosala, Videha, and Madra?

1. Ajatashatru
2. Bimbisara
3. Udayin
4. Nandivardhana

25. Who among the following were the special custom officers during the period of Mahajanpadas, as mentioned in Buddhist sources?

1. Kammikas 2. Pettanikas
3. Gahapatis 4. Kammakaras

26. Which of the following correctly identifies the political structure of the region that lay to the north of the river Champa, west of Anga, south of the Chotanagpur plateau, and east of the rivers Son and Ganga during the early historic period?

1. Republic of Malla
2. Monarchy of Magadha
3. Republic of Vajji
4. Monarchy of Kosala

27. At which of the following Harappan sites did houses discharge wastewater into jars placed outside, with no street-side drainage system, likely due to the region's arid climate?

1. Kalibangan 2. Mehrgarh
3. Mohenjodaro 4. Harappa

28. Which of the following terms best describes the Harappan Civilisation?

1. Mesolithic 2. Neolithic
3. Paleolithic 4. Chalcolithic

29. Which of the following features is depicted by the post-Harappan cultures like 'Cemetery H' and 'Ochre Coloured Pottery'?

1. Terracotta figurines
2. Complete cultural discontinuity
3. Selective continuity in pottery and burial practices
4. Influence of Mesopotamian styles

30. Which of the following was a republic in ancient India?

1. Kosala 2. Avanti
3. Magadha 4. Vajji

31. Which of the following sites is identified from Ashokan edicts as the southern provincial capital of the Mauryan Empire?

1. Taxila 2. Suvarnagiri
3. Ujjain 4. Tosali

32. During which approximate period did the Mature Harappan Phase, marked by urban planning, standardised material culture, and long-distance trade, flourish?

1. 1900 BC to 1400 BC
2. 2600 BC to 1900 BC
3. 3500 BC to 2600 BC
4. 1400 BC to 600 BC

33. Which Harappan artifact exemplifies the early use of the 'lost wax' (cire perdue) technique in metallurgy, a method that continued in Indian metal casting traditions?

1. The bust from Dholavira
2. The mother goddess from Harappa
3. The Priest-King statue from Mohenjo Daro
4. The 'Dancing Girl' figurine from Mohenjo Daro

34. Which ruler of Magadha, referred to in Greek sources as Agrammes or Xandrames, was contemporaneous with Alexander's invasion of north-western India?

1. Kaivarta
2. Mahapadma Nanda
3. Dhana Nanda
4. Dashasiddhaka

35. In which year did Alexander the Great defeat King Porus?

1. 312 BCE
2. 326 BCE
3. 321 BCE
4. 330 BCE

36. Which of the following Harappan sites, being exceptional, had middle town along with citadel and lower town?

1. Chanhudaro
2. Kalibangan
3. Dholavira
4. Allahdino

37. Which of the following Mahajanpadas was NOT situated in Central and Deccan regions?

1. Chedi
2. Panchala
3. Assaka
4. Avanti

38. At the time of Alexander's invasion of India Ambhi was the ruler of:

1. Kashi
2. Anga
3. Vaishali
4. Taxila

39. Which of the following urban centres was located within the territorial extent of Magadha during its early historic phase, apart from Rajagriha and Pataligrama?

1. Kannauj
2. Ujjayini
3. Gaya
4. Vaishali

40. In the context of early Buddhist texts, what was the role of a kammika?

1. Customs official responsible for collecting tolls and taxes
2. Head of a monastic council
3. Military commander of a janapada
4. Royal priest responsible for sacrificial rituals

41. Which Ashokan inscription first revealed that the practice of inscribing edicts on Dhamma began twelve years after Ashoka's coronation?

1. Minor Rock Edict at Maski
2. Rock Edict 13
3. Pillar Edict 6
4. Bhabru Edict

42. Which of the following sources attests to the historicity of king Ramagupta?

1. Allahabad Prashasti
2. Devichandraguptam
3. Nitisara
4. Mandsor Inscription

43. Chandragupta Maurya's empire extended in the northwestern region from:

1. Sindh to Punjab
2. Afghanistan to Balochistan
3. Iran to Kazakhstan
4. Uzbekistan to Kyrgyzstan

44. Which of the following correctly represents the categories of spies deployed under the Mauryan espionage system, whose eventual failure was seen as one of the factors leading to administrative decline during the later Mauryan period?

1. Amatyas, Rajukas and Pradesikas
2. Kumaramatyas, Sthanikas and Gopas
3. Gudhapurushas, Vyayamikas and Udasthitas
4. Dhamma Mahamatras, Yuktas and Samahartas

45. Who killed the last Mauryan king Brihadratha, thus bringing the Maurya dynasty to an end?

1. Pushyamitra Shunga
2. Kharavela
3. Vasudeva Kanva
4. Agnimitra

46. As a result of the treaty with Seleucus Nicator, which of the following regions did Chandragupta Maurya acquire?

1. Ujjain, Taxila, Pataliputra, Balkh
2. Sindh, Gujarat, Bengal, Kabul
3. Magadha, Kosala, Anga, Herat
4. Kabul, Kandahar, Herat, Balkh

47. Which of the following dynasties replaced the Mauryan empire after killing the last ruler Brihadratha?

1. Satvahanas 2. Shungas
3. Kanvas 4. Pahlavas

48. Who ascended the throne of the Gupta Empire after the death of Samudragupta in 375 CE?

1. Kumaragupta 2. Ramagupta
3. Chandragupta I 4. Chandragupta II

49. Which group of deities was Samudragupta compared with in the Allahabad Prasasti inscription, highlighting his unmatched power and sovereignty?

1. Agni, Vayu, Soma and Surya
2. Yama, Chandra, Mitra and Pushan
3. Brahma, Vishnu, Shiva and Saraswati
4. Dhanada, Varuna, Indra and Antaka

50. After which ruler did the decline of the powerful and vast Gupta Empire begin?

1. Skandagupta 2. Samudragupta
3. Chandragupta II 4. Shri Gupta

51. Which of the following statements about Ashoka is INCORRECT?

1. Rajatarangini – Initially, Ashoka's favoured deity was Brahma.
2. Dipavamsa and Mahavamsa – Ashoka was a religious scholar who later adopted the teachings of Buddhism.
3. Sarnath Minor Pillar Edict – Ashoka referred to himself as the 'protector of the Sangha'.
4. Bhabru Edict – Ashoka was a devotee of the Buddha, Dhamma, and the Sangha.

52. Which ancient Indian drama, attributed to a classical Sanskrit playwright, narrates the account of Chandragupta II killing his elder brother Ramagupta to protect royal honour and the kingdom?

1. Abhijnanasakuntalam by Kalidasa
2. Mudrarakshasa by Vishakhadatta
3. Mricchakatika by Shudraka
4. Devi Chandraguptam by Vishakhadatta

53. Bhitari Pillar inscription provides crucial information about which of the following Gupta kings?

1. Ramagupta 2. Skandagupta
3. Kumaragupta 4. Chandragupta II

54. Which of the following historical sources mentions Ramagupta as a Gupta ruler?

1. Arthashastra
2. Devi-Chandragupta
3. Bhavabhuti
4. Allahabad Pillar Inscription

55. Which of the following titles mentioned in Greek sources has been associated with Chandragupta Maurya?

1. Amitrokhates 2. Alitrokhates
3. Antiochus 4. Sandracottus

56. Whom did Pushyamitra Shunga assassinate to bring an end to the Maurya Empire?

1. Brihadratha 2. Shatadhanvan
3. Dasharatha 4. Kunala

57. The Mehrauli Iron Pillar, which bears a Sanskrit inscription referring to King Chandra, is located in which part of the country?

1. Delhi 2. Rajasthan
3. Uttar Pradesh 4. Madhya Pradesh

58. Who among the following was NOT a ruler of the Gupta dynasty?

1. Maharaja Gupta 2. Samudravarman
3. Ghatotkacha 4. Chandragupta I

59. Which inscription provides the only definite epigraphic reference to Chandragupta Maurya, attributing the commencement of the Sudarshana lake project to his reign?

1. Hathigumpha Inscription of Kharavela
2. Nasik Inscription of Satavahana and early Kshatrapa rulers
3. Besnagar Inscription of Heliodorus
4. Junagarh Inscription of Rudradaman I

60. From which inscription do we learn that, on the orders of Mauryan Emperor Chandragupta Maurya, his governor Pushyagupta constructed the Sudarsana Lake?

1. Junagadh Inscription
2. Bhitari Pillar Inscription
3. Prayag Prashasti
4. Nasik Inscription

61. Which of the following emperors promoted Murshid Quli to governor of Bengal?

1. Bahadur Shah I 2. Aurangzeb
3. Farukkhsiyar 4. Muhammad Shah

62. Who among the following authored the book 'The Crisis of Empire in Mughal North India'?

1. CA Bayly
2. Susan Bayly
3. Muzaffar Alam
4. Sanjay Subrahmanyam

63. In the context of the Mughal administration, which source, by its author, refers to crop-sharing (batai) as the most equitable method of revenue assessment, highlighting shared risk between the state and the peasantry?

1. Nigarnama-i-Munshi by Malikzada
2. Muntakhab-ul Lubab by Khafi Khan
3. Chahar Gulshan by Rai Chaturman
4. Ain-i-Akbari by Abul Fazl

64. Which coins, refined under Akbar's reign, facilitated long-distance trade and enhanced revenue collection through monetised taxation?

1. Dinar and Dirham
2. Tanka and Jital
3. Rupiya and Dam
4. Mohur and Ashrafi

65. Which of the following statements about the Gupta ruler Chandragupta I is INCORRECT?

1. According to inscriptions, the Gupta dynasty was founded by Shri Gupta.
2. Samudragupta was the son of Chandragupta I and Kumaradevi.
3. Chandragupta I started the Gupta Era in memory of his marriage to Kumaradevi.
4. Chandragupta I's wife, Kumaradevi, was a princess of the Licchavi dynasty.

66. Which Mughal ruler introduced month-scale in the *Mansabdari* System to make a difference between *Jama* (estimated income) and *Hasil* (actual income)?

1. Shah Jahan 2. Humayun
3. Jahangir 4. Akbar

67. The Battle of Jajau was fought between:

1. Bahadur Shah and Jahandar Shah
2. Bahadur Shah I and Muhammad Azam Shah
3. Muhammad Azam Shah and Farukkhsiyar
4. Muhammad Shah and Bahadur Shah I

68. According to the Mehrauli Iron Pillar inscription, which ruler was defeated by King Chandra, who is widely identified with Chandragupta II?

1. Rudrasena of the Vakataka dynasty
2. Vahlikas, identified with the Bactrian rulers
3. Mihirakula of the Huna lineage
4. Yashodharman of Malwa

69. Who among the following has propounded the 'Great Firm' theory in relation with the decline of Mughal empire?

1. CA Bayly 2. Muzaffar Alam
3. M Athar Ali 4. Karen Leonard

70. Which of the following statements about the Jizya tax is INCORRECT?
1. It was a type of religious tax levied on non-muslims.
2. Akbar abolished it in 1564 CE.
3. Aurangzeb reimposed it in 1679 CE.
4. In 1720 CE, Jahandar Shah abolished it permanently.

71. Bilsad inscription belongs to which of the following rulers?
1. Chandragupta I 2. Kumaragupta I
3. Narasimhagupta 4. Purugupta

72. Which Mughal emperor earned the nickname 'Rangila', meaning 'the colourful'?
1. Bahadur Shah I 2. Farrukhsiyar
3. Shah Alam II 4. Muhammad Shah

73. Which source provides important insights into the administrative disorder and fiscal crisis faced by the later Mughal Empire during the reign of Muhammad Shah?
1. Muntakhab-ul Lubab by Khafi Khan
2. Siyar-ul-Mutakhkhirin by Ghulam Husain Tabatabai
3. Tarikh-i-Firuz Shahi by Ziauddin Barani
4. Maasir-i-Alamgiri by Saqi Mustaid Khan

74. Which administrative system is considered one of the factors that contributed to the decline of the Gupta Empire, as it allowed minor rulers to consolidate power and exercise increasing autonomy from the central authority?
1. Rajuka System
2. Mandala System
3. Samanta System
4. Gana-Sangha System

75. Which of the following departments of Mughal administration was under the jurisdiction of Mir Bakhshi?
1. Charity 2. Justice
3. Military 4. Revenue

76. Which historian, in an influential study, attributed the decline of the Mughal Empire to the argument that Indian states before the colonial period were oligarchic in nature, organised around patron-client relationships, lacking both social commitment and legitimacy?
1. Satish Chandra 2. William Irvine
3. Jadunath Sarkar 4. MN Pearson

77. Which of the following Jagirs was non-transferable?
1. Tankha Jagir 2. Qila Jagir
3. Mashrut Jagir 4. Watan Jagir

78. Which Mughal emperor issued the famous Farman to the British East India Company in 1717 granting them trade privileges in Bengal?
1. Shah Alam II
2. Farrukhsiyar
3. Muhammad Shah
4. Bahadur Shah I

79. In the context of the Mughal administration, which statement best reflects Abul Fazl's justification for the imposition of taxes as mentioned in the Ain-i-Akbari?
1. Taxes were seen as arbitrary exactions imposed by the emperor without justification.
2. Taxes were considered temporary measures during times of famine or natural calamities.
3. Taxes were levied solely to fund imperial military campaigns and expansionist wars.
4. Taxes were justified as the remuneration of sovereignty, paid in return for protection and justice.

80. Which of the following was the major economic cause of the decline of the Mughal Empire?
1. Growth in trade
2. Gold and silver coins
3. Long and expensive wars
4. Lack of agricultural taxes

81. Which of the following was a significant factor contributing to the decline and eventual dissolution of the Maratha Confederacy in the early 19th century?

1. The British use of subsidiary alliances, diplomatic pressure, and military campaigns
2. The Marathas' refusal to expand beyond the Deccan region
3. The military alliance between the Marathas and Tipu Sultan during the Mysore Wars
4. The unification of all Maratha chiefs under the absolute leadership of the Chhatrapati at Satara

82. Which historian argued that the emergence of Maratha Swarajya was not a revolt against the Mughal Empire but a direct consequence of Mughal expansion, and that the Marathas largely retained the status of zamindars?

1. Gordon Stewart 2. Audrey Truschke
3. Jadunath Sarkar 4. Andre Wink

83. Which of the following correctly represents the sequence of key administrative offices under the Bahmani Sultanate, reflecting the model adopted from the Delhi Sultanate?

1. Sultan → Ariz-i-Mamalik → Wazir → Muhtasib → Qazi
2. Sultan → Vakil → Wazir → Bakhshi → Qazi
3. Sultan → Naib → Diwan → Sadr → Qazi
4. Sultan → Diwan-i-Riyasat → Wazir → Ariz → Qazi

84. Which later Mughal ruler's inability to effectively control the rise of regional powers, such as the Marathas, Sikhs and Jats, is often cited by historians as a key reason for administrative fragmentation?

1. Ahmad Shah (1748-1754)
2. Bahadur Shah I (1707–1712)
3. Muhammad Shah (1719–1748)
4. Farrukhsiyar (1713–1719)

85. Who among the following was blinded by Humayun in 1553 AD?

1. Askari 2. Islam Shah Suri
3. Hindal 4. Kamran

86. The last Mughal emperor, Bahadar Shah Zafar, was exiled by the British to:

1. Rangoon
2. Nepal
3. Tibet
4. Andaman and Nicobar

87. The Battle of Talikota, fought between the Vijayanagara Empire and the Deccan Sultanates, took place in which year?

1. 1526 2. 1556
3. 1572 4. 1565

88. Which of the following systems was the assignment of revenue of a particular territory to the nobles for their services under the Mughals?

1. Jagirdari system
2. Forty system
3. Amara-Nayaka system
4. Ashtasprashna system

89. Which Mughal ruler was the first to become a pensioner of the East India Company?

1. Akbar Shah II 2. Farrukhsiyar
3. Shah Alam II 4. Bahadur Shah I

90. After the conquest of which region did Babur assume the title of 'Padishah' in 1507?

1. Ferghana 2. Kabul
3. Herat 4. Samarkand

91. Consider the following sentences as the cause of the Maratha rise and select the correct option.

A. Natural topography of the Maharashtra region.
B. French support to the Marathas.
C. Strong personality of Shivaji.
D. Effect of Hindutva on the Marathas.

1. Only statements B, C and D are correct.
2. Only statements A, B and C are correct.
3. Only statements A, B and D are correct.
4. Only statements A, C and D are correct.

92. Who among the following has propounded the theory of 'Agrarian Crisis' in relation with the decline of Mughal empire?

1. Iqtidar Alam Khan
2. Irfan Habib
3. Shireen Moosvi
4. CA Bayly

93. Which of the following is a correct combination of the Akbar's military campaign?

1. Gujarat conquest – 1570-1571 AD
2. Merta conquest – 1559 AD
3. Gondwana conquest – 1560 AD
4. Ranthambore conquest – 1568 AD

94. Under Akbar's reign, in which year was the fort of Ahmadnagar captured, leading to the arrest of Bahadur Nizam Shah and the annexation of the Ahmadnagar kingdom?

1. 1600 2. 1596
3. 1601 4. 1597

95. Which of the following statements is correct about the Marathas?

1. Shivaji's first loot of Surat was not in 1660.
2. Shivaji was crowned as Chhatrapati at Raigad in 1672.
3. Shivaji established the concept of Hindavi Swaraj to free the land from Mughal and Adil Shahi control.
4. The Tulughma military tactic is used by Shivaji.

96. Under whose leadership did the Marathas suffer a major defeat in the Third Battle of Panipat?

1. Sadashivrao Bhau 2. Madhavrao I
3. Baji Rao II 4. Mahadji Scindia

97. Who among the following has authored 'Parties and Politics at the Mughal Court (1707-1740)'?

1. Satish Chandra 2. William Dalrymple
3. Muzaffar Alam 4. SP Verma

98. The policy 'sulh-i-kul', meaning 'peace with all', was a form of an expansionist policy. It was adopted by which Mughal ruler?

1. Akbar 2. Babur
3. Ibrahim Lodhi 4. Humayun

99. Which historian attributed the decline of the Mughal Empire to the influential role of banking houses known as 'great firms' in their relationship with the imperial state?

1. Muzaffar Alam 2. Karen Leonard
3. Satish Chandra 4. Irfan Habib

100. Within the confederacy of Marathas, who among the following were ruling Indore and Malwa?

1. Gaekwads 2 Bhonsles
3. Sindhias 4. Holkars

101. For effective governance, how many administrative divisions known as sarkars did Sher Shah Suri establish across his empire?

1. 54 2. 47
3. 32 4. 61

102. Which of the following wars in India was a direct result of the Seven Years War (1756–1763) in Europe?

1. First Anglo-Dutch War
2. First Carnatic war
3. Second Carnatic war
4. Third Carnatic war

103. Which of the following was the main reason for the introduction of the Dagh and Chehra systems in the Mughal Mansabdari administration?

1. To regularise land revenue collection
2. To prevent duplicacy in troops and horses maintained
3. To promote trade and commerce through military patrols
4. To maintain hereditary control over jagirs

104. Which Persian chronicle, composed in the late 16th century, provides an estimate of approximately 120 large cities and 3,200 qasbas in India during Akbar's reign?

1. Akbarnama 2. Ain-i-Akbari
3. Tarikh-i-Firishta 4. Tabqat-i Akbari

105. Which of the following historians, while describing the Mughal revenue system, noted that "Collection should begin for rabi from Holi and for kharif from Dashehra. The officials should not delay it for another crop"?

1. Khafi Khan 2. Yusuf Mirak
3. Abbas Khan 4. Abul Fazl

106. Who among the following was the chief superintendent of ports under Mughals?

1. Karori 2. Mushrif
3. Tahwildar 4. Mutasaddi

107. Who divided his whole empire into 47 divisions called 'Sarkars' which were again subdivided into smaller administrative units called 'Parganas'?

1. Shah Jahan 2. Sher Shah
3. Humayun 4. Aurangzeb

108. When was Awadh annexed by the British East India Company during the reign of Wajid Ali Shah?

1. March 1854 2. August 1857
3. February 1856 4. June 1855

109. Which administrative system introduced during Babur's reign involved officers being assigned a fixed sum of revenue from their jurisdiction, rather than a specified territory, with the surplus deposited in the imperial treasury?

1. Mansabdari system 2. Wajah system
3. Iqta system 4. Saranjam system

110. In the Mansabdari System, eventually the rank of a mansabdar came to be denoted by two numbers, namely Zat and Sawar. These two numbers are referred to which of the following?

1. Personal rank (status and salary) and size of contingents maintained by the mansabdar
2. Revenue collected and size of contingents maintained by the mansabdar
3. Land seized and size of contingents maintained by the mansabdar
4. Land collected and size of contingents maintained by the mansabdar

111. Who appointed Shiqdars as executive officers for the administration of criminal justice?

1. Akbar 2. Alauddin Khalji
3. Sher Shah Suri 4. Aurangzeb

112. In which year was Mysore Anche, the postal system of the Princely Mysore State, established by Maharaja Chikka Devaraya Wodeyar?

1. 1665 2. 1672
3. 1652 4. 1658

113. Carolina coins issued by the East India Company were basically made of:

1. Copper 2. Lead
3. Silver 4. Gold

114. Which of the following statements is INCORRECT about the Maratha Village Administration?

1. Village watchmen were known as Mahar.
2. The head of grain storage in the village was known as Phadnis.
3. Each village had a headman known as the Patel.
4. The village clerk and record-keeper is known as the Kulkarni.

115. What was Sarkar in Sher Shah's administration?

1. A committee for religious decisions
2. A Judicial department
3. A type of land revenue
4. An administrative division

116. What was Vijayanagara Empire's provincial administration system where land was assigned to officials in lieu of pay known as:

1. Ryotwari system
2. Jagirdari system
3. Nayankar system
4. Mansabdari system

117. Sher Shah Suri abolished all the previous mixed metal coins and introduced new coins. The Dam coins were made up of which of the following metals?

1. Gold
2. Silver
3. Copper
4. Bronze

118. Which ruler introduced the practices of maintaining descriptive rolls (huliya) of soldiers and branding (dagh) of horses to regulate the quality of cavalry during his reign?

1. Alauddin Khalji
2. Muhammad bin Tughlaq
3. Iltutmish
4. Balban

119. What does the term 'talab khasa' refer to in the context of the mansabdari system?

1. Expected net revenue realisation
2. Personal salary of a mansabdar
3. Number of soldiers under a mansabdar's command
4. Amount received for the maintenance of horsemen

120. Which official communication articulated the British policy of maintaining ethnic divisions within the Indian army by recommending that adjacent regiments remain "so alien that it would be ready to fire into it", following the 1857 rebellion?

1. The Charles Wood Despatch, 1861
2. The Peel Commission Report, 1859
3. The Eden Commission Recommendations, 1879
4. The Kitchener Reforms Memorandum, 1904

121. Who among the following coined the term, 'Pakistan', in 1933?

1. Chaudhry Rehmat Ali
2. Muhammad Iqbal
3. Agha Khan
4. MA Jinnah

122. In which year was the resolution on 'Swaraj' first passed in the Calcutta session of the Indian National Congress?

1. 1907
2. 1911
3. 1909
4. 1906

123. Guru Nanak's birth year, as generally accepted by most Sikh traditions, is:

1. 1441
2. 1475
3. 1469
4. 1459

124. What is the significance of the Uttaramerur inscriptions dated 919 CE and 921 CE during the reign of Chola king Parantaka I?

1. They provide evidence of India's early trade with Southeast Asia
2. They describe the military conquests of Parantaka I in Sri Lanka
3. They are key records of Chola village assemblies and early democratic practices
4. They contain hymns written by Tamil Bhakti poets

125. Which of the following sentences is correct about Dr. B.R. Ambedkar?

1. The temple entry movement was launched by him in 1930 at the Kalaram temple.
2. In 1925, he led the Mahad March at the Chowdar Tank at Colaba, near Bombay.
3. In 1931, Poona Pact was signed between BR Ambedkar and Mahatma Gandhi
4. In 1923, he set up the 'Bahishkrit Hitkarini Sabha'.

126. Which of the following movements marked the first organised effort led by Dr. BR Ambedkar to secure civic rights for the Depressed Classes in India?

1. Mahad Satyagraha
2. Dalit Federation Movement
3. Temple Entry Movement
4. Poona Pact Movement

127. Lord Macaulay's Minute of 1835 brought significant change to the Indian Education system. Which of the following points was NOT a part of Macaulay's Minute report?

1. The medium of Education will be English.
2. Western Science and literature were to be promoted.
3. The focus will be on Modern Education.
4. The medium of Education will be vernacular languages.

128. When did the Constituent Assembly finalise the Indian Constitution?

1. 16 January 1950
2. 16 November 1949
3. 16 January 1951
4. 26 November 1949

129. At which session of the Indian National Congress did the ideological rift between the Moderates and Extremists become most pronounced, leading to a formal split over the issue of constitutional methods versus self-reliance in achieving self-government?

1. Surat Session, 1907
2. Allahabad Session, 1899
3. Calcutta Session, 1906
4. Lucknow Session, 1916

130. In the context of tribal anti-colonial movements in eastern India, which of the following terms was commonly used to refer to exploitative outsiders such as zamindars and moneylenders?

1. Raiyats 2. Dikus
3. Mahajans 4. Talukdars

131. Which of the following statements about Indo-Islamic elements in temple and court architecture is INCORRECT?

1. Islamic-style tombs were a regular feature of Hindu temple complexes.
2. Royal platforms like Mahanavami Dibba had influences from both Hindu and Muslim designs.
3. The arch in Indo-Islamic buildings was often used decoratively.
4. The Lotus Mahal in Hampi shows a mix of arches and pyramid-shaped roofs.

132. Who among the following did Guru Nanak appoint as his successor?

1. Sri Chand 2. Bhai Mardana
3. Bhai Lehna 4. Baba Buddha

133. Which woman social reformer in colonial India was associated with the founding of the Women's Indian Association (WIA)?

1. Pandita Ramabai 2. Kamini Roy
3. Annie Besant 4. Sarojini Naidu

134. Which category of peasants owned their land and paid revenue directly to the state under the Mughals?

1. Pahi 2. Khudkasht
3. Raiyat 4. Muzari

135. Which of the following branches of *Vaishnavism* was founded by Madhvacharya in the 13th century?

1. Sri Vaishnavism
2. Gaudiya Vaishnavism
3. Warkari Vaishnavism
4. Sadh Vaishnavism

136. The Temples of Khajuraho are an example of which architectural type?

1. Kalinga style 2. Dravidian style
3. Nagara style 4. Vesara style

137. Which author, while serving as a British civil servant, observed in 1864: "The testimony of a single one of our countrymen has more weight with the court than that of any number of Hindus, a circumstance which puts a terrible instrument of power into the hands of an unscrupulous and grasping Englishman", thereby highlighting judicial discrimination that contributed to the rise of national consciousness in India?

1. James Mill 2. William Hunter
3. GO Trevelyan 4. AO Hume

138. Lala Lajpat Rai was assaulted by the Britishers for protesting against _____.

1. Campbell Commission
2. Hartog Commission
3. Simon Commission
4. Sadler Commission

139. During the Mughal Era, peasants were divided into three kinds: Khud-Kasht, Pahi-Kasht and Mujariyan. The term Khud-Kasht refers to:

1. someone working on others land
2. land owner is the cultivator and has the right to inherit or sell the land
3. land owner is not the cultivator and has the right to inherit or sell the land
4. someone holding land in partnership

140. Which of the following sentences is correct about the Indian National Congress?

1. AO Hume played an important role in the starting phase of the Indian National Congress.
2. The first session of the Congress took place under the leadership of Dadabhai Naoroji.
3. The first session of the Indian National Congress was held at Gokuldas Tejpal Sanskrit College, Poona.
4. The Indian National Congress was established in December 1884.

141. Which policy, adopted during the Second Five-Year Plan (1956-1961), reflected India's strategic shift toward import-substitution industrialisation by prioritising heavy industries and public sector expansion?

1. National Development Council Framework of 1952
2. Bombay Plan of 1944
3. Industrial Policy Resolution of 1948
4. Industrial Policy Resolution of 1956

142. Which of the following Articles of Indian Constitution provides for the creation of All India Services in India?

1. Article 370 2. Article 305
3. Article 355 4. Article 312

143. Which country's repeated assertion of dominance over Vietnam across centuries involved military, administrative, and cultural control?

1. United States 2. China
3. Japan 4. France

144. Some scholars like Robert Adams have question Gordon Childe's essential features of beginnings of civilisations. On what basis does he question Childe's analysis?

1. Childe ignored the role of divine kingship in early civilisations.
2. Childe failed to use textual sources from ancient civilisations.
3. Childe failed to understand that there were civilisations without metals and writing.
4. Childe did not recognise the importance of Greek and Roman contributions.

145. Which 15th century treaty is often viewed by historians as an early legal foundation for European imperialism, as it divided newly discovered lands outside Europe between two major powers (Spain and Portugal)?

1. Treaty of Picquigny (1475)
2. Treaty of Tordesillas (1494)
3. Treaty of Granada (1491)
4. Treaty of Alcáçovas (1479)

146. Which of the following concepts of Christianity stresses on the responsibility of human to preserve natural resources?

1. Trinity 2. Imago Die
3. Absolution 4. Stewardship

147. Which European city was a key hub for commercial capitalism in the 16th century?

1. Antwerp 2. Vienna
3. Berlin 4. Toledo

148. The rise of commercial capitalism significantly weakened the traditional structure of:

1. Market 2. Feudalism
3. Democracy 4. Industrial capitalism

149. The Supreme Soviet of National Economy in Soviet Union was called:

1. Duma
2. Glavki
3. Glasnot
4. Vesenkha

150. The book 'Environmentalism' is authored by:

1. Ramchandra Guha
2. DK Chakrabarti
3. Ranajit Guha
4. Daniel B Botkin

151. Who among the following is considered as the 'Mad King' of Roman empire?

1. Tiberius
2. Titus
3. Caligula
4. Claudius

152. Who among the following is recognised as the first economic theorist of capitalism?

1. Thomas Aquinas
2. Adam Smith
3. David Ricardo
4. Jean-Baptiste Colbert

153. Who among the following is NOT associated with the dependency 'Theory of Development'?

1. Hans Singer
2. Andre Gunder Frank
3. Adam Smith
4. Raúl Prebisch

154. During which of the following periods did the second urbanisation in India take place?

1. Later Vedic Age
2. Age of Guptas
3. Mauryan Age
4. Age of Mahajanpadas

155. The Treaty of Tordesillas (1494) divided overseas territories between:

1. Spain and Portugal
2. Britain and France
3. the Dutch and Portuguese
4. Italy and the Holy Roman Empire

156. What was the percentage of the population residing in urban areas in India, according to the 1901 Census?

1. 10.5%
2. 11.4%
3. 13.5%
4. 12.8%

157. What is Rajni Kothari's perspective on how the Congress system functioned in post-independence India?

1. A decentralised Panchayati Raj-based polity
2. A two-party federal coalition system
3. A one-party authoritarianism
4. A one-party dominant system with democratic functioning

158. Which political party initiated the replacement of the Planning Commission with the NITI Aayog as part of its institutional reforms?

1. Bharatiya Janata Party
2. Indian National Congress
3. Aam Aadmi Party
4. Janata Dal (United)

159. Which of the following statements is correct about environmental movements in India?

1. The Narmada Bachao Andolan demanded a large dam construction.
2. The Silent Valley Movement opposed a dam project in Assam.
3. The Appiko movement began in 1976.
4. The Chipko Movement involved women-led protests to save forests.

160. Which of the following polities is generally regarded as one of the earliest examples of a territorial state in ancient India during the 6th century BCE, marking a shift from tribal polities to organised state formation?

1. Kuru Kingdom
2. Matsya Kingdom
3. Magadha Kingdom
4. Avanti Kingdom

161. Which of the following best describes Chang'an's layout under the Sui dynasty (581–618 CE)?

1. Religious core and decentralised
2. Mixed zones and loose layout
3. Market grid and no central administration
4. Planned wards and central palace

162. Which of the following items of Nepal was highly valued in India, as mentioned by Kautliya?

1. Lapis Lazuli 2. Silk
3. Wool 4. Leather

163. Which of the following pre-modern Indian philosophers composed the 'Tattvacintamani' around the early 14th century CE, contributing significantly to the Nyaya school of logic?

1. Madhvacharya
2. Ramanujacharya
3. Shankaracharya
4. Gangesha Upadhyaya

164. Which book, published in 1994, critically examines how colonial authorities systematised Indian knowledge traditions to legitimise their rule, particularly through codification of law and education?

1. Orientalism and the Postcolonial Predicament
2. The Discovery of India
3. Textures of Time: Writing History in South India
4. The Colonial State and Forms of Knowledge: The British in India

165. In the context of the New Culture Movement, what was Hu Shi's principal intellectual argument?

1. Return to Buddhist values
2. Revival of Daoist metaphysics
3. Rejection of all Western influence
4. Literary and linguistic modernisation through vernacular Chinese

166. Which West Asian ruler captured Constantinople in 1453 CE, marking the end of the Byzantine Empire?

1. Saladin 2. Hulagu Khan
3. Mehmed II 4. Timur (Tamerlane)

167. In which year did Australians vote in a referendum to amend the Constitution to count Aboriginal Australians as part of the population?

1. 1962 2. 1967
3. 1972 4. 1976

168. Which of the following Christian principles is related to a responsible and caring relationship with the Earth?

1. Dominion 2. Stewardship
3. Sacrament 4. Divine Providence

169. Which West Asian reformer is credited with issuing the Tanzimat Fermani (Imperial Edict of Gülhane) in 1839, initiating comprehensive administrative modernisation in the Ottoman Empire?

1. Sultan Selim III
2. Mustafa Reşid Pasha
3. Sultan Mahmud II
4. Midhat Pasha

170. Which British official consolidated trade routes in Nepal through the Residency system?

1. Warren Hastings 2. Brian Hodgson
3. Lord Canning 4. Thomas Munro

171. Which ruler of the Mali Empire is historically noted for his pilgrimage to Mecca in 1324 CE, which significantly enhanced the empire's international prestige?

1. Mansa Musa
2. Sundiata Keita
3. Sunni Ali
4. Askia Muhammad I

172. Who among the following advocated radical ideas and asked his pupils to question all authority?

1. Henry Vivian Derozio
2. Swami Vivekanand
3. Dayanand Saraswati
4. Ishwar Chandra Vidyasagar

173. The concept of 'Li' and 'Qi' in Chinese cosmology was systematised by which philosopher?

1. Mozi
2. Zhu Xi
3. Wang Yangming
4. Laozi

174. Who among the following was an influential intellectual behind the shaping of Meiji Restoration in Japan?

1. Sakuma Shozan
2. Chong Ta San
3. Chen Duxiu
4. Mao Zedong

175. In which year did the Portuguese first establish control over the coastal areas of Sri Lanka?

1. 1565
2. 1545
3. 1505
4. 1500

176. Which ancient Chinese city is one of the earliest known walled cities, dating to around 1900 BCE?

1. Erlitou
2. Anyang
3. Liangzhu
4. Banpo

177. In which of the following countries is the cult of Kumari Virgin worship found?

1. Sri Lanka
2. Vietnam
3. Cambodia
4. Nepal

178. Who among the following is known as the father of modern absolutism?

1. Plato
2. Benedict de Spinoza
3. Thomas Hobbes
4. Aristotle

179. How does Emma Tarlo describe the emergence of Welcome locality as a 'site of history-making' in her study of urbanisation in '*Unsettling Memories*'?

1. Its layout was based on Mughal urban planning principles.
2. It was the first planned city built entirely after Partition.
3. Its residents produced narratives that counter official histories of displacement.
4. It hosted multiple museums preserving emergency documents.

180. Which Bronze Age city is considered to have the first known evidence of formal Chinese writing?

1. Anyang
2. Chengziya
3. Erlitou
4. Panlongcheng

181. What is the main purpose of role play in education?

1. To develop acting careers
2. To memorise textbook definitions
3. To entertain during school functions
4. To encourage active participation and empathy

182. As per NEP, 2020, what is the full form of GIF, the term meant especially for girls and transgender students to provide them equitable quality education?

1. Gender Inclusion Fund
2. Gender Increment Fund
3. Girls Inclusion Fund
4. Gender Identification Fund

183. What does 'language across the curriculum' mainly promote?

1. Teaching only language subjects
2. Using local language in exams
3. Developing language skills in all subjects
4. Teaching grammar in every lesson

184. Cognitive development refers to the:

1. Growth of motor skills
2. Social and emotional growth
3. Changes in physical appearance
4. Development of intellectual abilities and thinking processes

185. Why is subject content analysis important in lesson planning?

1. To avoid using teaching aids
2. To memorise textbook content
3. To shorten the syllabus
4. To align objectives with what is taught

186. Enabling democratic participation in classroom means:

1. allowing politicians to enter the classroom
2. empowering privileged students
3. empowering the weak and marginalised students
4. uncontrolled situation in classroom

187. Which factor is most important when selecting learning resources for a diverse classroom?

1. Cost of the resource
2. Length of the content
3. Popularity of the material
4. Cultural relevance and inclusivity

188. A student following deep approach of learning has the following characteristics, EXCEPT:

1. that it searches for the meaning inherent in the task
2. that it integrates aspects or parts of the task into a whole
3. that it sees the different aspects or parts of the task as unrelated to other tasks
4. that it is interested in the academic task and derives enjoyment from carrying it out

189. In teaching-learning, the use of real objects such as tools, utensils, art objects and clothing, that are made and used by people in a given culture or society is known as:

1. Chart 2. Model
3. Realia 4. Diorama

190. Which discipline deals with the study of human behaviour and mind?

1. Psychology 2. Zoology
3. Physiology 4. Linguistics

191. During the development of a child, 'synthesis' is the cumulative process which involves four basic elements namely, _____, _____, _____ and _____.

1. experience; maturation; equilibration; social transmission
2. language development; intellectual development; emotional development; physical development
3. intellectual development; social development; moral development; emotional development
4. experience; motivation; reward; punishment

192. Which of the following is NOT true about the Memory Level of Teaching?

1. It facilites rote memorisation of facts and concepts.
2. John F Herbart is the exponent of this level.
3. Under this system, pupil and teacher are the main members.
4. It emphasises critical thinking and analysis.

193. Which government initiative in India first operationalised support services for children with special needs within mainstream education?

1. Unnat Bharat Abhiyan
2. Operation Blackboard
3. Mid-Day Meal Scheme
4. Integrated Education for Disabled Children (IEDC) Scheme

194. Which of the following is an example of a teaching strategy?

1. Distributing report cards
2. Lecture
3. Project-based learning
4. Writing on the board

195. Which of the following can be considered a focused form of socialisation through which children of different sexes are socialised into their gender roles and taught what it means to be male or female?

1. Media socialisation
2. Peer group socialisation
3. Gender socialisation
4. Moral socialisation

196. Which curriculum development approach prioritises the active engagement of students by focusing on their individual needs, interests, and prior experiences?

1. Administrative approach
2. Content-centered approach
3. Learner-centered approach
4. Subject-centered approach

197. Which of the following tests is used to identify misconceptions the students may have and enables the teacher to build on their students' strengths?

1. Summative test
2. Standardised test
3. Diagnostic test
4. Achievement test

198. Which of the following will develop through social science teaching?

1. Nationalism
2. Favour of certain culture
3. Favour of certain region
4. Favour of certain religion

199. Which of the following is a quick and easy assessment technique in which students work in pairs to answer questions posed by the teacher?

1. One minute paper
2. Concept mapping
3. Think-pair-share
4. Jigsaw

200. Which discipline studies Human Behaviour and Society?

1. Biology
2. Chemistry
3. Mathematics
4. Sociology

ANSWERS

1	**2**	**3**	**4**	**5**	**6**	**7**	**8**	**9**	**10**
4	1	2	3	3	4	2	3	4	1
11	**12**	**13**	**14**	**15**	**16**	**17**	**18**	**19**	**20**
3	3	1	1	3	2	2	1	4	4
21	**22**	**23**	**24**	**25**	**26**	**27**	**28**	**29**	**30**
1	1	2	2	1	2	1	4	3	4
31	**32**	**33**	**34**	**35**	**36**	**37**	**38**	**39**	**40**
2	2	4	3	2	3	2	4	4	1
41	**42**	**43**	**44**	**45**	**46**	**47**	**48**	**49**	**50**
3	2	2	3	1	4	2	4	4	4
51	**52**	**53**	**54**	**55**	**56**	**57**	**58**	**59**	**60**
1	4	2	2	4	1	1	2	4	1
61	**62**	**63**	**64**	**65**	**66**	**67**	**68**	**69**	**70**
3	3	4	3	3	1	2	2	4	4
71	**72**	**73**	**74**	**75**	**76**	**77**	**78**	**79**	**80**
2	4	1	3	3	4	4	2	4	4
81	**82**	**83**	**84**	**85**	**86**	**87**	**88**	**89**	**90**
1	4	2	2	4	1	4	1	3	2
91	**92**	**93**	**94**	**95**	**96**	**97**	**98**	**99**	**100**
4	2	4	1	3	1	1	1	2	4
101	**102**	**103**	**104**	**105**	**106**	**107**	**108**	**109**	**110**
2	4	2	4	4	4	2	3	2	1

111	**112**	**113**	**114**	**115**	**116**	**117**	**118**	**119**	**120**
3	2	4	2	4	3	3	1	2	1
121	**122**	**123**	**124**	**125**	**126**	**127**	**128**	**129**	**130**
1	4	3	3	4	1	4	4	1	2
131	**132**	**133**	**134**	**135**	**136**	**137**	**138**	**139**	**140**
1	3	3	2	4	3	3	3	2	1
141	**142**	**143**	**144**	**145**	**146**	**147**	**148**	**149**	**150**
4	4	2	3	2	4	1	2	4	1
151	**152**	**153**	**154**	**155**	**156**	**157**	**158**	**159**	**160**
3	2	3	4	1	2	4	1	4	3
161	**162**	**163**	**164**	**165**	**166**	**167**	**168**	**169**	**170**
4	3	4	4	4	3	2	2	2	2
171	**172**	**173**	**174**	**175**	**176**	**177**	**178**	**179**	**180**
1	1	2	1	3	1	4	3	3	1
181	**182**	**183**	**184**	**185**	**186**	**187**	**188**	**189**	**190**
4	1	3	4	4	3	4	3	3	1
191	**192**	**193**	**194**	**195**	**196**	**197**	**198**	**199**	**200**
1	4	4	3	3	3	3	1	3	4

EXPLANATORY ANSWERS

1. The Jambudvipaprajnath, a 12th-century text based on an earlier Prakrit source, provides a list of 18 recognized guilds (śreņis) representing various social and occupational groups. Among these, the Bhillas (Bhils) — a tribal community traditionally associated with forest regions — are notably included. Their inclusion indicates the economic and social significance of tribal and semi-tribal communities in early medieval Indian society, as they were integrated into recognized guild structures.

2. The concept of the "public/private dichotomy" in feminist theory explores how gender relations are structured by dividing social life into public (political/economic) and private (domestic/family) spheres, often marginalizing women by confining them to the latter. Carole Pateman, a British feminist scholar, developed this idea extensively in her work "The Sexual Contract" (1988), arguing that liberal social contract theories ignored the subordination of women and the patriarchal nature of the private sphere.

3. The chronology of the Harappan Civilization (Indus Valley Civilization) has been debated among archaeologists. John Marshall, who supervised the excavations at Harappa and Mohenjo-Daro, suggested that the civilization flourished between c. 3250 and 2750 BCE. His dating, though later revised by more scientific methods such as radiocarbon dating, was among the earliest scholarly attempts to establish a chronological framework for the Harappan culture.

4. The Bloody Sunday incident occurred during the Russian Revolution of 1905, when unarmed demonstrators marching to present a petition to Tsar Nicholas II were fired upon by soldiers in St. Petersburg. This massacre marked a turning point, sparking widespread strikes, protests, and unrest that collectively became known as the 1905 Revolution.

5. Jakob Burckhardt, a 19th-century Swiss historian, authored "The Civilization of the Renaissance in Italy" (1860), a seminal work that portrayed the Italian Renaissance as the birth of modern individualism and secular culture. Burckhardt's analysis is foundational in Renaissance studies, emphasizing art, humanism, and political transformation during the period.

6. The auxiliary science of history that studies the physical remains of human civilization—such as tools, pottery, buildings, and monuments—is Archaeology. It provides material evidence that helps historians reconstruct past societies, their cultures, economies, and technological developments. Archaeology thus serves as a crucial complement to textual and oral sources in historical research.

7. The phrase "wie es eigentlich gewesen" (translated as "to show how it actually happened") is associated with the German historian Leopold von Ranke. He emphasized the use of primary sources and objectivity in historical writing, advocating that historians should describe the past as it truly occurred without imposing moral or philosophical judgments. His approach laid the foundation for modern empirical historical methodology.

8. The oldest inscription of India is attributed to Ashoka's Rock Edicts, dating to the 3rd century BCE. These inscriptions, written in Prakrit, Greek, and Aramaic (depending on the region), were engraved on rocks and pillars across the Indian subcontinent. They represent the earliest deciphered written records of Indian history, providing valuable insight into Mauryan administration, Buddhism, and Ashoka's moral and ethical policies.

9. The core political doctrine underlying nationalism is the belief that each distinct nation should pursue self-governance and prioritize its own values, interests, and identity above external influences. Nationalism is rooted in the idea of sovereignty — that the political and cultural unity of a people should be expressed through an independent state.

10. The Hakra ware culture is associated with a distinctive ceramic assemblage discovered at the beginning of the fourth millennium BCE. It represents a pre-Harappan culture centered in the Ghaggar-Hakra region, showing early developments in pottery, settlement organization, and trade that later evolved into the mature Harappan (Indus Valley) civilization.

11. The work authored by Bayazid Bayat that provides a narrative of events from the reign of Humayun to Akbar (1542–43 to 1590–91) is the Tadhkira-i Humayun o Akbar. Bayazid Bayat, an official in Akbar's administration, recorded his personal observations and experiences, making this text a valuable source for understanding Mughal court life, politics, and administration during the mid-16th century.

12. The cotton gin, a machine that revolutionized cotton production by efficiently separating cotton fibers from seeds, was invented in 1793 by Eli Whitney. This invention drastically increased the profitability of cotton farming in the American South and played a major role in the expansion of slavery due to increased labor demand on plantations.

13. Francesco Petrarch is regarded as the 'Father of Humanism' for his pivotal role in reviving classical learning and promoting human-centered philosophy during the Renaissance. He emphasized the study of classical texts and moral philosophy, inspiring a cultural movement that focused on human potential and achievements rather than purely religious concerns.

14. Aristotle is not associated with the Social Contract Theory of the origin of the state. The social contract tradition is primarily linked with Thomas Hobbes, John Locke, and Jean-Jacques Rousseau, who proposed that political authority arises from an implicit agreement among individuals. Aristotle, on the other hand, viewed the state as a natural institution arising from human sociability and the need for a good life, not a contractual arrangement.

15. According to Jansen (1989), approximately 700 wells existed in the ancient city of Mohenjodaro. This remarkable number highlights the sophisticated urban planning and water management systems of the Indus Valley Civilization, ensuring a consistent supply of water for domestic and public use.

16. The ruler known for patronising the observatory at Jaipur is Sawai Jai Singh II. A visionary astronomer and ruler of Amber (later Jaipur), he built several observatories known as Jantar Mantars in cities like Delhi, Jaipur, Ujjain, Varanasi, and Mathura during the 18th century. These observatories were equipped with large stone instruments for precise astronomical observations and calendar calculations.

17. The term 'Decolonise' refers to the process of releasing a country or region from being a colony and granting it independence. It involves the end of foreign domination and the restoration of political, economic, and cultural autonomy to the formerly colonised nation. The term is also used metaphorically in modern contexts to describe efforts to remove colonial mindsets and power structures.

18. The standard proportion of baked bricks used in the construction of Mohenjodaro and other Harappan cities was 4 : 2 : 1 (length : breadth : height). This uniform ratio demonstrates the Harappans' advanced understanding of measurement and standardization, contributing to their well-planned urban architecture and durability of structures.

19. The Harappans most commonly used copper for crafting artefacts such as tools, weapons, vessels, and ornaments. While bronze (an alloy of copper and tin) was also utilized, copper was more abundant and widespread across Harappan sites, being the primary metal used for everyday objects. The presence of copper artifacts across many settlements indicates that the Harappans had well-developed metallurgy and extensive trade networks to procure raw materials.

20. The refrain "Charaiveti Charaiveti", meaning "Keep moving, keep moving," occurs at the end of each verse in the Aitareya Brahmana. This ancient Vedic text emphasizes the importance of continuous effort, movement, and progress — both in the physical and spiritual sense — reflecting the dynamic worldview of early Indian philosophy.

21. According to Buddhist tradition, the Buddha attained enlightenment after 49 days of continuous meditation under the Bodhi tree at Uruvela (modern Bodh Gaya). During this period, Siddhartha Gautama remained in deep contemplation, overcoming temptations and distractions, ultimately attaining Bodhi (enlightenment) and becoming the Buddha — the "Awakened One."

22. In Puranic tradition, Mahapadma Nanda is described as the "exterminator of all Kshatriyas." He was the founder of the Nanda dynasty and is portrayed as having destroyed many Kshatriya lineages to consolidate his power. This depiction reflects his rise from non-Kshatriya origins and the establishment of a strong centralized monarchy in Magadha.

23. Apart from Uttarapatha (the northern route) and Dakshinapatha (the southern route), the Rajapatha was another major trade route that contributed to the economic expansion of Magadha during the early historic period. These routes facilitated commerce, cultural exchange, and the movement of goods such as metals, grains, and textiles across the subcontinent, strengthening Magadha's economic base.

24. The Magadhan ruler Bimbisara strategically reinforced his kingdom's power through multiple matrimonial alliances. He married Kosala Devi of Kosala, Chellana of Videha (a Lichchhavi princess), and Khema of Madra. These alliances enhanced Magadha's political influence, secured peace with neighboring states, and contributed to its territorial expansion.

25. The Pettanikas were special custom officers mentioned in Buddhist sources during the period of the Mahajanapadas. Their role was to collect customs and trade duties on goods entering and leaving city gates or marketplaces, reflecting the organized economic administration and trade regulation of that era.

26. The region lying north of the river Champa, west of Anga, south of the Chotanagpur plateau, and east of the rivers Son and Ganga corresponds to Magadha during the early historic period. Magadha was a monarchy, and under rulers like Bimbisara and Ajatashatru, it became the most powerful Mahajanapada, eventually forming the nucleus of later empires such as the Mauryan Empire.

27. At the Harappan site of Kalibangan, located in Rajasthan, houses discharged wastewater into jars placed outside rather than into street drains. This feature is attributed to the arid climate of the region, which made elaborate drainage systems unnecessary. Unlike cities such as Mohenjodaro, Kalibangan's drainage arrangement reflects environmental adaptation and regional variation within Harappan urban planning.

28. The Harappan Civilization is best described as Chalcolithic, meaning it belonged to the Copper-Stone Age, where people used both stone tools and copper/bronze implements. This stage marked a transition between the Neolithic and the Iron Age, characterized by urbanization, metallurgy, trade, and complex social structures.

29. Post-Harappan cultures such as Cemetery H and Ochre Coloured Pottery (OCP) display selective continuity in cultural elements like pottery designs and burial practices, while other features of the Mature Harappan phase disappeared. This indicates a gradual cultural transformation rather than a complete break, showing that elements of the Harappan tradition persisted into later regional cultures.

30. The Vajji Confederacy (also known as the Vrijji Sangha) was a republic in ancient India. Centered around Vaishali in present-day Bihar, it consisted of several clans, including the Lichchhavis. The Vajji polity functioned through a ganasangha (republican) system, with collective decision-making and assemblies representing the people — a contrast to the monarchical states of the period.

31. According to Ashokan edicts, Suvarnagiri was identified as the southern provincial capital of the Mauryan Empire. It was one of the four provincial centers along with Taxila (northwest), Ujjain (west), and Tosali (east). Suvarnagiri, located in present-day Karnataka, served as the administrative hub for the southern regions, reflecting the empire's efficient governance system.

32. The Mature Harappan Phase, characterized by urban planning, standardized brick architecture, script development, and long-distance trade (with regions like Mesopotamia), flourished approximately between 2600 BCE and 1900 BCE. This was the peak period of the Indus Valley Civilization, with major centers such as Mohenjo Daro, Harappa, Dholavira, and Kalibangan thriving.

33. The 'Dancing Girl' figurine from Mohenjo Daro exemplifies the early use of the lost-wax (cire perdue) technique in metallurgy. This bronze statue, depicting a young woman in a confident stance with one hand on her hip, demonstrates the Harappans' advanced metal casting skills. The same method continued in later Indian artistic traditions, such as Chola bronze sculptures.

34. The ruler of Magadha referred to in Greek sources as Agrammes or Xandrames was Dhana Nanda. He was the last ruler of the Nanda dynasty and was contemporaneous with Alexander's invasion (326 BCE). Greek historians described him as a powerful but unpopular ruler, overthrown later by Chandragupta Maurya with the guidance of Chanakya (Kautilya).

35. Alexander the Great defeated King Porus in 326 BCE at the Battle of the Hydaspes (modern Jhelum River). Despite Porus's eventual defeat, his bravery impressed Alexander, who reinstated him as ruler of his territory. This battle marked Alexander's farthest advance into the Indian subcontinent before his troops refused to march further east.

36. The Harappan site of Dholavira, located in present-day Gujarat, is exceptional because it had a unique threefold urban layout — consisting of a citadel, a middle town, and a lower town. Unlike other Harappan sites that generally had only two divisions (citadel and lower town), Dholavira's sophisticated town planning, water conservation system, and monumental architecture mark it as one of the most remarkable urban centers of the Indus Valley Civilization.

37. Among the Mahajanapadas, Panchala was not situated in the Central or Deccan regions. It was located in the northern part of India, between the Ganga and Yamuna rivers (in modern Uttar Pradesh). In contrast, Chedi lay in central India, Assaka in the Deccan region (modern Maharashtra and Telangana), and Avanti in western-central India (modern Madhya Pradesh).

38. During Alexander's invasion of India (326 BCE), Ambhi was the ruler of Taxila. He allied with Alexander and surrendered without resistance, seeking to strengthen his position against his rival, King Porus of the Punjab region. This alliance provided Alexander with strategic support and facilitated his advance into northwestern India.

39. During the early historic phase of Magadha, the city of Gaya was located within its territorial extent, apart from Rajagriha and Pataligrama (Pataḷiputra). Gaya held religious and cultural importance, associated with sacred sites like Bodh Gaya where the Buddha attained enlightenment, and was integrated into Magadha's political domain as the kingdom expanded.

40. In the context of early Buddhist texts, a kammika was a customs official responsible for collecting tolls and taxes at trade routes or city gates. These officials played a key role in regulating commerce and maintaining state revenue, reflecting the organized economic administration of the period.

41. The Ashokan inscription that first revealed that the practice of inscribing edicts on Dhamma began twelve years after Ashoka's coronation is the Pillar Edict 6. This edict provides chronological information about the evolution of Ashoka's Dhamma policy, indicating that he started issuing and inscribing edicts to spread his moral and ethical principles only after the twelfth year of his reign, reflecting a matured phase of his rule and religious transformation.

42. The historicity of King Ramagupta is attested by the Sanskrit drama Devichandraguptam, attributed to Vishakhadatta. The text narrates the story of Ramagupta, his brother Chandragupta II (Vikramaditya), and the latter's eventual usurpation of the throne after rescuing Ramagupta's queen from the Shakas. Although partly legendary, this literary source provides indirect historical evidence of Ramagupta's existence.

43. The empire of Chandragupta Maurya extended in the northwestern region from Afghanistan to Balochistan. After defeating Seleucus Nicator, Chandragupta gained territories including Arachosia (Kandahar), Gedrosia (Balochistan), and parts of Paropamisadae (Afghanistan), consolidating Mauryan control over a vast and strategic frontier region.

44. Under the Mauryan espionage system spies were organized into distinct categories such as Gudhapurushas (secret agents), Vyayamikas (roving spies or informants), and Udasthitas (stationary or resident spies). These agents collected intelligence on administration, military affairs, and public sentiment. However, in the later Mauryan period, the weakening of this espionage network contributed to administrative decline and loss of central control.

45. The last Mauryan king, Brihadratha, was killed by Pushyamitra Shunga, the commander-in-chief of the Mauryan army, during a military parade. This assassination around 185 BCE marked the end of the Mauryan dynasty and the beginning of the Shunga dynasty, which established its capital at Pataliputra.

46. As a result of the treaty with Seleucus Nicator, Chandragupta Maurya acquired the regions of Kabul, Kandahar, Herat, and Balkh. This agreement followed Seleucus's unsuccessful attempt to reclaim northwestern territories. In exchange for these provinces, Chandragupta presented Seleucus with 500 war elephants, and the treaty was further strengthened through a marital alliance, marking a significant diplomatic achievement in Mauryan foreign policy.

47. The Shunga dynasty replaced the Mauryan Empire after Pushyamitra Shunga assassinated the last Mauryan ruler, Brihadratha, around 185 BCE. Pushyamitra, who was the commander-in-chief (Senapati) under Brihadratha, established the Shunga rule with its capital at Pataliputra, marking a shift toward Brahmanical revivalism following the Mauryan period.

48. After the death of Samudragupta in 375 CE, his son Chandragupta II (Vikramaditya) ascended the throne of the Gupta Empire. Chandragupta II expanded the empire to its greatest territorial extent, defeating the Shakas in western India and promoting cultural and economic prosperity. His reign is often considered the zenith of the Gupta Golden Age.

49. In the Allahabad Prasasti inscription, composed by Harisena, Samudragupta is compared with the deities Dhanada (Kubera), Varuna, Indra, and Antaka (Yama). This comparison underscores his supreme wealth, power, sovereignty, and the ability to bestow or take away life, symbolizing his unmatched authority among rulers of his time.

50. The decline of the Gupta Empire began after the reign of Skandagupta. Although he successfully repelled invasions by the Hunas (White Huns), the prolonged wars exhausted the empire's resources. Following his reign, internal weaknesses and external pressures accelerated the disintegration of Gupta political power.

51. The incorrect statement about Ashoka is that according to the Rajatarangini, Ashoka's favoured deity was Brahma. The Rajatarangini (by Kalhana) actually describes Ashoka as a devotee of Buddha, not Brahma. It portrays him as a deeply religious king who promoted Buddhism in Kashmir. The other statements — his being called 'protector of the Sangha' in the Sarnath Minor Pillar Edict, his devotion to the Buddha, Dhamma, and Sangha in the Bhabru Edict, and his Buddhist faith as described in the Dipavamsa and Mahavamsa — are correct.

52. The ancient Indian drama Devi Chandraguptam, attributed to Vishakhadatta, narrates the story of Chandragupta II killing his elder brother Ramagupta to protect royal honour and the kingdom. Although the play survives only in fragments, it is an important literary source confirming the existence of Ramagupta and the dramatic events leading to Chandragupta II's rise to power.

53. The Bhitari Pillar Inscription provides crucial information about Skandagupta. This inscription, discovered in modern Uttar Pradesh, records his achievements, including his victories over the Pushyamitras and the Hunas, and highlights his efforts in maintaining the stability of the Gupta Empire during a period of external invasions and internal challenges.

54. The historical source that mentions Ramagupta as a Gupta ruler is the Devi-Chandragupta. This Sanskrit drama by Vishakhadatta (also the author of Mudrarakshasa) depicts Ramagupta as the elder brother of Chandragupta II, whose weak rule led to his downfall. The text is a vital literary reference corroborating Ramagupta's brief and controversial reign.

55. In Greek sources, Chandragupta Maurya is referred to as Sandracottus (or Androcottus). These accounts, mainly by Megasthenes, provide valuable details about the Mauryan Empire, including its administration, economy, and the grandeur of the capital, Pataliputra. This identification is key to synchronizing Greek and Indian historical chronologies.

56. Pushyamitra Shunga assassinated Brihadratha, the last ruler of the Maurya Empire, thus bringing it to an end around 185 BCE. The incident occurred during a military parade where Pushyamitra, serving as the commander-in-chief (Senapati), killed Brihadratha and established the Shunga dynasty, marking a shift toward Brahmanical dominance in post-Mauryan India.

57. The Mehrauli Iron Pillar, which bears a Sanskrit inscription referring to King Chandra (identified by many historians as Chandragupta II of the Gupta dynasty), is located in Delhi. The pillar is renowned for its rust-resistant iron composition and stands as a remarkable example of ancient Indian metallurgical skill and craftsmanship.

58. Samudravarman was not a ruler of the Gupta dynasty. The known early rulers include Maharaja Gupta (the probable founder), Ghatotkacha, Chandragupta I, Samudragupta, and Chandragupta II. The name Samudravarman does not appear in Gupta genealogies or inscriptions, and therefore does not belong to the dynasty's lineage.

59. The Junagarh (Junagadh) Inscription of Rudradaman I provides the only definite epigraphic reference to Chandragupta Maurya. It records that the construction of the Sudarshana Lake in Gujarat was initiated during Chandragupta's reign by his governor Pushyagupta, later repaired by Ashoka and again by Rudradaman I during the 2nd century CE.

60. The Junagadh Inscription also informs us that, on the orders of Mauryan Emperor Chandragupta Maurya, his governor Pushyagupta constructed the Sudarshana Lake. This inscription, written in Sanskrit by Rudradaman I, highlights the lake's long history of maintenance and the continuity of hydraulic engineering across dynasties.

61. The Mughal emperor Farrukhsiyar formally promoted Murshid Quli Khan to the position of Subedar (Governor) of Bengal in 1717.

Although Aurangzeb had earlier appointed him as the Diwan (chief revenue officer) of Bengal in 1700, and later as Deputy Subedar, it was under Farrukhsiyar that Murshid Quli Khan received full authority as the governor. This marked the beginning of Bengal's transformation into a semi-autonomous state, with Murshidabad as its capital.

62. The book The Crisis of Empire in Mughal North India was authored by Muzaffar Alam. This influential work analyzes the decline of the Mughal Empire in the 18th century, focusing on the political, social, and administrative changes in North India. Alam examines how regional powers emerged and how the Mughal state adapted to internal and external pressures, offering a nuanced understanding of the empire's transformation rather than a simple narrative of collapse.

63. The source that refers to crop-sharing (batai) as the most equitable method of revenue assessment is the Nigarnama-i-Munshi by Malikzada. In this work, Malikzada emphasizes that the batai system ensured fairness by allowing both the state and the peasantry to share the risks and rewards of agricultural production. This approach was viewed as a balanced method of revenue collection, reflecting a concern for agrarian justice and sustainability within the Mughal administrative framework.

64. During Akbar's reign, the refinement of the Rupiya and Dam coinage system facilitated long-distance trade and monetised taxation. The Rupiya (silver) and Dam (copper) became standardized currency units that improved fiscal management and enhanced commercial efficiency across the empire, laying the foundation for a stable Mughal monetary economy.

65. The incorrect statement about Chandragupta I is that he started the Gupta Era in memory of his marriage to Kumaradevi.

While Chandragupta I's marriage to Kumaradevi, a Licchavi princess, was politically significant and strengthened Gupta power, there is no evidence that he initiated the Gupta Era to commemorate it. The Gupta Era (beginning in 319–320 CE) is generally associated with his reign but its exact origin remains uncertain.

66. The Mughal ruler Shah Jahan introduced the month-scale (Mahana Jagir) system in the Mansabdari System to address the gap between Jama (estimated income) and Hasil (actual collection or realization). This reform aimed to ensure greater fiscal discipline and fairness by adjusting the payments of mansabdars according to the actual revenue collected rather than estimated income. It reflected Shah Jahan's efforts to bring financial stability and administrative efficiency to the Mughal Empire.

67. The Battle of Jajau was fought in 1707 CE between Bahadur Shah I (Prince Muazzam) and his brother Muhammad Azam Shah, following the death of Emperor Aurangzeb. Bahadur Shah emerged victorious, securing the Mughal throne. The battle was one of the major succession conflicts in Mughal history after Aurangzeb's long reign.

68. According to the Mehrauli Iron Pillar inscription, King Chandra (widely identified with Chandragupta II Vikramaditya) defeated the Vahlikas, who are identified with the Bactrian rulers of the northwest. This victory demonstrates the Gupta Empire's military strength and its extended influence beyond the Indian subcontinent.

69. The 'Great Firm Theory', which explains the decline of the Mughal Empire in terms of the weakening of large commercial houses (great firms) that managed state finances and trade networks, was propounded by Karen Leonard. She argued that these firms were crucial intermediaries between the state and the economy, and their decline undermined Mughal fiscal stability and political cohesion.

70. The incorrect statement about the Jizya tax is that Jahandar Shah abolished it permanently in 1720 CE. In fact, the Jizya, a religious tax levied on non-Muslims, was abolished by Akbar in 1564 CE, reimposed by Aurangzeb in 1679 CE, but there is no record of Jahandar Shah abolishing it in 1720 CE. His reign (1712–1713 CE) was short-lived and did not witness such a reform.

71. The Bilsad inscription belongs to the reign of Kumaragupta I. Discovered in Uttar Pradesh, this inscription records the installation of a pillar in honor of a victory during Kumaragupta's rule.

It helps confirm his authority and the continuation of Gupta administrative and religious practices during the mid-5th century CE.

72. The Mughal emperor Muhammad Shah was nicknamed 'Rangila', meaning "the colourful," due to his love for luxury, art, music, and culture. His reign (1719–1748 CE) is remembered for cultural revival and artistic achievements but also for political decline, as seen in events like Nadir Shah's invasion of Delhi in 1739.

73. The source that provides important insights into the administrative disorder and fiscal crisis of the later Mughal Empire, specifically during the reign of Muhammad Shah, is the Muntakhab-ul Lubab by Khafi Khan.

This historical chronicle offers a vivid account of the decline in administrative efficiency, corruption among officials, and the financial instability that plagued the empire during the early 18th century. Khafi Khan's observations are crucial for understanding the weakening of Mughal central authority and the onset of regional fragmentation.

74. The Samanta System is considered one of the factors that contributed to the decline of the Gupta Empire. Under this system, regional governors and local rulers (samantha) were granted autonomy in return for allegiance to the emperor. Over time, these local chiefs consolidated power and asserted independence, weakening the central administration and fragmenting imperial authority.

75. The Mir Bakhshi was the head of the military department in the Mughal administration. He was responsible for maintaining army records, appointing and reviewing mansabdars, managing military payments, and supervising intelligence officers (barids). The position was crucial in ensuring the empire's military efficiency and organization.

76. The historian M.N. Pearson, in an influential study, argued that the decline of the Mughal Empire stemmed from the oligarchic nature of Indian states before the colonial period. According to him, these states were organized around patron-client relationships, lacked social commitment, and suffered from weak legitimacy. This framework suggested that Mughal political culture was inherently fragile and could not sustain a centralized, legitimate order over time.

77. The Watan Jagir was a non-transferable jagir under the Mughal administrative system. It was usually assigned to Rajput chiefs or hereditary nobles in their ancestral territories as a recognition of loyalty and service to the Mughal emperor. Unlike transferable tankha jagirs, watan jagirs remained permanently attached to the holder's family and region.

78. The Mughal emperor Farrukhsiyar issued the famous Farman of 1717 to the British East India Company, granting it extensive trade privileges in Bengal. This Farman allowed the Company duty-free trade in Bengal, Bihar, and Orissa, and the right to rent additional lands, which significantly expanded its economic power and laid the groundwork for later political dominance.

79. In the Ain-i-Akbari, Abul Fazl justified the imposition of taxes as the remuneration of sovereignty, arguing that subjects paid taxes in return for protection and justice provided by the ruler. This philosophical justification linked fiscal obligations to moral and political legitimacy, framing taxation as a reciprocal duty within a just and ordered state.

80. The major economic cause of the decline of the Mughal Empire was its series of long and expensive wars — especially under Aurangzeb, including the Deccan campaigns. These wars drained the imperial treasury, disrupted trade and agriculture, and overextended administrative and military resources, ultimately leading to fiscal exhaustion and economic stagnation.

81. A significant factor contributing to the decline and eventual dissolution of the Maratha Confederacy in the early 19th century was the British use of subsidiary alliances, diplomatic pressure, and military campaigns. Through a combination of treaties, divide-and-rule tactics, and decisive wars (notably the Anglo-Maratha Wars, 1775–1818), the British systematically weakened the independent Maratha states, culminating in the defeat of Peshwa Bajirao II in 1818.

82. The historian Andre Wink argued that the emergence of Maratha Swarajya was not a revolt against the Mughal Empire, but rather a direct consequence of Mughal expansion. According to him, the Marathas largely retained their status as zamindars, integrating into the Mughal framework while simultaneously asserting regional autonomy — a process shaped more by imperial policies than outright rebellion.

83. The correct sequence of key administrative offices under the Bahmani Sultanate, following the model of the Delhi Sultanate, is:
Sultan → Vakil → Wazir → Bakhshi → Qazi. The Sultan was the supreme ruler; the Vakil acted as deputy or regent; the Wazir oversaw revenue and administration; the Bakhshi handled military affairs and personnel; and the Qazi served as the chief judicial authority.

84. The reign of Muhammad Shah (1719–1748) is often cited as the period during which the Mughal Empire's inability to control rising regional powers — including the Marathas, Sikhs, and Jats — led to severe administrative fragmentation. His reign witnessed internal inefficiency, factional court politics, and external invasions such as Nadir Shah's sack of Delhi in 1739, symbolizing Mughal decline.

85. In 1553 CE, Humayun ordered the blinding of his brother Kamran Mirza. Kamran had repeatedly rebelled against Humayun and sought alliances with Afghan and Persian forces, posing a persistent threat to Mughal stability. Despite family ties, Humayun's decision to blind Kamran was a measure to neutralize his political challenge permanently.

86. The last Mughal emperor, Bahadur Shah Zafar, was exiled by the British to Rangoon (present-day Yangon, Myanmar) after the Revolt of 1857. Following the fall of Delhi, he was captured and tried by the British for treason. He spent his remaining years in captivity in Rangoon, where he died in 1862, marking the formal end of the Mughal dynasty.

87. The Battle of Talikota was fought in 1565 CE between the Vijayanagara Empire and a coalition of the Deccan Sultanates — Bijapur, Ahmadnagar, Golconda, and Bidar. The defeat of Vijayanagara led to the sacking of its magnificent capital Hampi, signaling the decline of one of South India's greatest empires.

88. The Jagirdari System was the assignment of revenue from a particular territory (jagir) to nobles or mansabdars in exchange for their services under the Mughals. Jagirdars collected revenue from the assigned area to maintain troops and meet administrative expenses. This system was central to Mughal administrative and military organization.

89. The first Mughal ruler to become a pensioner of the East India Company was Shah Alam II. After the Battle of Buxar (1764), he granted the Diwani of Bengal, Bihar, and Orissa to the Company in 1765 and became dependent on British support. In return, he received an annual pension, symbolizing the beginning of Mughal subordination to British power.

90. After the conquest of Kabul in 1507, Babur assumed the title of 'Padishah' (meaning "Emperor" or "Great King"). This marked his assertion of full sovereignty and imperial ambition, distinguishing him from local Central Asian rulers and establishing the foundation for his later campaigns in India.

91. The correct option is: 4. Only statements A, C and D are correct.

A. Natural topography of Maharashtra (Correct): The hilly terrain and strong forts of the Western Ghats provided natural defense and supported guerrilla warfare (ganimi kava), aiding Maratha resistance.

B. French support (Incorrect): The Maratha rise under Shivaji was indigenous; the French became involved only in later 18th-century politics.

C. Strong personality of Shivaji (Correct): Shivaji's leadership, courage, and administrative skill united the Marathas and established the foundation of Swarajya.

D. Effect of Hindutva (Correct): The idea of Hindavi Swarajya gave ideological strength and cultural unity to the Maratha movement.

92. The theory of the 'Agrarian Crisis' in relation to the decline of the Mughal Empire was propounded by Irfan Habib. He argued that excessive land revenue demands, peasant revolts, and rural distress weakened the Mughal agrarian economy, causing administrative and military decline in the 17th and 18th centuries.

93. The correct combination of Akbar's military campaign is the Ranthambore conquest - 1568 AD. This victory followed his conquest of Chittor (1567–68) and consolidated Mughal authority in Rajasthan, breaking the Rajput strongholds and expanding the empire in northwestern India.

94. The fort of Ahmadnagar was captured in 1600 CE under Akbar's reign, marking the defeat and arrest of Bahadur Nizam Shah and the annexation of the Ahmadnagar kingdom into the Mughal Empire. This campaign extended Mughal control deep into the Deccan region.

95. The correct statement about the Marathas is that Shivaji established the concept of "Hindavi Swaraj" — self-rule of the native land — aimed at freeing the Deccan from Mughal and Adil Shahi control. This ideal became the ideological foundation of Maratha resistance and state formation.

96. The Marathas suffered a major defeat in the Third Battle of Panipat (1761) under the leadership of Sadashivrao Bhau. The battle was fought against Ahmad Shah Abdali (Durrani) and marked a devastating blow to Maratha power, leading to massive losses in men and prestige.

97. The author of the book 'Parties and Politics at the Mughal Court (1707–1740)' is Satish Chandra. This classic historical study provides an in-depth analysis of the factional struggles, court intrigues, and administrative weaknesses that characterized the Mughal Empire after the death of Aurangzeb, marking the beginning of its political decline.

98. The policy of Sulh-i-Kul, meaning 'peace with all', was adopted by Emperor Akbar. It emphasized religious tolerance, equal treatment of subjects regardless of faith, and harmony among different communities—forming a cornerstone of Akbar's inclusive governance and imperial ideology.

99. The historian Karen Leonard attributed the decline of the Mughal Empire to the role of influential banking houses ('great firms') whose financial control and weakening ties with the Mughal state undermined imperial stability and fiscal strength.

100. Within the Maratha Confederacy, the Holkars ruled over Indore and the Malwa region. Founded by Malhar Rao Holkar, this branch became one of the most powerful Maratha houses, playing a key role in central Indian politics during the 18th century.

101. For effective governance, Sher Shah Suri divided his empire into 47 administrative divisions known as sarkars. Each sarkar was further subdivided into parganas for efficient revenue collection and local administration. This reorganization strengthened the central authority and improved administrative efficiency.

102. The Third Carnatic War (1757–1763) in India was a direct result of the Seven Years' War (1756–1763) in Europe between Britain and France. The conflict decided the fate of colonial dominance in India, ending with British victory and the collapse of French political ambitions in the subcontinent.

103. The Dagh and Chehra systems were introduced in the Mughal Mansabdari administration primarily to prevent duplicacy in troops and horses maintained by mansabdars. Under this system, horses were branded (dagh) and soldiers' descriptions (chehra) were recorded to ensure authenticity and curb corruption.

104. The Persian chronicle that provides an estimate of approximately 120 large cities and 3,200 qasbas (small towns/townships) in India during Akbar's reign (around 1592–1593) is the Tabqat-i-Akbari. Authored by Nizamuddin Ahmad, this chronicle offers valuable statistical and administrative insights into the Mughal Empire, complementing other contemporary works such as the Ain-i-Akbari and Akbarnama.

105. The historian Abul Fazl, in his work Ain-i-Akbari, noted that "Collection should begin for rabi from Holi and for kharif from Dashehra. The officials should not delay it for another crop." This statement reflects the systematic and seasonal approach of Mughal revenue collection under Akbar's administration.

106. The chief superintendent of ports under the Mughals was known as the Mutasaddi. He was responsible for overseeing port administration, managing customs duties, regulating maritime trade, and ensuring smooth commercial operations at major ports like Surat, Cambay, and Hooghly.

107. The ruler who divided his empire into 47 administrative divisions called "Sarkars," which were further subdivided into smaller units called Parganas, was Sher Shah Suri. This administrative reorganization strengthened central control and enhanced efficiency in revenue collection.

108. The British East India Company annexed Awadh (Oudh) in February 1856 during the reign of Wajid Ali Shah, citing alleged misrule. This annexation became one of the immediate causes of resentment leading to the Revolt of 1857.

109. During Babur's reign, the Wajah system was introduced, wherein officers were assigned a fixed sum of revenue from their jurisdiction rather than a specific territory, and any surplus was deposited into the imperial treasury. This ensured accountability and limited corruption among officials.

110. In the Mansabdari System, the rank of a mansabdar was indicated by two numbers — Zat and Sawar. The Zat denoted the officer's personal rank, status, and salary, while the Sawar indicated the number of cavalrymen he had to maintain for imperial service.

111. The ruler who appointed Shiqdars as executive officers for the administration of criminal justice was Sher Shah Suri. The Shiqdar was responsible for maintaining law and order, overseeing criminal justice, and implementing the ruler's authority at the sarkar (district) level.

112. The Mysore Anche, the postal system of the Princely State of Mysore, was established by Maharaja Chikka Devaraya Wodeyar in 1672. This system helped improve administrative communication and trade within the kingdom, showcasing Mysore's early administrative sophistication.

113. The Carolina coins issued by the East India Company were made of gold. These coins, named after Queen Caroline, were minted for trade purposes and symbolized the Company's growing commercial and monetary influence in India.

114. The incorrect statement about the Maratha Village Administration is:

"The head of grain storage in the village was known as Phadnis."

In reality, the Phadnis was an assistant to the village accountant (Kulkarni) and dealt with administrative records, not grain storage. The Patel was the village headman, Kulkarni the record-keeper, and Mahar served as the village watchman.

115. In Sher Shah's administration, a Sarkar was an administrative division. Each Sarkar consisted of several Parganas and was governed by officials such as the Shiqdar (for law and order) and Munsif (for revenue). This division enhanced administrative control and efficiency.

116. In the Vijayanagara Empire, the provincial administration system where land was assigned to officials in lieu of pay was known as the Nayankar system (also called Amara-Nayaka system). The Nayakas were military chiefs granted land revenue rights in exchange for maintaining troops and ensuring local governance and security.

117. Sher Shah Suri introduced a uniform coinage system by abolishing mixed metal coins. His Dam coins were made of copper, while the Rupiya was of silver and the Mohur of gold. This reform standardized currency across the empire and enhanced trade efficiency.

118. The ruler who introduced the practices of maintaining descriptive rolls (huliya) of soldiers and branding (dagh) of horses to regulate cavalry quality was Alauddin Khalji. These measures were aimed at preventing corruption and ensuring that soldiers and horses registered with the state were genuine and well-equipped.

119. In the Mansabdari system, the term 'talab khasa' referred to the personal salary of a mansabdar. This was the amount received directly by the mansabdar from the imperial treasury, distinct from allowances for maintaining troops and horses.

120. The official communication that articulated the British policy of maintaining ethnic divisions within the Indian army, recommending that adjacent regiments remain "so alien that it would be ready to fire into it," was the Peel Commission Report of 1859. Issued after the Revolt of 1857, it aimed to prevent unity among Indian soldiers by emphasizing ethnic and regional segregation.

121. The term 'Pakistan' was first coined in 1933 by Chaudhry Rehmat Ali, a Cambridge student and prominent nationalist thinker. He introduced the term in his pamphlet "Now or Never: Are We to Live or Perish Forever?" published in London. The name represented the initials of Muslim-majority regions — Punjab, Afghania (North-West Frontier Province), Kashmir, Sindh, and Baluchistan — and symbolized the idea of a separate homeland for Muslims in the Indian subcontinent.

122. The resolution on 'Swaraj' (self-rule) was first passed at the 1906 Calcutta Session of the Indian National Congress, presided over by Dadabhai Naoroji. This session marked a major ideological shift as the Congress officially declared Swaraj as its ultimate goal. Naoroji's address clarified that Swaraj means self-government or independence like that of the United Kingdom or its colonies. This set the foundation for future demands for complete independence.

123. Guru Nanak Dev Ji, the founder of Sikhism, was born in 1469 CE at Rai Bhoi di Talwandi (now Nankana Sahib in Pakistan's Punjab province). He preached the message of equality, unity of God (Ik Onkar), and service to humanity (Seva). His spiritual teachings, expressed through hymns, are preserved in the Guru Granth Sahib, the central scripture of Sikhism.

124. The Uttaramerur inscriptions of 919 CE and 921 CE, issued during the reign of the Chola king Parantaka I, are some of the most important records of village self-governance in South India. They detail the functioning of the village assemblies (sabhas), including methods of election, qualifications for members, and procedures for disqualification. These inscriptions demonstrate a highly organized and democratic local administration, unique in the ancient world.

125. Dr. B.R. Ambedkar established the 'Bahishkrit Hitkarini Sabha' in 1923 to promote education and socio-economic reform among the Depressed Classes (Dalits). The organization's motto was "Educate, Agitate, Organize", which became a guiding principle of Ambedkar's social and political activism. Through this Sabha, he worked to uplift marginalized communities and laid the groundwork for future movements against caste discrimination.

126. The Mahad Satyagraha (1927) marked the first organized movement led by Dr. B.R. Ambedkar to secure civic rights for the Depressed Classes (Dalits) in India. It was held at Chavdar Tank in Mahad (Maharashtra), where Dalits asserted their right to draw water from a public tank. The event symbolized their fight against caste discrimination and social exclusion, and became a defining moment in the Dalit liberation movement.

127. Lord Macaulay's Minute on Education (1835) revolutionized the Indian education system by advocating English as the medium of instruction and emphasizing Western science, literature, and modern knowledge over traditional Indian learning. The statement that was not part of Macaulay's Minute is the proposal that "The medium of education will be vernacular languages", since Macaulay argued strongly against using Indian languages as the primary medium of higher education.

128. The Constituent Assembly of India finalized the Indian Constitution on 26 November 1949 after nearly three years of deliberation (from December 1946 to November 1949). The Constitution officially came into effect on 26 January 1950, celebrated as Republic Day. The adoption on 26 November marked the completion of India's constitutional framework and democratic foundation.

129. The ideological rift between the Moderates and Extremists in the Indian National Congress became most evident at the Surat Session of 1907. The conflict arose over methods to achieve Swaraj — the Moderates favored constitutional reforms and dialogue, while the Extremists, led by Bal Gangadhar Tilak, advocated direct action and self-reliance. The session ended in a formal split, weakening the nationalist movement temporarily.

130. In the context of tribal anti-colonial movements in eastern India, particularly in regions like Chota Nagpur, Santhal Parganas, and Orissa, the term "Dikus" was used by the tribal communities to refer to outsiders such as zamindars, moneylenders, and British officials who exploited them through unfair taxation, land grabbing, and debt bondage.

131. The statement "Islamic-style tombs were a regular feature of Hindu temple complexes" is incorrect. Hindu temples did not traditionally include tombs, as they are contrary to Hindu ritual and cosmological beliefs. However, during the Indo-Islamic architectural synthesis, certain features like arches, domes, and decorative motifs were adopted in secular and royal architecture. Examples include the Mahanavami Dibba and Lotus Mahal at Hampi, which reflect a fusion of Hindu and Islamic design styles.

132. Guru Nanak Dev Ji, the founder of Sikhism, appointed Bhai Lehna as his successor, who later became Guru Angad Dev Ji, the second Sikh Guru. Guru Nanak recognized Bhai Lehna's devotion, humility, and understanding of spiritual truth, and renamed him Angad, meaning "a part of his own body."

133. The Women's Indian Association (WIA) was founded in 1917 by Annie Besant, along with Margaret Cousins and Dorothy Jinarajadasa. It was one of the earliest women's organizations in colonial India, working for women's education, political rights, and social reform. Annie Besant's leadership made it a powerful platform for promoting women's suffrage and equal opportunity.

134. Under the Mughal agrarian system, Khudkasht peasants were resident cultivators who owned and tilled their own land, paying revenue directly to the state or through intermediaries. They were considered more secure and stable tenants compared to Pahi (non-resident cultivators) or Muzari (tenant farmers).

135. The Sadh Vaishnavism branch of Vaishnava philosophy was founded by Madhvacharya in the 13th century. He propounded the doctrine of Dvaita (dualism), emphasizing a clear distinction between the individual soul (jiva) and God (Vishṇu). His teachings countered the Advaita (non-dual) philosophy of Shankaracharya and greatly influenced devotional traditions in southern India, especially in Karnataka.

136. The Temples of Khajuraho, built between the 10th and 12th centuries CE by the Chandela rulers, are prime examples of the Nagara style of temple architecture, which is predominant in northern India. This style is characterized by curvilinear shikharas (spires), high plinths, and intricate sculptural decorations depicting deities, celestial beings, and human figures.

137. The statement highlighting judicial discrimination — that "the testimony of a single one of our countrymen has more weight with the court than that of any number of Hindus" — was made by George Otto Trevelyan (G.O. Trevelyan) in 1864. He criticized the racial bias and inequality within British colonial administration, which contributed to growing Indian resentment and early nationalist awakening.

138. Lala Lajpat Rai was brutally assaulted by the British police while leading a peaceful protest against the Simon Commission in Lahore on 30 October 1928. The Commission, appointed by the British government, excluded Indian members, sparking widespread outrage. Lajpat Rai's injuries from the lathi charge led to his death, and he became a martyr for India's independence movement.

139. During the Mughal period, Khud-Kasht referred to resident cultivators who owned and tilled their own land, holding hereditary rights of ownership and sale. They were permanent settlers, distinct from Pahi-Kasht (non-resident cultivators) or Mujariyan (tenant cultivators). Their secure status made them a stable base of the rural agrarian system.

140. The Indian National Congress (INC) was founded with the help of Allan Octavian Hume (A.O. Hume), a retired British civil servant, who played a key role in organizing early Indian political dialogue. The first session of the Congress was held in Bombay (not Poona) at Gokuldas Tejpal Sanskrit College from 28–31 December 1885, under the presidency of W.C. Bonnerjee.

141. The Industrial Policy Resolution of 1956 marked India's clear shift toward import-substitution industrialisation (ISI) during the Second Five-Year Plan (1956–1961). It emphasized the development of heavy industries, machine-building, and public sector enterprises to reduce dependence on foreign goods and strengthen domestic production. This policy reflected India's socialist and self-reliant development vision under Prime Minister Jawaharlal Nehru and the influence of P.C. Mahalanobis.

142. The creation of All India Services (AIS) — such as the Indian Administrative Service (IAS) and Indian Police Service (IPS) — is provided under Article 312 of the Indian Constitution. This article empowers Parliament to create new All India Services if the Rajya Sabha passes a resolution with a two-thirds majority, deeming it necessary for national interest.

143. Over the centuries, China repeatedly sought to assert military, administrative, and cultural control over Vietnam. From the Han dynasty (2nd century BCE) through various later dynasties, China attempted to sinicize Vietnamese culture and governance, though Vietnam maintained a strong sense of national identity and resisted domination, eventually achieving independence in the 10th century CE.

144. The archaeologist Robert Adams critiqued V. Gordon Childe's definition of early civilisations, arguing that Childe's model was too narrow and Eurocentric, as it emphasized urbanization, metallurgy, and writing as universal traits. Adams pointed out that some civilisations, such as those in the Americas or sub-Saharan Africa, flourished without metals or writing systems, challenging Childe's "Urban Revolution" criteria.

145. The Treaty of Tordesillas (1494) is regarded as a foundational moment in European imperialism. It was an agreement between Spain and Portugal, mediated by the Pope, dividing the non-European world along a meridian 370 leagues west of the Cape Verde Islands. Lands to the west went to Spain, and those to the east to Portugal — legitimizing their colonial ambitions and shaping early modern imperial boundaries.

146. The concept of Stewardship in Christianity emphasizes the human responsibility to care for and preserve God's creation, including natural resources. It teaches that humans are caretakers (stewards) of the Earth, entrusted by God to use its resources wisely and sustainably — not exploitatively. This forms the foundation of many Christian environmental ethics today.

147. During the 16th century, Antwerp (in modern-day Belgium) was one of Europe's most important commercial and financial centers, serving as a hub for international trade, banking, and early capitalist activity. Its bustling port attracted merchants from across Europe, Asia, and the Americas, marking it as a focal point of commercial capitalism before the rise of Amsterdam.

148. The rise of commercial capitalism — based on trade, profit-making, and accumulation of capital — significantly weakened feudalism, the medieval system that tied peasants to land and lords. As trade and money economy expanded, urban merchant classes grew powerful, reducing the dominance of land-based aristocracy and hereditary hierarchies.

149. The Supreme Soviet of the National Economy in the early Soviet Union (1917–1932) was known as Vesenkha (abbreviation for Vysshiy Sovet Narodnogo Khozyaystva). It was established to oversee state economic planning, industrial production, and resource allocation during the formative years of the socialist economy under Lenin.

150. The book "Environmentalism: A Global History" was authored by Ramachandra Guha, a prominent Indian historian and environmental thinker. The book traces the evolution of environmental movements across the world, exploring how concerns for nature, ecology, and sustainability shaped modern political and social thought.

151. The 'Mad King' of the Roman Empire refers to Caligula (Gaius Julius Caesar Augustus Germanicus), who ruled from 37 to 41 CE. He is infamous for his erratic behavior, cruelty, and extravagance, including declaring himself a god and engaging in acts of tyranny. His unpredictable rule led to his assassination by members of the Praetorian Guard.

152. Adam Smith is widely regarded as the first economic theorist of capitalism. His seminal work, "An Inquiry into the Nature and Causes of the Wealth of Nations" (1776), laid the foundation for classical economics, introducing concepts such as the invisible hand, free markets, and division of labor — all central to capitalist thought.

153. The Dependency Theory of Development emerged in the mid-20th century, critiquing global economic inequalities between developed (core) and developing (peripheral) nations. Its key proponents include Raúl Prebisch, Hans Singer, and Andre Gunder Frank. Adam Smith, however, belongs to the classical school of economics and is not associated with dependency theory.

154. The second urbanisation in India occurred during the Age of Mahajanapadas (6th century BCE). This period saw the rise of urban centres like Rajagriha, Vaishali, and Kashi, linked to trade, craft specialization, and political consolidation. It followed the decline of the earlier Harappan urban centres and coincided with the spread of iron technology and monetisation.

155. The Treaty of Tordesillas (1494) was signed between Spain and Portugal, under papal mediation, to divide newly discovered lands outside Europe. The line of demarcation was set approximately 370 leagues west of the Cape Verde Islands, granting Spain territories to the west (the Americas) and Portugal to the east (Africa and Asia).

156. According to the Census of India, 1901, only about 11.4% of the Indian population lived in urban areas. The vast majority of Indians continued to reside in rural regions, dependent on agriculture, reflecting the limited urban and industrial development under British colonial rule.

157. Political scientist Rajni Kothari described post-independence India's Congress system as a "one-party dominant system with democratic functioning." According to him, the Indian National Congress acted as a broad-based umbrella organization representing diverse social groups, ideologies, and interests, allowing democratic competition within its structure rather than through opposition parties.

158. The Bharatiya Janata Party (BJP) government, under Prime Minister Narendra Modi, initiated the replacement of the Planning Commission with the NITI Aayog (National Institution for Transforming India) in 2015. This reform aimed to promote cooperative federalism, decentralised planning, and a shift from rigid top-down economic control to policy think-tank-based governance.

159. The Chipko Movement, which began in the 1970s in Uttarakhand (then part of Uttar Pradesh), was a women-led environmental movement that involved villagers embracing trees ("chipko" means "to hug") to prevent deforestation. It was led by activists like Gaura Devi and Chandi Prasad Bhatt, symbolizing grassroots ecological resistance.

160. The Magadha Kingdom is generally regarded as one of the earliest and most prominent examples of a territorial state in ancient India during the 6th century BCE, marking the Second Urbanisation. Under rulers like Bimbisara and Ajatashatru, Magadha expanded through conquest and diplomacy, laying the foundation for future empires like the Mauryan Empire.

161. Under the Sui dynasty (581–618 CE), the Chinese capital Chang'an was built as a planned city with wards and a central palace complex. Its design reflected strict urban planning principles, featuring rectangular wards separated by walls and gates, with the imperial palace located centrally to symbolise political authority and cosmic order. This layout later influenced Tang dynasty capitals and even Japanese urban design.

162. According to Kautilya's Arthashastra, wool from Nepal was highly valued in India. The text mentions fine-quality woolen fabrics and blankets as luxury items imported from Himalayan regions, highlighting Nepal's role in trans-Himalayan trade and its contribution to early Indian textile culture.

163. The 'Tattvacintamani' was composed by Gangesha Upadhyaya in the early 14th century CE. This monumental work laid the foundation for the Navya-Nyaya (New Logic) school of Indian philosophy, systematising principles of logic, epistemology, and metaphysics. His ideas profoundly shaped later Indian scholastic thought.

164. The book "The Colonial State and Forms of Knowledge: The British in India" (1994) critically examines how British colonial authorities codified Indian knowledge systems—in law, education, and administration—to establish intellectual and political dominance. Edited by Bernard S. Cohn, it explores how the colonial state transformed indigenous epistemologies into tools of control.

165. In the New Culture Movement (early 20th-century China), Hu Shi argued for literary and linguistic modernisation through vernacular Chinese (baihua) instead of classical Chinese. He believed that using a simple, spoken language would democratise education, encourage creativity, and align Chinese culture with modern, rational, and scientific ideals.

166. The West Asian ruler who captured Constantinople in 1453 CE was Sultan Mehmed II, also known as Mehmed the Conqueror. His conquest of the Byzantine capital marked the end of the Byzantine Empire and the rise of the Ottoman Empire as a dominant power in both Europe and Asia. Constantinople was renamed Istanbul, becoming a key cultural and political center of the Islamic world.

167. In 1967, Australians voted overwhelmingly in a national referendum to amend their Constitution so that Aboriginal Australians would be counted in the national census and the federal government could make laws for them. This event marked a major milestone in Australia's civil rights movement and the recognition of Indigenous Australians.

168. The Christian principle of Stewardship emphasizes responsible and caring management of God's creation, including the Earth and all living beings. It teaches that humans are caretakers, not exploiters, of natural resources, accountable to God for how they treat the environment. This idea forms a theological foundation for modern Christian environmental ethics.

169. The Tanzimat Fermani (Imperial Edict of Gülhane) was issued in 1839 by Mustafa Reşid Pasha, a leading Ottoman reformer and statesman. It marked the beginning of the Tanzimat Era (1839–1876) — a period of comprehensive administrative, legal, and educational reforms aimed at modernising the Ottoman Empire along European lines and curbing corruption and decentralisation.

170. Brian Houghton Hodgson, a British official and scholar, played a major role in consolidating trade routes and diplomatic relations with Nepal through the Residency system during the early 19th century. Stationed as the British Resident at Kathmandu, Hodgson promoted trade, ethnographic studies, and zoological research, strengthening the British-Nepalese relationship.

171. The ruler of the Mali Empire renowned for his pilgrimage to Mecca in 1324 CE was Mansa Musa. His journey, one of the most famous in history, displayed the empire's immense wealth — particularly in gold — and brought global recognition to Mali as a powerful and prosperous African state. His pilgrimage also strengthened Islamic scholarship and architecture in West Africa, especially in Timbuktu and Gao.

172. Henry Vivian Derozio, founder of the Young Bengal Movement, encouraged his students at Hindu College, Calcutta, to question all forms of authority — religious, social, and political. He promoted rationalism, scientific thinking, and individual freedom, inspiring a generation of young Indians to embrace reform and modern ideas in early 19th-century Bengal.

173. The concepts of 'Li' (principle) and 'Qi' (vital force or material energy) in Chinese cosmology were systematised by the Song dynasty philosopher Zhu Xi (1130–1200 CE). Zhu Xi's synthesis of Confucianism, metaphysics, and ethics became known as Neo-Confucianism, profoundly influencing East Asian thought for centuries.

174. Sakuma Shozan was a leading Japanese intellectual and reformer whose ideas helped shape the Meiji Restoration. He advocated the principle of "Eastern ethics and Western science" (Wakon Y□sai) — arguing that Japan should modernise through adopting Western technology while preserving Eastern moral values. His thought deeply influenced Japan's transformation into a modern nation-state in the late 19th century.

175. The Portuguese first established control over the coastal areas of Sri Lanka in 1505 CE. Led by Lourenço de Almeida, they initially arrived for trade but soon gained political control over key ports like Colombo, laying the foundation for European colonial dominance in the Indian Ocean region.

176. The ancient Chinese city considered one of the earliest known walled cities, dating to around 1900 BCE, is Erlitou. Associated with the Xia dynasty or early Shang culture, Erlitou represents the emergence of urbanism and state formation in early China. Archaeological evidence includes palatial structures, bronze workshops, and defensive walls, suggesting an early centralised authority.

177. The cult of the living virgin goddess, Kumari, is found in Nepal, particularly in Kathmandu Valley. The Kumari is a prepubescent girl worshipped as the living embodiment of the goddess Taleju (Durga). This tradition combines Hindu and Buddhist beliefs and remains a unique cultural-religious practice of Nepal to this day.

178. Thomas Hobbes is known as the father of modern absolutism. In his seminal work Leviathan (1651), he argued that to prevent chaos and civil war, individuals must surrender their freedoms to an absolute sovereign who maintains order and security. Hobbes's theory laid the philosophical groundwork for modern political absolutism and the social contract theory.

179. In Emma Tarlo's anthropological study "Unsettling Memories: Narratives of the Emergency in Delhi", the Welcome locality is described as a "site of history-making" because its residents produced their own narratives of displacement, challenging official state accounts of urban resettlement during the Emergency (1975–77). Tarlo highlights how everyday memories and oral histories contested bureaucratic narratives of "progress" and "rehabilitation."

180. The Bronze Age city of Anyang (capital of the late Shang dynasty, ca. 1300–1046 BCE) provides the first known evidence of formal Chinese writing. The discovery of oracle bones inscribed with early Chinese characters at Anyang represents the origins of Chinese script and the earliest direct record of Chinese civilisation.

181. The main purpose of role play in education is to encourage active participation and empathy among learners. It helps students understand different perspectives, develop communication skills, and apply theoretical knowledge in real-life or simulated situations. Role play also enhances critical thinking and emotional intelligence.

182. As per the National Education Policy (NEP) 2020, GIF stands for Gender Inclusion Fund. This fund aims to ensure that girls and transgender students receive equitable quality education by supporting gender-sensitive interventions and inclusive educational practices at all levels.

183. The concept of 'language across the curriculum' mainly promotes the development of language skills in all subjects. It recognises that language is not confined to language classes but is a tool for thinking, learning, and expressing ideas in every discipline, thereby improving comprehension and communication.

184. Cognitive development refers to the development of intellectual abilities and thinking processes. It includes aspects such as reasoning, memory, problem-solving, perception, and decision-making, forming the foundation of how learners understand and interact with the world.

185. Subject content analysis is important in lesson planning because it helps teachers align instructional objectives with what is taught. By analysing content, educators can identify key concepts, organise material logically, and ensure that learning outcomes are achieved effectively and coherently.

186. Enabling democratic participation in the classroom means empowering the weak and marginalised students. It ensures that every learner, regardless of background or ability, has an equal voice and opportunity to contribute. This promotes inclusivity, respect, cooperation, and shared responsibility—key elements of a democratic learning environment.

187. The most important factor when selecting learning resources for a diverse classroom is their cultural relevance and inclusivity. Resources should reflect varied cultural, social, and linguistic backgrounds, ensuring that all students feel represented and valued while promoting equity in learning.

188. A student following a deep approach to learning seeks meaning, understanding, and integration of ideas. However, the characteristic that does not fit this approach is viewing different aspects of a task as unrelated to other tasks — this reflects a surface approach instead.

189. In teaching-learning, the use of real objects—such as tools, utensils, art pieces, or clothing—from a specific culture or society is known as Realia. These tangible materials make learning concrete, experiential, and engaging, helping students connect theory with real-life contexts.

190. The discipline that deals with the study of human behaviour and mind is Psychology. It explores cognitive processes, emotions, motivation, personality, learning, and social interactions to understand how humans think, feel, and act individually and collectively.

191. During the development of a child, 'synthesis' is a cumulative process that involves the integration of various factors shaping learning and growth. The four basic elements in this process are experience, maturation, equilibration, and social transmission — as proposed in Jean Piaget's theory of cognitive development.

192. The Memory Level of Teaching, proposed by John F. Herbart, focuses primarily on rote memorisation of facts, information, and definitions. It is teacher-centred and emphasises recall rather than higher-order thinking. Therefore, the statement that it emphasises critical thinking and analysis is NOT true.

193. The Integrated Education for Disabled Children (IEDC) Scheme, launched in 1974, was the first government initiative in India to operationalise support services for children with special needs within mainstream education. It aimed at inclusive education through aids, resource support, and teacher training.

194. A teaching strategy refers to a structured plan or approach used by teachers to facilitate learning effectively. Among the given options, project-based learning is an example of a teaching strategy, as it involves experiential learning, collaboration, and problem-solving to deepen understanding.

195. Gender socialisation is a focused form of socialisation through which children learn and internalise gender roles, behaviours, and expectations associated with being male or female. It occurs through family, school, media, and peer influence, shaping identity and social norms.

196. The learner-centered approach to curriculum development prioritises the active engagement of students by focusing on their individual needs, interests, abilities, and prior experiences. It encourages autonomy, critical thinking, and experiential learning, making education more meaningful and personalized.

197. A diagnostic test is used to identify students' misconceptions, learning difficulties, and strengths. It helps teachers understand specific problem areas and design targeted remedial instruction to improve learning outcomes.

198. Social science teaching aims to develop nationalism, civic awareness, and responsible citizenship. It encourages understanding of cultural diversity, democratic values, and social justice — fostering unity and national identity among students.

199. The Think-Pair-Share technique is a quick and interactive assessment method where students first think individually about a question, then discuss it in pairs, and finally share their responses with the class. It promotes participation, collaboration, and reflection.

200. The discipline that studies human behaviour and society — including social structures, institutions, relationships, and interactions — is Sociology. It explores how societies function and how individuals and groups relate within them.

Previous Paper (Solved)

Delhi Subordinate Services Selection Board

DSSSB–PGT (History) Recruitment Exam, 2021*

Subject Knowledge – History & Teaching Methodology

1. Which inscription of Rudradamana testifies to the annexation of Sourastra in western India by Chandragupta?
A. Junagadh B. Deccan
C. Konkan D. Malwa

2. Which daughter of Seleukas did Chandragupta marry?
A. Phila B. Apama
C. Laodice D. Helena

3. Name the tributary of Indus that dried soon after the Harappan Civilisation, preserving its remains from the annual floods.
A. Hakra B. Soan
C. Luni D. Suru

4. Most of the inscription engraved on an Ashokan pillar are written in which script?
A. Nagari script
B. Devanagari script
C. Prakrit script
D. Brahmi script

5. Which of the following is not a distinct zone of the Mauryan realm?
A. peripheral areas of the kingdom
B. core area in the Ganga valley
C. the metropolitan area around Magadha
D. Deccan area

6. Which book of Panini offers valuable glimpses of socio-economic, cultural and political life of 5th century BC?
A. Sutta Nipata
B. Samyuttanikaya
C. Ashtadhyayi
D. Vinaya Pitaka

7. Who was the last Nanda king?
A. Mahanandin
B. Mahapadma Nanda
C. Pandhukananda
D. Dhana Nanda

8. Ziya Barani was a counsellor in the court of which Sultan?
A. Sultan Ala uddin Khalji
B. Sultan Muhammad bin Tughlaq
C. Sultan Firoz Shah Tughlaq
D. Sultan Shams al-Din Iltutmish

9. The Malfuzat-I-Timuri was written in which language?
A. Kurdish B. Mongolian
C. Persian D. Arabic

10. Which of the following dynasties did not contribute in the rise of the Magadh empire?
A. Mauryan dynasty
B. Haryanka dynasty
C. Gupta Dynasty
D. Shaishunaga dynasty

11. Who was the court poet of Samudragupta?
A. Achyuta
B. Ganapatideva
C. Harisena
D. Nagasena

* Online exam held on 10/07/2021.

12. According to Puranas, Jain and Buddhist texts Mahapadma Nanda belonged to which varna?

A. Kshatriya B. Vaishya
C. Shudra D. Brahmin

13. What is Mahapadma Nanda not described as in the puranas?

A. Sarvakshatrantaka
B. Amitraghata
C. Second Parasurama
D. Ekrat

14. During the reign of which king did thirty-six republics including Vriji and Malla formed a confederacy and started war with Magadha?

A. Kalasoka B. Ajatasatru
C. Bimbisara D. Dhana Nanda

15. Which Gupta emperor is described as the 'Maharajadhiraja'?

A. Samudragupta
B. Chandragupta I
C. Ghatotkacha
D. Srigupta

16. Which of the following was not a metallurgical technique of Harappan civilization?

A. Two-piece stone moulds
B. Shallow casting
C. Cold hammering
D. Hydrometallurgy

17. Bimbisara belonged to which dynasty?

A. Haryanka dynasty
B. Nanda dynasty
C. Mauryan dynasty
D. Shaishunaga dynasty

18. Who wrote Kathasarit Sagar?

A. Kshemendra
B. Somdeva Bhatta
C. Kautilya
D. Vishakhadeva

19. Abul Fazl's elucidation of the principle of sovereignty is contained in which book?

A. Fatwa-i-Jahandari
B. Tarikh-i-Rashidi
C. Tarikh-i-Hukama
D. Akbarnama

20. Which was the main source of Harappan images and writing?

A. tomb paintings
B. rocks
C. seals
D. copper tablet

21. Name the book written by Fakhr-i Mudabbir.

A. Tarikh-i-Rashidi
B. Adab ul harb wa'sh Shujat
C. Fatawa-i-Jahandari
D. Malfuztl-Timuri

22. Who painted 'The Grand-Duke's Madonna' in 1505?

A. Giovanni Bellini
B. Giorgione
C. Raphael
D. Titian

23. Who founded the Brahmo Samaj?

A. Ramakrishna Paramhansa
B. Ishwar Chandra Vidyasagar
C. Dayananda Saraswati
D. Raja Ram Mohan Roy

24. Which of the following is not an ancillary discipline?

A. chronology
B. archaeology
C. philology
D. technology

25. Name the painter who painted 'The creation of Adam' in the Sistine Chapel

A. Michelangelo
B. Donatello
C. Raphael
D. Leonardo da Vinci

26. Which state was under Hyder Ali Khan and Tipu Sultan?

A. Hyderabad B. Bijapur
C. Mysore D. Awadh

27. To escape the problem of civic strife, most Italian cities adapted ....

A. aristocracy B. feudalism
C. republicanism D. signoria

28. Which Florentine scholar wrote 'The Prince' in 1513?
A. Desiderius Erasmus
B. Niccolo Machiavelli
C. Guillaume Bude
D. Giotto di Baondone

29. Under which act would India be governed directly by and in the name of the Crown, acting through a Secretary of State?
A. India Act of 1858
B. Act for the Better Government of India
C. Government of India Act, 1858
D. Indian Councils Act

30. What is Balkrishnabuva Ichalkaranjikar known for?
A. Dramatic Vocal music
B. Instrument music
C. Hindustani Music
D. Musical dramas

31. What is the science of language that deals with the patterns of sounds called?
A. philosophy B. phonology
C. physiology D. philology

32. The study of God and religious subjects is called ....
A. Theology B. idolatry
C. Mythology D. Philosophy

33. Where did the first serious mutiny break out in 1806?
A. Meerut B. Awadh
C. Vellore D. Jhansi

34. Which of the following factors do not determine the ability of a author of documents, to tell the truth about the source?
A. Alertness and the dexterity of attention
B. Rational approach
C. Prejudice
D. Keen observation

35. What does Renaissance mean?
A. Re-Birth
B. Determination
C. Enlightenment
D. Birth

36. When was the Clemency Resolution passed?
A. 31 July 1857
B. 15 March 1857
C. 30 June 1857
D. 31 May 1857

37. Who authored the Doctrine of Lapse?
A. Lord Dalhousie B. Lord Canning
C. Lord Acton D. Lord Curson

38. In which year did Aurangzeb die?
A. 1700 B. 1707
C. 1701 D. 1717

39. The British Parliament permitted uninterrupted flow of European missionaries in which act?
A. The Indian universities Act
B. Charter Act of 1813
C. India Act
D. Indian Council Act

40. Which of the following is not a category of devotion as referred by Rizvi?
A. mal B. jan
C. namus D. adab

41. What was the socio-religious reform movement also known as?
A. Indian National Movement
B. Indian Awakening
C. Indian Renaissance
D. Indian Nationalism

42. Name the volume on the history of Vijayanagara, written by Robert Sewell, that appeared in the year 1900.
A. Peasant State and Society
B. New Cambridge History of India
C. A History of South India
D. A Forgotten Empire

43. Who founded the Arya Samaj?
A. Atmaram Pandurang
B. Swami Dayananda Saraswati
C. Ramakrishna Gopal Bhandarkar
D. Mahadev Govind Ranade

44. When was Federation of Indian Chambers of Commerce and Industry (FICCI) established?
A. 1975 B. 1972
C. 1927 D. 1957

45. Who among the following is not a Nationalist Historian?
A. Ramakrishna Gopal Bhandarkar
B. Dadabhai Naoroji
C. Damodar Dharmananda Kosambi
D. Romesh Chunder Dutt

46. Which of the following periodicals did not become daily newspapers later?
A. Dnyanodaya
B. Hindupanch
C. Dnyan Prakash
D. Induprakash

47. Which movement was suddenly suspended following the mob-violence at Chauri Chaura in Uttar Pradesh?
A. Civil Disobedience Movement
B. The Non-Cooperation Movement
C. Peasants Movement
D. The Quit India Movement

48. Who was the first Indian woman socialist and also the first Indian woman revolutionary who fought for her motherland's freedom, after the 1857 uprising?
A. Sarojini Naidu
B. Kasturba Gandhi
C. Madam Bhikaji Cama
D. Dr. Annie Besant

49. Who among the following historians belonged to the Annales School of History?
A. Marc Bloch
B. Antonio Gramsci
C. David Arnold
D. John Stuart Mills

50. Which school of thought follows an approach to knowledge based on observation or experience but not theory?
A. Annales School
B. Subaltern School
C. Nationalist School
D. Empiricist School

51. Where was the first session of All India Kisan Sabha held?
A. Pune B. Bombay
C. Lucknow D. Mysore

52. When was Ramkrishna Mission established?
A. 15 May, 1899
B. 1 May, 1897
C. 15 May, 1897
D. 5 May, 1898

53. Who was the first president of the Indian National Congress?
A. Samuel Aaron
B. Jamnalal Baja
C. Mr. Womesh Chunder Bonnerjee
D. Dadabhai Naoroji

54. The Factory Act, that sought to limit the working hours of children and women was passed in which year?
A. 1891 B. 1898
C. 1888 D. 1890

55. In which year did the Indian Naval Mutiny take place?
A. 1946 B. 1944
C. 1945 D. 1947

56. Name the first Boarding House opened by Chhatrapati Shahu Maharaj.
A. Victoria Maratha Boarding
B. Shahu Boarding House
C. Chatrapati Shahu Boarding
D. Shri Prince Shivaji Maratha Boarding House

57. Name the official manual and gazetteer of Akbar's reign.
A. Akbarnama
B. Sulh-i-kul
C. Tarikh-i-Hukama
D. Ain-i-Akbari

58. Who founded the Theosophical Society?
A. Madame Blavatsky
B. Neili Sengupta
C. Annie Besant
D. Margaret Cousins

59. What ideology did Akbar follow to sustain the principle of authority and subordination in a hierarchical pattern?
A. Imperial ideology
B. Liberal ideology
C. Dominant ideology
D. Conservative ideology

60. Who had been the Secretary of State for India from 1874 and Prime-Minister from 1886 to 1892?
A. Lord Ripon
B. Lord Salisbury
C. Lord Dufferin
D. Lord Cross

61. Which country was labelled a "Garrison state" due to its lengthy trysts with military regimes?
A. Pakistan B. Bangladesh
C. India D. Nepal

62. Aurangzeb decided to streamline the revenue administration in Bengal to finance funds against whom?
A. Mongols B. Sikhs
C. Rajputs D. Marathas

63. Where was zabt not adopted in totality in 1600?
A. Gujarat B. Agra
C. Lahore D. Multan

64. According to the study of Toxic Wastes in the United States, who among the following was least likely to live in an area damaged by toxic wastes?
A. Latinos
B. African Americans
C. Whites
D. Native Americans

65. Where did the "Redwood Rabbis" of Jewish community engage in a public struggle to protect one of the areas last remaining stands of Redwood trees?
A. Colorado B. Texas
C. Florida D. California

66. Who is recognized as 'The Father of the Nation' or 'Father of the Republic of China'?
A. Mao Zedong
B. Sun Yat-sen
C. Chiang Kai-shek
D. Deng Xiaoping

67. Where did the May Fourth Movement start?
A. Shanghai B. Peking
C. Taipei D. Canton

68. When did the first Anglo-Burmese War take place?
A. 1829 B. 1822
C. 1820 D. 1824

69. The Antyaja constitute of which caste?
A. Kshatriya B. Dalit
C. Brahman D. Vaishya

70. When did Laos become a French protectorate?
A. 1867 B. 1875
C. 1899 D. 1893

71. Which resolution was adopted by the Muslim League demanding the formation of an independent Pakistan?
A. Multan Resolution
B. Lahore Resolution
C. Karachi Resolution
D. Islamabad Resolution

72. Which language was earlier known as Khas Kura?
A. Nepali B. Sinhala
C. Pali D. Bhutanese

73. What was the Mughal ranking system called?
A. Asrzi system
B. Jagidari system
C. Zabt system
D. Mansabdari system

74. Which party did Yuan Shi-kai form?
A. Kuomintang
B. Republican Party
C. Chinese Communist Party
D. Comintern

75. Which was the first commercial capital of Tokugawa Japan?
A. Osaka B. Kyoto
C. Tokyo D. Edo

76. Which of the following countries did not participate in the 'Slicing of the Chinese Melon'?
A. India B. Russia
C. France D. Japan

77. Who sold the island of Penang to the British in 1790?
A. Sultan of Kedah
B. Sultan of Johor
C. Sultan of Malacca
D. Sultan of Kelantan

78. Which of the following is not a registered political party of Maldives?
A. Maldivian Democratic Party
B. People's Democratic Alliance
C. Dhivehi Raiyyithunge Party
D. Adhaalath Party

79. The Shu Tzi organization, that helped recycle millions of pounds of paper and metal, belongs to which country?
A. Laos B. Philippines
C. Vietnam D. Taiwan

80. Which South Asian country is not within the confines of India's regional security framework?
A. Sri Lanka B. Pakistan
C. Nepal D. Bhutan

81. The Reserve Bank of India was set up on the basis of recommendations by which of the following Commissions?
A. National Statistical Commission
B. Hilton Young Commission
C. Barbington Smith Commission
D. Raleigh Commission

82. Which of the following Acts was not associated with "The Stolen Generation" phenomena caused by the Australian Federal and State government agencies?
A. The Native Administration Act (1936)
B. The Aboriginal Ordinance Act (1918)
C. The Aborigines Protection Act (1909)
D. The Aborigines Act (1934)

83. How many jatis are there according to the Varna-samkarah (mixture of varnas)?
A. 57 B. 62
C. 35 D. 75

84. The Vandalic or Vandal War was fought between which two Civilizations?
A. Byzantine - Kanem
B. Wadai - Shilluk
C. Byzantine - Carthage
D. Carthage - Shilluk

85. In which year did the British try to conquer the French colony of Haiti?
A. 1799-1804 B. 1791-1796
C. 1798-1803 D. 1793-1798

86. The concept of moksha or nirvana is linked with the perception of which God?
A. Brahma B. Vishnu
C. Ganesh D. Mahesh

87. Who is the author of the book "Indische Alterthumskunde" published in four volumes between 1847 and 1861?
A. Richard Fick B. Christian Lassen
C. Hegel D. Voltaire

88. Which aspect of Indian culture is divided into Natya, Nritya and Nritta?
A. Theatre
B. Dance
C. Art and Architecture
D. Music

89. Which of the following inventions produced in South India from about 300BCE was used for making "Damascus Swords" renowned for their toughness and sharpness?
A. Zinc B. Copper alloy
C. Wootz Steel D. Iron

90. The stone tool technology, "Acheulean" was developed by which hominid species?

A. Homo georgicus
B. Homo habilis
C. Homo erectus
D. Homo sapien

91. What is the language of Vedas?
A. Sanskrit B. Hindi
C. Prakrit D. Pali

92. Which period among the following is Known as the Golden Age of Indian coinage?
A. Mauryan period
B. Gupta period
C. Mughal Period
D. Chola period

93. Who authored the book "Indian Atheism" published in 1969?
A. Debiprasad Chattopadhyaya
B. Satish Chandra
C. Bipan Chandra
D. Ramakrishna Bhattacharya

94. Which of the following is not true about culture?
A. Culture is cumulative
B. Culture is learned and acquired
C. Culture is shared by a group of people
D. Culture is stagnant

95. Which of the following civilizations was not associated with the economy of the Indus valley civilization?
A. Mesopotamia
B. Southeast Asia
C. China
D. Persia

96. Which Indian Maharishi devised the concept of "anu" which is closely related to the atomic theory of John Dalton?
A. Sushruta B. Kanad
C. Chanakya D. Panini

97. Who among the following is the architect of the Red Fort?
A. Imad al-Din Riyadi
B. Abdul Hamid Muharrar Ghaznavi
C. Ustad Ahmad Lahouri
D. Abdul Khair Khairullah

98. Archaeological findings from which of the following sites in the IVC indicates that dentistry was practiced as early as 7000BCE by skilled Bead Crafters?
A. Lothal B. Mehrgarh
C. Dholavira D. Babar Kot

99. Which ruler introduced the concept of "rupee" or "rupaiyah"?
A. Babur
B. Bindusara
C. Sher Shah Suri
D. Shah Jahan

100. What is the earliest example of the use of gunpowder by the Ottoman Empire?
A. Battle of Chaldiran
B. Battle of Ankara
C. Seige of Constantinople
D. Battle of Varna

101. Which historian put forward the view that the Namahsudras have close relations with North Indian Brahmins?
A. Ramesh Chandra Majumdar
B. Niharranjan Ray
C. Bipan Chandra
D. Sarat Chandra Roy

102. "Pravasi Bharatiya Divas" is celebrated on ..... .
A. 19th June
B. 23rd November
C. 9th January
D. 2nd October

103. Who among these women wrote the "Stri Purush Tulana" (1882) which is considered to be India's first Feminist text?
A. Tarabai Shinde
B. Savitribai Phule
C. Jind Kaur
D. Kamini Roy

104. According to Megasthenes, which of these rulers first attempted to establish a navy?
A. Dasharatha
B. Chandragupta Maurya
C. Ashoka
D. Bindusara

105. Which of the following Indian rulers aided the British to quell the Santhal Rebellion?

A. Nawab of Awadh
B. Nawab of Murshidabad
C. Nizam of Hyderabad
D. Nawab of Ghazipur

106. Identify the traditional festival, largely celebrated in Odhisa, to commemorate the day traders and merchants set sail for Southeast Asia.

A. Boita Bandana
B. Magha Saptami
C. Rath Yatra
D. Nuakhai

107. Which of the following tribes originated in the Southern Chinese province of Yunnan?

A. Chakmas B. Ahoms
C. Garo D. Mundas

108. Anandibai Gopalrao Joshi (1865-87) was associated with which of the following professions?

A. Literature
B. Medicine
C. Social Reform
D. Music

109. Who was the editor of the periodical, "The Adyar Bulletin"?

A. Anne Besant
B. Savitribai Phule
C. Helena Petrovna Blavatsky
D. Krupabai Satthianadhan

110. The "Persons of Indian Origin" (PIO) card scheme was launched by the government in the year ....

A. 1998 B. 1990
C. 1999 D. 1996

111. The "Mundari" language of the Munda tribe falls under which language family?

A. Austronesian
B. Austro-asiatic
C. Dravidian
D. Afro-Asiatic

112. Which of these dynasties was actively involved in combating piracy in the Malacca strait in Southeast Asia?

A. Chola Dynasty
B. Pandyan Dynasty
C. Chalukya Dynasty
D. Pallava Dynasty

113. In which part of India are the "Onge" indigenous people settled?

A. Adirondack Mountains
B. Khasi-Jayantia Hills
C. Andaman islands
D. Chota Nagpur Plateau

114. "India : A Million Mutinies Now" is written by which of these diasporic writers?

A. Jhumpa Lahiri
B. Salman Rushdie
C. Vidiadhar Surajprasad Naipaul
D. Kiran Desai

115. In which of these periods do we observe considerable advantages for women in education, marriage, arts and even warfare?

A. Post Vedic Period
B. Early Vedic Period
C. Colonial Period
D. Mughal Period

116. Under which government act were the Santhal Paraganas declared to be "partially exclusive areas" where no act of legislature applied unless the Governor directed it by prior public notification?

A. Government of India Act, 1909
B. Government of India Act, 1858
C. Government of India Act, 1935
D. Government of India Act, 1919

117. The Chotanagpur Tenancy Act was passed in which of the following years:

A. 1900 B. 1905
C. 1908 D. 1901

118. In which of the following Harappan settlements was the first evidence of a dockyard found?

A. Lothal B. Malwan
C. Dholavira D. Babar Kot

119. "From the Caves to the Jungles of Hindostan" (1879-86) is the literary work of which of the following women?
A. Ismat Chughtai
B. Anne Besant
C. Helena Petrovna Blavatsky
D. Kamini Roy

120. Who was the leader of the Khasi Revolt?
A. Chattra Sing Syiem
B. Rajendra Sing Syiem
C. Prabhat Ray Syiem
D. Tirot Sing Syiem

121. The Green Revolution in India commenced under the leadership of which Prime Minister?
A. Morarji Desai
B. Indira Gandhi
C. Jawaharlal Nehru
D. Lal Bahadur Shastri

122. Which of these four schools of historiography downplays "ideology" in its approach?
A. Marxist School
B. Nationalist School
C. Cambridge School
D. Subaltern School

123. Under which operation did India deploy Indian Peace Keeping Force to Sri Lanka?
A. Operation Sahyog
B. Operation Vijay
C. Operation Pawan
D. Operation Woodrose

124. The "Indo-Soviet Treaty of Peace, Friendship and Co-operation" was signed in ....
A. August, 1971 B. April, 1976
C. August, 1951 D. April, 1975

125. "Oral Tradition" or "Oral Lore" can be classified as:
A. Tertiary Sources
B. Secondary sources
C. Primary Sources
D. Third-Party Sources

126. The "Apsara", India's oldest research reactor, was built with the assistance of which country?
A. United Kingdom
B. Soviet Union
C. United States of America
D. China

127. The book "Humanism : A New Religion" can be credited to which of the following Humanists?
A. Thomas Mann
B. John Dewey
C. Julian Huxley
D. Charles Francis Potter

128. Which of the following is not a cause of/ least affects Postmodern Scepticism?
A. Shifting terrain of power configurations
B. Simulational technologies
C. Radical changes in the nature of phenomena
D. Arbitrary linguistical hierarchies

129. Which of the following schools attached the "Aryan" label to Indian history?
A. Subaltern School
B. Nationalist School
C. Marxist School
D. Orientalist School

130. "Indian National Committee for Space Research" (INCOSPAR), which was dissolved with the formation of ISRO, was set up in the year:
A. 1962 B. 1965
C. 1960 D. 1969

131. The following argument: state making is similar to organized crime because it is a "quintessential protection racket with the advantage of legitimacy" was made by which scholar?
A. Daniel Bell
B. Michel Foucault
C. Auguste Comte
D. Charles Tilly

132. Which of the following treaties is one of the two treaties that compromise the "Peace of Westphalia"?
A. Treaty of Lyon
B. Treaty of Antwerp
C. Treaty of Münster
D. Treaty of Munich

133. "Descriptio Indiæ" is a source of Indian Historiography written by:
A. Roger Joseph Boscovich
B. Joseph Tiefenthaler
C. Albertus Magnus
D. Gregor Mendel

134. In which year was the Reserve Bank of India nationalised?
A. 1952 B. 1950
C. 1955 D. 1949

135. "Indian Numismatics" (1981) is written by which of the following historians?
A. R.S. Sharma
B. Irfan Habib
C. Damodar Dharmananda Kosambi
D. A. Aiyappan

136. Which of these historians was particularly averted to Hegel's "concept of philosophy" in history?
A. William Carrigan
B. Leopold von Ranke
C. John Lanigan
D. John Thomas Gilbert

137. The view that the top officials of the East India Company were responsible for plundering the Indian economy and society can be attributed to which of these following historians?
A. Gordon Johnson
B. Rajat Kanta Ray
C. Anil Seal
D. Romila Thapar

138. The term "Licence Raj" was coined by which one of the following:
A. B.N. Adarkar
B. Montek Singh Ahluwalia
C. Bhimrao Ramji Ambedkar
D. Chakravarti Rajagopalachari

139. The Battle of Diu, between the Portuguese and Gujarat being backed by Muslim allied forces, was fought in the year ....
A. 1500 B. 1524
C. 1516 D. 1509

140. What is epistemology?
A. Study of the nature, origin and limits of human knowledge.
B. The branch of metaphysics dealing with the nature of being.
C. Writing of history based on the critical examination of sources.
D. Science of phenomena as distinct from the nature of being.

141. The French established "French Indochina" in Southeast Asia after which of these wars?
A. Franco-Siamese War
B. Cambodian-Vietnamese war
C. Sino-French War
D. First Indochina War

142. The Italian Parliament passed the "Law of Guarantees" (Law of Papal Guarantees) in the year:
A. 1922 B. 1871
C. 1876 D. 1929

143. The Treaty of Portsmouth (1905) signed between Russia and Japan, gave Japan dominance over which of these Asian countries?
A. Korea B. Indonesia
C. Singapore D. Malaysia

144. Through which of these following Acts was one seat in the Governor Generals Executive Council reserved for an Indian?
A. Indian Councils Act, 1892
B. Indian Councils Act, 1909
C. Government of India Act, 1919
D. Government of India Act, 1935

145. Who among these explorers was successful in establishing the Spanish colony in the Philippines?

A. Hernan Cortez
B. Miguel Lopez de Legazpi
C. Ferdinand Magellan
D. Diego de Almagro

146. "A Discourse of Trade from England unto the East Indies", (1621) is the work of which of the following mercantilists?
A. Josiah Child
B. Thomas Mun
C. Charles Davenant
D. Jean Bodin

147. Between the 1960s and 1990s, the economies of the "Four Asian Tigers" underwent rapid industrialization. This group includes:
A. Singapore, Thailand, Burma, Indonesia
B. South Korea, Taiwan, Singapore, Hong Kong.
C. South Korea, Malaysia, Thailand, Singapore
D. Indonesia, South Korea, North Korea, Thailand

148. Which of these monarchs personally owned the "The Congo State" as a result of treaties signed by the Congo chiefs?
A. Leopold I B. Albert I
C. Albert II D. Leopold II

149. President's rule has never been imposed in which of the following states?
A. Assam B. Kerala
C. Chhattisgarh D. Nagaland

150. When was the Ministry of Development of North Eastern Region established?
A. September, 2011
B. September, 2001
C. September, 2008
D. September, 2007

151. "The Wealth of Nations" (1776) by Adam Smith, severely attacks which of these economic policies?
A. Capitalism B. Socialism
C. Mercantilism D. Laissez-faire

152. Which of the following is the world's oldest publicly listed company?
A. The Bombay Burma Trading Company
B. The Dutch East India Company (VOC)
C. Imperial Privilege Oriental Company
D. The East India Company

153. Which among the following was the hallmark of the French Colonial Mission?
A. Slave Trade
B. Mercantilism
C. Civilising mission
D. Spice Trade

154. When did the British take over Java from the Dutch?
A. 1811 B. 1829
C. 1824 D. 1814

155. Who was the Architect of the Second five year plan that laid special emphasis on Industrialization?
A. Prasanta Chandra Mahalanobis
B. K.N. Raj
C. Jawaharlal Nehru
D. Amartya Sen

156. The "Guelphs and the Ghibellines" during Renaissance refers to:
A. Mandates adopted by city states with regards to trade.
B. Warring factions siding with the Pope or the king.
C. Supporters of Humanism and Scholasticism respectively.
D. Italian city states

157. Japan began its imperialist pursuit during which of the following periods?
A. Azuchi-Momoyama Period
B. Edo Period
C. Muromachi Period
D. Meiji Period

158. Which of the following cases was a landmark judgement with regards to the imposition of "President's rule"?

A. M.C. Mehta Case
B. S.R. Bommai Case
C. Kesavananda Bharti Case
D. Golaknath Case

159. French colonial pursuit was successful in attempts to colonize:
A. Rio de Janeiro, Brazil
B. Florida, America
C. Nova Scotia, Canada
D. Sao Luis, Brazil

160. Which of the following aspects is not considered a cause of Industrial Revolution?
A. Government policy of "protectionism".
B. Surge in population.
C. The development of new methods of communication and banking.
D. The setting up of new commercial lines for steam engines.

161. Which amendment to the Indian constitution provides for the establishment of Metropolitan Planning Committees in urban Areas?
A. 74th Amendment
B. 54th Amendment
C. 62nd amendment
D. 43rd Amendment

162. Whose doctrinal system, among these listed philosophers, was adopted by the Roman Catholic Church as its official philosophy in 1917?
A. Thomas Aquinas
B. Pope Gregory X
C. Immanuel Kant
D. Albertus Magnus

163. The Bishnoi Movement of the 1700's took place in which Indian State?
A. Gujarat
B. Punjab
C. Maharashtra
D. Rajasthan

164. Which of the following was the first ever environmental law passed in the Indian subcontinent in 1865?
A. Forest Conservation Act
B. Indian Forests Act
C. Air (Prevention and Control of Pollution) Act
D. Wildlife Protection Act

165. Which part of the Indian Constitution relates to the Panchayat?
A. Part IX B. Part VI
C. Part V D. Part XI

166. When was "the Urban Land (Ceiling and Regulation) Act" (1976) repealed?
A. 2002 B. 1999
C. 2005 D. 2007

167. The "Jawaharlal Nehru National Urban Renewal Mission" was launched in the year:
A. 2002 B. 2008
C. 1999 D. 2005

168. The principle that, "it is the greatest happiness of the greatest number that is the measure of right or wrong", is associated with which of these English philosophers?
A. Jeremy Bentham
B. John Stuart Mill
C. John Locke
D. Thomas Hobbes

169. Who among these Indian political thinkers popularized and contributed most to the ideology of "Hindutva"?
A. Ram Manohar Lohia
B. Vivekananda
C. Vinayak Damodar Savarkar
D. Periyar

170. Which of the following cases is related to the "Anti-Defection Law"?
A. A.K. Gopalan Case
B. Shankari Prasad Case
C. Kihoto Hollohan Case
D. I.R. Coelho Case

171. Which of the following economists coined the phrase "Hindu Rate of Growth"?
A. Bhimrao Ramji Ambedkar
B. Raj Krishna
C. Shankar Acharya
D. Amartya Sen

172. The "Discourses on Livy" is the work of which political thinker?
A. Niccolo Machiavelli
B. Thomas Aquinas
C. Aristotle
D. Erasmus

173. Who among these female activists founded the "Arya Mahila Samaj"?
A. Margaret Cousins
B. Savitribai Phule
C. Pandita Ramabai
D. Dr. Vina Mazumdar

174. Which of these British Prime Ministers introduced the "Communal Award"?
A. Winston Churchill
B. Clement Attlee
C. Anthony Eden
D. Ramsay MacDonald

175. "Annihilation of Caste" by Bhimrao Ramji Ambedkar, was written in the year:
A. 1916 B. 1936
C. 1926 D. 1946

176. The following opening sentence belongs to which of the following works, "Man is born free; and everywhere he is in chains"?
A. Leviathan
B. The Social Contract
C. An Essay Concerning Human Understanding
D. A System of Logic

177. "The Closing Circle : Nature Man and Technology" (1971) was written by which of the following ecologists?
A. Barry Bishop
B. Rachel Carson
C. Robert Whittaker
D. Barry Commoner

178. "Sambad Kaumudi", the Bengali, pro-reformist, weekly newspaper was owned by which of these reformists?
A. Raja Ram Mohan Roy
B. Rabindranath Tagore
C. Debendranath Tagore
D. Bhabani Charan Bandopadhyay

179. When did Manabendra Nath Roy break off his association with The Communist International?
A. 1945 B. 1929
C. 1940 D. 1919

180. The Constitution of India describes India as a ....
A. Democratic Republic
B. Meritocratic Republic
C. Federal Republic
D. Presidential Democracy

181. .... retarded individuals have IQ scores of 20 to 40 and they may master very basic self-care skills and some communication skills.
A. Severe B. Profound
C. Mild D. Moderate

182. What does ICIDH stands for?
A. Integrated Classification of Impairments, Disabilities, and Handicaps
B. International Classification of Impairments, Disabilities, and Handicaps
C. Inclusive Classification of Impairments, Disabilities, and Handicaps
D. Indian Classification of Impairments, Disabilities, and Handicaps

183. Which gland is situated at the base of the brain and has two lobes named anterior and posterior?
A. Adrenal Gland
B. Pituitary Gland
C. Thyroid Glands
D. Endocrine Glands

184. .... is a fast and efficient way to provide immediate feedback to the learner, and to save time on tutor marking.
A. Continuous and Comprehension Evaluation
B. Computer Assisted Assessment
C. Essay type questions
D. Multiple Choice Questions

185. .... by a family member is a form of incest, and results in more serious and long-term psychological trauma.

A. Sexually explicit media contact
B. Verbal Comments
C. Sexual Abuse
D. Non-verbal actions

186. Who is the father of modern linguistics and one of the pioneers of Cognitive Science?
A. Ferdinand De Saussure
B. L.H. Clarke
C. Burrhus Frederic Skinner
D. Noam Chomsky

187. For Indian women, what was the Medieval India considered as?
A. Renaissance
B. Middle Age
C. Reform Age
D. Dark Age

188. Learning disability in writing is known as ....
A. Dyslexia
B. Dysgraphia
C. Dyscalculia
D. Dyspraxia

189. Concept mapping comes under which type of assessment?
A. Thinking skills assessment
B. Technology & Media-Based assessments
C. Activity based assessments
D. Art based assessment

190. Name the psychologist who accidently noticed secretion of saliva in the dog on the sight of food.
A. Burrhus Frederic Skinner
B. Sigmund Freud
C. Ivan Pavlov
D. Edward Lee Thorndike

191. .... is an imaginative activity, original and has a value.
A. Self-actualisation
B. Motivation
C. Attention
D. Creative work

192. Which inventory was originally devised by Hathaway and McKinley to aid clinical psychologists in the diagnosis of psychological disorders?
A. Millon Clinical Multiaxial Inventory
B. NEO-Personality Inventory
C. Minnesota Multi Phasic Personality Inventory
D. Bell Adjustment Inventory

193. The four types of non-verbal classroom communication are body language, eye contact, clapping and ....
A. smile
B. project
C. written test
D. assignment

194. .... is the capacity to think logically and solve problems in novel situations, independent of acquired knowledge.
A. Graphology
B. Fluid Intelligence
C. Elaboration
D. Crystallised Intelligence

195. Under which article The Right to Education Act (RTE), 2009 makes provisions for free and compulsory education for children between age 6 and 14 of the Indian Constitution?
A. Article 21 (A)
B. Article 15
C. Article 21
D. Article 12

196. With which sense is tactile stimuli associated?
A. tasting
B. hearing
C. feeling or touch
D. smelling

197. On what approach is critical pedagogy based on?
A. Pedagogical approach
B. Trait approach
C. Problem posing approach
D. Constructive approach

198. Which category of gender analysis refers to changes in social aspects of the participants lives as the result of the project?
A. Labour
B. Time
C. Cultural
D. Resource

199. Which type of text informs, explains, describes or defines that author's subject to the reader?
A. Transactional
B. Narrative
C. Expository
D. Reflective

200. Which principle of classical conditioning is the initial stage of learning when a response is first established and gradually strengthened?
A. Principle of Acquisition
B. Principle of Spontaneous recovery
C. Principle of Stimulus Generalisation
D. Principle of Extinction

ANSWERS

1	2	3	4	5	6	7	8	9	10
A	D	A	D	D	C	D	B	B	C
11	**12**	**13**	**14**	**15**	**16**	**17**	**18**	**19**	**20**
C	C	B	B	B	D	A	B	D	C
21	**22**	**23**	**24**	**25**	**26**	**27**	**28**	**29**	**30**
B	C	D	D	A	C	D	B	C	C
31	**32**	**33**	**34**	**35**	**36**	**37**	**38**	**39**	**40**
B	A	C	C	A	A	A	B	B	D
41	**42**	**43**	**44**	**45**	**46**	**47**	**48**	**49**	**50**
C	D	B	C	C	B	B	C	A	D
51	**52**	**53**	**54**	**55**	**56**	**57**	**58**	**59**	**60**
C	B	C	A	A	D	D	A	A	B
61	**62**	**63**	**64**	**65**	**66**	**67**	**68**	**69**	**70**
A	D	A	C	D	B	B	D	B	D
71	**72**	**73**	**74**	**75**	**76**	**77**	**78**	**79**	**80**
B	A	D	B	D	A	A	B	D	B
81	**82**	**83**	**84**	**85**	**86**	**87**	**88**	**89**	**90**
B	C	A	C	D	A	B	B	C	C
91	**92**	**93**	**94**	**95**	**96**	**97**	**98**	**99**	**100**
A	B	A	D	B	B	C	B	C	C
101	**102**	**103**	**104**	**105**	**106**	**107**	**108**	**109**	**110**
B	C	A	B	B	A	B	B	A	C
111	**112**	**113**	**114**	**115**	**116**	**117**	**118**	**119**	**120**
B	A	C	C	B	C	C	A	C	D
121	**122**	**123**	**124**	**125**	**126**	**127**	**128**	**129**	**130**
D	C	C	A	C	A	D	C	D	A

131	132	133	134	135	136	137	138	139	140
D	C	B	D	C	B	B	D	D	A
141	**142**	**143**	**144**	**145**	**146**	**147**	**148**	**149**	**150**
C	B	A	B	B	B	B	D	C	B
151	**152**	**153**	**154**	**155**	**156**	**157**	**158**	**159**	**160**
C	B	C	D	A	B	D	B	C	A
161	**162**	**163**	**164**	**165**	**166**	**167**	**168**	**169**	**170**
A	A	D	B	A	B	D	A	C	C
171	**172**	**173**	**174**	**175**	**176**	**177**	**178**	**179**	**180**
B	A	C	D	B	B	D	A	B	A
181	**182**	**183**	**184**	**185**	**186**	**187**	**188**	**189**	**190**
A	B	B	B	C	D	D	B	A	C
191	**192**	**193**	**194**	**195**	**196**	**197**	**198**	**199**	**200**
D	C	A	B	A	C	C	C	C	A

Previous Paper (Solved)

Delhi Subordinate Services Selection Board

DSSSB–PGT (History) Recruitment Exam, 2018*

Subject Knowledge – History & Teaching Methodology

1. The most important industry at Lothal and Chanu daro was:
A. Metallurgical products
B. Shipbuilding
C. Handlooms
D. Bead making

2. A central government Mauryan officer in charge of revenue collection was called:
A. Karmika B. Samaharta
C. Adhyaksha D. Sannidhata

3. Harappan weapons were made from:
A. All of the other options
B. Copper
C. Bronze
D. Stone

4. Harappan towns were divided into large _____ blocks.
A. semi-circular B. circular
C. rectangular D. square

5. Which of the following options represents two important Harappan crops?
A. Rice and lentils
B. Cotton and sugar cane
C. Sesame and mustard
D. Wheat and barley

6. Maurya chronology hinges around the date of:
A. Year of Asoka's coronation
B. Buddha's death
C. Alexander's invasion
D. Mahavira's death

7. How were the later-day Guptas related to the Imperial Guptas?
A. Through marriage
B. As a junior branch of the imperial family
C. As members of the same line
D. As feudatories

8. The state promoted trade in ancient India through:
A. All of the other options
B. Ensuring security on trade routes
C. Maintaining roads
D. Establishing market towns

9. Of the sixteen Mahajanapadas referenced, how many were located in the Ganga valley?
A. 15 B. 10
C. 4 D. 7

10. The entry port for trade between the Indus trading centres and Mesopotamia was:
A. Elam B. Bahrain
C. Oman D. Afghanistan

11. The inhabitants of Anga and Magadha Janapadas were held in contempt because:
A. They traded in certain articles not favoured by the Brahmanical law givers
B. They supported the Buddha
C. They were heretics
D. They were black-skinned

12. Which animals was engraved on most Harappan seals?
A. Bison
B. Humpless bull/Unicorn

* Online exam held on 05/07/2018.

C. Elephant
D. Tiger

13. The most important Harappan item(s) of export was/were:
A. Metals and precious stones
B. Foodgrains
C. Pottery
D. Textiles

14. Which city was the first metropolis of the Ganga civilisation?
A. Pataliputra B. Kausambhi
C. Vaishali D. Rajgriha

15. Which of the following was a reason for Harappans to move from their urban sites?
A. Hydrological changes
B. Foreign invasion
C. Demographic changes
D. Environmental changes

16. Any record pertaining to the Gupta empire is NOT available post which of the following dates?
A. 533 CE B. 535 CE
C. 500 CE D. 543 CE

17. Copper in Harappan times was obtained from:
A. Mesopotamia B. Baluchistan
C. Khetri mines D. Barbarikon

18. Which group first faced Samudragupta's imperial designs?
A. Maghas B. Shakas
C. Nagas D. Satavahanas

19. In ancient India, the largest urban centre of the following was:
A. Taxila B. Pataliputra
C. Kausambhi D. Champa

20. The Mauryan officer Dandapala was actually a:
A. Spy
B. Royal door keeper
C. Chief commandant
D. Chief punitive officer

21. Which of the following was one of the main elements of Akbar's Rajput policy?
A. All of the other options
B. Grant of full autonomy and protection to Rajput polities
C. Establishment of matrimonial alliances
D. Appointment of Rajput chief's as high officials of Mughal government

22. The Lodis were:
A. Of pure Afghan origin
B. Ottoman Turks
C. Of pure Turk origin
D. Timurid Turks

23. Babur wrote his autobiography *Babur Nama* in:
A. Persian B. Pashto
C. Arabic D. Turki

24. From Iltutmish's death until Balban's accession, actual power was wielded by:
A. Army
B. All of the other options
C. Theologians
D. Nobility

25. The sophisticated life style of elite urbanites described by Vatsayana indicates:
A. The rise of trade
B. The prevalence of port towns
C. The emergence of a rich urban class
D. The rise of fashion consciousness

26. Arikamedu and Barbaricum were:
A. Agrarian centres
B. Intermediate urban centres
C. Famous ancient port-towns
D. Industiral bases

27. Which sultan's territory was the largest in the Delhi Sultanate?
A. Alauddin Khilji
B. Muhammad bin Tughlaq
C. Firuz Shah Tughlaq
D. Sikander Lodi

28. Which was NOT an important constituent element of Mughal government?
A. Arabic B. Persian
C. Turki D. Indian

29. The socio-economic significance of the trading and craft guilds lay in their:

A. Evolving into castes
B. Enforcing social discipline
C. Maintaining business and occupational monopoly of particular *varnas*
D. Providing economic support and organisation to trade and crafts

30. At the time of his coronation at Kalanaur, Akbar's age was:
A. Fifteen B. Twenty
C. Eighteen D. Thirteen and half

31. Which ancient sect gave women an important place and instituted orders of female ascetics?
A. Tantrics B. Lokayatas
C. Virasaivites D. Ajivikas

32. The Jesuit missionary who held discussions with Akbar and wrote about them was:
A. William Rubruck
B. Thomas Roe
C. Antony Monserrate
D. John di Plan Carpini

33. The Mughals captured Chittor in 1568 after defeating:
A. Rana Amar Singh B. Rana Ram Singh
C. Rana Uday Singh D. Rana Pratap Singh

34. Dinara was a:
A. Type of doorway B. Dinarius coin
C. Silver coin D. Gold coin

35. The Bhakti movement was headed by leaders such as:
A. Bindusara
B. Ramanuja and Kabir
C. Makanda Ghosale
D. Sandrocottus and Seleucos

36. The first sovereign ruler of the Delhi Sultanate was:
A. Qutb ud din Aibak
B. Iltutmish
C. Nasiruddin Mahmud
D. Aram Shah

37. The dynasty founded by Khizr Khan, Timur's nominee, is known as the Sayyid dynasty because:
A. Khizr Khan was a descendant of the Prophet
B. The ruled under the title Sayyid
C. Khizr Khan was a distinguished scholar of theology
D. Khizr Khan belonged to the Sayyid tribe of eastern Turkestan

38. Which of the following is true about Sufism?
A. Sufism was against synthesis of Hindu and Muslim culture
B. Sufism made no distinction between creeds and faiths
C. Sufism supported the caste system actively
D. Sufism addressed iteself to specific occupational groups

39. After recapturing Delhi and his second coronation, Humayun could rule for only:
A. Six months
B. Two and Half years
C. Two years
D. Fourteen months

40. The ancient city of Muziris was situated in:
A. Kabul valley B. Khyber pass
C. Kerala D. Maharashtra

41. The largest bridge was built in Akbar's time at:
A. Jaunpur B. Delhi (Barapula)
C. Jajau D. Nurpur

42. From the _____ century, several of the mystical and protestant elements were recombined in the Bhakti or devotional movements.
A. late thirteenth B. early fourteenth
C. fourteenth D. fifteenth

43. Vasco da Gama was helped by _____ to reach the Malabar coast.
A. Ibn Khurdadhbhi
B. The merchant Suleiman al-Tajir
C. Ibn Majid
D. Ibn Saud

44. Who first translated that *Tota Maina* stories into Persian?
A. Jiya Naqshwi B. Amir Khusrau
C. Badauni D. Faizi

45. The *sufi* sect of the Chistis was active in _____ India.

A. North-west B. Eastern
C. North D. South

46. Who first divided the Mughal empire into provinces?
A. Babur B. Akbar
C. Jahangir D. Humayun

47. The European nation that first discovered the sea route to India was:
A. Netherlands under the Spanish Hapsburgs
B. Spain via Manila
C. Portugal under the Aviz dynasty
D. England under the Tudors

48. What stylistic novelty is found in the tomb of Khan-i-Jahan Telangani built in Delhi under the Delhi Sultanate?
A. Octagonal shape
B. True arch
C. Double dome
D. Use of white marble against red sandstone

49. Who discovered the passage to India by the Cape of Good Hope?
A. Niccolo Conti B. Bartolomeu Diaz
C. Marco Polo D. Vasco da Gama

50. Shia *sufi* teachings spread from Sindh and Punjab across north and central India from the _____ century.
A. thirteenth B. twelfth
C. eleventh D. fourteenth

51. The first Portuguese settlement in Bengal was at:
A. Baranagar B. Chandernagar
C. Bandel D. Hooghly

52. Buland darwaza was built at Fatehpur Sikri by Akbar to:
A. Celebrate the birth of Salim
B. Commemorate his victory of Gujarat
C. Commemorate the completion of twenty five years of rule
D. Celebrate his alliance with Amber and his marriage with Amber princess

53. What are the three Gs motivating the European discoveries?
A. God, gluttony and gold
B. God, gold and glory
C. Greed, gourmandise and glory
D. Greed, god and glory

54. The giant Qutb Minar within the Quwwat-ul-Islam mosque in Delhi consists of _____ tapering shafts with balconies supported on muqarnas corbels.
A. seven B. six
C. four D. five

55. The media used for engraving Sultanate inscriptions was:
A. Lead plates and stone
B. Stone and iron plates
C. Copper plate and stone
D. Copper and iron plates

56. The medieval *sufi* sects of the Suhrawardi were active in _____ and the Firdausi were active in _____.
A. Sindh; Bihar
B. Punjab; Bihar
C. East Bengal; Orissa
D. Punjab; Sindh

57. Akbar introduced the mansabdari system to:
A. Engender loyalty
B. Satisfy officer's egos
C. Distribute favours
D. Organise nobility and army

58. The Portuguese first arrived in India at:
A. Kochi B. Calicut
C. Mangalore D. Kappad

59. Which is the correct chronological order of these Bhakti preachers?
A. Nanak, Chaitanya, Kabir
B. Kabir, Nanak, Chaitanya
C. Kabir, Ramdas, Ramjas
D. Chaitanya, Kabir, Nanak

60. Foreign traveller(s) who visited during Jahangir's reign was/were:
A. Francisco Pelsaert
B. William Finch and Francisco Pelsaert
C. Ralph Fitch
D. William Finch

61. A former Brahmo, Shiv Narayan Agnihotri (1850-1929), formed the Dev Samaj in the Punjab in:

A. 1887 B. 1897
C. 1885 D. 1859

62. The French headquarters in South India was at:
A. Arcot B. Pondicherry
C. Arikamedu D. Tanjore

63. The greatest bankers in Bengal were:
A. Hazoorimull B. Gyanchand
C. Jagat Seth D. Alamchand

64. Which of the following is NOT true about the revolt of 1857?
A. It spread over much of North and Central India.
B. Leaders participating in revolt instituted command structures on the model of the company's army and administration.
C. Leaders participating in revolt established pan-Indian alliances.
D. Leaders participating in the revolt evoked Mughal forms of governance.

65. De-industrialisation referred to:
A. Decay of traditional urban centres
B. All of the other options
C. Decline of indigenous crafts
D. Deserted villages

66. Who wrote the book *The Indian Musalmans*?
A. Kevin MacDonald B. James Mill
C. S.S. Thorburn D. W.W. Hunter

67. Which successive order of Governor-Generals is correct?
A. Hastings, Cornwallis, Barlow, Amherst
B. Hastings, Shore, Cornwallis, Wellesley (Mornington)
C. Cornwallis, Bentinck, Auckland, Ellenborough
D. Warren Hastings, Cornwallis, Sir John Shore, Wellesley (Mornington)

68. Which historian claimed that 1757 impact the Indian economy and that the boom continued into the nineteenth century?
A. Morris D Morris B. Angus Maddison
C. C A Bayly D. B R Tomlinson

69. The Danes are famous for introducing into Bengal:
A. The printing press
B. Charity work
C. Evangelists
D. Missionary activities

70. The Dutch established themselves in Bengal at:
A. Bankibazar B. Serampore
C. Murshidabad D. Chinsurah

71. A famous French traveller who visited Chinsurah in the late seventeenth century was:
A. Jean Baptiste Tavernier
B. Robert Challes
C. Francois Bernier
D. Francois Beaulieu

72. What is NOT a true statement with regard to the eighteenth century India?
A. Indigenous trade and shipping increased.
B. Traditional towns in India were eclipsed by the dynamism of Calcutta, Madras and Bombay.
C. Towns such as Benaras, Pune, Lucknow, Hyderabad, Mysore or Jaipur experienced growth in the eighteenth century at the expense of Delhi, Agra and Lahore.
D. By 1800, commercially speaking, the capitals of most successor states were towns without a secure future.

73. Which of the following is NOT true with regard to the British impact on the Indian economy?
A. The terms of international trade, the conditions of production in India, and the regulations imposed by its European government all turned against Indian entrepreneurs and merchants.
B. Nineteenth-century colonial policy offered protection to Indian-owned and India-based enterprises.
C. In the 1900s, J.N. Tata, after large expenditure, sought to raise capital in London for a proposed steel works plant at Jamshedpur. He found London financiers unwilling to lend to a speculation under Indian management.

D. Secure, profitable and expensive state-backed loans for major railways and canals were raised internationally.

74. The first negative effect of British rule in Bengal was seen in:
A. The new market towns established by the British
B. The famine of 1769-70
C. Revenue farming
D. None of the other options

75. The first European steam-powered factory producing cotton yarn was established:
A. In Ahmedabad in 1853
B. In Bombay in 1856
C. In Bombay in 1854
D. Near Calcutta in 1817 or 1818

76. All European companies established themselves at Surat because:
A. It had a great market
B. It was a great emporium of trade
C. It had good transport links with the interior
D. It was a great emporium of trade and it had a great market

77. What was NOT a consideration for European companies to settle in Bengal?
A. Inexpensiveness of items for daily use
B. Power of the local court
C. Good transport links through rivers
D. Diversity and inexpensiveness of trading goods

78. The British East India Company could ultimately suppress the 1857 revolt because:
A. Company ships fired cannons on the Indians
B. The Company controlled all land routes
C. The revolt focused upon only a few hubs, such as Delhi or Lucknow, and the leaders failed to consolidate across wider areas except through alliance with lesser centres or power-brokers
D. The Company had large number of British troops

79. The French in Bengal reached great heights under:
A. Francis Hardancourt
B. Philippe Caron
C. Robert Lessier
D. Francois Dupleix

80. The Dutch lost to the English at the:
A. Battle of Plassey in 1757
B. Battle of Chinsurah or Battle of Biderra in 1759
C. Battle of Jugalkot in 1752
D. Battle of Hooghly in 1758

81. The East India Association (1855) was set up in:
A. Calcutta and Nagpur
B. Calcutta and Bombay
C. Madras and Bombay
D. London and Bombay

82. The earliest cities of southern Mesopotamia were:
A. Uruk and Kish
B. Nippur and Kish
C. Eridu, Uruk, Bad-tibira, Nippur and Kish
D. Eridu and Babylonia

83. In the more recent texts, Oman and the Indus region are known as:
A. Lugalzagesi and Lagash
B. Bad Kimbesh and Meluhha
C. Magan and Meluhha
D. Om Kippur and Tilgrath

84. After Dayanand's death, the Lahore Samaj and other societies he had formed across Northern India came together to establish a school in his memory at ____, which was called ____ and whose date of establishment was ____.
A. Lahore; The Dayanand Anglo-Vedic College; 1886
B. Lahore; The Dayanand Vedic College; 1887
C. Bombay; The Dayanand Shaka; 1887
D. Lahore; The Dayanand Vedic Association; 1890

85. Rowlatt in 1919, non-cooperation in 1920-22, civil disobedience in 1930-34 were:
A. Both mass movements by Gandhi, based on 'truth-force' (*satyagraha*) and a Jain-influenced non-violence (*ahimsa*) and

based on Gandhi's activism and idealism, which appealed to young volunteers, local leaders and many established all-India politicians as a means of confronting the British without risking violence or violent reprisals.

B. Mass movements by Gandhi, based on 'truth-force' (*satyagraha*) and a Jain-influenced non-violence (*ahimsa*)

C. Based on Gandhi's activism and idealism, which appealed to young volunteers, local leaders and many established all-India politicians as a means of confronting the British without risking violence or violent reprisals.

D. Urban protests

86. Later Mesopotamian urbanisation showed:

A. Small settlements

B. An alomst explosive increase in the size of the buildings

C. Presence of camels

D. Drainage canals

87. The raw material that epitomises Mesopotamian civilisation is:

A. Palm leaf   B. Stone

C. Clay   D. Wood

88. Jyotirao Phule established the _____ Samaj (truth-seeking society).

A. Satyapath   B. Satyagraha

C. Satyashodhak   D. Satyabhama

89. The surveys of Robert McCormick Adams and Hans Nissen showed:

A. How the relative size and number of Mesopotamian settlements gradually shifted: the number of small or very small settlements was reduced overall, whereas the number of larger places grew

B. Small or very small settlements grew fast

C. Mesopotamian settlements gradually shifted to urban conglomerates

D. Small settlements suddenly died out

90. Motilal Nehru's constitutional consultative committee report (1928) was rejected by the All Indian Muslim Conference in 1929 because the Conference thought that:

A. The Nehru Report generated the broadest possible consensus among Indian opinion and envisaged pan-Indian rights and structures, while the Muslim Conference felt that in view of India's vast extent and divisions, the only form of Government suitable to Indian conditions was a federal system with complete autonomy and residuary powers vested in the constituent states

B. It was too pro-British

C. It marginalised Muslims from decision making

D. It favoured Hindus and would create a Hindu state

91. Arya Samaj, which was started in erstwhile Bombay in 1875 and in Lahore in 1877 by Dayanand Saraswati, was also known as:

A. Noble Society

B. Honoured Society

C. Distinguished Society

D. Great Society

92. A trans-shipment point for Mesopotamian trade with the Oman coast and the Indus region was:

A. Nishapur

B. Barbarikon

C. The isle of Dilmun (modern Bahrain)

D. Barygaza

93. Brahma Sabha (1828), Dharma Sabha (1830) and Landholder's Society (1838) were ____ based societies.

A. Bombay   B. Calcutta

C. Patna   D. Delhi

94. The poem Vande Mataram was written by:

A. Aurobindo Ghosh

B. Bankim Chandra Chatterjee

C. Bipin Chandra Pal

D. Rabindranath Tagore

95. When did the Indian Constitution come into force?

A. 25th January, 1950

B. 25th January, 1949

C. 26th January, 1948

D. 26th January, 1950

96. The clearest sign of Mesopotamian urbanisation can be seen at:
A. Eridu
B. Uruk Levels VI to IV
C. Uruk and Kish
D. Nippur

97. A system of writing first developed by the ancient Sumerians of Mesopotamia is known as:
A. Cuneiform B. Cueniform
C. Cuneiformal D. Apsidal

98. Mesopotamian temples were:
A. Round in shape
B. Square in shape
C. Rectangular buildings, covering areas as large as 275 by 175 feet
D. Hexagonal in shape

99. Which political leader entitled his political autobiography, A Nation in Making (1925)?
A. Motilal Nehru
B. Dadabhai Naoroji
C. M.K. Gandhi
D. Surendranath Banerjee

100. Which of the following is a correct statement?
A. Untouchability was neither abolished nor removed under the schedules of the Constitution
B. Untouchability was removed under the schedules of the Constitution
C. Untouchability was declared a crime punishable by law, carrying a prison sentence under the schedules of the Constitution
D. Untouchability was officially abolished, though not removed under the schedules of the Constitution, reinforced by an Act of 1955.

101. The Hellenistic Age is the period during which:
A. Greek thought and culture became dominant in the regions under the rule of the four generals among whom Alexander's empire had been divided.
B. The Athenian Empire fought with the Sassanid Empire
C. The early Greeks fought with the Sassanians
D. The later Greeks fought with the Persians

102. The Peloponnesian League was:
A. A defensive alliance against the Delian League
B. A league formed to promote Greek commercial interests
C. An alliance of the Greek islands against mainland Greece
D. An offensive alliance of the Greek city states against the Persians

103. Which of the following was a city-state hostile to Athens?
A. Knossos B. Naxos
C. Sparta D. Rhodes

104. Which of the following work was NOT done by the Roman Empire?
A. Encompassing most of continental Europe, Britain, much of Western Asia, northern Africa and the Mediterranean islands
B. Following a mixture of paganism, philosophical beliefs and early Christianity
C. Introducing the western calendar
D. None of the other options

105. The year 2350 B.C. was a turning point in the history of Mesopotamia because:
A. Rivers dried up and trade was affected for the first time.
B. For the first time, an empire arose on Mesopotamian soil. The driving force of that empire were the Akkadians.
C. Floods destroyed all its cities.
D. The Mesopotamian civilisation faced constant invasions.

106. The power vacuum after the fall of Athens and Sparta was filled by:
A. Philip II of Macedon (382-336 BCE), after his victory over the Athenian forces and their allies at the Battle of Chaeronea in 338 BCE.
B. Alexander I of Macedonia after a devastating flood weakened Greece
C. Philip I of Macedon
D. Anaximander of Macedonia

107. The first Roman emperor was:
A. Nero B. Julius
C. Tiberius D. Augustus

108. The concept of an atomic universe was first posited in Greece through the work of:
A. Democritus and Leucippus
B. Heraclitus
C. Argon
D. Thales

109. The designation *Hellas* is derived from:
A. Hellen, son of Deucalion of Pyrrha, who features in Ovid's tale of the Great Flood in his *Metamorphoses*
B. Helios, the Sun God
C. Hellenic, a mountain in Central Greece
D. Hela, the Greek Goddess of Fortune

110. Greece was designated a Protectorate of Rome in:
A. 141 BCE B. 167 BCE
C. 168 BCE D. 146 BCE

111. In its character, Mesopotamia was a:
A. Homogeneous
B. Composite civilisation
C. Heterogeneous civilisation, containing many diverse elements and people
D. Centralised empire

112. Which civilisation was NOT a part of ancient Greece?
A. Aegean Civilisation
B. Minoan Civilisation
C. Cycladic Civilisation
D. Mycenaean Civilisation

113. Early work in physics and engineering was pioneered by:
A. Archimedes of the Greek colony of Syracuse
B. Euclid
C. Democritus
D. Themistocles

114. Which sea does NOT surround Greece?
A. Akkadian Sea B. Aegean Sea
C. Mediterranean Sea D. Ionian Sea

115. Which of the following is among the many legacies of Roman dominance?
A. The Rome-India trade
B. All of the other options
C. The widespread use of Romance languages (Italian, French, Spanish, Portuguese and Romanian) derived from Latin, the modern Western alphabet, the calendar and the emergence of Christianity as a major world religion
D. Capture of the Red Sea trade

116. The Archaic Period (800-500 BCE) in Greece is characterised by:
A. The introduction of republics instead of monarchies (which, in Athens moved towards Democratic rule) organised as a single city-state or polis as well as The institution of a legal framework
B. The introduction of republics instead of monarchies (which in Athens, moved towards Democratic rule) organised as a single city-state or polis
C. A highly statist rule
D. The institution of a legal framework

117. Augustus Caesar's original name was:
A. Marcus B. Octavian Caesar
C. Antonius Caesar D. Julius

118. In 31 BCE, Octavian Caesar annexed ____ as a province of Rome following his victory over Mark Antony and Cleopatra at the Battle of Actium.
A. England B. Greece
C. Germania D. Gaul

119. The Akkadians were contemporary to the:
A. Early Mesopotamians
B. Sumerians
C. Very early Harappans
D. Babylonians

120. The first ruler of the Akkadians was:
A. Heraclitus B. Eusebius
C. Sargon D. Tilgrath Pilser

121. The sharia (from *shar* or 'the way') is:
A. A system of faith
B. A set of laws
C. Laws inscribed permanently
D. The body of normative guidance that grew out of the original framework, during and after the time of Prophet Muhammad

122. The birthplace of the renaissance is:
A. Spain B. Germany
C. France D. Italy

123. The transition debate refers to:
A. The transition from feudalism to capitalism
B. The transition from republicanism to a monarchical system
C. The transition from agrarian capitalism to commercial capitalism
D. The transition from trade to agriculture

124. Ganshof wrote on:
A. The feudal economic structure
B. Feudal policy
C. The legal aspects of feudalism
D. Feudal religion and morality

125. The middle period of feudalism saw:
A. A monarchical revolution leading to the concentration of power
B. A transport revolution
C. A revolution in technology
D. The appearance of large-scale cities in Europe

126. The Prophet Muhammad (570-632 CE) was tasked with:
A. Putting into place Islam's ethical framework
B. Conveying the revelation
C. Providing economic support and organisation to trade and crafts
D. Conveying the revelation and putting into place Islam's ethical framework

127. The defining aspect(s) of the Prophet's ethical framework at large was/were:
A. The 'pillars' of the faith; bearing witness to God and his prophet, ritual prayer, alms-giving, fasting and pilgrimage
B. Jihad
C. The rule of a just king
D. Trade and commerce as a sacred duty

128. Which of the following monarchs was intimately associated with the early feudal system?
A. Charles V B. Henry Tudor
C. Charlemagne D. Barbarossa

129. The hunting and burning of witches at the stake reached its height during:
A. The late medieval period
B. The seventeenth century
C. The fifteenth century
D. The sixteenth century

130. The Mongols were:
A. Horse rearing nomadic people at inception
B. Horse rearing nomadic people at inception and Pastoralists
C. Pastoralists
D. Agriculturists

131. The renaissance put ____ at the centre of the world.
A. ideas of man B. discoveries
C. nature D. cities

132. Which author has written on Central Asian nomadic culture?
A. Mario Prato B. Owen Lattimore
C. Carlo Nicolo D. Philip Ashton

133. Constantinople fell to the Ottoman Turks on:
A. 3 November, 1492 B. 29 May, 1456
C. 2 June, 1204 D. 29 May, 1453

134. Which of the following books was written by Maurice Dobb?
A. *The Rise of Capitalist Agriculture*
B. *Commercial Capitalism in England*
C. *India in the World Economy*
D. *Studies in The Development of Capitalism*

135. The tax imposed by the medieval church was called:
A. Tithe B. Religiosa
C. Gabelle D. Imperium

136. Which of the following authors wrote on the transition from feudalism to capitalism?
A. Paul M Sweezy B. Fernand Braudel
C. Gabriel Ferrand D. Ronald La Haye

137. What is NOT true with regard to feudalism?
A. It had more villages than towns
B. It made land the basis of all relations
C. It made agriculture the chief activity
D. It adopted western philosophies of monarchism

138. The Arab occupation of ____ led to the crusades.
A. Lebanon B. Byzantium
C. Syria D. Jerusalem

139. Feudalism is:
A. A patrimonial system
B. A system where the king appropriates all control
C. A land-based social, economic and political system
D. Not hostile to mercantilism

140. Feudal relations encompass:
A. The republican spirit
B. Economic relations
C. Social, political, religious, legal and moral spheres
D. Economic relations; and social, political, religious, legal and moral spheres

141. Which of the following is true about the Reformation?
A. It heightened popular consciousness of the occult
B. It popularised witch hunting
C. It created many peasant leaders
D. It shaked people's faith in one, unitary Christian Church

142. Capitalism was first visible:
A. In Spain with bureaucratic capitalism
B. In France as the feudal system declined
C. In the Portuguese imperial system
D. In England with the rise of capitalist agriculture

143. Portugal's map and atlas making tradition was inherited from:
A. The Catalans of Mallorca by way of the Arabs
B. Mathematicians
C. Scientists at Sagres
D. Spain

144. Calvin was a ____ reformer.
A. English B. French
C. Swiss D. Belgian

145. Which authors coined the term 'proto-industrialisation'?
A. Peter Metcalfe and Hans Humperdink
B. Amos Vanderbilt and Michael Wood
C. Hans Medick, Peter Kriedte, Jurgen Schlumbohm
D. Peter Burke and C H Phillips

146. Industrial capitalism was based on:
A. High and protective tariffs
B. Centralised production, as in the factory system
C. High and protective tariffs; and centralised production, as in the factory system
D. Tax-free land

147. The Peasant's War in Germany lasted for the duration of:
A. 1524-1525 B. 1528-1530
C. 1525-1530 D. 1526-1530

148. Which one of the following is NOT a phase Capitalism?
A. Merchant Capitalism
B. Finance Capitalism
C. Imperial Capitalism
D. Industrial Capitalism

149. Which of the following is NOT true about the Protestant Reformation?
A. It believed in massive altar decorations
B. It dispensed with the pomp and pageantry of the Catholic Church
C. It attacked the corruption of bishops and cardinals
D. It believed in direct and personal communion with God

150. Mercantilism was:
A. An initial phase in merchant capitalism
B. Based on plunder and protectionism
C. All of the other options
D. A part of national economic strategies

151. The artist mantegna painted at the:
A. Sistine Chapel
B. Church in Padua
C. The cout of Gonzagas in Mantua
D. Vatican Church in Rome

152. Which of the following is TRUE with regard to the renaissance?

A. It was not hostile to religion but religion was left as a personal matter
B. Majority of renaissance art had a religious theme
C. Portraiture emerged as an art style during the renaissance
D. All of the other options

153. Prince Henry of Portugal set up a laboratory for the discovery project at:
A. Tagus B. Lisbon
C. Sagres D. Lagos

154. Agrarian capitalism was synonymous with:
A. Improvements in riverine traffic
B. The enclosure movement in the countryside
C. A big transport revolution
D. The use of steam

155. The initial preacher of the Protestant Reformation was:
A. Martine Luther B. John of Presbyter
C. John Knox D. Auguste Calvin

156. Proto-industrialisation is also known as:
A. Verlag system
B. Industrialisation before industrialisation
C. Kauf system
D. Putting out system

157. How is capital different from money?
A. Money is for spending while capital more money
B. Money is for hoarding, while capital is for spending
C. Money is for everyday use, while capital is only for investment
D. Money is for spending while capital creates more money; and Money is for everyday use, while capital is only for investment

158. The 'discoveries' of the world beyond Europe were led in the fifteenth century by:
A. Portugal B. Catalan
C. Portugal and Spain D. Spain

159. Christopher Columbus's voyage was financed by:
A. Calvi in Corsica
B. Queen Isabella and King Ferdinand of Spain
C. The republic of Genoa
D. King Ferdinand of Aragon

160. Merchant capitalism was based on:
A. Sea-borne commerce
B. Overseas trade
C. Trade, plunder and slavery
D. Trade and commerce as duty

161. The opium wars were followed by:
A. The Taiping Rebellion
B. The Boxer Movement
C. Muslim revolts in Xinjiang
D. The Hundred Flowers Reform Movement

162. Which of the following is NOT true regarding Japan's economy?
A. Japan is subject to earthquakes but has very little rainfall
B. It is the world's top fishing nation
C. It has the greatest number of ports for container and marine shipping concentrated in a small space
D. Rice is its chief crops

163. Commodore Perry first landed at Yedo Bay on:
A. 4 February, 1854 B. 21 August, 1853
C. 8 July, 1853 D. 3 July, 1853

164. The Sino-Japan war was:
A. A clash between China and Japan for the control of Korea and Manchuria
B. The Outcome of conflicts in Manchuria
C. A clash between China and Japan for the control of Korea
D. The result of an illegal railway line laid by Japan in Hunan

165. The immediate background to the establishment of Nationalist China was:
A. Military reforms between 1901-11
B. Anti-Qing feeling in cities
C. The October 1911 Wuhan uprising by the New Army whose officers did not support the Qings
D. Revolutionary Alliance of 1905 by Sun Yat-Sen

166. Which is NOT true with regard to the Taiping Rebellion?

A. Hardly any land tax was paid to the Qings after the rebellion
B. It captured all the coastal forts in China
C. It was an anti-imperialist movement
D. It saw the early tremors of Communist 'earthquake' that would engulf China in the 1940s

167. The reason(s) behind the Boxer Uprising is/are:
A. None of the other options
B. Imperial designs of Britan and Russia
C. Imperial designs of Britain and Russia, and Severe drought and the disruption caused by the growth of foreign spheres of influence
D. Severe drought and the disruption caused by the growth of foreign spheres of influence

168. Which of the following is true about the Anglo-Chinese opium wars?
A. They broke the myth of China's invulnerability
B. They broke the myth of China's invulnerability; and They opened up China, saw inflation and protection to missionaries
C. They opened up China
D. They opened up China, saw inflation and protection to missionaries

169. The Taiping movement rose in:
A. Kwangtan province, a remote Southwest corner of China
B. Gansu province
C. The heart of China
D. Szechwan province

170. The Eight-Nation Alliance – an international military coalition set up in response to Boxer Rebellion in summer of 1900 – was composed of:
A. Japan, Russia, Britain, France, United States, Germany, Italy and the Portuguese Empire.
B. Japan, Russia, Britain, France, United States, Germany, Italy and the Austro-Hungarian Empire.
C. Japan, Russia, Britain, France, United States, Germany, Italy and Austria.
D. Japan, Russia, Britain, France, United States, Germany, Italy and Spain.

171. China faced ____ opium war(s).
A. Two
B. None of the other options
C. Three
D. One

172. The leaders of the Taiping Rebellion were:
A. Li Tong and the Society of Righteous Fists
B. None of the other options
C. Li Huang Cho and the Society of the Harmonius Hand
D. Hung Hsiu Ch'uan and his Society of God Worshippers

173. Japanese emperor who assumed the title of Meiji, or Enlightened Ruler; was:
A. Mutsuhito
B. Masahiro
C. Shigeru Okinawa
D. Hirohito

174 The Qings crushed the Taiping rebellion on:
A. 27th July, 1863
B. 19th July, 1864
C. 18th February, 1865
D. 20th July, 1864

175. Which of the following is NOT true with regard to Japan?
A. It transformed from a feudal agricultural society to an industrialised society within a little over 100 years.
B. It adopted western philosophies of liberalism.
C. It adopted western science, technology, constitutional monarchy and military on western lines.
D. It is poor in natural resources, yet it could rise from defeat in World War II through rapid economic development.

176. Which is NOT true as regard the May Fourth Movement of 1917-23?
A. It was a peasant movement seen chiefly in the countryside
B. It saw a move from anti-Qing feelings to anti-imperialism

C. It was a precursor of communism with its anti-warlord activities
D. It was a reaction to Treaty of Versailles and the Allies' favourable treatment of Japan

177. The Treaty of Kanagawa, signalling the 'opening up' of Japan, was signed on:
A. 28 March, 1854
B. 31 March, 1854
C. 30 March, 1854
D. 2 April, 1854

178. Between which duration did the Boxer Uprising take place?
A. 1899-1901 B. 1900-1901
C. 1898-1900 D. 1898-1899

179. The Taipings were:
A. Linked with secret societies such as The Triad
B. All of the other options
C. Intent on retaking Nanking as the Treaty of Nanking 1842 was a symbol of Chinese humiliation
D. Influenced by Confucian and Christian doctrines

180. Japan consists of 4 large island: Honshu, Hokkaido, Shikoku and Kyushu. Which among them is the seat of Japanese culture and contains its main cities?
A. Honshu B. Kyushu
C. Hokkaido D. Shikoku

181. Which of the following distinguishes inclusion from integration?
A. Fitting the child into the system,
B. Modifying the curriculum and setup to suit the child's needs
C. Giving additional information
D. providing material

182. According to Bronfenbrenner, government and education council form an important element in this level ____ of child's eco-system.
A. Mezosystem
B. Endosystem
C. Chronosystem
D. Exosystem

183. Complete the sentence choosing the correct option.
Simulations as a teaching method allows:
A. Imagination
B. Experiencing a given situation
C. Reading a story
D. Playing a role

184. Radha wants children to develop appropriate tone and modulations. Which method should she employ?
A. Listening
B. Singing
C. Simulations
D. Part taking in drama

185. Conveying messages through circulars is which form of communication?
A. Oral communication
B. Non-verbal communication
C. Mass communication
D. Personal communication

186. Emphasis of curriculum is on the:
A. Material provided
B. Process and skills to be developed
C. Process followed
D. Content to be taught

187. A Science teacher of grade 7 wants to state instructional objectives at the Analysis level of Bloom's Taxonomy. What is the correct action word that he/she needs to use?
A. Identify B. Justify
C. Relate D. Describe

188. What does the transferability feature of learning improve?
A. Enhances vertical structure of learning
B. Gives scope for spiral structure of learning
C. Makes learning difficult
D. Increases horizontal span of learning

189. One of the basic scientific skills is:
A. Observation B. Teaching
C. Listening D. Narrating

190. Special educators help the school in implementing inclusion by:
A. Bringing new admissions
B. Providing material for play

C. Creating awareness about the different types of special needs
D. Providing reading activities

191. Which one is an example of a URL leading to Search engine?
A. Index.html
B. http.rediff.com
C. Html. google.com
D. www.yahoo.com

192. What would Harish endusre by using rubrics to assess reading skills?
A. Validity B. Scaffolding
C. Reliability D. uniformity

193. Illustrating boys as active and girls as passive was done in:
A. Policy documents in the 70's
B. In the rural settings
C. Government initiatives in the 80's
D. Textbooks in the 80's and 90's

194. Introduction of pre-matric scholarship is an initiative for "Education for Women's equality" proposed by:
A. UNESCO B. NPE
C. ICDS D. UGS

195. Online exams are preferred because:
A. They save time
B. Administration is easy
C. Objective tests
D. Malpractices are diminished

196. Sheela wants to conduct extra classes for students who scored below 50% in Science. In order to find out who are such students, she would list their information and use the Excel command:
A. Sort B. Sum
C. Average D. Format

197. Staying update with current affairs is best possible through:
A. TV and newspapers
B. Gossiping
C. Telephonic conversations
D. TV, internet and newspapers

198. Language development starts with:
A. Imitation
B. Cooing
C. Sound discrimination
D. Reading

199. What is the right sequence if Rohan wants to add sound effects to his power point presentation?
A. Select picture – insert – clipart
B. Open the slide – animation – custom animation – sound effects
C. Open the slide – animation – transition sound – applause
D. Place the cursor on the content – review – track changes

200. What does maintaining a reflective diary help teachers in?
A. Planning lessons
B. Professional development
C. Talking to parents
D. Reporting to management

ANSWERS

1	2	3	4	5	6	7	8	9	10
D	B	A	C	D	B	D	A	B	B
11	**12**	**13**	**14**	**15**	**16**	**17**	**18**	**19**	**20**
A	B	A	D	A	D	C	C	B	C
21	**22**	**23**	**24**	**25**	**26**	**27**	**28**	**29**	**30**
A	A	D	D	C	C	B	A	C	D
31	**32**	**33**	**34**	**35**	**36**	**37**	**38**	**39**	**40**
A	C	C	D	B	B	A	B	A	C

41	**42**	**43**	**44**	**45**	**46**	**47**	**48**	**49**	**50**
B	C	C	A	C	B	C	A	B	C
51	**52**	**53**	**54**	**55**	**56**	**57**	**58**	**59**	**60**
D	B	B	D	C	A	D	D	B	B
61	**62**	**63**	**64**	**65**	**66**	**67**	**68**	**69**	**70**
A	B	C	C	B	D	D	C	A	D
71	**72**	**73**	**74**	**75**	**76**	**77**	**78**	**79**	**80**
A	A	B	B	D	D	B	C	D	B
81	**82**	**83**	**84**	**85**	**86**	**87**	**88**	**89**	**90**
D	C	C	A	A	B	C	C	A	A
91	**92**	**93**	**94**	**95**	**96**	**97**	**98**	**99**	**100**
A	C	B	B	D	B	A	C	D	D
101	**102**	**103**	**104**	**105**	**106**	**107**	**108**	**109**	**110**
A	A	C	D	B	A	D	A	A	D
111	**112**	**113**	**114**	**115**	**116**	**117**	**118**	**119**	**120**
C	A	A	A	B	B	B	B	B	C
121	**122**	**123**	**124**	**125**	**126**	**127**	**128**	**129**	**130**
D	D	A	C	C	D	A	C	B	B
131	**132**	**133**	**134**	**135**	**136**	**137**	**138**	**139**	**140**
A	B	D	D	A	A	D	D	C	D
141	**142**	**143**	**144**	**145**	**146**	**147**	**148**	**149**	**150**
D	D	A	C	C	C	A	C	A	A
151	**152**	**153**	**154**	**155**	**156**	**157**	**158**	**159**	**160**
C	D	C	B	A	B	D	C	B	C
161	**162**	**163**	**164**	**165**	**166**	**167**	**168**	**169**	**170**
A	A	C	C	C	B	C	B	A	B
171	**172**	**173**	**174**	**175**	**176**	**177**	**178**	**179**	**180**
A	D	A	B	B	A	B	A	B	A
181	**182**	**183**	**184**	**185**	**186**	**187**	**188**	**189**	**190**
B	D	B	D	C	B	B	B	A	C
191	**192**	**193**	**194**	**195**	**196**	**197**	**198**	**199**	**200**
D	C	D	B	D	A	A	C	C	B

Previous Paper (Solved)

DSSSB—HISTORY TEACHER (PGT) Recruitment Exam, 2015*

POST SPECIFIC SUBJECT-RELATED QUESTIONS

1. The first thing that primitive man learnt was:
A. To make a wheel
B. To domesticate animals
C. To lead a settled life
D. To make fire

2. Men of the modern type— "Homo Sapiens" appeared in the:
A. Mesolithic period
B. Upper Palaeolithic period
C. Middle Palaeolithic period
D. Lower Palaeolithic period

3. The Palaeolithic man lived on:
1. Hunting
2. Fishing
3. Cultivation
4. Food-gathering

Choose the correct answer group:
A. 1, 2, 3 B. 1, 2, 4
C. 2, 3, 4 D. 1, 3, 4

4. Rober Bruce Foote discovered Palaeolithic stone tool in:
A. 1857 B. 1862
C. 1863 D. 1821

5. Match the following:

(*a*) Palaeolithic age	1. Stone-copper tools
(*b*) Mesolithic age	2. Polished stone tools
(*c*) Neolithic age	3. Chipped stone tools
(*d*) Chalcolithic age	4. Microliths

Codes:

	(*a*)	(*b*)	(*c*)	(*d*)
A.	3	2	4	1
B.	2	3	4	1
C.	2	3	1	4
D.	3	4	2	1

6. Which of the following is **not** correctly matched?
A. Mesolithic period – Microlith industry
B. Palaeolithic period – Wandering life
C. Neolithic period – Settled life
D. Chalcolithic period – Food-producing stage

Directions: *The following questions consists of two statements one labelled as Assertion (A) and the other as Reason (R). You have to examine these two statements carefully and decide if the Assertion (A) and the Reason (R) are individually true and if so, whether the Reason is a correct explanation of the Assertion. Select your answer to these items using the code given below:*

A. Both (A) and (R) are true and (R) is the correct explanation of (A)
B. Both (A) and (R) are true but (R) is not the correct explanation of (A)
C. (A) is true but (R) is false
D. (A) is false but (R) is true

7. Assertion (A) : The Himalayas are responsible for making the Indo-gangetic plains a vast well watered garden, swarming with population.

* Tier-I

Reason (R) : This was the reason for Asian nomadism.

8. **Assertion (A)** : In Bronze age the urbanisation took place

Reason (R) : The disparity between the rich and poor grew.

9. **Assertion (A)** : Ahar practically did not use microlithic tools, stone axes or blades but copper objects.

Reason (R) : Art of smelting and metallurgy was known to the people of Ahar from the very beginning as copper was locally available.

10. **Assertion (A)** : The Indus people did not use metal money.

Reason (R) : They did not have the technology to make metallic coins.

11. **Assertion (A)** : The Indus people worshipped Mother Goddess.

Reason (R) : Excavations at several Indus sites reveals that Indus people worshipped figures of terracota representing Mother Goddess.

12. In which of the following respects, the various Harappan sites have marked uniformity?
A. Agricultural practices
B. Crafts
C. Town planning
D. Seals

13. The largest number of Harappan sites in post independence India have been discovered in:
A. Gujarat
B. Punjab and Haryana
C. Rajasthan
D. N.W. Uttar Pradesh

14. The metal most widely used by the Indus Valley people was:
A. Copper B. Bronze
C. Gold and Silver D. Tin

15. Who worked on the decipherment of the Indus Script?
A. I. Mahadevan B. H.D. Sankalia
C. V.D. Smith D. B.B. Lal

16. Which of the following was **not** a contemporary of the Indus or Harappan Civilization?
A. Egypt B. Mesopotomia
C. Sumer D. Greek

17. One aspect of the Harappan life which formed the basis of the Harappan system, but about which very little or nothing is known as:
A. Rural life
B. Cattle breeding
C. Transport and communication
D. Demographic patterns

18. Who of the following suggested that Aryans originally lived in Central Asia?
A. Prof. Macdonell B. Bradenstein
C. Max Muller D. Sir William Jones

19. The Battle of Ten Kings was fought on the bank of:
A. Sutlej B. Jhelum
C. Sindhu D. Ravi

20. 'Askini' is the ancient name of which river?
A. Saraswati B. Beas
C. Chenab D. Ghaggar

21. Which of the following Vedas is the oldest?
A. Rig Veda B. Sama Veda
C. Yajur Veda D. Atharva Veda

22. Match the following:

Vedanga	**Subject**
(*a*) Kalpa	1. etymology
(*b*) Nirukta	2. grammar
(*c*) Vyakarana	3. ritual
(*d*) Siksha	4. pronunciation

Codes:

	(*a*)	(*b*)	(*c*)	(*d*)
A.	2	3	1	4
B.	1	2	3	4
C.	4	3	2	1
D.	3	4	1	2

23. The term "Vedanta" is used for which Vedic text?

A. Aranyakas B. Upanishads
C. Brahmanas D. Smritis

24. The name "Aghnya" (not to be killed) mentioned in many passages of the Rig Veda applies to:

A. Priest B. Women
C. Cows D. Brahmanas

25. Which Sutra deals with the rules relating to big sacrifices?

A. Dharmasutra B. Grihyasutra
C. Srautasutra D. Sulvasutra

26. Match the following:

Officer	**Function**
(*a*) Suta	1. Treasurer
(*b*) Samgrahitri	2. Carpenter
(*c*) Bhagadugha	3. Collector of taxes
(*d*) Takshan	4. Charioteer

Codes:

	(*a*)	(*b*)	(*c*)	(*d*)
A.	1	3	4	2
B.	3	2	1	4
C.	4	1	3	2
D.	2	4	3	1

27. The ploughed land in the vedic period was termed as:

A. Urvara B. Yava
C. Dhanya D. None of the above

28. The four fold division of society is expressly mentioned in:

A. Yajur Veda
B. Satapatna Brahmana
C. Hiranyagarbha-sukta
D. Purusha-sukta of Rig Veda

29. Prof. Jacobi is of the view that Rig Veda must have been written in:

A. Before 1000 B.C.
B. 2nd Century B.C.
C. 1200 B.C.
D. Third millennium B.C.

30. In which book the lending of money on interest is condemned?

A. Dharmasutra B. Ritisutra
C. Buddhist text D. Jain text

31. According to Puranas who was the founder of the Magadhan dynasty?

A. Bimbisara B. Shishunaga
C. Brihadratha D. None of these

32. Who was the last ruler of Nanda dynasty, defeated by Chandragupta Maurya?

A. Ugrasena
B. Dhan Nanda
C. Das Siddhak
D. Mahapadmananda

33. Where was the first Jain Council held around the third Century B.C.?

A. Vallabi B. Vaishali
C. Pataliputra D. Jrimbhikagrama

34. According to the Jaina tradition Neminatha the 22nd Tirthankara was related to:

A. Krishna B. Udayana
C. Paraswara D. Bimbisara

35. The strict followers of Mahavira were known by which name?

A. Digambaras B. Svetambaras
C. Brahmacharya D. None of the above

36. Which of the following was the real name of Lord Buddha?

A. Siddhartha B. Tathagata
C. Gautama D. Boudhayan

37. The first royal king to patronise Buddhism was:

A. Bindusara
B. Chandragupta Maurya
C. Ashoka
D. None of the above

38. The Abhidhamma Pitaka was composed in which Council?

A. Kashmir Council
B. Rajgriha Council
C. Vaishali Council
D. Pataliputra Council

39. How is Buddha's first sermon at Saranath described?

A. Dharma Pravarthan

B. Dharma Chakra Pravarthan
C. Dharma Samagam
D. Madhya Samagam

40. Which state was not situated in the South during Ashokan empire?
A. Chola B. Pallav
C. Pandya D. All of these

41. Who was Mauryan King who left the throne and became Jaina?
A. Bindusara
B. Chandragupta Maurya
C. Dasarath
D. Kunal

42. Which of the following statements about Arthashastra is/are correct?
1. It is a treatise on Mauryan political economy and administration.
2. Its date and authorship is a fully eastablished fact beyond any controversy.
3. It is divided into 15 Adhikarnas.
4. Its evidence is unfortunately not corroborated by any other source.

Select the correct answer from the codes given below:
A. 2 and 4 B. 3 and 4
C. 1 and 2 D. All of the above

43. The Mauryan Civil Servants were called by the general name of:
A. Amatyas B. Rajukas
C. Mahamatras D. Lipikaras

44. Mark the correct number of spokes in Dhamma Chakra.
A. 20 B. 32
C. 30 D. 24

45. The term "Dharmasthiya" used by Kautilya denoted:
A. Educational institution
B. Religious institution
C. Judicial court
D. Department of revenue

46. Evidence of Roman trade with South India is available from the excavations at:
A. Arikamedu and Alagangulam
B. Arikamedu and Kanyakumari
C. Kanyakumari and Kodungallur
D. Alagangulam, Arikamedu and Kodungallur

47. Match the following authors with their literary works:
(*a*) Ashwaghosha 1. Gathasapthasati
(*b*) Patanjali 2. Sariputraprakarana
(*c*) Hala 3. Mahabhashya
(*d*) Bhasa 4. Swapnavasavadatta

Codes:

	(*a*)	(*b*)	(*c*)	(*d*)
A.	1	2	3	4
B.	2	1	3	4
C.	3	2	1	4
D.	2	3	1	4

48. The first epigraphic reference of committing Sati (of A.D. 510) has been found from:
A. Erau (M.P.) B. Prayaga (U.P.)
C. Bhital (U.P.) D. Vidisha (M.P.)

49. Which secular work describes Rama's invasions of Ceylon?
A. Gadhayuddha B. Setu Bandu
C. Shapatashataka D. Karpoora Manjari

50. The language of the Sangam literature was:
A. Sanskrit B. Telugu
C. Tamil D. Brahmi

51. Two-storeyed vihar of the rock-cut order was made at:
A. Karle B. Bedsa
C. Bhaja D. Nasik

52. What is a Prashasti?
A. Private endowment B. Eulogy of a king
C. Royal charter D. Copper plate

53. The common coins used in Gupta age, due to the decline in trade were:
A. Copper B. Iron
C. Cowries D. Silver

54. Who built the Sudharshan lake of Saurashtra?
A. Chandragupta Maurya
B. Pushpagupta
C. Ashoka
D. Tushashp

55. Which Vakataka ruler married the daughter of Chandragupta II?
A. Rudrasena II B. Rudrasena I
C. Narendrasena D. Pravarasena

56. Forced labour during the Gupta period is referred to as:
A. Vishti B. Shudra
C. Vaisheshika D. Vali

57. Kalhana's Rajatarangini is a historical work on:
A. Malwa B. Kashmir
C. Vaishali D. Pataliputra

58. Name the river, on whose bank was the city of Vijayanagara located.
A. Kaveri B. Krishna
C. Wainganga D. Thungabhadra

59. The founder of the Satavahana dynasty is:
A. Simukha
B. Yajnashri Satakarni
C. Pulamayi I
D. Sri Shatakam

60. The Pandyan empire was finally absorbed into the:
A. Sultanate of Delhi B. Vijayanagara
C. Chera D. Mughal empire

61. The Rashtrakutas were the successors of the:
A. Vakatakas
B. Chalukyas of Kalyani
C. Chalukyas of Badami
D. Pallavas of Kanchi

62. The temples found in Aihole are:
1. Meguti Shivalaya
2. Ladhkhan temple
3. Jain temple
4. Durga temple
5. Huchimalligudi
Choose the correct answer group:
A. 1, 2, 5 B. 2, 3, 4 and 5
C. 1, 2 and 4 D. 2, 3 and 5

63. The Khajuraho temples were built by:
A. Chalukyas B. Chauhans
C. Paramaras D. Chandellas

64. Alberuni visited India with which Muslim invader?
A. Mohammud of Ghazni
B. Mohammad Ghori
C. Mohammad-bin-Qasim
D. None of the above

65. Raziya was close to which of these nobles?
A. Qubacha
B. Jalaluddin Yakut
C. Nasiruddin Mahmud
D. None of these

66. When Taimur invade, which dynasty ruled over India?
A. Lodhi B. Tughlaq
C. Sayyid D. Khilji

67. Sher Shah is considered to be the fore-runner of Akbar in administration because:
A. his administrative policies were adopted by Akbar
B. he ruled before Akbar
C. he trained Akbar in administration
D. he supervised Akbar's administration

68. Who built the precious Pillar of Chittor (Kirti Stamba)?
A. Rana Kumba B. Rana Sanga
C. Rana Maldev D. None of these

69. Lakh Baksh was the title of:
A. Aibak B. Balban
C. Iltutmish D. Jalal-ud-din-Yakut

70. Ahmed Shah Abdali belonged to which clan?
A. Irani B. Turani
C. Afghani D. Durani

71. Krishnadevaraya belonged to the:
A. Sangam dynasty B. Saluva dynasty
C. Tuluva dynasty D. Aravidu dynasty

72. The Bahmani Sultan who shifted the capital from Gulbarga to Bidar was:
A. Muhammad Gawan
B. Ahmad Shah
C. Nizam Shah
D. Mahmud Shah

73. Put in correct chronological sequence, the successors of Shivaji:

1. Sahu
2. Shivaji II
3. Rajaram
4. Sambhaji
5. Ram Raja

Choose the correct answer group:

A. 4, 3, 2, 1, 5 B. 2, 1, 5, 3, 4
C. 5, 4, 2, 1, 3 D. 1, 2, 3, 5, 4

74. Which of the following was the founder of the house of the Peshwas?

A. Parashurama Trimbak
B. Ramachandra Pant
C. Balaji Vishwanath
D. Balaji Bajirao

75. Under Zabti System the most fertile land was classified as:

A. Polaj B. Parauti
C. Chachar D. Banjar

76. Vasco da Gama reached Calicut in:

A. 1498 A.D. B. 1480 A.D
C. 1492 A.D. D. 1463 A.D.

77. Match the List-I with List-II.

List-I	List-II
(*a*) Francisco de Almeida	1. Encourage his fellow countrymen to marry Indian women
(*b*) Alfenso de Albuquerque	2. Blue-water policy
(*c*) Nino da Cunha	3. Transferred Portuguese capital from Cochin to Goa
(*d*) Martin Alfonso de Souza	4. Famous Jesuit Saint Francisco Xavier accompanied him to India

Codes:

	(*a*)	(*b*)	(*c*)	(*d*)
A.	2	1	4	3
B.	3	2	1	4
C.	1	2	3	4
D.	4	2	1	3

78. Guru Nanak's concept of religion was:

A. Severely practical B. Ethical
C. Both (A) and (B) D. Purely spiritual

79. Who built the Jama Mosque of Delhi?

A. Akabar
B. Qutub-ud-din-Aibak
C. Jahangir
D. Shahjahan

80. What was the original name of Tansen?

A. Makaranda Pande B. Baz Bahadur
C. Lal Kalwant D. Ramtanu Pande

81. Who is the author of 'My Experiments with Truth'?

A. Jawaharlal Nehru
B. Mahatma Gandhi
C. Rajendra Prasad
D. Sardar Vallabhabhai Patel

82. Who started the Modern Local Self-Government?

A. Lord Irwin B. Lord Ripon
C. Lord Curzon D. Lord Auckland

83. In whose tenure the capital of India was transferred from Delhi to Calcutta?

A. Lord Minto
B. Lord Hardings
C. Lord Curzon
D. Viscount Chelmsford

84. The Royal Indian Navy was established in:

A. 1930 B. 1931
C. 1934 D. 1936

85. The play Neel Darpan was written by:

A. M.G. Ranade
B. Deenbandhu Mitra
C. Rajaram Mohan Roy
D. Ishwar Chandra Vidyasagar

86. The Strachy Commission was connected with:

A. The Vernacular Press
B. Famine
C. Education
D. Local Self-Government

87. Who said "Go back to the Vedas"?

A. Dayananda Saraswati

B. Rajaram Mohan Roy
C. Vidyasagar
D. Ishwar Chandra Vidyasagar

88. The Trade Union Act was passed in:
A. 1926 B. 1930
C. 1939 D. 1941

89. Queen's Proclamation was passed in which month of 1858?
A. April B. June
C. August D. September

90. How many Home Rule Leagues were formed in India in 1916?
A. 2 B. 4
C. 5 D. None

91. Match the following:

(*a*) Quit India Movement	1.	1927
(*b*) Simon Commission	2.	1920
(*c*) Khilafat Movement	3.	1942
(*d*) Montague Chelmsford	4.	1919

Codes:

	(*a*)	(*b*)	(*c*)	(*d*)
A.	1	2	3	4
B.	3	1	2	4
C.	4	3	2	1
D.	3	4	2	1

92. Where was the historical case settled upon INA?
A. In the Fort William, Calcutta
B. In the Red Fort of Delhi
C. In the Central Hall of Parliament
D. In a Warship Near Bombay

93. The main inspiration behind Five Year Plan was:
A. USSR B. USA
C. UK D. None

94. Match List I with List II:

List-I		**List-II**
(*a*) NAM	1.	U.K.
(*b*) Non-Aggression Pact	2.	U.S.A.
(*c*) Unipolar World	3.	U.S.S.R.
(*d*) Commonwealth	4.	Yugoslavia

Codes:

	(*a*)	(*b*)	(*c*)	(*d*)
A.	1	2	3	4
B.	3	4	2	1
C.	2	3	4	1
D.	4	3	2	1

95. In which year China usurped Tibet?
A. 1950 B. 1957
C. 1959 D. 1960

96. Nationalism of Banks was done in:
A. 1969 B. 1965
C. 1970 D. 1971

97. Who wrote 'Hind Swaraj'?
A. Bal Gangadhar Tilak
B. Vinobha Bhave
C. Chandra Shekhar Azad
D. M.K. Gandhi

98. Pandit Nehru was a believer in:
A. Isolation B. Adult Franchise
C. Hindu State D. None of the above

99. India Agriculture can be characterised as:
A. Progressive
B. Subsistence based
C. Technically rich
D. Production for market

100. Which was the area of dispute between India and China?
A. Burma B. Uttar Pradesh
C. Tunjun pass D. Tibet

ANSWERS

1	2	3	4	5	6	7	8	9	10
D	B	B	A	D	D	B	B	C	A
11	**12**	**13**	**14**	**15**	**16**	**17**	**18**	**19**	**20**
C	D	B	A	A	D	A	C	D	C

21	22	23	24	25	26	27	28	29	30
A	B	B	C	C	D	A	D	A	A
31	**32**	**33**	**34**	**35**	**36**	**37**	**38**	**39**	**40**
B	B	C	A	A	A	C	D	B	B
41	**42**	**43**	**44**	**45**	**46**	**47**	**48**	**49**	**50**
B	A	A	D	C	A	D	A	B	C
51	**52**	**53**	**54**	**55**	**56**	**57**	**58**	**59**	**60**
A	B	C	B	A	A	B	D	A	A
61	**62**	**63**	**64**	**65**	**66**	**67**	**68**	**69**	**70**
A	B	D	A	B	C	A	A	A	D
71	**72**	**73**	**74**	**75**	**76**	**77**	**78**	**79**	**80**
C	D	A	C	A	A	A	C	D	D
81	**82**	**83**	**84**	**85**	**86**	**87**	**88**	**89**	**90**
B	B	B	C	B	B	A	A	B	A
91	**92**	**93**	**94**	**95**	**96**	**97**	**98**	**99**	**100**
B	B	A	D	C	A	D	B	B	D

HISTORY

1. HARAPPAN CIVILIZATION

1.1 INTRODUCTION

In 1924, scholars in history were roused by the announcement of Sir John Marshall that his Indian aides, particularly R.D. Banerjee, discovered (1922-23) at Mohenjo-daro in the Larkana district of Sind, now in Pakistan, the remains of a civilisation, one of the oldest of the world. A few hundred miles towards the north of Mohenjo-daro, four or five superimposed cities were excavated at Harappa in the Montgomery district of the Punjab, now in Pakistan. Recently, excavations carried out on the site of Kalibangan have revealed a third city as large as Harappa and Mohenjo-daro. That the civilisation was not confined to the limits of the Indus Valley can be understood from the finds of relics of the same civilisation at Sutkagendor on the sea board of south Baluchistan, in the west of Alamgirpur in the Uttar Pradesh in the east; and from Ropar in the Himalayan foothills in the north to Bhagatrav on the river Kim in between the Narmada and Tapti in the South. This civilisation belonged to the Chalcolithic i.e. Copper Bronze Age of history; no trace of iron has been found.

Until the discovery of the remains of the Indus Civilisation, it was believed by scholars that the history of India practically began with the coming of the Aryans. But this theory is an exploded one and the pre-historic civilisation of India, that is, the Indus Civilisation is contemporaneous with the civilisations of Mesopotamia, Egypt, etc.

MAJOR HARAPPAN SITES AND THEIR EXCAVATORS

Name of Sites	Year of Excavation	Excavators	Region/River	Features
Harappa	1921	Daya Ram Sahni	Montgomery district of Punjab (Now in Pak) on the left bank of Ravi.	- City followed grid planning. - Row of six granaries. - Only place having evidences of coffin burial. - Evidence of fractional burial and coffin burial - Cemetery-H of alien people.
Mohenjo-daro	1922	R.D. Banarjee	Larkana district in Sind on the right bank of Indus. (Now in Pak).	- City followed grid planning. - A large granary and Great Bath, a college. - Human skeletons showing invasion and massacre. - Evidence of horse comes from superficial level. - A piece of woven cotton alongwith spindle whorls and needles - A bearded man in steatite and a bronze dancing girl are found. - Town was flooded more than seven times. - A seal representing Mother Goddess with a plant growing from her wombe and a woman to be sacrificed by a man with a knife in his hand.
Chanhu-daro	1931	N. Gopal Majumdar, Mackey	Situated in Sind on the bank of Indus.	- The city has no citadal. - Famous for bead makers shop. - A small pot, possibly an inkpot. - Foot prints of a dog chasing a cat. - Evidence of copper or bronze tools of carts with seated drivers. - Three different cultural layers- Indus, Jhukar and Jhangar.

Kalibangan	1953	A. Ghosh	Situated in Rajasthan on the Bank of Ghaggar.	- Shows both Pre-Harappan and Harappan phase. - Evidence of furrowed land. - Evidence of seven fire altars and camel bones. - Many houses had their own well. - Kalibangan stands for black bangles. - Evidnce of a wooden furrow - Evidences of two types of burials: (1) burials in a rectangular grave and; (ii) burials in a circular grave.
Lothal	1953	S.R. Rao	Situated in Gujarat on Bhogava river near Gulf of Cambay.	- A tiled floor which bears intersecting design of circles. - Remains of rice husk (Rungpur is the only other Harappan city where the rice husk has been found) - Evidence of horse from a terracotta figurine. - A ship designed on a seal - A terracotta ship - An instrument for measuring angles, pointing to modern day compass - Houses with entrances on the main street a unique feature as the houses of all other Harappan cities had side entries. - First man-made port in the world and a dock. - Evidence of joint burial.
Banwali	1974	R.S. Bisht	Situated in Hissar district of Haryana.	- Shows both Pre-Harappan and Harappan phase. - Good quantity of barley found here.
Surkotada	1964	J.P. Joshi	Situated in Kutch (Bhuj) district of Gujarat	- Bones of horses, Bead making shops.
Sutkagendor	1927	Stein, R.L.	Situated in Baluchistan on Dast river.	- Trade point between Harappa and Babylon, belong to mature phase. - Evidence of horse
Amri	1935	N.G. Majumdar	Situated in Sind on the bank of Indus.	- Evidence of antelope.
Dholavira	1985-90	R.S. Bisht	Situated in Gujarat in Rann of Kutch.	- Seven cultural stages. - Largest site. - Three parts of city. - Unique water management.
Rangpur	1953	M.S. Vats, B.B. Lal & S.R. Rao	Situated on the bank of Mahar in Gujarat.	- Rice was cultivated.
Kot Diji	1953	Fazal Ahmed	Situated on the bank of Indus.	- Wheel made painted pottery. - Traces of a defensive wall and well aligned streets. - Knowledge of metallurgy, artistic toys etc. - Five figurines of Mother Goddess discovered.
Ropar	1953	Y.D. Sharma	Situated in Punjab of the banks of Sutlej.	- Evidence of burying a dog below the human burial. - One example of rectangular mudbrick chamber was noticed. - Five fold cultures- Harappan, PGW, NBP, Kushana-Gupta and Medieval.
Balakot	1963-76	George. F. Dales	Situated on the Arabian Sea.	- Remain of pre-Harappan and Harappan civilisation. - The mounds rise to the height of about 9.7mts and are spread 2.8 sq hectare of area.
Alamgirpur	1958	Y.D. Sharma	Situated on Hindon in Ghaziabad	- The impression of cloth on a trough is discovered. - Usually considered to be the eastern boundary of the Indus culture.

1.2 GEOGRAPHICAL EXTENT

The Harappan culture was the most extensive of the ancient civilizations in area, including not only the Indus plain (the Punjab and Sind), but also northern Rajasthan and the region of Kathiawar in western India. It was essentially a city culture and among the centres of authority were the two cities of Mohenjo-daro and Harappa. The 1400 settlements, discovered so far are distributed over a very wide geographical area. Its known extent in the west is upto Sutkagendor in Baluchistan: Alamgirpur in Meerut district (Uttar Pradesh) in the east, Daimabad (Ahmadnagar district, Maharashtra) in south; and Manda (Akhnoor district, Jammu and Kashmir) in the north, covering an area of almost 1600 km. east-west and 1400 km. north-south. The total geographical area over which this civilization flourished is more than 20 times of the area of Egyptian and more than 12 times of the area of Egyptian and Mesopotamian civilizations combined. It covers an area of about 12,50,000 sq. km. Harappan settlements are mostly located on river banks of Indus and Saraswati.

SOME NEW FINDS

Site	Location	Discovered by
Ganverivala	Pakistan	Rafeeq Mugal
Rakhi Garhi	Jind (Haryana)	Rafeeq Mugal

1.3 TOWN PLANNING

The first thing that strikes us with regard to Harappan culture is the town planning and urbanisation. Mohenjo-daro, Harappa, Lothal or Sutkagendor were built on similar plan. To the west of each was a citadel built on a high platform. It was defended by wall and on it were constructed the public buildings. Below this citadel was the town proper. Everywhere, the main streets ran from north to south and other streets ran at right angles to the main streets. Houses, residential or others, stood on both sides of the streets. Both at Harappa and Mohenjo-daro, houses were built of kiln-burnt bricks. At Lothal and Kalibangan, residential houses were made of sun-dried bricks. The drains, wells and bathing platforms were made of kiln-burnt bricks. An average house had, besides kitchen and bath, four to six living rooms. Large houses with thirty rooms and staircases suggest that there were large two or three storyed buildings. Most of the houses had wells within them and a drainage system carried the waste water to the main underground drain of the street. There were also public baths with wells. The covered drains of the streets had soak-pits and manholes for clearing. There were also arrangements for street lighting.

TOWNS ASSOCIATED WITH DIFFERENT INDUSTRIES

Levan	Stone tools factory
Sukar	Stone tools factory
Lothal	Stone tools factory Factory for metallic finished goods
Balakot	Factory for pearl finished goods, Bangle's factory
Chanhudaro	Beads factory Pearl finished goods factory Metallic finished goods factory Bangle's factory

EVIDENCE FROM CHIEF SITES

Cemetry H & R-37	Harappa
Prepared Garments	Mohenjodaro
Lower fortified town	Kalibangan
Port town	Lothal
Evidence of Rice	Lothal, Rangpur
Coffin Burial	Harappa
Horse Bone	Surkotada
Fire Altar	Kalibangan & Lothal
Temple like palace	Mohenjodaro
Horse's tooth	Rana Ghundai
Pashupati Seal	Mohenjodaro
Goddesses	Mohenjodaro
Copper Rhino	Diamabad
Copper Chariot	Diamabad
Copper Elephant	Diamabad
Granery	Moehnjodaro & Harappa
Bronze Female Dancer	Mohenjodaro
Granery outside fort	Harappa
Beads factory	Lothal & Chanhudaro
Copper ox	Kalibangan
Bangles factory	Chanhudaro, Balakot
Graveyard	Harappa, Lothal
Phallus Worship	Harappa
Bronze Bufallo	Diamabad

Evidence of Earthquake	Kalibangan
Evidence of Plough	Kalibangan
Balance made up of Ivory	Lothal & Mohenjodaro
Copper dog	Lothal
Camel's Bone	Kalibangan
Boustrephedon Style	Kalibangan
Stone Covered Grave	Surkotada
Canals	Malavan
Wooden Drainage	Kalibangan

At Harappa, a great granary has been discovered. It was built on a raised platform to protect it from floods. The granary was divided into storage blocks for storing of corn collected from the people as land tax.

1.4 ECONOMIC LIFE

The discovery of granaries and the urban lifestyle of the people proves that the Harappan people were undoubtedly 'comfort loving' and were prosperous.

(i) Agriculture : The Indus people sowed seeds in the flood plains in November, when the flood water receded, and reaped their harvests of wheat and barley in April before the advent of the next flood. The Harappans probably used the wooden plough with wooden or copper ploughshare. *Gabarbands or nalas* enclosed by dams for storing water were a feature in parts of Baluchistan and Afghanistan, but channel or canal irrigation seems to have been absent.

The Indus people produced wheat, barley, peas, kodon, sanwa, jowar, ragi, etc. They produced two types of wheat and barley. A good quantity of barley has been discovered at Banwali. In addition to this, they produced sesame and mustard. The Indus people were the earliest people to produce cotton.

(ii) Domestication of Animals : Although the Harappans practised agriculture, animals were kept on a large scale. Oxen, buffaloes, goats, sheeps domestic fowls and pigs were domesticated. The humped bulls were favoured by the Harappans. From the very beginning, dogs were regarded as pets. Cats were also domesticated, and signs of the feet of both dogs and cats have been noticed. They also kept asses and camels, which were possibly used as beasts of burden. Elephants were well known to the Harappans, who were also acquainted with the rhinoceros, spotted dear, sambhar deer, hog deer, wild pig, etc.

(iii) Trade and Commerce: The thriving agricultural economy supported a flourishing trade both within the northern and western areas of the sub-continent and between the people of this culture and those of the Persian Gulf and Mesopotamia. The products of Indus have been found in Mesopotamia. Its seals and produce were also discovered at Sumer. The findings of Indus seals suggest that merchants from Indus actually resided in Mesopotamia. Their chief merchandise was probably cotton exported from probably Lothal harbour. The Mesopotamian records from about 2350 BC refer to trade relations with Meluha, which was the ancient name given to the Indus region. There were two intermediate trading stations called Dilmun and Makan which lay between the regions of two civilisations.

EVIDENCES HARAPPAN'S EXTERNAL TRADE

— Mention of '*Meluha*' in Sumerian literature

— Evidence of trade between 'Magan'

— Seals of Indus Valley have been noticed from Ur, Kis, Susa and Logas towns of Mesopotamia.

— Like Mesopotamian, Cylindrical seals have been found from Mohenjodaro.

— Use of Mesopotamian cosmetics products by the Harappans.

— Coffin made burials have been a foreign phenomenon which were too frequent in Harappa and Mesopotamia.

— Figure of humped bull on Mesopotamian seals.

MAJOR IMPORTS BY THE HARAPPANS

Material	Source
Gold	Afghanistan, Persia, Karnataka
Silver	Afghanistan, Iran
Copper	Baluchistan & Khetri (Rajasthan)
Tin	Afghanistan, Central Asia
Agates	Western India
Chalcedony	Saurashtra
Lead	Rajasthan, South India, Afghanistan, Iran
Lapis Lazuli	Badakashan and Kashmir
Turquoise	Central Asia, Iran
Amethyst	Maharashtra
Jade	Central Asia
Carnelian	Saurashtra

(iv) Crafts and Industries: Mohenjo-daro was a great industrial centre. Weaving was probably the chief industry. Harappans were also acquainted with the art of dyeing. Pottery was an important industry. Harappans used to export these pots made on potter's wheel and burnt in kilns not only to nearby areas but also to the far-flung places. The art of smelting metals was well-known to the people of Harappa. The use of lead, bronze and tin was rampant. Huge brick structures suggest that brick-laying was an important craft. They also attest to a class of masons. The Harappans also practised boat-making, seal-making and terracotta manufacturing. The Harappans were also experts in beadmaking.

(v) Weights and Measures: The regulation of weights and measures forms the basis of trade and Harappans were very accurate in this respect. The sexagesimal system and the decimal system were known to the Harappans. The weights were of cubical and spherical in shape and were made of chert, jasper and agate and sometimes of grey stone and were in a series, first doubling from 1, 2, 4, 8 to 64 then going to 160, 320, 640 and so forth. The unit of ratio was 16 equivalent to 13.64 grams.

The measurement as per the discovery of the bronze rod was divided accurately into units of 0.264 inches with an error of .003 inches. Another scale on a shell was on the decimal system of 1.32 inches forming a foot of 13.2 inches.

16 *Chhatank* made a *ser* and 16 *annas* made one rupee.

(vi) Communications: Transport and communications are a major part of trade and commerce. Harappans also had good transporting system for their internal and external trade. Representation of ships and boats are found on some seals and as graffiti on pottery. For onland journey and transport, they relied upon the bullock carts and rarely horse carts. They practised navigation on the coast of the Arabian Sea.

(vii) Arts : The Harappans were utilitarians although not completely devoid of artistic sense. They were well-acquainted with the manufacture and use of bronze. Bronze-smiths produced images and utensils. They also made several kinds of tools and weapons, namely, axes, saws, knives and spears. Jewelleries of silver, gold and copper were also made on a large scale.

The most notable artistic achievement of the Harappans was in their seal engravings, especially those of animals (also see box)

The red sandstone torso of a man seems to show an attempt at portraiture. However, the bronze dancing girl, found in Mohenjo-daro, is perhaps among the most striking Harappan figurines, Naked but for a necklace and a series of bangles, she stands in a provocative posture.

The pots were beautifully painted in several colours such as red, black, green and rarely yellow. The terracotta figurines, both human and animal, and toys prove that the Harappa people, enjoyed the work of art. Statues made of bronze, stone and sandstone represent their high sense of art. But they obvoiusly seemed to have less painting skills as apart from painted pots they have not left any proof of it.

The artistic skills of the Harappan people were also manifested in their pottery making (see box).

HARAPPAN POTTERY

- Harappan pottery is bright or dark red and is uniformly sturdy and well baked.
- It is chiefly wheel made, and consists of both plain and painted ware, the plain variety being more common.
- Harappan people used different types of pottery such as glazed, polychrome, incised perforated and knobbed. The glazed Harappan pottery is the earliest example of its kind in the ancient world.
- On the whole, Harappan pottery was highly utilitarian in character, though the painted designs on some pieces show a remarkable artistic touch.

HARAPPAN SEALS

- Most commonly made of steatite (soft stone).
- The technique of cutting and polishing these seals with white luster was a unique invention of the Harappans.
- The majority of the seals have an animal engraved on them with a short inscription.
- Unicorn is the animal most frequently represented on the seals.
- Main types : (a) the square type with a carved animal and inscription. (b) the rectangular type with inscription only.

Bronze Art : The Harappan culture belongs to Bronze Age. Bronze was made by smiths by mixing tin with copper. A woman dancer made of bronze is the best specimen. It has right arm poised on the hip with few bracelets covered with left arm on a bent left leg, a necklace and well-braided hair, the ankles and feet are missing.

Late Harappan Pottery Culture

❖ **Cementary H. Culture** - (Harappa) Black and Red Polished ware

❖ **Jhukar Culture** -Chanhudaro (yellow pottery) coloured with violet and black also

❖ **Jhangar Culture** - Chanhudaro, Greyware

Black and Redware

❖ internally black-coloured, red coloured outside

❖ Painting on potteries found in Bihar, Rajasthan, Madhya Pradesh, West Bengal

❖ Paintings absent in potteries found in Doab area.

❖ White paintings on potteries from Ahar and Gilund

❖ Atranjikhera, Hastinapur, Alamgirpur and Jodhpur are some important sites.

O.C.P. (Ochre-Coloured Pottery) 2000 BC.

❖ **Chief Areas** - Ganga-Yamuna doab

❖ **Structure of Potteries** - Orange coloured

❖ **Chief Cities** - Hastinapur, Ahichchatra, Lalkila Rajapur

(viii) Currency : Thousands of seals have been discovered not only from the Harappan sites but also from the remains of other world civilisations. Every merchant and his family had a seal bearing an emblem and a brief inscription. But it is still unknown whether they used these seals as currency or not. In absence of evidence, it is safe to assume that the Harappans practised barter system and got goods they need in exchange of their articles.

1.5 SOCIAL AND RELIGIOUS LIFE

The social life of the Harappans can be arranged into following categories :

(i) Class: It is not proved if there existed any classes or caste as the Aryan's varna system. Based upon the mounds we can assume that there were classes if not castes according to the occupation of the people.

(ii) Dress and Ornaments: As far as their dress is concerned, one cannot say anything definitely, because all information about their dress is based on inferences arrived at from two types of materials: firstly, on the basis of spindles discovered and secondly from the dress of statues and carvings on different seals found in those cities. Ornaments were also popular among both men and women. Necklaces, fillets, armlets, finger-rings and bangles were probably used by both the sexes. Girdles, nose studs, ear-studs, anklets etc. may have been worn by women only as are proved by the statues.

The seals bearing figures, hair-pins, combs and a few statues also have been discovered in Harappa and Mohenjo-daro, which tells us about the hair-dressing of the people of those days. It is quite interesting to know that these people, also knew the use of some sorts of collyrium, face-powders, lip-sticks, face paints and perfumary, which were also exported.

(iii) Religion : Following were the highlights of the religious life of the Harppans :

- The chief male deity was the *Pashupati Mahadeva* (Proto-Siva), represented in seals as sitting in a yogic posture on a low throne and having three faces and two horns. He is surrounded by four animals (elephant, tiger, rhino and buffalo), each facing a different direction, and two deers appear at his feet.

- The chief female deity was the Mother Goddess, who has been depicted in various forms.
- There is sufficient evidence for the prevalence of phallic worship. Numerous stone symbols of female sex organs (yoni worship) , besides those of the phallus, have been discovered.
- The worship of fire is proved by the discovery of fire altars at Lothal, Kalibangan and Harappa.
- Indus people also worshipped Gods in the form of trees (pipal, etc.) and animals (unicorn etc.).
- They believed in ghosts and evil forces and used amulets as protection against them.

(iv) Script: The script of the Harappan people had 400 to 500 signs and it were not alphabetic but was **logosyllablic** writing system. Although the Harappan script is yet to be deciphered, overlaps of letters on some of the potsherds from kalibangan show that the writing was from left to right and from right to left in alternate lines, i.e. **'boustrophedon'**.

(v) Games : The Harappans preferred indoor hobbies to outdoor amusements. Dance and music were their popular amusements. Some tubular and conical dices discovered in these cities show that the evil of gambling is as old as history. Another game which they played resembles our modern chess. Marble dolls and animals toys show that the children of Mohenjodaro were well supplied with playthings. Fishing and hunting animals were other source of entertainment.

(vi) Disposal of the Dead : No definite proof is available regarding the disposal of the dead bodies yet. It is believed that the dead were either burnt completely, cremation followed by burial of ashes and rarely the burial of the dead after exposure to birds and beasts.

THE DECLINE OF INDUS VALLEY : THEORISTS AND THEORIES

Theorists	Reasons of Decline
1. Gorden Childe, Stuart Piggot	External aggression
2. H.T. Lambrick	Unstable river systems
3. K.U.R. Kenedy	Natural calamity
4. Orell Stein and A.N. Ghosh	Climate change
5. R. Mortimer Wheeler	Aryan invasion
6. Robert Raikes	Earthquake
7. Sood and Aggarwal	Dryness of river
8. Walter Fairservis	Ecological imbalance

INDUS VALLEY–FACTS AT A GLANCE

- The state which has accounted for highest number of Harappan sites after independence: *Gujarat*
- Three Harappan sites that have yielded three stages of Harappan civilization (Pre-Harappan, Harappan and post-Harappan : *Rojde, Desalpur and Surkotada.*
- Most commonly engraved animal on Harappan seals: *Humpless bull or unicorn*
- Sites which have yielded evidence of a pre-Harappan settlement: *Kot-Diji, Kalibangan and Harappa*
- Time span of the Harappan civilization as fixed on the basis of radio-carbon dating: *2300 BC–1750 BC.*
- Major Harappan cities that acted as ports: *Lothal, Balakot, Suktagendor and Allahdin (Pakistan).*
- The geometric shape of the region covered by the Indus civilization: *Triangle*
- The Harappan city with most impressive drainage system: *Mohenjo-daro.*
- Most common materials used for the Harappan stone sculpture: *Limestone and steatite.*

• Two most useful sources for understanding the religious and social life of the Harappan people: *Terracotta figures and seals.* • Mound at Harappa was discovered by *Charles Mason* in 1826. • *Wheeler* said, Indus Valley was a colony of Sumerians • Lions have not been found anywhere in Harappa. • Wider road of Harappa was 30 foot. • A Kushana period Stupa has been found from Mohenjodaro. • Mother goddess was not worshipped at Rangpur. • Evidence of cultivation of peas. Till has been traced from Harappa, paddy from Lothal. • Harappans had trade relations with Mesopotamians around 2300 B.C. • Largest Harappan site in India is situated in Haryana Rakhigarhi, second largest is Dholavira in Gujarat.	• Dimension of Brick-length 11 inches, width -5.5 inches, depth-2.75 inches, ratio 4 2 : 1 • Harappan wheels were axeless. • Sutkegendor, Balakot, Lothal, Allahadino and Sutaka-koh were coastal/port towns. • Mohenjodaro had 10.5 mt. wide road. • At Kalibangan, the lanes and roads of the city were built in a definite proportion. Lanes were 1.8 mt wide and roads were 3.6, 5.4 & 7.2 mtrs. wide. • In Mohenjodaro the length of the Great Bath was 12 mtrs, breadth 7 mtrs, depth 2.8 mtrs. • In the South-West of Mohanjodaro, there was a granery which covers 55x37 mtrs. It is surrounded by verandah's on four sides. There are 27 blocks of solids bricks in grannery. • In Harappa, perhaps because of the river Ravi the Granery is outside the fort. • In the Lothal port, there was a dockyard which is 216 mtrs. in length and 37 mtrs. in breadth.

VEDIC AGE

1.6 INTRODUCTION

The Vedic age began in India in about 1500 BC with the coming of the Aryans, who scattered on the plains of northern India. Max Muller believes it an anomaly to regard the race as Aryan because scientifically Aryan connotes nothing but language. The relationship between the race and language of these people with the classical languages of Europe was established by a Bavarian Franz Bopp in 1816.

Aryans developed Vedic culture based on Vedas. The meaning of the word Veda is "knowledge", the best of all knowledge in the eyes of Hindus. It is a collection of hymns, prayers, charms, litanies and sacrificial formulae. There are four Vedas, namely, *Rig Veda, Sam Veda, Yajur Veda* and *Atharva Veda.*

1.7 ORIGIN OF THE ARYANS

Some scholars, such as Max Muller and Dr. Thapar, believe that originally, the Aryans seem to have lived somewhere in the area east of the Alps, in the region known as Eurasia, the region of the Caspian Sea and the southern Russian steppes, and gradually dividing into a number of tribes migrated in search of pasture, to Greece and Asia Minor, to Iran and to India. By that time, they came to be known as Aryans. This is proved by some Aryan names mentioned in the **Kassite** inscriptions of 1600 BC. and the **Mitanni** inscriptions of the fourteenth century BC. found in Iraq which suggest that from Iran a branch of the Aryans moved towards the west.

ORIGINAL HOME OF ARYANS

REGION	THEORIST
ASIA	
Central Asia	Max Muller
Tibet	Dayanand Saraswati
Pamirs	Mayor
Turkistan	Hurz Feld
Bactria	J.C. Rod
Steppes	Brandstein

EUROPE	
Germany	Penka and Hert
Hungary	Giles
Southern Russia	Nehring
West Baltic	Mach
Arctic Region	B.G. Tilak
Russian Steppes	Prof. Belfy
INDIA	
Central India	Rajbali Pandey
Kashmir	L.D. Kala
Sapta Sindhu	A.C. Das
Himalayan Foothills	Pt. Laxmidhar Shastri

Others scholars, such as Ganganath Jha, A.C. Das, Dr. Sampurnanand etc established the **Sapta-Sindhu** theory of Rig Veda which believ that Aryans were not foreigners but were indigenous people residing in the region comprising modern Punjab and Sindh. This theory has met with criticism, as the historians argue over the vast differences of culture between the Harappans and the Aryans.

Another theory propounded by Lokmanya Tilak suggests the Polar region as the original homeland of Aryans. This view is corroborated by ***Zend Avesta*** and ***Rig Veda***.

1.8 ARYANS' ARRIVAL IN INDIA

The Aryans came to India in several waves. The earliest wave is represented by the *Rig Vedic* people who appeared in the subcontinent in about 1500 BC. They came into conflict with the indigenous inhabitants called the Dravidians mentioned as *dasa* or *dasyus* in *Rig Veda*. The *Rig Veda* mentions the defeat of Sambara by Divodasa, who belonged to the Bharata clan. Possibly the *dasyus* in the *Rig Veda* represent the original inhabitants of the country, and an Aryan chief who overpowered them was called *Trasadvasyu*. The Aryan chief was soft towards the *dasas*, but strongly hostile to the *dasyus*. The term *dasyuhatya*, slaughter of the dasyus, is repeatedly mentioned in the *Rig Veda*.

Some of the chief tribes of the period were *Yadu, Turvasu, Druhyu, Anu Puru, Kuru, Panchala, Bharata* and *Tritsu*. Among the inter-tribal conflicts the most important was the 'Battle of the Ten Kings.'

DRAVIDIANS

- ❖ It is believed that before the coming of the Aryans in India, the greater part of Northern and North-Western India was inhabited by a group of people known as Dravidians.
- ❖ On arrival of the Aryans, unable to meet their challenge, they gradually moved southwards.
- ❖ Perhaps, in India, they were first to use rivers for navigation and irrigation.

ARYANS

- ❖ The group of Indo-Europeans who moved to Persia and India are known to Aryans
- ❖ The Aryans are the original inhabitants of Central Asia.
- ❖ They arrived in India around 1500 BC
- ❖ The region where the Aryans settled in India was called Sapta Sindhu (also referred to as the Brahmavarta)
- ❖ The Aryans established themselves in India by defeating the natives whom they called **Dasas** or **Dasyus**
- ❖ The period when the Aryans first settled in India, is known as Early Vedic Period
- ❖ The Aryans spread to Indo-Gangetic plains in the later Vedic Period and this region came to be known as Aryavarta
- ❖ The Aryans were the first people in India to know the use of iron and brought horses along with them

1.9 RIG VEDIC POLITY

The administrative machinery of the Aryans in the Rig Vedic period worked with the tribal chief in the centre. He was called *rajan*. Although his post was hereditary, we have also some traces of election by the tribal assembly called the *samiti*. The king was called the protector of his tribe. He protected its cattle, fought its wars and offered prayers to gods on its behalf.

Several tribal assemblies, such as the *sabha, samiti, vidatha,* and *gana* mentioned in the *Rig*

Veda exercised deliberative, military and religious functions. Even women attended the *sabha* and *vidatha* in Rig Vedic times. But from the political point of view important were the *sabha* and *samiti.*

In the day-to-day administration, the king was assisted by a few functionaries. The most important functionary seems to have been the *purohita.* The two priests who played a major part in the time of *Rig Veda* were Vasishtha and Visvamitra. The next important functionary seems to be the *senani. Princes* received from the people voluntary offering called *bali.*

There were cases of theft and burglary, and especially we hear of the theft of cows. Spies were employed to keep an eye on such unsocial activities. The officer who enjoyed authority over the pasture ground was called *vrajapati*. He led the heads of the families called *Kulapas,* or the heads of the fighting hordes called *gramanis* to battle. The king did not maintain any regular or standing army, but in times of war he mustered a militia whose military functions were performed by different tribal groups called *vrata, gana, grama, sardha.*

TRIBAL POLITY

- The chief was the protector of the tribe or *Jana.*
- However, he did not possess unlimited powers for he had to reckon with the tribal assemblies.
- *Sabha, Samiti, Vidhata* and *Gana* were the tribal assemblies. Of these, *Vidhata* was the oldest. These assemblies exercised deliberative, military and religious functions.
- The two most important assemblies were the *Sabha* and *Samiti. Samiti* was general in nature and less exclusive than *Sabha.*
- Women attended *Sabha* and *Vidhata* in *Rig Vedic* times.
- A few non-monarchical states (*ganas*), are described whose head was *Ganapati* or *Jyestha.*

1.10 SOCIO-ECONOMIC LIFE IN RIG VEDIC PERIOD

Tribal Organization : Kinship was the basis of social structure. People gave their primary loyalty to the tribe, which was called *jana.* Another important term which stands for the tribe in the *Rig Veda* is *vis.* Probably the *vis* was divided into *grama* or smaller tribal units meant for fighting. When the gramas clashed with one another, it caused *samgrama* or war. The term for family (*kula*) is mentioned rarely in the *Rig Veda.* It seems that family in early Vedic phase was indicated by the term *griha.* Differentiation in family relationships leading to the setting up of separate households had not proceeded far, and the family was a very large joint unit. It was obviously a patriarchal family headed by the father. Since it was a patriarchal society, the birth of a son was desired again and again.

PURUSHASUKTA THEORY

Purushasukta is a late hymn (of Mandal X) of the *Rig Veda.* The hymn says that when the gods divided *purusha* or the Primeval creator, the Brahman was his mouth; Kshatriya (rajanys) was made his arms; the Vaishya was his thighs; and the Shudra sprang from his feet. This is the only hymn in the *Rig Veda* in which the names rajanya, vaishya and shudra occur.

Marriage and Status of Women : The institution of marriage was established, although symbols of primitive practices survived. We also notice the practice of levirate and widow remarriage in the *Rig Veda.*

The status of women was equal to men and they received *Upanayana* and education, studied *Vedas* and some of them even rose to the rank of seers composing Vedic hymns. Monogamy was established, though polygamy and polyandry were also known.

Varna System : *Varna* was the term used for colour, and it seems that the Aryans were fair and the indigenous inhabitants dark in complexion. The *dasas* and *dasyus,* who were conquered by the Aryans, were treated as slaves and sudras. Gradually, the tribal society was divided into three groups—warriors, priests and the people. The fourth division called the *Shudras* appeared towards the end of the *Rig Vedic* period. In the age of the *Rig Veda,* divisions based on occupations had started. But this division was not very sharp.

Occupation : Their earliest life seems to have been mainly pastoral, agriculture being a secondary occupation. The Aryans did not lead a settled life. Although they used several animals, the horse played the most significant role in their life.

The *Rig Vedic* people possessed better knowledge of agriculture. Ploughshare is mentioned in the earliest part of the *Rig Veda* though some consider it an interpolation. Possibly, this ploughshare was made of wood.

They were acquainted with sowing, harvesting and threshing, and knew about the different seasons. Inspite of all this, there are so many references to the cow in the *Rig Veda* that the *Rig Vedic* Aryans seem to have been a pastoral people. The term for war in the *Rig Veda* is ***gavisthi*** or 'search for cows'. Whenever we hear of gifts made to priests, it is stated in terms of cows and women slaves and never in terms of the measurment of land. The *Rig Veda* mentions such artisans as the carpenter, the chariot-maker, the weaver, the leather worker, the potter, etc. This indicates that they practiced all these crafts. The term, *ayas* used for copper or bronze shows that metal working was known.

Metals Known to Rig Vedic People	
Gold	*Hiranya*
Iron	*Shyama (Krishna Ayas)*
Copper	*Ayas*

Diet: The Indo-Aryans, while sharing the ancient Iranian veneration for the cow, felt no scruple about sacrificing both bulls and cows at weddings or on other important occasions. The persons who took part in the sacrifice ate the flesh of the victim, whether bull, cow, or horse. But meat was eaten only as an exception. Milk was an important article of food, and was supplemented by cakes of barley or wheat (*yava*), vegetables, and fruit.

Strong Drinks : The people freely indulged in two kinds of intoxicating liquor, called *soma* and *sura*. *Sura* probably was a kind of beer. *Soma* juice was considered to be particularly acceptable to the gods, and was offered with elaborate ceremonial. The *Sama Veda* provides the chants appropriate for the ceremonies.

Amusements: Amusements included dancing, music, chariot-racing, and dicing. Gambling with dice is mentioned so frequently in both the *Rig Veda* and the later documents that the prevalence of the practice is beyond doubt.

RIVERS MENTIONED IN RIG VEDA

Rig Vedic Name	New Name
Gomati	Gomal
Krumi	Kurram
Kubha	Kabul
Suvastu	Swat
Sindhu	Indus
Drishadvari	Ghaghar/Chitang
Satudri	Satluj
Vipas	Beas
Parushni	Ravi
Asikni	Chenab
Vitasta	Jhelum

FREQUENCY OF IMPORTANT WORDS MENTIONED IN RIG VEDA

Word	Times Mentioned
Om	1028
Pita	335
Ashva	315
Jana	275
Mata	234
Indra	250
Gau	176
Vish	171
Vidata	122
Brahmana	14
Surya	10
Kshatriya	9
Yamuna	3
Yamuna	3

Raja	1
Sudra	1
Vaishya	1
Rajya	1
Kulpa	1
Ganga	1
Samudra	1

1.11 RIG VEDIC GODS

Indra He was the most important divinity. He played the role of a warlord, leading the Aryan soldiers to victory against the demons. 250 hymns are devoted to him in the Rig Veda. He was associated with thunder and storm and is addressed by various names: *Ratheshtha, Jitendra Somapa, Purandra, Varitrahan and Maghayam*

Agni He was the second important divinity. He was intermediary between Gods and men. 200 hymns of the Rig Veda are devoted to him.

Varuna He was the upholder of *Rita* or cosmic order or natural order. He personified water.

Soma He was considered to be the god of plants. An intoxicant drink was also called *soma*.

Yama He was the guardian of the world of dead.

Surya Similar to that of the Greek God Helios.

Savitri The famous Gayatri *mantra* is addressed to Savitri.

Pusan Lord of jungle path, main function was that of guarding of roads, herdsmen and cattle.

Vishnu A relatively minor God at that time.

Vayu Wind God

Dyaus Father of Heaven

Aditi Goddess of Eternity

Maruts Storm Spirits

Gandharvas Divine Musicians

Ashvins Healers of diseases and experts in surgical art

Ribhus Gnomes

Apsaras Mistresses of Gods

Rudra An archer God, whose anger brought disease

Vishvadeva Intermediate Deities

Aranyani Goddess of Forest

Usha Goddess of Dawn

Prithvi Goddess of Earth.

Note : Surya, Savitri, Pusan and Vishnu were also called ***Sun Gods.***

1.12 later Vedic phase : PERIOD AND SPREAD

The Later Vedic Age extends from 1000 BC to 600 BC when the three later Vedas, *Yajur, Sama* and *Atharva*, the *Brahmanas* and few early Upanishads were composed. After the Upanishads, the age of Epics followed.

The later Vedic texts show that the Aryans expanded from Punjab over the whole of western Uttar Pradesh covered by the Ganga-Yamuna doab. South was penetrated many centuries later. The *Ramayana* has partly unfolded the tale of the Aryan advent into the south. In the beginning, they cleared the land by burning and later with the use of iron tools (which became common by 1000-800 BC).

1.13 LATER VEDIC POLITY AND ECONOMY

Political Organisation : In later Vedic times, the *vidatha* completely disappeared. The *sabha* and *samiti* continued to hold the ground, but their character changed. Women were no longer permitted to sit in the *sabha*, and it was now dominated by nobles and Brahmanas. The formation of wider kingdoms made the king more powerful. Tribal authority tended to become territorial. The term *rashtra,* which indicates territory, first appears in this period. The King performed the *rajasuya* sacrifice, which was supposed to confer supreme power on him. He performed the *asvamedha*, which meant unquestioned control over an area in which the royal horse ran uninterrupted. He also performed the *vajapeya* or the chariot race, in which the royal chariot was made to win the race against his kinsmen. During this period collection of taxes and tributes seems to have become common. They were probably deposited with an officer called *sangrihitri*. In the discharge of this duties, the king was assisted by the priest, the commander, the chief queen and a few other high functionaries. At the lower level the administration was possibly carried on by village assemblies, which may have been controlled by the chiefs of the dominant tribes. Even in later Vedic times the king did not possess a standing army. Tribal units were mustered in times of war, and, according to one ritual for success in war, the king had to eat along with his people (*vis*) from the same plate.

REGIONS AND KINGS

Eastern king	*Samrat*
Western king	*Suvrat*
Northern king	*Virat*
Southern king	*Bhoja*
King of middle country	*Raja*

IMPORTANT RATNINS / OFFICIALS IN THE LATER VEDIC PERIOD

Purohita	Chief Priest, in also sometimes refered to as *Rastragopa*.
Senani	Supreme Commander of army
Vrajapati	Officer-in-Charge of pasture land
Jivagribha	Police officer
Spasas/Dutas	Spies who also sometimes worked as messengers
Gramani	Head of the village
Kulapati	Head of the family
Madhyamasi	Mediator on disputes
Bhagadugha	Revenue collector
Sangrahitri	Treasurer
Mahishi	Chief queen
Suta	Charioteer and court minstrel
Govikartana	Keeper of games and forests
Palagala	Messenger
Kshatri	Chamberlain
Akshavapa	Accountant
Sthapati	Chief Judge
Takshan	Carpenter

KINGDOMS IN THE LATER VEDIC AGE

	Kingdom	Location
(j)	**Gandhar**	Rawalpindi and Peshawar districts of Western Punjab
(ii)	**Kekaya**	On the bank of River Beas, east of Gandhar kingdom
(iii)	**Uttar Madra**	Kashmir
(iv)	**Eastern Madra**	Near Kangra
(v)	**Southern Madra**	Near Amritsar
(vi)	**Kushinagar**	Nurthern region of modern Uttar Pradesh
(vii)	**Panchal**	Bareilly, Badayun and Farrukhabad districts of modern Uttar Pradesh
(viii)	**Kashi**	Modern Varanasi
(ix)	**Koshal**	Faizabad region of today's Uttar Pradesh

Occupation : The Aryans now lived a sedentary life, domesticated animals and cultivated on a greater scale than earlier sugar-cane. Cattle still constituted the principal form of movable property. Elephants were tamed. However, the idea of private possession of land gradually began to crystallize. Wheat was also cultivated during this period along with barley. Rice is mentioned in sources but was not an important crop at this time. Beans and Sesame and pulses such as Moong, Urad etc. were also known. New arts, artists and craftsmen also emerged i.e. smelters, ironsmiths, carpenters, weavers, leather workers, jewellers, dyers and potters. Trade was also boosted.

Pottery: The later Vedic Aryans used four types of pottery - Black and Red Ware, Black Slipped Ware, Painted Grey Ware (PGW), and Red Ware. The black and red earthen pots were used around 600 BC by the people of Koshala. The Aryans knew copper or bronze (*lohitayas*) and Iron (*Krishna ayas*). They introduced the PGW in northern India. It consisted of bowls and dishes, which were used either for rituals or for eating or both. These were mostly found to the upper Gangetic basin.

Currency: A gold piece of specific weight called *Satamana* is mentioned in *Sathapatha-Brahmana*. *Nishka* was the popular currency. *Suvarna* and *Krishnala* were two other classes of coins in circulation. Barter system still continued in spite of the presence of metallic coins. Money-lending was a lucrative trade and the interest on loan was moderately charged. The usurer is mentioned as *Kusidin*.

CHARACTERISTICS
❖ Growth of kings power, ❖ Its priests arrogating themselves ❖ Its religious outlook rapidly changing, ❖ Rigidity in caste-system. ❖ The term '*Rashtrya*' meaning territory first appeared. ❖ Growth of king's power. ❖ Samiti lost its importance and Sabha developed into council of ministers *i.e., Mantriparishad*. ❖ Women were not permitted to sit in sabhas.

1.14 LATER VEDIC SOCIETY

Social Organisation: The later Vedic society came to be divided into four varnas called the *Brahmanas*, rajanyas or kshatriyas, vaisyas and shudras. Brahmanas conducted rituals and sacrifices for their clients and for themselves, and also officiated at the festivals associated with agricultural operations. They prayed for the success of their patron in war, and in return the king pledged not to do any harm to them. Sometimes, the brahmanas came into conflict with the rajanyas, who represented the order of the warrior-nobles, for position of supremacy. The vaisyas constituted the common people and they were assigned the producing functions such as agriculture, cattle-breeding etc. Some of them also worked a artisans. Towards the end of the Vedic period, they began to engage in trade. All the three higher varnas shared one common feature, they were known as *Dvijas* (twice born), i.e., they were entitled to *upanayana* or investiture with the sacred thread according to the Vedic mantras. The fourth verna was deprived of the sacred thread ceremony, and with this began the imposition of disabilities on the shudras. Outside the caste-system, there stood two important bodies of men, namely, *Vratyas* and *Nishadas*.

According to the *Aitareya Brahmana*, in relation to the prince, the brahmana is described as a seeker of livelihood and an acceptor of gifts but removable at will. A vaisya is called tribute-paying, meant for being beaten, and to be oppressed at will. The worst position is reserved for the *shudra*. He is called the servant of another. Certain sections of artisans such as *rathakara* or chariot-maker enjoyed a high status, and were entitled to the sacred thread ceremomy. In the family, we notice the increasing power of the father, who could even disinherit his son. In later Vedic age, polygamy was prevalent, instances of child-marriage were also there. The term *Nagara* appears for the first time showing joint beginnings of town life. Women were generally given a lower position. Although some women theologians took part in philosophic discussions and some queens participated in coronation rituals, ordinarily women were thought to be inferior and subordinate to men.

Marriage : Eight types of marriages were prevalent in the later Vedic age (described in box). Of these, four (*Brahma, Daiva, Arsa* and *Prajapati*) were generally approved and were permissible to Brahmans. These were religious marriages and were indissoluble.

TYPES OF MARRIAGES IN THE LATER VEDIC AGE

1.	***Brahma***	:	Marriage of a duly dowered girl to a man of the same varna with Vedic rites and rituals.
2.	***Daiva***	:	Father gives the daughter to the sacrificial priest as part of fee or *dakshina*.
3.	***Arsa***	:	A token bride-price of a cow and a bull is given.
4.	***Prajapati***	:	Marriage without dowry and bride-price.
5.	***Gandharva***	:	Marriage by the consent of two parties, often clandestine. A special form of it was *swayamvara* or self choice.
6.	***Asura***	:	Marriage by purchase.
7.	***Paisacha***	:	It is the seduction of a girl while asleep, mentally deranged or drunk hence, it can hardly be called a marriage.
8.	***Rakshasa***	:	Marriage by capture.

***Anuloma Marriage* :** Marriage of a man below his varna was called Anuloma. It was sanctioned by the sacred texts.

***Pratiloma Marriage* :** Pratiloma marriage was the marriage of a girl or women to one lower than her own varna. It was not sanctioned by the sacred texts.

Gotra System : The institution of *gotra* appeared in later Vedic times. Literally, it means the cow-pen or the place where cattle belonging to the whole clan are kept. The *gotra* has been regarded as a mechanism for widening the socio-political ties, as new relationships were forged between hitherto unrelated people. People began to pracitse *gotra* exogamy. No marriage could take place between persons belonging to the same *gotra* or having the same ancestor.

Ashrama System : *Ashramas* or four stages of life were not well established in early Vedic times. In the post-Vedic texts, we hear of four *ashramas* : that of *brahmachari* or student, *grihastha* or householder, *vanaprastha* or partial retirement and *sanyasa* or complete retirement from the world. But only three are mentioned in the later Vedic texts. The last or the fourth stage had not been well established in later Vedic times.

Food and Drinks: The staple diet was milk and *ghee*, vegetables, fruit and barley. Wheat was rarely eaten. On ceremonial occasions at a religious feast or the arrival of a guest, a more elaborate meal usually including the flesh of ox, goat, sheep and birds were taken after being washed with *sura*. Fish and other river animals were also relished upon. The guests were never served vegetarian foods, or at least one non-vegetarian food was compulsory. The eating of cow's beef had become a taboo. *Sura* was a favourite drink for both sexes.

Dress: Clothes were simple. Two-piece clothes were normally worn : *uttariya* or the upper garment and *antariya* or the lower garment. There was no diffrence between the clothes of male and female. Ornaments were used by both the sexes and bangles were worn by privileged few, Shoes were used. Use of oil, comb, mirror, razors, hair ointment and a few cosmetics was known.

Amusements: Music, both vocal and instrumental, was the major source of amusements. Playing of veena, drum flute, harp and cymbals were more common, also were dance. Chariot-racing and gambling were other sources of entertainment.

Education: It was for a privileged few. Only Brahamanas and Kshatriyas were allowed to get education. Even women education was discouraged and the study of the Vedic literature was forbidden to women in spite of the fact that a few gifted women scholars were present at the time and female teachers were also there.

The subjects taught were *veda, itihasa,* grammer, mathematics, ethics, dialectics, astronomy, military science, fine arts, music and medical science.

1.15 RELIGION IN LATER VEDIC PERIOD

The two outstanding Rig Vedic gods, Indra and Agni, lost their former importance. On the other hand Prajapati, the creator, came to occupy the supreme position in the later Vedic pantheon. Rudra, the god of animals, became important in later Vedic times and Vishnu came to be conceived as the preserver and protector of the people. In addition, some symbolic objects began to be worshipped, and we notice signs of idolatry. Pushan, who was supposed to look after cattle, came to be regarded as the god to the *sudras*. Important female deities during the Later Vedic Age were : Usha (goddess of Dawn), Aditi (Mother of Gods), Prithvi (Earth Goddess), Aryani (Forest Goddess) and Saraswati (River deity). The mode of worship changed considerably. Prayers continued to be recited, but they ceased to be the dominant mode of placating the gods. Sacrifices became far more important, and they assumed both public and domestic character. The guest was known as *goghna* or one who was fed on cattle. The priests who officiated at sacrifices were rewarded generously and given *dakshinas* or gifts. The sacrificer was known as the *yajamana*, the performer of *yajna*, and much of his success depended on the magical power of words uttered in the sacrifices.

IMPORTANT VEDIC RITUALS

- ***Rajasuya*** **:** The king's influence was str4engthened by rituals. He performed this sacrifice, which was supposed to confer supreme power on him.
- ***Asvamedha*** **:** A king performed the *Asvamedha*, which meant unquestioned control over the area in which the royal horse ran uninterrupted. The ceremony lasted for three days at the end of which horse sacrifice was performed.
- ***Vajapeya*** **:** A king performed the *Vajpeya* or the chariot race, in which the royal chariot was made to win the race against his kinsmen. The ritual lasted for seventeen days and was believed not only to restore the strength of the middle-aged king but also to elevate him from the position of *raja* to that of *samrat*.
- ***Garbhadhana :*** A ceremony which is performed to promote conception in women.
- ***Pumsayam*** **:** This ritual is performed to procure a male child.
- ***Semontonayam*** **:** It is a ritual performed to ensure the safety of the child in the womb.
- ***Jatkarma*** **:** It is a birth ceremony performed before the cutting of the umbilical cord.
- ***Culakarma*** **:** It is a ritual, also known as tonsure, performed for boys in their third year.
- ***Upanayana*** **:** It is an initiation ceremony to confor ***dvija*** (twice-horn) status to boys of the highter varnas in their eighth year.

CHIEF PRIESTS

The chief priests who were engaged in performing the sacrifices were -

(i) ***Hotri*** -The invoker, he recited hymns from *Rig Veda*.

(ii) ***Adhvaryu*** - the executor, he recited hymns from *Yajur Vada*.

(iii) ***Udgatri***-the singer, he recited hymns from *Sama Veda*.

The chief priest received voluntary offerings from the people called *Bali*.

1.16 VEDIC LITERATURE

The vast literature of the Aryans is divided into two parts—*Sruti* and *Smriti*.

(i) Sruti Literature : The word ***Veda*** has been derived from the Sanskrit word *Ved*, which means 'spiritual knowledge'. The Vedas are four in number—*Rig Veda*, *Samaveda*, *Yajurveda*, and *Atharvaveda*. The *Rig Veda* contains a references only to the first three ***Vedas***, which suggests that the fourth ***Veda*** was composed at some later date.

HIGHLIGHTS OF THE FOUR VEDAS

SAMVEDA

- Rythmic compilation of hymns for Rigveda
- has only 75 fundamental hymns
  (a) Karnataka - Jaiminiga
  (b) Gujarat - Kanthun
  (c) Maharashtra - Ranayaniya
- sung by Udgatri

RIGVEDA

- Collection of hymns
- Oldest of all vedas
- Associated with 'Sakel' community
- Collection of 1017 hymns after adding "Blhilya Sukta" number is 1028
- Compiled in 10 'mandalas' & 8 'Ashtaks'.
- II, III, IV, V, VI & VII are oldest mandalas
- I, VIII, IX, X are latest mandalas
- Mandala IX is completely devoted to 'Soma'
- Mandala II to VII were created by Grita Samada, Vishwamitra, Vamadeva, Atri, Bharadwaj, Vashistha, VIII Kanwa and Angira, IX Soma

YAJURVEDA

- Rituals of yajnas
- Is sung by priest "Adhavaryu"
- has been compiled in "fourty path"
- has been divided into, Krishna Yajurveda & Shukla Yajurveda
- prose text

ATHARVAVEDA

- mantras for magic spells
- populate ritualistic systems & superstitions
- associated with 'Saunkiya' and 'Paiplad' community
- collection of 711/73/760 hymns
- not included in "Trai"
- has been divided in 20 "Kandas"
- 18th, 19th & 20th 'Kandas' are later works
- provides freedom from evil spirits
- oldest text on Indian Medicine.

BRAHMANA

- Detailed Literature
- Interpretation of vedic hymns
- A type of religious philosophy
- Seven in number

ARANYAKA

- Literarily, it means 'Jungle'
- Provides description of Moral Science and Philosophy
- Provides details of hermits and saints who lived in Jungles
- Gives stress on meditation
- Protests the systems of 'Yajnas'

UPANISHADA

- Literary meaning is 'satra' (to sit near masters' feet) in which Guru offers band of knowledge to their disciples
- Is a combination of Tatva-mimansa and philosophy
- They are also called 'vedanta'
- Primitive upanishada are 'Brahadaranyaka' and 'Chandogya'
- Later Upnishada like '*Katha*' and *Swetaswatar*' have been written in poetic forms.
- 'Brahma' is the summary of philosophy, which is the only a 'truth' in the world
- Knowledge awards salvation says Upanishadas
- Oldest possibility Narsinghpurvatapani
- Latest possibility Allopanishada in Akbar's reign

VEDAS AND THEIR BRAHMANAS

1. *Rigveda* : *Aitereya and Kaushitaki*
2. *Samaveda* : *Tandya and Jaiminiya*
3. *Yajurveda* : *Tattiriya and Satpatha*
4. *Atharvaveda* : *Gopatha*

(ii) Smriti Literature : *Smriti* is traditional knowledge and designates almost the entire body of post-Vedic classical Sanskrit literature. *Smriti* literature generally includes the following overlapping subjects:

(a) ***The Vedangas*** **:** They refer to certain branches of post-Vedic studies regarded as auxiliary to the *Vedas*. The *Vedangas* are conventionally divided into six headings, namely :(i) '***Kalpa***' or the ritual canon, including the ***dharma shastras*** or legal codes (ii) '***Jyotisha***' or astronomy (iii) '***Siksha***' or phonetics (iv) '***Chhanda***' or metre (v) '***Nirukta***' or etymology (vi) ***Vyakarana*** (Grammar).

(b) The '***Shad-Darsana***' **:** Six orthodox schools of Hindu philosophy, namely '*Nyaya*' '*Vaiseshikha*', *Sankhya*', '*Yoga*', '*Mimamsa*, and *Vedanta*'.

(c) '***Itihasa***' : 'Legendary' or 'semi-legendary' works, specifically the *Ramayana* and *Mahabharata* and often extended to the *Puranas*.

(d) '***Puranas***' : Being a fairly late description of ancient legends, they are heavily coloured with superstitions. The *Puranas* represent the most corrupt form of Hinduism. They are 18 in number (see box).

THE EIGHTEEN PURANAS

(i)	*Brahma Purana*	(ii)	*Vishnu Purana*
(iii)	*Shiva Purana*	(iv)	*Padma Purana*
(v)	*Shrimad Bhagwat Purana*	(vi)	*Agni Purana*
(vii)	*Narad Purana*	(viii)	*Markandey Purana*
(ix)	*Bhavishya Purana*	(x)	*Ling Purana*
(xi)	*Varah Purana*	(xii)	*Vaman Purana*
(xiii)	*Brahm Vaivertya Purana*	(xiv)	*Skanda Purana*
(xv)	*Surya Purana*	(xvi)	*Matsya Purana*
(xvii)	*Garuda Purana*	(xviii)	*Brahmand Purana*

(e) ‘***Upaveda***’ : Also known as the auxiliary Vedas, they deal with medicine, architecture, erotics, archery and various arts and crafts. These were partly derived from original Vedic texts and were traditionally associated with one or other of the *Vedas*. Thus (i) ‘*Ayurveda*' or medicine is an ‘*Upaveda*' of the ‘*Atharva Veda*'; (ii) ‘*Dhanurveda*' or archery is said to be a part of the ‘*Yajur Veda*'; (iii) ‘*Gandharva Veda*', the science of singing, is part of the ‘*Sama Veda*'.

(f) ‘***Tantras***’ : *Tantras* are the writings of *Shakta* or *Shaivite* sects and also of certain antinomian Buddhist scholars.

(g) ‘***Agamas***’ : They are scriptures of sectarian Hindus like Vaishnavites, Shaivites and *Shaktas*.

(h) ‘***Upangas***’ : They are a generic name for any collection of treatises although traditionally confined to the philosophical systems of ‘*Nyaya*' and ‘*Mimansa*" — the ‘*Dharma Sutras*' the ‘*Puranas*' and the ‘*Tantras*.'

(iii) Epics : Some historians regard the Later Vedic Period as the Period of Epics. The *Mahabharata* and the *Ramayana* are the two great epics of this period.

(a) *Ramayana*: It is said to have been composed by the sage, Valmiki. The incident related in it precedes the *Mahabharata* by about a hundred and fifty years. The story of Ramayana is of indigenous origin and had existed in ballad form in Prakrit, in more than one version. It was rewritten in Sanskrit and augmented with many ‘*shlokas*'. The epic was given a Brahmanical character which was not visible in the original work. It is also known as *Adi Kavya*. It contains 2,400 verses and is divided into seven books. The central theme of this epic is the conflict between Rama, a representative of the Aryan civilisation, and Ravana, a representative of the non-Aryan civilisation. Evidence places the oldest part of the Ramayana to before 350 BC. The reference in the epic to the mingled hords of Yavanas and Shakas suggests that it received accretions in the Graeco-Scythian period and may have acquired its final shape by about AD 250.

(b) *Mahabharata*: The Mahabharata is the bulkiest epic consisting of 100,000 verses and is divided into 18 paravas (books). This book is usually assigned to Rishi Ved Vyas, but scholars have expressed doubts if such a great work could have been accomplished by one single person. The story itself occupies only about one-fourth of the poem. It is a tale about conflict between Aryans—Kaurava and Pandava. The rest is episodical comprising cosmology, theogony, state craft, the science of war, ethics, legendary history, mythology, fairy tales and several digressional and philosophical interludes, of which the best known is the *Bhagvad Gita*.

1.17 ORIGIN OF HINDU PHILOSOPHY

By the end of the later Vedic Age, six prominent schools of Hindu Philosophy had been established. They are as follows:

1. ***Sankhya*** of **Kapila :** According to *Sankhya* philosophy, the world was created and it has evolved more by *prakriti* (nature) than by God.
2. ***Yoga*** of **Patanjali :** This school says a person can attain salvation through mediation and physical application.
3. ***Nyaya*** of **Gautama :** Nyaya, the school of analysis, says that salvation is attainable through the acquisition of knowledge.
4. ***Vaisheshika*** of **Kanada :** According to this school, earth, water, fire, air and ether (sky), when combined together, give rise to new objects.
5. ***Mimamsa*** of **Jaimini :** According to *Mimamsa* philosophy, the Vedas contain the eternal truth. It recommends the performance of Vedic sacrifices to attain salvation.
6. ***Vedanta*** of **Badarayan :** It says, *Brahma* is the reality and everything else is unreal **(*Maya*).** The self (soul) is identical with brahma.

VEDIC CIVILISATION

- **Origin of Indian Music** - Samveda
- **Mention of Word 'Shudra'** - Rigveda 10th Mandala
- **Gayatri Mantra** - Rigveda
- **Mention of 'Gotra'** - Atharvaveda
- **Mention of word 'Yajna'** - Brahmana
- **Somaras (drink)** - Rigveda (9th Mandala)
- Varna - Rigveda
- **Four fold division of Society** - Rigveda 10th Mandala
- **Mention of four Ashrams** - Jabala Upanishada
- **Mention of Upanayan** - Satpatha Brahmana
- **War between Aryan & Dasas** - Rigveda
- **Transmigration of soul** - Brahadaranyka Upanishada
- **Five divisions of India** - Aiteraya Brahamana
- **Wife and Husband are complementary** - Satapathabrahmana
- **Battle of Ten kings** - Rigveda (7th Mandala)
- **Superiority of Brahmins** - Aiteraya Brahmana
- **Rajanaya** - Rigveda 10th Mandala
- **Marut as Agriculturist** - Satpatha Brahmana
- **Satyameva Jayate** - Mundaka Upanishada
- **Pashupath Shiva** - Atharveda
- **Vishnu** - Satapatha Brahmana
- **Conversation between Yam & Nachiketa** - Katha Upanishada

2. RISE OF MAGADH IN RELATION TO 16 MAHAJANPADAS

2.1 MAHAJANPADAS

In the later Vedic period, the tribal organisations changed its identity and gradually shifted to the territorial identity, and the area of settlement were now regarded as *janapadas* or states. In transition from tribe to monarchy, they lost the essential democratic pattern of the tribe but retained the idea of government through an assembly representing the tribes. These states consisted of either a single tribe such as the *Shakyas*, *Kolias*, *Mallas* etc. or a confederacy of tribes such as the *Vrijis*, *Yadavas*, *Parchala* etc.

The people in the lower Ganges Valley and Delta, which were outside the Aryan pale, were regarded as M*lecchas*. There was, therefore, a strong consciousness of the pure land of the Aryans called *Aryavarta*. Each *janapada* tried to dominate and subjugate other *janapadas* to become *Mahajanapadas*.

According to *Anguttara Nikaya,* there were about sixteen *Mahajanapadas* in the sixth century BC. Their capitals and locations are given in a table on the 16 *Mahajanapadas*.

2.2 IMPORTANT REPUBLICS

The kings in these states had the supreme authority. The *Mahajanapadas* of Vrijji, Malla, Kuru, Panchal and Kamboj were republican states and so were other smaller states like Lichhavi, Shakya, Koliya, Bhagga, and Moriya. These republican states had a *Gana-parishad* or an Assembly of senior and responsible citizens. This *Gana-Parishad* had the supreme authority in the state. All the administrative decisions were taken by this *Parishad.* Again, the republics were basically of two types: (a) the republics comprising a single tribe like those of the Sakyas, the Kolias and the Mallas, and (b) the republics comprising a number of tribes or the republics of confederacy like the Vrijjis.

THE 16 MAHAJANAPADAS

Mahajanapadas	Capitals	Locations
1. **Gandhara**	Taxila	Covering the region between Kabul and Rawalpindi in North Western Province
2. **Kamboja**	Rajpur	Covering the area around the Punch area in Kashmir
3. **Asmaka**	Potana	Covering modern Paithan in Maharashtra; on the bank of River Godavari
4. **Vatsa**	Kaushambi	Covering the modern districts of Allahabad and Mirzapur
5. **Avanti**	Ujjain	Covering modern Malwa (Ujjain) region of Madhya Pradesh
6. **Surasena**	Mathura	Located in the Mathura region at the junction of the Uttarapath & Dakshinapath
7. **Chedi**	Shuktimati	Covering the modern Budelkhand area
8. **Malla**	Kushinara, Pawa	Modern districts of Deoria, Basti, Gorakhapur in eastern Uttar Pradesh

9. **Kurus**	Hastinapur/Indraprastha	Covering the modern Haryana and Delhi area to the west of River Yamuna
10. **Matsya**	Virat Nagari	Covering the area of Alwar, Bharatpur and Jaipur in Rajasthan
11. **Vajjis**	Vaishali	Located to the north of the River Ganga in Bihar
12. **Anga**	Champa	Covering the modern districts of Munger and Bhagalpur in Bihar
13. **Kashi**	Banaras	Located in and around present day Varanasi in Uttar Pradesh
14. **Kosala**	Shravasti	Covering the present districts of Faizabad, Gonda, Bahraich, etc
15. **Magadha**	Girivraja/Rajgriha.	Covering modern districts of Patna, Gaya and parts of Shahabad
16. **Panchala**	Ahichhatra (W. Panchala) Kampilya (S. Panchala)	Present day Rohilkhand and part of Central Doab in Uttar Pradesh

DIFFERENCES BETWEEN REPUBLICS AND MONARCHIES

- In republics, every tribal oligarch claimed share in revenues from peasants. In the monarchies, the king claimed to be the sole recipient of such revenues.
- In a tribal oligarchy or republic, each raja (tribal oligarch) was free to maintain his own little army under his *senapati*. In a monarchy, the king maintained his regular standing army. He did not permit any other armed forces within his boundaries.
- Republics functioned under the leadership of the oligarchic assemblies, while a monarchy functioned under the individual leadership of the king.
- The Brahamanas had a considerable influence on the monarchial administration, while they were relegated to the background in the republics.

2.3 RISE OF MAGADHA

The Haryankas : Magadha came into prominence under the leadership of **Bimbisara** (542-493 BC), who belonged to the ***Haryanka dynasty.*** He strengthened his position by marriage alliances. He took three wives. His first wife was the daughter of the king of Kosala and the sister of Prasenajit. His second wife Chellana was a *Lichchhavi* Princess from Vaishali, and his third wife was the daughter of the chief of the Madra clan of Punjab. Marriage relations with the different princely families gave enormous diplomatic prestige and paved the way for the expansion of Magadha westward and northward.

The earliest capital of Magadha was at Rajgir, which was called Girivraja at that time. It was surrounded by five hills, the openings in which were closed by stone walls on all sides. This made Rajgir impregnable.

Bimbisar was succeeded by his son **Ajatasatru** (492-460 BC). Ajatasatru killed his father and seized the throne for himself. Throughout his reign, he pursued an aggressive policy of expansion.

Ajatasatru was succeeded by **Udayin** (460-444 BC). His reign is important because he built the fort upon the confluence of the Ganga and Son at Patna. This was done because Patna lay in the centre of the Magadhan kingdom.

The Sisunagas : Udayin was succeeded by the dynasty of ***Sisunagas***, who temporarily shifted the capital to Vaishali. Their greatest achievement was the destruction of the power of Avanti with its capital at Ujjain. This brought to an end the 100 years old rivalry between Magadha and Avanti.

The Nandas : The *Sisunagas* were succeeded by the *Nandas*, who proved to be the most powerful rulers of Magadha. So great was their power that Alexander, who invaded Punjab at that time, did not dare to move towards the east. The Nandas added to the Magadhan power by conquering Kalinga from where they brought an image of the Jina as a victory trophy. All this took place in the reign of **Mahapadma Nanda**. He claimed to be *ekarat,* the sole sovereign who destroyed all the other ruling princes.

The Nandas were the first non-kshatriya rulers. The last Nanda ruler was defeated by Chandragupta Maurya who founded the Maurya Empire.

CAUSES FOR THE RISE OF MAGADHA

1. Advantageous geographical location with both Rajgir and Pataliputra situated at strategic locations.
2. Abundance of natural resources, such as iron, enabled Magadhan rulers to equip with effective weapons.
3. The alluvial soil of the Gangetic plains and sufficient rainfall were very conducive for agriculture produces.
4. Rise of town and use of metallic money boosted trade and commerce. The princes could levy tolls and accumulate wealth to pay and maintain their army.
5. Use of elephants on a large scale in wars.
6. Unorthodox character of Magadhan society.
7. Contribution of several enterprising and ambitious rulers.

IRANIAN INVASION

❖ In 516 B.C. Darius sent a naval expedition to explore the valley of the river Indus.

❖ The province of Indus Valley was annexed by him by about 519 B.C. as is mentioned in his inscriptions.

❖ He divided the province in 20th Straphy, which was considered to be the richest and the most populous province of the Persian empire.

❖ Its annual tribute amounted to 360 Euboic talents of gold-dust.

❖ The Kharosthi script was used on the north-western frontier since then uptil about 4th century A.D.

CHRONOLOGY OF FOREIGN INVASIONS

❒ 518-486 B.C. : King Darius or Darus invaded India.

❒ 326 B.C. : Alexander invaded India.

❒ 190 B.C. : Indo-Greeks or Bactrians invaded India.

❒ 90 B.C. : Sakas invaded India.

❒ 1st Century A.D. : Pahalavas invaded India.

❒ 45 A.D. : Kushanas or Yue-chis invaded India.

EFFECTS OF PERSIAN INVASION

- Introduction into India the Aramic form of writing, which later developed into the Kharoshthi alphabet.
- Promotion to Indo-Iranian trade.
- Geographical exploration of the Indus and the Arabian Sea, leading to opening of a new water route.
- Fusion of Iranian/Persian features in the Mauryan art.
- Impact of Buddhism on the Zoroastrian religion of ancient Persia.

ALEXANDER INVASION

❖ Alexander marched to India through the Khyber Pass in 326 B.C.

❖ He was bravely checked by the local chieftains despite the fact that they had no chance of success.

❖ He was even checked by the queens of the vanquished and dead chiefs.

❖ His advance was checked on the bank of the Beas because of the mutiny of his soldiers.

❖ In 325 B.C., he began his homeward journey.

- ❖ In 324 B.C., he reached Susa in Persia and died the next year.
- ❖ The Greek invasion of India opened the trade route between north-west India and Western Asia.
- ❖ Eastwards trade went through the Ganga delta to the coast of Northern Burma and south along the east coast.
- ❖ Guilds (*Shreni*) came into existence.
- ❖ Money was introduced. Punch-marked coins in gold and silver and of copper cast have been discovered.
- ❖ Introduction of money facilitated the trade.

EFFECTS OF ALEXANDER'S INVASION

- Establishment of direct contact between India and Greece in different fields.
- Opening up of four distinct routes between India & Greek by land and sea paving way for increased trade and cultural contacts between the two regions.
- Establishment of more Greek settlements in north-western region.
- Establishment of the coast and search for harhours from the mouth of the Indus to that of the Euphrates.
- Promotion to expansion of the Mauryan empire in north-west India due to destruction of local powers by Alexander.

2.4 SOCIO-ECONOMIC CONDITIONS DURING MAHAJANAPADAS

Besides, the establishment of big empires, another important feature of the age was increased prosperity and the growth of towns. The primary reason of increased prosperity of India was its growth of foreign trade with the countries of the North West, Western countries and several countries of Asia.

There were several trade routes and roads connecting different parts of India in all directions. One trade route was from Kosambi, through Gangetic plain, to Punjab and then Taxila joining the routes to Iran, Central Asia, European countries and several countries of Asia. Another route started from Rajagriha and, passing through Kosambi and Ujjaini, was connected with the port of Baroach from where the trade was carried on with western countries through sea-route. One important route passed through the entire Gangetic plain and reached the boundary of Burma and, yet, another route connected northern plain with the sea-coast of south-east. These routes developed because of increased trade and, in turn, helped in enhancing internal as well as external trade.

The increased prosperity of the Indians affected their social structure as well. Towns became not only the centres of trade but centres of industries as well. Various goods were produced on a large scale to feed the foreign trade and that could be possible only in towns or *vice versa,* towns grew up where goods were produced on a large scale. By that time, Indian rulers had started minting good coins of different metals. It helped in the development of trade and growth of industries because coins proved to be a good medium of exchange and, thus, facilitated transactions. The growth of trade and industry formed rich trading and industrial communities which concentrated themselves in towns. We find existence of different guilds formed by traders and industrialists during this period. It created various organised and consciously awakened groups in towns which, finally, resulted in the formation of several sub-castes.

2.5 RELIGIOUS CONDITIONS DURING *MAHAJANAPADAS*

The changed economic and social circumstances influenced contemporary religious thought. The formation of awakened groups of traders, industrialists and labour resulted in putting a challenge to the supremacy of the *Brahmanas.* The formation of sub-castes also did the same. Several of these groups were rich as well which gave them an advantageous position in the society. It led to religious awakening in the society which resulted in formation of several religious sects. There is no doubt that the rise of Jainism and Buddhism during this age was a result of the changed economic and social circumstances also. We also find that both of these religious sects got support from the neo-rich trading and industrial classes which were eager to get a better social status so far denied to them. The same way, both Jainism and Buddhism drew large converts from new sub-castes who were interested in getting equal status for all castes thereby getting the facility of having better social status for themselves.

3. RISE OF HETERODOX SECTS WITH SPECIAL REFERENCE TO BUDDHISM, JAINISM

Numerous religious sects arose in the middle Gangetic basin in the sixth century BC. We hear of as many as 62 religious sects in this period. Of these sects, Jainism and Buddhism were the most important, and they emerged as the most potent religious reform movements.

3.1 CAUSES OF RISE OF RELIGIOUS MOVEMENTS

In post-Vedic times, society was clearly divided into four varnas: *brahmanas*, *kshatriyas*, *vaisyas* and *shudras*. Each varna was assigned well-defined functions, although it was emphasized that varna was based on birth and two higher varnas were given some privileges.

Naturally the varna-divided society seems to have generated tensions. The *kshatriyas*, who acted as rulers reacted against the domination of the priestly class called *brahmanas*, who claimed various privileges. It was one of the causes of the origin of new religions. Vardhamana Mahavira, who founded Jainism, and Gautama Buddha, who founded Buddhism, belonged to the *kshatriya* clan, and both disputed the authority of the brahmanas.

But the real cause of the rise of these new religions lay in the introduction of a new agricultural economy in north-eastern India. The period saw the rise of a large number of cities in north-eastern India. The earliest coins belonged to the fifth century BC, and they are called punch-marked coins. The use of coins naturally facilitated trade and commerce, which added to the importance of the *vaisyas*. In the brahmanical society, the *vaisyas* ranked third. Naturally they looked for some religion which would improve their position.

The trade of money-lending was established in the Vedic age. The practice of providing loans on interest was also legal but the trade was generally looked down upon by the *brahmans*. The *vaisyas* who practised this trade wanted to raise their social position in the eyes of religion. So, the *vaisyas* extended generous support to both Mahavira and Gautama Buddha. The merchants, called the *setthis,* made handsome gifts to Gautama Buddha and his disciples.

The *Vedic* practice of killing cattles in sacrificial rituals was inimical to the emerging agricultural economy. Besides, the Sanskrit language was the knowledge of a chosen few while the common masses spoke Prakrit. The inferior position of women also facilitated the growth of new religions which had actually started off the reform in Hinduism.

3.2 JAINISM

The Founder : Rishabha, who was the father of king Bharata, the first *chakravarti* king of India, founded Jainism. The *Vishnu Purana* and *Bhagavat Purana* describe Rishabha as an incarnation of Narayana. Risabha was succeeded by 23 other *Tirthankaras*. Parsvanatha (850 BC) was the 23rd *Tirthankara.* Jainism became a major religion under Vardhamana Mahavira, the 24th Tirthankara.

JAINISM IN THE PAST

- The name of Jaina *Tirthankaras Rishabha* is found in the Rig Veda.
- The *Vishnu Purana* and the *Bhagavat Purana* describe *Rishaba* as an incarnation of Narayana.
- The male nude torso discovered from the Indus Valley culture has something to do with the *tirthankaras.*
- There were twenty-four tirthankaras, all *kshatriyas* and belonging to the royal family. *Parsavanath* was the 23rd *tirthankara.*

24 TIRTHANKARAS		
	Name	**Symbol**
1.	*Rishabha*	Bull
2.	*Ajitnath*	Elephant
3.	*Sambharanath*	Horse
4.	*Abhiaandam Swamy*	Monkey
5.	*Sumathinath*	Curlew
6.	*Padamprabhu*	Red Lotus
7.	*Suparaswanath*	*Swastik*
8.	*Chandraji Prabhu*	Moon
9.	*Suvidhinath*	Crocodile
10.	*Shitalnath*	*Srivatsa*
11.	*Shregansnath*	Rhinoceros
12.	*Vasupujya*	Buffalo
13.	*Vimalnath*	Boar
14.	*Ananthnath*	Falcon
15.	*Dharamnath*	*Vajra*
16.	*Shantinath*	Deer
17.	*Kuntunath*	He-Goat
18.	*Arnath*	Fish
19.	*Mallinath*	Water Pot
20.	*Muniswasth*	Tortoise
21.	*Naminath*	Blue Lotus
22.	*Neminath*	Conch Shell
23.	*Parswanath*	Serpent
24.	*Mahavir*	Lion

According to Jainism, the Tirthankaras descended on earth from time to time to guide the masses.

Vardhamana Mahavira : Vardhamana Mahavira was born in 540 BC in a village (Kundagrama) near Vaishali. His father was the head of a famous kshatriya clan (Inatrika), and his mother a Lichachhavi princess. They were also connected with the royal family of Magadha. In the beginning Mahavira led the life of a householder, but in the search for truth, he abandoned the world at the age of thirty and became an ascetic. He kept on wandering for twelve years from place to place. During the course of his long journey, it is said, he never changed his clothes for twelve years, and abandoned them altogether when he attained perfect knowledge or *kaivalya* at the age of 42. Through *kaivalya,* he conquered misery and happiness. Because of this conquest, he is known as Mahavira or the great hero or *jina,* i.e., the conqueror, and his followers are known as *Jainas.* He propagated his religion for thirty years, and his mission took him to Kosala, Magadha, Mithila, Champa, etc. He passed away at the age of 72 in 468 BC at a place called Pavapuri near modern Rajgir in Bihar.

Teachings : Jainism taught five doctrines: (i) do not commit violence, (ii) do not speak a lie, (iii) do not steal, (iv) do not acquire property, and (v) observe continence (*brahmacharya).* It is said that only the fifth doctrine was added by Mahavira, the other four being taken over by him from Prasavanath.

Jainism recognized the existence of the gods but placed them lower than the *jina.* It did not condemn the varna system. According to Mahavira, a person is born in a high or in a lower varna in consequence of the sins or the virtues acquired by him in the previous birth. In his opinion, through pure and meritorious life, members of the lower castes can attain liberation.

Jainism rejected the authority of the *Vedas* and *Vedic* retrials. It did not believe in the existence of God, but it believed in *Karma* and the transmigration of soul (Nirvana).

THREE GEMS OR *RATNAS* OF JAINISM

According to Jainism, attainment of *Moksha* or *Nirvana* was the most important human desire. It says that *Moksha* can be attained through practising the following three *ratnas* or gems:

I. Right Faith (***Samyak Vishwas***) in the omniscient Lord Mahavira

II. Right Knowledge (***Samyak Jnan***) of the doctrines of Jainism

III. Right Conduct (***Samyak Karma***), ie, fulfillment of the great five vows of Jainism (a) *ahimsa* (b) truthfulness (c) no stealing (d) no attachment of property and (e) Chastity or *Brahmacharya*

Sects : Although Parsva, the predecessor of Mahavira, had asked his followers to cover the upper and lower portions of their body, Mahavira asked them to discard clothes completely. On account of this, in later times, Jainism was divided into two sects: *Svetambaras* or those who put on white dress, and *Digambaras* or those who keep themselves naked.

SOME MORE JAINA SECTS
• **Yapaniyan** - Karnataka, impact of Tantricism – Came out of Swetambara – Finds mention in inscription of Vikramaditya VI • **Pujiramat** – Came out of Swetambara – Supported Idol Worship • **Terapainthi** - Came out of Swetambara • **Sammiya** - Came out of Digambara • **Bispanthi** - Came out of Digambara - Supported idol worship

Sacred Literature : According to *Svetambaras*, the original doctrine taught by Mahavira was contained in 14 old texts called *Purvas*, which were passed orally and were compiled later as twelve *Angas*.

The sacred literature of the *Svetambaras* is written in a form of Prakrit called *Ardhamagadhi* and may be classified as follows: (i) The twelve *Angas*, (ii) The twelve *Upangas*, (iii) The ten *Parikaranas*, (iv) The six *Chhedasmras*, and (v) The four *Mulasutras*. *Niryuktis* and *Churini* are the Comments on 14 *Purvas*.

This literature is not accepted by *Digambaras*, but *Svetambaras* accept it.

TWELVE ANGAS OF JAINISM	
1. *Acharanga*	2. *Sutrakruthanga*
3. *Sthananga*	4. *Somavayanga*
5. *Vakyaprainapti*	6. *Dharma-Kathanga*
7. *Upaska-Adhyananga*	8. *Anthakrudasanga*
9. *Anuttarapada Kanga*	10. *Prashnavyakaranaka*
11. *Vipakasutranga*	12. *Drustipravadanga*

Jaina Philosophy : The Jaina philosophy may be studied under the following heads :

***Syadvada* :** All our judgements are necessarily relative, conditional and limited. According to *Syadvada* (the theory of may be, seven modes of predication (*saptabhangi)* are possible. Absolute affirmation and absolute negation both are wrong. All judgements are conditional.

***Anekantavada* :** The Jaina metaphysics is a realistic and relativistic pluralism. It is called *Anekantavada* or the doctrine of the 'manyness of reality'. Matter (*Pudgala)* and Spirit (*Jiva*) are regarded as separate and independent realities.

***Instruments of Knowledge* :** According to Jaina philosophy, the following are the main instruments of knowledge :

(i) *Matijnana:* Perception through activity of sense organs, including the mind.

(ii) *Srutajnana:* Knowledge revealed by scriptures.

(iii) *Avadhijnana*: Clairvoyant perception.

(iv) *Manahparyayajnana:* Telepathic knowledge.

(v) *Kevalajnana:* Temporal knowledge or Omniscience.

Jaina Councils

First Council was held at Pataliputra by Sthulabahu in the beginning of the third century BC and resulted in the compilation of 12 *Angas* to replace the lost 14 *Purvas*.

Second Council was held at Valabhi in the 5th century AD under the leadership of Devaradhi Kshamasramana and resulted in final compilation of 12 *Angas* and 12 *Upangas*.

SPREAD OF JAINISM
❒ Jains built stupas with railings, pillars, and gateways. The Hathi Gumpha, Udaigiri and Khandagiri caves of Orissa conain Jain relics and inscriptions ❒ Mathura became a centre of Jain art during the Kushana period ❒ The statue of Gomatesawara and Karakala testify to the excellence of Jain architecture ❒ Dilwara temple at Mt. Abu and temples a Ranakpur are example of suberb workmanship.

IMPACT OF JAINISM
⇨ Jainism made the first serious attempt to mitigate the evils of varna order and ritualistic vedic religion.
⇨ The early Jainas discarded the Sanskrit language mainly patronized by Brahmans and adopted Prakrit language
⇨ Their religious literature was written in Ardhamagadhi and the texts were finlly compiled in the sixth century A.D. in Gujarat (Vallabhi).
⇨ The Jainas composed the earliest important works in *Apabhramsha* and prepared its first grammer.

FIVE CATEGORIES OF SIDDHAS
❖ ***Tirthankara,*** who has attained salvation.
❖ ***Arhat,*** who is about to attain Nirvana.
❖ ***Acharya,*** the head of the ascetic group.
❖ ***Upadhyaya***, teacher or saint, and
❖ ***Sadhu***, which includes the rest.

3.3 BUDDHISM

Gautama Buddha : Gautama Buddha or Siddhartha was a contemporary of Mahavira. He was born in 563 BC in a Shakya (kshatriya) family in Lumbini near Kapilavastu, which is situated on the foothills of Nepal. Gautama's father (Shudhodana) seems to have been the elected ruler of Kapilavastu, and headed the republican clan of the Shakyas. His mother (Mahamaya) was a princess from the Kosalan dynasty. From his early childhood, Gautama showed a meditative bent of mind. **Alara Kama** was his teacher of meditation. His charioteer was **Channa**, while his horse's name was **Kanthaks.** He was married early, but married life did not interest him. At the age of 29, he left home. He kept on, wandering for about seven years and then attained knowledge at the age of 35 at Bodh Gaya under a *pipal* tree, From this time onwards, he began to be called the Buddha or **The Enlightened.**

Gautama Buddha delivered his first sermons at Sarnath in Banaras. Gautama Buddha passed away at the age of 80 in 483 BC at a place called Kusinagar, identical with the village called Kasia in the district of Deoria in eastern Uttar Pradesh.

FIVE GREAT EVENTS IN BUDDHA'S LIFE AND THEIR SYMBOLS	
● Birth	- Lotus and bull
● Great renunciation	- Horse
● Nirvana	- Bodhi tree
● First Sermon	- Wheel (Dharma Chakra)
● Parinirvana/Death	- Stupa

Teachings : Buddha said that the world is full of sorrows and people suffer on account of desires. If desires are conquered, *nirvana* will be attained. He recommended an **eight-fold path** (*astangika marga)* for the elimination of human misery. It comprised : Right Observation, Right Determination, Right Speech, Right Action, Right Livelihood, Right Exercise, Right Memory and Right Meditation. Buddha also laid down a code of conduct for his followers. The main items in this social conduct are: (i) do not covet the property of others, (ii) do not commit violence, (iii) do not use intoxicants, (iv) do not tell a lie, and (v) do not indulge in corrupt practices.

Buddha (The Entightened), ***Dhamma*** (The Doctrine) and ***Sangha*** (The order) are **three jewels of Buddhism.**

Buddhism does not recognize the existence of god and soul (*atman*). It particularly won the support of the lower orders as it attacked the varna system. Women also were admitted to the *sangha* and thus, brought at a par with men.

Dissention in Buddhism: Like Jainism, Buddhism also faced dissention. It was divided into three main sects:

BODHISATTVA

Bodhisattva means one whose essence is *bodhi* (enlightenment). In Buddhism, the term refers to the historical Gautam Buddha, prior to his Enlightenment. Bodhisattva also refers to other individuals who are destined to become Buddhas in this or in another life. The number of possible *Bodhisattva* in the world is theoretically limitless. *Bodhisattvas* postpone their own final entrance into *Nirvana* in order to alleviate the suffering of others. The aspirant *Bodhisattva* must be a male, but may live the life of a householder and need not be a monk. The title has been frequently applied to Buddhist kings, scholars and teachers in South-East Asia.

The celestial *Bodhisattvas* are considered to be manifestations of the eternal Buddhas. Foremost among the celestial *Bodhisattvas* is *Avalokitesvara.* In China, the most widely worshipped *Bodhisattvas* are *Manjusri* (representing wisdom), *Ksitigarbh* (the saviour of the dead, *Samantabhadra* (representing happiness) and *Kuan-yin* (Chinese name of Avalokitesvara). In Tibet, *Avalokitesvara, Manjusri* and *Vajrapani* form a popular trinity. *Maitreya* is represented both as a future Buddha and as a *Bodhisattva.*

***Hinayana* or Lesser Vehicle :** (i) Its followers believed in the original teachings of Buddha. (ii) They sought individual salvation through self-discipline and meditation. (iii) They did not believe in idol-worship (iv) *Hinayana* is a religion without God, *Karma* taking the place of God. (v) *Nirvana* is regarded as the extinction of all. (vi) The oldest school of *Hinayana Buddhism* is the *Sthaviravada (Theravada* in Pali) or the 'Doctrine of the Elders'. (vii) Its Sanskrit counterpart, which is more philosophical, is known as *Sarvastivada* or the doctrine which maintains the existence of all things, physical as well as mental. (viii) From *Sarvastivada* or *Vaibhasika* branched off another school called *Sautantrika,* which was more critical in outlook.

***Mahayana* or Greater Vehicle :** (i) Its followers believed in the heavenliness of Buddha and sought the salvation of all through the grace and help of Buddha and Bodhisattavas. (ii) It believes in idol-worship. (iii) It believes that *Nirvana* is not a negative cessation of misery but a positive state of bliss. (iv) *Mahayana* had two chief philosophical schools: the *Madhyamika* and the *Yogachara.* (v) The former took a line midway between the uncompromising realism of *Hinayanism* and the idealism of *Yogachara.* (vi) The *Yogachara* school, founded by Maitreyanatha, completely rejected the realism of *Hinayana* and maintained absolute idealism.

***Vajrayana* or Vehicle of Thunder Bolt :** (i) Its followers believed that salvation could be best attained by acquiring the magical power, which they called *Vajra.* (ii) The chief divinities of this new sect were the *Taras.* (iii) It became popular in Eastern India, particularly Bengal and Bihar. (iv) It was a form of Buddhism, which appeared in eastern India in the 8th century and was finally established in Tibet in 11th century, as a result of mission sent from the great *Vajrayana* monastery of Vikramshila.

Buddhist Scriptures : Buddhist Scriptures include the following:

- ***The Vinaya Pitaka:*** (i) It mainly deals with rules and regulations, which the Buddha promulgated. (ii) It describes in detail the gradual development of the *Sangha.* (iii) An account of the life and teaching of the Buddha is also given.
- ***The Sutta Pitaka:*** (i) It consists chiefly of discourses delivered by Buddha himself on different occasions. (ii) Few discourses delivered by Sariputta, Ananda, Moggalana and others are also included in it.
- ***The Abhidhamma Pitaka:*** (i) It contains the profound philosophy of the Buddha's teachings. (ii) It investigates mind and matter, to help the understanding of things as they truly are.
- ***The Khandhakas:*** (i) They contain regulations on the course or life in the monastic order and have two sections—the *Mahavagga* and the *Cullavagga.* The third part, the *Parivara,* is an insignificant composition by a Ceylonese monk.
- Among the non-canonical literature, *Milindapanho, Dipavamsa* and *Mahavamsa* are important. The later two are the great chronicles of Ceylon.

THE IMPORTANT BUDDHIST WRITERS

Some of the prominent Buddhist writers were :

- **Asvaghosha :** Contemporary of Kanishka. He was poet, dramatist, musician, scholar and debator.
- **Nagarjuna :** He was a friend and contemporary of Satavahana king Yajnasri Gautamiputra of Andhra. He propounded the *Madhyamika* School of Buddhist philosophy, popularly known as *Sunyavada.*
- **Asanga and Vasubandhu :** Two brothers who flourished in the Punjab region in fourth century A.D. Asanga was the most important teacher of the *Yogachara* or *Vijnanavada* School founded by his guru, Maitreyanatha. Vasubandhu's greatest work, *Abhidharmakosa* is still considered an important encyclopaedia of Buddhism.
- **Buddhaghosha :** Who lived in the fifth century AD was a great Pali scholar. The commentaries and the *Visuddhimaga* written by him are a great achievement in the Post-Tripitaka literature.
- **Dinnaga :** The last mighty intellectual of the fifth century, is well known as the founder of the Buddhist logic.
- **Dharmakirti :** Lived in the seventh century AD; was another great Buddhist logician; a subtle philosophical thinker and dialectician.

BUDDHIST COUNCILS

No.	Venue (Year)	Presiding Priest	King	Major Outcomes
First	Satparni Rajagriha (483 BC)	Mahakassapa	Ajatashatru	Upali recited the *Vinaya Pitaka* which contains the rules of the Buddhist order; Anand, the other disciple of the Buddha, recited *Suttapitaka*, containing the great collection of Buddha's sermons on matters of doctrine and ethical beliefs.
Second	Vaishali (383 BC)	Sabakami	Kalasoka	Split of the Buddhist order into *Sthaviravadins* or *Theravadins* and Mahasanghikas over small points of monastic discipline.
Third	Pataliputra (250 BC)	Mogaliputta Tissa (also known as Upagupta)	Ashoka	Establishment of the *Sthaviravada* school as an orthodox school; Codification of *Abhidhamma Pitaka*, which deals with philosophy of Buddhism, in Pali
Fourth	Kundalvana, Kashmir (72 AD)	Vasumitra; Asvaghosha was the deputy of Vasumitra	Kanishka	Division of Buddhism into the *Mahayana* and *Hinayana* sects.

CONTRIBUTIONS OF BUDDHISM

- The doctrine of *ahimsa* (non-violence) is one of the main contributions of Buddhism.
- It gave India a religion devoid of complicated and incomprehensible rituals and symbols.
- It laid the foundation of image worship in the country.
- The *Mahayana* Buddhists started the practice of worshipping personal gods and erecting temples.
- Buddhism made perhaps the finest contribution in the realm of art and architecture: stupas, stone pillars, caves, and development of Gandhar art by the Indo-Greek sculptors are some of the striking examples.
- Buddhism enriched the Pali language immensely.
- Buddhism led to the establishment of residential universities: Nalanda and Vikramashila in Bihar; Vallabhi in Gujarat and Taxila in the north west frontier region
- Through its missionaries in different countries of the world, Buddhism broke the isolation of India and established an intimate relationship between India and the rest of the world.
- It promoted trade and commerce.

3.4 AJIVIKAS

It was an ascetic sect that emerged in Indian about the same time as Buddhism and Jainism. It was founded by Gosala Maskariputra, who was a contemporary and early friend of Mahavira, the founder of Jainism. Maskariputra died shortly before the Buddha (probably about 484 BC) after a quarrel with Mahävira.

The Ajivika sect professed a total determinism in the transmigration of soul, or series of rebirths. It held that the affairs of the entire universe were ordered by a cosmic force called **niyati** (which in Sanskrit means rule, destiny"), which determined all events and thus man's fate to the last detail. Unlike other contemporary sects, it did not believe that man himself could better his lot in the course of his transmigration.

The Ajivikas went about naked and claimed special strictness in their rules as to means of livelihood.

3.5 MATERIALISTIC SECTS

Though the Buddhism, Jainism and Ajivika sect ignored the gods, they were not atheists and materialists in true sense as all of them admitted the existence of supernatural beings. They all accepted the fundamental doctrine of transmigration of soul. However, there were some thinkers who rejected all immaterial categories completely.

A list of important materialistic sects that arose in the 6th century BC is given in the following table.

IMPORTANT MATERIALISTIC SECTS

Sect	Founder	Philosophy
(i) **Annihilationism or Uchchedavada**	Ajita Kesakambalin, a contemporary of Buddha	The concept of rebirth and life after death is false, and hence there is no life after the present one.
(ii) **Antinomianism**	Purana Kassapa	There is nothing like bad consequences of bad works and good consequences of good works. There is nothing like a pious work or a sin.
(iii) **Atomism**	Pakuda Katyayana	Just as earth, water, air and light are indestructible elements, so are sorrow, happiness and life. The later Vaisheshika school originated from this idea.
(iv) **Lokayat**	Charvak	One should lead a lustful life even if it entails being in debt. God is non-existent.
(v) **Scepticism**	Sanjaya Bellathiputta	The existence of heaven, soul, god, virtue, sins, etc cannot be determined with certainty.

3.6 HINDU REVIVALIST MOVEMENTS

(a) ***Bhagavatism* or *Vaishnavism***: This cult was propounded by Vasudeva. The faith in the *Puranas*, the *Ramayana*, the *Mahabharata*, the *Bhagwat Gita*, theory of incarnations of God, attainment of Salvation or *Nirvana* by *bhakti*, idol-worship, chanting of prayers etc., were popularised by Vasudeva.

Types of Vaishnavism: On the basis of period, *Vaishnavism* can by classified into three types :

(i) ***Bhagwata*** : Originated in about second century BC and were made popular by 12 Alvars in South.

(ii) ***Pancharatras*** : Systematised in about 1st century AD by Sandilya.

(iii) ***Vaikhanasas*** : Initially a part of *Yajurvedic philosophy* of *Taittiriya* School, it was founded anew by *Vikhanas*. Its main text is *Vaikhana Sutra* which is based on the five-fold concept of Vishnu, such as (i) *Brahman* (ii) *Achutya*, (iii) *Purush*, (iv) *Satya* and (v) *Anirudha*.

(b) Saivism : The other popular sect of Hinduism is Saivism. The origin of Siva can be traced to the concept of *Rudra* in the *Rig Veda.* Probably, he found his place among Aryan Gods because of the influence of the Dravidians, who had a similar god among them called *Pasupati.* In the *Yajur Veda,* he is referred to as *Sambhu* or *Shankar.* In the *Atharva Veda,* he is regarded as the Supreme God while in the *Svetasvatara Upanishad*, his spouse Uma or Parvati is provided a similar position. Thus, Siva rose into prominence with the passage of time. However, the rise of Saivism, with a philosophy and organization of its own, cannot be traced back earlier than about the beginning of the Christian era. The sect, probably, was started by a person called Lakulin or Nakulin near about the beginning of the second century AD. Afterwards, Saivism was divided into four important schools, viz. *Pasupata, Saiva, Kapalika* and *Kalamukha.* However, Siva is worshipped most in the form of the *Linga* (Phallus) because of the influence of another sect of Saivism called *Lingayat*. Saivism is now a part of Hinduism and the worship of Siva is most popular among the Hindus.

BUDDHISM, JAINISM AND HINDUISM : A COMPARISON

Points of Similarity

1. All the three religions are tender to human life, the Jaini being over-scrupulous in this respect.
2. They believe in the transmigration of the soul.
3. They aim at *Mukti* (or salvation), complete deliverance from human cares and anxieties.
4. They all attach importance to *Karma* (action).
5. Both Buddhism and Jainism deny the authority of the *Vedas*.
6. Both grew of Brahmanical Hinduism.
7. Both were preached at the same time and in the same region, i.e., Magadha.
8. Both abhor bloody sacrifices.
9. Both rely on the system preaching through monks.

Points of Difference

1. The Brahmans acknowledge caste, but the Buddhists reject it.
2. The Brahmans worship vedic gods, while the Buddhists respect twenty-four Buddhas, and Jains their 24 Tirthankaras
3. The Jains retain the caste system and believe in the Brahmanical gods but subordinate to their own saints, called *Tirthankaras,* but they deny the divine authority of the Vedas and the exclusive claim of the Brahmans.
4. The Buddhists and Jainas have more respect for animal life than the Brahmans.
5. The Brahmans have great respect for fire, while the Jainas and the Buddhists have none.
6. The Brahmans have no respect for the relics of their saints, but the Buddhists have great respect for them.
7. The Brahmans believe in the scriptural character of the *Vedas*, but the Buddhists reject them.
8. The Brahmans enjoin bloody sacrifices, but the Jainas and the Buddhists are opposed to them.

4. THE MAURYAS

4.1 SOURCE MATERIALS

There are two main literary sources for the Mauryan period. One is the '*Arthashastra*', written by Kautilya or Chanakya, the Prime Minister of Chandragupta Maurya, which explains how a good government should be organised. The other source is '*Indica*', written in Greek by Megasthenes, the ambassador of Seleucus Nicator at the court of Chandragupta. Megasthenes wrote not only about the capital city of Pataliputra but also about the Maurya empire as a whole and about the society. The history of Ashoka's reign can be constructed mainly on the basis of his edicts.

ARTHASHASTRA

- Written by Chankaya/Vishnugupta/Kautilya
- Divided in 15 Adhikarnas and 180 Prakarnas
- is related to money and politics
- is divided into fifteen parts
- six thousand sholakas
- comment - Pratipada Panchika commented by-Bhataswamy
- Manuscript discovered by Arya Sharma Shastri in 1904

'*Mudrarakshasa*', written by Vishakhadatta in 5th century AD, gives an interesting account of how Chandragupta with the help of Kautilya overthrew the Nandas. Jain and Buddhist traditions also throw sidelight on the history of the Mauryas. Jain scriptures refer to Chandragupta's death and the Buddhist work, '*Mahavamsa*', relates an account of the life and work of the king Ashoka. *Malvikagnimitram,* written by Kalidasa, throws enough light on the last years of the Mauryan rule and the ascendance of Pushyamitra Sunga.

Apart from the above literary sources, inscriptions of Junagarh and other inscriptions of Ashoka on rocks and pillars help us much in building the story of this age. The monuments belonging to the Mauryan period speak of the culture and civilisation of this period. The stupas, viharas, and caves tell us about the development of art and architecture of this period.

DIFFERENT VIEWS ON THE ORIGIN OF THE MAURYAS

- **Buddhist Sources:** They connect them with the tribe of sakyas whose region ws full of peacocks i.e. Moriyas and they mention Chandragupta as a Kshatriya.
- **Jain Sources:** They link Chandragupta to *Moriya* tribe of peacock tamers.
- **Brahmaical Sources:** They describe Mauryas as Shudra.
- **Greek Sources:** They mention that Sandrokottas (Chandragupta) was born of humble origin.

4.2 CHANDRAGUPTA MAURYA (321-293 BC)

The Maurya dynasty was founded by Chandragupta Maurya. He took advantage of the growing weakness and unpopularity of the Nandas in the last days of their rule. With the help of Chanakya, who is known as Kautilya, he overthrew the Nandas and established the rule of the Maurya dynasty.

Chandragupta built up a vast empire which included not only Bihar and good portions of Bengal, but also western and north-western India, and the Deccan. Leaving Kerala, Tamil Nadu and parts of north-eastern India, the Mauryas ruled over the whole of the subcontinent. In the north-west, they held sway over certain areas which were not included even in the British empire.

Chandragupta, according to the Jaina literature, in his last days converted into Jainism and abdicating his throne in favour of his son Bindusara became a monk.

VARIOUS NAMES OF CHANDRAGUPTA MAURYA	
Name	**Source**
Palibrothus	Strabo
Androcotus	Arien, Plutarch
Piyadamas	*Mudraraksha*
Vrishal	*Mudraraksha*
Chandrasiri	*Mudraraksha*
Kulihin	*Mudraraksha*

4.3 BINDUSARA (293-273 BC)

He was son of Chandragupta and was known as *Amitraghta* (slayer of foes) by the Greek writers. He continued his friendly links with the Syrian King Antiochus I and is stated to have requested him for a present of figs and wine together with a sophist. Antiochus sent figs and wine but replied that Greek philosophers were not for export. He received a Greek ambassador, Daimachos, from Antiochus I. Pliny tells that Ptolemy II Philadelphus of Egypt sent an envoy, Dionysios, to Bindusara's court.

VARIOUS NAMES OF BINDUSARA	
• Amitraghat	Sanskrit Literature
• Amitchetas	Strabo which was Greek version of Sanskrit 'Amitraghata'
• Seemseri	Rajvalli Katha
• Bindupala	Fa-Feenchulin or slayer of foes

4.4 ASHOKA (273-232 BC)

Ashoka was the third and the greatest of the Mauryan rulers. He occupies a high position not only in the history of India but in the world history also. He was coronated four years after the death of his father, Bindusara (273BC). The gap is interpreted differently by different historians.

We have scanty and unreliable sources to know the early life of Ashoka. From the Buddhist traditions we learn that he was originally called 'Chandasoka' or the fierce Asoka owing to his many evil deeds, but afterwards he became Dharmasoka i.e., pious Asoka. Scholars regard it a fabrication by the Buddhists as they were eager to emphasize the effects of one's conversion to their faith which they called the 'True Religion.' From Rock Edict No. XIII, we learn that after Kalinga War (261BC) Ashoka was a thoroughly changed man. He discarded *Digvijay* and followed *Dharmavijay*. Due to this policy, his name shines with unique brilliance.

Like his predecessors. Ashoka assumed the title of *Priyadarshi* (pleasing to look at) and *Devanampriya* (beloved of Gods). In the Sarnath inscription, he adopted the third title i.e., *Dharmasoka*.

ASHOKA'S HELLENISTIC CONTEMPORARIES		
Antiochus II Theos	-	Syria
Ptolemy II Philadelpus	-	Egypt
Magas	-	Cyrne
Antigonus Gonatas	-	Macedonia
Alexander	-	Epirus

VARIOUS NAMES AND EPITHETS OF ASHOKA	
• **Devanamkpriya**	Monarchial Epithet
• **Ashokavardnan**	Purana
• **Piyadassiraja**	Barabar cave inscription
• **Ashoka Maurya**	Junagarh Inscription
• **Piyadasi**	Kandhar inscription

Ashoka's Dhamma: There was a great difference between Ashoka's personal religion and the religion he preached. His personal religion was, of course, Buddhism as he frankly admitted in the *Bhabru Edict* that he believed in the principles of Buddhism. In several of his edicts, in the capacity of the defender of the faith, he prescribed rules of punishment for those *Bhikshus* (monks) who violated the principles of Buddhism. He undertook journeys to the holy places of Buddhism and also called a Buddhist Council to meet in his time. However, the greatness of the Ashoka lies in the fact that he never thrusted his own religion upon anyone else. The *Dhamma* he placed before the world to follow was not pure Buddhism but it was the essence of all religions.

He appointed a new class of officers called *dharmayuktas, dharma-mahamatras* and *stri-adhyaksha* for the moral and spiritual uplift of the subjects.

According to Ashoka, the true spirit of religion does not lie in or is not fulfilled by keeping fasts or singing hymns or reciting prayers. He was, on the contrary, quite sure that true religion consisted in leading a pure and pious life. Asoka's dhamma comprised all the good qualities of the religions of the world, which he was convinced, were not exclusively the monopoly of Buddhism alone.

4.5 LATER IMPERIAL MAURYAS

Ashoka, according to Buddhist texts, ruled for twenty-seven years. The disintegration of the Mauryan empire seemed to have set in immediately after Ashoka's death. So long he lived, he maintained his effective hold over the entire empire, extending in the north from the foot of the Hindukush to the border of the Tamil country in the south.

The tenth and the last of the Mauryas was Brihadratha, who, according to the testimony of Banabhatta, was murdered by his general Pushyamitra Sunga who ascended the throne in 187 BC. The empire founded by Pushyamitra is known as **Sunga Dynasty**. With Brihadratha's death (185 BC), the historic rule of the Mauryas came to an end within less than half a century of Ashoka's death and 137 years since its foundation by Chandragupta Maurya.

4.6 CAUSES OF THE DECLINE OF THE MAURYANS

Following factors are held responsible for the decline of the Mauryan empire.

- Weak successors of Ashoka
- Militant Brahmanical reactions to Ashoka's religious policy which was closer to Buddhism
- Ashoka's pacifist policy aiming at *Dharamvijay* instead of *Digvijay*.
- Financial crisis owing to the enormous expenditure on the army and large bureaucracy.
- Highly centralised character of the Mauryan government
- Greek invasion on the north-west.

4.7 MAURYAN ADMINISTRATION

Central Administration

The Mauryan rule was vast and highly centralized bureaucratic rule with the king as the fountain head of all powers. The king claimed no divine rule; rather it was paternal despotism, Kautilya called the king "*dharmapravartaka*" or promulgator of social order.

MAURYAN *MANTRIPARISHAD*	
Mantrin	- Chief Minister
Purohita	- High Priest
Senapati	- Commander-in-charge
Yuvaraj	- Crowned Prince
Samaharta	- Collector of Revenue
Yukta	- Subordinate Officer-in-Charge of Revenue of the King
Prashasti	- Head of Prisons
Sannidata	- Head of Treasury
Nayaka	- Head of City Security
Paur	- City Police
Vyabharika	- Chief Judge
Karmantika	- Head of Industries and Factories
Dandapala	- Head of Police
Durgapala	- Head of Royal Fort
Annapala	- Head of the Food Grains Department
Rajjukas	- Officers responsible for land measurement and fixing its boundary.
Pradesika	- Head of District Administration

The highest functionaries at the centre were called *Tirthas*. There was also the *mantriparishad* to assist the king in day-to- day administration. Kautilya mentions 27 superintendents (*adhyakshas*) mostly to regulate economic activities.

The following *Tirthas* were the parts of the Mauryan administration.

TIRTHAS OF MAURYAN EMPIRE	
Matriparishad Adhyaksha	-Head of the Council of Minister.
Koshadhyaksha	- Treasury officer.
Akaradhyaksha	- Mining officer.

Lauhadhyaksha	- Metallurgy officer
Lakshanadhyaksha	- Officer-in-charge of Coin-minting.
Lavanadhyaksha	- Officer of Salt department.
Swarnadhyaksha	- Officer of gold department.
Koshthagaradhyaksha	- Manager of the royal treasury.
Panyadhyaksha	- Officer of the Commerce department.
Kunyadhyaksha	- Officer of forest.
Ayudhadhyaksha	- Officer of weapon manufacturing and defence department.
Pautavadhyaksha	- Officer for weights and measurements.
Manadhyaksha	- Officer of time and place determining department.
Shulkadhyaksha	- Officer-in-charge of royal income, punishment etc.
Sutradhyaksha	- Textile Department Officer.
Sitadhyaksha	- Manager of the royal farming.
Suradhyaksha	- Custom department officer.
Sunadhyaksha	- Slaughter-house officer.
Mudradhyaksha	- Officer of royal symbol, coin and passport department.
Vivitadhyaksha	- Officer of the pasture land.
Dyutadhyaksha	- Officer of the gambling department.
Bandhanagaradhyaksha	- Officer of the prison department.
Navadhyaksha	- Inspector of animal husbandry.
Naukadhyaksha	- Officer of the shipping department.
Pattanadhyaksha	- Officer of the port.
Sansthadhyaksha	- Manager of the trade.
Sainya Vibhagadhyaksha	- Officers of infantry, cavalry, elephants & chariots department.

Provincial Administration: Except the capital Pataliputra, the whole empire was divided into four provinces controlled by a viceroy—either a prince or a member of royal family.

MAURYAN PROVINCES AND THEIR CAPITALS

	Province	Capital
I.	**Uttarapatha (North)**	Taxila
II.	**Dekshinapatha (South)**	Suvarnagiri
III.	**Avantipatha (West)**	Ujjain
IV.	**Prachyapatha (East)**	Toshali or Kalinga
V.	**Central Province**	Pataliputra

District Administration : Each district had three main officers-*Pradeshikas, Rajukas* and *Yuktas*.

Sub-district administration: Sub-districts were administered by *Gopa* (account) and *Sthanika* (tax collector). The villages were administered by village headmen.

City Administration: The administration of capital Pataliputra has been described by Megasthenese. According to him, the capital was administered by six board consisting of five members each, being entrusted with matters relating to industrial arts, care of foreigners, registration of birth and death, regulation of weights and measures, public sale of manufactured articles and last with collecting toll on the articles.

Judicial Administration: Justice was provided by the king, *Pradeshika* and *Rajukas*. At lowest level, the justice was administered by the village headman. There were two types of courts : (i) *Dharmasthas*: The civil courts redressing cases of marriage, contracts etc. and (ii) *Kantakasodhana*: the criminal courts which tried criminal cases and tax evasion.

Army: Mauryas had a big army, According to Pliny, Chandragupta maintained 600,000 foot soliders, 30,000 cavalary and 900 elephants. According to Meghasthenese, the army was administered by six committees consisting of five members each, taken from a board of 30 officers.

Espionage: It was integral to the Mauryan administration; Speis were of two types : *Santha* and *Sanchar*; the former worked by remaining stationed at a public place and the latter by moving from place to place. The spies were the ears and eyes of the king. They were also called "*Gudhapurshas*."

DHAMMA MAHAMATTAS

Dhamma Mahamattas were the officials appointed by Ashoka in the 14th year of his reign to supervise the practical working of the king's Dhamma policy. In the beginning, they were concerned with promoting general welfare while putting emphasis on the practice of ***Dhamma***. To perform their duties, these officials could enter the houses of all classes and sects of people, including the royal relatives. However, their power to interfere in the lives of the people gradually increased later. They were active not only within the empire but also in the frontier areas and neighbouring regions.

Revenue Administration : There were different sources of state revenues : cities (*durga*), rural areas (*rashtra*), mines (*khan*), road and traffic (*vanikpatha*), pastures (*Vraja*), Plantations (*setu*) and forests (*vana*).

Land Taxes : Different types of taxes were levied upon the rural areas (*rashtras*) for the extraction of land revenue. Kautilya gives a detailed account of these taxes. These were as follows:

- ***Bhaga***: The chief source of revenue levied at the rate of 1/4th or 1/6th.
- ***Pindakara***: Assessed on group of villages and paid by husbandsmen.
- ***Kara***: Taxes levied on fruits and flower garden.
- ***Hiranya***: taxes levied in cash on special class of crops.
- ***Pranaya***: Imposed by the state during emergency periods. It amounted to 1/3rd or 1/4th of the produce according to the nature of the soil.
- ***Bali***: A tax known since the Vedic period continued under the Mauryans.

Import Duties: *Prabeshya* or import duties were fixed at 20 per cent of the cost price. *Panyadhyaksha* and *Pattanadhyaksha* were responsible to verify every import to the state. They were also responsible for the export of each article from the state and collected the revenue known as *nishkramya*.

Sales Tax: Taxes were imposed on every article before it was sold or purchased by *Sulkadhyaksha* : 9.5 per cent on items sold on the basis of calculation, 5 per cent on the items sold on the basis of measurement, and 6.5 per cent on the goods sold on the basis of weight.

Besides these, there were many other taxes collected by the state, such as taxes on artisans and artists, taxes on animal slaughter-houses, taxes on manufacturing houses, taxes on gambling houses, on prostitutes, on the income of temples and on the additional incomes of the wage earners.

4.8 SOCIO-ECONOMIC AND RELIGIOUS CONDITIONS UNDER THE MAURYAS

Kautilya's *Arthasastra* and contemporary literature throw a flood of light on political, religious, social and economic conditions of the Mauryan Period. The establishment of a strong and large empire ensured peace and security. Therefore, people could pay greater attention to economic growth. There also flourished internal trade. Various contemporary literature confirm that the state controlled and organised the agriculture, industry, trade, animal husbandry, cattle-breeding and commerce of the country. The main livelihood of the people was agriculture. The state directly controlled the agriculture of the crown lands.

It is also evident that the Mauryan rulers maintained ship building as a state monopoly. Trade and commerce with the foreign countries were strictly regulated. Textile manufacture was one of the major industries. Kautilya also leaves many details of metallurgical interest and discusses about manufacture of copper, lead, tin, bronze, iron, etc. Many other industries including dyes, gums, drugs, perfumes, potteries, developed considerably. War equipment like swords, shields, armours, war-chariots and many *jantrani* (machine) were manufactured in large quantities. The state owned many industrial and trading units.

Kautilya's *Arthasastra* and Megasthene's accounts also give evidence of the society and social condition of the people. *Varna* or the caste-system and stages of religious discipline took a definite shape, which corresponds to Hindu caste-system. Slavery was an established institution. Women were placed in high esteem. Yet, prostitution was an established institution. *Ganikadhyaksha* was the officer-in-charge of its periodical supervision. Festivals and merry gatherings were common. The people led a simple and unostentatious life and were inspired by the sense of morality and idealism.

4.9 MAURYAN ART

The age of Mauryas contributed significantly to the development of arts, including architecture, sculpture, engineering, polishing, etc. Chandragupta Maurya built his capital and palace at Pataliputra. The wonderful palace was made of wood. Ashoka further improved the wooden walls and buildings of the capital and added many attractive edifices, which could be traced from the site at Kumrahar on outskirts of Patna. The 80-pillared hall found at Kumrahar in Patna represents the masterpiece of Mauryan sculpture. Each pillar is made of single piece of sandstone.

Ashoka built a large number of *stupas*. According to the Buddhist tradition, Ashoka built as good as 84,000 stupas. These structures were solid and domic, made of rock or bricks. The art of sculpture or rock cutting also reached its zenith during Ashoka's time. Seven rock-cuts sanctuaries lying about 25 miles north of Gaya, Bihar–four on the Barabar hills and three on the Nagarjuna hills–belong to the time of Ashoka and his successors. The caves are also fine examples of Mauryan art. They were used for religious ceremonies and also, as assembly halls.

Another noticeable feature was art of polishing the monuments, pillars, caves made of hard rocks. Art of engineering equally flourished. Civil engineering was in highly advanced state and, therefore, so many spectacular buildings, stupas, pillars could be constructed with perfection and efficiency. Also, the art of jewellery attained a remarkable progress.

Single-bull capital of Rampurva, single-lion capital at Lauriya Nandangarh and four-lion capital at Sarnath and Sanchi are another examples of Mauryan art.

The punched-marked silver coins of the Mauryas which carry the symbols of the peacock, and the hill and crescent were also a part of Court Art.

The second category of art i.e. popular art included the folk tradition of arts represented by figures of Yaksha and Yakshinis found from Besnagar, Didarganj etc. The abundance of beautiful pottery called Northern Black Polished Ware (NBPW) and terracotta figurines were another item of popular art.

7.10 ASHOKAN INSCRIPTIONS/EDICTS

A brief description of Ashokan inscriptions is given as under:

(i) The Major Rock Edicts: They are a set of 14 inscriptions found at eight places: Dhauli, Girnar, Jauguda Kalsi, Mansehra, Shahbazgarhi, Sopara and Yerragudi. The Major Rock Edicts also include two separates edicts found at Kalinga. The Major Rock Edicts deal with administration and ethics.

(ii) The Minor Rock Edicts: The Minor Rock Edicts are spread on 13 places: Bairat, Brahmagiri, Gavimath, Gujarra, Jatinga-Rameshwar, Maski, Palkigundu, Rajula-Mandagiri, Rupanath, Sasaram, Siddapur, Survrnagiri and Yerragudi.

The Minor Rock Edicts include the following:

a. ***The Queen's Edict*** : It was located at Allahabad-Kosam.

b. ***Barabar Cave Inscriptions*** : Located in Bihar, these inscriptions speak of Ashoka's donation of the cave to the Ajivikas.

c. ***Kandahar Inscriptions*** : They are located at Shar-i-Quna in southern Afghanistan.

d. ***Bhabru Inscriptions*** : It has been found at Bairat in Rajasthan. It deals with Ashoka's conversion to Buddhism.

(iii) The Major Pillar Edicts : They are a set up of seven edicts found at Allahabad-Kosam, Merrut (now in Delhi), Topran (now in Delhi), Lauriya Areraj, Lauriya Nandangarh and Rampurva (all three in Bihar).These edicts are engraved on monolithic pillars.

(iv) **Minor Pillar Edicts :** These include:

(a) ***Rummindei Pillar Inscription :*** It mentions the exemption of Lumbini, birth place of Lord Buddha, from tax.

(b) ***Nigalisagar Pillar Inscription*** **:** Originally located year Kapilvastu, now near Rummindei or Lumbini. It says the Asoka increased the stupa of Buddha Konakamana to double its former size

(c) **Schism Edict :** Found at Kausambi, Sanchi and Sarnath, this edict appeals for maintaining unity in the Buddhist order.

Language of Inscriptions : Ashokan inscriptions use three different languages –Prakrit, Greek and Aramaic–and four scripts–Brahmi, Kharoshthi, Greek and Aramaic. Prakrit inscriptions are written in Brahmi and Kharoshthi. Rest inscriptions are written in Greek and Aramaic scripts. The Kandahar Rock inscription is bilingual, using Greek and Aramaic languages. Inscriptions in Kharoshthi are all clustered in the north-west.

5. THE GUPTAS

5.1 INTRODUCTION

It was, perhaps, sometimes late in the obscure period of the third century AD that the Gupta dynasty emerged. One Sri Gupta, who brought Magadha under his control, was the founder of the Gupta dynasty. Sri Gupta was succeeded by Ghototkacha Gupta. The first two kings of the dynasty were described as *Maharajas*. It is generally believed that first two rulers of the dynasty ruled before 320 AD. They were followd by some of the mighty rulers of ancient Indian history.

5.2 CHANDRAGUPTA I (320 AD-335 AD)

Chandragupta I, grandson of Sri Gupta and son of Ghatotkacha Gupta, was the first great ruler of the line. He increased power and prestige of the empire to a great extent by matrimonial alliance and conquests. He married Kumaradevi, the Lichchavi princess. His empire included modern Bihar, Oudh, Allahabad, Tirhut, in addition to Magadha. He assumed the title of *Maharajadhiraj*. He started the Gupta Era in AD 320, which marked the date of his accession.

5.3 SAMUDRAGUPTA (335 AD-375 AD)

Samudragupta ascended the throne in 335 AD. The basic information about his reign is provided by an inscription *Prayaga Prasasti* composed by **Harisena**, the poet at his court, and engraved on an Ashokan pillar at Allahabad. The places and the countries conquered by Samudragupta can be divided into five groups. Group one includes princes of the Ganga-Yamuna doab who were defeated. Group two includes the rulers of eastern Himalayan states and some frontier states, such as princes of Nepal, Assam and Bengal. It also covers some republics of Punjab. Group three includes the forest kingdoms situated in the Vindhya region and known as '*atavika rajyas*'. Group four includes twelve rulers of the eastern Deccan and South India, who were conquered and liberated. Group five includes the names of the Sakas and Kushanas.

Samudragupta embarked upon a policy of conquest. In fact, *Digvijaya* became the ultimate goal of his life. For his military achievements, he has been aptly complimented by the historian V.A. Smith as the ***Indian Napoleon.*** He has described Samudra Gupta as the ***'Hero of a Hundred Battles'.***

5.4 CHANDRAGUPTA II (380 AD-412 AD)

The reign of Chandragupta II saw the highest watermark of the Gupta empire. He extended the limits of the empire by marriage alliance and conquests. Chandragupta I married his daughter Prabhavati with a Vakataka prince who belonged to the Brahmana caste and ruled in central India. The prince died and was succeeded by his young son. So, Prabhavati became the virtual ruler. Chandragupta exercised indirect control over the **Vakataka Kingdom**. This afforded a great advantage to him. With his great influence in this area, Chandragupta II conquered western Malwa and Gujarat, which had been under the rule of the Saka *Kshatrapas* for about four centuries. The conquest gave Chandragupta the eastern sea coast, famous for trade and commerce. This also contributed to the prosperity of Malwa, and its chief city Ujjain. Ujjain seems to have been made the second capital by Chandragupta II.

CHANDRAGUPTA II'S NINE GEMS

Person (Field)	Famous Works
1. Amarsimha (Lexicography)	*Amarkosha*
2. Dhanvantri (Medicine)	*Ayurveda*
3. Harisena (Poetry)	*Allahahad Inscription*
4. Kalidasa (Drama and Poetry)	*Abhijnanashakuntalam, Meghdrot etc.*
5. Kahapanaka (Astrology)	*Jyothisyashastra*
6. Sanku (Architecture)	*Shilpashastra*
7. Varahamihira (Astrology)	*Brihadsamhita*
8. Vararuchi (Grammar)	*Vyakarana (in Sanskrit)*
9. Vetalabhatta (Magic)	*Mantrashastra*

The exploits of the king called Chandra are glorified in an iron pillar inscription fixed near Qutub Minar in Delhi. But the epigraphic eulogy seems to be exaggerated.

Chandragupta II adopted the title of *Vikramaditya* which had been first used by an Ujjain ruler in 57 BC as a mark of his victory over the Saka Kshatrapas of western India. The court of Chandragupta II at Ujjain was adorned by numerous scholars such as Kalidasa and Amarasimha.

It was in Chandragupta's reign that the Chinese pilgrim **Fa-Hien (399-414)** visited India and wrote an elaborate account of the life of its people.

5.5 KUMARAGUPTA I, MAHENDRADITYA (415-455 AD)

Chandragupta II was succeeded by his son, Kumaragupta I. Nothing is known about his political career, but numismatic and epigraphic evidence indicates that the strength, unity, and prestige of the empire remained unshaken in his reign. Towards the close of his reign, the Gupta power was seriously menaced by the new invaders called the *Hunas*. Kumaragupta died during the war with the Hunas.

5.6 SKANDAGUPTA VIKRAMADITYA (455-467 AD)

Skandagupta, the last great ruler of the Gupta dynasty, probably came to the throne when the war with Pushyamitra was still going on. His victory saved the Gupta empire. He succeeded in defeating the Hunas and in maintaining the integrity of his ancestral empire. Success in repelling the Hunas seems to have been celebrated by the assumption of the title *Vikramaditya*. The decline of the empire began soon after his death. The Hunas later became the rulers of Punjab and Kashmir.

5.7 DECLINE OF THE GUPTA EMPIRE

Though Gupta rule lingered till the middle of the sixth century AD, the imperial glory had ended a century earlier. The reasons were : (i) invasion by the Hunas, (ii) rise of feudalism, (iii) weak successors, (iv) financial difficulties, (v) decline of foreign trade, and (vi) absence of large professional army to maintain vast empire.

5.8 GUPTA ADMINISTRATION

In contrast to the Mauryas, the Gupta kings adopted pompous titles such as *parameshvara, maharajadhiraja* and *paramabhattaraka* which signify that they ruled over lesser kings in their empire. Kingship was hereditary, but royal power was limited by absence of a firm practice of primogeniture.

The Gupta bureaucracy was not as elaborate as that of the Mauryas. The most important officers in the Gupta empire were the *kumaramatyas*. They were appointed by the king in the home provinces and possibly paid in cash. The Guptas organized a system of provincial and local administration. The empire was divided into *bhuktis* and each *bhukti* was placed under the charge of an *uparika*. The *bhuktis* were divided into *vishayas* (districts), which were placed under the charge of *vishyapati*. In eastern India, the *vishayas* were divided into *vithis*, which again were divided into villages. The village headman became more important in Gupta times.

Since much of the imperial administration was managed by feudatories and beneficiaries, the Gupta rulers did not require as many officials as the Mauryas did. They did not require too many officers also because, unlike the Maurya state, the Gupta state did not regulate economic activities on any big scale. The participation of leading artisans, merchants, elders, etc. in rural and urban administration also lessened the need for maintaining a large retinue of officers.

IMPORTANT GUPTA OFFICIALS AT THE CENTRAL LEVEL

(i)	***Mahabaladhikrita***	Commander-in-Chief.
(ii)	***Mahadandanayak***	Chief justice.
(iii)	***Mahapratihar***	An official to maintain the royal palace.
(iv)	***Mahasandhivigrahak or Sandhivigrahak***	An official for post-war conciliation.
(v)	***Dandapashika***	Head of the police department.
(vi)	***Bhandagaradhikreta***	Head of the royal treasury.

(vii)	***Mahapaksha-Patalik***	Head of the account department.
(viii)	***Vinaysthitisansathapak***	Head of the education department.
(ix)	***Sarvadhyaksha***	Inspector for the all central departments.
(x)	***Mahashwapati***	Controller of cavalry.
(xi)	***Mahamahipilapati***	Controller and executor of elephantry.
(xii)	***Vinaypura***	Official to present different guests at king's court.
(xiii)	***Yuktapurusha***	Office to keep account of war booty.
(xiv)	***Khadyatpakika***	Inspector of royal kitchen.
(xv)	***Ranabhandagarika***	Officer-in-charge of army stores.
(xvi)	***Mahanarpati***	Head of foot soldiers (infantry).

5.9 ECONOMIC AND SOCIAL DEVELOPMENTS

Revenue and Trade : A study of the inscriptions of the Gupta period reveals that eighteen different taxes were levied at that time. Land revenue was the chief source of income. Land tax was between 1/4 to 1/6 of the produce. It is known from the inscriptions of Pallavas and Vakatakas that taxes were enforced on buffalo milk, curd and also on fruits and flowers. The forests, meadows and salt mines, added to the income of the state.

Land taxes increased while those on trade and commerce decreased; *Visthi* (forced labour) prevailed. Religious functionaries were granted land called *Agrahara*.

Trade through rivers proved quite cheap and comfortable. During this period, the ship-building industry greatly flourished. Tamralipti, a port in Bengal, was an important trade centre and from there trade was carried on with the eastern countries like China, Ceylon, Java and Sumatra. In Andhra, there were many ports on the banks of the rivers, Godavari and Krishna; Tondai was a famous port of Chola state. Kalyana, Chol, Broach and Cambay were the important ports of the South.

The Guptas issued the largest number of gold coins, which were called *dinaras* in their inscriptions.

Emergence of Priestly Landlords : The striking development of the Gupta period, especially in Madhya Pradesh, was the emergence of priestly landlords at the cost of local peasants. Land grants made to the priests certainly brought many virgin areas under cultivation. But these beneficiaries were imposed from above on the local tribal peasants, who were reduced to a lower status. In central and western India, the peasants were also subjected to forced labour (*Visthi*).

TYPES OF TAXES DURING THE GUPTAS

Kalpita/Upkilpta	Sales Tax and Purchase Tax
Halivakar/Halidanda	Tax on Ploughing
Bali	An additional oppressive tax on people
Prataya	Toll tax
Bhog	King's share of produce
Bhoga	General Tribute
Bhag Bhagkar	Combination of Bhog and Bhaga
Bhatta	Police tax
Chat	Security tax
Charasana	Grazing tax
Hiranya	Tax on special produce taken in cash
Udakabhag	May be water tax
Uparikar	Tax collected from all subjects
Taradaya	Tax on navigation
Rajju	Tax for Measurement of land
Sarvarishti	Forced tax
Bedakbhog	Irrigation tax
Uparnik	Tax taken from border area

Land grants to the brahmanas on a large scale suggest that the brahmana supremacy continued in Gupta times. The Guptas who were originally *vaishyas* came to be looked upon as *kshatriyas* by the *brahmanas*. The *brahamans* presented the Gupta kings as possessing the attributes of gods. All this helped to legitimise the position of the Gupta princes, who became great supporters of the *brahmanical* order. The *brahmanas* accumulated wealth on account of numerous land grants. So they claimed many privileges, which are listed in *Law Book of Narada*, a work of about the fifth century AD.

Caste Systems : The castes proliferated into numerous sub-castes as a result of two factors. A large number of foreigners had been assimilated into the Indian society, and each groups of foreigners was considered a kind of Hindu caste. The other reason for the increase in the number of castes was the absorption of many tribal peoples into brahmanical society through the process of land grants. The tribal chiefs were given a respectable origin. But most of their ordinary kinsmen were given a low origin, and every tribe became a kind of caste in its new incarnation.

The position of shudras improved in this period. They were now permitted to listen to the epics and the *Puranas*. They could also worship a new god called *Krishna*. All this can be attributed to a change in the economic status of the shudras as from the seventh century onwards, they were mainly represented as agriculturists. During this period, the untouchables, especially the *chandalas*, increased in number.

Position of Women : In the Gupta period, women were also allowed to listen to the epics and the *Puranas*, and advised to worship *Krishna*. But women of higher orders did not have access to independent sources to livelihood in pre-Gupta and Gupta times. The main reason for the subordination of women belonging to the upper *varnas* was the complete dependence on men for their livelihood. They lacked proprietary rights. However, the gifts of jewellery, ornaments, garments, and similar other presents made to the bride on the occasion of her marriage were considered her property. Gupta and post-Gupta law books substantially enlarged the scope of these gifts which were known as *Stridhana*.

Katyayana, a law-giver of the sixth century, holds that she could sell and mortgage her immovable property along with her *stridhana*. This clearly implies that women received shares in landed property but generally a daughter was not allowed to inherit landed property in the patriarchal communities of India.

In the Gupta age, there was a growing tendency to lower the marriageable age of girls. According to *Vishnu Purana*, the age of bridegroom should be three times that of the bride. According to *Angas*, the difference in age of the groom and the bride during marriage should be considerably less. *Grihya Sutras* forbids the marriage with the girl reaching the age of puberty.

5.10 RELIGION : THE REVIVAL OF HINDUISM

Bhagavatism centred around the worship of Vishnu or Bhagavat, and originated in post-Mauryan times. Vishnu was a minor god in Vedic times. He represented the sun and also the fertility cult. By the second century BC he was merged with a god called Narayana. He was also called Bhágavat, and his worshippers were called Bhagavatas.

Narayana was supposed to bestow shares or good fortune (*bhagya*) on his *bhakta* or worshippers. In returñ, the worshippers or *bhaktas* offered their loving devotion or *bhakti* to him. The worshippers of Vishnu and those of Naranyana were brought under one umbrella by merging Vishnu with Narayana. The former was a Vedic god and the latter was of Dravidian origin. But the two cultures, the two types of peoples and the two gods mingled with each other.

The great epic *Mahabharata* was recast to show that Krishna was identical with Vishnu. So by 200 BC the three streams of worshippers and their gods merged into one. This resulted in the creation of **Bhagavatism** or **Vaishnavism**. Several religious recitations, including the *Vishnusahastranama,* were composed for the benefit of the Vishnu worshippers. By the sixth century, Vishnu became a member of the trinity of gods along with Shiva and Brahma.

5.11 GUPTA ART

In art, architecture, sculpture, painting and terracotta figurines, the Gupta period witnessed unprecedented activities and development all over India. That is why the period is also referred to as the 'Golden Age of Ancient India'. In architectural types, it ushered in a new age which is particularly noticed in the architectural style of the temples. In fact, it initiated a creative and formative period for the foundation of a typical Indian temple architecture.

Architecture : In the rock-cut architecture, the conventional types reached their culmination. The rock-cut caves, mostly Buddhist, but also Hindu and Jaina, had the conventional two parts : (i) the proper shrine called the *Chaitya* and (ii) the monastery, i.e., the *Vihara* or *Sangharama*. The most notable of these are to be found in Ajanta, Ellora, Aurangabad and Bagh. Brahmanical rock-cut shrines, although lesser in number than those of the Buddhists, were not rare either. Reference may be made in this connection to the Udaygiri series of shrines, near Bhopal. The shrines are also to be found at Badami in the Bijapur district. Jaina caves are to be found at Badami as also at Aihole.

Structural buildings in altogether new style were initiated. Contemporary epigraphic evidence refers to the building of numerous temples and cities with lofty edifices with the new materials. Flat-roofed temples, temples with *Sikhars*, rectangular temples, circular and square temple survive today as specimens of the new architectural style and system. Sanchi temple, Parvati temple, Meguti temple and Baigram temples may be mentioned in this connection. The temples at Sanchi, Tigawa, and Eran are the best preserved among the structural temples of the period. The most well known *Sikhara* temple is that of Dasavatara at Deogarh. Brick temple of Bhitargao in Kanpur may be referred to as one of the new cultural temples built with the new material— bricks.

FAMOUS TEMPLES OF THE GUPTA AGE

Vishnu Temple	Tigawa (Jabalpur)
Shiva Temple	Bhumara (Nagaud)
Parvati Temple	Nachria Kuthara
Dasavtar Temple	Deogarh (Jhansi)
Shiva Temple	Koh (Nagaud)
Bhitragaon Temple	Bhitragaon
Lakshman Temple	Kanpur (Brick made)
Lakshman Temple	Sirpur (Raipur)
Mukund Darra Temple	Kota
Dhammekh Stupa	Sarnath
Jarasangh's Sitting	Rajgrih (Bihar)

Sculpture : It may be mentioned that the Gupta plastic conception had its birth at Mathura and spread to Sarnath, Shravasti, Prayag, and other places. At Sarnath, the plastic conception of Mathura school with all its elegance reached perfection in figure of seated Buddha in *Dharma-Chakra-Pravarthana* attitudes. The perfection is also noticed in a few specimens found in the figures of Siva, Kartikeya, etc., at Malwa, and partly noticed in the *Durgamahishamardini* and bust of Siva at Bhumara.

GUPTA ARCHITECTURE

- Gupta age marks the beginning of the main styles of temple architecture in India namely the *Nagara style* and *Dravida Style*
- The finest example of temple architecture is the **Dasavatara temple at Deogarh.** It is also an example of early stone temple with a Shikara.
- It has a square *grabhagriha* with exquisitely carved doorway.
- The **Bhitragaon temple of Kanpur** is made entirely of bricks.
- Other examples of temple architecture are *Parvati temple* at Nachna Kuthira, *Shiva temple* at Khoh, *Cave temple* at Udayariti etc.

AJANTA PAINTINGS

- The greatest specimen of Buddhist art in Gupta times is provided by Ajanta paintings. They depict the various events in the life of Gautama Buddha and previous Buddhas, of Jataka stories.
- Bagh caves had the folk culture as the basic theme.
- The paintings in the cave no. 9 and 10 belong to the first and second century B.C.
- Cave no.10 belongs to the early Gupta Age, approximately 350 A.D.
- Paintings in the cave no. 16, 17 and 19 belong to the later period approx to 650 A.D.
- Painting of the Cave no.1 and 2 belong to the post-Gupta period.
- The finest examples of paintings of this period are found in the rock-cut cave number 1, 16 and 19 at Ajanta
- The wall painting of the Bodhisattava in cave 1 is the finest example of Gupta art.
- The outstanding examples are the frescoes or wall-paintings.

Painting : The art of painting, including terracotta and clay modelling, assumed a secular character during this period and became more popular than stone sculpture. Vatsyayana's work *Kamasutra* includes painting as one of the sixty-four *kalas* i.e., arts. Yasodhara, commentator of Vatsyayana refers to *Shadanga* i.e., six limbs of art distinction : type (i) (*rupabheda*), (ii) ideal proportions (*pramanas*), (iii) expression of mood (*bhava*), (iv) embodiment of charm (*lavany-yojana*), (v) points of view (*sadrisya*), and (vi) preparation of colours (*varnakabhanga*).

All this and other references prove the intellectual ferment of the Gupta period and the detailed thinking about the theory and technique of painting. The best specimens of painting of the period are to be found on the walls of the Ajanta caves, Bagh cave in Gwalior, Settannavasal temple at Puddukkottai and at Badami. Incidents of life of Buddha were the subject matter of the Gupta painters. The painting *Dying Princess* in one Ajanta cave has earned the admiration of Burgess, Fergusson, Griffiths and many others. The Gupta art of painting has been praised by art critics for its brilliance of colour, richness of expression and delicacy of execution.

IMPORTANT LITERARY WORKS DURING THE GUPTA PERIOD

Works	Creators
I. Epics	
*Ramayan**	— Valmiki
*Mahabharat**	— Ved Vyasa
Raghuvansa, Ritusamhara, Meghaduta	— Kalidasa
Ravanabadha	— Batsabhatti
Kavyadarshana and *Dasakumarcharita*	— Dandin
Kiratarjuniyam	— Bharavi
Nitishataka	— Bhartrihari
II. Dramas	
Vikramovarshiya, Malvikagnimitra and	— Kalidasa
Abhijnanasakuntalam Mrichchakatika	— Sudaraka
Swapnavasavadatta, Charudatta and *Pratignayaugandharayana*	— Bhasa
Mudrarakshasa and *Devichandraguptam* — Vishakhadatta	
III. Eulogy	
Prayag-Prasasti	— Harisena
IV. Philosophy	
Sankhyakarika (based on *Shankhya* philosophy)	— Ishwar Krishna
Padartha Dharmasangraha (based on *Vaisheshika* philosophy)	— Acharya Prashastipada
Vyasa Bhasya (based on *Yoga* philosophy)	— Acharya Vyasa
Nyaya Bhasya (on *Nyaya* philosophy)	— Vatsyayana
V. Grammar	
Amarakosha	— Amarsimha
Chandravyakarana	— Chandragomin
Kavyadarsha	— Dandin
VI. Narrative Story	
Panchatantra and *Hitopadesha*	— Vishnu Sharma
VII. Mathematics and Astronomy	
Aryabhattiya	— Aryabhatta
Brihatsamhita and *Panchasidhantika*	— Varahmihira
Suryasidhanta	— Brahmagupta
VIII. Miscellaneous Works	
Nitisastra	— Kamandaka
Kamsutra	— Vatsyayana
Kavyalankara	— Bhamah

**Ramayana* and *Mahabharat* were given the final shape during this period.

5.12 DEVELOPMENT OF SCIENCE AND TECHNOLOGY

Mathematics and Astronomy : In the field of mathematics, we come across during this period a work called *Aryabhatiya* written by Aryabhatta, who belonged to Pataliputra. It seems that this mathematician was well versed in various kinds of calculations. A Gupta inscription of Allahabad suggests that the decimal system was known in India at the beginning of the fifth century AD. In the field of astronomy a book called *Romaka Sidhanta* was compiled. It was influenced by Greek ideas, as can be inferred from its name.

WHY IS THE GUPTA DYNASTY CALLED THE GOLDEN AGE IN ANCIENT INDIA

The Gupta period is called the Golden Age in the ancient Indian history owing to the following factors:

- Establishment of political unity with peace and prosperity; complete removal of foreign rule
- Light taxes and mild punishment
- Establishment of religious tolerance
- Unprecedented growth in architecture, painting and literature
- Great advancement in science and technology
- Improvement in conditions of women and Shudras.

Aryabhatta was the first to use the decimal system. He formulated the rule for finding out the area of triangle which led to the origin of trigonometry and calculated the value of pie (π). He laid the foundation of algebra in his *Aryabhatiya*. The most famous work of this time was *Suryasiddhanta*. *Brahmagupta* in 7th century AD began to apply algebra to astronomical problems. The three major contributions of the Gupta period in the field of mathematics were: **the notational system, the decimal system and the use of zero.**

CONTEMPORARIES OF THE GUPTA KINGS		
	Dynasty	**Region**
I.	**Kushanas and Shakas**	Sindh, Sakastan and Bactria
II.	**Madras**	Between Lahore and Sialkot
III.	**Yaudheyas**	Ludhiana to Saharanpur
IV.	**Nagas**	Upper Gangetic Plain
V.	**Maghas**	Rewa-Kausambi
VI.	**Vakatakas**	Vidarbha and southern Maharashtra
VII.	**Abhiras**	Deccan
VIII.	**Traikutakas**	Parts of Gujarat, Konkan and some districts of northern Maharashtra
(IX)	**Bhojas**	Berar region
(X)	**Suras**	Districts of Durg, Raipur, Bilaspur and Sambalpur
(XI)	**Sarahhapurujas**	Raipur district
(XII)	**Panduvamais**	Amarkantak region
(XIII)	**Nalas**	South-eastern area of Kosala which included Bastar district
(XIV)	**Anandas**	Andhra
(XV)	**Salankayanas**	Region between the lower courses of rivers Krishna and Godavari.
(XVI)	**Kadambas**	South-west Deccan

Astronomy: Prominent astronomers were **Aryabhatta** and **Varahamihir**. The former found out the causes of lunar and solar eclipses; calculated the circumferences of earth; was first to reveal that the sun is stationary and the earth revolved round the sun. Varahamihir's well known works are *Brihatsamhita* and *Panch Siddhantika*. Brahmagupta, wrote the *Brahma Sphutic Siddhanta* in verse and laid the foundation of the law of gravitation.

Medicine : The two great physicians of this period were **Sushruta** and **Charaka**. The *Sushruta Samhita* describes the methods of operating cataracts, stone diseases and various other ailments. Charaka is considered to be the father of Indian medicine. Vrihad Vagabhatta, a well-knonw physician, wrote *Astanghridaya.*

6. SOCIETY & ECONOMY—FROM VEDIC TILL 7TH CENTURY

6.1 SOCIAL AND ECONOMIC CHANGES

The central factor that ultimately transformed the ancient Indian society into medieval society was the practice of land grants. This practice came into being because of a serious crisis that affected the ancient social order. Contemporary *Puranic* texts complain of a situation in which *varnas* or social classes discarded the functions assigned to them. This led to the origin of '*varna-sankar*' or intermixture of social classes. The crucial step to meet the situation was to grant land to priests and officials in lieu of salaries and remuneration. Land grants became frequent from the fifth century AD. According to this, the brahmanas were granted villages free from taxes.

We notice an important change in the agrarian economy. Landed beneficiaries could not cultivate lands by themselves, nor could they collect revenues by themselves. The actual cultivation was entrusted to peasants or sharecroppers who were attached to the land but did not legally own it. Frequent seizures of power and land grants gave rise to several categories of landed people. Formerly, all things in society were graded according to the *varnas*, but now they also came to be determined according to the landed possessions of a person.

A *Purana* of the eighth century states that thousands of mixed castes were produced by the connection of *vaishya* women with men of lower castes. This implies that *shudras* and untouchables were divided into countless subcastes. Every tribe or clan was now given the status of a separate caste in the Hindu society.

From eighth century onwards '*samanta*' '*ranak*' '*rautta*' (rajput) etc. class of people grew in power. Some were government officers who were paid not in cash but by assigning to them revenue bearing villages. Thus we can trace the growth of feudalism from this period onwards. The hereditary chiefs gradually began to assume many of the functions of the government. They assumed the right to sublet their lands to the followers without the prior permission of the ruler, thus increasing the number of people who drew sustenance from land without working on it themselves.

6.2 TRADE AND COMMERCE

From the 6th century AD. onwards, there started a sharp decline in trade. The decline of trade led to the decay of towns. In northern India, from 8th century onwards, there was a period of stagnation and even of decline. The main reason for this was the setback to trade and commerce.

The decline in trade and commerce was due to the collapse in the West of the Roman empire with which India had flourishing and profitable trade. The rise of Islam leading to the collapse of old empires, such as the Sassanid (Iranian) empire, also affected India's foreign trade, particularly the overland trade. As a result, there was remarkable paucity of new gold coins in north India between the eight and the tenth centuries.

However, foreign trade and commerce in northern India began to revive gradually from the tenth century onwards. Malwa and Gujarat benefitted most from the revival of this trade. There was also the decline of internal trade which led to the languishing trade guilds called *shrenis and sanghas* in north India. With the decline of the Roman empire, China had become a main focus of trade in the Indian Ocean. Thus, while India's trade with the western areas declined, trade with South-East Asia and China grew steadily till the Twelfth century. The lead in this trade was taken by South India and Bengal.

6.3 CULTURAL DEVELOPMENT

In about the 6-7th centuries started the formation of cultural units, which later, came to be known as Karnataka, Maharashtra, Orissa, Rajasthan, Tamil Nadu, etc. The identity of the various cultural groups is recognized by both foreign and Indian sources. The Chinese traveller Hieun Tsang mentions several nationalities. The Jaina books of the late eighth century notice the existence of 18 major peoples or nationalities. It describes the physical features of 16. It produces samples of their language and says something about their character. Vishakhadatta, an author of about the ninth century AD, speaks of different regions inhabited by people, different in customs, clothing and language.

The 6-7th centuries are equally important in the history of Sanskrit literature. Sanskrit continued to be used by the ruling class from about the second century AD. onwards. As the rulers came to live in pomp and splendour, the style of their language became verbose and ornate. The ornate style in Sanskrit prose and poetry also became common since the seventh century, and the traditional Sanskrit pandits still love to write in it. The best example of verbose in prose is found in the writings of Banabhatta. Although the prose of Bana was not easy to imitate, it continued to serve as a model for Sanskrit writers in the medieval period.

From the seventh century AD. a remarkable development took place in the linguistic history of India. Buddhist writings from eastern India show the faint beginning of Bengali, Assamese, Maithili, Oriya and Hindi. Similarly, the Jaina works of the same period show the beginning of Gujarati and Rajasthani. In the south Tamil was the oldest language but Kannada came to grow at about this time. Telugu and Malayalam developed much later. It seems that each region came to develop its own language on account of its isolation from the others. On the break-up of the Gupta empire, there arose several independent principalities, which naturally hindered country wide contacts and communications The decline of trade meant lack of communication between the various regions, and this promoted the growth of regional languages.

Regional scripts became more prominent in the seventh century AD, and later. From Maurya to Gupta times, although the script underwent changes, more or less the same script continued to obtain throughout the country. Thus, a person who has mastered the script of the Gupta age can read inscriptions from different parts of the country in that period. But from the seventh century every region came to have its own script, and hence one cannot read post-Gupta inscriptions found in different parts of the country unless he has the knowledge of regional scripts.

6.4 RELIGIOUS MOVEMENTS AND BELIEFS

South India tended to become the land of stone temples. Stone and bronze were the two main medias in which divinities were represented.

We also notice some religious changes in post-Gupta times. Hindu divinities came to be arranged according to their grades in the hierarchy. Just as society was divided into unequal classes based on rituals, landed property, military power, etc., so the divinities were also divided into unequal ranks. *Vishnu, Shiva* and *Durga* appeared as supreme deities, presiding over many other gods and goddesses. We find the practice of worshipping *Brahma, Ganapati, Vishnu, Shakti* and *Shiva*. They were called *panchadeva* or five divinities. The chief god *Shiva* or some other deity was installed in the main temple, around which four subsidiary shrines were erected to house the other four deities. Such temples were known as *panchayatana*. The Vedic gods *Indra, Varna* and *Yama* were reduced to the position of *lokapalas* or security guards. Early medieval pantheons give us a good idea of divine hierarchy based on wordly hierarchy. In many of them, the supreme mother goodess was represented in a dominating posture in relation to several deities.

The monastic organisation of the Jainas, Shaivites, Vaishnavites, etc., also came to be divided into about five ranks. The highest rank was occupied by the *acharya*, whose coronation took place in the same manner as the coronation of the prince.

From the seventh century AD onwards, the *Bhakti* cult spread throughout the country, and especially in the south, *Bhakti* meant that people made all kinds of offerings to the god in return for which they received the *prasada* or the favour of the god. It meant that the devotees completely surrendered to their god. This practice can be compared to the complete dependence of the tenants on the landowners. Just as the tenants offered and rendered various services to the lord and then received land and protection as a kind of favour from him, a similar relation came to be established between the individual and his god. Since elements of feudalism persisted in the country for a very long time: *Bhakti* came to be deeply embedded in the Indian ethos.

The most remarkable development in the religious field in India from about the sixth century AD was the spread of tantricism. In the 5-7th centuries, many brahmanas received land in Nepal, Assam, Bengal, Orissa, Central India and the Deccan, and it is about this time that tantric texts, shrines and practices also appeared. Tantricism admitted both women and shudras into its ranks and laid great stress on the use of magic rituals. Some of the rituals may have been in use in earlier times, but they were systematized and recorded in the tantric texts from about the sixth century AD onwards. They were intended to satisfy the material desires of the devotees for physical possessions and to cure the day-to-day diseases and injuries. Obviously tantricism arose as a result of the large-scale admission of the aboriginal peoples in brahmanical society. The brahmanas adopted many of the tribal rituals, charms and symbols, which were now officially compiled, sponsored and fostered by them. In course of time, these were distorted by the brahmanas and priests to serve the interests of their rich patrons. Tantricism permeated Jainism, Buddhism, Shaivism and Vaishanavism. From the seventh century onwards, it continued to hold ground throughout the medieval age. Many medieval manuscripts found in different parts of the country deal with tantricism and astrology, and the two are completely mixed with each other.

The period from late 8th century onwards was marked by a revival and expansion of Hinduism, and a continued decline of Buddhism and Jainism. Buddhism did not so much decline, as it assumed forms which made it indistinguishable from Hinduism. Jainism continued to be popular, particularly among the trading communities.

6.5 EDUCATION, SCIENCE AND LEARNING

The system of education which developed in the earlier period continued without much change. There was no idea of mass education at that time. People learnt what they felt was needed for their livelihood. Sometimes, temples made arrangements of education at a higher level as well. The main subjects studied were the various branches of the vedas and grammar. Education of a more formal kind, with greater emphasis on secular subjects, continued to be provided at some of the Buddhist *viharas* (monasteries). Nalanda in Bihar was the most famous of these. Kashmir was another important centre of education.

India made an important contribution to science. In ancient times, religion and science were inextricably linked together. Astronomy made great progress in the country because the planets came to be regarded as gods, and their movements began to be closely observed. Their study became essential on account of their connection with changes in seasons and weather conditions which were important for agricultural activities. The science of grammar and linguistics arose because the ancient brahmanas stressed that every Vedic prayer and every *mantra* should be recited with meticulous correctness. In fact, the first result of the scientific outlook of Indians was the production of Sanskrit grammar. In the fourth century BC Panini systematized the rules governing Sanskrit and produced a grammar called the *Astadhyayi*.

By the third century BC, mathematics, astronomy and medicine began to develop separately. In the field of mathematics the ancient Indians made three distinct contributions : **the notation system, the decimal system and the use of zero**. The earliest epigraphic evidence for the use of the decimal system is in the beginning of the fifth century AD. The Indian notational system was adopted by the Arabs who spread it in the Western world. The Indian numerals are called Arabic in English, but the Arabs themselves called their numerals *hindsa*. Before these numerals appeared in the West, they had been used in India for centuries. They are found in the inscriptions of Ashoka, which were written in the third century BC.

The Indians were the first to use the decimal system. The famous mathematician *Aryabhata* (AD. 476-500) was acquainted with it. The Chinese learnt this system from the Buddhist missionaries, and the Western world borrowed it from the Arabs when they came in contact with India. Zero was discovered by the Indians in about the second century BC. Since the time of its discovery, the Indian mathematicians considered zero as a separate numeral, and it was used in this sense in sums of arithmetic. In Arabia, the earliest use of zero appears in AD 873. The Arabs learnt and adopted it from India and spread it in Europe. Although both the Indians and the Greeks contributed to the discipline of algebra, in Western Europe its knowledge was borrowed not from Greece but from the Arabs who had acquired it from India. Aryabhata formulated the rule for finding the area of a triangle, which led to the origin of trigonometry. The most famous work of this time is the *Suryasiddhanta*, the like of which is not found in contemporary ancient East.

The most renowned scholars of astronomy were Aryabhata and Varahamihira. *Aryabhata* belonged to the fifth century, and Varahmihira to the sixth. Aryabhata calculated the position of the planets according to the Babylonian method. He discovered the cause of lunar and solar eclipses. The book of Aryabhata is called the *Aryabhatiya.* Varhamihira's well-known work is called the *Brihatsamhita*, which belongs to the sixth century AD.

The ancient Indian physicians studied anatomy. They devised methods to diagnose diseases and prescribed medicines for their cure. The earliest mention of medicines is in the *Atharva Veda*. But as in other ancient societies, the remedies recommended were replete with magical charms and spells, and medicine could not develop along scientific lines.

In the sixth century AD., India produced two famous scholars of the Ayurveda, Sushruta and Charaka. In the *Sushrutasamhita,* Sushruta describes the method of operating cataract, stone disease and several other ailments. He mentions as many as 121 implements to be used for operations. In the treatment of diseases he lays special emphasis on diet and cleanliness. Charaka's *Charakasamhita* is like an encyclopaedia of Indian medicine. It describes various types of fever, leprosy, hysteria (*mirgi*), and tuberculosis. Possibly Charaka did not know that some of these are infectious. His book contains the names of a large number of plants and herbs which were to be used as medicine. The book is thus useful not only for the study of Indian medicine but also for that of ancient Indian flora and chemistry. In subsequent centuries, Indian medicine developed on the lines laid down by Charaka.

LITERARY ACTIVITIES IN ANCIENT INDIA

Astadhyayi : by Panini (5th century BC), the earlier grammar called Bhagavati sutra.

Mahabhashya : by Patanjali, a commentary on Astadhyayi.

Manu Smriti : by law book composed between 200 B.C. and 200 AD.

Arthashastra : by Kautilya deals with statecraft, a major source of Mauryan administration.

Indica : by Megasthenese, a source of Maurayan society and administration.

Chandasutra : by Pingala.

Buddhacharita : by Asvaghosha, life history of Buddha in Pali.

Saundarnanda : by Asvaghosha.

Sariputra Prakarana : By Asvaghosha.

Vajrasuchi and Sutralankara : by Asvaghosha.

Kumar Sambhav : by Kalidas, the theme is the marriage of Lord Siva and Uma and the birth Kartikeya.

Raghuvamsa : by Kalidas, an epic based on Mahabharat.

Naisad Charita : by Sri Harsha, contains story of Nala and Damayanti.

Shishupal Vadha : by Magha.

DRAMA

Natyashashtra : by Bharat, earliest known work Sanskrit.
Malvikagnimitra : by Kalidas
Vikramurvashi : by Kalidas
Abhigyanshakuntalam : by Kalidas
Ratnavali, Priyadarshika and Nagananda : by Harshavardhan.
Mahaviracharita, Uttarramacharita and Maltimadhava : by Bhavabhutt.

LYRIC POETRY

Meghadutam: by Kalidas
Sringarshataka, Nitishataka and Vairagyashataka: by Bhartrihari.
Chaura Panchasikla : by *Bilhana*.
Gita Govinda : by *Jayadeva*

HISTORICAL WRITING

Harshacharita ; by Banabhatta
Gaudavaho : by Vakpati, written in Prakrit.
Uttara Ramacharita : by Sandhyakar Nandi, deals with conflict between Kaivarta peasants and Pala prince Rampala.
Vikramankadeva Charita : by Bilhana.

PROSE LITERATURE

Daskumaracharita : by Dandin
Vasvadatta : by Subhandu
Brihat Kathamanjari : by Kshemendra
Kathasaritasagar : by Somadeva.
Panchatantra : by Vishnu Sharma
Hitopdesha : by Narayan Pandit.

OTHERS

Kamasutra and Arya Manjushree : by Vatsyayana
Pavandhoot : by Dhoyi.
Swapnavasvadatta : by Bhasa
Matavilasa Prahasana : by Mahendravarman-I.
Si-yu-ki by Hiuen Tsang
Fo-Kuoki : by Fa-hien.
Pancha Sidhantika : Varahmihir.
Surya Sidhantika and Aryabhattiyam : Aryabhatt.
Nitisara : Kamandaka
Charak Samhita : Charaka
Hastayurveda : Palkapya
Mitakshara : a commentary on law book of Yajnavalkya by Vignaneswara.
Dayabhaga : a treatise on inheritance by Jimutvahana
Sidhanta Siromani : by Bhaskarcharya
Nighantu : by Dhanvantri.
Mudrarakshasha : by Vishakhadatta.
Prabhanda Chintamani : by Merutunga
Geography of India : Ptolemy
Parshistaparvana : by Hemachandra
Brihat Katha Kosh : by Harisena
Kavyamimansa and Prabandhakosha : by Rajshekhar.
Mrcihkatika : by Sudraka
Prithviraya Vijaya : by Jayanak
Nala Vemba : by Pugalendi.

7. SULTANATE ERA—THE DEFEAT OF HINDU KINGDOM AND ESTABLISHMENT OF DELHI SULTANATE

7.1 INTRODUCTION

The defeat of Prithviraj Chauhan in the second battle of Tarain in 1192 by Shahabuddin Muhammad Ghori inaugurated an era of Muslim rule in India.

The sudden death of Muhammad Ghori in 1206 and his failure to specify succession procedures pitted his three slaves Tajuddin Yalduz, Nasiruddin Qubacha and Qutbuddin Aibak against each other. The internal dissension and strife led many Ghurid possessions in India to revolt and proclaim independence. Meanwhile, Qutbuddin Aibek succeeded both in capturing the throne of Delhi and to retain over Indian territories.

The period between 1206 and 1526 in the Indian history is known as the '***Period of the Sultan Rulers.***' During this period, rulers belonging to five different dynasties—the Slaves, the Khiljis, the Tughlaqs, the Sayyids and the Lodhis—ruled over India.

7.2 THE SLAVE DYNASTY (1206-1290 AD)

All the Muslim rulers that ascended the throne of Delhi after the death of Muhammad Ghori in 1206 till 1290 were either themselves slaves or the descendants of these slave rulers. That is why the rulers belonging to this dynasty are generally known as the **'Slave Rulers'** or the **'Mameluk Sultans'** and the dynasty is called the **'Slave Dynasty'.** Muhammad Ghori had left his Indian possessions in the care of his former slave, Qutb-ud-din Aibak, who on the death of his master, severed his links with Ghazni and asserted his independence.

Qutb-ud-Din Aibak (1206-1210 AD)

Qutb-ud-din had played a vital role under his chief in extending the authority of the Ghoris. Qutb's achievements as monarch were, however, a mere shadow of his achievements as Viceroy. Within the brief span of four years he was destined to reign and live, his work was naturally concerned with retention of what he had acquired rather than with expansion. His devotion to Islam is attested by two mosques built by him at Delhi and Ajmer. The fact that Aibak could not sufficiently consolidate his position is borne out by the fact that his nominee and adopted son, Aram Shah, was driven out from the throne by the Turkish nobles of Delhi who replaced Aram by their own nominee Shamsuddin Iltutmish. In 1210, Aibak died from the effects of a fall from his horse while playing polo.

Iltutmish (1210-1236 AD)

Iltutmish was the son-in-law of Aibak. He rendered great service to the Islamic empire in India. He secured a letter of investiture from the Caliph of Baghdad in 1229 which bestowed him the title of **Sultan of Hindustan**. He not only suppressed the rebellious chiefs and nobles but also his powerful rivals like Yaldoz and Qubacha and the Khiljis of Bengal to protect the Muslim Empire in India from various challenges. He destroyed the power of Rajput princes and brought the whole of North India under his control. Instead of Lahore, he made Delhi the capital and centre of the Muslim Empire.

Iltutmish organised the *iqtas* (administrative units), the army and the currency. The *iqta* was the grant of revenue from the territory in lieu of salary. The larger *iqtas* carried administrative responsibilities. The *iqta* system linked the farthest part of the empire to the Centre. Iltutmish introduced the silver *tanka* and the copper *jital*—the two basic coins of the Sultanate period, with a standad weight of 175 grains.

ILTUTMISH

- Organisation of a group of 40 loyal nobles—***Turkan-i-Chahalgani*** or ***Chalisa*** or ***Forty***.
- Introduction of the silver coins called *tanka* and copper coins called *jitals*.
- Introduction of ***Iqtadari*** system: division of empire into **Iqtas**, which were assigned to the nobles and officers in lieu of salary.
- Refusal to provide shelter to Jalal-ud-din the Khwarizm ruler–who fled to Punjab following the attack of Chengiz Khan.
- Completion of the construction of **Qutb Minar** in Delhi.

Raziya Sultan (1236-1239 AD)

Razia, the daughter of Iltutmish, assumed the reigns of the government in 1236. She was the first and last woman among the Muslim rulers who sat on the throne of Delhi. However, the Pathan nobles regarded it below their dignity to pay obedience to a woman. On the other hand, the traditional Muslims resented her public appearances without covering her face with *'burqa'* or a veil. Also, the appointment of an Abyssinian slave named **Jamat-ud-din Yakut** as superintendent of the stables was resented by the **Chahalgani** Turks or ***Chalisa***, a group of nobles.

Raziya was murdered near Kaithal in 1240. She was succeeded by several of her kins till 1266 when Balban emerged as a powerful sultan. Though Balhan formally become the ruler in 1266, the period 1246-1287 is known in history as the age of Balhan due to the dominant role he played at Delhi at the time.

Balban (1266-1285 AD)

Ghiyasuddin Balban ascended the throne in February 1266. He first executed the survivors of the *Chalisa* and relieved himself of the dangers of rivalry. He suppressed with an iron hand the hillmen whose forays were a terror in the suburbs of Delhi. He cleared the forests around Delhi and 'at a sacrifice of 100,000 men turned a haunt of bush-rangers into a peaceable agricultural district.' He freed the roads from brigands by killing and burning without mercy. He built forts and established Afghan garrisons to guard communications with Bengal. The titles of Turkish Khans for vast estates were strictly examined and he took back the lands from which no adequate military service was received and, thus, reduced the power of the nobles. He maintained pomp and dignity at his court. He ensured security by an efficient system of espionage and severely punished spies for their defaults.

Balban died in 1286, after nominating Kai Khusroo, the son of Muhammad, as his successor. The nobles, however, raised his grandson Kaikubad, the seventeen year old son of Bughra Khan, to the throne. Kaikubad gave rein to pleasure and the guidance of government was entrusted to his vizir. During his short reign of three years, Kaikubad became a hopeless paralytic.

BALBAN

- Declaration that the Sultan was the representative of God on earth–forwarding the Iranian **Divine Right Theory'** of Kingship.
- Introduction of the practice of ***sijda*** (under this practice, people would kneel and touch the ground with their head to greet the Sultan) and *pabos*.
- End of the influence of *Chalisa*.
- Ereation of the department of military affairs (***Diwan-i-arz)***
- Abolition of the post of *naik*.
- Royal instruction to the *ulemas* to confine themselves to religious affairs.

7.3 THE KHILJIS (1290-1320 AD)

The Khiljis, wrongly believed to be Afghans, were actually Turks who had for a long time settled in the region of Afghanistan, called Khalj and adopted Afghan manners and customs. The Ghaznavi's and Ghori's invasions, and Mongol pressure from Central Asia had pushed them into India.

Jalal-ud-Din Khilji (1290-1296 AD)

Jalal-ud-Din was the founder and the first king of the Khilji dynasty. He followed mild and generous policies. This generous policy of the Sultan affected his foreign policy as well. In 1290, he invaded the fort of Ranthambhor.

In 1294, Ala-ud-Din Khilji, a nephew of Jalal-ud-Din, invaded Ramchandra, the ruler of Devagiri in the South. Ramchandra was defeated and Ala-ud-Din returned with an immense booty. Jalal-ud-Din himself advanced to Kara to give warm welcome to his nephew who got him treacherously murdered and himself usurped the throne in 1296.

Ala-ud-Din Khilji (1296-1316 AD)

The history of Alauddin's reign had three features of permanent interest. Firstly, he was the first Muslim ruler of Delhi to create an empire embracing the larger portion of India; political unity was restored after many centuries of disintegration. Secondly, he gave some sort of administrative cohesion to the Sultanate which had so long been little more than a collection of military fiefs. Thirdly, he was a bold innovator in respect of the relation between the state and the *Shariat* or Islamic law.

The most important experiment undertaken by the Alauddin was the attempt to control the markets. Alauddin sought to control the prices of all commodities, from foodgrains to horses, and from cattle and slaves to costly imported cloth. He was the first monarch in the Sultanate to establish direct relations with the peasants to know the actual amount they paid by way of land revenue. He also built up an efficient espionage system.

ALA-UD-DIN KHALJI

His Conquests

(i) Ranthambor (1301), (ii) Mewar (1303), (iii) Jalar (1311), (iv) Conquest of the Deccan (1305), (vi) Devagiri (1307), Telengana (1310), (vii) Dwarasamudra (1311), (viii) Pandya Kingdom (1311), (ix) Devagiri

Economic Reforms

- Introduction of Dagh or branding of horses and *Chehra* (descriptive role of soldier)
- Confiscation of the religious endowments and free grants of lands.
- Creation of a new department, viz. *Diwan-i-Mustakhraj* to enquire into the revenue arears and to collect them
- Establsihment of separate markets for foodgrains cloth, horses, fruits etc.
- The check on markets was kept by two officers-*diwan-i-Riyasat* and *shahna-i-Mandi*

Administrative Reforms

- Reorganised the Spy system
- Prohibition on use of wine
- Nobles should not intermarry without his permission.

Military Reforms

- Abolition of *Iqtas* of royal troppers and the payment of their salaries in cash
- Regular muster of the army.

7.4 THE TUGHLAQ DYNASTY (1320-1399 AD)

Ghiyasuddin Tughlaq (1320-1325 AD)

Ghiyasud-din Tughlaq was the founder of the Tughlaq dynasty. From an ordinary person, he rose to the position of provincial governor of Dinapur under Ala-ud-Din Khilji. He repelled the Mongol invaders several times. He killed Khusro Khan, the usurper, and became the Sultan. He was a wise and generous ruler.

ACHIEVEMENTS OF GHIYAS-UD-DIN TUGHLUQ

- Reintroduced the food laws of Ala-ud-Din
- Suppressed the rebellions in the distant provinces with strong hand and restored the peace and order
- Organised better postal systems
- Encouraged agriculture

In 1323, he defeated the ruler of Warrangal and annexed his territory. A war of succession was going on in Bengal. Ghiyas-ud-Din took an advantage of such a situation and invaded Bengal. He suppressed the rebels and in this way Bengal also became a part of his empire. On his way back to Delhi, he defeated the ruler of Tirhut which he also annexed.

Muhammad-bin-Tughlaq (1325-1351 AD)

Muhammad-bin-Tughlaq is best remembered as a ruler who undertook a number of bold experiments, and showed a keen interest in agriculture. He was deeply read in religion and philosophy and had a critical and open mind. He had deep interest in philosophy, astronomy, logic and mathematics. He conversed not only with the Muslim mystics, but also with the Hindu *yogis* and Jain *saints* such as Junaprabha Suri. He was also prepared to give high offices to people on the basis of merit, irrespective of whether they belonged to noble families or not.

MUHAMMAD BIN TUGHLAQ

- Transfer of the capital from Delhi to Devagiri.
- Introduction of token copper currency to replace gold and silver coins.
- Unsuccessful expedition to subjugate Quarajal–the region identified as the modern Kulu in Kangra district of Himachal Pradesh.
- Futile plan to conquer Khurasan and Iraq.
- Creation of ***Diwan-i-Kohi*** (department of agriculture).
- Formulation of the 'Famine code' for relief to the famine-affected people.
- Independence of Deccan and Bengal.
- Introduction of ***dinar*** (a gold coin) and ***adl*** (a silver coin).
- Establishment of the city of **Jahanpanah.**
- Appointment of Ibn Batutah, a Moroccon, as the head **qazi** of Delhi.
- Arrival of an envoy from the Chinese ruler, Toghan Timur (1341)

MONGOL INVASIONS DURING THE DELHI SULTANATE

	Sultan	Events
1.	**Iltutmish**	In 1221, Genghis Khan came up to the bank of river Indus. But he did not enter India.
2.	**Balban**	Prince Muhammad of Multan, Bughra Khan from Samana, and Malik Mubarak joined hands to defeat the Mongols.
3.	**Jalal-ud-din Khilji**	In 1292, Mongols under Abdullah invaded India, but they were repulsed.
4.	**Ala-ud-din Khilji**	In 1299, Ala-ud-din personally marched against the Mongol leader, Qutlugh Khwaja, and defeated him. He also defeated the Mongol leader Ali Beg in 1304.
5.	**Muhammad bin Tughlaq**	In 1329, Tazmashirin Khan reached near Delhi, but was defeated by Sultan Muhammad bin Tughlaq.

Firoz Shah Tughlaq (1351-1388 AD)

The nobles and theologians at the court selected Muhammad's cousin Firoz Shah as the next Sultan. He gave a number of important concessions to the theologians. He tried to ban practices with the orthodox theologians considered un-Islamic. Thus, he prohibited the practice of Muslim women going out to worship at the graves of saints. He persecuted a number of Muslim sects which were considered heretical by the theologians. He refused to exempt the brahmanas from the payment of *Jaziya* since this was not provided for in the *shariat*. Worse, he publicly burnt a brahmana for preaching to the Muslims, on the ground that it was against the *shariat*.

FEROZ SHAH TUGHLAQ

- Establishment of ***Diwan-i-Khairat*** (department for poor and needy people) and ***Diwan-i-Bundagan*** (department of slaves).
- Making **Iqtadari** system hereditary.
- Construction of canals for irrigation: (i) from Yamuna to the city of Hissar; (ii) from the Sutlej to the Ghaggar; (iii) from the Ghaggar to Firuzabad; and (iv) from Mandvi and Sirmour Hills to Hansi in Haryana.
- Establishment four new towns; Firuzabad, Fatehabad, Jaunpur and Hissar.

- Imposition of *jaziya* on the Brahmans for the first time.
- Arrival of the two Ashokan pillar edicts/ inscriptions from Khizrabad and Meerut to Delhi.
- Establishment in Delhi a hospital described variously as **Dar-ul-Shifa**, **Bimaristan** or **Shifa Khana.**

Successors of Firoz Shah : Firoz Shah died in 1388. His successors were weak and incompetent. They were merely kings in name and acted as puppets in the hands of their ministers. Consequently, the Tughlaq empire went rapidly down the path of decay. Firoz Shah was followed by Tughlaq Shah, Abu-Bakar and Nasir-ud-din Mahmud Shah. **It was during the reign of Nasir-ud-din Mahmud Shah that Timur invaded India in 1398.**

INVASION OF TIMUR

Conqueror of Persia, Afghanistan and Mesopotamia, Amir **Timur** or **Timurlane** invaded India in 1398. He had no intention of annexing India to his empire in Samarqand, but to loot its rich booty. Following his invasion, there was disorder and confusion in the country. Delhi was ruined and depopulated. His invasion widened the gulf between the Hindus and the Muslim. Indian art found its way in Central Asia as he took a large number of skilled artisans as captives. Timur's invasion paved the way for Mughal conquest. Babur was a descedant of Timur and he claimed the throne of Delhi partly on that account.

7.5 SAYYID DYNASTY (1414-1450 AD)

Khizr-Khan, a lieutenant of Timur, was a Sayyid and so his dynasty is called the Sayyid Dynasty. Khizr Khan ruled till 1421, but his whole reign was marked by utter chaos and disorder. He was succeeded, after his death, by his son **Mubarak Shah** (1421-1434). During his reign the *subedars* of Punjab, Bhatinda and Doab broke out in revolt and the whole of his period was spent in trying to suppress them. He died in 1434 and was succeeded by his son **Mohammad Shah** (1434-1445). During his reign, the ruler of Malwa invaded Delhi, which was however, saved by the valiant Subedar of Lahore, **Bahlol Lodhi**. After Mohammad Shah's death, his son Ala-ud-Din Alam Shah (1445-1451) proved incompetent. He himself handed over the reigns of his kingdom to Bahlol Lodhi and retired to Badaun.

7.6 LODHI OR PATHAN SULTANS (1451-1526 AD)

Bahlol Lodhi (1451-1488 AD)

Lodhi Sultans were the members of the first Pathan dynasty in India. Sher Shah Suri founded the next.

Bahlol Lodhi was the founder of the Lodhi dynasty. He founded the rule of the Lodhi dynasty by usurping the throne from the last of the Sayyid rulers, Ala-ud-Din Alam Shah. He was a strong and brave ruler. He tried to restore the glory of Delhi by conquering territories around Delhi and after continuous wars for 26 years, he succeeded in extending his authority over Jaunpur, Rewail, Itawah, Mewar, Sambhal, Gwalior etc. He was a kind and generous ruler. He was always prepared to help his subjects. Though he was himself illiterate, he extended his patronage to art and learning. He died in 1488.

Sikandar Lodhi (1488-1517 AD)

Bahlol Lodhi was succeeded by his son Nizam Khan who ascended the throne in 1488 as Sikander Lodhi . Like his father, he was a brave and able ruler. He extended his empire by conquering Dholpur, Chanderi and Jaunpur. **He shifted his capital to Agra.** He kept strict vigilance on his nobles and jagirdars whom he strictly suppressed. He introduced several reforms and provided an efficient administration. He was a staunch Sunni and a Muslim fanatic. He lacked religious tolerance. In the name of religion, he perpetuated untold cruelties on the Hindus. He was a great lover of art and learning. He was just and believed in the well-being of his subjects. During his reign, prices were low and people were happy.

SIKANDAR LODHI
• Establishment of a new city called Agra.
• Transfer of capital from Delhi to Agra.
• Demolition of the famous Jwalamukhi temple at Nagarkot.
• Imposition of **Jaziya** and pilgrim's tax on the Hindus.
• Introduction of ***Gaz-i-Sikandari*** (Sikandar's yard) of 32 digits for measuring cultivated land.

Ibrahim Lodhi (1517-1526 AD)

Sikander Lodhi was succeeded by his son Ibrahim Lodhi who ascended the throne in 1517. He was obdurate and haughty. His ill-treatment turned the loyal Afghan noble against him. They hatched a conspiracy to declare his uncle, Jalal Khan, as the ruler of Delhi, but they failed. Thereafter, Ibrahim crushed his nobles very cruely. He was so whimsical that the honour of his nobles was never safe. Tired of his continuous ill-treatment, **Daulat Khan Lodhi**, the governor of Punjab, invited Babur to invade India. Babur took advantage of the opportunity and defeated Ibrahim Lodhi in 1526 in the **Battle of Panipat**. Ibrahim Lodhi was killed in the battle-field and Babur founded the famous Mughal Dynasty. Ibrahim was unique in chivalry, courage and determination. In the words of Niamatullah : "No Sultan of India except Sultan Ibrahim had been killed on the battle field."

7.7 GENERAL ADMINISTRATION OF THE SULTANATE

- The Turkish Sultans in India declared themselves *Lieutenant of the faithful* i.e. of the Abbasid Caliphate of Baghdad and included his name in *Khutba,* it did not mean that the Caliph became the legal ruler. The Caliph had only a moral position.
- Political, legal and military authorities were vested in the Sultan. He was responsible for administration and was also the commander-in-chief of the military forces. He was also responsible for the maintenance of law and justice.
- No clear law of succession developed among Muslim rulers. Thus, military strength was the main factor in succession to the throne.
- When the Turks conquered the country, they divided it into a number of tracts called ***Iqtas***, which were assigned among the leading Turkish nobles. The holders of the office were called *Muqti* or *Walis*. It was these tracts, which later became province or *Subah*.
- Below the province were the ***Shiqs*** and below them the ***Paragana***. We are told that the villages were grouped into units of 100 or 84 traditionally called ***Chaurasi***. The *Paragana* was headed by ***Amil***. The most important people in villages were the ***Khuts*** (Landowners) or ***Muqaddam*** or headman. The village accountant was called ***Patwari***.

IMPORTANT CENTRAL DEPARTMENTS

Department	Function
Diwan-i-Risalat	Department of appeals
Diwan-i-Ariz	Military department
Diwan-i-Bandagan	Department of slaves
Diwan-i-Qaza-i-Mamalik	Department of justice
Diwan-i-Isthiaq	Department of pensions
Diwan-i-Mustakhraj	Department of arrears
Diwan-i-Khairat	Department of charity
Diwan-i-Kohi	Department of agriculture
Diwan-i-Insha	Department of correspondence

Important Central Officials : Important central government officials under the Sultanate system were as follows :

(i) *Wazir*—The chief minister of the State-in charge of revenue and finances, controlled by other departments.

(ii) *Ariz-i-Mamalik*—Head of Miltary department

(iii) *Qazi* – Legal officer (dispensed civil law based based on Muslim law ***Shariat***)

(iv) *Wakil-i-dar*—Controller of the royal house hold.

(v) *Barid-i-mumalik*—Head of the state news agency.

(vi) *Amir-i-majlis*—Officer-in-charge of royal feasts, conferences and festivals.

(vii) *Majlis-i-am*—Council of friends and officers consulted on important affairs of the state.

(viii) *Dahir-i-mumalik*—Head of the royal correspondence.

(ix) *Sadr-us-sudur*—Dealt with the religious matters and endowments.

(x) *Sadr-i-jahan*—Officers-in-charge of religious and charitable endowment.

(xi) *Amir-i-dad*—Public prosecutors.

(xii) *Naib wazir*—Deputy minister.

(xiii) *Mushrif-i-mumalik*—Accountant general.

(xiv) *Mustauf-i-mumalik*—Auditor general.

(xv) *Amir-i-hazib*—Officer-in-charge of the royal court.

(xvi) *Kazi-i-mumalik*—Chief Justice.

(xvii) *Kazi-ul-kazat*—Head of the Central Judicial department.

7.8 PROVINCIAL ADMINISTRATION

The provinces were under governors called *Amirs.* Control from the centre was lax especially over distant provinces. The local officials were mostly Hindus who played an important part in the rural life of the period. The Hindu rulers held tributary status in different parts of the realm. The unit of administration continued to be the village with its headman and accountant. Peace was maintained by garrisoning strategic centre and by improving communications. The peasant's ownership of land was recognized and large loans were advanced to the peasants. It may be mentioned that Firuz Shah wrote off all loans given by Muhammad-bin-Tughlaq as they could not be easily collected.

Officials of the Provinces : Important officials at the provincial level were as follows :

(i) ***Amir*** - governor.

(ii) ***Mukti/Wali*** - responsible for law and order and collection of taxes in their *iqtas.*

(iii) ***Nazir/Wakuf*** - Officials responsible for collecting revenue in the provinces.

(iv) ***Sahib-i-diwan*** - maintained accounts of the provinces and sent them to the central administration.

(v) ***Mushrif*** - Officer-in-charge.

(vi) ***Shiqdar*** - Officer-in-charge of land measuring a *shiq.*

IMPORTANT ARMY OFFICIALS		
(i)	***Ariz-i-Mumalik***	A head of the diwan-i-arz department responsible for the recruitment, payment and inspection of troops.
(ii)	***Amir-i-Akhur***	Officer commanding royal horses.
(iii)	***Shahna-i-pil***	Superintendent of royal elephants.
(iv)	***Amir-i-bahr***	Officer-in-charge of police and transport.

7.9 REVENUE ADMINISTRATION AND CLASSIFICATION OF LAND

REVENUE ADMINISTRATION

The sources of revenue were two-fold : religious, and secular. The former, called ***zakat,*** was due only from the Muslims, the latter included land tax and ***Jaziya*** which the non-Muslims had to pay. One fifth of the spoils of war, known as ***Khams*** or ***Ghamnish,*** belonged to the State. The heirless property was taken over by the state. In effect, non-Muslims had to pay much more than the Muslims. The main heads of expenditure were the royal household, the administration, the army, the pious and charitable organizations, social services, public works including irrigation and the rewards, gifts and presents bestowed by the Sultan. ***Kharaj*** or land revenue was one-third of the gross produce and was raised to half by Alauddin. ***Ushra*** was one-tenth of the gross produce on land held by Muslims. ***Transit*** and ***Octroi*** duties were income from mines, forests, treasure trove and heirless property.

TYPES OF LAND

(A) Khalisa : It was the class of land which was directly administered by the central government. Revenue from such land was collected by the officials appointed by the central government.

(B) Muqtis or Walis : This was the category of land which was in the hands of provincial governors. The provincial administration collected the revenue from this land and, after meeting the collection charges, deposited the surplus in the central treasury.

(c) *Inam* or *Waqf* : *Inam* or *Waqf* was the land given to the people especially the Muslim saints and scholars, in gift or charity. This class of land had no tax liabilities.

(d) Land of Feudatory Hindu Chiefs From such land, the Sultan got fixed annual tributes.

7.10 SOCIO-ECONOMIC LIFE DURING SULTANATE ADMINISTRATION

SOCIAL LIFE

(i) Caste System : The Hindu society was divided into four castes. The coming of Muslims and their constant condemnation of the caste-system made the system more rigid. The Hindu society in order to strengthen itself recasted the *Smritis* and tried to bring back from the Islamic fold those Muslims who were converts from Hinduism.

(ii) Position of Women : The Hindu women were given inferior position in society and their educational development was prevented since the Gupta age. Her condition deteriorated and she became a victim of many social evils such as *sati*, *Jauhar*; The ***Devadasi system*** had become prevalent and widow-remarriage illegal. The introduction of dowry system in the name of *stridhana* further depreciated her position in the household. The position of Muslim women though not very much different was yet better. She had the privilege to education and could remarry.

(iii) Slave System : It was a common practice among the Sultans and the nobles to maintain a large contingency of slaves—both males and females. The prisoners of wars were generally the main constituent of this system. They were supposed to perform every task free of cost. But they were not subject to torture.

(iv) Dress, Food and Manners : *Achakan* and *Salwar* were introduced in the Northern India under the Muslim influence. The high-class women's dress was copied by almost all in the society. The food and social manners and ceremonies were copied. The vices of gambling and drinking, which were prevalent among the Muslims of the age, were also adopted by the Hindus. The Muslims took to Indian spices and eventually some deeply ingrained Hindu customs.

(v) Relation between the Hindus and the Muslims : The rulers generally kept themselves aloof from the general masses. The masses–whether Hindu or Muslim–were subjected to similar exploitation. The common people lived a harmonious life and influenced each other in different fields of life. They were averse to the upper class conflict of the ruling class and the *Ulema*.

ECONOMIC LIFE

Indian industries were quite advanced in that period. Textile industry was the primary industry of India at that time. Silk, cotton and woollen clothes of different quality and varied colours were produced in large quantity. The clothes were studded with gold, silver, pearls, diamonds and other precious articles. Textiles were exported. Sugar industry, paper industry, metal work, stone-cutting, pearl from the sea, ivory and sandal-wood work etc were other important industries of India of that period.

The Sultans of Delhi and other rulers of provincial dynasties had their own workshops (*Karkhanas*) to manufacture different articles to fulfill the needs of Sultans, nobles and other rich people. The traders and industrialists were organised into guilds which helped them in many ways and, thus, helped in the growth of trade and industry of the country.

India carried brisk trade–both internal and foreign. Ibn Batutah describes Delhi as the foremost trading centre of the world. Daulatabad was famous for its pearl trade. One noticeable feature of Indian foreign trade was that prior to the coming of the Portuguese in India, the monopoly of importing and exporting goods from India was in the hands of Persian and Arab Merchants except in Malabar Coast. India had trade relations with Europe, Malaya, China, Central Asia, Afghanistan, Persia, Tibet and Bhutan.

Besides the prosperous trade, the fertile land added to the economic prosperity of India. The Persian irrigation wheel swelled the yield of Indian crops. The agricultural production and the foreign trade of India remained good throughout the period of Sultanate and India, thus, enjoyed prosperity during this period.

CAUSES FOR THE DISINTEGRATION OF THE SULTANATE

The causes for the decline of the Sultanate, which lasted for 320 years, were as follows:

- Inherent weakness of the system of government: As the governance depended on the ability and personal character of the king, it was bound to disintegrate under weak rulers.
- Thoughtless actions of Muhammad bin Tughlaq and the appeasement policies of Firoz Tughlaq.
- Invasion of Timur.
- Degeneration in the general character of the nobility.
- Lack of a clear-cut succession policy.

8. MUGHALS PERIOD (1526 to 1707)

8.1 INTRODUCTION

The Mughal era, which began with the Babur's victory over Ibrahim Lodi in the **First Battle of Panipat (1526)** is often perceived as marking a new beginning in the history of Muslim rule in India. Unlike the fractious Sultanate period when the state resembled a theatre of war, the Mughal rule is regarded as a time when contentious issues of religion and politics were placed on the backburner and the splendour of monarchy took centrestage.

8.2 BABUR (1526-1530)

Babur was the first Mughal emperor of India. He was born in the Ferghana, Central Asia, in the princely family of mixed Mongol and Turkish blood. Failure to recover his father's land caused him to turn reluctantly to south-east. After defeating Ibrahim Lodhi with the support of Punjab's governor, Daulat Khan Lodhi, Babur turned his attention to the Rajput confederacy and defeated Mewar ruler Rana Sanga in the **Battle of Khanwa** in 1527. This victory secured Babur's position in the Delhi-Agra region. Babur's reign ended in 1530 and he was succeeded by his son Humayun.

REASONS OF BABUR'S INDIAN EXPEDITIONS

There were various reasons for Babur's Indian expedition.

- The Ottomans defeated the Safavids and the Uzbegs controlled Transoxiana forcing Babur's imperial impulses towards India.
- Meagre income of Kabul
- Desire to emulate Timur
- Punjab was part of the Timurid province and hence was considered a legal partrimony of the Timurids
- Apprehension of Uzbeg attacks At Dik Khat, Babur had heard an eye witness account of Timur's invasion of India from a 111 year old woman.

Babur's Five Expeditions : Bahur's five famous expeditions were as follows :

First Expedition : In 1519, he stormed Bajaur which fell after a spirited struggle in which Babur's artillery played a decisive part. Babur occupied Bhira where gunpowder was used for the first time.

Babur quit India, leaving Bhira in the charge of Hindu Beg; but the latter was soon (1519) expelled by the natives.

Second Expedition : The same year, in September, Babur again marched through the Khyber, in order to subdue the Yusufzai and make Peshawar fort as a .base for future operations in Hindustan But he was recalled by disturbing news from Badakhshan, which came into Babur's possession in 1520.

Third Expedition : For the third time Babur marched in 1520, through Bajaur towards Bhira. Subduing the recalcitrant Afghan tribes on the way, he proceeded to Sialkot, which submitted without striking a blow. The people of Saiyidpur defied Babur, but were easily subdued. However, Babur had to hastily retrace his steps again to fight Shah Beg Arghun, ruler of Kandahar.

After two unsuccessful efforts, Babur finally acquired Kandahar, in 1522, through the treachery of its Governor, Maulana Abdul Bagi. Shah Beg established himself in Sindh, and Kamran (Babur's second son) was put in charge of Kandhar.

Fourth Expedition : Thus, thoroughly secure at home, Babur for the fourth time invaded India, in 1524. Daulat Khan, Governor of the Punjab, was growing very powerful. Sultan Ibrahim had summoned him to Delhi. But Daulat Khan offended him by not appearing in person. To protect himself from the Sultan's wrath, Daulat Khan sent his son Dilawar Khan, toinvite Babur to dethrone Ibrahim Lodi in favour of his uncle Alam Khan (or, Ala-ud-din).

Babur readily fell in with this invitation, and marched once more into the valleys of the Jhelum and the Chenab. Lahore and Dipalpur soon fell into his hands. Daulat Khan was defeated by the Delhi forces and driven into exile. But he came back and sought reinstatement at the hands of the invader. Babur, however, offered him only Jalandhar and Sultanpur instead. Daulat Khan felt disappointed, and the fiefs were bestowed upon his more reliable son Dilawar Khan. Dipalpur was given to Alam Khan.

Daulat Khan and his second son, Ghazi Khan, fled to the hills, only to return in the wake of Babur's withdrawal. They recaptured Sultanpur from Dilawar, and Dipalpur from Alam Khan. Ibrahim's attempt to subdue Daulat Khan proved unsuccessful. But Babur's Lahore detachment inflicted a defeat upon him.

On account of this unsettled state, Alam Khan fled to Kabul and once again sought Babur's aid to seat himself on the throne of Delhi. In return Babur was promised sovereignty over Lahore and the West Punjab.

Alam Khan returned to India with this understanding. But the wily Daulat won him over. The two Khans accordingly marched on Delhi, only to be disgracefully routed by the Sultan.

Fifth Expedition : Babur now crossed the frontier for the last time (Nov., 1525), with the largest army he had ever led into Hindustan. Humayun was with him with a contingent from Badakhshan. Crossing the Jhelum, the Lahore army also joined him. All told, his followers numbered not more than 12,000 of whom perhaps only 8,000 were effectives.

Sialkot had been lost. His generals in India had gathered together at Lahore. But Daulat Khan alone had taken the field with not less than 40,000 men. Ibrahim Lodi was soon to confront him with 1,00,000 men and a large number of war-elephants.

However, Daulat Khan's forces melted away at Babur's mere approach. Babur had nothing more to do with him than upbraid him for his treacherous conduct. Death soon snatched away Daulat Khan altogether from the field.

On February 26, 1526 Humayun won his spurs for the first time, against an advance division of the Imperial forces.Ibrahim was coming from Delhi, and Babur from Sirhind and Ambala. On April 1, again Babur's men encountered a cavalry division of the Sultan and crushed it. From April 12 to 19, one whole week, the two armies faced each other, with little action, near Panipat, the plain intended by Nature to be the battle-field of nations.

IMPORTANT BATTLES FAUGHT BY BABAR

Battle of Panipat (1526): He defeated Ibrahim Lodhi. This was his fifth expedition in India in which he was successful.

Battle of Khanwa (1527): He defeated Rana Sanga of Mewar.

Battle of Chanderi (1528): Babur defeated Medini Rai. He was the first to entitle himself as the 'Padshah'. After the Kushanas, he was the first to bring Kabul and Kandhar into the Indian empire.

Battle of Ghaghra (1529): He fought against the allied forces of Afghans in Bihar and Bengal. Sultan Nusrat Shah of Bengal faced crushing defeat.

8.3 HUMAYUN (1530-1556)

Humayun succeeded Babur at the young age of 23. When he occupied the throne, he found himself surrounded by enemies on all sides. In the east were Mahmud Lodhi and other Afghans under Sher Khan. In the south was Sultan Bahadur Shah, the ruler of Gujarat, and in the North-West, Kamran, the younger brother of Humayun. Humayun's early expeditions were against Kalinjar, Jaunpur and Chunar. He waged a war with Bahadur Shah of Gujarat in 1533-1536, and conquered the provinces of Sarangpur, Mandesar, Mandu, Champaner and Diu. About the same time he built *Dinpanah* at Delhi as his second capital.

HUMAYUN'S EXPEDITIONS

Humayun's famous expeditions may be listed as follows *:*

Expedition of Kalinjar (1531) : Humayun besieged the fort of Kalinjar in Bundelkhand. Humayun was forced to make peace and accept a huge indemnity from the Raja

Battle of Daurah (1532) : Humayun defeated Mahmood Lodi, the Afghan of Bihar.

Siege of Chunar (1532) : Humayun besieged the fort of Chunar under Sher Shah, who offered nominal submission. It proved to be mistake on the part of Humayun to accept it.

Wars with Bahadur Shah (1535-1536) : Bahadur Shah annexed Malwa in 1531, Captured the fort of Raisin and defeated the chief of Chittor in 1533. No wonder Humayun marched against him. Bahadur Shah has seiged Chittor. Rani Karnawati appealed to Humayun for help by sending him a *Rakhi.* Humayun did not attack Bahadur Shah as long as siege of Chittor lasted. It was only after the fall of Chittor that Humayun started his operations against Bahadur Shah, who had escaped to Mandi. Humayun captured the Fort of Mandu, Champaner and Mandsor. With the conquest of Gujarat in 1535, Humayun completed his conquest in Central India. But due to mismanagement of Askari, Bahadur Shah recaptured large part of Gujarat.

Battle of Chausa (1539) : Humayun's return to Agra was blocked by Sher Khan. Both armies delayed the attack and rains started, leaving the Mughal encampment flooded. Humayun was defeated.

Battle of Kanauj, (1540) : After reaching Agra, Humayun and his brother Kamran decided to fight Sher Shah but due to the differences between the brothers, Humayun fought the Battle of Kanauj alone and lost. Humayun became a fugitive and Sher Shah became the ruler of Agra and Delhi.

8.4 AFGHAN INTERRUPTION : RISE OF SHER SHAH SURI (1540-1555)

Humayun was defeated by Afghan ruler Sher Shah Suri at the **Battle of Chausa** (near Buxar in Bihar) in 1539. Following this defeat, he was driven into exile in Persia. He regained his kingdom in 1555 after the end of the rule of the Suri dynasty.

An Afghan of humble origin, Sher Shah had risen through military service so he was well placed to take advantage of temporary Mughal weakness. After defeating Humayun twice in Chausa and Kanauj (1539 and 1540), he made himself emperor of Delhi, extending his control to Gwalior and Malwa. He carried out innovations in the land revenue system and the army which were subsequently built on by the great Mughal emperor, Akbar.

Sher Shah was a great expansionist and wanted to expand his kingdom. In 1544, he invaded the fort of Kalinjar, which was ruled by Kirti Singh and laid a siege of the fort. During this siege, one of the cannons accidentally went off killing him on 26th May, 1545. His dead body was taken to Sasaram, where he had already built a mausoleum for himself, and was buried. Successors of Sher Shah were weak. The Suri dynasty's rule ended in 1555.

Sher Shah's Administration

(i) Administrative Units : For administrative convenience, Sher Shah divided his kingdom into 47 divisions called ***Sarkars***. *Sarkars* were divided into ***parganas***. *Parganas*, under the charge of ***Shiqdar*** or ***Shiqdar-i-Shiqdaran,*** were consisted of a number of villages. While *Shiqdar* looked after the law and order and general administration of his ***Pargana, Munshif*** or ***Munsif-i-Munsifan*** collected the land revenue in the *Pargana.*

(ii) Central Administration : Sher Shah divided the government under several departments, each under the charge of a minister, who was assisted by other high officers. The finance minister was called *Wazir*. He personally supervised all the departments. His important departments were as follows :

1. ***Diwan-i-Wazarat*** : Department of revenue and finance.
2. ***Diwan-i-Ariz*** : Military Department.
3. ***Diwan-i-Rasalatmuhtasib*** : Foreign Affairs department which was also incharge of appointing Ambassadors.
4. ***Diwan-i-Insha*** : Custodian of all government documents and papers. It was also incharge of government dispatches.
5. ***Diwan-i-Quza*** : Justice department.

6. ***Diwan-i-Barid*** : Intelligence department.
7. ***Diwan-i-Saman*** : Department in-charge of royal household.

(iii) Justice: Civil cases of *pargana* were heard by *Amir* and criminal cases by a *Qazi* or *Mir-i-Adal.* Sher Shah introduced the principle of local responsibility for local crimes. *Muqqadams* were punished for failure to find culprits.

(iv) Land Revenue: Sher Shah had fixed the land revenue after getting the whole of the land measured through the agency of Raja Todar Mal. He got an accurate survey of all the agricultural land and fixed a definite revenue for each unit of land (normally, one-third of produce). For the measurement of land, ***Sikandari gaja*** (32 points) was made the base. The farmers were allowed to make revenue payments directly to the government treasury in order to eliminate their exploitations by the intermediaries. The area sown, the type of crops cultivated and the amount each peasant had to pay was written down on a paper called *patta* and each peasant was informed of it. He also introduced the system of *qabuliyat* (deed of agreement) with the peasants to discourage *jagir system.*

Peasants had also to pay survey charge (***Jaribana***) and tax collection charge (***Muhasilans***) which were 2.5 per cent and 5 per cent respectively.

(v) Military Reforms : Sher Shah effected many military reforms in order to save the country from foreign invasions and internal revolts. With the object of organizing the army, Sher Shah began to pay the soldiers their salaries in cash; maintained their descriptive rolls (*chehra)* and brandised (*dagh*) the horses, etc. He set up cantonments in different parts of the empire and a strong garrison was posted in each of them.

(vi) Roads and Trade : Sher Shah made many roads to encourage trade, to provide comfort and convenience to the travellers, to facilitate the movement of troops from one place to another and to carry on the administration systematically and properly. Of these roads, four are very important—(i) the **Grand Trunk Road,** which lays between Sunargaon in East Bengal and Attock in the North-West boundary of India, (ii) a road from Agra to Burhanpur in the Deccan, (iii) a road between Agra and Jodhpur and Chittor in Rajputana, and (iv) a road between Lahore and Multan. On either side of these roads, shady trees were planted, *sarais* were built at the interval of two *koses* (about three miles) from each other where separate arrangements for lodging and boarding for the Hindu and Muslim existed.

(vii) Coins: Sher Shah also reformed the coins and struck many kinds of coins of pure gold and silver. He struck copper-coins such as *dam*, a half *dam*, a quarter *dam* and gave the name of rupee to the silver coin. This rupee (*rupia*) coin of Sher Shah remained in use throughout the Mughal period.

Sur Architecture : The following are the highlights of Sur architecture :

- Sur Architecture forms the climax of Pre-Mughal style of architecture.
- Sur built tombs of Sasaram which were octagonal. Most outstanding was **Sher Shah's Mausoleum** built on a huge plinth, amidst a lake and is multi-storeyed.
- He also built the Purana Qila whose surviving monuments are **Qila-i-Kuhna Masjid** and the **Sher Mandal** library.

Restoration of Humayun (1556-1556)

During his exile in Persia, Humayun was given military help by King Shah Tahmasp to conquer Kabul and Kandhar from his brother Kamran, After that he turned to India to regain his lost throne. With the help of an able officer, Bairam Khan, Humayun defeated the weak rulers of the Suri dynasty and took control over Agra and Delhi in 1556. He died from the effects of an accidental fall from the staircase of his library at Delhi in AD 1556.

His reign is significant mainly because of the introduction of Persian influences into India when he returned from exile accompanied by Persian scholars and artists. Persian became the court language and pockets of Shiite religious influence grew up in India.

8.5 AKBAR (1556-1605)

Though Humayun reconquered his empire, he was not destined to reap the fruits of his success. He fell from the staircase of his library and died soon due to its effect. The death of Humayun placed the responsibility of the kingdom over the young shoulders of Akbar.

Akbar was crowned at Kalanaur at the young age of thirteen years. Bairam Khan, the tutor of the prince, became the *Wakil* of the kingdom with the title of *Khan-i-khana* and rallied the Mughal forces.

Second Battle of Panipat: Akbar's earliest conflict was with Hemu, a general of Adil Shah. Hemu proceeded to Delhi where the Mughal governor, Tardi Beg Khan, offered a feeble resistance and suffered defeat (October, 1556). On receipt of the news of the fall of Agra and Delhi, Bairam Khan marched to meet Hemu. The two armies met at Panipat (5th November 1556). Hemu fought bravely but was defeated and Akbar reoccupied Delhi and Agra.

Military Conquests of Akbar: In 1560, Akbar ended the regency of Bairam Khan and took the reins of government into his own hands. But the initial phase of conquest had begun during the regency of Bairam Khan. Gwalior, Ajmer and Jaunpur were occupied. The conquest of Malwa was achieved in 1561. The independent Sultan of Malwa, Baz Bahadur, was indifferent to politics and war. The struggle ended with Baz Bahadur's submission in 1570 and his enrolment as a *mansabdar* in Akbar's court. In 1564, Asaf Khan conquered the independent Hindu principality of Garh Katanga. This was a Gond Kingdom comprising the northern districts of modern Madhya Pradesh.

Akbar's first victory in Rajasthan was won without bloodshed. In 1562, he made his first pilgrimage to the mausoleum of the Sufi Saint, Sheikh Moin-ud-Din Chishti, at Ajmer. On the way, he received Raja Bhar Mal of Ajmer who made his submission without fighting. In 1570, Akbar received the submission of the rulers of Marwar and Bikaner. There was only one Rajput state which continued to offer opposition—Chittor. The siege of Chittor had begun in 1567. Udai Singh of Chittor sought safety in the Aravali Hills, leaving the defence of the fort to two gallant chiefs, Jaimal Rathor and Patta. In 1568, the great fort fell. Akbar was able to cement his alliance with Rajputs.

Akbar conquered Gujarat (1572-1573) and Bengal (1574-1576). In 1591, Akbar sent four missions to the rulers of Khandesh, Ahmadnagar, Bijapur and Golconda, calling upon them to recognize his suzerainty and pay him tribute. Khandesh ruler offered his submission. Ahmednagar was captured in 1600. By 1595, Akbar's armies had conquered Kashmir, Sindh, Orissa, Central India and Qandhar.

AKBAR'S NINE JEWELS OR *NAV-RATNAS*

1. **Abdul Rahim:** A celebrated Hindi and Turki scholar; remembered for a collection of *dohas, Rahim Satsai* and translation of *Babarnama* into Turki; conferred the title of ***Khan-e-Khana*** by Akbar.
2. **Abul Fazal:** Known for *Akbarnama* and *Ain-i-Akbari*.
3. **Birbal:** Known for his humour and wits; original name Mahesh Dass; died while fighting with the Yousuf-zai tribe in the north-west.
4. **Faizi:** Credited with the translation of *Leelawati* into Persian.
5. **Hamim Humam:** A close friend of Akhar; chief of royal school or ***pathasala***.
6. **Raja Man Singh:** A great Rajput general; helped the emperor in the Battle of Haldighati and in the battle against the Afghans.
7. **Shaikh Mubarak:** A sufi; brain behind Akbar's *Mahzar.*
8. **Tansen:** Court singer of Akbar; known as *sangeet samrat.*
9. **Todar Mal:** Known for his expertise in land revenue matters; his revenue policy was adopted by Sher Shah and Akbar.

8.6 JEHANGIR (1605-1627)

Jehangir was not without the imperial ambition of his father and early years of his reign saw some important military successes. Bengal had never been reconciled to the vassalage of Delhi and the frequent change of governors gave the local Afghans opportunity to rebel. In 1612, Jehangir saw the need of earning the goodwill of the Afghans in order to disarm them against the Mughals. He, therefore, followed a conciliatory policy.

Most noteworthy military success of Jehangir was his triumph over the Rajputs of Mewar. In 1613, Jehangir personally proceeded to Ajmer to guide the expedition, the supreme command of which was given to Prince Khurram. Though the Rajputs displayed dauntless heroism, they suffered heavy losses. The treaty that was signed between the Rana and the Emperor (1615) recognized Jehangir as the suzerain of Mewar.

At the end of his reign, his son, Shah Jehan, rebelled against him. Another crucial event of his reign was that when he fell ill, his queen, Nur Jehan, took active interest in the matters of state. Even the coins were issued jointly in the names of Jehangir and Nur Jehan. A skilled connoisseur of Persian art and painting, Jehangir patronised the best painters of the period like Abul Hasan and Mansur who laid unprecedented emphasis on scenic beauty, birds and beasts.

8.7 SHAH JEHAN (1628-1658)

After putting an end of the short reign of his nephew, Dawar Bakshi, the son of Khusru, Shah Jehan found himself in undisputed possession of the throne in 1628 when he was at the age of thirty-six. After he became emperor, he exhibited geniality and moderation as a ruler.

He had to face two revolts, at Bundelkhand and Deccan. Jujhar Singh, the son of Bir Singh Bundela, revolted in ***Bundelkhand***, a difficult region to the south of the Yamuna. Unable to stand against the imperial forces, he made his submission to Mahabat Khan. The Gond Raja's son appealed to Shah Jehan who sent Prince Aurangzeb to suppress the new revolt (1634). The Bundela strongholds were captured one by one.

Shah Jehan pursued the Mughal designs of the complete conquest of the Deccan. However, it could not be completed during Shah Jehan. Shas Jehan's policy towards central Asia was to secure a possession of Qandhar which the Persians had re-occupied during the Jehangir's reign. He occupied Badakshan and Balkh in 1646.

During his reign, the authority of the Emperor was not seriously challenged and there was no foreign invasion. In the history of Indian art, it was a golden age. In religion, Shah Jehan's intolerance destroyed the political solidarity of the empire in Aurangzeb's reign. Administration as also economic conditions were deteriorating. Although the imperial system looked imposing, there was laxity in central supervision and control. Foreign trade was prosperous, but its profits were enjoyed by a very small class.

8.8 AURANGZEB (1658-1707)

Aurangzeb ruled for almost fifty years. His empire stretched from Kashmir in the north to Jinji in the south, and from the Hindukush in the west to Chittagong in the east. Within the empire, he had to deal with a number of difficult problems, such as the problems of the Marathas in the Deccan, the Jats, and Satnamis and Rajputs in north India, and that of the Afghans and Sikhs in the north-west.

Aurangzeb's direct attention was concentrated on the affairs of North India. During 1681, the affairs of the South centred around the rise of the Maratha power under Shivaji. For about 25 years (1682-1707), he made desperate efforts to crush the Marathas, exhausting himself and his empire in the process.

HIGHLIGHTS OF AURANGZEB'S REIGN

- The second coronation of Aurangzeb took place when he defeated Dara (1659).
- He took the title of ***'Alamgir'*** in 1659.
- He was also called as ***Zinda Pir***, the living saint.
- In 1662, ***Mir Jumla***, Aurangzeb's ablest general, led the expedition against Ahoms.
- He forbade **inscription** of ***Kalma*** on the coins.
- He ended the celebration of ***Navroz*** festival.
- ***Muhtasibs*** (regulators of moral conduct) were appointed by him.
- He **forbade music** in the court.
- He ended ***Jarokha Darshan***, use of almanacs and weighing of the emperor.
- Aurangzeb compiled *Fatwa-i-Alamgir*.
- *Jaziya* was re-introduced. However, the Hindu mansabdars maintained their high proportion during his rule.
- The Mughal conquests reached a climax during his reign, as Bijapur and Golconda were annexed in 1686 and 1687 respectively.

8.9 LATER MUGHALS

Bahadur Shah I (1707-1712) : Aurangzeb died in 1707. A war of succession started amongst his three surviving sons — Muazzam. Azam and Khan Baksh. Muazzam defeated Azam and Khan Baksh and ascended the Mughal throne with the title of Bahadur Shah. He pursued pacifist policy and was, therefore, also called *Shah Bekhabar.* He also assumed the title of Shah Alam I. He made peace with Guru Gobind Singh and Chatrasal. He granted *Sardeshmukhi* to Marathas and also released Shahu. He forced Ajit Singh to submit, but later recognised him as the Rana of Marwar.

Jahandar Shah (1712-13) : Ascended the throne with the aid of Zulfikhar Khan. His nephew, Farrukhsiyar, dethroned him.

Farrukhsiyar, (1713-19) of Ascended the throne with help of **Sayyid brothers**, Abdullah Khan and Hussain Khan, who were Wazir and Mir Bakshi respectively. Farrukhsiyar was killed by the Sayyid brothers in 1719. Sikh leader **Banda Bahadur** was captured at Gurdaspur and executed.

Mohammad Shah (1719-48): During his reign, Nadir Shah raided India and took away the peacock throne and the *Kohinoor* diamond. He was a pleasure loving king and was nicknamed ***Rangeela***. During Muhammad Shah's reign, autonomous states of Hyderabad, Bengal and Awadh were established by Nizam-ul-mulk, Murshid Quli Khan and Saddat Khan Burhan-ul-Mulk respectively.

Ahmed Shah (1748-1754) : During his reign Ahmed Shah Abdali (one of the ablest generals of Nadir Shah) marched towards Delhi and the Mughals ceded Punjab and Multan.

Alamgir (1754-1759) : During his reign, Ahmed Shah Abdali occupied Delhi. Later, Delhi was also plundered by the Marathas.

Shah Alam II (1759-1806) : During his reign, Najib Khan Rohilla became very powerful in Delhi, so much so that Shah Alam II could not enter Delhi. The **Battle of Buxar** (1764) was fought during his reign.

Akbar Shah II (1806-37) : During his reign, Lord Hastings ceased to accept the sovereignty of Mughals and claimed an equal status.

Bahadur Shah II (1837-1862) : The last Mughal king, who was confined by the British to the Red Fort. During the revolt of 1857, he was proclaimed the Emperor by the rebellions. He was deported to Rangoon following the 1857 rebellion.

CAUSES OF THE DECLINE OF THE MUGHAL EMPIRE

- Worthless and negligent later Mughal emperors.
- Absence of a definite law of succession, leading to the instability of the government and growth of partisanship at the cost of patriotism.
- A heterogeneous and non-hereditary nobility.
- Degeneration of the nobility with factious quarrels and intrigues.
- Vast expansion of the empire making it difficult for the weak rulers to control it.
- Deterioration of the army.
- Revolts of Rajputs, Sikhs, Jats and Marathas due to Aurangzeb's religious policy
- Failure of Aurangzeb's Deccan policy
- Invasion of Nadir Shah and Ahmed Shah Abdali.

8.10 INVASIONS OF NADIR SHAH AND AHMAD SHAH ABDALI

Nadir Shah : Nadir Shah of Persia was very ambitious. He captured Qandhar and eyed the Afghanistan territory on the Mughal border. The Mughal *Subedar* Nasir Khan failed to receive any help from the court and, therefore, without posing any resistance he fled. From Afghanistan, Nadir Shah entered Punjab through Peshawar. He met the royal Mughal army at Karnal on 24 February in 1739. The royal army's main contingent under the Emperor Muhammad Shah and Nizam-ul-Mulk did not join the battle. As as a result, the army under Sadat Khan, Khan-i-Dauran and Nasir Mohammad signed the treaty with Nadir Shah accepting to give Nadir two crore rupees in lieu of protecting their territory.

During his invasion, Nadir Shah ordered a general massacre in which about 20,000 citizens were killed. The property was ransacked and every part of the city was looted. Nadir Shah remained in Delhi upto May 15. When he returned to Persia, he had collected huge booty including the famous Peacock Throne and *Kohinoor* diamond.

Nadir's attack paved way for further foreign invasions into India. The next invader was Ahmad Shah Abdali.

THE STORY OF KOHINOOR DIAMOND

After the battle of Panipat, Babur ordered his son Humayun to secure the treasures at Agra, which had been the capital of the Lodhi dynasty since 1502.

When Babur joined Humayun at Agra, Humayun presented him with a magnificent diamond. It has always been a matter of some dispute, but it seems almost certain that this splendid gem was the ***Kohinoor*** (mountain of light), making its first appearance in history. The ***Kohinoor*** was given to Humayun by the family of the **Raja** of **Gwalior,** whom he had given protection. Humayun later gave the diamond to **Shah Tahmasp** of Persia. The Shah sent it as a present to **Nizam Shah** in the Deccan. Somehow, the gem returned during the 17th century into the treasury of the Mughal emperor, **Shah Jahan.** When **Nadir Shah** plundered Delhi in 1739, he seized the diamond along with the other Moghul jewels and named it *Koh-i-noor.* The Kohinoor passed through several hands before finally resting in the **Tower of London,** where it remains on display even today.

Ahmad Shah Abdali's Invasion and the Third Battle of Panipat : Ahmed Shah Abdali, the successor of Nadir Shah, launched his first invasion at Punjab in 1748. It was followed by another invasion in 1749 in which he defeated Moin-ul-Mulk, the Governor of Punjab. In 1752, Abdali invaded Punjab for the third time and fourth time in 1756. In the fourth invasion, he reached upto Delhi and looted Indian territory as far as Mathura and Agra. In course of all these invasions; he did not meet with any resistance.

However, the Marathas posed a stiff resistance to him during his fifth invasion. He was enraged when Rohilla chief Najib-ud-Daulah and the Nawab of Awadh, Shuja-du-Daulah, established by him, were defeated by the Marathas. He also felt humiliated when his son Timur Shah was ousted from Punjab. He invaded India for the sixth time in 1759 and regained Punjab.

A fierce battle was fought, on 14 January 1761, between the forces of Ahmad Shah Abdali and Marathas at Panipat. After initial success in what is known as the **Third Battle of Panipat,** the Marathas suffered a crushing defeat. In all, the Marathas lost 28,000 soldiers in this encounter. The sense of defeat was so great that the Peshwa Balaji Baji Rao (Nana Saheb) died of shock.

The major causes of Ahmed Shah Abdali's success were the faulty war strategy of the Marathas, the lack of homogeneity and absence of popular local support from Rajputs, Jats, Sikhs etc. Lack of national feeling and weakness of the Indian soldiers also contributed towards the defeat of the Marathas in the battle.

8.11 MUGHAL ADMINISTRATIVE STRUCTURE

The centre of the whole structure of government was the sovereign. Before the sovereign, all important matters relating to appointments, increments, *jagirs, mansabs,* government grants, orders of payment, petitions of princes, governors, *bakhshis, diwans, faujdars,* and private petitions sent through nobles were submitted. Even when the sovereign was on the move, the daily routine was observed.

Central Administration

Wazir was the most important functionary. The unrestricted use of the powers of a *Wazir* by Bairam Khan was a warning against the appointment of an all-powerful *Wazir.* The office of the *Vakil* was retained, but none of the *Vakils* after Bairam Khan exercised the powers and influence of a prime minister.

Provincial Administration

Mughal empire was divided into *subah* or province which was further subdivided into *sarkars, parganas* and villages. However, it also had other territorial units as '*Khalisa'*, (royal land), *Jagirs* (autonomous rajas) and *Inams* (gifted lands, mainly waste lands). There were 12 territorial units (*subah*) during Akbar's reign, which increased to 21 under Aurangzeb's reign. The administrative agency in the provinces under the Mughal was an exact miniature of that of the central government. The provincial administration was based on the principles of "uniformity" and "**Check and Balance**".

Judicial Administration

The Mughals efficiently carried on the judicial administration with the help of *Qazi-ul-Quzat*. He was the chief justice of the state and decided the religious and criminal cases. Local *Qazis* were appointed by him. He also used to supervise the law courts within the empire. He could also hear appeals against local law courts. At the provincial level, *Sadr, Kotwal, Muqaddam* and *Chowkidar* heard the cases. The consumer cases were heard by *amil*.

MUGHAL OFFICIALS	
A. CENTRE	
Wazir	Akbar abolished the post of all-powerful *Wazir*; became the head of the revenue department; also known as ***Diwan-i-ala.***
Diwan	Responsible for all income and expenditure and had control over *Khalisa* and jagir land.
Mir Bakshi	Headed military department, nobility, information and intelligence agencies.
Mir Saman	Incharge of imperial household and *Karkhanas*.
Kiwan-i-Bayutat	Maintained roads, government buildings etc. and worked under *Mir Saman*.
Mir Munshi	Incharge of royal correspondence.
Sadr-us-Sadr	Incharge of charitable and religious endowments.
Qazi-ul-Quzat	Headed the judiciary department.
Muhtasib	Censor of public morals.
Mushrif-i-Mumalik	Accountant-general
Mustauf-i-Mumalik	Auditor-general
Daroga-i-Dak-Chauki	Officer in charge of imperial post, equivalent to today's post master-general
Mir-i-arz	Officer in charge of petition
Waqia Navis	News reporters/writers
B. PROVINCE	
Sipahsalar	The head executive (known as Sipahsalar under Akbar and later known as *Nizam* or *Subedar).*
Diwan	Incharge of revenue department.
Bakshi	Incharge of military department.
Sadr	Incharge of judicial department.
C. DISTRICT/SARKAR	
Fauzdar	Administrative head.
Amal/Amalguzar	Revenue collection.
Kotwal	Maintenance of law and order, trial of criminal cases and price regulation.
D. PARGANA	
Shiqdar	Administrative head combined in himself the duties of '*fauzdar* and *kotwal*'.
Amin, Qanungo	Revenue officials.
E. VILLAGE	
Muqaddam	Headman.
Patwari	Accountant.
Chowkidar	Watchman.

Mansabdari System

Mansabdari system, introduced by Akbar in 1595-96, was the steel-frame of the emperor's military policy. The term ***mansab*** means an officer or rank. The *Mansabdar*, i.e, the holder of the ***mansab***, was an official who, out of his pay, was expected to furnish a certain number of cavalry to the imperial army.

Salient features of the Mansabdari system were as follow:

- Mansabdars were graded into 39 classes, ranging from commanders of 10 to 10,000.
- Twin ranks—*Zat* and *Sawar*–were allotted. The former indicated a noble's personal status, while the latter, the number of troops he had to maintain.
- *Mansabdari* had three scale gradations : (i) *Mansabdar* (500 *zat* and below). (ii) *Amir* (between 500-2500 *zat*). and (iii) *Amir-i-Umda* (2,500 *zat* and above).
- *Mansab* was not an hereditary system. Mansabdars were paid through revenue assignments (*jagirs*).

Reforms in Mansabdari : An important change in Mansabdari in Jehangir's reign was the introduction of the ***du-aspa-sih-aspa*** rank. This was made part of the *sawar* rank. The mansabdari *sawar* obligations and the payment made for them were both doubled.

Shah Jehan introduced the ***Month-Ratio*** or ***Month-Scale*** system in Mansabdari. Under this system, salaries of Mansabdars were fixed on a month scale: ten months, eight months and so on. The obligations of maintaining ***sawars*** were brought down accordingly.

Land Revenue System

Land was classified into four types : ***Polaj*** (continuously cultivated), ***Parauti*** (left fallow for a year or two to recover productivity), ***Chachar*** (left fallow for three or four years) and ***Banjar*** (uncultivated for five years or more).

During the early years of Akbar's reign, several revenue experiments were made. There were three principal revenue systems in the Mughal empire, which may be described as follows :

(i) ***Ghallabaksh*** or crop division: Under this system, a share of each crop was taken by the State. This system prevailed in lower Sind, a part of Kabul and Kashmir.

(ii) ***Zabti system*** Todar Mal, who was appointed Akbar's finance minister (***diwan-i-ashraf***) in 1582, set up a regulation or standard system of revenue administration known as the Zabti system. This system was applied from Multan to Bihar and in large parts of Rajputana, Malwa and Gujarat. Under this system, lands were accurately surveyed. ***Polaj*** and ***Parauti*** lands were subdivided into three grades (good, mild and bad). The average produce was calculated from the mean of the three grades. The demand of the state was one third of average produce. The settlement under the ***Zabti*** system was made directly with the cultivator.

Under the ***Zabti*** system, the cash rates were fixed on the average of ten years' actual i.e, from the past experience of ten years. That is why this system is also called ***Dahsala*** system.

ADVANTAGES OF DAHSALA SYSTEM

- It enabled the administrators to guess fairly the revenue of the state.
- Cultivators knew what they were required to pay.
- The government also promised to reduce the revenue in case of unforeseen circumstances of natural calamities.
- The state advanced loans to the cultivators.
- Remissions of revenue was granted in bad seasons.

(iii) ***Nasaq*** **or Estimate :** Past assessment determined the present. Todar Mal collected the accounts of the *Qanungos* and in some places ascertained their accuracy by local enquiries. From these accounts he prepared the rent roll of the *Subah.* The *Nasaq* system did not depend upon survey or seasonal records of produce. It resembled the *Zamindari* settlement.

CATEGORIES OF AGRICULTURISTS DURING THE MUGHAL RULE

The agriculturists in the Mughal period were grouped into the following three categories on the basis of availability of land :

(i) ***Khudkashta***: Also known as *Malik-i-Jamin*, *Khudkashta* were peasants who cultivated own land. Also known as ***Mirasdars*** (in Maharashtra) and ***Gaveti*** (in Rajasthan), *Khudkashta* were the original settlers of the village.

(ii) ***Muzarian***: Muzarian or tenants were the agriculturists who lived in their own villages, but cultivated the land taken on ***batai*** (rent) from the ***Khudkashta***. The Muzarians were of two types: (a) tenants-at-will, and (b) tenants who had hereditary tenancy rights.

(iii) ***Pahikashta***: The peasants who lived in other villages on temporary basis were called ***Pahikashta***. They were given a share in their produce as a remuneration.

OCCUPANCY RIGHT AND TYPES OF LAND

The Pands in the Mughal period was divided into the following four categories on the basis of authority.

(i) ***Jagir***: It was a class of land whose revenues were assigned to a ***jagirdar*** or ***mansabdar***: Jagirs were of two types: (a) ***tankhwah jagirs*** which were assigned in lieu of salary, and (b) watan jugirs which were hereditary possessions of the autonomous chiefs.

(ii) ***Khalsa***: It was a class of land which was in direct control of the central administration.

(iii) ***Madad-i-mash***: It was a category of land which was granted to scholars, religious persons for their maintenance. In Rajusthan, such a land was called *sasan*.

(iv) ***Paibaki*** : It was a class of land which was theoretically under the centre. However, its incomes were not earmarked for the central government's works. The revenues from such land were used for the compensation of loss of jagirdars.

8.12 RAJPUT POLICY OF THE MUGHALS

The mutual relations of the Mughals and the Rajputs have a great importance in the history of the Mughal Period. As long as the Mughal emperors maintained friendly relations with the Rajputs, their empire went on flourishing and making progress day by day. Conversely, however, when they turned them into their foes, their empire also began to decay.

Babur could not frame any fixed Rajput policy due to his early death in 1530 AD. **Humayun** was caught in countless wars with Sher Shah Suri and Bahadur Shah. So, the Rajputs recovered their lost territories and improved their military position during his rule.

Akbar made the Rajputs not only his friends but also contracted relationships with them. He established matrimonial alliances with the royal families of the Rajput states, such as Amber, Bikaner and Jaisalmer. He granted the Rajputs equal rights with the Muslims and appointed them on high and elevated positions. However, he surely carried on wars against those Rajput rulers who did not accept his authority. He fought continuous battles against Rajput states like Gondwana, Ranthambhor, Kalinjir and Mewar. When a conquest was completed, he treated the subdued Rajput ruler with utmost politeness and due honour. Actually, the essence of Akbar's Rajput policy was that at first they should be brought under his control, and thereafter they should be treated with due regards and friendliness.

RAJPUT POLICY OF AKBAR

- Many Rajputs were taken into the Mughal Service.
- Many were created Mansabdars.
- *Jaziya* was abolished. Pilgrimage tax was also abolished.
- Akbar took many Rajput princesses as his bride.

Jehangir followed his father's policy only. The greatest achievement of Jehangir, as regards Mughal-Rajput relation, was the subjugation of Mewar.

Shah Jehan modified somewhat the Rajput policy of his ancestors but he did not try to reverse it entirely. He did not remove the Rajputs from their high offices and never tried to re-impose the oppressive taxes like *jaziya* and pilgrimage tax on Hindus.

Aurangzeb altogether gave up the policy of toleration and forbearance followed by his forefathers and thus the Mughal lost the trusted friends like Rajputs. He was a bigot *Sunni Mussalman* and wished to set up a purely Muslim state in India. He tried to get rid of Raja Jai Singh of Amber and Raja Jaswant Singh, the ruler of Marwar, in order to end the influence and power of the Rajputs. Aurangzeb's Rajput policy proved to be utterly fatal to the Mughal empire and was the main cause of its downfall. In fact, Aurangzeb failed altogether to understand the importance of the Rajputs.

8.13 DECCAN POLICY OF THE MUGHALS

The Deccan was divided into about 87 small kingdoms at the time of **Babur's** invasion. In 1590, when **Akbar** turned his attention to the Deccan only four states existed : 1. Farukhshahi State of Khandesh; 2. Nizamshahi State of Ahmadnagar; 3. Adilshahi State of Bijapur; and 4. Qutabshahi State of Golconda.

Akbar had two chief objects in conquering the Deccan. First of all, he wished to annex the Deccan to his empire to be profited by its wealth and other resources. His second object was that he wished to drive the Portuguese out of India, because he thought that they were terrible foes of the Mughal empire as they were making raids upon the economic resources of the country.

The Mughal subjugated at first Daulatabad in 1599 and Ahmadnagar in 1600. The Mughals did take possession of Ahmadnagar but they could not annex it to the Mughal empire completely. Akbar divided his newly-conquered Deccan region into three provinces–Berar, Khandesh and Ahmadnagar and placed them under the control of prince Daniyal.

Jehangir wished that the Mughal control over Ahmadnagar should be further confirmed and, if possible, the kingdoms of Bijapur and Golconda might be brought under the Mughal subjugation. But, the boundaries of the Mughal empire continued to be the same in the Deccan as they were in 1605. Jahangir faced still opposition from Malik Ambar of Ahmeednagar. One after another important Mughal commanders failed against Malik Ambar. However, in 1621, Malik had to sign a peace treaty with the Mughal and kingdoms of Ahmadnagar, Bijapur and Golconda agreed to pay tributes of twelve lakhs, eighteen lakhs and twenty lakhs to the emperor, respectively.

Shah Jahan followed the policy of the complete conquest of the Deccan. In 1636, the Sultans of Bijapur and Golconda acknowledged the Mughal suzerainty.

During **Aurangzeb**, the kingdom of Ahmadnagar became an unshaken and solid part of the Mughal empire. The emperor himself went to the Deccan and annexed Bijapur and Golconda to the Mughal empire in 1686 and 1687 respectively.

The Mughal policy of expansion towards the Deccan proved to be very fatal to the Mughal empire. First, these long wars of the Deccan spelled the bankruptcy of the Mughal empire from the economic view point. Secondly, the administration received a setback by Aurangzeb's continuous absence (for 25 years) from the capital. Consequently, there were risings and revolts against the Mughal empire in all sides.

8.14 FOREIGN POLICY OF THE MUGHALS

The Mughals refused to be drawn in a tripartite Ottoman– Mughal–Uzbek alliance against the Persians as it would have upset the Asian balance of power and left them alone to face the might of the Uzbeks. Alliance with Iran was also helpful in promoting trade with Central Asia.

The territorial power of the Uzbeks grew rapidly in the seventeenth century under the Abdullah Khan Uzbek. In 1572-1573, Abdullah seized Balkh which, along with Badakhshan, had served as a kind of buffer between the Mughals and the Uzbeks. In 1577, Abdullah Khan sent an embassy to **Akbar**, proposing to partition Iran. Akbar was not moved by this appeal to sectarian narrowness. A strong Iran was essential to keep the restless Uzbeks in their place. At the same time, Akbar had no desire to get embroiled with the Uzbeks, unless they directly threatened Kabul or the Indian possessions. This was the key to Akbar's Central Asia policy.

Jahangir's policy towards Central Asia resulted in loss or Qandhar to the Iranian king, Shah Abbas, in 1622.

Shah Jehan's North West Frontier policy consisted in expanding the Mughal influence in that direction and annexing the lost territory of Qandhar to the Mughal Empire. He did not achieve any success in it.

During **Aurangzeb**, Mughal attained its territorial climax in the north-west (as in other parts), stretching up to the Hindukush.

8.15 RELIGIOUS POLICY OF THE MUGHALS

Babur proclaimed *jihad* or religious war against the Hindus especially Rana Sanga and he called the Hindus *Kafirs* in order to excite his soldiers. He levied the stamp duties on the Hindus alone but remitted them in case of the Muslims. Besides it, it is said that he demolished numerous temples at Chanderi and it was under his orders that one of his officers, Mir Baqa, razed to the ground a sacred temple built at the birth place of Shri Ramchandra at Ayodhya and raised a mosque in its place. Similarly, he got many Jain temples demolished. **Humayun** too adopted his father's policy as far as his relations with Hindus were concerned.

The credit of establishing a '**Secular State**' in India goes to **Akbar** alone.

Highlights of Akbar's religious policy are as follows:

- He abolished *Jaziya* and pilgrimage tax and forcible conversion of prisoners of war.
- He built an *Ibadat Khana* at Fatehpur Sikri to discuss religious matters. He invited many distinguished person at the ***Ibadat Khana***.
- To curb the dominance of Ulema, Akbar introduced a new *Khutba,* written by Faizi, and proclaimed *Mahzarnama* in 1579, which made him the final interpreter of Islamic law (*Mujtahid Imam-i-Adil*) in case of any controversies. It made him *Amir-ul-Momin* (leader of the faithful) and *Amir-i-Adil* (a just ruler).
- His religious liberalism is reflected again in the pronouncement of ***Tauhid-i-Ilahi*** or ***Din-i-Ilahi,*** which propounded Sufi divine monotheism.

TENETS OF *DIN-I-ILAHI* (1582)

- It could be adopted on Sunday by performing *paibos*. (the emperor placed his feet on the head of the initiated), following which Akbar gave *Shat* (formula).
- The initiated had to express greeting in the form of *Allah-o-Akbar* and *Jalle-Jalalhu.*
- He had to abstain from meat and give alms.
- There were no scriptures and priests.
- *Tauhid-i-Ilahi* had four grades of devotion in the ascending order—sacrifice of property, life, honour and religion.
- Birbal, Abul Fazl and Faizi joined the order.
- Badauni believed that Akbar was creating a new religion but contemporary historians believe that he was only trying to attain the status of *Insaan-i-Kamil*.

Jehangir, of course, continued to follow his father's liberal policy and refused to play in the hands of the Muslim Ulemas. He put an end to the practice of contracting marriages between Hindu men and Muslim women so commonly prevalent in Rajouri in Kashmir. However, he adopted a harsh policy towards Gujarat. He was moved by religious ends to some extent in adopting an oppressive policy towards Guru Arjun Dev. Thus, some of his acts certainly show that Jehangir was disposed to bigotry in a small measure but, he could not manifest it openly owing to the then prevailing atmosphere and the rapid movement of the time.

Like his father, **Shah Jehan** pursued a tolerant religious policy, although there were aberrations at times.

Aurangzeb was a bigoted Sunni Musslman who wanted to establish a Muslim state in India. He demolished countless temples and erected mosques in their places. He slaughtered cows in temples and confiscated lands previously endowed on them. He issued royal edicts to the effect that the Hindus should not open any school for their children, He reimposed *jaziya* and pilgrimage tax on Hindus. Octroi taxes were collected from the Hindus very strictly and severely. The celebration of Hindu festivals like Dussshera, Diwali etc. in the Royal Court was absolutely stopped. Many Hindus who had held elevated positions under the government were removed from their high posts and many other wrongs were perpetrated on the Hindus. Many allurements and temptations were offered to the Hindus in order to convert them to Islam. Thus, under Aurangzeb, the Mughal empire was turned into a fully Islamic State.

8.16 SOCIO-ECONOMIC CONDITIONS UNDER MUGHALS

The socio-economic conditions under the Mughals can be studied under the following headings :

(i) Feudal Society: The medieval Indian society was organised on a feudal basis. The emperor, as the absolute ruler, was the head of the social system.

(ii) The Aristocracy: The Mughal nobility or the ruling elite, collectively styled as *umara* (pl. of *amir*), who belonged to the first category of the mansabdari system, and the feudatory chietains, who owned allegiance to the Mughal crown, comprised the aristocracy. The latter were also graded as *mansabdars.* The aristocracy was composed of Muslims as well as Hindus, although the number of the latter was small.

(iii) The Middle Class: The middle class, though extensive, was heterogeneous in character. It was composed of junior *mansabdars,* middle-level civil and judicial officials, big landlords, merchants, bankers and professional men, including the priests, men of letters, and artists. Social stratification of the Hindus being based on the hereditary caste system, only the prosperous and influential among the high borns found their way into the middle class. Nevertheless, the Muslims also tended to determine social status on the basis of birth and racial considerations.

(iv) The Masses: They included the peasantry—small peasant proprietors as well as the agricultural labourers—soldiers, artisans, craftsmen, shopkeepers, lower level government servants, menials, slaves and millions of the self-employed persons.

(v) Wealth and General Prosperity: Uninterrupted peace, freedom from foreign invasions and good government enriched the Mughal treasury and ushered in an era of prosperity and material well-being for the people.

(vi) Status of Women: The Mughal period produced several capable and intelligent women who influenced the politics of their times–Rani Karnavati, Rani Jodha Bai, Rani Durgavati, Rani Rupmati, Chand Bidi, Nur Jehan, and her mother Asmat Begum, Mumtaz Mahal, Jahanara, Roshanara, Jaibunisa, Jija Bai (mother of Shivaji). Tara Bai (wife of Raja Ram) and Bibi Sahiba (wife of Subedar of Kabul). However, in general, the women suffered from all sorts of handicaps. Women were not given education, they did not command respect in the society and they had no independent existence. The laxity in morals of the emperors, nobles and rich people had reduced their position to articles of pleasure.

The emperors and their nobles kept a large number of wives, concubines and slave girls in their *harems.* Besides, both Muslim and Hindu women suffered from certain social evils. Sunni Muslims could have four wives at a time while a Shia Muslim had the liberty to have even more wives than four. The Muslim women had to observe *purdah* most strictly. That virtually meant slavery to them. The impact of the Islam and the insecurity of honour of women due to constant wars and battles further affected adversely the condition of Hindu women. Many social evils like *purdah* system, child marriages, prohibition on widows' marriages, the practice of Sati, polygamy etc. had crept up in the Hindus society and these continued during the rule of the Mughals. Akbar tried to mitigate the evils of *sati* and child marriage, but he did not succeed much.

(vii) Fairs and Festivals: Indian social life was very colourful and busy; it was full of hustle and bustle because of numerous social functions and rituals, fairs and festivals, most of which were accorded religious sanction. The Hindus celebrated the festivals of *Holi, Basant-Panchami, Dussehra, Diwali, Shivaratri and Makar Sankranti* with great zest and gusto, while the Muslims celebrated *Id-uz-zuha, Idil-Fitr, Shab-i-Barat, Muharram and Milad-un-Nabi.*

(viii) Education and Learning: The imperial Mughals were highly educated and cultured. Princes of their times extended liberal patronage to education and learning. **Babur** was a scholar of Persian and Turki languages. He is said to have invented a new style of verse in Persian, known as *mubaiyan.* He has made his name immortal in the history of literature by his memories, entitled *Tuzuk-i-Baburi,* which constitutes a first-rate authority on his own career and the history of his times. **Humayun** was well-read in Turki, Persian and Arabic languages; he showed special interest in religious studies, mathematics, astronomy and fine arts. Though a failure as a ruler and administrator, he retained his literary taste till the very end of his life. A magnificent personal library was attached to his royal palace, called *Din Panah* or *Sher Mandal,* in Delhi.

Akbar was the first among the Muslim rulers of India who made a serious attempt to reform the educational system to suit the national aspirations of people. As mentioned earlier, the Indo-Islamic system of education as introduced by the Sultans of Delhi was based on orthodox Islamic concepts and was very limited in its scope. Its two-fold object was to produce priests for the propagation of Islam and bureaucracy to run the administration of the Islamic state in accordance with the *sharait.* The Hindus found no place in that educational system although some of them, called the *kayasthas,* had taken to the study of Persian to seek employment under the sultans. The traditional aim of the Indo-Islamic system of education carried no weight with Akbar who wanted education to serve as a vehicle for national progress. Change in the educational policy of the state was necessitated by the grant of religious freedom to all the Indians and change in the nature of recruitment to the imperial bureaucracy which was made secular in personnel and functions. From a close scrutiny of Abul Fazal's monumental works *Akbarnama* and *Ain-i-Akbari,* we come to the conclusion that Akbar, though personally not interested in academic exercises, was fully conscious of the importance of education for the socio-cultural and material advancement of the people. **He brought about several reforms in the field of education.**

Firstly, he provided a secular base to it by making a distinction between the Arabic and Persian studies. The Arabic studies, which dealt almost exclusively with the Islamic scriptures and theology, were allowed to flourish as ever before, although the curricula and scope of Persian studies were broad-based to include many secular subjects, including natural sciences and medical studies, to attract Hindus and Muslims alike. The study of Persian language and literature was popularised on an all-India basis.

Secondly, Akbar expanded elementary education to raise the percentage of general literacy among the masses. He introduced a new curriculum of studies for the *makhtabs* and suggested improved methods of instruction to the children. The educational institutions, mosques, *khanqahs* and Hindus temples were the places where the books were usually preserved. That is why the historians of the day do not say much about the libraries of the period.

Thirdly, historiography itself constituted one of the most popular branches of learning and a major occupation for the ambitious scholars eager to secure royal favours. The art of medieval Indian historiography reached its perfection during the reign of Akbar under whose liberal patronage the Indian scholars, Hindus and Muslims both, cherished and cultivated it as a full fledged discipline in its own right.

Fourthly, Akbar's reign is also notable for the introduction of *maqulat* or rational sciences as a subject of study in the *madrasas* and encouragement to industrial and technical education in the state-run *karkhanas.* This step was taken by Akbar on the advice of Mir Fathullah Shirazi, a Persian scholar and scientist who excelled in all branches of *maqulat,* including physics, chemistry and mechanics.

Jahangir and **Shah Jehan,** the worthy successors of Akbar, were equally great patrons of learning and literature. The liberal educational policy adopted by Akbar for the intellectual and cultural advancement of the Indians remained in full force till the end of Shah Jehan's reign. The literary movement born during Akbar's time showed unabated zeal during the period of Shah Jehan's rule. The educational institutions established during the reign of Akbar flourished and their number increased manifold with the liberal financial aid from the government.

8.17 CULTURAL DEVELOPMENTS UNDER THE MUGHALS

The Mughal emperors were very fond of art. Under their patronage, all arts, particularly architecture, painting and music made special progress and all kinds of artists used to receive encouragement from state. Aurangzeb was the Mughal emperor who considered it more creditable to finish art altogether instead of encouraging it. In reality, he was completely deficient in the natural inclination towards art, otherwise, all other Mughal emperors exhibited their particular tendency towards the development of art and tried their utmost to advance it.

ARCHITECTURE

The Mughal emperors were great builders and that is why the Mughal period is called the '*Golden Age of Architecture*' in the Indian history. The Mughal rulers were very fond of building great mansions. The mansions built by them astonish many a visitors even today owing to their vastness, durability, beauty and delicacy.

Mughal architecture was the admixture of various influences— foreign and Indian, Muslim and Hindu. Babur and Humayun had a great liking for the Persian style but by the passage of time during the reign of Akbar some Indian elements got blended in it, while in the time of his successors, slowly and slowly, the Persian style was altogether abandoned and the Mughal style entirely became Indian. Hence, any particular style cannot be designated as the Mughal style because there was a great difference between the ratio of influences during the reigns of different monarchs.

Architectural developments in the period stretching from the rule of Babur to Aurangzeb are discussed as follows :

Babur : He built two mosques : one at Kabulibagh in Panipat and the other at Sambhal in Rohilkhand.

Humayun : Architectural highlights of his reign may be listed as follows :

- He laid the foundation of the city *Din Panah* at Delhi.
- **Humayun's Tomb is called the prototype of Taj Mahal**. It has a double dome of marble, while the central dome is octagonal. It was built by his widow Haji Begum.

Akbar : Architectural highlights of his reign may be listed as follows:

- Buildings built by Akbar are : **Agra Fort** (1565), **Lahore Palace** (1572), **Fatehpur Sikri, Buland Darwaza** and **Allahabad Fort** (1583).
- The architecture at Fatehpur Sikri is an excellent blending of Persian, Central Asian and various Indian (Bengal and Gujarat) styles. It is also known as **Epic Poem in Red Sandstone**. Indian tradition includes deep eaves, balconies and kiosks. Central Asian Style is evident in the use of glazed blue tiles.
- Two unusual buildings at Fatehpur Sikri are **Panch Mahal** and **Diwan-i-Khas.**
- The **Panch Mahal** has the plan of **Buddhist Vihara.**
- **The Jodhabai's Palace, Diwan-i-Aam** and, **Diwan-i-Khas** are Indian in their plan.
- **Buland Darwaja** (built after Gujarat victory), formed the main entrance to Fatehpur Sikri. It is built in the **Iranian style** of half dome portal.

- **Salim Chishti's Tomb** (redone in marble by Jahangir is the first Mughal building in pure marble), **palaces of Birbal**, ***Anup*** **Talao, Mariyam Mahal are also inside** the Fatehpur Sikri.
- He built the **Jahangiri Mahal** in Agra fort according to Hindu design based on ***Man Mandir.***
- **Haroon Minar**— Tower built by Akbar in memory of his elephant (*Horoon*).
- He also began to build his own tomb at Sikandara which was later completed by Jahangir.

Jahangir : Architectural highlights of his reign may be listed as follows :

- The style of architecture used by both Jahangir and Shah Jahan is known as Indo Persian. Important features of this style are curved lines, bulbous dome, foliated arches, vigorous use of marble instead of red sandstone and use of *pietra dura* for decorative purposes.
- Nur Jahan built **Itimad-ud-Daula's** (another name of Mirza Ghiyas Beg) **Marble tomb** at Agra, which is noticeable for the first use of *pietra dura* (floral designs made up of semi-precious stones) technique.
- He built **Moti Masjid** *in* Lahore and his own **Mausoleum at Shahdara** *(*Lahore).
- He also changed the plan of **Akbar's Tomb at Sikandara**. It is an unusual tomb as it is not surmounted by a dome and built on the model of *a Buddhist Pagoda.*

Shah Jehan : Architectural highlights of his reign may be listed as follows :

- He was the most prolific and magnificent builder.
- Mosque building activity reached its climax in **Taj Mahal** at Agra. Ustad Isa was the master architect under whose guidance, the Taj Mahal was designed and constructed in Agra. Its construction took 22 years. He also built the **Jama Masjid** (sand stone) in Delhi.
- Some of the important buildings built by Shah Jehan at Agra are **Moti Masjid** (only mosque of marble), **Khaas Mahal, Musamman Burz** (Jasmine palace where he spent his last years in captivity) and **Sheesh Mahal** with mosaic glasses on walls and ceilings.
- Many stone buildings were destroyed by him and replaced by marble.
- He laid the foundations of **Shahjahanabad** in 1637 where he built the Red Fort and *Taqt-i-Taus* (Peacock throne).
- Most richly ornamented buildings in Red Fort was the **Diwan-i-Khas** or **Rang Mahal**.
- Shah Jehan built **Nahar-i-Faiz.**

Aurangzeb : Architectural highlights of his reign may be listed as follows :

- Only building built by Aurangzeb in the Red Fort is **Moti Masjid.**
- Only monument associated with Aurangzeb is **Bibi Ka Makbara** which is the tomb of his wife **Rabbia-ud-Daura** in Aurangabad.
- He also built the **Badshahi Mosque** *in* Lahore.

GARDENS

Laying out of beautiful gardens was the special contribution of the Mughals. The **Nur-i-Afshan** in Agra was laid by the founder of the Mughal rule, Babur. Jahangir is famous for the **Shalimar Garden** at Srinagar. Nur Jahan's brother, Asaf Khan, laid out the famous Nishat Bagh. In fact, the garden and the gateway can be found in almost all Mughal-style tombs.

PAINTINGS

The **Mughal Art of Painting,** like the Mughal architecture, was the outcome of many influences. In the beginning, during the reign of Babur and Humayun, it was affected altogether by the Persian influence. During the reign of Akbar, the policy of religious toleration and the mutual feelings of friendship between Hindus and Muslims deeply affected the art of painting also and in this way it became an admixture of the Persian and the Indian influences. Thus, slowly and slowly, the Persian influence began to decrease, so much so that in the reign of Jahangir, this art became really Indian and the Persian influence on it was insignificant.

Following are the highlights of the Mughal paintings :

- The Mughals introduced new themes depicting the court, battle scenes and the chase and added new colours (Peacock blue and Indian red).
- Humayun had taken into his service two master painters Mir Syed Ali and Abdus Samad. These two painters were ordered to paint the famous ***Dastan-i-Amir Hamzah***.
- Basawan, Daswanath, Haribans, Abdus Samad and Farruk Beg were the famous painters in Akbar's court.
- Apart from illustrating Persian books of fables (*Humzanama),* the painters illustrated *Razmnamah* (*Mahabharata*) and *Akbaranama.*
- Under Akbar, European painting was introduced at the court by the Portuguese priests.
- Jehangir was a connoisseur of art. During his period, purely Indian style of painting developed. **Portrait painting** reached a climax during Jehangir. Aga Raja, Muhammad Nadir, Muhammad Murad, Manohar, Bishan Das and Goverdhan were famous painters during Jahangir

Besides the Mughal painting, there grew up in this age two more schools of painting: (a) Rajput School of Painting, and (b) Kangra School of Painting.

The **Rajput School of Painting** was developed in Rajputana, particularly Jaipur, in the 18th century. In it, familiar and popular themes have been taken and an effort has been made to show or depict an ordinary citizen, his religious rites and amusements. Religion and art are very closely related to each other in it and the spiritual themes have special importance in this school of painting.

Towards the end of the 18th century, another kind of painting was developed in Northern India, particularly kangra, known as the **Kangra School of Painting**. The theme relates to Hindu gods and goddesses in this art. Many subjects were selected from the Hindu religious books like the *Ramayana*, the *Mahabharata*, the *Ram Mala*, *Geet Govind* etc. and they were depicted beautifully in pictures. Similarly, beautiful paintings (portraits) of *Shiva-Parvati*, *Radha-Krishna* etc. were produced.

MUSIC

The Mughal kings, except Aurangzeb, had a great attachment with music. However, it was due to Akbar's interest and patronage of this art that both kinds of music—instrumental and vocal—made unusual advancement in his time. In his time, the 'National Indian Music' took its birth by the blending of the Hindus and Muslims types of music. Akbar extended patronage to singers like Tansen, Baiju Bawra, Abdus Rahim Khan Khana, Raja Bhagwan Das and Raja Man Singh.

Shah Jehan had patronised many singers. Of these, Jagannath, Janardhan Bhatt, Ram Das, Maha Patra etc. were particularly famous. It is said that once Shah Jehan was so pleased with the singing of Jagannath, the royal poet of Sanksrit, that he weighed him against gold and gave him the whole of this gold as a prize.

LITERATURE

The Mughals gave great patronage to literature : Persian, Hindi and Sanskrit.

(i) Persian Literature: During the Mughal period, Persian was the state language and, therefore, most of the literatures—prose, poetry, history—were written in this language.

Babur's autobiography, *Tuzuki-i-Baburi,* written in Turkish is an invaluable gem of literature. In it, Babur has described each event and subject in a very interesting way and in simple language without exaggeration.

Humayun's sister, Gulbadan Begum, too was a well-educated woman, who wrote '*Humayun Nama*'. Though Akbar was himself illiterate, yet he encouraged the production of literature very much. He was the patron of many scholars, poets and historians. As a result of it, literature made wonderful progress in his time. The Persian literature produced in his reign can be divided into three parts : (i) historical books (ii) translated books, and (iii) original literary books.

In the reign of **Akbar**, many famous books of different languages were translated into Persian and a separate 'Translation Department was opened. This work of translation was entrusted to many learned scholars, such as Abdur Rahim Khan Khana, Badauni, Abul Fazl, Faizi, Naqib Khan, Ibrahim Sarhindi.

TRANSLATION OF SOME FAMOUS SANSKRIT WORKS INTO PERSIAN DURING AKBAR

(i)	*Ramayana*	–	Badauni
(ii)	*Lilavati*	–	Faizi
(iii)	*Atharva Veda*	–	Hazi Ibrahim Sarhindi
(iv)	*Mahabharata* was translated and renamed as *Razmnamah*		

Jehangir maintained a large number of writers and poets at his court, of whom Mirza Ghias Beg, Naqib Khan, Mutamid Khan, Niamtullah, Abdul Haq Dehlvi etc. were specially prominent.

In **Shah Jehan's** reign, important historical works were produced, such as '*Padshah Nama*', '*Shahjehan Nama*' and '*Alami-i-Salih*. Dara, Shah Jehan's eldest son, was the greatest literary and learned man of that time. He compiled several philosophical books like '*Majmua-ul-Bahrin*' '*Safnat-ul-Aulia*' etc. Not only this but he translated very important sanskrit works into Persian, such as, the '*Upanishads*', the '*Bhagwad Gita*' and '*Yog Vashisht*.'

During **Aurangzeb's** reign, many historical books were written, though compilation of such books was prohibited by law.

(ii) Hindi Literature: Malik Mohammad Jayasi wrote a poetical composition *Padamavat* on Padmani, the queen of Mewar in 1540. This composition has an exalted place in Hindi literature.

Akbar's reign was the golden age of the Hindi poetry because it was in his time that some Hindi poets of immortal fame, such as Tulsi Das, Sur Das, Mira, Rahim and Ras Khan lived. The greatest Hindi poet of Akbar's time was Sant Tulsi Das (1532-1623) whose name has been rendered immortal for ever by his most renowned book the '*Ramacharitmanas*'. Sur Das has elucidated in very beautiful words of **Brij Bhasha** in his book, *Sur Sagar,* the childhood of Lord Krishna and the true love of Krishna and Radha.

Keshav Das was another noted poet of this age, who was the author of several books, such as '*Kavi Priya*', '*Ram Chandrika*' '*Rasik Priya*', '*Alankri*', '*Manjari*' etc. During the Shah Jehan period, great poets like Sunder, Senapati, Bhushan and Behari lived who wrote very good books. Sunder wrote a book named '*Sunder Sringar*' in 1634. Shah Jehan decorated him with the distinctions of '*Kaviraj*' and '*Maha Kavi*'.

HINDI LITERATURE

• Ramanuja	*Brahmsutra*
• Parhasarthi	*Karma Mimansa*
• Jayadeva	*Gita Govinda*
• Vijnansvara	*Mitakshara*
• Jimuta Vahna	*Dayabhaga*
• Chand Bardoi	*Prithviraj Raso*
• Jaisi	*Padmavat*
• Salibhadra	*Bharata Bahuholi*

(iii) Sanskrit Literature: Akbar was the first Mughal monarch who patronized Sanskrit as well as Hindi. During his reign, many Hindi writers were also writers of Sanskrit. In his time, the first-Sanskrit-Persian dictionary, named '***Parsi Prakash***' was compiled. Jehangir too extended royal patronage to Sanskrit writers and kept them in his court. Jagannath Pandit, Kavindra, Acharya Saraswati and Vedangacharya were famous writers of his court. Jagannath was the Royal poet of Sanskrit in Shah Jehan's Court.

MAJOR BOOKS OF THE MUGHAL ERA

Book	Author	Book	Author
Tuzuki-i-Baburi	Babur	*Ain-e-Akbari*	Abul Fazl
Humayun Nama	Khwand Amair	*Muntakhab-ui-Tawarikh*	Badauni
Danun-i-Himayun	Gulbadan Begum	*Nuriyya-e-Sultaniyya*	Abdul Haqq
Akbar Nama	Sheikh Abul Fazal	*Waqt-e-Hyderabad*	Nimat Khan Ali
Tabaqat-i-Akbari	Khwajah Nizamuddin Ahmad Baksh	*Futuhat-e-Alamgiri*	Ishwar Das
Muntakhabut-ul-Tawarikh	Abdul Qadir Badauni	*Nuskha-e-Dilkusha*	Bhimsen
Tuzuk-i-Jahangiri	Jahangir	*Khulasat-ul-Tawarikh*	Sujan Rai Khatri
Tarikh-i-Alfi	Mulla Daud	*Padshah Namah*	Abdul Hamid Lahori
Masnavi Nala-i-Daman	Faizi	*Padshah Namah*	Mumahad Waris
Iqbalnama-i-Jahangiri	Muhammad Khan	*Shahjahan Namah*	Muhammad Salih
Chahar Chaman	Chandra Bhan Brahman	*Shahjahan Namah*	Inayat Khan
Padshahnama	Abdul Hamid Lahori	*Hamlai-Haidri*	Muhammad Rafi Khan
Alami-i-Salih	Mohamanad Salih	*Namah-e-Alamgiri*	Aquil Khan Zafar
Majmua-ul-Bahrin	Dara Shikoh	*Salinat-ul-Auliya*	Dara Shikoh
Alamgirnama	Munshi Mirza Muhammad Kazin	*Safinat-ul-Auliya*	-do-
Massir-i-Alamgiri	Saqi Mustaid Khan	*Najma-ul-Bahrain*	-do-
		Raqqat-e-Alamgiri	Aurangzeb
		Hasmat-ul-Arifin	Dara Shikoh
		Muntkhbi-ul-Lubat	Kafi Khan

9. MEDIEVAL PERIOD—BHAKTI MOVEMENT AND SUFISM

The arrival of Islam in Indian resulted in a unique mingling of cultural traditions. This mingling led to the growth of a composite culture in the country. Evidences of this contact can be seen in religion, architecture, literature, music and painting.

9.1 SUFISM OR THE SUFI MOVEMENT

Sufism represents the spiritual and mystical dimensions of Islam. The term *Sufi* probably came from the Arabic word *Sof* (wool). This was perhaps due to the result of the old ascetic practice of wearing only a coarse woollen garment.

This movement was first born in Iran when some of the religious scholars and liberal thinkers in that country realised that there was little difference among the various beliefs, such as the *Shia* and the *Sunni* sects. In the realm of ideas, it marks the end of the domination of the *Mutazila* or rationalist philosophy, and the rise of orthodox schools based on the *Quran* and *Hadis (Traditions* of the Prophet and his companions) and of the *Sufi* mystic orders.

SUFISM

- *Sufism* springs from the doctrine of *Wahadat-ul-wajud* or unity of being. This doctrine was propounded by **Ibn-ul-Arabi** *(*1165-1240).
- One of the earliest *Sufis* was a woman saint **Rabia of Basra** who laid great emphasis on love as bond between god and individual soul.
- The *Sufi* orders are widely divided into two : *Ba-Shara,* that is, those who followed the Islamic law and *Be-Shara,* that is, those who were not bound by it. Of the *Be-Shara* movement, only two acquired significant influence : the *Chishti* and *Suhrawardi Silsilas.*

9.2 BHAKTI MOVEMENT

The concept of the *Bhakti* was nothing new to Indians. It is old as the Hindu religion offers three paths for attaining salvation—the *Gyan Marg* or the path of knowledge, *Dharma Marg* or the path of law and the *Bhakti Marg* or the path of devotion to a personal god. There is evidence of this path in holy scriptures like the *Upanishads, Ramayan, Mahabharata, Gita* etc. These scriptures distinctly refer to the two chief principles of unity of God and devotion to a personal god. But it was in the 11th and 12th centuries that the *Bhakti* Movement rose and grew stronger.

The basic principles of the *Bhakti* movement was the loving relationship between the devotee and his personal god. The *Bhakti* saints discarded rituals and sacrifices as modes of worship. Instead, they emphasized the purity of heart and mind as also kindness and love to all as the simple way to the realisation of god. They also discarded the castes, creed and gender based discrimination in the society.

The Bhakti exponents were divided into two groups: *Nirguna Bhakti* and *Saguna Bhakti.*

Main charactcristics of the ***Nirguna Bhakti*** are :

(i) Belief in one Supreme god

(ii) Self surrender to god

(iii) Faith in ***guru*** (master)

(iv) No belief in caste system, idol worship and ritualism;

(v) No attachment to any particular language.

Main characteristics of the ***Saguna Bhakti*** are :

(i) Belief in a particular form of god

(ii) Non-belief in caste system and rituals

(iii) Belief in idol worship

(iv) Popularisation of local languages.

MAIN SUFI ORDERS IN INDIA

Order	Founder	Region	Features
Chisti Order	Shaikh Moin-ud-in Chisti (Hamid-ud-din Nagauri, Qutub-ud-din Bakhtiyar Kaki, Nizam-ud-din Auliya Shaikh Salim)	Ajmer, Uttar Pradesh, Punjab, Bihar, Bengal, Orissa, Deccan	Believed in simplicity and poverty; lived mainly on charity; adotping musical recitations called *sama*; create a mood of nearness to god.
Suhrawardi Order	Shaikh Shihab-ud-din Suhrawardi (Baha-udi-din Zakariya Rukn-ud-din Abul Fath)	North-west India	They did not believe in leading a life of poverty accepted direct service of the state; holding posts ecclesiastical department.
Qadri Order	Shaikh Abdul Qadir Jilani (Shah Nizamat Ullah, Nasir-ud-din Muhammad Jilani)	Sind, Lahore	This order was dominant in Sind and Lahore; Prince Dara Shikoh was its follower.
Naqshbandi Order	Khwaja Baqi Billah, Shaikh Ahmad Sarhindi		They tried to harmonise the doctrines of mysticism; teachings of orthodox Islam.
Other Muslim Sects	Muhammad Madhi, Bayazid Ansri Abdullah Shattari	Jaunpur, Jullunder,	These three sects laid greater stress on the religion rathre than India its form.

PROMINENT EXPONENTS OF NIRGUNA BHAKTI

(i) Guru Nanak : Nanak was born in a Khatri family at Talwandi in the Lahore district in 1469. He spent his life preaching the gospel of tolerance. In order to put an end to the religious conflicts, he laid stress on moral virtues.

TEN SIKH GURUS

(i) Guru Nanak (1469-1539)
(ii) Guru Angad (1539-1552)
(iii) Guru Amardas (1552-1574)
(iv) Guru Ram Das (1574-1581)
(v) Guru Arjun Dev (1581-1606)
(vi) Guru Har Gobind (1606-1644)
(vii) Guru Har Rai (1645-1661)
(viii) Guru Har Kishan (1661-1664)
(ix) Guru Tegh Bahadur (1664-1675)
(x) Guru Gobind Singh (1675-1708)

On his teachings, his followers founded a new religion known as **Sikhism**. Sikh means disciple. Sikhism conceives god as *nirakara* (formless) and recognises god by various names—Rama, Rahim, Rab, Hari, Govinda and Murari. Nanak preached his ideals through *kirtans,* which are collected in the form of a book called *Adi Granth.* He asked his followers to wear ***five K's***—(a) *Kesh* (long hair), (b) *Kangha* (comb), (c) *Kaccha* (a pair of shorts), (d) *Kara* (iron bracelet), and (e) *Kripan* (sword or dagger).

(ii) Kabir : Kabir, a Muslim weaver, was one of the greatest pupils of Ramananda. According to tradition, he was the abandoned child of a Brahmin widow. He grew up as the foster-child of the weaver Niru and his wife. He flourished, most probably, in the end of the fourteenth and early fifteenth century. He composed beautiful verses in Hindi which are still familiar in Northern India. His followers are called *Kabirpanthis* meaning, 'the travellers in the path of Kabir'.

(iii) Raidas : He was a contemporary of Kabir and a fellow-disciple of Ramananda. A cobbler by caste, Raidas composed songs brimming with love and devotion.

(iv) Namdeva: Namdeva was born in 1270. Some of his *abhangas* are included in Guru Granth Sahib.

(v) Ramananda: Ramananda was a great devotee of Sri Rama. He opened his doors to all-upper castes, untouchables, Muslims etc.

FAMOUS DISCIPLES OF RAMANANDA	
Kabir	A weaver
Ravidas or Raidas	A cobbler
Sena	A barber
Sadhana	A butcher

PROMINENT EXPONENTS OF SAGUNA BHAKTI

(i) **Ramanuja :** In 11th century, Ramanuja tried to assimilate Bhakti to the tradition of Vedas. He argued that grace of God was more important than knowledge about him in order to attain salvation. The tradition established by Ramanuja was followed by number of thinkers such as Madhvacharya, Ramananda, Vallabhacharya and others.

(ii) **Jnandeva :** He was progenitor of Bhakti movement in Maharashtra.

(iii) **Ekanath :** He was opposed to caste distinction and evinced greatest sympathy for men of low caste.

(iv) **Tukaram :** He was a farmer's son and a great devotee of *Vitthal.*

(v) **Ramdas :** He established *ashramas* all over India. It was from him that Shivaji received the inspiration to overthrow Muslim authority and found the kingdom.

(vi) **Surdasa :** He was a disciple of famous religious teacher Vallabhacharya. He sang the glory of Krishna's childhood and youth in his *Sursagar*.

(vii) **Tulsi Das :** He composed the famous *Ramacharitamanas.*

NAYANARS AND ALVARS

In South, the *Bhakti* movement was led by a series of popular saints called *Nayanars* and *Alvars.* The chief object of their worship was Shiva and Vishnu respectively. They spoke and wrote in Tamil and Telugu.

10. MEDIEVAL ARCHITECTURE

10.1 ARCHITECTURAL DEVELOPMENTS

The Indo-Islamic architecture manifested the aesthetic heritage of the new Sultans. It included both religious and secular structures. While indigenous architecture is trabeate i.e. the space is spanned by means of beams laid horizontally; the Islamic form is arcuate, whereby arches are used to bridge a space. The dome is the prominent feature of the mosque in contrast to the *Sikhar* of Hindu temples. The Turkish rulers used both the dome and arch method as well as the slab and beam method in their buildings.

In the beginning, the Muslims converted temples and other existing buildings into mosques. Examples of this are the *Quwwat-ul-Islam* mosque near the *Qutab Minar* in Delhi and *Adhai Din ka Jhonpra* at Ajmer. The only new construction in Delhi, was a facade of three elaborately carved arches in front of the deity room (*garbha griha)* which was demolished. For the style of decoration on these arches, they used scrolls of flowers and verses of the *Quran* which were intertwined in a very artistic manner.

The most magnificent building constructed by the Turks in the thirteenth century was the *Qutab Minar.* This tapering tower, originally 71.4 metre high, built by Iltutmish, was dedicated to the Sufi saint, Qutab-ud-Din Bakhtiyar Kaki, who was greatly venerated by the people of Delhi.

The Khalji period saw a lot of building activitis . Alauddin built his capital at Siri, a few kilometres away from the site around the *Qutab.* He added an entrance door to the *Qutab.* This door, which is called the *Alai Darwaza,* has arches of very pleasing proportions. It also contains a dome which, for the first time, was built on correct scientific lines. Ghiyasuddin and Muhammad Tughlaq built the huge palace-fortress complex called *Tughlaqabad.* By blocking the passage of the Yamuna River, a huge artificial lake was created around it.

A striking feature of the Tughlaq architecture was the sloping walls. This is called "batter" and gives the effect of strength and solidity to the building. A second feature of the Tughlaq architecture was the deliberate attempt to combine the principles of the arch and the lintel and beam in their buildings. This is found in a marked manner in the buildings of Firuz Tughlaq.

ARCHITECTURAL LANDMARKS OF THE SULTANATE PERIOD

Structure	Location	Builder
Quwwat-ul-Islam Mosque	Delhi	Qutub-ud-din Aibak
Adhai Din Ka Jhonpra	Ajmer	Qutub-ud-din Aibak
Qutub Minar	Delhi	Iltutmish (founded by Qutub-ud-din Aibak)
Tomb of Hazarat Nizamuddin Aulia	Delhi	Ala-ud-din Khilji
Alai Darwaja	Delhi	Ala-ud-din Khilji
Jamaat Khana Masjid	Delhi	Ala-ud-din Khilji
Tomb of Ghiyas-ud-din Tughlaq	Delhi	Muhammad bin Tughlaq
Tughlaabad Fort	Delhi	Ghiyas-ud-din Tughlaq
Moth Ki Masjid	Delhi	Prime Minister of Sikandar Lodi

HIGHLIGHTS OF SULTANATE ARCHITECTURE

I. The new architecturai features introduced in India by the Turkish Sultans were: (a) dome; (b) the true arch without the support of beam; (c) lofty towers; and (d) the vault.

II. The usage of voussoired arch and dome was established once and for all in the Khilji period. However, the first example of voussoired arch is the tomb of Ghiyas-ud-din Balban.

III. The Tughlaq architecture shows stark simplicity and sobriety with the following features; thick and battered or sloping walls, squich arches for supporting domes, tapering minaret-like buttresses or supports and multi-domed roofs.

IV. Blue-enamelled tiles, the lotus-motif covering the dome and free use of ***guldastas*** are special characteristics of the Lodhi architecture.

PROVINCIAL KINGDOMS DURING AND AFTER THE SULTANATE		
Kingdom	**Capital**	**Founder/Most Important Ruler**
1. Shah Mir dynasty in **Kashmir**	Kashmir	Shah Mirza or Sams-ud-din : Zainul Abidin
2. Sisodia dynasty in **Mewar**	Chittor	Rana Hamir : Rana Kumbha
3. Rathore dynasty in **Marwar**	Jodhpur	Rao Chunda: Rao Jodha and Maldeva
4. Kachhawaha dynasty of **Amber** or **Amer**	Ajmer	Dullah Rao: Hammir Deva
5. Muzaffarshahi dynasty in **Gujarat**	Anhilvada (later Ahmedahad)	Zafar Khan or Muzaffarshah: Ahmad Shah I, Mahmud Begra (Mahmud I) and Bahadur Shah
6. Sultanate of **Bengal**	Gaud	Ilyas Shah: Ala-ud-din Shah
7. Suryavansi or Gajapati dynasty in **Orissa**	Jajnagar	Kapilendra: Kapilendra
8. Khalji dynasty in **Malwa**	Mandu	Dilawar Khan Ghori: Mahmud Khalji
9. Sharqi dynasty in **Jaunpur**	Jaunpur	Malik Sarwar: Ibrahim Shah Sharqi
10. Ahom dynasty in **Kamrup** and **Assam**	Charaideo (later Charqua)	Sukapha: Suhungmung
11. Farukki dynasty in **Khandesh**	Burhanpur	Malik Raja Farukki: Malik Raja Farukki
12. **Bahmani** in **Karnataka**	Gulbarga (later Bidar)	Hasan Gangu Bahman Shah: Firuz shah, Ahmad Shah I
13. **Vijaynagar**	Hastinavati or Hampi	
(i)	**Sangam dynasty**	Harihara I : Harihara I
(ii)	**Suluva dynasty**	Narasimha Suluva: Narasimha Suluva
(iii)	**Tuluva dynasty**	Vira Narasimha: Krishnadeva Raya
(iv)	**Aravidu dynasty**	Penugonda Thirumala: Thirumala

10.2 BAHMANI KINGDOM

The Bahmani kingdom was founded in 1347 by Hasan Gangu, who proclaimed his independence from the sultanate. He reigned under the title of Alu-ud-din Bahmani or Bahman Shah. Gulharga was the capital of Bahmani kingdom. Some of the other notable Bahmani Sultans were: Muhammad Shah I, Firuz Shah, Ahmad Shah (also known as **Wali** due to his association with a *sufi*, Gesu Daraz), Humayun (famous for his minister **Mahmud Gawan**) and Muhammad Shah III. Ahmad Shah shifted the capital from Gulbarga to Bidar.

By the end of the 15th century, Bahmani Kingdom had split in five independent kingdoms: Bijapur, Ahmadnagar, Berar, Bidar and Golconda.

Administration

Mahmud Gawan proved to be the most efficient administrator of the Bahmani kingdom. Gawan founded the four provinces of Gulbarga, Daulatabad, Telengana and Berar to administer efficiently. He divided each of the four provinces into two divisions, placing each division under a separate governor. Thus, the entire kingdom was divided into eight *tarafs,* each governed by a *Tarafdar.*

To strengthen the central administration, Gawan curtailed the powers of the *Tarafdars* or the Governors. Many parganas were converted into crown lands and special district collectors were appointed to collect revenues from central places. Henceforth, all local appointments of consequence were to be made by the Sultan. The provincial armies, too, were to be regularly scrutinised by the Centre. Moreover, only one fort in each province was left in the charge of the Governors, the remaining forts were entrusted to officers and troops appointed by the Sultan. A systematic survey and assessment of the land revenue was ordered to improve the revenue system. The army allowances were increased.

MAHMUD GAWAN

He was the Prime Minister or the Peshwa of Muhammad Shah III between 1463-81. The Bahmani kingdom saw a resurgence under his guidance. His military conquests included Konkan, Goa and the Krishna-Godavari delta. During the reign of Muhammad Shah III, Muhammad Gawan expanded the Bahmani Kingdom as never before.

However, he was a Persian by birth, hence an ***Afaqi*** or ***Gharib***. ***Afaqis*** or ***Gharibs*** were the nobles who were of foreign origins and had migrated from Arab or elsewhere. The rise of *Afaqi* noble was resented by the ***Deccani*** nobles, ie, those who were of indigenous origin. Hence, the Deccani conspired against him and got him executed in 1481.

DECCAN SULTANATE

Following the downfall of the Bahmani kingdom, the following five independent kingdoms emerged inthe Deccan.

1. The Imad Shahi Dynasty of Berar: It was the first principality to defect from the Bahmani dominions. In 1484. Fatullah Khan, Imad-ul-Mulk, the governor of Gawilgarh, one of the two divisions of Berar, proclaimed independence and soon occupied the whole of Berar. He founded the Imad Shahi dynasty which continued to rule, with Elichpur as its capital, till in 1595. It was annexed by the Mughals.

2. The Nizam Shahi Dynasty of Ahmednagar: In 1490, Malik Ahmad, the governor of Junnar, successfully revolted, and established himself as an independent sovereign. He founded the Nizam Shahi dynasty. Frequently embroiled in wars with Bijapur and Golconda, it formed a *Subha* of Akbar's Empire and was finally annexed to the Mughal 1637 under Shahjahan.

3. The Qutb Shahi Dynasty of Golconda: The Golconda kingdom comprised the ruins of the Kakatiya principality of Warangal, and was extensive, fertile and rich in territory. It was founded in 1518 by a Turkish officer, Sultan Quli Qutb Shah, who was appointed the Governor of Golconda by Muhmud Gawan. He moved the capital from Warangal to Golconda. Initially, in spite of the incessant warfare between Bijapur and Ahmednagar, it enjoyed a comparative seclusion. Gradually, however, Golconda too got embroiled in the Deccan politics, fought serious wars against Bijapur and in 1565 joined the Muslim confederacy against the Vijayanagar kingdom.

4. The Barid Shahi Dynasty of Bidar: The kingdom comprised the territory around the Bahmani capital. Qasim Barid, a former minister of Mahmud Gawan, had become its *de facto* ruler as early as 1492. But he and his successor hesitated from assuming formal ranks until 1527. The dynasty lasted till 1619 when, it was annexed by Bijapur.

5. The Adil Shahi Dynasty of Bijapur: The most important of the five kingdoms, Bijapur became an independent kingdom in 1489 AD when its Governor, Yusuf Adil Khan declared independence. He and his successors consistently waged wars against Vijayanagar and the other Muslim neighbours, till his efforts were rewarded in the Battle of Talikota in 1565, AD which rendered a death blow to Vijayanagar.

FIVE INDEPENDENT KINGDOMS IN THE DECCAN

Kingdom	Year	Founder	Dynasty	Annexation
Berar	1484	Fataullah Imad	Imad Shahi Shah	1574 (Ahmednagar)
Bijapur	1489	Yusuf Adil Khan	Adil Shahi	1686 (Mughal)
Ahmadnagar	1490	Malik Ahmad	Nizam Shahi	1633 (Mughal)
Golconda	1518	Quli Shah	Qutb Shahi	1687 (Mughal)
Bidar	1526-1527	Amir Ali Barid	Barid Shahi	1618 (Bijapur)

10.3 Vijayanagar kingdom

Vijayanagar kingdom and the city was founded by **Harihar-I and Bukka-I** (sons of Sangama), who were feudatories of **Kakatiyas** and later became ministers in the court of Kampili. Harihar and Bukka were brought to the centre by Mohammed-bin-Tuglaq, converted to Islam and were sent to south again to control rebellion. Harihara and Bukka founded the Vijayanagar empire in 1336 on the advice of **Vidyaranya.**

Vijayanagar's arch rival was Bahmani with whom it fought over Tungabhadra doab (between Krishna and Krishna-Godavari delta) and Marathwada. Vijayanagar-Bahmani contest was started by Bukka I in 1367 when he attacked the Bahmani fortress at Mudkal. Vijayanagar was ruled by the following four dynasties:

THE SANGAMA DYNASTY (1336-1485)

Harihara I (1336-1356) laid the foundations of Vidyanagar. Bukka I (1356-1379) strengthened the city of Vidyanagar and renamed it Vijayanagar. He restored harmony between the warring *Vaishnavs* and the *Jains*. The Rais of Malabar, Ceylon and other countries kept ambassadors at his court. The greatest achievement of **Deva Raya I** (1406-1422) was his irrigation works, where a dam was built across the Tungabhadra, with canals leading to the city. **Deva Raya II** (1423-1446) was the grandson of Deva Raya I. Ahmad Shah I Bahmani invaded Vijayanagar and exacted a war indemnity. Deva Raya II, the greatest ruler of the Sangama dynasty, began the practice of employing Muslim cavalrymen and archers in the army. He allotted them jagirs, constructed a mosque in Vijayanagar and ordered that a copy of the *Quran* be placed before his throne for the benefit of the Muslims.

Deva Raya II was called *Immadi Deva Raya.* In his inscriptions, he has the title of '*Gajabetekara*' (the elephant hunter). Ceylon paid a regular tribute to him. He had leanings for *Vira Saivism,* yet he tolerated other religions and had members of other sects as his ministers. **Dindima** was his court poet, whereas **Srinatha** was given the title of *Kavi-Sarvabhauma.* Thirty four poets received his patronage.

Abdur Razzak, the envoy of Shah Rukh, visited Vijayanagar during his reign. He is the author *of two Sanskrit works: Mahanataka Sudhanidhi* and a commentary on the *Brahmasutras of Badrayana.*

FIRST USURPATION : THE SALUVA DYNASTY (1485-1505)

Vijayanagar witnessed chaos and disorder after 1465 due to weak rulers. However, the situation was saved by the governor of Chandragiri, Narasimha Suluva, who seized the throne in about 1485 in what is known in history as the **First Usurpation**. Narsimha was succeeded by Timma and Imadi Narsimha who were minors at the time of their coronation. The real power was in the hands of **Narsa Nayak**, who was the Reagent.

SECOND USURPATION : THE TULUVU DYNASTY

Following the death of Narsa Nayak in 1505, his son, Vira Narasimha, succeeded as the reagent. He deposed the Suluva ruler and laid the foundation of the Tuluvu dynasty by what is known in history as the **Second Usurpation**.

Krishnadeva Raya (1509-1529) was the greatest ruler of the Tuluva dynasty. Some of the highlights of his rule are as follows:

- Krishnadeva Raya maintained friendly relations with Albuquerque, the Portugese governor, whose ambassador **Friar Luis** resided in Vijayanagar. He gave Albuquerque permission to build a fort of Bhatkal.
- He built the *Vijaya Mahal* (House of Victory) and expanded the Hazara Rama temple and the Vithal Swami Temple. He took the titles of *Yavanaraja Sthapanacharya* (restorer of the Yavana Kingdom, i.e. Bahmani) and *Abhinava Bhoja.* He is also known as *Andhra-Pitamaha* and *Andhra Bhoja.*
- He was a gifted scholar in both Telugu and Sanskrit, of which only two works are extant: the Telugu work on polity *Amuktamalyada* and the Sanskrit drama *Jambavati Kalyanam.*

THIRD USURPATION : THE ARAVIDU DYNASTY

The Aravidu dynasty was founded by Thirumala II, the brother of Rama Raja, who ruled in the name of Sadasiva Raya. On his failure to repopulate Vijayanagar, he shifted the capital to Penugonda. During his rule, the *Nayaks* became independents. Tirumala then divided his empire into three practically linguistic sections and placed them under his sons.

THE BATTLE OF TALIKOTA (1565)

After the death of Krishnadeva Raya, power passed into the hands of his son-in-low, Rama Raja. An able and ambitious but tactless administrator, he took active interest in the politics of Muslim states of Bijapur, Golconda and Ahmednagar. He supported the one against the other according to his interest. This incensed the Muslim rulers of Ahmednager, Bijapur and Golconda and they jointly fought battle against Vijaynagar in **Talikota or Raksha Tangadi** in February 1565. Ramaraja was defeated and killed. The Battle of Talikota brought an virtual end to the Vijaynagar empire.

REASONS FOR GROWTH OF VIJAYANAGAR EMPIRE

- Growth in agriculture and trade in the territories of Karnataka.
- Chola state was finished. The re-emergence of powerful cheiftainships over portions of Tamil country outside of Cholamandalam firmly established independent bases of competitive power.
- Early Vijayanagar expansion came at the expense of great Hindu kingdoms such as the Hoysala states of Karnataka and the Reddi kingdom of Kondavidu in Andhra.
- These northern warriors drew resources from the newly overrun areas by way of tributes.
- Small warriors of *nayakas* were the leading political figures in the Vijayanagar states and European sources refer to the acquisition and shifting of some part of the resources commanded by them to the capital city in the form of tribute.

FAMOUS TRAVELLERS TO VIJAYANAGAR KINGDOM

Abu Abdullah/Ibn Batuta: A Moroccan traveller, left account of Harihara I's reign in his book *Rehla* also called *Tuhfat-un-Nuzzar fi Gharaib-ul-Amsar Wa Ajaib-ul-Assar.*

Nicolo de Conti: An Italian traveller who visited during the time of Deva Raya I. Left an account in *Travels of Nicolo Conti.*

Abdur Razzak : Ambassador of Shah Rukh of *Samarqand* at the Court of the Zamorin of Calicut. He gives an account of the reign of Devaraya II, in his *Matla us Sadain Wa Majma ul Bahrain.*

Athanasius Nikitin *:* A Russian merchant who described the conditions of the Bahmani kingdom under Muhammad III in his *Voyage to India.*

Ludvico de Vorthema *:* An Italian merchant who visited India in 1502-1508 and left his memoirs in *Travels in Egypt, India, Syria etc.*

Duarte Barbosa (1500-1516): A Portugese, who has given a vivid account of the Vijayanagar government under Krishna Deva Raya in his famous book-*An Account of Countries Bordering the Indian Ocean and their Inhabitants.*

Dominigos Paes: Portugese who spent a number of years at Krishna Deva's court and has given a glowing account of his personality.

Fernao Nuniz: A Portugese writer of 16th century who spent three years in Vijayanagar. (1535-37).

11. THE ADVENT OF EUROPEANS AND THE ESTABLISHMENT OF BRITISH RULE

11.1 THE PORTUGUESE

Vasco-da-Gama Discovers Sea Route to India : India had commercial relations with the countries of the west from time immemorial. But from the seventh century AD, her sea borne trade passed into the hands of the Arabs, who began to dominate the Indian Ocean and the Red Sea. It was from then that the enterprising merchants of Venice and Genos purchased Indian goods. The geographical discoveries of the last quarter of the fifteenth century deeply affected the commercial relations of the different countries of the world and produced far-reaching consequences in their history. Bartholomew Diaz doubled the Cape of Good Hope, or the Stormy Cape, as he called it, in 1487; and Vasco da Gama found out a new route to India and reached the famous port of Calicut on the 17th May, 1498.

On his arrival at Calicut, Vasco da Gama was received by its Hindu ruler, known by the title of Zamorin. The arrival of Vasco da Gama led to the establishment of trading stations at Calicut.

PORTUGUESE CHRONOLOGY

1498: Vasco da Gama found a new route to India and reached the port of Calicut.

1502: Vasco da Gama established a factory at Cochin.

1505: Francis co de Almeida became the first Portuguese governor in India.

1509: Albuquerque succeeded Almeida as governor. Defeat of the combined fleet of Gujarat, Egypt and Zamorin at the hands of Almeida.

1510: Albuquerque captured Goa from Bijapur ruler.

1530: Governor Nino da Cunha transferred his capital from Cochin to Goa.

1534: Diu and Bassein were acquired from Bahadur Shah of Gujarat.

1535: Subjugation of Diu.

1542: Martin Alfonso de Souza became new governor during his governorship. The famous Jesuit Saint Francisco Xaveir arrived in India.

1559: Subjugation of Diu

1612: Loss of Surat to the English

1631: Loss of Hugli to Qasim Khan, a Mughal noblc

1661: Portuguese King presents Bombay to his son-in-law Prince Charles II of England as dowry.

1739: Salsethte and Bassein are lost to the Marathas

Vasco-da-Gama established a factory at Cochin in 1502. He was followed by Alfonso de Albuquerque in 1503. In 1505, the Portuguese decided to appoint a governor to look after their Indian affairs. Francisco de Almeida became the first governor. Albuquerque succeeded him in 1509. Albuquerque was the real founder of the Portuguese empire in the east.

After Albuquerque, the Portuguese began to decline and in the end, they were left only with Goa, Diu and Daman, which they retained till 1961.

11.2 THE DUTCH

The lucrative trade which prospered the Portuguese merchants compelled the jealous Dutch to get direct access to the spice markets in South-East Asia. After undertaking a series of voyages since 1596, they set up a small commercial organisation, named the **United East India Company** in 1602.

- **Formation of the Company :** The Dutch East India Company was formed with powers to make wars, conclude treaties, acquire territories and build fortresses in March, 1602, by a Charter of the Dutch Parliament,
- **Establishment of Factories:** The Dutch set up factories at Masulipatam (1605), Pulicat (1610), Surat (1616), Bimilipatam (1641), K.Arikal (1645), Chinsura (1653), Kasimbazar, Barangore, Patna, Balasore, Negapatam (all in 1658) and Cochin (1663).
- The Dutch replaced the Portuguese as the most dominant power in European trade with the East, including India.
- Pulicat was their main centre in India till 1690, after which Negapatam replaced it.
- The Dutch conceded to English after their defeat in the Battle of Bedera in 1759.

CAUSES OF THE DECLINE OF PORTUGUESE AND DUTCH COMPANIES

A. *Portuguese*

(i) Inefficient successor of Albuquerque
(ii) Corruption in Portuguese administration
(iii) Religious intolerance of the Portuguese
(iv) Rise of Dutch, French and the British

B. *Dutch*

(i) Increasing Anglo-French rivalry
(ii) Growing interference from the Dutch government in the internal affairs of the company
(iii) Dutch government's stress on maintaining its primacy over the affairs of the company rather than focussing on carrying trade
(iv) Unsatisfactory behaviour of the Dutch

11.3 THE FRENCH

In the middle of the seventeenth century Louis XIV's finance minister Colbert formed a **French East India Company** named **Compagnie des Indes Orientales** in 1664. Louis XIV provided the Company with an interest-free loan of 3 million livre. The Company was thus, created and financed by the State. After initial attempts made to colonise Madagascar had proved a failure, the Company undertook a fresh expedition in 1667 under the command of Francis Caron accompanied by Marcara, a native of Ispahan reached India and set up the first French factory at Surat in 1668. The second factory was set up at Masulipatnam in 1669. A factory was also developed at Chandernagar (Bengal) between 1690 and 1692. Two major French trading posts in India were Pondicherry, established in 1674 by Francis Martin, and Chandernagar.

In 1693, the newly built French factory at Pondicherry was captured by the Dutch but by the Treaty of Ryswick between the European powers, there was restoration of mutual conquests and the Dutch returned Pondicherry to the French in 1697.

During the first quarter of the eighteenth century, however, the French Company suffered serious setback for lack of resources and the factories at Surat, Masulipatam and Bantam had to be abandoned. This condition of the French Company continued till 1720.

From after 1742, when Dupleix become Governor of Pondicherry, there was a change in the character and objective of the French Company motive of imperial expansion replaced their former commercial motive. This naturally opened a new chapter in the Anglo-French conflict in India.

11.4 THE ENGLISH

Before the East India Company established trade in India, *John Mildenhall,* a merchant adventurer, was the first Englishman who arrived in India in 1599 by the over land route, ostensibly for the purpose of trade with Indian merchants.

On 31st December, 1600, Queen Elizabeth granted a Charter to the Company named 'The Governor and Company of Merchants of London Trading in the East Indies' the rights to carry on trade with all countries of the East. This company is commonly known as the English East India Company.

CHRONOLOGY OF ENGLISH EAST INDIA COMPANY

1600 - Establishment of the English East India Company.

1608 - Captain William Hawkins visited the Mughal Court of Jehangir.

1609 - Emperor Jehangir issued *farman* permitting the English to establish a factory at Surat.

1613 - The English East India Company's factory was set up at Surat.

1615 - Sir Thomas Roe was successful in obtaining two *farmans* from the Mughal Court confirming free trade with exemption from inland toll.

1616 - The East India Company established its branch factory at Masulipatanam.

1632 - The English obtained the Golden *Farman* with the right to trade in the kingdom of Golkunda for a fixed customs duty, from the Sultan of Golkunda.

1633 - The eastern branch factory of East India Company was established in Hariharpur, Balasore.

1639 - The local king of Madras granted the Company a lease.

1651 - Nawab Shuja-ud-din of Bengal granted the English, the right to carry on their trade on payment of a fixed duty.

1662 - King Charles II of England was given Bombay as dowry after marrying the Portuguese princess.

1667 - The English obtained the royal *farman* to trade in Bengal from the Mughal Emperor Aurangzeb.

1687 - The English East India Company replaced its headquarters from Surat to Bombay.

1691 - The Governor of Bengal gave the English Company *Dastaks* (Free trade passes) on the payment of a fixed duty.

1717 - English obtained a number of trade concessions from the Mughal Emperor Farrukhsiyar after the Emperor was cured of a painful disease by the English Surgeon William Hamilton.

For a few years, the English East India Company confined its activities to the spice trade with Java, Sumatra and the Moluccas. But in 1608 **Captain William Hawkins** came to the court of Jehangir with a letter from James I, king of England, requesting permission for the English merchants to establish in India. But due to vehement opposition of the Portuguese and the Surat merchants, Emperor Jehangir had to change his mind and Hawkin's mission failed. Next year, Jehangir issued a *farman* permitting the English to establish a factory permanently at Surat. In 1615, a British mission under Sir Thomas Roe succeeded in obtaining *firmans* from the Mughal court confirming free trade without liability to pay inland toll. In 1632, the English obtained from the Sultan of Golconda the *Golden farman* granting them the right to trade throughout the kingdom of Golconda on payment of a fixed customs duty of 500 *pagodas* per year. This *farman* was renewed in 1634.

The Company obtained from the Nawab Shuja-ud-din a *farman* in 1651 granting the English the right to carry on their trade on payment of a fixed duty of Rs. 3,000 per year.

12. BRITISH RULE AND ITS IMPACT ON INDIAN ECONOMY

12.1 INTRODUCTION

The commercial rivalry, jealousy, desire to expand their sphere of dominion coupled with the hatred for other nations and the confrontation of these nations in Europe embittered the relations of the trading companies in India. Each of them was trying to expel the other so as to avoid competition for the markets. These commercial enimity soon plunged these European companies into direct conflict with one another. The decline of ruling power of the native Indian kingdom accelerated their desire and they came into open battles against rival companies. For that, they also manipulated the help of the Indian princes who were weak but were still an important head of their states.

12.2 ANNEXATION POLICIES OF THE COMPANY

Doctrine of Lapse : Lord Dalhousie devised a Doctrine of Lapse, according to which if a ruler of the protected state died without leaving a natural heir, his adopted son was not allowed to rule. His state was to be annexed by the British.

Subsidiary Alliance: It was used by Lord Wellesley. Under the Subsidiary Alliance, a king was provided with military security. The Princely states used to remain independent so far as internal matters were concerned but it was not possible to have any outside interference. The British Company's Resident was kept in the court of the Indian king and the Princely states had to pay an annual amount. The Indian ruler could not employ any European to his service without prior approval of the British nor could he negotiate with any other Indian ruler without consulting the governor-general.

ACQUISITIONS OF INDIAN STATES IN BRITISH EMPIRE

(1) **Under Subsidiary Alliance:** Hyderabad (1798), Mysore (1799), Awadh (1801), Peshwa (1802), Bhonsle and Scindia (1803), Udaipur, Jodhpur and Jaipur (1818).

(2) **Under Doctrine of Lapse:** Satara (1848), Jhansi, Sambhalpur of Orissa (1849), Baghat (1850), Jaitpur of Bundelkhand (1849), Udaipur in Rajputana (1852), Jhansi (1853) and Nagpur (1854)

12.3 ANGLO-FRENCH RIVALRY

The trading company's rivalry ousted the Dutch and the Portuguese from the Indian scene. Now, only the English and the French were left to compete with each other for the Indian markets. Between 1740-1760 European wars in which France and England were opponents brought them into conflict in India as well. The political disorders and the decline of imperial authority facilitated their ambition. This was more true for the South India. The Coromandal Coast and its hinterland which was referred to as Carnatic by the Europeans became the scene of a long-drawn contest between the French and the English.

THE CARNATIC WARS

Taking advantage of the mutual discords and selfish motives among the Indian rulers, the English successfully adopted all types of fraudulent means to achieve victory over India. But before it the French and the English were locked in a struggle for economic and political fortune in India, which unfolded in the form of three Carnatic wars between 1740 and 1763 in Southern India.

First Carnatic War (1744-1748) : The hostilities between the English and the French began in the late 18th century.The First Carnatic War was the fallout of the Austrian war of succession, in which France and England were in opposite camps. The English navy under Barnett captured a few French ships. The French Governor, Dupleix, besieged Madras, in 1746 both by land and sea.

The French also unsuccessfully tried to capture Fort St. David, an English possession to the south of Pondicherry. The Nawab of Carnatic sided with the English and sent a large army under Mahfuz Khan to force the French to evacuate Madras. However, a small French army under Captain Paradise defeated the Nawab's army in what is called the Battle of St. Thome.

In 1748, the general war between the England and French ended and, as a part of the peace settlement, Madras was restored to the English by the **Treaty of Aix-la-Chapelle** in 1748 which ended the Austrian war of succession. Under the terms of Treaty Madras was handed back to the English much to the disgust of Dupleix. Though the First Carnatic war ended, the rivalry in trade and over the possessions in India continued and had to be decided one way or the other.

Second Carnatic War (1749-1754) : The Second Carnatic War was closely linked with the dispute of succession in the Nizam Hyderabad and over the Nawabship of Carnatic. The establishment of Chanda Sahib, ally of the French, on the throne of Carnatic was bound to have adverse effect on English trade since the hinterland of Madras would be in the hands of their enemies. Clive was sent with 200 European and 300 Indian soldiers. He captured Arcot, the capital of Carnatic, Chanda Sahib sent about half of his army under his son Raja Sahib to take back Arcot and Clive was besieged there. The timely arrival of Muran Rao, a Maratha chief, enabled Clive to defeat Raja Sahib. Then, Chanda Sahib was forced to raise the seige of Trichinopoly. He fled away and was put to death by the Raja of Tanjore. Thus, Muhammad Ali became the Nawab of Carnatic. Dupleix tried to recover his position but could not do anything. He was recalled in 1754. His successor, Godheau, began to negotiate for peaceful relations with the English and ended warfare with them in 1754 A.D. and he signed the **Treaty of Pondicherry.**

TREATY OF PONDICHERRY, 1754

The Treaty of Pondicherry which brought an end to the Second Carnatic War had the following provisions:

I. Promise of the English and the French companies not to interfere in the internal affairs of Indian rulers.

II. Acceptance to stay of the French army under Bussy at Hyderabad.

III. Return by the English and the French companies of the conquered parts of each other.

IV. Treaty to be finalised only after the approval of the respective governments of the two companies at home.

Third Carnatic War (1756-1763) : The Treaty of Pondicherry proved to be very short-lived. In, 1756, there broke out the well-known Seven Years' War in Europe and before long the two nations began to fight in India also. Thus, the Third Carnatic War was merely an echo of the Seven Years' War in Europe.

The French Government sent a powerful army under the command of Count-de-*Lally* to mitigate the influence of the British in India. Lally captured Fort St. George and decided to attack Madras, but by this time the English had won name and fame by winning the Battle of Plassey in 1757.

In January 1760, the English General, Sir Eyre Coote, defeated the French army under Lally in the **Battle of Wandiwash**. The English captured Pondicherry and Mahe, badly defeating the French.

The war ended in 1763 with the signing of the Treaty of Paris. The third Anglo French conflict proved to be decisive. Although French factories in India were restored, they could no longer be fortified or even adequately garrisoned with troops.

ANGLO-CARNATIC (ARCOT) WARS

- An instance of Anglo French Rivalry.
- First (1746-48). The French besieged Madras. At St. Thome battle, the Nawab of Carnatic's army was defeated by French under Dupliex.
- Treaty of *Aix-La-Chapelle* (1748) ended the War of Austrian Succession.
- Second War (1749-54). Dupleix aligned with Muzaffar Jung (Hyderabad) and Chanda Sahib (Carnatic)
- After initial victoires, Robert Clive emerged victorioius.
- Third War (1758-63) French, Count de Lally captured 'Fort St. David'.
- French were defeated at *Wandiwash (1760)*
- Pondicherry was returned to French by the *Treaty of Paris.*

REASONS FOR THE ENGLISH SUCCESS

I. Naval superiority of the British, facilitating swift movement of the English to and from India

II. Comparatively secure geographical position of England

III. Home government's complete approval to the policies and programmes of the English; little interest of the French government in Indian affairs

IV. Stronger financial position of the British

V. Establishment of the English control over Bengal, one of the richest and most prosperous regions of India then

VI. English control over Bombay and Madras

VII. Lack of coordination between the policy of Dupleix and the French government

VIII. Recall of Bussy from Hyderabad.

12.4 THE BRITISH CONQUEST OF BENGAL

The East India Company secured valuable privileges in 1717 under a royal *farman* by the Mughal Emperor, which had granted the Company the freedom to export and import their goods in Bengal without paying taxes and right to issue passes or *dastaks* for the movements of such goods. The Company servants were also permitted to trade but were not covered by this *farman.* They were required to pay the same taxes as Indian merchants. This *farman* was a perpetual source of conflict between the Company and the Nawabs of Bengal. All the Nawabs of Bengal from Mushid Quli Khan to Alivardi Khan, had objected to the English interpretation of the *farman* of 1717. They had compelled the Company to pay the lump sums to their treasury, and firmly suppressed the misuse of *dastaks.*

Situation was worsened in 1756, when the young and quick tempered Siraj-ud-Daulah succeeded his grandfather, Alivardi Khan.

When the Nawab ordered the English to demolish their fortifications at Calcutta, the British refused to do so. English joined a conspiracy organised by the enemies of the young Nawab to place Mir Jafar on the throne of Bengal, they presented Siraj-ud-Daulah with an impossible set of demands. Both sides realised that a war to the finish would have to be fought between them. They met for the battle on the field of Plassey, 20 miles from Murshidabad, on 23rd June 1757.

BLACK HOLE TRAGEDY, 1756

It is said that 146 English prisoners, held by the Mughals, were crowded into a small chamber that had a single, small window on a June night in 1756. Several of prisoners died of suffocation and wounds. This aroused the indignation of Englishmen in India. However, historians treat this tragedy as a myth rather than reality.

THE BATTLE OF PLASSEY (1757)

The Battle of Plassey was a battle only in name. The major part of the Nawab's army led by the traitors Mir Jafar and Rai Durlabh, took no part in the fighting. The Nawab was forced to flee and was captured and put to death by Mir Jafar's son Miran. The English proclaimed Mir Jafar, the Nawab of Bengal and set out to gather the reward. The

Company was granted undisputed right to free trade in Bengal, Bihar and Orissa. It also received the zamindari of the 24 Parghanas near Calcutta. Mir Jafar paid a sum of Rs. 1,77,00,000 as compensation for the attack on Calcutta to the Company and the traders of the city.

Mir Jafar's treasury was soon emptied by the demands of the Company's officials for presents and bribes. When Mir Jafar hesitated to fulfill their all expectations they forced him in October 1760 to leave the throne in favour of his son-in-law, Mir Qasim, who rewarded his benefactors by granting the Company the zamindari of the districts of Burdwan, Midnapur, and Chittagong and giving handsome presents, totalling 29 lakhs of rupees to the high English officials.

THOSE WHO BETRAYED SIRAJ-UD-DAULA
Jagat Seth : a rich banker **Khadim Khan**: a powerful noble **Manik Chand** : officer in charge of Calcutta **Mir Jaffar** : Commander-in-chief **Omi Chand** : a famous merchant of Calcutta **Rai Durlabh** : Treasurer of Nawab

THE BATTLE OF BUXAR (1764)

Mir Qasim belied English hopes and soon emerged as a threat to their position and designs in Bengal. Mir Qasim was defeated in a series of battles in 1763 and fled to Avadh, where he formed an alliance with Shuja-ud-Daulah, the Nawab of Avadh, and Shah Alam, the fugitive ruler of Mughal Empire. The three allies crashed with the English army under Major Munro at Buxar on 22nd October, 1764 and were thoroughly defeated.

Company became the real master of Bengal atleast from 1765. Its army was in sole control of its defence and the supreme political power was in its hands. The Nawab depended for his internal and external security on the British. As the *Diwan*, the East India Company directly collected its (Bengal, Bihar, Orissa) revenues, while through the right to nominate the Deputy Subedar, it controlled the *Nizamat* or the police and judicial powers.

In May 1765, Robert Clive became the Governor of Bengal for the first time.

Political Implications of the Battle of Buxar: The Battle of Buxar proved to be decisive resulting in the establishment of British sovereignity in Bengal. This battle brought out the political weaknesses and military shortcomings of the Indians and the hollowness of the Mughal Empire.

THE TREATY OF ALLAHABAD (1765)

The Treaty of Allahabad was concluded by Clive with Shuja-ud-Daula and the Mughal Emperor Shah Alam II, according to which the British got the right of free trade in Awadh and they were allowed to keep a British army at the expense of the Nawab of Awadh. Shah Alam II got the districts of Kora and Allahabad and was also given an annual pension of Rs. 26 lakh. In return for this favour, Shah Alam gave the Diwani of Bengal, Bihar and Orissa to the British.

The company, by another treaty, also agreed to pay a sum of 53 lakh rupees per annum in lieu of the right of Nizamat to the minor *Nawab*.

Thus, the company acquired both the *Diwani* as well as *Nizamat* rights over Bengal, Bihar and Orissa.

ROBERT CLIVE
Robert Clive began his career in Madras on an annual salary of 5 pounds per annum. His presence in the successful siege of Arcot gained him adulation and his involvement in the conquest of Bengal made him a cynosure of the British public. He was made the Governor of Bengal twice—from 1757-1760 and 1765-1767. As the Governor of Bengal, he made huge fortunes. He established a Dual System of Government for the Bengal province.

DUAL SYSTEM OF ADMINISTRATION IN BENGAL (1765-1772)

Under this system, the administration was divided between the Company and the Nawab but the whole power was actually concentrated in the hands of the Company. This complex system remained in practice during the period from 1765 to 1772.

Under this system, Clive gave the responsibility of collecting *Diwani* to the Indians and appointed two deputy *diwans* (Mohammad Raza Khan for Bengal and Raja Shitab Roy for Bihar). For *Nizamat* functions (police and judicial) the British gave the additional responsibility of deputy *Nazim* to Mohammad Raza Khan. The deputy *Nazim* could not be remove without the consent of the company. Thus, although the responsibility for administration—*Diwani* as well as *Nizamat*–was exercised through Indian agencies, the company acquired real power. Under dual system, the administration was theoretically divided between the company and the Nawab but the whole power was actually concentrated in the hands of the company. Thus the system was very advantageous for the company: *it had power without responsibility.*

In 1772, Warren Hastings put an end to this Dual System.

12.5 THE ANGLO-MARATHA RIVALARY

The third Peshwa Balaji Baji Rao could not withstand the shock of the defeat of the Marathas in the **Third Battle of Panipat** and died on June 23, 1761. He was succeeded by his son Madhav Rao. He kept in check the ambition of his brother Raghunath Rao, maintained unity among the Maratha chiefs and nobles and very soon recovered the power and prestige of the Marathas which they had lost in the Third Battle of Panipat. The English became conscious of the growing power of the Marathas and wanted to crush their re-establishment. They got this opportunity very soon after the death of Madhav Rao in 1772.

THE FIRST ANGLO-MARATHA WAR (1775-1782)

The primary cause of the first Maratha war was the interference of the English in the internal affairs of the Marathas. Peshwa Madhav Rao was succeeded by his younger brother, Narain Rao. His uncle, Raghunath Rao, wanted to become the Peshwa and got him murdered. The great Maratha chiefs took up the cause of Madhav Rao Narain, the posthumous son of Narain Rao. Raghunath Rao, approached the English for help.

Raghunath Rao or Raghoba concluded with the Bombay council, the **Treaty of Surat** in March 1775. Under this treaty Raghoba promised to hand over Bassein and **Salsette** and a few islands near Bombay to the British. **This treaty** was not approved by the Calcutta Council and a new treaty – **Treaty of Purandar** – was signed in 1776. This treaty accepted Madhav Rao II as new Peshwa. This was followed by the **Treaty of Salbai** (1782) and the **Treaty of Bassein.**

Treaty of Salbai : This treaty was signed between Warren Hastings and Mahadji Scindia . Under this treaty Salsette and Bassein were given to the British. Raghunath Rao was pensioned off. The treaty established the British influence on Indian politics.

The Treaty of Bassein is regarded as a very important step towards the establishment of the English dominance over India. This treaty was made between the last Peshwa of the Marathas, Baji Rao II and the English on December 31, 1802. The main provisions of this Treaty were the recognition of Peshwa's claim in Poona, acceptance of Subsidiary Alliance by Baji Rao II and reliquishing of all rights to Surat by Baji Rao to the British.

THE SECOND ANGLO-MARATHA WAR (1803-1805)

For Marathas, Treaty of Bassein was nothing short of surrender of national honour. Holkar and Scindia stopped fighting. Scindia and Bhonsle combined but Holkar and Gaikwad remained aloof. Scindia and Bhonsle were asked by the English to withdraw their troops to the north of the Narmada River but they refused. It led to war. Both Scindia and Peshwa had accepted the sovereignty of the English. The Scindia and the Bhonsle entered into the subsidiary alliance by concluding the **Treaty of Surje-Arjangaon** and the **Treaty of Deogaon** respectively. Now Holkar alone was left in the field who still avoided their supremacy. Wellesley, now turned his attention towards Holkar, but Yeshwant Rao Holkar proved more than a match for the British. The company made peace with Holkar in January 1806 by the **Treaty of Rajghat** giving back to the latter the greater part of his territories.

THE THIRD ANGLO-MARATHA WAR (1817-1818)

Marathas made a desperate last attempt to regain their independence and old prestige in 1817. This led in organising a united front of the Maratha chiefs and was taken over by the Peshwa who was smarting under the rigid control exercised by the British Resident. However, once again the Marathas failed to evolve a concerted and well-thought out plan of action. The Maratha confederacy was altogether destroyed. Now the British Government became the supreme and paramount authority in India.

ANGLO-MARATHA TREATIES AT A GLANCE

Treaty of Surat, 1775; was signed by Raghunath Rao wherein he promised to hand over Bassein and Salsette and a few islands near Bombay to the British.

Treaty of Purandhar, 1776; was signed by Madhav Rao II. The Company got a huge war indemnity and retained Salsette.

Treaty of Salbai, 1782; was signed by Mahadji Scindia whereby the British influence in Indian politics and mutual conflicts increased amongst the Marathas.

Treaty of Bassein, 1802; was signed between Baji Rao II. This treaty gave effective control of not only Maratha but also Deccan regions to the Company.

Treaty of Deogaon, 1803; by Bhonsle assured British supremacy over the Maratha kingdom.

Treaty of Surji-Arjangaon, 1803 by Daulat Rao Scindia assured the same.

CAUSES OF THE DEFEAT OF THE MARATHAS

There were several reasons for the defeat of the Marathas in their war against the English. Important among them are as follows:

I. Lack of capable leadership

II. Military weakness of the Marathas

III. Mutual bitterness and lack of cooperation among Maratha chiefs.

IV. Lack of a sound economic system; no provision for the proper collection of *Chauth* and *Sardeshmukhi*

V. Lack of cohesive political outlook

VI. Taking the assistance of the Pindaris

VII. Non-involvement in public welfare activities in the conquered territories

VIII. Lack of cordial relations with other princes and Nawabs of India

IX. Failure in estimating correctly the political and diplomatic strength of the British.

12.6 CONQUEST OF MYSORE

The First Anglo-Mysore War (1766-1769) : The English were Conscious of Hyder Ali's increasing power in the south. Therefore, they joined hands with the Nizam of Hyderabad and the Marathas, who were also jealous of Hyder's growing strength. The English forces attacked Mysore simultaneously from Bombay and Madras. But they were defeated by Hyder and forced to sign the **Treaty of Madras** in 1769. Under this treaty, both sides restored each other's conquest and promised mutual help in case of attack by a third party. When Hyder Ali was attacked by the Marathas in 1771, the English, according to the promise they had made, did not come to former's help. This led Hyder Ali to distrust and dislike them.

The Second Anglo-Mysore War (1780-1784) : In 1778, English in India seized the French settlements including Mahe, a port which was very useful to Hyder Ali for the entry of supplies. He prompted Hyder Ali to declare war. He inflicted a severe defeat on the English forces compelling them to flee Madras with French assistance. The port of Kadnoor was captured.

Luckily for the English, Hyder Ali died in December 1782. He was succeeded by his son Tipu Sultan who carried on the war and captured the Fort of Badnur in 1783.

The second Anglo-Mysore War, in which the English forces were led by **Sir Eyre Coote**, ended inconclusively with the signing of the **Treaty of Mangalore** in 1784. Under this treaty both parties agreed to return the conquered land of each other.

HIGHLIGHTS OF THE REIGNS OF HYDER ALI AND TIPU SULTAN

Hyder Ali

I. Hyder become the Sultan of Mysore after the death of Nanjaraj, who had usurped power reducing its king Chikka Krishna Raj (belonging to the Wodeyar dynasty).

II. He took steps to train his army on European lines and preferred infantry to equestrian troops.

III. He set up a modern artillery.

IV. He won Sera, Hoskote, Dod, Bellapur, Nandidurg, Gudi Banda, Kodi Konda, Bednur (renamed as Haider Nagar) and Sunda (which included two coastal cities of Coonoor and Mangalore.)

Tipu Sultan

I. Introduction of a new system of coinage, new scales of weights and measures.

II. Improvisations in the fields of agriculture, trade and commerce.

III. Abandonment of the custom of giving *jagirs* and reduction in the hereditary possessions of the *poligars*.

IV. Missions to France and Constantinopoe to manage some aid for the state but without success.

V. Organisation and training to army on European lines; Arming the infantry with rifles.

VI. Attempt to establish a navy on modern lines for which two dockyards were established.

VII. Check on the *jagirdars* and *poligars* by reducing the jagirs

VIII. Collection of many books on diverse subjects and setting up a big library

IX. Support to the French soldiers in setting up a Jacobin club in Serinagpatnam in 1797.

X. Setting up of a Board of Admiralty

XI. Plantation of the Tree of Liberty at Serinagpatnam

XII. Grant of funds for the repair of Sringeri Temple and installation of the image of Goddess *Sharda*

The Third Anglo-Mysore War (1789-1792): War between the two again began in 1789 and ended with Tipu's defeat in 1792. Even though, Tipu fought with exemplary bravery, Lord Cornwallis, the then Governor General, had succeeded through shrewd diplomacy in isolating him by winning over the Marathas, the Nizam, and the rulers of Travancore and Coorg.

The Third Mysore War came to an end by the **Treaty of Srirangapatam** in March, 1792. Tipu Sultan had lost half of his territory as a result of Third Mysore War and was burning with revenge. He wanted to get back his territory and, to achieve that objective, he carried on negotiations with the French and Zanuan Shah of Kabul.

The Fourth Anglo-Mysore War (1799): After making Subsidiary Alliance with the Nizam, Wellesley asked Tipu Sultan to accept the same but he refused. This led to war, Mysore was attacked from two sides. The main army under General Harris supported by Nizam's subsidiary force under Arthur Wellesley attacked Mysore from the east, while another army advanced from Bombay. Tipu died defending Seringapattam in 1799, making the English the master of Mysore. As a matter of formality, prince Krishna, a boy of the Wodeyar family, was placed on the throne and a subsidiary alliance was imposed.

TREATIES SIGNED BY HYDER ALI AND TIPU SULTAN

❖ **Treaty of Madras,** 1769, restored the conquered territories to their respective owners.

❖ **Treaty of Mangalore,** 1784, restored the conquered territories mutually and liberated war prisoners.

❖ **Treaty of Srirangapatanam,** 1792 was signed by Tipu Sultan by which he had to cede half of his territory to the Company and paid a huge war reparation.

12.7 ANNEXATION OF PUNJAB

Ranjit Singh, the chief of the *Sukarchakiya misl* (one of the 12 *misls* or confederations of Punjab), conquered Lahore in 1799. In 1805, he also snatched Amritsar from the Bhangi *Misl.* He attacked the areas across the river Sutlej and brought many sikh chieftains under his suzerainty. Soon Ranjit Singh took over Multan, Kashmir and Peshawar also. However, he signed the **Treaty of Amritsar,** also called the **Treaty of Perpetual Friendship,** in 1809 under which he accepted the East India Company's greater right over the cis-Sutlej territories.

HIGHLIGHTS OF RANJIT SINGH'S ADMINISTRATION
I. Training of army on European lines with the help of French officers Ventura and Allard.
II. Setting up an artillery unit.
III. Introduction of payment of monthly salary to the soldiers.
IV. Appointment of Fakir Aziz-ud-din, a Muslim, as Foreign Minister.
V. Appointment of Dina Nath, a Hindu, as Finance Minister.
VI. Establishment of a special court at Lahore where Maharaja himself heard cases and passed judgements.
VII. Establishment of a well organised state.
VIII. Shelter to the Afghan King. Shah Shuja, who had been pushed out of his country (the Afghan king gave ***Kohinoor*** diamond to Ranjit Singh.)

The death of Maharaja Ranjit Singh in June 1839 was followed by political instability and rapid changes of government in the Punjab. Selfish and corrupt leaders came to the front. Ultimately, power fell into the hands of the brave and patriotic but utterly indisciplined army. This led the British to look greedily across the Sutlej upon the land on the five rivers even though they had signed a treaty in 1809.

The First Anglo-Sikh War (1845-1846) : The decisive battle was fought at Sobraon on February 10 1846 and the Sikhs under Ranjit Singh Majithia were routed. The English then crossed the Sutlej on February 13 and captured the capital of Lahore on February 20.

The Sikhs were defeated due to treachery and half heartedness of their leaders.

The war came to an end by the **Treaty of Lahore** which was signed on 9th March, 1846. This treaty left the Sikhs with no capacity for resisting the English. Another treaty was made with the Sikhs on 16th December, 1846, this treaty is known as **'Second Treaty of Lahore'** or the **Treaty of Bhairowal.**

THE TREATY OF LAHORE (1846)
I. The territories lying to the south of the river Sutlej were given to the company.
II. The Sikh committed to pay 1.5 crore rupees to the company as war indemnity.
III. The company was given control over the mountainous areas between the Beas and the Indus rivers which included Kashmir and Hazarah.
IV. **Rani Jindan Kaur** was made the Regent of the state and **Lal Singh** as the *Wazir* of the Maharaja. Sir Henry Lawrence was appointed as the Resident of Lahore.

The Second Anglo-Sikh War (1848-1849) : The second Anglo-Sikh war began in 1848 as the Sikhs were feeling humiliated due to their defeat in the first Anglo-Sikh war. However, the immediate cause was the rebellion of Mulraj, Governor of Multan, against the company. This provided the new Governor-General Lord Dalhousie, a chance to interfere in the affairs of Punjab and annex Punjab in the British empire.

The English and the Sikh forces fought at Ramnagar, Chillianwala and Gujarat. The battle at Gujarat under the command of Sir Charles Napier was decisive. Punjab was annexed to the British dominion in March 1849. Dalip Singh, the minor son of Ranjit Singh, and his mother, Rani Jindan, were pensioned off and sent to England.

12.8 THE ANGLO-NEPAL RELATIONS

The British acquired the districts of Gorakhpur and Basti from the *Nawab* of Awadh in 1801. This brought the boundary of Nepal, a powerful *Gurkha* state, to touch the British frontier. Several battles were fought between the British and the *Gurkha* in 1814. The Gurkhas were forced to sign the **Treaty of Sagauli (1816).** Under the Treaty, the *Gurkhas* gave up their claim over the Tarai region and ceded the Kumaon and Gurwal areas to the British. They also agreed to keep a British Resident at Kathmandu and not to employ any other foreigner in their services other than the English.

Another treaty, the **Treaty of Chogyal (1817)** was signed between the English and Nepal. Governor-General Lord Hastings handed over the territory lying between the Tista and the Mechirivers to Nepal. This created an effective barrier between the British territories and Nepal. The treaty also ended the domination of Nepal over Sikkim for the future.

12.9 THE ANGLO-BURMA RELATIONS

Two Anglo-Burma Wars were fought in the first half of the 19th century.

First Anglo-Burmese War (1824-26) : The Burmese subjugated Assam in 1821-22 and confronted the British all along their north-east frontier. In 1824, Lord Amherst declared war on Burma which lasted for two years. The peace was conclued in 1826, when the Burmese king ceded the provinces of Arakan and Tenasserim, withdrew from Assam and recognised the independence of Manipur. The king also agreed to admit a British envoy at his court.

Second Anglo-Burmese War (1852) : The new Burmese king Tharrawaddy, who usurped the throne in 1837, adopted an unfriendly attitude towards the British and started violating the agreements reached after the first war. In 1852, British forces under the General Godwin, reached Rangoon before storming many cities. Dalhousie himself went to Rangoon later that year and occupied Pegu or Lower Burma. Hostilities ended with the accession of king Mindon in 1853. Burma opened herself to British trade and admitted a British Resident.

12.10 THE ANGLO-PINDARIS WAR

The Pindaris were a group of free-booters who survived mainly on systematised plunder. They were mostly active in the areas of Rajputana and the Central Provinces. After the end of the Anglo-Nepalese war, Lord Hastings turned to deal with these disturbing elements, mostly because the Pindaris had recently carried their raids into British territory and were also enlisted as mercenaries in the armies of the hostile Maratha chiefs.

Under the command of Thomas Hislop and Lt. John Malcolm, the British troops succeeded in expelling the Pindaris from Malwa and across the Chambal in the end of 1817. Its important leaders like Karim Khan surrendered on 18th February, 1818.

12.11 THE SUPPRESSION OF PATHANS

Pathans were more organised than Pindaris, who were banded together for the purpose of preying on government and powerful chiefs. They grew in power under the leadership of Amir Khan and Muhammad Shah Khan and had also served some of the Rajputs and Maratha chiefs of the time. The Company's Government decided to detach this powerful Pathan chief from the other predatory bands, and after some negotiations, persuaded Amir Khan on 9th November 1817. He was recognised as the Nawab of Tonk and was brought to the Company's side and was a helpful ally of the English for the suppression of Pindaris.

12.12 THE ANNEXATION OF AVADH

The Nawab of Avadh had many heirs and could not therefore be covered by the Doctrine of Lapse. Some other pretext had to be found for depriving him of his dominions. Nawab Wajid Ali Shah was accused of having misgoverned his state and of refusing to introduce reforms. His state was therefore annexed in 1856.

GOVERNOR-GENERALS AND VICEROYS

12.13 INDIAN UNDER GOVERNOR-GENERALS

Warren Hastings (1772-1785) : Highlights of his regime are as follows :

Administrative Reforms: End of the Dual System; shifting of treasury from Murshidabad to Calcutta.

***Revenue Reforms*:** Collection of revenue was taken over by the Company.

Judicial Reforms: Zamindars were deprived of their judicial powers; establishment of civil and criminal courts in each district.

Social Reforms: In 1781, he founded the Calcutta Madrasa for promotion of Islamic studies.

This was the first educational institution established by the Company's Government.

Impeachment: Warren Hastings tendered his resignation in protest against the Pitts India Bill in 1785. He was accused for the Rohilla War; Nand Kumar's murder; the case of Chet Singh and accepting of bribes. His impeachment lasted for seven years from 1788 to 1795. He was exonerated of all charges.

Sir John Macpherson, (1785-1786): He held the post temporarily.

Lord Cornwallis (1786-1793). Highlights of his regime are as follows :

Permanent Settlement of Bengal The land was given on permanent basis to the *zamindar* in 1793, instead of giving it to the highest bidder each year. This system brought prosperity to both the Company and the zamindars at the cost of the common peasantry.

Judicial Reforms: Reorganisation of the Revenue Courts; reorganisation of the Criminal Courts; depriving the Collectors of the judicial functions; compilation of the Cornwallis Code.

Police Reforms: Depriving *zamindars* of their police functions; establishment of the *thanas.*

Sir John Shore (1793-1798): He followed a policy of non-intervention.

Sir A. Clark (1798): He held the post temporarily.

Lord Wellesley, 1798-1805: He is famous for introducing *Subsidiary Alliance System*. He opened a college to train the Company's servants in Calcutta. That is why he is also called the *Father of the Civil Services in India.*

Lord Cornwallis (1805): Appointed for another term, he, however died very soon.

Sir George Barlow (1805-1807) : An important event was the Mutiny of Vellore in 1806 in which the Indian soldiers killed many English officers.

Lord Minto I (1807-1813) : His rule is famous for a treaty with Shah of Persia and Treaty of Amritsar (1809) with Ranjit Singh. He sent Sir Charles Metcalfe to the court of Ranjit Singh.

Marquess of Hastings (1813-1823): He was the first to appoint Indians to the high jobs of responsibility. The first vernacular newspaper *Samachar Patrika* began to be published during his time.

John Adam (1823): He held the post temporarily.

Lord Amherst (1823-1828): His reign is known for the first Anglo-Burmese War (1824-26) and Mutiny of Barrackpur (1824).

William Bayley (1818): He held the post temporarily.

Lord William Bentinck (1828-1835): Following are the highlights of his regime :

Administrative and Judicial Reforms: Abolition of provincial courts of appeal and circuit; powers of the Magistrates increased; appointment of Indians as judges; replacement of Persian by vernaculars as court language; introduction of the jury system; Sadar Diwani Adalat and Sadar Nizamat Adalat at Allahabad; codification of laws.

Educational Reforms: English accepted as the medium of instruction after the famous Macaulay's recommendation; Medical College at Calcutta in 1835.

Social Reforms: Abolition of *sati* in 1829; suppression of *thuggee* in Central India; banning of female infanticide; banning of human sacrifice; reform in the Hindu Law of Inheritance.

By the Charter Act of 1833, the Governor-General of Bengal was made the Governor-General of India. Thus, Bentinck became the first Governor-General of India.

Sir Charles Metcalfe (1835-36): He held the post temporarily. He removed the restrictions on the vernacular press.

Lord Auckland (1836-42): Important events of his regime included the outbreak of first Afghan War and the signing of a Tripartite Treaty among the English, Ranjit Singh and Shah Shuja of Afghanistan.

Lord Ellenborough (1843-1844): His period is known for the end of the First Afghan War, annexation of Sindh to the British Empire (1843).

William Bird (1844): He held the post temporarily.

Lord Hardinge (1844-1848): The most important event of his period is First Sikh War (1845-1846).

Lord Dalhousie (1848-1856): He was the youngest to hold the office of the Governor-General. He is famous for the *Doctrine of Lapse*. The Second Burmese War, 1852, took place because of Lord Dalhousie's desire to exclude all European power from Burma. The Second Anglo-Sikh War ended Sikh power and Punjab was annexed.

Highlights of his regime are :

Administrative Reforms: Separate Lieutenant-Governor appointed for Bengal; Simla made the summer capital.

Military Reforms: Artillery Headquarters moved from Calcutta to Meerut; Army Headquarters shifted to Simla; formation of Gurkha Regiments.

Railways: First Railway line was laid from Bombay to Thana, in 1853.

Post and Telegraph: Reforming the defects of the Postal System and linking all the important towns telegraphically.

Education: Sir Charles Wood's Despatch on Education (1854) recommended the setting up of universities in Calcutta, Bombay and Madras. In 1853, competitive examination for the Indian Civil Services began.

Lord Canning (1856-1858): Annexation of Avadh; enactment of Hindu Widow Remarriage Bill, 1857; establishment of universities at Calcutta, Madras and Bombay; the revolt of 1857 were some of the important events during his stint as Governor-General.

12.14 INDIA UNDER VICEROYS

Lord Canning (1858-1862) : Following the Queen's proclamation of 1858, transferring the Government from the company to the British Crown, Lord Canning was made the first viceroy of India.

Important developments in his regime were as follows :

Financial Reforms: A 5% income tax was imposed on all earning beyond five hundred rupees a year.

Judicial Reforms: Penal Code was prepared by incorporating the suggestions earlier made by the First Law Commission headed by Lord Macaulay. High Courts were set up at Calcutta, Bombay and Madras under the provisions of the Indian High Courts Act of 1861. By a special Act passed in 1861, a separate Police Department was set-up in every province.

Lord Elgin (1861-1863): The most important event of his time was the suppression of the *Wahabi* Tribe of the fanatic Muslims inhabiting the North-West Frontier.

Lord John Lawrence (1864-1869): An important event of his time was war against Bhutan in 1865. The Punjab and Oudh Tenancy Act, 1868, was enacted. Two severe famines hit India; first in 1800 in Orissa and the second in 1868-69 in Bundelkhand and Rajputana. A Famine Commission was set up under the chairmanship of **Sir Henry Campbell**. The Afghan policy of Lord Lawrence is commonly known as the *Policy of Masterly Inactivity*. Submarine, telegraphy system was opened in 1865 between India and Europe.

Lord Mayo (1869-1872): For the first time in the Indian history a census was held in 1871. A college was set up at Ajmer to impart suitable education to the sons of the Indian princes. Subsequently, this college came to be known as the 'Mayo College'. An Agricultural Department was set-up. In 1872, a convict, Sher Ali, stabbed him to death at Port Blair.

Lord Northbrooke (1872-1876): The main events of his period were : desposition of Gaekwad in 1874; the Kuka movement; visit of Prince of Wales; abolition of income tax; famine in Bihar and Bengal in 1873-1874.

Lord Lytton (1876-1880): Main events of his viceroylty were (i) Famine of 1876-1878; Famine Commission was appointed in 1878 headed by **General Richard Strachey**. (ii) The Delhi Durbar, January 1, 1877, was held to decorate Queen Victoria with the title *Kaiser-i-Hind.* (iii) The Vernacular Press Act, 1878 was passed, putting several curbs on the vernacular newspapers; (iv) Indian Arms Act, 1878, forbade the Indian people from keeping or dealing in arms without the permission of the Government. (v) Foundation of the Mohammedan Anglo-Oriental College was laid by Lord Lytton in 1877 at Aligarh. (vi) Statutory Civil Service in 1879. It was also laid down that the candidates had to appear and pass the civil service examination which began to be held in England. The maximum age for these candidates was reduced from 21 to 19 years.

Lord Ripon (1880-1884) : Important events during Ripon's stint as viceroy were as follows: (i) Repeal of Vernacular Press Act, 1882, (ii) Resolution in 1882 for institution of local self-government in India; (iii) constitution of the Hunter commission on education (1882); (iv) the maximum age for admission to civil service raised to 21; (v) Enactment of the first factory Act (1881); and (vi) Introduction of the Ilbert Bill which would authorize Indian judges to hear cases against the Europeans as well.

Lord Dufferin (1884-1888): His period witnessed the third Anglo-Burmese War which led to annexation of upper Burma. Three Tenancy Acts were passed to give greater security of tenure to the tenants.

Lord Lansdowne (1888-1894): Major developments during his regime are: (i) Enactment of second Factory Act (1891), (ii) Demarcation of the Indo-Afghan border (Durand Line); and (iii) Second Indian Council Act (1892).

Lord Elgin II (1894-1899): A bubonic plague in Bombay in 1896 and severe drought at Bikaner and Hissar district were some of the important events of his period.

Lord Curzon (1899-1905): Highlights of his viceroylty are as follows : (i) Lord Curzon set up a Famine Commission (ii) The Punjab Land Alienation Act of 1900, prohibited the sale of agricultural lands or its attachment in execution of a decree. (iii) Agricultural banks were established. (iv) In 1904, the Co-operative Credit Societies Act was passed. (v) The Department of Agriculture was established in 1901. (vi) He founded an Agricultural Research Institute at Pusa (vii) A Commission was appointed in 1901 to consider the problem of irrigation. (viii) In order to preserve and protect ancient monuments of India, he passed the Ancient Monuments Protection Act, an Archaeological Department was established in 1901. (ix) He set-up a Police Commission under the Chairmanship of Sir Andrew Frazer in 1902. (x) A Criminal Investigation Department was opened in each province. In 1901, the Imperial Cadet Corps was set up. (xi) Lord Curzon appointed a University Commission under the Chairmanship of his Law Member, Sir Thomas Raleigh, and passed the Indian Universities Act of 1904. (xii) The most controversial decision of Curzon was the partition of Bengal in 1905.

Lord Minto II (1905-1910) : His stint as viceroy is famous for the Minto-Morley Reforms of 1909 which provided for separate electorate to Muslims.

Lord Hardinge II (1910-1916): In honour of King George V and Queen Mary of England, a Coronation Darbar was held at Delhi. In 1911, the capital of the country was announced to be shifted from Calcutta to Delhi. In 1912, Delhi became the new capital. When Lord Hardinge was heading a procession through the Chandni Chowk in his new capital, some extremist revolutionaries threw a bomb on him. The Viceroy himself escaped unhurt. The First World War broke out in 1914. In 1916, Lord Hardinge laid the foundation of the Benaras Hindu University. Madan Mohan Malaviya was the Founder-Chancellor of this university.

Lord Chelmsford (1916-1921): Enactment of the Government of India Act, 1919 (Montague-Chelmsford Reforms) which introduced dyarchy in the provinces; enactment of Rowlatt Act (1919); the Jallianwala Bagh Tragedy (1919); and the beginning of the Non-Cooperation Movement were some of the important events of his period.

Lord Reading (1921-26) : End of the Non-Cooperation Movement (1922); arrival of the Prince of Wales (1921); and outbreak of the Moplah Revolt (1921) were some of the important events of his period.

Lord Irwin (1926-31) : The Viceroylty of Irwin is known for: (a) appointment of Simon Commission in 1928; (b) passing of the resolution for complete independence (*purna swarajya*) in 1929; (c) launching of the civil Disobedience movement; (d) Gandhi-Irwin Pact in 1931; (e) first Round Table Conference (1930).

Lord Wellingdon (1931-1936): Important events were : The Second Round Table Conference, 1931; restarting of the Disobedience Movement, 1931; the Communal Award, 1932; the Poona Pact, 1932; the Third Round Table Conference; 1932, the Government of India Act of 1935; earthquake in Bihar on January 15, 1934.

Lord Linlithgow (1936-43): Highlights of his reign are: (i) beginning of the Second World War; (ii) longest reign as viceroy of India; (iii) coming into force of the Government of India Act 1935 with provinces going to elections; (iv) arrival of the Cripps Mission; (v) beginning of the Quit India Movement; and (vi) Great Famine of Bengal (1943)

Lord Wavell (1943-1947): His period is famous for : the Simla Conference, 1945: arrival of the Cabinet Mission, 1946; the Constituent Assembly boycotted by the Muslim League which launched the heinous 'Direct Action Day' on August 16, 1946; the Interim Government under Pt. Jawaharlal Nehru's leadership; Attlee's Declaration that his government was intended to hand over the administration of India to her people before June 1948, even if no agreement was reached between the Congress and the Muslim League.

Lord Mountbatten, March 1947-June 1948. Declaration of 3rd June, 1947; Indian Independence Act; Partition of the country between two independent states of India and Pakistan with Lord Mountbatten and Mr. M.A. Jinnah as their respective Governor-Generals.

THE BRITISH ADMINISTRATIVE STRUCTURE IN INDIA

12.15 ACTS FOR EAST INDIA COMPANY'S ADMINISTRATION IN INDIA

Until 1765, the East India Company was functioning under the Royal charter issued by Queen Elizabeth in 1600. There were two committees in England—'Court of Proprietors' and 'Court of Directors'–to run the affairs of the company smoothly. The court of Proprietors comprised all the shareholders of the company. Of the members of the court of Proprietors, 24 members constituted the Court of Directors, which executed all the rules and regulations framed by the Court of proprietors.

The situation, however, changed with the signing of Treaty of Allahahad (1765), which gave the company the Diwani of Bihar, Bengal and Orissa. With the acquisition of this right, the Company also became a political power. Lord Clive established Dyarchy or Dual Government in Bengal which lasted till 1772. After the end of the Dual Government system, the British Parliament began to enact laws from time to time defining administrative set up of the company. A brief description of these law is given as under.

(i) Regulating Act, 1773: This Act made changes in the Constitution of the Court of Directors of the Company and subjected their actions to the supervision of the British Government. It was an Act to regulate the affairs of the Company in India. Through this Act, the Governor of Bengal was given the new title of 'Governor-General' for all the British territories in India. Provision was made for an Executive Council of four members to aid and advise the Governor-General who was to carry out the decisions taken by the majority of his Council. A Supreme Court was set up at Calcutta, directly under the British Crown.

(ii) Pitts' India Act of 1784 : The Act of 1784 concerned itself mainly with the Company's Home Government in London. It established a Board of Commissioner's to supervise the civil and military government of the Company (Board of Control) which consisted of Chancellor of Exchequer, a Secretary of State and four Privy Councillors appointed by the King. The Governor-General was to have three Councillors, one of whom was to be the Commander-in-Chief. The Board of Control had no independent executive power. The Act placed the civil and military government of the Company in due subordination to the Government in England. Lord Cornwallis, a personal friend of Pitt the Younger who surrendered Yorkshire to the rebellious Americans was appointed the Governor-General in 1786.

(iii) Charter Act, 1793 : After this Act, the Company got monopoly of trade with India, for another twenty years. The salaries of the members of the Board of Control and other functionaries of the Company were to be drawn from the Indian Exchequer. The Governor-General was given greater control over the Governors of Bombay and Madras. Stress was laid on the policy of non-intervention in the internal affairs of the native states.

(iv) Charter Act, 1813 : This Act put an end to the commercial activities of the Company. Indian trade was thrown open to all the British merchants. But the Company was allowed to enjoy monopoly trade with China and in tea trade. But the government and the revenues of India continued to be in their hands.

(v) Charter Act, 1833 : Through this Act, the Company became a political agent of the Crown. It also provided for a single Central Legislative Council instead of three. A code of Civil and Criminal Laws, which was effective throughout the British territories in India was drawn. This Act marked the beginning of the Indian Legislature. The policy of free trade was introduced by ending the Company's trade monopoly. It centralized the whole administration.

(vi) Charter Act, 1853 : By this Act, the number of Directors was reduced from 24 to 18, six being nominees of the Crown. The position of the President of the Board of Control was equalised with that of a Secretary of State. It laid the foundation of the parliamentary system of government in India. The legislative and the executive councils were separated. The deliberations of the legislative council were to be public. This Council could not play any effective part.

12.16 CIVIL SERVICES SET UP

The Civil Service was the 'steel-frame' of British administration. Lord Clive was the first to pay attention to the civil services. He prohibited the employees of the company from undertaking any private trade or accept any gift. Cornwallis adopted the policy of Europeanisation of the civil services which was a bane for the Indians as they could not be appointed to higher posts. The highest post that an Indian could aspire to go was that of **Munsif, Sadar Amin** or Deputy collector. Then credit for introducing the first steps towards training of the company's civil servants to improve their efficiency goes to Lord Wellesley, who founded the Fort William College at Calcutta in 1800. Till 1853, all appointments to the Civil Services were made by the directors of the East India Company. The Charter Act of 1853, decreed that all recruits were to be selected through a competitive examination. In the days of Cornwallis, the Indians were completely excluded from the Civil Services which was a deliberate policy.

CIVIL SERVICES

(a) Failure of the attempts of *Clive and Warren Hastings* to put an end to corruption among officials.

(b) Introduction of Civil Services by *Cornwallis* and his reforms to purify and improve administration.

(c) Establishment of the *College of Fort William* at Calcutta by *Wellesley* to train the young Civil Servants, and its replacement by *East India College* at Haileybury in England.

(d) Discontinuation of the practice of appointing Civil Servants by the Court of Directors and starting of the practice of selecting Civil Servants through a competitive exam with the passing of the *Charter Act of 1853*.

A *special feature* of Indian Civil Service was the *exclusion of Indians* from it. *Reasons for this* (a) The belief that an administration based on British model could be firmly established only by English personnel. (b) Lack of trust in the ability and integrity of the Indians. (c) A deliberate policy - because the task of establishing and consolidating British rule in India could not be left to Indians. (d) The desire of the influential class of British society to preserve the lucrative posts in Civil Service for their sons.

However, Indians were recruited in large numbers to fill subordinate posts as they were cheaper and much more readily available than Englishmen.

Sir Charles Aitchison Commission, 1886 : Lord Dufferin appointed this Commission in 1886 to consider the demand for simultaneous examination and the lowering of maximum, age. It recommended :

(1) Dropping the term 'covenanted' and 'unconvenanted' and divided the sources into three classes-Imperial Indian Civil Services, the Provincial and the Subordinate Service. The first was to be recruited in England and the latter in India exclusively from Indians.

(2) It suggested the age limit to be 19 and 23 as the minimum and maximum age limits.

(3) It rejected the idea of simultaneous examination and advised the abolition of statutory civil services.

The Montagu Chelmsford Report 1918: The report's recommendations with regard to civil services are as follows :

(i) The holding of simultaneous examination in India and in England.

(ii) One-third of the superior posts in the Indian Civil Service were to be recruited in India and this percentage to be increased annually by 1.5 per cent.

(iii) There should be no racial descrimination in matter of appointments.

Lee Commission, 1923 : Another Royal Commission on Superior Civil Services in India, was appointed in June 1923 with Lord Lee as its chairman. Its recommendations were :

(i) The Secretary of State should continue to recruit the Indian Civil Service, the Irrigation Branch of the Service of Engineers and the Indian Forest Services.

(ii) On the basis of the Government of India Act 1919, it recommended the establishment of a Public Service Commission.

(iii) 20 per cent of the officers should be recruited by promotion from Provincial Civil Services and of the remaining 80 per cent, half should be Indian and half British.

The Government of India Act, 1935 : The Act, provided for the establishment of a Federal Public Service Commission and Provincial Pubilc Service Commissions. However the main grievance of the educated Indians remained that they were not freely and impartially admitted to office.

12.17 ARMY STRUCTURE

The bulk of the Company's army consisted of Indian soldiers. In 1857, the strength of the army in India was 311,400 of whom 2,65,900 were Indians. Its officers were British. The highest Indian officer was a '*Subedar*'. The British mantained a large hired army, with least expenditure. Lord Dalhousie thought of reducing the number of Indians in the army. He used to state that the British soldiers were an essential element of their power in India.

WHITE REVOLT

The 'White Revolt' refers to the revolt by the British army officers in India against Lord Clive's order to stop the practice of paying extra allowance to them during the period of war. The revolt was, however, suppressed.

12.18 POLICE STRUCTURE

The police system really began with Cornwallis. He appointed a superintendent (*daroga*) of police for Calcutta in 1791 and extended this system to the districts in the next years. He established a system of circles or '*thanas*'. The hereditary village police became '*chowkidars*' or watchmen. Later, the post of district superintendent of police was created to head the police organisation in a district.

12.19 JUDICIARY STRUCTURE

A supreme court was for the First time established at Calcutta by the Regulating Act in 1773. The system of granting justice through a hierarchy of civil and criminal courts was stabilised by Cornwallis in 1793. A *Diwani Adalat*, or civil court was established in each district, which was presided over by the District Judge who would be a Civil Servant. In 1865, High Courts were established at Calcutta, Madras and Bombay to replace the *Sadar* courts of *Diwani* and *Nizamat*. The British also established a new system of laws through the process of enactment and codification of old laws, as many laws were based on the '*shastras*' and '*shariat*' as well as on imperial authority. The Charter Act of 1833 delegated the power of framing laws to the Governor-General in Council. The first Law commission was constituted under Lord Macaulay to codify and improve upon various rules and regulations prevalent in India.

12.20 LOCAL SELF-GOVERNMENT

Local self-government means management of local affairs by such local bodies as have been elected by the people living in that particular locality. The Indian Council Act of 1861, inaugurated the policy of legislative devolution and Mayo's Resolution of 1870 on financial decentralisation was a natural corollary. The provincial governments were authorised to resort to local taxation to balance their budgets.

Lord Ripon honestly and sincerely strove for colonial self-government. His views on it got expressed in 1852 in a pamphlet entitled '*The Duty of the Age*' in which he maintained that democracy had two postulates–first, that every man so far as he is a man has a claim to share in the government of his country, in all its duties, responsibilities and charges and secondly, that self-government is the highest and noblest principles of politics, the safest foundation on which the state can rest. Thus, Ripon insisted on the growth of local bodies throughout the country like the Municipal Committees and City Bodies in the towns and the Subdivision, *Talukas* and *Tehsils* in the villages, which would be given executive powers with financial resources of their own. It was perhaps the desire of Ripon that power in India should be gradually transferred to the educated Indians. Ripon insisted on election of the local bodies as against selection by the Government. In all these measures, his concern was not so much for efficiency in administration as popular education in the science of government.

In 1908, the entire subject of self-government was reviewed by the **Royal Commission on Decentralisation** and important recommendations were made almost in every sphere. The Commission laid emphasis on the development of village panchayats and sub-district boards. Regarding municipalities, the Commission urged the withdrawal of existing restrictions on their powers of taxation and also stoppage of regular grants-in-aid from provincial governments except for undertaking large projects such as those concerning drainage or water supply. It suggested that municipalities might undertake the responsibility for primary education, hospitals, famine relief, etc.

With the coming of the Government of India Act 1919, local self-government became a 'transferred' subject under popular ministerial control. Each province was allowed to develop local self-governments according to their needs and requirement. By the Government of India Act, 1935 further impetus was given to the development of local self-government.

IMPACT ON INDIAN ECONOMY

12.21 INTRODUCTION

The victory of the East India Company in the Battle of Buxar in 1764 started the process which culminated in the transformation of India's economy into a colonial economy. The trade and industry of the country received a severe jolt of a result of the policies of the foreign rule. Britain looked upon India as her colony which had to be developed in the imperial interests.

12.22 PHASES OF ECONOMIC POLICY IN INDIA

R.P. Dutt, a Marxist scholar and dialectician, has explained economic exploitation of Indian economy under the following three heads:

(i) Phase of Merchant capital or Mercantilism (1757-1813)

(ii) Phase of Industrial capitalism or Free Trade Capitalism (1813-1858)

(iii) Phase of Finance capital or Finance Colonialism (1860 on wards)

(i) *THE MERCANTILIST PHASE (1757-1813)*

- The East India Company monopolized trade and began direct plunder of India's wealth.
- They could impose their own prices that had no relation to the costs of production. This was the phase of *buccaneering capitalism* whereby wealth flowed out of the barrel of the trader's guns.

- The Company used its political power to monopolize trade and dictate terms to the weavers of Bengal.
- The Company used revenue of Bengal to finance exports of Indian goods.

(ii) *THE INDUSTRIAL PHASE (1813-1860)*

- The commercial policy of the East India Company after 1813 was guided by the needs of the British industry.
- The British mercantile industrial capitalist class exploited India as Industrial Revolution in Britain completely transformed Britain's economy.
- *Charter Act of 1813* allowed one way free trade for British citizens resulting in Indian markets flooded with cheap and machine made imports. Indians lost not only their foreign markets but their markets in India too.
- India was now forced to export raw materials consisting of raw cotton, jute and silk, oilseeds, wheat, indigo and tea, and import finished products.
- Indian products had to compete with British products with heavy imported duties on entry into Britain.

(iii) *FINANCE COLONIALISM (1860-1947)*

- The essence of 18th and 19th century colonialism lay in the transformation of India into a supplier of foodstuffs and raw materials to the metropolis, a market for metropolitan manufactures and a field for investment of British capital.
- Started with the emergence of the *phase of Finance Capitalism* in Britain. The rebellion of 1857 was the key factor in the change of the nature of the colonialism.
- The British introduced roads and railways, post and telegraph, banking and other services under the '*guaranteed interests*' schemes (government paid minimum dividend even if profits were non-existent). Various investments by the British capitalists were also made in India.
- As a result of this, the burden of British public debts kept on increasing and India became, in the real sense, a colony of Britain.

12.23 AGRARIAN POLICY

LAND REVENUE POLICY

Land revenue was the main source of revenue of the provinces. It was partly in the nature of a rent and partly a tax. The following four systems were adopted during the British rule to collect land revenue.

(i) ***Itaredari System***: In 1773, the Company introduced the system of auctioning the right of collecting revenue from an area to the highest bidder.

(ii) ***Permanent Settlement***: The settlement was divised by **Cornwallis** in 1793. According to it, the zamindars, who formerly collected land revenue only were recognized as the landlords. Their right of ownership was made hereditary and transferable. Cultivators were reduced to low status of mere tenants and were deprived of long-standing rights to the soil and other customary rights. In 1799, zamindars were given power to evict or confiscate their tenants, property for non-payment of rent. Under the Permanent Settlement, a zamindar was required to pay about 89 percent, i.e, 10/11, of what he received as land revenue to the government and retain 11 per cent, i.e 1/11, with himself for his service. The land revenue was fixed for ten years on a permanent basis.

(iii) ***Ryotwari Settlement***: The land settlement in Madras (i.e. South and South Western) was called *Ryotwari* ***Settlement*** and was connected with the name of ***Thomas Munro***. In this system, rent was directly settled with the *ryots*. Real motive behind this system was to realise the maximum from the land in shape of revenue. The revenue was fixed for a period not exceeding thirty years on the basis of the quality of the soil and the nature of the crop. The government share was about half of the net value of the crop.

(iv) ***Mahalwari System***: It was a modified version of the zamindari system. Under it, settlements were made estate (*mahal*) by estate or village by village. The village community was the owner of the land, the village community was technically called 'co-sharers'.

A SURVEY OF BRITISH LAND REVENUE POLICY			
Land Revenue System	**Originator**	**Year**	**Area**
(i) ***Itaredari System***	Warren Hastings	1773	Bengal
(ii) ***Permanent Settlement***	Lord Cornwallis	1793	Bengal, Varanasi division of U.P., Bihar, North Karnataka and Orissa.
(iii) ***Ryotwari Settlement***	Sir Thomas Munroe	1820	Madras, Coorg, East Bengal, Berar, Bombay and Assam.
(iv) ***Mahalwari Settlement***	Holt Mackenzie	1822	Punjab, Central Provinces, Upper Provicnes including Agra, Avadh and Delhi.

Impact of Colonial Land Revenue Systems

Following were the main impacts of colonial land revenue systems :

- The land settlements introduced market economy and did away with customary rights. Cash payment of revenue encouraged money-lending activity.
- It sharpened social differentiation. The rich had access to the courts to defend their property.
- Forcible growing of commercial crops proved hazardous for the peasants because they had to buy food grains at high prices and sell cash crops at low prices.
- The stability of the Indian villages was shaken and the entire setup of the rural society began to break up.

12.24 IMPACT OF COLONIALISM ON INDIAN ECONOMY

(i) Impoverishment of the Peasantry: High revenue demands led to devastation, as it led to poverty and the deterioration of agriculture in the 19th century. It forced the peasant to fall into the clutches of the money-lender. If the peasant could not pay the money, his land was sold-off. Gradually more land passed into the hands of money-lenders, merchants, rich peasants and other rich classes.

(ii) Disruption of Traditional Economy and the Decline of Artisans and Craftsmen : The policies of the East India Company not only snatched the foreign markets but also its internal markets by a system of inland custom and transit duties. Besides the import of foreign manufacture on a large scale resulted in a steep decline in the sale of Indian products. The decline of the traditional industries with the absence of new industries to take its place worsened the economic life of the country. This deprived millions of workers of employment. These workers fell upon agriculture as other avenues of employment were not availahle.

Another reason of the decline of the indigenous industries was that while the English market for Indian manufactures was progressively narrowed through prohibitions and extremely high tariffs, the Indian markets were thrown wide open to British manufactures by imposing free trade on India.

Before the advent of the British, indigenous industries did not have any fear of competition. Hence, upgrading of production technology on a continuous basis did not take place in India as it did in Europe making the Indian products less competitive. This led to the process of deindustrialisation in India.

(iii) Changes in Agrarian Life: The condition of the peasantry was affected by several factors. **First**, there was a steady increase in population "due to the establishment of peaceful conditions amongst a people used to war, and possessing high natural fertility." This led to increasing pressure on land, which was accelerated by the ruin of cottage industries resulting from the growing import of British manufacturers. The average size of the holdings was reduced. **Secondly**, the revenue systems pressed heavily on the peasantry. **Thirdly**, the introduction of sophisticated law, the establishment of regular law courts, the improvement of communications, the increasing flow of British goods, etc. exposed the rural areas to steadily increasing interference from outside. The net results were the gradual disappearance of economic self-sufficiency and "the gradual transfer of authority within the village from the village elders to the agents of the Government." Their gradual disappearance led to a radical socio-economic transformation of rural life.

(iv) Disintegration of Village Communities and Emergence of the Indian Middle Class : The land revenue system, established by the British in India, led to the break-up of that ancient social framework within which the agricultural population had lived for centuries. Co-operation was replaced by competition and a new middle class emerged due to all these processes. The opening of the village to foreign imports gave a deadly blow to the village crafts and industries.

(v) Growth of Rural Indebtedness: There was progressive increase in indebtedness of Indian agriculturists. One of the most important reasons for the growth of rural indebtedness was that over 75 per cent of the peasants could not earn even bare minimum livelihood from land. Under the new system, land became a marketable commodity. While giving the peasant the freedom to mortgage or sell his land, it also gave the creditor of the indebted peasant freedom to seize the latter's land. In the conditions of poverty engendered by the new economic environs, more and more land came to be transferred to the money-lender in lieu of the debt the peasant owed to him. Large-scale expropriation of the Indian peasantry leading to the widespread growth of absentee landlordism also took place.

(vi) Commercialisation of Agriculture: Under the new system, the peasant produced mainly for the market, which with the steady improvement of means of transport and expanding operations of trading capital under British Rule, became available to him. He did so with a view to realising maximum cash, primarily to pay land revenue to the state which was fixed fairly high. This led to the practice of growing specialised crops by the peasants. Thus, the land in groups of villages came to be solely used because of its special suitability, for the cultivation of a single agricultural crop such as cotton, jute, wheat, sugarcane, oil-seeds, indigo, opium, etc. Further, the commercialisation made the agriculturist dependent on the middleman for the sale of his product, i.e., the merchant. The merchant by his superior economic position took full advantage of the poverty of the peasant.

(vii) Rise of Modern Industries and Growth of Foreign Capital in India: In terms of chronology, the plantation industries of indigo, tea and coffee were the first to be introduced in India. . They were exclusively European in ownership, and did not entirely depend on modern mechanical contrivances. The coming of railways heralded the entry of modern machines in India and during the 1850's cotton textile, jute, and coal mining industries were started in India. The two fields were primarily exclusive preserve of European capital.

The railways comprised the single biggest item of British capital investment in India, but much of its burden was shifted to the Indian taxpayers through the peculiar system of 'private investment at public risk'. The bulk of railway equipment was imported from England and about 90 per cent of the superior railway posts were manned by the British. A substantial part of the income generated through railway and other industrial investment in plantations, mines, banking and insurance, shipping, jute mills, etc. was siphoned out. It has been estimated that before 1914 nearly 97% of British capital investments in India was diverted towards completion of government projects (railways, road transport, etc.), plantation industry (tea, coffee, rubber, etc), and development of financial houses (banks, insurance companies, etc.). The foreign banks in India held nearly three-fourths of the total bank deposits. Many multinationals operated their subsidiary companies in India, and penetrated into almost every sector of the Indian economy.

(viii) Change in the Structure of India's Trade: The expansion of British trade in India not only proved ruinous to Indian trade and industry, but also radically changed the structure of India's trade. India was forced to admit British imports either free or at nominal rates of duties, while Indian manufactures of products continued to be subjected to high import duties in England. India, which was the world's principal producer and exporter of fabrics in the first half of the eighteenth century, was in the next century reduced to the position of one of the largest consumers of foreign manufactures—cotton textiles being the major item of import. Silk and woollen fabrics, machinery and metal manufactures were some of the other commodities of import into India. On the other hand, the exports which came to consist of raw cotton, raw silk, food grains, opium, indigo, and jute, denuded the country of her agricultural surplus, raised the prices of raw materials and "laid the foundation of future agricultural shortage and famines.

(ix) Drain of Wealth Theory: R.C. Dutt and Dadabhai Naoroji first cited the Drain of Wealth Theory. Naoroji brought it to light in his book titled *Poverty And Un-British Rule in India.*

Drain of Wealth refers to a portion of national product of India, which was not available for consumption of her people. Drain of Wealth began in 1757, after Battle of Plassey when the Company's servants began to export fortunes from Indian rulers, zamindars, merchants and common people and send home.

CONSTITUENTS OF THE DRAIN OF WEALTH

Following were the different ways by which the company drained the wealth of India.

- **Home Charges:** Home Charges refer to the expenditure in England by the Secretary of State on behalf of India. It included : Costs of the Secretary of State's India Office, East India Company's military adventures, cost of suppressing the Mutiny of 1857 and the compensation of the Company's share holders, pensions to the British Indian officials and army officers, costs of army training, transport, equipments and campaigns outside India and guaranteed interests on railways.
- **Remittances:** To England (a part of their salaries, incomes and savings) by English civil servants, military and railway employee's, lawyers, doctors etc.
- **Foreign Trade:** The phase of finance imperialism entered India with the introduction of railways, development of plantations, mines, banking and factories faced through British capital. Much of the burden of the expanding railway network was met by the Indian taxpayer through the guaranteed interest scheme.

12.25 DEVELOPMENT OF TRANSPORT

The British felt the need of a cheap and easy system of transport for making large scale export to Indian market and securing raw materials for British industries. They introduced steamships. They improved the roads and thus, work on a Grand Trunk Road from Calcutta to Delhi began in 1839 and was completed in the 1850's. But real improvement in transport came with the coming of railways. The first railway line running from Bombay to Thane was opened to traffic in 1853. By the end of 1869 more than 6,000 kms of railways had been built by the guaranteed companies, but this system proved very costly and slow, therefore in the same year Government of India decided to build new railways as State enterprises. By 1905, nearly 45,000 kms of railways had been built.

12.26 DEVELOPMENT OF MODERN INDUSTRIES UP TO 1947

We can demarcate the following three distinct phases in the growth and development of modern industries in India :

(i) First Phase (up to 1914) : An important development in the second half of the 19th century was the establishment of large scale machine-based industries in India. The 1850s and 1860s also witnessed the growth of plantation industries' (i.e. indigo, tea, coffee, rubber, etc.), jute mills and coal mines. Most of the industries were started and managed, by British capitalists under encouragement from the Government of India.

A significant development in this phase was the setting up of the first-ever Tata Iron and Steel company (TISCO) at Jamshedpur by Jamsedji Tata in 1907. It produced pig iron in 1911 and steel by 1913.

(ii) Second Phase (1914-1939): The main feature of this phase was the production of consumer goods for the mass market within India. Foreign imports fell to a very low level while there was increase in Government purchases for war purposes.

CHALLENGES TO INDIAN COTTON TEXTILE INDUSTRY DURING COLONIAL RULE

I. Competition from Lancashire and Manchester textile products.

II. Discriminatory tariff and excise policies

III. Absence of long-term credit facilities from European-owned and European-dominated banking industry.

IV. Dependence on imported plant and equipment

V. Absence of government protection

VI. Expansion of railway system and concessional freight rates favouring movement of goods with port towns against linkages between inland centers.

From 1920s onwards, the established industries like cotton, jute, tea and coal did not yield good profits, whereas paper, glass, sugar, cement, matchboxes and even steel, magnesium chloride and sulphuric acid industries got firmly established.

The inter-war period showed a sharp conflict between foreign capital and indigenous enterprises. In 1917, a Munitions Board was established to control the purchase and manufacture of Government Stores and munitions of war. In 1921, the Government appointed a Fiscal Commission under the chairmanship of **Sir Ibrahim Rahimtoola**.

RAHIMTOOLA FISCAL COMMISSION

The commission submitted its report in 1923. It recommended a policy of protection for industries in the initials stage of development. It laid down a **Triple Formula** for industries claiming fiscal protection: It includes :

I. The industry should have natural advantages, such as adequate supply of raw material, labour, cheap power and a ready home market.

II. The industry cannot develop without protection as rapidly as is desirable.

III. The industry must be able to eventually face world competition without protection.

The Commission also recommended the establishment of a **Tariff Board** to consider applications for fiscal protection.

The Government accepted the recommendation of the commission and protection was granted to steel industry in 1924, paper industry in 1925, matchbox in 1918, cotton and textile industry in 1930, and sugar industry in 1932.

(iii) Third Phase (1939-1947) : This phase marked the production of capital goods for the domestic market. It was a process of import substitution. The enormous needs of global war shortened the gestation period for this phase of production considerably and India embarked on the production of heavy chemicals (Caustic Soda), sophisticated machinery, aircrafts, automobiles, locomotives, ships and a variety of other heavy and capital goods. The near stoppage of industrial imports created favourable circumstances for the growth and consolidation of Indian capitalism.

Another significant development was the growing collaboration between Indian and foreign capitalists as was evident in a number of joint Indo-British ventures as managing agencies and joint industrial enterprises. The capitalist class drew strength from the nationalist movement and in turn sustained it by financial assistance. India thus, slowly graduated from a colony supplying raw materials to become one of the outer satellites in the capitalist planetary system, with the U.S.A. as the central star.

12.27 FAMINES DURING COLONIAL RULE

India witnessed a series of famines and scarcities. The nationalists believed that export of food grains was a cause of scarcity and famine because India sent out not its surplus of foodgrains but the stock which were required to meet its daily needs.

(i) Famine Under Company's Rule: During the rule of the East India Company India suffered in one part or another from 12 famines and 4 severe scarcities. Some of the major are as under :

- The first famine was the dreadful Bengal famine of 1769-1770, which claimed a third of the population of the province.
- The years 1781-1782 were the years of scarcities in Madras, while in 1784 a severe famine afflicted the whole of northern India.

- In 1792, there was a famine in Madras.
- During 1803, famine occurred in NWFP and Avadh.
- In 1833, the Guntur Famine took place in which 2 lakh persons died out of a total population of 5 lakhs.
- In 1837, there was a severe famine in upper India.

(ii) Famine Under the Crown Administration: Under the Crown, there were ten severe famines besides a large number of scarcities. Some of them are as follow:

- The first famine occurred in 1860-1861 in the areas of Punjab, Rajasthan, Kutch and Uttar Pradesh. It is reported that 20 lakhs people perished.
- In 1866-1867, there occurred famine in which following areas like Orissa, Madras, Northern Bengal and Bihar were affected. The calamity was most severe in Orissa hence it is popularly known as Orissa Famine. It was estimated that 13 lakh persons died in Orissa alone.
- A great famine occurred in 1876-1878, in which Madras Bombay, Uttar Pradesh and Punjab were affected with a population of more than 58 millions. R.C. Dutt has estimated that 5 million persons perished in a single year.
- Orissa, Madras and Bihar witnessed a devastating famine during 1888-89. Nearly 1.5 lakh people lost their lives in it.
- In 1896-97, a catastrophic famine occurred in Rajasthan, Western Uttar Pradesh, Bombay, Hyderabad Madras and Madhya Pradesh. It is estimated that 51.5 lakh people lost their lives in this famine.
- The famines of 1899-1900 affected an area of 1,89,000 square miles and population of 28 million in Madhya Pradesh, Bombay, Hyderabad, Rajasthan, Eastern Punjab and princely states of Western India.
- The Great Bengal Famine of 1942-1943 took a heavy toll of life. In this famine, it is reported that nearly 20 lakhs people died.

FAMINE COMMISSIONS

I. **Strachey Commission, 1880:** In 1880, Viceroy Lytton appointed under the presidency of Sir Richard Strachey to formulate general principles and suggest measures for fighting famine in response to the recommendation of the commission, in 1883, a provisional **Famine Code** was formulated. The Famine code formed a guide for the various provincial famine codes which were subsequently formulated.

II. **MacDonnell Commission, 1901** Lord Curzon appointed a Famine Commission under the chairmanship of Sir Anthony MacDonnell. The commission submitted its report in 1901. It emphasised the benefits of a policy of "moral strategy". Another important recommendation of the commission was the appointment of a Famine Commissioner in a province where relief operations were expected to be extensive.

13. THE REVOLT OF 1857

The Revolt of 1857, a watershed in the history of British rule in India, shook the very foundation of the British empire in India. It changed the character of British rule, marking the end of the rule of the East India Company and bringing British India directly under the British Crown.

NATURE AND CHARACTER OF THE REVOLT

Even since the book, 'First War of Indian Independence' by the distinguished revolutionary V.D. Savarkar was published in London in 1909, the nature and character of the Revolt of 1857 has been hotly debated among the nationalists and historians. The debate centres round three main views: (*i*) that the revolt was a Sepoy Mutiny; (*ii*) that it was a national struggle or War of Independence; and (*iii*) that it was a mere manifestation of feudal unrest and reaction.

Sepoy Mutiny: British historians and certain observers of the 19th century saw it merely as a "Sepoy Mutiny". Sir John Seeley described the event as a "wholly unpatriotic and selfish Sepoy Mutiny with no native leadership and no popular support". This view is based on the assumption that the so-called Mutiny was started by soldiers discontented with their service conditions. But the fact is that though the rebellion began as a military uprising, its leadership was in the hands of civilians, and a very large number of civilians, including peasants, joined it. Besides, the military discontent was just on the causes for the outbreak of the Revolt of 1857.

War of Independence or Nationalist Struggle: At the beginning of the present century the nationalists interpreted the Revolt as a War of Independence. The lead in this direction was given by V.D. Savarkar, who described it as "a planned war of national independence". Dr. S.N. Sen, in his book Eighteen Fifty Seven, partially agrees with this view and says: "What began as a fight for religion ended as a war of independence." Disagreeing, Dr. R.C. Majumdar maintained that "the so called First National War of Independence of 1857 is neither first nor National war of Independence". It certainly was not a "War of Independence", because the larger part of the country and large sections of the people took no part in it. Besides, various leaders of the revolt had no identity of purpose.

Feudal Unrest: Marxist historians have interpreted the Revolt of 1857 as the struggle of the soldier peasant democratic combine against foreign as well as feudal bondage". This view, again is contrary to facts, particularly given that the leaders of the rebellion themselves belonged to a feudal back ground. Another historian, Dr. S.B. Chaudhari, who is closer to this view, maintains that the Revolt of 1857 can be bifurcated into mutiny and rebellion. It was the outcome of the coming together of two series of disturbances, military and civil, each provoked by independent grievances.

It would be difficult to precisely categorise the rebellion. It was undoubtedly anti-imperialist and nationalist, because both Hindus and Muslims participated in equal measure and in close cooperation and both the sepoys and the civilians wanted to throw out the imperial rulers. The concept of common nationality and nationhood was, however, completely missing.

CAUSES OF THE REVOLT

As about the nature of the rebellion, there is also considerable controversy regarding its actual causes. Historians, both British and Indian, have over emphasised the importance of military grievances and the greased cartridges affair. But recent research has established beyond doubt that the "greased cartridge" was not the only cause nor even the most important. On the contrary, there were a variety of causes—political, social, religious and economic—which combined to produce the rebellion.

Political Causes: The British policy of annexations had disturbed the political equilibrium in the country. The indiscriminate application of the "Doctrine of Lapse" by Lord Dalhousie had caused widespread discontent. The overthrow of Nawab Wajid Ali Shah of Awadh, annexation of several Hindu principalities and forfeiture on the ex-Peshwa's pension had alarmed the Princely States. The annexation of Princely States was not a blow to the princely families alone, but to their dependent subjects as well.

On the eve of the rebellion, Indians believed that the existence of all states was threatened and annexation of the remaining states was a question of time. The absentee sovereigntyship of the British rule in India was an equally important political factor. The Indians felt that they were being ruled from England and the country was being drained of her wealth.

Administrative and Economic Causes: The annexation of Indian states produced startling economic and social consequences under the British rule. Not only was the Indian aristocracy deprived of power and position, but all high posts, civil and military, were reserved for the Europeans. Racial discrimination was evident everywhere.

The administrative machinery of the East India Company was inefficient and inadequate. The land revenue policy was most unpopular. Many districts in the newly annexed states were in permanent revolt. Many taluqdars (hereditary landlords) were deprived of their position and resources. Large estates were confiscated and auctioned off. Thus the new land revenue settlements made by the East India Company in the newly annexed states, made the aristocracy poor without benefiting the peasantry, who fell into the clutches of unprincipled money-lenders and groaned under the weight of heavy assessments and excessive duties. The judicial system that the Company introduced in India became an instrument of oppression.

Social and Religious Causes: The Traditional Indian social system and culture appeared to be in danger under the reformist zeal of the British administrators. The sway of leaders of orthodoxy both maulvis and pandits regarding common law in matters of succession, inheritance, etc. was challenged. The missionaries were given ample facilities for the propagation of Christianity. The Religious Disabilities Act of 1856 modified Hindu customs; a change in religion did not debar a son from inheriting the property of his heathen father. The Indian mind was getting increasingly convinced that the English were conspiring to convert them into Christianity.

Military Causes: There was widespread discontent amongst the Indian soldiers serving in the British army, in which the majority of the soldiers and junior officers were Indians. The Indian soldiers resented their low pay and poor prospects of promotion. Campaigns in strange lands outside the boundaries of India were unpopular with them, on account of the great hardships involved. Indian soldiers serving overseas were either not given overseas allowances (bhatta) at all or paid much lower than the European soldiers serving in the British army, which was one of the major causes of discontent among Indian soldiers.

Another cause of military discontent was the General Service Enlistment Act, which made it compulsory for all recruits to cross the seas whenever ordered to do so. The details of the "greased cartridge" issue, which, however, was not the main cause of discontent, are as follows: Shortly before the Revolt of 1857 the new Royal Enfield rifle had been introduced. The new type of cartridge used with it had caps allegedly greased with the fat of cow or pig. Before loading the cartridge, the cap had to be removed with the teeth. This issue is said to have agitated both Hindu and Muslim soldiers.

BEGINNING AND SPREAD OF THE REVOLT

The Revolt was sparked off on March 29, 1857 when a section of Indian soldiers of the 19th and 34th Native Infantry posted at Barrackpur near Kolkata mutinied and a Brahmin soldier, Mangal Pandey, killed two British army officers. The mutiny was suppressed, Mangal Pandey tried and executed and the 19th and 34th Native Infantry disbanded. About two months later, on May 10, 1857 the soldiers of the 3rd Cavalry Regiment at Meerut refused to touch the greased cartridges and broke out in open rebellion. Next day the rebellious soldiers of Meerut marched to Delhi and proclaimed the old Mughal emperor Bahadur Shah II as the King Emperor of Hindustan. The success of the rebellion in Delhi created a sensation in various parts of North and Central India and rebellions broke out in Awadh,

Ruhelkhand, West Bihar and many other towns and cities of the North-Western Provinces.

On June 4, the soldiers of the 2nd Cavalry and 1st Native Infantry mutinied at Kanpur and killed several British men, women and children. The leader of the revolt at Kanpur was Dhondu Pant alias Nana Saheb, the adopted son of Peshwa Baji Rao II who was living in exile at Bithur near Kanpur. Nana Saheb, assisted by his devoted follower Tantiya Tope, assumed the role of a conquering hero and was proclaimed the Peshwa. At Jhansi Rani Lakshmibai, the widowed queen of Raja Gangadhar Rao, the last Maratha ruler of Jhansi, led the rebellion. At Lucknow Begum Hazrat Mahal, the queen of Nawab Wajid Ali Shah of Awadh declared her 11 year old son Birjis Qadar as Nawab and the whole of Awadh rallied round her authority. In Bihar a local Rajput Zamindar Kunwar Singh, an old man of eighty, who held extensive estates in Arrah, raised the banner of rebellion, which soon spread to many parts of Bihar, including Danapur near Patna, Chotanagpur, Ranchi, Palamu etc. The tribals of the region also joined the rebellion. Kunwar Singh provided the longest, most valiant and spirited resistance to the British and after nearly ten-month-long successful battles against the British died on May 9, 1858, from wounds received in action. Several towns of North-Western and Central Provinces, such as Aligarh, Etawah, Farrukhabad, Bareilly, Banda, Hamirpu etc. also rose in rebellion and independent governments were setup there under the former local chiefs.

SUPPRESSION OF THE REVOLT

The rebel leaders could not consolidate their initial gains, while the Governor General, Lord Canning took all possible steps to gather the forces from Bombay, Madras, Calcutta and Punjab to quell the rebellion. On July 16, 1857 Bithur and Kanpur were captured from Nana Saheb, who probably escaped to Nepal. Nana Saheb's Prime Minister Tantia Tope with his soldiers then joined Rani Lakshmibai at Jhansi. On September 20, 1857, the British troops captured Delhi. Bahadur Shah II surrendered to the English on the sole condition that his life should be spared. Thereupon he, along with his favourite Queen Begum Zinnat Mahal and her son, were made captives in the palace of the fort. On September 2, three young sons of Bahadur Shah II were shot dead publicly. Emperor Bahadur Shah was tried by a court martial, found guilty and sentenced to imprisonment for life. He was exiled to Rangoon with his queen Zinnat Mahal, and died after four years, on November 7, 1862.

In Awadh, Begum Hazrat Mahal and Maulvi Ahmadullah gave stiff resistance to the British. After the fall of Lucknow in March 1858, Begum Hazrat Mahal escaped to Nepal and Maulvi Ahmadullah was killed in an encounter (June 1858). Even thereafter, the Taluqdars of Awadh continued the bitter struggle till the end of 1858.

On May 30, 1858, Rani Lakshmibai of Jhansi assisted by Tantia Tope, attacked Gwalior. The Sindhia ruler of Gwalior was defeated and escaped to Agra. The rebel troops entered the fort of Gwalior and seized the treasury and the arsenal. Rani Lakshmibai's objective in capturing Gwalior was to cut off the direct communication of the British in North India with Bombay, while it also provided a brilliant opportunity of rallying the whole Maratha country in the south against the British. The seizure of Gwalior created a sensation throughout India. The British, greatly alarmed, prepared a comprehensive plan to retake Gwalior, with Sir Hugh Rose, Commander of the British Army himself taking the command of the British troops at Gwalior. In the ensuing battle on the range of hills between Gwalior and Kotah-Ki-Sarai, the Rani of Jhansi, attired as a man and mounted on horseback, fought valiantly against the British army in spite of being greatly outnumbered and lacking resources. She fell on the battlefield on June 17, 1858. Tantia Tope escaped into the jungles of Central India where he carried on a bitter guerrilla warfare until April 1859 when he was betrayed by a Zamindar friend and captured while asleep. He was tried and sentenced to death on April 15, 1859. By the end of 1859 all the great leaders of the Revolt, such as Kunwar Singh, the Ruhela leader Khan Bahadur Khan of Bareilly, Maulvi Ahmadullah of Awadh, Tantia Tope etc. were dead and Begum Hazrat Mahal and Nana Saheb had escaped to Nepal leading to the restoration of the British authority in India fully and firmly.

LEADERS OF THE REVOLT

Nana Saheb: Actual name Dhondu Pant, he was the adopted son of the last Peshwa Baji Rao II. He lived with his family at Bithur (Kanpur District U.P.) at the time of the Revolt. Nana Saheb was the leader of the Revolt in Kanpur and was actively supported by Tantia Tope. After facing successive defeats, he escaped to Nepal and till his death continued to defy the English and defiantly told them: "There will be war between me and you as long as I have life, whether I be killed or imprisoned or hanged. And whatever I do will be done with the sword only.

Rani Lakshmibai: She was the widow of Raja Gangadhar Rao, the last Maratha King of Jhansi. When he died without heir, Dalhousie, in contravention of the Treaty at of 1817, annexed the principality. On June 4, 1858, Rani Lakshmibai was proclaimed the head of the State and she provided spirited lead to the rebels and fought heroically against the British forces. She and her companion Tantia Tope made the most imaginative and heroic resolve to capture Gwalior, where she was killed in action. Her devoted followers, determined that the British should not boast that they had captured her even dead, burned her body. Sir Hugh Rose, who led the British forces against her, described her as "the best and bravest military leader of the rebels."

Emperor Bahadur Shah II: The last Mughal emperor, he was the leader of the revolt in Delhi and was declared the King emperor of Hindustan. He was then over eighty years of age. He was a poet of considerable merit in both Hindi and Urdu and a patron of poets and literary men. He wrote under the pen-name 'Zafar'.

During the revolt he exerted himself to the outmost to hold together his people belonging to different faiths, to maintain order in the besieged city of Delhi, to sustain the morale of his subjects and to encourage his forces to continue the fight till the bitter end. He banned cow slaughter in Delhi. His greatest remorse before death was: "How unfortunate is Zafar that he could not secure even two yards of land for his burial in his motherland."

Begum Hazrat Mahal: The wife of Nawab Wajid Ali Shah of Awadh, who had been deposed by the English in 1856, played a memorable part in raising the banner of rebellion in Awadh. She ruled on behalf of her 11 year old son Birjis Qadar with great wisdom and reorganised the machinery of administration. She directed the attack on the Residency at Lucknow. After the fall of Lucknow, she joined Maulvi Ahmadullah at Shahjahanpur, but was defeated and escaped to Nepal. She refused to accept the pension offered to her by the British and chose to die unmourned in Nepal.

Maulvi Ahmadullah: He is son of the best known Muslim Maulvis who prepared the ground for the popular revolt against the British. A native of Arcot (Tamil Nadu), he had settled down at Fayzabad. He called upon "all true believers to rise against the English in fidels and to drive them out of India." This leading spirit of the Revolt of 1857 in Awadh was recognised even by the English enemy as "a man of great abilities of undaunted courage and of stern determination and by far the best soldier among the rebels." After the fall of Lucknow, he escaped to Ruhelkhand and gave a tough fight to the British at many places. He inspired so much terror by his activities that the Governor General offered a reward of Rs. 50,000 to anyone who could capture him. On June. 5, 1858, he was shot dead at Powain, on the Awadh-Ruhelkhand border.

Kunwar Singh: A leading Rajput Zamindar of Arrah district in Bihar, with his home at village Jagdishpur, he was eighty year old when he raised the banner of revolt against the British. Gifted by nature with undaunted courage, chivalry and qualities of generalship, he was rightly regarded as the "Lion of Bihar" during the Revolt. He over threw the British authority in Shahabad district and established his own government. He marched to Kalpi to help Nana Saheb for a joint attack on Kanpur. He carried the torch of rebellion to Rohtas, Mirzapur, Rewa , Banda and Lucknow, where he was received with great honour. His last exploit was to inflict a severe defeat upon the English near his hometown of Jagdispur. In this war the British suffered very heavy losses and their Commander and a number of officers and soldiers, lost their lives. Kunwar Singh also was wounded severely and died on April 26, 1858. After him his brother Amar Singh continued the fight against the English till December 1859.

Khan Bahadur Khan: This grandson of the Ruhela leader Hafiz Rahamat Khan raised the banner of rebellion in Ruhelkhand with epicentre at Bareilly (U.P.). Though seventy year old at the time, he defended Ruhelkhand with skill and undaunted courage, defeating four columns of British troops which had converged upon Bareilly, before he was forced to retreat into the forests of the Himalayan foothills. He assumed the office of Viceroy under the Mughal emperor Bahadur Shah and treated Hindus and Muslims with equality and statesmanlike wisdom. He was captured by treachery, tried and hanged.

Tantia Tope: Actual name Ramchandra Panduranga, he was an indomitable fighter well versed in the original Maratha guerrilla tactics. He helped Nana Saheb in the revolt at Kanpur and Rani Lakshmibai of Jhansi in her attack on the fort of Gwalior. After her death he kept large British forces engaged in chasing him across Central India and Rajputana. Finally he was betrayed by his friend into the hands of the British. He was tried and sentenced to death. Brave man that he was, he put the noose round his neck with his own hands and with unfaltering steps ascended the gallows on April 18, 1859.

The capture of Tantia Tope was the last important act in the suppression of the Revolt in Central India. The remarkable guerilla warfare which he had carried on for ten months against enormous odds elicited administration even from his opponents and may be looked upon as a fitting end to the struggle.

WHY THE REVOLT FAILED

The failure of the Revolt was a foregone conclusion. Some of the important factors for its failure are described as under :

(*i*) The Revolt was not inspired by any positive and creative idea. It had no vision of a higher social order or higher political system. It lacked plan, programme and funds. The only thing which united the rebels was their desire to eliminate the British rule. However, elimination of foreign rule was equated with the physical destruction of foreign personnel and independence identified with restoration of the personal rule of those deprived of their rights and privileges by the foreigners.

(*ii*) The Revolt remained confined to a small part of North India, primarily Ruhelkhand, Awadh, Delhi and parts of Central India and Bihar. The whole of Rajputana, Punjab, Eastern India including Bengal and the entire South India remained totally unaffected. The Sikhs, Marathas, Rajputs and the ruling chiefs of eastern India did not take any part in the Revolt.

(*iii*) The rebel leaders lacked political leadership, military experience and strategic perception. None of them realised the consequences of the fall of Delhi and took no measures for its joint defence.

(*iv*) There was little discipline among the rebels and their loyalties were fragile. Intellectually, too, they were no match to their adversary, whose military techniques were based on modern science and technology.

(*v*) In strategy and tactics the British forces were far superior to the Indian rebels and worked under the orders of a highly organised Government in India which was backed by ample resources in men and resources of the British empire.

(*vi*) There was no single great leader who could fuse the scattered elements into a consolidated force of great momentum, with a definite policy and action. The activities of the rebel leaders were also confined within the narrow limits of self-interest.

(*vii*) The lack of interest shown by the intellectuals in the movement was also a serious drawback.

AFTERMATH OF THE REVOLT

Even though the Revolt of 1857 ended in failure, it was the first great and direct threat to British rule in India. In the aftermath of the Revolt, the leaders of the Revolt and the mutinous Indian soldiers paid with their lives; their liberty and their property were forfeited as the penalty of failure. The victorious English troops committed inhuman atrocities upon the Indian people. Thousands of rebels were hanged publicly after a mock trial. In meting out punishment they were humiliated and degraded. The rebel villages were destroyed wholesale. Indians were more alienated than ever from their British rulers.

The Revolt of 1857 brought about fundamental changes in the character of the British administration. Some of these were :

(*i*) The Queen's Proclamation: This was the most significant development. The Proclamation was read out by Lord Canning at a Durbar held on November 1, 1858 at Allahabad. The Proclamation announced the end of the rule of the East India Company and assumption of the Government of India directly by the Crown. Under the Proclamation, Lord Canning became the first Viceroy and Governor-General.

(*ii*) The Proclamation also declared the end of the era of further expansion of the British empire in India. It also promised non-interference in the religious affairs of the people, grant of equal protection of law and respect for ancient rights and customs of the people.

(*iii*) The Act for the Better Government of India, 1858 was passed, which terminated the process commenced by the Pitts India Act, 1784. The Act of 1858 ended the dualism in the control of Indian affairs and made the Crown directly responsible for the management of Indian affairs. Following this, fundamental changes in the administrative set-up were made in the executive, legislative and judicial administration of India by passing the Indian Council Act of 1861, the Indian High Court Act of 1861 and the Indian Civil Service Act of 1861.

(*iv*) Indians were associated with legislative matters and administration, and a humble beginning in this direction was made by the Indian Councils Act of 1861.

(*v*) The British Army was recognised, increasing the proportion of the Europeans in the army. The field and other artillery was to be manned entirely by the Europeans. Pursuing a conscious policy of "divide and rule", regiments were created on the basis of caste, community and regions to prevent the emergence of nationalist feeling among soldiers.

(*vi*) The policy of "divide and rule" was also pursued towards the Indian people. Appeasement of Muslims was introduced, with disastrous consequences for Indian nationalism.

(*vii*) The policy towards the Princely States also changed radically and the States were treated as the bulwark of the empire against future contingencies. The policy of annexation was now completely given up and the rulers of Princely States were allowed to adopt heirs. But the status of these rulers was reduced to privileged subordinates and dependents.

(*viii*) Reactionary and backward looking elements like the Princes, zamindars, landlords and merchants were patronised to promote the interests of the British.

(*ix*) The Revolt ended the era of territorial expansion and ushered in the era of economic exploitation. It opened India to the British merchant and capitalist class for India's further economic exploitation.

(*x*) The Revolt left terrible financial scars on the Indian soil. Village along the line of march of the British army were burnt to ashes and cultivators fled to save their lives. A severe famine broke out in Agra in 1861. Kanpur and Lucknow were gutted and Delhi was virtually depopulated. The entire burden of the outbreak and suppression of the Revolt was thrown on the Indian people. The public debt of India increased by about 98 million sterling, adding thereby to the annual interest charged by 2 million sterling.

(xi) The Revolt left a legacy of racial bitterness. "The entire Indian people were dubbed as unworthy of trust and subjected to insults, humiliations, and contemptuous treatment."

(xii) It has been said that Julius Caesar dead was more powerful than Julius Caesar alive. The same may be said about the Revolt of 1857. Whatever might have been its original character, it soon became a symbol of challenge to the mighty British empire in India and remained a shining star for the rise and growth of the Indian national movement. The leaders of the Revolt of 1857, such as Rani Lakshmibai, Bahadur Shah, Kunwar Singh, Nana Saheb, etc. became national heroes and champions of national freedom, and stories of their heroic struggle animated the fighters for freedom more than half a century later.

14. THE SOCIO—RELIGIOUS REFORM MOVEMENTS AND THE RISE OF NATIONALISM

14.1 SOCIAL AND CULTURAL POLICY OF THE BRITISH

Till 1813, British followed a policy of non-interference in the religious, social and cultural life of the country, but after 1813 they took active steps to transform Indian society and culture. The 18th and 19th centuries witnessed a great ferment of new ideas in Britain and Europe which influenced the British outlook towards Indian problems. The Christian missionaries and religious minded persons wanted to spread Christianity in India. They supported a programme of westernization in the hope that it would eventually lead to the country's conversion to Christianity, whereas, Radicals wanted to introduce western sciences, philosophy and literature in India. Radicals were given strong support by Raja Ram Mohan Roy (1774-1883) and other like-minded Indians, who believed that the salvation of India lay in science and humanism.

Enlightened British public opinion was also helpful to curb some of the social evils of the Indian society. The practice of *sati* was the most important of all. Regulation XVII of December 1829, declared the practice of *sati* or burning or burying alive of widows illegal and punishable by criminal courts as culpable homicide. The evil of infanticide was done with by the **Bengal Regulations XXI of 1795 and III of 1804.** It declared the infanticide to be illegal and equivalent to committing a murder. Furthermore, the Act of 1870, made it compulsory for the parents to register the birth of babies and provided for the verification of female children for some years after birth was able to curb the evil practice.

The Act XV of 1856 or Hindu Widows' Remarriage Act legalised marriage of widows and declared the issues from such marriages as legitimate.

Legislative action in prohibiting child marriage came in 1872 by the **Native Marriage Act or Civil Marriage Act**. The marriages of girls below the age of 14 and boys below 18 years were forbidden. Moreover, the enactment of the **Age of Consent Act in 1891**, forbade the marriages of girls below the age of 12 years. The **Sharda Act of 1930** further pushed the marriageable age for boys to 18 years and girls to 14 years.

Act V of 1843, declared slavery illegal. The **Penal Code of 1860** put a restraint on the slavery trade.

In 1872, government sanctioned the inter-caste and inter-communal marriage.

14.2 TRENDS AND CAUSES OF REFORM MOVEMENTS

The reform movements in the 19th century fell in two broad categories : (i) Reformist movements like the Brahmo Samaj, the Prathana Samaj and the Aligarh Movement. (ii) Revivalist movements like the Arya Samaj, the Ramakrishan Mission and the Deoband Movement. The only difference between one reform movement and the other lay in the degree to which it relied on tradition or on reason and conscience.

The socio-religious reform movements may be broadly identified with four major trends which are (a) reforms from within (b) reforms through legislation; (c) reform through symbols of change; and (d) reform through social work. These movements were influenced by two intellectual criteria-rationalism and religious universalism. But a trend of revivalism was also present. There was a tendency in the wake of the colonial subjugation to hark back the 'golden' Indian Past. These movements played an important role in creating cultural consciousness and rootedness among western liberal educated Indian people while arousing the patriotic feeling among Indians.

Following factors were responsible for the social and cultural awakening in 19th century:

I. Establishment of British rule and its deep influence on the political, economic, social and cultural life of the country

II. Orientalists painstaking efforts to bring into limelight India's past.

III. Creative literature by scholars and writers

IV. Popularity of the Christian missionaries

14.3 REFORM MOVEMENTS AMONG THE HINDUS

THE BRAHMO SAMAJ : Raja Rammohan Roy was a man of extraordinary intellect. He fought vehemently against the custom of *sati* prevalent in the contemporary society. In 1815, Rammohan founded the *Atmiya Sabha.* On 20th August 1828, he founded the *Brahmo Samaj.* The principal aim of the *Samaj* was to eradicate the evils from the Hindu society, to check the growing influence of Christianity and establish fundamental unity among all religions. In essence, the *Brahmo Samaj* mainly concentrated on the non-dualistic aspect of the Hindu faith.

SOME IMPORTANT DATES IN RAJA RAMMOHAN'S LIFE	
1772:	Birth in the village of Radhanagar in Bengal
1809:	Publication of *Gift to Monothiests* (*Tuhfat-i-Muwahidin*)
1815:	Foundation of the *Atmiya Sabha*
1817:	Establishment of Hindu College in Calcutta.
1820:	Writing of a treatise based on the *Bible* and rejection of the plea of a Christian friend for conversion to Christianity
1821:	Publication of *Sambad Kaumadi*
1825:	Establishment of the Vedanta College
1828:	Establishment of *Brahmo Samaj*
1829:	End of the practice of *Sati*
1833:	Death

The *Brahmo Samaj* led a crusade against *sati*, polygamy, child-marriage, caste-system, *purdah* system, untouchability, use of intoxicants etc. The leaders of Brahmo Samaj also worked for the welfare of peasants, liberty of press, social legislation.

The *Brahmo Samaj* participated in building up national sentiment by glorifying the Indian culture.

After the demise of Raja Rammohan Roy in 1833, the leadership of *Brahmo Samaj* was passed on to the hands of Debendranath Tagore.

In 1866 the *Brahmo Samaj* was split into the *Brahmo Samaj* of India headed by Keshav Chandra Sen and the *Adi Brahmo Samaj,* which remained under the guidance of Devendranath Tagore. The cause of the split in the Brahmo Samaj was the difference of opinion between Tagore and Sen over the age of marriage of boys and girls. Sen advocated marriage in higher age. It was with Sen's active support that the **Native Marriage Act** was passed in 1872, raising the marriageable age of girls to 14 and that of boys to 18.

There was yet another split in the *Brahmo Samaj* in 1878 when Keshab Chandra Sen got his underage daughter married with the Maharaja of Cooch-Behar, violating the Brahmo Marriage Act of 1872. The opponents of Sen formed the *Sadharan Brahmo Samaj*.

VEDA SAMAJ AND PRATHANA SAMAJ : Formed along the lines of the *Brahmo Samaj*, the *Veda Samaj* of Madras and the *Prathana Samaj* of Bombay were founded in 1864 and 1849 respectively. Main figure in *Veda Samaj* was K. Sridharalu Naidu and in Prathana Samaj were M.G. Ranade (1842-1901), R. Banderkar (1837-1925) and N.G. Chandravakar (1855-1923). The *Prathana Samaj* laid more emphasis on social reform, upon works rather than faith. The *Veda Samaj* condemned casteism and did much for improving the lot of women in society.

RAMAKRISHNA MISSION AND VIVEKANANDA : Ramakrishna Parmahansa's (1836-1886) teachings are based on ancient and traditional concepts amidst increasing westernization and modernization. However, Ramakrishna put his emphasis on the essential spirit, not the symbols or rituals. The *Ramakrishna Mission* was conceived and founded by his disciple, Narendra Nath Dutta, better known as Swami Vivekananda, in 1897, eleven years after the death of Ramakrishna. Swami Vivekananda (1863-1902) popularized Ramakrishan's religious message.

RAMKRISHAN MATH : POINTS TO REMEMBER

- The first *Ramakrishan Math* was established by Swami Vivekananda at Baranagore in 1897, while the *Ramkrishna Mission* was founded in 1909.
- By pointing the weaknesses of Hindu religion and society, their degraded position was realised by the Hindus.
- The Mission regarded education, emancipation of women and removal of poverty as absolutely necessary for pursuing religion.
- It emphasized upon self-realisation of individuals which would in the long run lead to social and national upliftment.
- Thus, Vivekananda and Ramkrishan Mission made useful contribution to Hindu religion, culture, society and Indian nationalism.

Vivekananda also known as 'stormy Hindu', emerged as a preacher of **neo-Hinduism** and attended the Parliament of Religions held at Chicago in 1893. He decried untouchability and the caste-system. He was not only concerned with spirituality, but called for social action to remove squalor and poverty. The Mission carried on humanitarian relief and social work. The Mission had many branches in different parts of the country.

IMPORTANT EVENTS IN VIVEKANANDA'S LIFE

1863:	Born in Calcutta
1880:	First contact with Ramkrishna Paramhansa
1891:	Travelled all alone across the country and witnessed galling poverty, misery and suffering of the common people
1893:	Address to the Parliament of Religions in Chicago.
1897:	Establishment of the Ramkrishna Mission in Belur (near Calcutta) and Mayavati (near Almora in Uttaranchal)
1902:	Death

ARYA SAMAJ : The *Arya Samaj* movement, launched in Bombay in 1875, was revivalist in form though not in content. The founder, **Swami Dayanand**, rejected Western ideas and sought to revive the ancient religion of the Aryans. The headquarters of the Arya Samaj was later shifted from Bombay to Lahore. Dayananda's motto was '*Go back to the Vedas*'. He gave his own interpretation of the *Vedas*. He disregarded the authority of later Hindu scriptures like the *Puranas.* Dayanand condemned idol worship and preached unity of God. He decried untouchability and casteism was not sanctioned by the *Vedas*. He advocated widow remarriage and a high status for women in society. His views were published in his famous work *Satyartha Prakash.*

The *Samaj* based its social programme on 'Ten Principles,' entirely on the authority of the *Vedas*, conditioned by rationalism and utilitarianism. The *Arya Samaj* lays great emphasis on education. The Dayananda Anglo-Vedic (D.A.V.) institution, spread all over the country, is a standing proof of the educational achievements of the *Samaj*. Swami Dayananda stressed on *swadeshi, swadharma, swabhasha* and *swarajya.* He was perhaps the first messenger of *Swaraj.* The most distinctive feature of the Samaj was its emphasis on *Shuddhi. Shuddhi* was a device for effecting the religious, social and political unity of people. *Arya Samaj* inspired patriotism and influenced several national leaders and thus contributed towards arousing national consciousness.

ARYA SAMAJ : POINTS TO REMEMBER

- *Arya Samaj* was first established at Bombay in 1875, with the mission to spread true Hindu religion.
- It provided equal status to its members and completely discarded casteism.
- It fought against all social evils of the Hindu society such as *sati*, polygamy, child-marriage, *Purdah*.
- The Arya Samaj established a large number of educational institutions.

- The most distinctive feature of the Samaj was its emphasis on *Shuddhi. Shuddhi* was a device for effecting the religious, social and political unity of people.
- *Arya Samaj* inspired patriotism and influenced several national leaders and thus contributed towards arousing national consciousness.
- Dayanand Saraswati was the first to preach *Swadeshi.* Thus reviving pride in Indian culture and tradition.

The orthodox opinion in the *Arya Samaj* set up the *Gurukula Pathasla* at Haridwar in 1902. The Samaj always remained in the forefront of political movement and produced leaders of the eminence of Lala Hans Raj, Pandit Guru Dutt and the Lala Lajpat Rai. Dayanand's political slogan was 'India for the Indians.' Perhaps the most phenomenal achievement of the *Arya Samaj* was in the field of social reform and spread of education. Unfortunately its revivalist tendency such the *shuddhi movement* to convert non-Hindus to Hinduism, helped in raising communal feelings.

Ishwar Chandra Vidyasagar : Pandit Ishwar Chandra Vidyasagar made important contributions towards making of modern India. He opposed child marriage and polygamy and laid great stress on women's education and women upliftment. The success of his countrywide movement for widow remarriage was seen in the enactment of a law in 1856, which legalised remarriage of widows. Interestingly, the first widow remarriage under this law was celebrated under the direct supervision of Vidyasagar. Other than widow remarriage, Vidyasagar also campaigned valiantly against polygamy and child marriage. He established Bethune School in 1849 in Calcutta for women's education.

SOCIAL REFORMS IN WESTERN INDIA : Western India in Maharasthra also witnessed some social reforms. Jagannath Shankar Saheb, Bal Shastri Jambhekar, Vishnu Shastri Bapat and Krishan Shastri Chaplunkar were some of the pioneers of the new reform movement. Jambhekar attacked Brahmanical orthodoxy and tried to reform popular Hinduism. In 1832, he started a weekly '*The Darpan*'.

In 1849, the *Paramahansa Mandali* was founded. Its founders believed in one God and were primarily interested in breaking caste rules. In 1848, several educated youngmen formed the Student's Literary and Scientific Society, which had two branches, the Gujarati and the Marathi '*Dnyan Prasarak Mandalis*'. In 1851, Jyotiba Phule and his wife started a girls' school at Poona. Vishnu Shastri Pundit, founded the Widow Remarriage Association in the 1850's. Karsondas Mulji started the '*Satya Prakash*' in Gujarat in 1852 to advocate widow remarriage.

An outstanding champion of new learning and social reform in Maharashtra was Gopal Hari Deshmukh, who became famous by the pen name of '*Lokahitawadi*'. Dadabhai Naoroji was also a social reformer who was among the founders of an association to reform the Zoroastrian religion and the Parsi Law Association which agitated for the grant of a legal status for women and for uniform laws of inheritance and marriage for the Parsis.

The Bharat Dharma Maha Mandala : In defence of orthodox Hinduism and against the teachings of the Arya Samaj, the Ramakrishna Mission, etc., orhtodox educated Hindus organised themselves. Among them were the Dharma Maha Parishad in South India, the Dharma Maha Mandali in Bengal etc.

Dharma Sabha : This was another orthodox society, founded in 1830 by Radhakant Deb (1794-1876). Members of the Sabha defended the socio-religious *status quo* against newspapers. The Sabha played an active role in promoting western education, even among girls.

14.4 REFORM MOVEMENTS AMONG THE MUSLIMS

THE WAHABI MOVEMENT: The Wahabi movement was launched by Shah Walliullah (1702-62); who was the first Indian Muslim leader to express concern at degeneration among the Muslims due to Western influences. The Wahabi movement was essentially a revivalist movement. Walliullah urged the desirability of creating a harmony among the four schools of Muslim jurisprudence. He emphasised the role of individual conscience in religion.

Later, Shah Abdul Aziz and Syed Ahmed Barelve popularized the teachings of Walliullah. They also gave political colour to his teachings and aimed at creating a homeland for the muslims.

SYED AHMAD KHAN AND THE ALIGARH MOVEMENT: The most important reformer among the Muslims was Syed Ahmad Khan (1817-1898). He tried to modernize the outlook of the Muslims. He tried to reconcile his co-religionists to modern scientific thought and to the British rule and urged them to accept services under the Government. Reforms started with the foundation of Mohammedan Literary Society at Calcutta in 1863. This Society promoted discussion of religious, social and political questions in the light of modern ideas and encouraged upper and middle class Muslims to take to western education.

Sir Syed also tried to reform the social abuses in the Muslim community. He condemned the system of '*piri*' and '*muridi*'. He also condemned the institution of slavery and described it un-Islamic. His progressive social ideas were propagated through his magazine '*Tazhib-ul-Akhlaq*' (Improvement of Manners and Morals). In '*Commentaries of the Quran*' he criticized the narrow outlook of traditional interpreters.

Syed Khan opposed the participation of Muslims in the activities of Indian National Congress. He wanted more time for the Indian Muslims to organise and consolidate their position which he thought could be best done through education for which he regarded maintaining good relations with the British very essential. But he emphasised the unity between Hindus and Muslims.

MAJOR EVENTS IN SIR SYED'S LIFE	
1817:	Born in New Delhi
1864:	Foundation of a scientific society
1870:	Publication of a Urdu journal, ***Tahzib-al-Akhlaq***
1875:	Foundation of Aligarh School, which was converted into the **Mohammadan Anglo-Oriental College** in 1877. (The college was finally converted in Aligarh Muslim University in 1920).
1878:	Membership of the Imperial Legislative Council
1888:	Conferred Knighthood

THE DEOBAND SCHOOL : The ulema under the leadership of Muhammad Qasim Nanautavi (1832-1880) and Rashid Ahmad Gangohi (1828-1905) founded the School of Islamic theology at Deoband in the Saharanpur district of the Uttar Pradesh in 1866. The object was to train religious leaders for the Muslim community. The school curricula shut out English education and Western culture. The instruction imparted was in original Islamic religion and the aim was moral and religious regeneration of the Muslim community. In contrast to the Aligarh Movement which aimed at welfare of the Muslim community through Western education and support of the British Government, the *Deoband* school did not prepare its students for government jobs or worldly careers but for preaching of Islamic faith. It was for its religious instruction that the *Deoband* school attracted students not only from all parts of India but from the neighbouring Muslim countries also. In politics, the *Deoband* school welcomed the formation of the Indian National Congress in 1885.

Maulana Abul Kalam Azad, Mahmud ul-Hasan and Shibli Numani were some of the noted followers of this school.

THE AHMADIA MOVEMENT : Mirza Ghulam Ahmad (1839-1908) was the founder of this movement. The movement, formed in 1889, believed in universal religion, encouraged fraternal unity and opposed sacred wars. Mizra Ghulam proclaimed himself as a **Messiah** and an incarnation of Krishna.

TA'AYUUNI MOVEMENT : The Ta'ayuuni movement was led by Karamat Ali Jaunpuri. The movement, based on the teaching of Shah Waliullah, opposed innovations and syncretistic practices.

14.5 SIKH REFORM MOVEMENTS

SINGH SABHA MOVEMENT : The rationalist and progressive ideas of 19th century also influenced the Sikh community. In 1873, the *Singh Sabha* movement was founded at Amritsar. Its objective was twofold. It planned to bring to the Sikh community the benefits of Western enlightenment through modern education. It also countered the proselytizing activities of the Christian missionaries as well as Hindu revivalists. The Sabha opened a network of *Khalsa* schools and colleges throughout Punjab.

THE AKALI MOVEMENT : The *Akali* Movement was an offshoot of the *Singh Sabha* movement. The *Akali* movement aimed to liberate the Sikh *Gurdwaras* (temples) from the control of corrupt *mahants* who enjoyed the support of the government. In 1921, the *Akalis* launched a non-violent, non-cooperation satyagraha movement against the *mahants.* The Government resorted to repressive measures but had to bow before popular opinion and pass the Sikh Gurdwaras Act in 1922, which was later amended in 1925.

The *Akali* movement was a sectarian or a regional movement but not a communal movement. The *Akali* leaders played a notable role in the national liberation struggle though some dissenting voices were heard occasionally.

14.6 PARSI REFORM MOVEMENT

REHNUMAI MAZDAYASNAN SABHA : The Parsi community could not remain unaffected by the wind of change that swept India. In 1851, a group of English educated Parsis set up the *Rahnumai Mazdayasnan Sabha* or Religious Reform Association for the object of "the regeneration of the social condition of the Parsis and the restoration of the Zoroastrian religion to its pristine purity." Naroaj Furdonji, Dadabhai Naoroji, K.R. Cama were in the forefront of the movement. The newspaper *Rast-Gofter* (Truth-Teller) propagated the message of the Association. Parsi religious rituals and practices were reformed and Parsi creed redefined. In the field of social reform, attention was focused on improvement of lot of Parsi women in society like removal of *purdah* system, raising the age of marriage and education of women. Gradually the Parsis emerged as the most Westernised section of Indian society.

14.7 INDEPENDENT REFORM MOVEMENTS

Derozio and Young Bengal: A radical trend arose among the Bengali intellectuals during the late 1820's and the 1830's. Henry Vivian Derozio, a native of Scotland had special love for India and her people. Derozio and his followers were known as the Derozians and Young Bengal, and were fiery patriots. He expressed his love for India in his poetry. Derozio promoted radical ideas through his class lectures and by organising student societies for debates and discussions on literature, history, philosophy and science. However, they did not succeed in creating a long movement.

Theosophical Society : The Theosophical Society was founded in the United States by Madam H.P. Blavatsky and Colonel H.S. Olcott, who later came to India and founded the headquarters of the Society at Adyar near Madras in 1886. The Theosophist Movement soon grew in India as a result of the leadership given to it by Mrs. Annie Besant who had come to India in 1893. The Theosophists advocated the revival and strengthening of the ancient religions of Hinduism, Zoroastrianism, and Buddhism. They recognized the doctrine of the transmigration of the soul. They also preached the universal brotherhood of man. As religious revivalist the Theosophists were not very successful, but they helped Indians recover their self-confidence, even though it tended to give them a sense of false pride in their past greatness.

14.8 LOWER CASTE MOVEMENTS

In the 19th and 20th centuries, a number of circumstances created class consciousness among the lower castes. Under the new circumstances—the British policy of divide and rule, spread of western education, introduction of a common Indian Penal Code and Code of Criminal Procedure, the growth of national consciousness, the extension of railway networks and popularity of modern political concepts, such as equality and social egalitarianism–lower castes took upon themselves to struggle for caste equality. Their efforts resulted in the organisation of several lower caste movements, especially in South India and Western India.

In the South and the West, the lower caste movements were a direct revolt against the Brahmanical domination. Grievances nurtured by the educated section of the low and backward castes were a major cause for the rise of caste movements.

JUSTICE MILLER COMMITTEE

The British Government appointed a committee on Backward Castes under the Chairmanship of Lesley Miller, Justice of the Mysore High Court. The Miller Committee emphasized on professional education for backward classes. It recommended 50 per cent reservation in government jobs for seven years for backward classes. It also recommended free education, free books and relaxed conditions for admission to government and government-aided schools for backward class students. These recommendations were strongly opposed by Brahmin. However, they were implemented by the first non-Brahmin *Diwan* of Mysore, Kantharaja Urs, in 1919.

A brief survey of the caste movements, along with other socio-religious reform movements, in the late 19th and early 20th centuries is given ahead on separate tables.

14.9 EFFECTS OF SOCIO-RELIGIOUS REFORM MOVEMENTS

The various reform movements had similarities. They provided the much needed confidence to educated Indians. They laid stress upon rational understanding of social and religious ideas encouraging a scientific and humanitarian outlook. Thus, their moorings of superior western culture gave way to confidence in their rich cultural heritage.

Almost all of them, voiced against the obsolete rites, practices and social evils which were against humanity. Enough importance was attached with the emancipation of women through female education, abolition of child-marriage, widow re-marriage, abolition of *Purdah-system*. There was an unequivocal demand for the abolition of caste-system and loathesome practice of untouchability.

The socio-religious reform movements paved the way for the national movement in several ways. A wide nationalist attitude was cultivated. The movements promoted the feelings of self-confidence, self-respect and patriotism and thereby developed a feeling of national consciousness. On the negative side, these movements created feelings of mutual competition, rivalry and hatred among different communities, which encouraged communalism, violence and growth of divisive organisations that helped the British to carry out their policy of '*divide and rule*' with dexterity.

SOCIO-RELIGIOUS REFORM MOVEMENTS OF THE 19TH-20TH CENTURIES

Hindu Socio-Religious reform Movements and Organizations

Movement/Organisation	Year	Place	Founder	Objectives
Swaminarayan Sampraya		Gujarat	Swami Sahjananda (original name Ghanshayama)	Protest against epicurean and luxurious practices of Vaishnavism.
Atmiya Sabha (later Brahmo Samaj)	1815-1828	Calcutta	Raja Ram Mohan Roy	To propagate monotheism & reforms in the Hindu society
Brahmo Samaj	1828	Calcutta	Raja Ram Mohan Roy, Keshab Chandra Sen, Debenbranath Tagore	Emphasized on human dignity, opposed idolatry and criticized social evils as *sati*
Young Bengal	1826-1832	Calcutta	Derozio, Rasik Krishna Mullik, Tarachand Chuckervarty, Krishnamohan Banerjee	Opposed vices in the society; believed in truth, freedom, & reason; social reform.
Dharma Sabha	1830	Calcutta	Radha Kanta Deva	Founded to counter Brahmo Samaj Movement Opposed to liberal and radical reforms, including *Sati.*
Namdhari/ Kuka Movement	1841-1871	NWF (Ludhiana, Punjab)	Bhai Balak Singh and Baba Ram Singh	Spread the true spirit of Sikhism, opposed to all caste distinctions.
Rahanumai Mazdayasan Sabha	1851	Bombay	S.S. Bangali, Naoroji, Fundonji, J.B. Nacha, etc.	A socio-religious organization of the Parsis founded for the restoration of Zoroastrian religion to its pristine glory and social regeneration of the Parsi community through modern education and emancipation of women.
Radha Swami Satsang	1861	Agra	Tulsi Ram also known as Shiv Dayal Saheb	Belief in one Supreme Being, religious unity, emphasis on simplicity of social life and social service.
Prarthana Samaj	1867	Bombay	Dr. Atmaram Pandurang	Reforming Hindu religious thought and practice in the light of modern knowledge.
Indian Reform Association	1870	Calcutta	Keshab Chandra Sen	Create public opinion against child marriages & for legalizing the Brahmo form of (Civil) marriage. Promote the intellectual and social status of Indian women.
Arya Samaj	1875	Bombay	Swami Dayananda Saraswati	To reform Hindu religion in North India.
Theosophical Society	1875	New York	Madam H.P. Blavatsky & Col. H.S, Olcott	Advocated the revival & strengthening of ancient religions of Hinduism, Zoroastrianism & Buddhism.
Deccan Education Society	1884	Pune	M.G.Ranade, V.G. Chibdonkar, G.G.Agarkar. etc.	To contribute to the cause of education and culture in Western India. The Society founded the Ferguson College, Pune in 1885.
Seva Sadan	1885	Bombay	Behramji, M. Malabari	Campaign against child marriage and enforced widowhood and care for socially exploited women.
Ramakrishna Mission	1887	Calcutta	Swami Vivekananda	To carry on humanitarian relief and social work.

Indian National Social Conference	1887	Bombay	M.G. Ranade and Raghunath Rao	To focus attention on matters relating to social reforms. It was the social reform cell of the Indian National Congress.
Deva Samaj	1887	Lahore	Shiva Narain Agnihotri	Ideas closer to Brahmo Samaj, asked his followers to follow social code of conduct and ethics, as not to accept bribe, indulge in gambling and consume intoxicants and non-vegetarian food.
Madras Hindu Association	1892	Madras	Viresalingam Pantalu	Movement concerned with the plight of widows and combat Devadasi system.
Bharat Dharma Mahamandala	1902	Varanasi	Pandit Madan Mohan Malaviya and Pandit Din Dayal Sharma	Organization of the orthodox Hindus, also known as Sanatana dhamis, to counter the teachings of the Arya Samaj.
The Servants of India Society	1905	Bombay	Gopal Krishna Gokhale	To work for social reforms, & train "national missionaries for the service of India."
Poona Seva Sadan	1909	Pune	G.K.Devadhar and Ramabai Ranade (wife of M.G. Ranade)	Establish institutions for the economic uplift and useful employment of women.
Niskam Karma Math (The monastery of disinterested Work)	1910	Pune	Dhondo Keshav Karve	Work for social reform, selfless service to mankind and educational progress of women. Founded India's first women's University in Pune,1916.
The Bharat Stri Mandal	1910	Calcutta	Saralabala Devi Choudharani	First women's organization on all-India basis to further the cause of Women's education and emancipation of women.
Social Service League	1911	Bombay	Narayan Malhar Joshi	Social service and improve the conditions of the common masses by opening schools, libraries, dispensaries.
Seva Samiti	1914	Allahabad	Pandit Hridayanath Kunzru	Organize social service, promote education and reform criminal and fallen elements in society
The Indian Women's Association	1917	Madras	Mrs. Annie Besant	Work for uplift of Indian women and "to secure a larger a free and fuller life for them".

Muslim Socio-religious Movements and Organizations

Movement/Organization	Year	Place	Founder	Objectives
Faraizi or Faraidi Movement	1804	Faridpur, Bengal	Haji Shariatullah and Dudhi Miyan	Emphasis on strict monotheism and to rid the Muslim Society of non-Islamic social customs, rituals and practices. It was an anti-landlord & anti-British movement.
Wahabi Movement	1820	Rohikhand	Syed Ahmed of Rae Bareilly	Popularized the teachings of Waliullah; stressed role of individual conscience in religion.
Taayuni Movement	1839	Dacca	Karamati Ali Jaunpur	Opposed to the Faraizi Movement and supported the British rule.
Deoband Movement (A school of Islamic Theology at Deoband, Saharanpur, UP)	1867	Deoband	Muhamman Qasim Nanautavi and Rashid Ahmed Gangohi	Improve the spiritual and moral conditions of Indian Muslim. It supported the INC and was opposed to the Pro-British Aligarh movement.
Aligarh Movement	1875	Aligarh	Sir Syed Ahmed Khan	Liberalization of Indian Islam and modernization of Indian Muslims through religious reinterpretation, social reform and modern education.

Ahmadiya Movement	1889-90	Faridkot	Mirza Ghulam Ahmad of Qadiyan	Universal religion of all humanity, opposed to Islamic orthodoxy and spread of western liberal education among Indian Muslims.
Nadwatal Ulema	1894-95	Lucknow	Maulana Shibli Numani	To reform the traditional Islamic system of education, to strengthen Hindu-Muslim unity and to arouse nationalism among Indian Muslims.
Ahrar Movement	1910	Aligarh	Riza Khan & Ali Brothers	Against Aligarh Movement.
Khudai Khidmatgar Movement	1929	NWFP	Khan Abdul Ghaffar Khan	Upliftment of people of Frontier & prepare them for attainment of independence,

Lower Caste/Caste Movements and Organizations

Movement/Organization	Year	Place	Founder	Objectives
Satya Shodhak Samaj	1873	Maharashtra	Jyotiba Phule	Opposed to untouchability, priestly or Brahmin domination, belief in social equality and uplift of the lower castes by educating them.
Aravippuram Movement	1888	Aravippuram, Kerala	Shri Narayan Guru	Opposed to religious disabilities against lower castes, believed in social equality, attacked Brahmin domination and worked for the uplift of lower castes by educating them. Demanded free entry of the people of lower castes to the temples.
Shri Narayan Dharma Paripalana Yogam or S.N.D.P. Movement	1902-03	Kerala	Shri Narayan Guru, Dr. Pilau and Kumaran Asan	Same as above. In 1920, T.K. Madhavan launched the Temple Entry Movement.
The Depressed Class Mission	1906	Bombay	V.R. Shinde	Launched by the Prathana Samaj as an independent association to organize education facilities for lower castes.
Bahujan Samaj	1910	Satara, Maharashtra	Mukundrao Patil	Opposed to exploitation of the lower castes by the upper caste Brahmins, landlords, merchants and money lenders.
Justice (Party) Movement	1815-16	Madras	C.N. Mudaliar, T.M. Nair and P.Tyagaraja Chetti	Opposed Brahmin predominance in education, services and politics.
Depressed Classes Welfare Institute (Bahiskrit Hitkarini)	1924	Bombay	Dr. B.R. Ambedkar	To Propagate the gospel of social equality among caste Hindus and untouchables, Demanded constitutional safeguards for the depressed classes.
Self-Respect Movement	1925	Madras	E.V.Ramaswami Naicker'Periyar'	Anti-Brahmin and Hindu orthodoxy radical movement, advocated weddings without priests, forcible temple entry, total defiance of Hindu social laws and also theism.
Harijan Sevak Sangh	1932	Pune	Mahatma Gandhi	Organization for removal of untouchability & social discriminations against untouchables and other lower castes. Provide medical, educational and technical facilities to untouchables.
Dravida Munetra Kazhagam	1944	—	C.N. Annaduari & Ramaswamy Naicker	Social equality.

15. THE INDIAN FREEDOM MOVEMENT

TRIBAL MOVEMENTS

According to the 1991 census, Scheduled Tribes formed 7.85% of the total population of India. They have been divided by anthropologists into two categories (*i*) the non-frontier tribes, which constitute 89 per cent of the total tribal population and (*ii*) frontier tribes, of the seven North-eastern frontier states of Nagaland, Arunachal Pradesh, Meghalaya, Assam, Manipur, Mizoram and Tripura.

These two areas were differently placed geographically, economically and historically, in relation to the surrounding non-tribal society as well as the penetration of their social structures by outsiders, especially under colonialism. This difference was reflected in the different issues agitated and types of movements that arose in the tribal areas.

Tribals, adivasis or aboriginals were usually the original inhabitants of vast tracts in western, central, southern, eastern and north-eastern parts of the country. With the exception of the North-east, they had been reduced to a minority with the influx of outsiders and exposed to rapid changes. They were groups of people bound together by blood relationships and socially organised differently from 'caste' society, though often forming its lowest stratum. They subsisted on shifting cultivation combined with hunting and fishing. With the onset of colonialism they were often reduced to being agricultural labourers on their own land and increasingly recruited as coolies to work in distant mines, plantations and factories.

Tribal movements in colonial India were distinguished from the movements of other communities in that they were the most militant, most isolated (at least initially) and most frequent. There were about 70 listed tribal revolts from 1778 to 1947. The tribal uprisings were marked by immense courage on the part of the tribals and their butchery by the official machinery of suppression.

CAUSES OF THE TRIBAL MOVEMENTS

Some of the important causes of tribal movements were :

(*i*) The British land settlements in India had eroded the tribal traditions of joint ownership and sharpened tensions within the tribal society.

(*ii*) The activities of the Christian missionaries in the tribal areas created varied reactions amongst the tribal.

(*iii*) The tightening of governmental control over the forest zones, creation of reserved forests and attempts to monopolise forest wealth through curbs on the use of timber and grazing facilities, caused great unrest among the tribals on account of dislocation in the tribal economy.

(*iv*) The tribals also resented the introduction of general laws which they considered as intrusions into their personal lives.

(*v*) The tribals were also greatly influenced by movements of internal religious and socio-cultural reform.

(*vi*) Some of the tribal uprisings took place in reaction to the efforts of the landlords to enhance taxes on timber and grazing, police exactions, new excise regulations, exploitation by low-country traders and money-lenders and restrictions on shifting cultivation in forests.

MOVEMENTS OF THE NON-FRONTIER TRIBES

The major movements that occurred among the non-frontier tribes were mainly confined to Central India, West-Central India and Andhra, becauses tribes down south were too primitive, too small in number and too isolated to organise movements, in spite of their exploitation and resultant discontent. Among the tribes that participated in these movements were Khond, Savara, Santhal, Munda, Oraon, Koya, Kol, Gond and Bhil.

The situation among the non-frontier tribes was complex. The relatively homogeneous and egalitarian tribal culture of various tribal areas was already breaking up with the penetration of outsiders even before the advent of colonialism. The resulting social differentiation and exploitation were greatly aggravated by British rule and its accompanying commercialisation. Outsiders from the plains—money-lenders, traders, land grabbers and contractors—were joined by the British administrators and local landlords (a result of the British legal conceptions that argued for absolute private property) in sucking dry the tribals, as well as eroding traditions of joint ownership and sharpening tensions within the tribal society. Christian missions were active in many tribal areas, bringing education and promise of social ascent, but also exploiting the tribals in their own manner and often speaking and acting against their traditional belief systems. They elicited a variety of responses from the tribals, ranging from hostility to an attempt to use Christianity in antiforeign ways. British attempts to reserve forests and monopolise forest wealth by banning shifting cultivation and restrict cattle grazing and firewood collection from the 1860s added fuel to the fire, as did new taxes on toddy etc.

The rebellions by the non-frontier tribals were usually reactions against outsiders (the hated diku), local landlords and rulers, the support provided to the latter by the British administration and intervention by them in the life of the tribals. The indigenous names for these tribal movements were ***meli, hool*** and ***ulgulan***.

Despite their common background, these movements tended to differ both overtime and in the issues that they tackled. Kr. Suresh Singh divides tribal movements into three phases. The first was between 1795 and 1860, which coincided with the rise, expansion and establishment of the British empire. The second coincided with the intensive phase of colonialism and covered the period 1860-1920 when "merchant capital penetrated into tribal economy affecting their relationship with land and forest." The third phase covers the period from 1920 to the achievement of independence in 1947. During this phase tribals not only launched so-called separatist movements but also participated in the nationalist and agrarian movements. While the leadership of the first phase emerged from the upper crust of tribal society, that of the second rose from the lowest rung of it. In the third phase, as tribal movements acquired a tendency of getting linked with wider movements, leadership was often provided either by those tribals who had the benefit of education or by outsiders ranging from Gandhian social workers to Alluri Sitaram Raju. On the basis of issues their typologies may be constructed as (*i*) ethnic or cultural movements; (*ii*) reform or Sanskritisation movements; (*iii*) agrarian and forest based movements and (*iv*) political movements. These are tentative and overlapping divisions, one often leading to the other.

FIRST PHASE

The first phase of these movements was sparked off by the British attempts to penetrate tribal areas and introduce reforms there. These tribal movements frequently tended to be restorative in character, led by traditional sections whose privileges had been undermined by colonisation of India.

Pahariyas Uprisings: Thus the Pahariyas, a martial tribe occupying the Raj Mahal Hills, waged a long and bloody struggle from 1778 under their Sardars to resist encroachment on their territory. The British were compelled to make peace with them and declare it ***damni-kol*** area.

Khond Uprising: The Khond lived in vast hill tracts stretching from Tamil Nadu to Bengal and covering Central Provinces, in virtual independence due to the mountainous terrain. Their uprisings from 1837 to 1856 were directed against the British, in which the tribals of Ghumsar, ***China-Ki-Medi***, Kalahandi and Patna actively participated. The movement was led by Chakra Bisoi in the name of the young Raja. The main issue was the attempt by the government to suppress human sacrifice, introduction of new taxes by the British and the influx of zamindars and ***Sahukars*** into their areas, which was causing the tribals untold misery. The British formed a Mariah Agency, against which the Khonds fought with tangi—a kind of battle axe-bows, arrows, even swords. Later Savaras and some local militia clans also joined in, led by Radhakrishna Dandasena. Chakra Bisoi disappeared in 1855, after which the movement petered out.

Kol and Ho Uprisings: The Kolarian tribes of Chotanagpur, ruled by Petty Chieftains called Raja, resented the gradual extension of British authority in their territory. The British occupation of Singbhum was much resented by the Raja of Parahat. His subjects, the Hos, zealously guarded the frontiers and would not allow officials to enter into their territory. It was only in 1827, after many villages were burnt and a large number of Hos were killed, that they submitted, biding their time.

The Mundas of Chotanagpur broke out in revolt in 1831, the Hos joining them. This uprising was caused by the new policy of farming revenue to outsiders and the introduction of the Bengalis into their country. The rebellion soon spread over a considerable area, including Ranchi, Hazaribagh, Palamau and Manbhum. Violence and pillage was universal and indiscriminate. The wrath of the rebels was specially vented upon the foreign settlers, about a thousand of whom were slaughtered in their homes. After extensive military operations the uprising was suppressed in March 1832. The Hos continued to be refractory and military operations were undertaken in 1836 and 1837 before they submitted to the British authority.

Santhal Rebellion: The Santhal rebellion of 1855-56 was marked by some of the worst features of elemental tribal passions and open denunciation of British rule. The rebellion, covering the districts of Birbhum, Singbhum, Bankura, Hazaribagh, Bhagalpur and Monghyr in Orissa and Bihar, was precipitated mainly by economic causes. The money-lenders and colonial administrators both exploited them. The ***diku*** merchants charged interest on loans, ranging from 50 to 500 per cent and exploited and cheated the tribals in many other ways, often grabbing their lands. The tribals turned against the British Government when they found that the British officers, instead of redressing their grievances, were more anxious to protect their oppressors from the tribals wrathful vengeance. Under the leadership of two Santhal brothers, Siddhu and Khanhu, more than ten thousand Santhals assembled in June 1855, when a divine order was issued asking the Santhals to get out of the control of their oppressors and take possession of the country and set up a government of their own." Within a month, the rebellion had assumed a formidable shape. The rebels cut of the postal and railway communications between Bhagalpur and Rajmahal, proclaimed the end of the Company's rule and commencement of the Santhal regime. They attacked the houses of money-lenders, zamindars, white planters, railway engineers and British officials. The open war with the British continued till February 1856, when the rebel leaders were finally captured and the movement was put down with a great deal of repression.

Other tribal rebellions during this period were ***Tomar*** revolt in Chhotanagpur (1795); ***Koli*** disturbances in Maharashtra (1784-85); ***Chauri*** movement in Bihar (1798); Panchet estate revolt (1809-28); Bhil revolt in Gujarat; Munda uprisings (1820-1832 and 1837); ***Kherwar*** uprising under Bhagirath in Bihar; Bhumij uprising; Gond uprising in Bastar (1842); Bhil revolt under Kunwar and Jivo Vasuo revolt in Gujarat (1850 and 1857-58).

SECOND PHASE

But these measures, apart from being "too little and too late" were followed by a phase from 1860 to 1920 when colonialism tightened its hold on India. By combining both foreign and indigenous exploitation, it affected the internal structure of the tribals, their relation with land and forests and increased their dependence on the diku. Alongside, there was intensified Christian missionary activity that represented another form of penetration of indigenous society, while simultaneously giving hope of reform and change. This gave the movements from 1860 to 1920 a double purpose—to fight against exploitative outsiders on the one hand, and to reform their own societies on the other. Thus, apart from violent outbursts, there were also movements for revitalisation promising miraculous entry into a Golden Age, or millenarianism. These often combined a peculiar mixture of Sanskritisation tendencies (a tendency to adopt the culture of the upper castes) with tribal beliefs and a desperate hope of better times. Their leadership was no longer the monopoly of old chieftains, whose defeat climaxed in 1857. They often followed in the wake of older movement.

Kharwar Uprising: The crushing of the Santhal rebellion (1855-56) was followed by the Kharwar uprising of the 1870s, which preached monotheism and internal reform at first but had begun to turn into a campaign against revenue settlement operations just before it was suppressed.

Khonda Dora Uprising: This phase saw the birth of many charismatic leaders, rebellious prophets claiming magical powers. The Khonda Doras of Dabur in

Visakhapatnam Agency in 1900 followed Korra Mallaya who claimed to be an ***avatar*** of the Pandavas and promised that he would by magic turn the tribals' bamboos into guns, and the government's weapons into water. Then he would drive out the English and rule himself. The police shot dead 11 of the rebels and hanged two.

Naikada Movement: The Naikada forest tribes in Madhya Pradesh and Gujarat, similarly, launched movements against British officers and caste Hindus with religious fervour, and attacked police stations in 1868 in a bid to establish a *dharmaraj* under their Charismatic leaders.

Bhil Uprisings: Slightly later in southern Rajasthan the Bhils of Banswara, Sunth and Dungarpur States were stirred to action by a reform movement under Govind Guru, who was a bali or bonded labourer. By 1913 it developed into a bid to set up a Bhil Raj. Four thousand Bhils assembled on Mangad Hill, and the British were able to disperse them only after considerable resistance in which 12 tribals were killed and 900 taken prisoner.

Bhuyan and Juang Uprisings: These uprisings took place in Keonjhar (Orissa) in 1867-68 and again in 1891-93. The first was led by Ratna Nayak. The main participants were Bhuyans, who were later joined by Kals and Juangs. The main cause was the hurt pride of Bhuyans who held important positions in the administration of Keonjhar— the presence of their Sardar was essential at the time of the coronation. After the death of Raja in 1867 there was a dispute over succession and the British put their protege on the throne, without consulting the Bhuyans. This enraged them and sparked off a rebellion broadly followed the pattern of the first phase being led by traditional chiefs and having restorative aims.

The second uprising of 1891-93 was against the feudal and oppressive regime of the king who had been installed by the British. Led by Dharni Dhar Nayak, it had a wider and larger support among the population. It completely paralysed the state administration and the Raja was forced to seek refuge in Cuttack. The rebellion was ultimately put down with the help of the local administration.

Bastar Uprisings: In 1910, the British troops suppressed an uprising in the Jagdalpur region against the Raja of Bastar. Though partly provoked by a succession dispute the main cause was the recent imposition of forest regulations and feudal levies. The rebels disrupted communications, attacked police stations and forest outposts, burnt schools and even tried to besiege Jagdalpur town.

Koya Rebellion: It occurred in 1879-80 in the eastern Godavari tract of present-day Andhra Pradesh and also affected some portions of Malkangiri district in Orissa. Its heart lay in the "Rampa Cauntry" of Chodavaram where tribal Koya and Konda Sara hill chiefs had risen against their overlord in 1803, 1840, 1845, 1858, 1861 and 1862. The 1879-80 rebellion was led by Tomma Sora and reflected problems faced by tribals like erosion of customary rights over forests, police exactions, exploitation by money-lenders, and new excise regulations restricting domestic production of toddy. Tomma Sora was hailed as the King of Malkangiri. The rebellion at its height affected 5,000 square miles and the peasants took over a police station. Sora was shot dead by the police and the movement collapsed, but only with the use of six regiments of the Madras infantry. In 1886 another uprising took place here. The rebels, led by Raja Anantayyar, formed themselves into a Ram Sandu (Ram's Army) and appealed to the Maharaja of Jaypore to help them in throwing out the British.

Munda Uprisings: The Ulgulan of Birsa Munda in the region south of Ranchi in 1899-1900 is the best known tribal rebellion of this period. The transformation of the Mundari agrarian system into non-communal feudal, zamindari or individual tenures was the key to the agrarian disorders that climaxed in the religious-political movements of Birsa. Money-lender and merchant ***thekeddars*** (forest contractors) added to the Munda woes. The conversion of some Mundas to Christianity appeared to promise help and from 1858 there are references to Christian tribals resisting the oppressive zamindars. In March 1879 Mundas claimed that Chhotanagpur belonged to them.

Birsa Munda was the son of a share-cropper who had received some education from the missionaries and then came under Vaishnava influence. In 1893-94 he had participated in a movement to prevent village wastelands being taken over by the Forest Department. His initial popularity was based on medicinal and healing powers, by which Birsa claimed to make his followers invulnerable. The Mundas envisaged an ideal and just society which would be free from internal as well as European exploiters. Women also participated in the movement.

In 1899 Birsites shot arrows and tried to burn down churches. Police became their target in 1900, but on 9th January the rebels were defeated in a fight at Sail Rakeb hill, and Birsa died in jail. Nearly 350 Mundas were tried, of whom three were hanged and 44 transported for life. There was some belated relief in the Chhotanagpur Tenancy Act of 1908 with recognition to joint farming rights and ban on beth begari or forced labour. Though the claim that Birsa was a full-fledged nationalist is a bit far-fetched, a primitive but basic anti-imperialist thrust cannot be denied to his movement.

Khond Uprising: As the 20th century advanced, certain "proto-nationalist" appeals could be discerned in the anti-imperialist content of some tribal movements. News of the First World War in the Orissa feudatory state of Saspalla in October 1914 gave an ongoing Khond rebellion the hope that there would be no Sahibs left in the country and the Khonds would have an autonomous government. The uprising was put down with the burning of Khond villages.

British efforts to recruit tribal labour for menial work on the western front led to a Santhal uprising in Mayurbhanj.

THIRD PHASE

Tana Bhagat Movements: After the First World War there were a number of bhagat (religious mendicant or prophet) movements amongst the Mundas and Oraons of Chhotanagpur. These movements, led by the tribal bhagats, were a kind of Sanskritisation movements. The Oraons called these movements Kurukh dharman or the real and original religion of the Oraons.

After the emergence of these nationalist religious tribal movements the Gandhian workers took interest in launching constructive work amongst the tribals. By the 1920s the Congress had established strong ties with the Tana Bhagats and preached them the lesson of nationalism. Under its leadership they took part in the freedom struggle by picketing liquor shops, holding demonstrations and staging satyagrahas and dharnas.

The religiosity of these movements had a "profound bearing" on the state of consciousness of the Adivasis and provided them with a code of political ethics to resist and struggle against their exploitation. From the 1920s it also gave them aspirations and solidarity that sometimes led to linking their local grievances with the national movement. This was more true of forest-based grievances that were purely against British administration than agrarian grievances which were often against the local zamindars.

There were a number of these bhagat movements like that of Jara Bhagat, Balram Bhagat, Gau Rakshini Bhagats and even a woman ***bhagat*** named Devamenia. While these movements combined some form of Sanskritisation, like asking followers to give up meant and drink, from the later part of 1915 these began to converge into a large powerful messianic movement which went under the name of 'Tana Bhagat Movement'. Its message was that God would send a most powerful and benevolent delegate down to earth to redeem the Oraons from their miserable state. Sometimes this Messiah was identified with Birsa, Munda or with the German Kaiser-Baba—who would expel all foreigners from their land. This soon became a powerful movement for internal reforms and overthrow of outsiders.

The Government often used repressive methods against these movements. Their adherents were jailed and their lands confiscated. These hardships, however, did not deter the bhagats followers. In fact they even inspired the Mos, a neighbouring Munda tribe, to begin a similar bhagat movement in the 1930s under Hari Babu.

Chenchu Tribals Movement: The Chenchu tribals of Guntur district in Andhra Pradesh launched a powerful forest Satyagraha during the Non-Cooperation movement. The links were provided by leaders like Venkattappaya and even Gandhi visited Cuddapah in September 1927. The Congress wanted to confine the movement to social boycott of forest officials, but the peasants began sending cattle into the forest without paying grazing fees. Some villagers in Palnad proclaimed Swaraj and attacked police parties and the forest administration virtually collapsed for some time. Similarly the Bhil movement under Motilal Tejawat got a more millenarian flavour in 1921-22, though the Congress itself refuted any links with it.

In Bengal at Jalpaiguri in February 1922, the police were attacked by Santhals wearing Gandhi caps which they claimed made them immune to bullets.

Rampa Rebellion: A unique example of tribal militancy came from the 'Rampa' region north of Godavari, which had witnessed various uprising in the 19th century. In 1916 it saw a revolt that was a prelude to veritable guerrilla warfare in the region between August 1922 and May 1924. Their grievances as earlier, were against money-lenders and forest laws. An unpopular tahsildar, Bastian of Gudem, provided the immediate spark by trying to construct forest roads with unpaid labour. The movement was led by an outsider, Alluri Sitaram Raju, claiming astrological and healing powers who has become a folk hero in Andhra Pradesh. He was inspired by the Non-Cooperation movement and admired Gandhiji, though he considered violence necessary to win tribal goals. He claimed to be bullet proof. Sitarama Raju was a formidable tactician and his band of rebels enjoyed the confidence of the surrounding population of about 2,500 square miles. Raju was captured and killed in May 1924 after immense effort, which finally ended the massive rebellion which cost the Madras Government 15 lakh rupees.

Forest Satyagrahas: Such links between nationalism and tribal movements continued and were strengthened during phases of mass movements like the Civil Disobedience of 1930-32. Thus in Maharashtra, Central Provinces as well as Karnataka, forest Satyagrahas among poor peasants and tribals became the most widespread and militant form of civil disobedience with peaceful violations by villagers, who sometimes numbered a lakh. But the movement often went beyond the limits set by Gandhian non-violence with attacks on forest guards and police and leaders emerging from among the tribals themselves, like Ganjan Korku of the Gonds in Betul. There were even some attempts at no revenue movements.

While in some areas like Begal, the earlier fervour was missing, the Chhotanagpur tribal belt was active. In Hazaribagh, Bonga Majhi and Somra Majhi led a movement that combined socio-religious reform along Sanskritisation lines with Congress sympathies. Meanwhile, Santhals everywhere were said have taken to liquor brewing, claiming Gandhiji as their leader. The Kharwars of Palamau, Bihar, participated in forest Satyagrahas in the 1930s, demanding restoration of their customary rights to extract timber and collect forest produce for consumption. The tribals of Garhwal region launched a movement against forest contractors in the 1930s.

Not all tribal movements were connected with the national movement. There were some isolated, localised movements, like those of the Andamanese tribals from 1925. Others tended to get linked with the Communist movement, the most striking example of which was the Telengana movement. In this movement, the tribals of Andhra Pradesh participated from 1946 onwards and fought against landlords and the forced labour that they imposed.

There were also movements during this phase for separate political autonomy among tribals. Thus in the 1940s the Gonds, led by their ex-ruler, made an effort to mobilise people professing Gond-dharma though the unrest was related to land-based issues. This later was transformed into a demand for a separate Gond land for Chhattisgarh tribes. In the 1940s and early 1950s a woman social reformer arose among them, Raj Mohini Devi by name, who preached against drinking and other social evils.

Jharkhand Movement: The movement for a separate Jharkhand State compring 16 districts in Bihar, Orissa, West Bengal and Madhya Pradesh is over six decades old. It originated in the 1920s with the formation of Chhotanagpur Unnati Samiti with a view to drawing government attention to tribal problems. Its political base widened with the formation of the Adivasi Mahasabha after the first elections of 1937. There were a series of violent incidents between 1938 and 1947. Subsequently the Mahasabha was wound up and a new Regional Jharkhand Party was formed in 1949.

MOVEMENTS OF FRONTIER TRIBES

The other region to have witnessed tribal movements of considerable proportions was the north-eastern frontier. The region differed substantially from the rest of tribal India in two basic aspects. Here the tribals formed an overwhelming majority and thus were relatively economically and socially secure. The other factor was that because of their geo-political situation and historical background of living in the vicinity of the international border in relative isolation, this region was not completely integrated within the politico-economic system of colonialism and remained somewhat cut off from the cultural patterns of the mainland.

These characteristics effected the type of movements that occurred here. In the first place, with one striking exception, these movements tended to remain aloof from the freedom struggle, often incorporating a demand for political autonomy either within the Indian Union or as a separate unit. This was also because many of the tribes were living on the international frontier, sharing ethnic and cultural affinities with tribesmen across the border. Similarly, in contrast to Central India, there was hardly any agrarian and forest-based movement as the tribals remained in possession of land and surrounding forests except in Tripura.

Some scholars point to another difference between the tribal movements in the two regions; the movements in the North-east were by and large revolutionary or revivalistic, rather than having a 'Sanskritising' tendency, which the plains tribal movements often incorporated. This again was partly on account of their relative isolation from Hindu society and a strong Christian missionary influence in their modernisation. The movements in the North-east tended to be political and secular, with a definite continuity, unlike those of Chhotanagpur which were often followed by long periods of dormancy or even extinction.

These factors have led to a different typology being suggested for the tribal movements along the frontier from that of the non-frontier tribes. These are (*a*) religious and social reform movements; (*b*) movements for separate statehood within the Indian Union or more autonomy for tribal areas; (*c*) insurgency and (*d*) assertion of cultural rights. There is a very thin dividing line between (*b*), (*c*) and (*d*). These types of movements became important largely after 1935 and it is in the present context that they are cited rather than as full-fledged pre-independence phenomena.

This does not mean that there was no anti-imperialist tinge to the movements in this region. The British were the first to impose, in many areas, territorial authority over hitherto free tribals that weakened the traditional structure. Most of the tribes fought this onslaught though rather tentatively (as they were not tightly knit and organised) under their traditional chiefs or other men from the influential strata.

Khasi Uprising: As a result of the Burmese war the British got possession of the Brahmputra Valley and conceived the idea of linking up this territory with Sylhet by a road passing through the entire length of the Khasi domain. Conscriptions of labourers for road construction led the Khasis to revolt under the leadership of Tirut Singh, a Khasi chief. The Garos joined them. The long and harassing warfare with the Khasis continued for four years and was finally suppressed in early 1833.

Singphos Rebellion: While the British were engaged in a harassing warefare with the Khasis, the Singphos broke into open rebellion in early 1830, which was suppressed after three months. But the Singphos remained in a mood of sullen discontent and again rose in rebellion in 1839 when they killed the British Political Agent.

Minor Tribal Movements: In 1835 the Saflas raided British plains subjects and the British took to reprisals to avenge this. In 1836 the Mishimis killed a botanist, Griffith, suspecting his intentions. Between 1839 and 1842 there was a Khampti uprising in Assam when they attacked and killed British Agent Adam White and 80 other officers and soldiers. In 1842 the Lushais raided British territory of Arakan, Sylhet and defeated the British forces. In 1843 the Singpho Chief Nirang Phidu attack the British garrison and killed several soldiers.

In 1844 the Lushais attacked Manipuri villages. Reprisals by the British followed. The Lushai leader Sukla was arrested and transported for life. In 1849 Khasma Singpho attacked British villages in Assam and was captured in 1855. There was a punitive mission led by Eden against the Mishimis to avenge the killing of two missionaries. In 1860 the Lushai chief raided British Tripura and killed 186 British subjects. Between 1860 and 1862 there was a revolt of Syntengs of Jaintia Hills. In 1861 the Phulaguri uprising of tribal peasants took place. In 1872-73 the Saflas had to be quelled by a British military expedition. In 1882 the Kacha Nagas of Cachhar attacked the whites under a miracle worker named Sambhuden who claimed that his magic had made his followers immune to bullets. In Manipur there was a Nupital or a "women's war" in

1904 against the order issued by the Political Agent to rebuild the Assistant Political Agent's bungalow by forced labour.

Two aspects may be noted in these movements which differentiate them from the anti-British movements in the plains. First, tribals deeply resented British penetration of their areas, which took place somewhat later than in the plains. The British penetrated the area during the First Anglo-Burmese War (1824-26), annexed the Jaintia Hills in 1832, including the earlier 25 Khasi states, set up British administrative centre at Kohima in 1876, formed a Naga Hill district in 1881. Each of these events was followed by revolts. Second, these movements under the traditional chiefs continued much later than in the plains, the last major one being the Kuki revolt, which carried on for two years between 1917 and 1919.

Kuki Revolt: The Kukis had migrated to Manipur in the 18th century. The British policy of recruitment for coolie labour during World War I seriously affected the stability of the labour-short Kuki economy in general and their agriculture particularly. Guerrilla war under their chiefs went on for two years, fuelled also by other grievances like ***pothang*** (tribals being made to carry baggages of officials without payment) and government efforts to stop shifting cultivation or jhum. The rebellion could be put out only after a long time and lot of effort.

Tribal Uprisings in Tripura: The tribal chiefs also became instruments of stratification of hill society, by acquiring feudal interests with the help of the British, which alienated the common tribals. This was most noticeable in Tripura, the only region to witness large scale agrarian and forest-based movements. Here the demographic profile of tribals changed from 64 per cent in 1874 to 36 per cent in 1911 because the Raja of Tripura invited Bengalis to settle in Tripura for economic reasons. This led to loss of land and control over forest by tribals and their relegation to lower rungs of society. A number of tribal uprisings took place in reaction to these developments. Parikshit Jamatia led a movement against arbitrary rate of house tax in 1863. There was an armed rebellion in 1942-43 in the southern subdivision of Tripura where Reangs rose under the leadership of Ratnamani, who declared himself king and proclaimed independence. The British forced the Maharaja to deploy adequate forces to take the tribals to task. Revolutionary activities were started in Tripura by the Bharati Sangh in the mid-1920s. With the formation of Tripura State Congress, an organised attempt at responsible government was made in 1936. It also gave expression to the public resentment against the feudal privileges of the rulers. A Gana Parishad was formed in 1937 on the lines of the State People's Conferences in other Princely States.

Zeliangsong Movement: The only other important tribal movement of the frontier to have made some link with the national movement was the Zeliangsong movement among the Nagas of Manipur belonging to the Zemi, Liangmei and Rongmei tribes.

After the British conquered Manipur in 1891, the hill tribes were directly administered by the British officials, which increased their exploitation manifold and included arbitrary exactions like a new house tax, forced labour and provision of travelling allowances in the form of food and cash for touring officials. The Manipur tribals submitted without protest but when the British failed to protect them from the wrath of the Kukis during the Kuki rebellion (1917-19), the tribals revolted. They also resented the preaching of Christianity against their traditional faith.

Rani Gaidinliu's Naga Movement: Jodnang (1905-31), a young Rongmei leader, came to the fore to bring about social unity and to revitalise the age old religion by abolishing irrational customs. From this internal reform and unity the movement turned outward during its second phase to become a political struggle against British rule and for the establishment of a Naga Raj. Jadonang was captured and hanged on August 29, 1931.

After his execution the movement was carried on by 17-year old Gaidinliu till it was suppressed in 1932. She integrated the tribal movement with the Civil Disobedience movement and preached disobedience to oppressive laws and non-payment of house tax. The movement used Gandhi's name and the Indian National Army called Gaidinliu 'Rani'. This link, however, remained weak and the Congress could not enter the hills, except the municipal jurisdiction of Shillong, before independence. Jadonang's religious ideas crystallised in the Heraka Cult led by Gaidinliu. After the movement was finally suppressed, it was converted into a peaceful movement with the establishment of tribal organisations like Kabui Samiti (1934), Kabui Naga Association (1946), Zeliangsong Council (1947 and Manipur Zeliangong Union.

De-Sanskritisation Movement: A feature peculiar to the frontier tribal movements was the movement for de-sanskritisation. In Manipur, a 'De-Sanskritisation' movement was begun among the Meiteis, some of whom rebelled against the corrupt malpractices of the neo-Vaishnavite Brahmins during the rule of the Churchand Maharaja (1891-1941). They felt that a combination of Brahmins, the Maharaja and the British were spoiling their society and wanted to return to the nativistic Sanmali Cult. In 1939 they led a movement and in 1946 the State Congress was formed by Rajkumar Bhubansena. Hijan Irbot formed the Krishak Sena and later the Communist Party. On the whole, there were no Sanskritisation movements in this region. Even the Brahma movement of the Bodo Kacharis stopped short of the hills. And despite certain opposition, the colonial phase saw large scale conversion to Christianity among Nagas, Mizos, Khasis, Garos and reforms associated with Christianity.

Quest for Autonomy: Another feature of the tribal movements of this region was their quest for autonomy. While administrative unification helped in the formation of tribal identity, their sense of isolation from the mainstream was aggravated by the entire system of non-regulative administration under which the North-east hills had functioned in some guise or the other since the 1830s. Till 1937 the North-east Hills were uniformly administered as 'backward tracts' exclusively under the Chief Commissioner's jurisdiction exercised by British district officers. This sense of isolation led to political movements, especially from the 1920s seeking goals ranging from autonomy to independence and relying on means ranging from constitutional agitation to armed insurgency, though the latter became prominent only after independence.

Tribal Movements, 1935-47: Contributing to the development of a sense of larger tribal identity were (*a*) the Government of India Act 1935, (*b*) the rise of modern education and (*c*) gradual emergence of a small and educated middle class among the tribes of the hills and plains.

The importance of the Government of India Act, 1935 in this process was two-fold. First under the Act, the administrative pattern of the region was bifurcated from April 1937. The Mizo Hills, Naga Hills, North Cachar Hills and North East Frontier tracts were called "excluded areas"—that is, excluded from ministerial jurisdiction and the Garo Hills, the British Portion of Khasi Jaintia Hills and Mikir Hills were termed "partially excluded" areas. The "excluded areas" were guarded by an "inner line" which prevented the entry of outsiders without permit. There was, besides, a twilight zone of British power, i.e. two princely states (Manipur and Tripura) with which the relations were maintained through the agency of the Government of Assam and an "unadministered Naga Tribal area". Such bifurcation of administration gave the hill districts a special kind of identity which was crucial to subsequent political events. Secondly, the 1935 Act marked a major beginning in the growth of tribal alliances. In this period the major tribes of the hills and the plains such as the Nagas, Khasis, Bodos, Miris, Kacheris and Seweris pressed their demands through various organisations such as the Nága Club, Seng Khasi Club (founded in 1911, for association of Angamas, Senas, Rengamas), Khasi Darbar, Tribal League and Ahom League. Many leaders of these groups, such as Rup Nath Brahma, Karo Chandra Boley and Jadav Chandra Khaklari were members of the Legislative Assembly.

The second state in the growth of tribal alliances ranges from 1945 to 1947. In its background lay the impact of World War II, the policy of British administration, the growing nationalist movement and the certainty of freedom, the communal riots of 1946-47, the Cabinet Mission proposals, a growing sense of ethnic identity and a fear of losing it. All these factors contributed to ethno-political movements in Garo Hills, Khasi and Jaintia Hills, Lushai Hills and Naga Hills.

World War II, during which these hills had become important theatres of war, had penetrated their isolation due to world events. Many tribals feared that their cherished ancient laws, customs and village organisations would be destroyed by non-tribal rulers after independence. In the shadow of new hopes and fears, the Naga Hill District Tribal Council was organised by Charles Pawsy, Deputy Commissioner of the Naga Hills district, in 1945. In part it was formed to attend to the task of postwar reconstruction. In April 1946 at Wokha this organisation was renamed the Naga Nationalist Council and the idea of ethnocentric nationalism emerged. During the first half of 1946 two other prominent organisations were formed—the Garo National Council (February 1946) and the Mizo Union.

At the time of independence there were two major political trends among the frontier tribes. The first was in favour of asserting more tribal autonomy within the Indian Union. This was visible in the politics of the Mizo Union, Garo National Council, East Indian Tribal Union and All Party Hill Leaders Conference. The second trend was towards complete independence for tribal areas. Its protagonists were the Naga Nationalist Council, the United Mizo Freedom Organisation and the Mizo National Front.

PEASANT MOVEMENTS

British rule had far-reaching impact on rural India. Under the new administrative measures, the old agrarian system collapsed, new land tenures were created, new social classes emerged and the peasantry came under the iron grip of zamindars, money-lenders, tax collectors and parasitical intermediaries. Within a few decades of the British rule, the Indian peasantry came to be oppressed and exploited not only by the foreign rulers and their agents, but also by the native exploiters and urban based capitalists.

The protests, revolts and movements launched by the exploited and oppressed peasants were mainly direct against enhancement of rent, evictions, usurious practices of money-lenders and exploitation and oppression of the plantation owners. These were mainly anti-landlord, anti-money-lender and anti-foreign. They did not gain class consciousness and did not become class movements, because they grew out of local grievances, remained localised and had no regular organisation and leadership.

The Champaran and Kaira satyagrahas under the leadership of Mahatma Gandhi in 1918 opened up possibilities of organising the peasants and under the aegis of the Indian National Congress, Kisan-Sabhas were organised in the 1920s. But the Kisan Sabhas sought relief only against excessive land revenue demand and did hardly anything to rescue the peasantry from the clutches of the zamindars, landlords and money-lenders. Nevertheless, though the peasantry was disorganised and leaderless, there were numerous peasant uprisings during the British rule in India, exhibiting the courage and determination of the illiterate and poor Indian peasants to rise and fight against their exploitation and oppression. Peasant participation in the Revolt of 1857 too indicates their anti-foreign leanings.

Nature of Peasant Movements: Over three-fourths of the population of India was at that time involved in agricultural pursuits or related activities. The nature and content of this occupation underwent far reaching changes under colonialism which, beginning with the Diwani of Bengal in 1765, radically transformed the agrarian system and improverished the peasantry. With it came new land revenue and colonial administrative and judicial systems. These effective changes created new social classes ruining the handicrafts sector and leading to stagnation.

The structural changes brought about by colonialism resulted in severe famines during the second half of the 18th century, leading to great misery among the peasantry. Periodically occurring economic depression also led to great hardships among them. It was against this background that numerous movements were launched against enhancement of rent, forcible cultivation of a particular crop such as indigo, forcible evictions, usurious practices of money-lenders and exploitation and oppression of plantation owners.

Under colonial India, essentially three types of agrarian zones were created. These were :

(*i*) Zamindari areas of Bengal and Taluqdari areas of U.P. where the tenants were left without any legal protection at the mercy of the zamindars who, apart from appropriating a large rent, also compelled them to pay illegal dues or ***nazrana*** and perform ***begar*** or forced labour; (*ii*) ryotwari areas in the Madras Presidency, where the government itself acted as the landlord, extracting a very high revenue, forcing the peasants into debt and ultimate reducing them to tenants-at-will, share-croppers and landless labourers; (*iii*) tribal zones, which have been discussed in the previous chapter.

An earlier generation of scholars held that peasant rebellions in India were infrequent mostly ineffective, disorganised, localised and spontaneous or prepolitical in nature. They attributed this weakness of the peasant movement to the "degraded character" of the peasantry and its peculiar social structure of caste.

Recent scholar has challenged this characterisation. It is pointed out that peasant revolts took place during the past two centuries in every state of peasant day India. There is empirical evidence of over 75 of them. Nor were they spontaneous or lacking in organisation or leadership. They however, did tend to have limitation of class consciousness or a broader social understanding till at least some of them merged with the national movement. The character of the peasant movements differed from region to region and from time to time. They sometimes assumed semi-political or communal complexion, such as the Moplah rebellion, under the developing political situation.

We may broadly divide the peasant struggles into three chronological though overlapping phases : (*i*) protest movements based on caste or religious identity and consciousness, but primarily a response generated by the emerging colonial exploitation; (*ii*) secular movements arising out of the same reasons but rejecting caste identity and consciousness; (*iii*) the national movement culminating in radical political consciousness with the platform of Kisan Sabhas, Congress Socialist Party (CSP), etc.

SOME IMPORTANT PEASANT UPRISINGS AND MOVEMENTS

Indigo Riots (1859-60): The largely European planters used totally arbitrary and ruthless methods to force peasants to grow the unremunerative indigo crop on a part of their land in eastern India. Peasants were kidnapped, illegally confined, women and children were attacked, cattle were lifted and crops were looted, burnt and destroyed if the peasants were recalcitrant. The privileges and immunities enjoyed by the British planters placed them above the law and beyond all judicial control.

Finally, in 1860 the terribly oppressed indigo peasants launched "non-cultivation of indigo" movements. Beginning with the ryots of Govindpur village in Nadia district, the indigo strikes rapidly spread to other areas and by the spring of 1860, encompassed all indigo districts of Bengal. Factories were attacked as were policemen and police posts. The peasants even went on a strike, raised funds to fight the court cases filed against them and initiated legal action on their own against the planters. Household servants of the planters were pressurised to leave the service of their employers through social boycott and caste pressures used by the indigo agitators.

The indigo peasants got tremendous support from the intelligentsia and the press as well as the missionaries of Bengal. Outstanding in this respect was the role of Harish Chandra Mukherji, editor of Hindu Patriot. Deen Bandhu Mitra's play, Neel Darpan was to gain great fame for vividly portraying the oppression by planters.

The ryots themselves showed tremendous courage and initiative as well as cooperation, organisation and discipline. There was also complete Hindu Muslim unity. Not being able to withstand the many sided, united resistance, the planters began to close their factories—a process that was speeded up by the Government notification of November 1860, that the ryots could not be compelled to grow indigo and that it would ensure that all disputes were settled by legal means. The ryots had soon a great victory, though for a limited and immediate cause.

This was the first strike of the Indian peasants and it succeeded. The same story was repeated in 1867-68 in Champaran (Bihar). The indigo riot proved a source of great inspiration during India's struggle for freedom.

Deccan Riots (1874-75): In ryotwari areas of the (Deccan) district of Pune and Ahmadnagar in Maharashtra, the land revenue was already very high, which had to the paid even when a succession of bad harvests followed. In addition, the cotton boom which had provided some prosperity to the peasants in the early 1860s disappeared overnight with the ending of the American Civil War in 1864 and the resumption of cotton supplies from that continent to Europe. The result was an acute depression in cotton exports from India and a crash in prices. In these circumstances the peasants had nowhere to turn except money-lenders, most of whom were outsiders, Marwaris or Gujaratis. The latter exploited this situation to their advantage and obtained mortgage of a very large portion of land against rural loans. The situation became more and more explosive as the peasants were faced with the brutal alternative of mortgaging land or eviction. Some unscrupulous money-lenders even went to the extent of inducing or compelling the debtor-peasants to compromise the honour of their women to get relief from the crushing burden of debts.

The Maratha peasants finally gave vent to their feelings and, beginning with Sirur taluk in December 1874, by May-September 1875 the anti-Sahukar (money-lender). Deccan riots affected 33 places in six taluks. There was However, very little actual violence except the forcible seizure of debt bonds led by their traditional headmen (Patels). In almost every caste the object of the rioters was to obtain and destroy the debt-bonds, decrees etc. in the possession of their creditors. Personal violence against them was used only when they refused to hand over these documents.

The uprising was completely crushed by the police assisted by the military and nearly a thousand peasants were arrested. The Government of India also appointed a Commission to inquire into the nature and cause of these riots. The Commission unanimously held that poverty and consequent indebtedness of the cultivators were the real causes of the riots. Following the Commission's recommendations, the Government passed the Agriculturists' Relief Act, 1879 which imposed restrictions on alienation of peasants' lands and on the operations of the Civil Procedure Code. Consequently, the peasant could not be arrested and sent to civil jail for failure to pay debts.

Revolt of the Ramosis: The Ramosis of Maharashtra once served in the inferior ranks of police in the Maratha administration. After the fall of the Maratha kingdom, as a result of the Anglo-Maratha wars, they reverted back to their lands and had to face considerable distress. Chittur Singh, who revolted in Satara in 1822 as a protest against heavy assessment, gathered these Ramosis under his banner and they played a prominent part in plundering the country and destroying its forts. In 1825 chronic scarcity in the Deccan further distressed them and they broke into revolt in 1826 under the leadership of Umaji. For three years they scourged the countryside. Ultimately the British Government condoned their crimes, gave them land grants and recruited them as hill police.

Wasudeo Balwant Phadke's Uprising: Later on, Wasudeo Balwant Phadke raised a force of Ramosis peasants. Phadke's feelings were deeply stirred by the devastations caused in Western India by the terrible famine of 1876-77 and he was convinced that the miseries of India were the consequence of foreign rule. With the support of backward communities like this Ramosis and simple sturdy peasants of Maharashtra villages, Phadke organised social banditry or political dacoities on a significant scale. He was arrested in 1880 and died three years later (1883) in prison. His band of Ramosis remained active till 1887.

Pabna Agrarian Unrest: In the Permanent Settlement Areas of East Bengal (now in Bangladesh), the zamindars used crafty methods to deprive the ryots of their occupancy rights, which had been granted by the Act of 1859. Among these methods were enhancing rents beyond legal limits through a variety of cesses (abwab), short changing in measurement. Costly litigation and forced eviction. In reaction to this high-handedness of the zamindars the peasants of a number of districts of East Bengal launched a movement between 1870 and 1885.

The storm centre of the movement was Pabna, a comparatively prosperous jute growing district where in May 1873, an Agrarian League or combination was formed to resist the unjust demands of the zamindars. The members of the Pabna League raised a litigation expenses fund, held mass meetings to which villagers were called by drumbeats and organised non-payment of rent campaign. The main form of resistance was legal and was generally peaceful.

The Pabna unrest had two noteworthy features. First, it provided a model for peasant combination at a time when there was no Kisan Sabha or political party to organise the peasantry. Secondly, it was non-communal, even though the majority of the zamindars were Hindu and Muslims formed a large part of the tenantry. Hindu peasants fought alongside Muslim peasants against the Hindu zamindars. Many newspapers of the region, like Hindoo Patriot and Anand Bazar, being pro-landlord, opposed the peasants limited demands and even tried to portray it as a communal struggle of Muslim tenants versus Hindu landlords. The three principal leaders of the League were Shah Chandra Roy, Shambhu Pal and Khoodi Mollah. Some others like R.C. Dutt and the Indian Association (founded in 1876), however, did come out in favour of the tenants.

The peasant discontent smouldered till 1885, resulting ultimately in the Bengal Tenancy Act of 1885. This Act, while it very imperfectly protected tenants from the worst aspects of zamindari oppression, also gave rise to the powerful ***jotedar*** groups, some of whom turned out to be as exploitative as the zamindars.

Pagal Panthis Uprisings: Pagal Panthi was a semi-religious sect. Its members came mostly from the primitive tribes, Hajong and Garo, living in the Mymensingh district of Bengal (now in Bangladesh). The founder of this sect was a ***darvesh*** or a mendicant called Karan Shah, whose son and successor Tipu, motivated by religious and political aims, organised an uprising of the Garo and Hajong peasants. Tipu openly took up their cause against the oppressions by the zamindars, who realised illegal cesses from the peasants. He gathered round him a band of armed followers and collected money by plunder. He asked his followers not to pay rent above a specified minimum. In January 1825, he led a mob of his armed brigands and attacked the houses of the zamindars of Sherpur, who had to take shelter with the British officials. The Government, alarmed by the strength of the Pagal Panthi uprising, conceded the justice of Tipu's demands and made a more equitable arrangement to protect the cultivators. The Pagal Panthi uprising continued for about ten years—1825-35—and was finally suppressed after massive military operations against them.

No-Revenue Movements: In the Kamrup and Darrang districts of Assam, attempts by the British to hike land revenue in temporarily settled areas by 50-70 per cent were resisted by an organisation of assemblies of villagers led by the rural elite. These enforced non-payment of revenue by using social boycott and ostracism against those who decided to pay. Eventually some concessions were gained. Similarly in Maharashtra, after the famines of 1896-97 and 1899-1900, a number of non-payment of revenue campaigns were launched under the auspices of the Poona Sarvajanik Sabha, which had recently been captured by Tilak. These spread to Surat, Nasik, Kheda and Ahmedabad on their own initiative. A revolt of peasants threatened with loss of their land took place in the Punjab in the last decade of the 19th century. To ease the situation, the government enacted the Punjab Alienation Act in 1902-03.

The no-revenue movements did not follow the pattern of other peasant struggles described above, because they were sparked off by particular grievances with specific and limited objectives and derived their leadership and much of their support from relatively better off sections of the peasants. There was a tradition of another type of rural out-breaks aiming at something like total changes, often with strong religious and millenarian overtones and rooted in the lower depths of Indian society—tribals and poor peasants.

Moplah Uprisings: In the Malabar region, the discontent of the Moplah Muslim peasants continued with a strong religious flavour to give a Hindu-Muslim angle to the expression of anti-landlord and anti-foreign discontent. Hindu upper caste Namboodari and Nair ***jenmis***, position had been reestablished, even vastly enhanced, by the British insistence on landlord rights. They were backed by the police and the law courts and the British tightened their grip over the Muslim Moplah peasantry. Retaliation and revolt became virtually endemic in many talukas of South Malabar and had a messianic tinge as the rebels courted death in the belief that as Ahadis they would go straight to heaven. Twenty two revolts were recorded between 1836 and 1854; more uprisings took place in 1882-85 and again in 1896. That its roots were clearly agrarian is indicated by the fact that there was an increase of 224 per cent in rent.

PEASANT MOVEMENTS IN THE FIRST HALF OF THE 20TH CENTURY

One of the major driving forces behind the 1857 rebellion had been peasant grievances against the British rule. The crushing of the revolt left most of these unresolved. The consolidation and expansion of British rule during the next half century gave birth to a host of new conflicts. These, however, tended to remain fairly localised and focused on particular grievances. Social and geographical conditions prevented the spread of such movements, more so because the colonial state had developed its repressive machinery and communication links. The colonial regime systematically disarmed the insurgents and those whom it could not crush, it coopted into the system before the insurgency could spread beyond a fairly localised area. The peasant struggles between 1858 and 1914 were, therefore, necessarily disjointed. Only with Gandhiji and the Congress championing peasant demands and attempting to join them with the broader national movement did peasant resistance begin to link up more systematically and became something more than a collection of local struggles. The man most responsible for providing this link was Mahatma Gandhi, under whose leadership the masses entered the all India national movement. The first two movements that Gandhiji led were, however, concerned with the local grievances of cultivators and their tremendous success propelled him to the centre stage.

Champaran Indigo Satyagraha: The first of these involved the woes of cultivators in Champaran, Bihar who in the 19th century had been forced by European planters to cultivate indigo on 3/20th of their holding- known as ***tinkathia*** system. With the declining market for indigo in the face of synthetic dyes, the planters were now willing to release the farmers from their irksome crop, but only by recurring enhancements in rent and other illegal dues. Persuaded by a local man, Raj Kumar Shukla, in 1917, Gandhiji offered civil disobedience and refused to leave the district when ordered. The Government capitulated and Gandhiji ordered an inquiry, which involved touring with men like Rajendra Prasad and J.B. Kriplani and recording statements of thousands of peasants. The result was the abolition of the ***tinkathia*** system and compensation to the peasants for illegal increase in their dues.

Kheda Satyagraha: Gandhiji's intervention proved much more of a permanent success at Kheda district of Gujarat, where he went to alleviate the Kunbi-Patidar peasants' distress due to failure of crops. Their appeals for remission of land revenue were being ignored by the Government. With the help of leaders like Indulal Yajnik and Vallabhbhai Patel, Gandhiji toured the district advising the peasants to stand firm and withhold payment of revenue. After a hard struggle, the Government issued secret orders directing that revenue should be recovered only from those peasants who could pay and Gandhiji withdrew the movement in 1918.

Kisan and Eka Movements: The 20th century witnessed not only the revolt of the peasantry against the excesses of the talukdari, ryotwari and zamindari systems but also the formation of peasants organisations like the Kisan Sabhas.

Some of the major grievances of the peasantry, reflecting their pathetic conditions were (*i*) lack of occupancy rights in many regions on land tilled by them; (*ii*) exaction by the landlords of tribute cesses, gifts and even forced labour, over and above the regular or even excessive rent; (*iii*) periodic revision of land revenue in ryotwari areas by the Government, which was usually steep and (*iv*) heavy indebtedness to the village landlords or money-lenders, leading to generational debt traps. The outbreak of World War I added to the miseries of the peasants. During this period there was a sharp increase in the price of foodgrains, benefiting middlemen and merchants at the cost of the poor.

During and after World War I, government encouragement to talukdari and zamindari made the lot of the peasantry miserable in UP. Some active members of Home Rule League (like Gauri Shankar Mishra and Indira Narayan Dwivedi, with the support of Madan Mohan Malviya) began organising the peasants of U.P. on modern lines into Kisan Sabha in 1918. But it was Baba Ramchandra, a Maharashtrian Brahmin, who took the initiative to organise the peasants of Awadh against the landlords. He had been wandering among the peasants since 1909, dressed like a Sanyasi quoting from the ***Ramcharitmanas*** to awaken them to a sense of dignity. He told the peasants that they were in bondage to the Government and taluqdars and could free themselves only by organising against the excesses of the system.

In June 1920, Baba Ramchandra and other tenants from Pratapgarh and Jaunpur districts went to Allahabad and persuaded Gauri Shankar Mishra and Jawaharlal Nehru to visit the villages and see the peasants misery for themselves. In 1920, the peasant movement get associated with the Non-Cooperation Movement launched by the Congress. Differences between Non-Cooperators and those who preferred constitutional agitation like Malviya led to an alternative Awadh Kisan Sabha being set up at Pratapgarh in October 1920. This Sabha united all 330 grassroots Kisan Sabhas of Awadh under its wings.

The Awadh Kisan Sabha asked the Kisans to refuse to till ***bedakhli*** land, not to offer unpaid labour, boycott those who did not accept these conditions and to solve their disputes through panchayats. It had both high and low caste kisans among its adherents. In 1921, the peasant movement became militant and spread to Rai Bareli, Faizabad and Sultanpur. The peasants held demonstrations demanding that evictions from land should stop. They raided the houses of landlords and money-lenders, looted bazars and granaries and clashed with the police, leading to firing and killing of many peasants.

The Congress tried to restrain the violent edge of the movement and the amendment to the Awadh Rent Act in 1921 also acted as a brake. But the peasants were not pacified and in late 1921 to early 1922, the movement emerged again in Hardoi, Barabanki and Sitapur districts, as a unity of ***Eka*** movements. The main grievance of the movement was extraction of rent, which was generally 50 per cent higher than the recorded rent. Its grassroots leadership came from Pasi and Ahir low-caste leaders unprepared to accept the non-violent limits set by mainstream nationalists. For this reason it got isolated by March 1922 and the repressive policy of the Government brought the Eka movement to its end.

Second Moplah Uprising: Already known for their rebellious tendencies combined with a strong religious fervour, the Moplahs were organised by the Congress and Khilafatists during the Non-Cooperation days. A tenant-rights agitation developing in Malabar from 1916, was taken up by the Khilafat movement after the Manjheri Conference of April 1920. Promises of a coming egalitarian Muslim State were made. The arrest of established Congress and Khilafat leaders like K. Mahadevan Nair, Gopala Menon, Yakub Hasan and P. Moideen Koya in February 1921 left the field clear for radical preachers.

On August 20, 1921, a police raid on Tiruraingadi mosque in search of arms sparked off a major rebellion with widespread attacks on police stations, public offices, communications and houses of oppressive landlords. Lenient landlords and poor Hindus were hardly touched.

The situation, however, changed when the British declared martial law. The Hindus, either under pressure or voluntarily, took a pro-authorities stance. The Moplahs became out and out anti-Hindu. They attacked and forcibly converted or murdered the Hindus. What started as largely an anti-government and anti-landlord affair, had thus assumed strong communal overtones.

The Congress had already distanced itself from the Moplahs for their use of violence. In British reprisals, by December 1921 unofficially over 10,000 Moplahs were killed and over 50,000 had either surrendered or were captured and the back of the revolt was broken.

Bardoli (Gujarat) Satyagraha: The Gandhian satyagraha and agitation contributed substantially to the spectacular success at Bardoli in Surat district in 1928. Here followers of Gandhiji, like the Mehta brothers, had carried out a sustained campaign since 1922. Not only the landowning peasants of Kunbi-Patidar castes but also the low caste untouchables and tribals like Kali-paraj (dark people) participated in the movement. They gave the tribals a less derogatory name of Raniparaj (inhabitants of the forest) and exhorted them against the ***hali*** system under which they laboured as hereditary labourers for upper-caste owners.

When the Bombay Government announced an enhanced revenue by 22 per cent, in spite of the fall in cotton prices, the Mehta bothers persuaded Vallabhbhai Patel to organise a sustained no-revenue campaign. Its success lay in the mobilisation of low caste audience along with the land owners. Skilful use was made of caste associations, social boycott, religious appeals and bhajans or devotional songs. Bardoli became a national issue and sustained pressure forced the Government to reach a settlement on the basis of a judicial inquiry and return of confiscated lands. A result of the Maxwell-Broomfield inquiry was that enhancement of land revenue in Bardoli was reduced from 22 per cent to 6.03 per cent.

Peasant Movements in the 1930s and 1940s: The success at Bardoli gave a tremendous fillip to the peasant movement. It was the time of the Civil Disobediences launched by the Congress in 1930, which elicited mass response. At the same time, the Great Depression of 1929-30 brought agricultural prices crashing down while rents and taxes remained high, impoverishing the peasants.

The struggle was most intense in U.P. where the peasants forced the Congress to go beyond its no-revenue campaign which asked the zamindars not to pay the Government. The movement spread to many districts of U.P. The Congress leaders asked the peasants to stop making any kind of payment. The Government tried to suppress the movement and declared the peasant union illegal.

The peasants of Gujarat, especially in Surat and Kheda, refused to pay taxes and went on Hijrat (migration) to Baroda State territory to escape repression. In Bengal and Bihar powerful movements were launched against the hated ***Choukidari*** tax. In Madras ryots held meetings and campaigned against land revenue, especially at Tanjore, Madurai and Salem. By 1931, grain riots started in some districts and the movement continued to grow.

By 1931, preparations for a no-revenue movement had started in some Karnataka districts as well. Attempts were made in Maharashtra to influence the village chiefs not to pay their revenue by including their tenants to withhold their rent. The popular agitation spilled over into the neighbouring Princely States. A powerful no-tax campaign developed in Chattarpur state of Bundelkhand. There were major elemental forest movements in Central Provinces. In the Punjab there were agitations against the Patiala Maharaja.

There were also a number of more or less spontaneous outbursts. Peasants in Hissar district refused rent and forcibly seized crops of landlords in April 1930. In Kangra (Himachal Pradesh) there was defiance of forest grazing regulations. In Rohtak there was widespread social banditry by Jats assisted by others from lower castes. In Bihar there was a very powerful no-***Chaukidari*** tax agitation. The provincial leadership, however, because of its small-landlord links, refused to take up no-rent movement despite growing distress from the great fall in the agricultural prices.

All-India Kisan Sabha: Kisan Sabhas continued to be formed in the U.P., Bihar, the Punjab etc. The United Provinces Kisan Sabha, founded in 1918, launched a formidable peasant movement in some districts of Awadh in 1920-21. The Andhra Provincial Ryots Association was started in 1928. The following year Bihar Kisan Sabha was founded by Swami Sahajanand Saraswati. Because these associations were scattered, an attempt was made after the Civil Disobedience movement to found an All-India Kisan Sabha, an apex organisation of the Indian peasants.

The Sabha was founded as a separate Congress outfit for two major reasons: (*i*) there was growing disenchantment with the Congress, with the peasant leaders keen on taking peasant struggles beyond no-revenue campaigns against indigenous exploiters, i.e. the zamindars and taluqdars; (*ii*) the growth of a new generation of young, militant broadly left-wing political cadres from the womb of the Civil Disobedience movement and the Congress itself wanted a new avenue of expression. With the decline of Civil Disobedience people began to search for new forms of agitation and found them in organising peasants. The formation of the Congress Socialist Party in 1934 also provided a platform for all left-wing communist and socialist elements to work openly and in a legal manner. The All-India Kisan Sabha was formed in April 1936 at Lucknow with Swami Sahajanand as President and N.G. Ranga as general secretary. The first session was addressed by Jawaharlal Nehru. Other participants included Ram Manohar Lohia, Sohan Singh Josh, Indulal Yagnik, Jai Prakash Narayan, Acharya Narendra Deva, Kamal Sarkar and others.

A Kisan Sabha manifesto was finalised, which considerably influenced the agrarian programme adopted by the Congress at the Faizabad session. The manifesto included: (*i*) protection of peasants from economic exploitation; (*ii*) demand for 50 per cent reduction in land revenue and rent; (*iii*) moratorium on debt; (*iv*) abolition of feudal levies; (*v*) security of tenure for tenants; (*vi*) a living wage for labourers and (*vii*) recognition of peasant unions. Other demands of the Kisan Sabha were even more radical like abolition of landlordism, licensing of money-lenders, minimum wages for agricultural labourers, fair prices for commercial crops etc. The Kisan Sabha held its second session along with the Faizpur Congress Session in 1932.

Peasant Movements During Congress Ministries (1937-39): A new atmosphere of increased civil liberties along with varying kinds of agrarian legislations for debt relief restoration of lands lost during the Depression and for securing of tenure for tenants were taken up when the Congress ministries came to power after 1937 and provided new hopes to the peasants. These were not, however, altogether fulfilled, because often the leaders in power were reluctant to touch the existing relations.

For instance in Bihar under its Kisan Sabha, a powerful bakasht (self-cultivated lands) movement was launched in 1937-38. The landlords evicted tenants from bakasht lands with the formation of the Congress ministry in 1937. Therefore, the Kisan Sabha thought that the time had come for redressal of grievances. The movement led to clashes with the zamindars and reached its peak in 1939, when a combination of concessions, legislations and arrests of 600 activists succeeded in temporarily quelling the movement.

In U.P. the Congress party was much more left oriented than its counterparts in Bihar. This was reflected in the legislation of Tenancy Bill, which was not given assent to by the Governor even after two years of its passage.

In Bombay Province, the Congress was successful in getting restored to their original owners those lands which had been sold as a result of the no-rent or revenue campaign during the Civil Disobedience movement.

In Kerala, through the efforts of the Congress Socialist Party and Communists, Krishak Sangathans (Peasant Associations) were set up all over, demanding an end to feudal levies, renewal fees, advancement evictions etc. They also organised a powerful campaign for amending the Malabar Tenancy Act.

In coastal Andhra, peasant marches were effectively used for peasant mobilisation. One of their main demands was for debt relief, which was incorporated in the legislation passed by the Congress ministry.

In Bengal Kisan Sabha activities included a successful agitation against Canal Tax in Burdwan and the Hat Tola movement in north Bengal. This was against a levy collected by the landlords from peasants at ***hat***.

Punjab was a hot-bed of nationalist activities. Here the Kisan Sabhas that had emerged in the early 1930s through the efforts of Naujawan Bharat Sabha, Kirti Kisan, the Congress and Akali activists, were given a new sense of direction and cohesion by the Punjab Kisan Committee, formed in early 1930s. The target attack was the Unionist Ministry dominated by big landlords of western Punjab. Two major issues were resettlement of land revenue and increase in canal tax or water rate. Peasants held demonstrations and marches. Hundreds of them courted arrest. As a result, many concessions were won.

In all the Provinces, efforts were made to protect the peasants from money-lenders and improve irrigation facilities. But in most areas the zamindars remained in a dominant position. This period too witnessed the mushrooming of Praja Mandals in many Princely States and major struggles broke out, especially after the Haripur Session of the Congress in 1938, in Jaipur, Kashmir, Rajkot, Patiala, Hyderabad, Mysore, Travancore, etc.

IDEOLOGIES AND PROGRAMMES OF INDIAN NATIONAL CONGRESS

Allan Octavian Hume (A.O. Hume), a retired British member of the Indian Civil Service who had settled at Simla, founded the Indian National Union the fore runner of the Indian National Congress, in 1884. After touring Calcutta, Bombay and Madras (Kolkata, Mumbai and Chennai), Hume announced that a conference of the Indian National Union would be held at Pune in December, which would be composed of educated delegates from all parts of the three presidencies. But cholera having broken out at Pune, the venue of the conference was shifted to Tejpal Sanskrit Pathsala, Bombay. The first session of the Indian National Union was held on December 28, 1885. At the suggestion of Dadabhai Naoroji the name of the organisation was changed to Indian National Congress (INC). Womesh Chandra Banerjee, a leading lawyer of Calcutta (Kolkata), was elected its president.

In its early years the Congress had no permanent organisation. "There were no paying members, no officials other than General Secretary, no Central Office and no funds." Every year a session was held in different city with a different President and it was managed by a local Reception Committee with locally collected funds. Yet the Congress went from strength to strength because it made itself the mouth piece of national aspirations and attracted the support of thousands who did not attend its sessions. The growing strength of the organisation was reflected in the growing number of attendance at the sessions itself. Thus, at the first session in Bombay, there were 72 delegates, about 38 of them from the Bombay Presidency and only 3 from Bengal. At the second session in Calcutta (1886)—in which Surendra Nath Banerjee and Anand Mohan Bose played an important role—there were 434 delegates; at the third session in Madras (Chennai) (1887) there were 607; and at the fourth session at Allahabad there were 1248.

Factors Responsible for the Foundation of I.N.C.: Several theories exist to explain why the Congress, from its modest beginning, went on to become the most powerful representative of the Indian people at large. Some of these theories are discussed here.

(*i*) Safety Valve Theory: That the INC was not founded by an Indian but by a retired English Civil Servant, A.O. Hume has led to speculation that Hume founded that INC to provide a 'safety valve' to the growing discontent against the British rule. It is also reported that Hume received from Viceroy Dufferin the idea of organising an annual conference of educated Indians for political discussions. This may be true as far as it goes; but there is no trustworthy evidence to show the Dufferin suggested the founding of the INC or that the INC was meant as a 'safety valve'. Had the INC been the 'safety valve' to safeguard British interests, it would not have faced rough weather from the British Government. Dufferin himself described the Congress as the mouthpiece of the 'microscopic minority' and charged it with inciting hatred against British officials. In 1888 the Viceroy formally warned some Princely States not to support the Congress. Far more effective was the alienation of the Muslims from the Congress through the policy of "divide and rule". Lord Curzon wrote to the Secretary of State in 1900; "The Congress is tottering to its fall and one of my great ambitions, while in India, is to assist it to a peaceful demise."

(*ii*) Rival Ambitions of Indian Elite: Some historians with neo-imperialist leaning, centred mainly at Cambridge, have argued that the Indian National Congress was not really national at all, but was a movement either of the frustrated job-hungry middle class or self-interested individuals with a lust for power and they used the Congress as a vehicle for the pursuit of their own rivalries. In particular individual cases, this may have been true enough. But generalising it, to the extent of playing down ideology and patriotic motivation, is not only cynical but misses the point that the articulation of such ideas influenced millions. More significantly, it slurs over the economic and racist dimensions of British imperialism, which were at the top of the agenda of the Indian National Congress from the very beginning. A closer look shows that India was a nation in the making whose aspirations and grievances were first articulated and represented by a small section of the educated middle classes like lawyers and journalists because they had the best opportunity and exposure to modern events to do so.

(*iii*) Need for an All-India Body: We have already discussed the growing resentment against the conditions of economic and political subjugation under British rule and the various organisations that had come up in response. In fact during the last ten days of 1885 as many as five conferences were held in different parts of the country. Given the emergence of an educated section all over the country it was only a matter of time before an all-India body to work together for political purposes came into being. Hume took advantage of the existing environment. He had the advantage that Indians found him free of regional loyalties. Even more importantly, the early nationalists hoped to use him as a 'lightning conductor' on an acceptable catalyst for their own aspirations which, as we shall see, were initially quite temperate.

MODERATE PHASE

In his first Presidential speech, W.C. Bannerjee, the first Congress President; explained the aims and objectives of the Congress as being the following: (*i*) the promotion of personal intimacy and friendship amongst the countrymen; (*ii*) eradication of all possible prejudices relating to race, creed, or provinces; (*iii*) consolidation of sentiments of national unity; (*iv*) recording of the opinions of educated classes on pressing problems of the day and (*v*) laying down of lines of future course of action in the public interest.

Bannerjee also made it clear that the educated Indians in general and the Congress in particular were thoroughly loyal well-wishers of the Government. The Congress was merely meant to be a forum to represent their views to the British authorities, in whose sense of justice they had tremendous faith. Bannerjee's opening statements defined the type of politics as well as the method and style of functioning of I.N.C. and underlined the hopes of the educated middle classes that were going to dominate this body till 1905 and then again from 1908 to 1915.

Objectives and Demands of the I.N.C.: In the early years, the I.N.C. also suffered from a blinkered conviction in the essential sense of justice and goodness of the British people they deluded themselves that all would be well if the British people could be acquainted with the true state of affairs. They had an equally deep-rooted belief that the Indian nation was one and that its suffering arose from the discriminatory behaviour of sundry bureaucrats. The resolutions passed at various Congress sessions reflected the twin factors. They were roughly similar from one session to the next and they dealt with three broad types of grievances, namely political, administrative and economic.

***(i)* Political Grievances:** In concrete terms, the demands of the Congress centred round the Legislative Councils. The Congress demanded expansion of their size, introduction of an elected element into their composition and enlargement of their functions. The emphasis was on the introduction of representative institutions. The leaders of the early Congress sincerely desired their country's progress along the lines laid down by the political thought and political experience of the West.

***(ii)* Administrative Grievances :**

(*a*) Under this head foremost was the demand for the Indianisation of the higher grades of services, particularly the Indian Civil Service through simultaneous I.C.S. examinations in England and India.
(*b*) Separation of the Judiciary from the Executive.
(*c*) Removal of restrictions on freedom of the press and speech.
(*d*) Abolition of discriminatory laws which restricted the freedom of the people (e.g. Arms Act).
(*e*) Higher jobs for Indians in the army.
(*f*) Protection of Indians settled in foreign countries.
(*g*) Raising of an Indian Volunteer Force.

These demands, it may be noted, combined pleas for racial equality with a concern for civil rights.

***(iii)* Economic Grievances:** All the economic demands raised were centred round the general poverty of India and the theme of drain of her wealth. Resolutions were regularly passed calling for :

(*a*) An enquiry into India's growing poverty and famines.
(*b*) Cuts in Home Charges and military expenditure.
(*c*) More funds for technical education to promote Indian industries. The nationalist blamed the British for the destruction of India's indigenous industries.
(*d*) An end to unfair tariffs and excise duties.
(*e*) Reduction of land revenue, extension of irrigation and development of agricultural banks which would free the agriculturists from the clutches of the money-lenders.
(*f*) Improvement of the condition of workers in plantations.
(*g*) An end to ill treatment of India coolies abroad.
(*h*) Abolition of the salt tax.
(*i*) An end to the sufferings caused by the Forest Law and forest administration.
(*j*) Reduction in the heavy military expenditure of the British Government in India.

Evaluation on Work: While the political demands of the early Congress were moderate, its economic demands were radical and anti-imperialist in nature. They laid bare the exploitative machinery through which the British State functioned and asked for basic changes in the economic relations between India and England. The Congress was also a truly national body with secular demands. Though it was mainly a political body its programme included the welfare of Indians in all walks of life, except religion. It provided a link between the government and the people, thus laying the foundation for the freedom movement. The passing of the Indian Councils Act of 1892, which provided some powers to elected local bodies, though it was highly unsatisfactory, was partly a result of the pressure put by the Moderates.

FACTS ABOUT CONGRESS

- Founded in 1885 by A.O. Hume.
- Venue of first session—Goku Tejpal Sanskrit School of Bombay (Mumbai).

- First President—W.C. Bannerjee.
- First Women President—Annie Besant (1917, Calcutta).
- First Indian Women President—Sarojini Naidu (1925, Kanpur).
- First English President—George Yule.
- First Muslim President—Badruddin Tyabji.
- Women President—Annie Besant (1917), Sarojini Naidu (1925) and Nalin Sengupta (1933).
- Thrice President (Maximum times)—Dadabhai Naoroji (1886, 1893, 1906), J.L. Nehru (1929, 1936, 1937).
- Only session to hold in a village—1937 (Faizpur).
- First Split of Congress—1907 (Surat).
- First Joint session of Congress and Muslim League Lucknow (1916).
- Word **Swaraj** was first used from Congress platform (1906) Calcutta.
- Only session presided over by Gandhi—Belgaon (1924).
- Complete Independence was demanded for the first time (1929), Lahore.
- For the first time National Anthem was sung in the Calcutta Session (1896) of I.N.C. i.e., Vande Mataram.
- For the first time National Anthem was sung in the Calcutta session (1896) of I.N.C. i.e., Vande Mataram. For the first time National Song (Jana Gana Mana) was sung in Calcutta session (1911) of I.N.C.
- Maulana Abul Kalam Azad was the youngest president of I.N.C..
- The first session of Congress (Bombay, 1885) was attended by 72 representatives.
- During the fourth session of I.N.C. (1888, Allahabad) emphasis was given on formation of its constitution.
- During Nagpur session (1891), the word 'National' was added to Congress.
- During Poona session (1895), representatives second time discussed on the formation of its constitution.
- During Calcutta session of 1906, its president for the first time used 'Swaraj' in his speech.
- In Lucknow session of Congress (1916) the two factions of Congress (Extremists and Moderates) reunited.
- During Special session of Congress in Calcutta (1920), Gandhi proposed to start Non-Cooperation movement. A 15-member executive council was organised. Membership fee was set up. Instead 'Swaraj' as its aim.
- During Ahmedabad session of I.N.C. (1921), C.R. Das was elected its President but Azmal Khan presided over the session because C.R. Das was in prison.
- During Gaya session (1922) differences arose over the issue of council entry, C.R. Das and Motilal Nehru organised Swaraj Party in 1922.
- During its Delhi session (1923), I.N.C. decided to establish All-India Khadi Board.
- Gandhi presided over only Belgaon session (1924) of I.N.C.
- During this session **knowledge of weaving** was fixed as minimum qualification for its members. Gandhi decided to set up 'All-India Charkha Association'. He declared '1926' as year of keeping silent.
- During Guwahati session of I.N.C. (1926), wearing of Khadi was made compulsory for its workers.
- During Madras session of I.N.C. (1927), proposals for independence and to boycott Simon Commission were passed—Gandhi did not participate.
- During Karachi session (1931) Fundamental Rights and Economic Policy Proposals Passed.
- During its 1932 and 1933 session Government had declared it an illegal organisation.
- During Lucknow session (1936), J.L. Nehru explained socialism for the first time.
- During Faizpur session (1937) Congress decided to take part in election of 1937.
- 1938 session of Congress held in a village Haripura.
- In Ramgarh session (1904), decision on Individual Satyagraha.
- The word "Congress" or I.N.C., was taken from the history of U.S.A. which means group of people.
- During Tripuri session of I.N.C. (1939) Subhash Chandra Bose defeated Pattabhi Sitaramaya (Gandhi's candidate in presidential election) but later resigned and Rajendra Prasad. became its President.

- During Calcutta session (1928) First All-India Youth Congress was established.

THE RISE OF NEO-NATIONALISM

The moderate policies of the early Congress disillusioned many of its younger leaders, known as Neo-nationalists or Extremists. Criticising the supplicant attitude of Congress, **Aurobindo Ghosh *published New Lamps for Old in* 1893-94**, in which he described the Congress leaders' pleas to the government on issues like Legislative Councils and simultaneous Civil Service examination in London and India, as "playing with bubbles". Ashwini Kumar Datta derided the Congress as a "three days tamasha". Bipin Chandra Pal mocked it as a "begging institution" (1902). Lala Lajpat Rai wrote a series of articles criticising the aims and methods of the Congress. He declared that political rights could not be won by an organisation which could not "distinguish between begging rights and claiming them". Bal Gangadhar Tilak, who was in the forefront of this new ideology, said that "Indians could not achieve any success if we croak once a year like a frog". In contrast to the older leaders of the Congress, who believed in appealing to the British nation and came to be known as 'Moderates', Tilak and his supporters came to be known as 'Extremists'.

Neo-Nationalism: The nationalisms of the Extremists was inspired by a newly rekindled pride in the glory of India's ancient culture. This new pride had been generated by the rediscovery and research of many western scholars. The great pioneer was Sir William Jones, founder of the Asiatic Society in Calcutta. Some German scholars interested themselves in Sanskrit studies. Max Muller went into raptures over the glories of ancient Indian civilisation and explained what India could teach the West. The western exploration of India's ancient heritage imbued educated Indians with a new self-confidence and they turned to the past for inspiration to restore national glory in literature, philosophy, art and policies.

The socio-religious reformers of the 19th century further fostered the growth of this cultural nationalism. Swami Dayanand forged a link between Hinduism and political liberation. He fostered the national pride of his countrymen by declaring that from the days of Manu to those of the Pandavas, the Aryans were the paramount power throughout the world. Vivekananda raised patriotism to a high spiritual level. He forged a link between religion, social service and politics. Bankim Chandra Chatterjee in his novel ***Anandamath***, published in 1882, containing the song ***Vande Mataram***, inspired the vision of Mother India. Aurobindo Ghosh in his work ***Bhavani Mandir***, wrote that "our mother country is not a piece of earth, not a figure of speech nor a fiction of mind. It is mighty ***Shakti*** composed of the ***Shaktis*** of all the millions of units that make up the nation". Bal Gangadhar Tilak, the greatest pillar of Extremism, identified nationalism with the feeling of Hindutva. He wrote: "The Hindus of the Punjab, Maharashtra, Telengana and Dravida are one and the reason for this is the only Hindu Dharma". Tilak was not a communalist. He used 'revivalism' for the political purpose of 'awakening' different sections of the people and strengthening their self-confidence by convincing them that they had a sound socio-religious base. Lala Lajpat Rai also was wedded to the idea of Hindu nationality; like Tilak, his conception of 'Hindu nationality' did not imply hostility to the Muslims.

CAUSES FOR THE RISE OF EXTREMISM

Some of the important causes for the rise of the extremist philosophy are :

1. The anti-people policies of the government, such as the withdrawal of cotton excise duties in 1896, the Universities Act of 1904 and the controversial partition of Bengal in 1905.
2. The policies of Lord Curzon, which provided immediate provocation for the rise of extremism. Curzon treated the Congress as an 'unclean thing', an 'seditious' organisation, etc.
3. The potential base for political activity was expanding rapidly with the increasing circulation of the vernacular newspapers. Some of the most popular journals like ***Calcutta Bangabasi***, and ***Kesari*** and ***Kal*** of Poona were very critical of the moderate politics of the Congress.
4. The achievements of the Moderates appeared frustrating to the young educated. Opportuni-

ties in the public services were strictly limited. For example in 1903 only 16,000 Indians held posts at salaries higher than Rs. 75 a month.

5. Some of the great thinkers and leaders like Vivekananda, Tilak, Aurobindo Ghosh, etc. of the period also stirred the people towards the path of the extremism. Vivekananda was the first to say openly, "Weakness is sin, weakness is death. When, O Lord, will our nation be free."
6. The external events exploding the myth of racial superiority of the whites also helped in the growth of extremism. The emergence of Japan as a modern powerful country after 1868, its victory over Russia in 1905 and similarly the defeat of Italy at the hands of Ethiopia in 1896 proved conclusively that all claims of racial superiority were false. The events in Ireland, Russia, Egypt, Turkey and China also instilled a new self-confidence in the Indian people.
7. Long before the launching of the Swadeshi movement as part of the agitation against the partition of Bengal, the seeds of ***swadeshi*** had been sown in Bengal by Ashwini Kumar Dutta and Rabindranath Tagore, who repeatedly called for ***atmasakti*** (self-reliance) through ***swadeshi*** enterprise and national education. Similarly in the Punjab, the cult of ***swadeshi*** was being propagated by Arya Samajists like Lala Lajpat Rai.
8. The torch of extremism was lit by Tilak who used religious orthodoxy (organisation of Ganapati festival from 1874 and Shivaji festival from 1896 onwards) to arouse national consciousness. He was the first to give the slogan of "Swarajya, Swadeshi and Boycott" and wrote in his paper ***Kesari***, "Our nation is like a tree, of which the original trunk was Swarajya and branches were Swadeshi and Boycott".
9. The three pillars of extremism were 'Lal, Bal and Pal' (Lala Lajpat Rai, Bal Gangadhar Tilak and Bipin Chandra Pal) who became the ideals of future nationalists. All of them through their newspapers (Tilak's ***Kesari***, Pal's ***New India*** and Lala's ***Punjabi***) launched vehement attacks on the British government.

SWADESHI MOVEMENT

The partition of Bengal officially came into effect on October 16, 1905. Its announcement set off a mighty upsurge which brought people and political leaders of all shades of opinion together. Numerous protest meetings were held. The student community joined the anti-partition movement with great enthusiasm. ***Vande Mataram*** overnight became the national song for the whole country. The day the partition came into effect (October 16, 1905) was observed in Bengal as a day of mourning. No cooking was done and all the shops and marketplaces were kept closed. On the suggestion of Rabindranath Tagore the day of partition was further observed as Rakhi Bandhan Day.

To offer more active resistance, it was decided to boycott goods. People vowed not to purchase British cloth, salt, sugar or anything else manufactured in England. This was the beginning of the ***Swadeshi*** movement, which within a few years transformed the Indian political scene. The ***Swadeshi*** movement quickly gathered force. Bonfires of British cloth demonstrated the people's determination not to rely on foreign products. The sale of English goods fell dramatically as Bombay mills worked overtime to meet the demand for ***swadeshi*** textiles. It became a matter of pride to wear coarse ***dhotis*** made on local handlooms rather than the fashionable Manchester textiles. The ***Swadeshi*** movement gave a tremendous impetus to Indian industry.

Students played a key role in the movement. The University of Calcutta, which supervised education in schools and colleges, was denounced as a ***gulam khana*** (house for slaves) and a 'National Council of Education' was established with a view to organising a system of education on national lines and under national management. Another unique feature of the ***Swadeshi*** movement was the large number of industrial strikes that took place during the period.

SIGNIFICANCE OF THE MOVEMENT

A remarkable feature of the ***Swadeshi*** movement was the "simultaneous presence in it, at least in germ, of so many of the tendencies and forces which went on shaping the life of our people till 1947 and even beyond". The ***Swadeshi*** movement was the beginning of the organised movement in India. It was the only movement which fully achieved its objective, in that partition of Bengal was revoked in 1911. It was the ***Swadeshi*** movement which "brought nationalism from a realm of theory and sentiments into the field of practical politics which leavened the life of India as a whole". According to Surendra Nath Banerjee, the ***Swadeshi*** movement was not "merely an economic or a political movement but an all-comprehensive movement coextensive with the entire circle of our national life". Mahatma Gandhi wrote that the real awakening of India "took place after the partition of Bengal." The spirit of ***Swadeshi*** percolated down to almost every walk of life—industries, education, culture, literature and fashion, and it became the symbol of national self-reliance. "No other phase of our national movement can boast of a cultural accompaniment as rich as ***Swadeshi***."

THE SURAT SPLIT

The ***Swadeshi*** movement also cast its shadow on the growing differences between the Moderate and Extremist groups in the Congress. The Varanasi session of the Congress, presided over by G.K. Gokhale in 1905, recorded its protest against the partition of Bengal. But the Moderates were not ready to extend open support to boycott which was in conflict with their policy of "petition and persuasion".

At the Calcutta session of the Congress, presided over by Dadabhai Naoroji in 1906, the Extremists were able to secure better terms from the Moderates, when the INC recognised the boycott as "legitimate" and accorded its most cordial support to the ***Swadeshi*** movement.

The growing differences between the Moderates and the Extremists came to the fore at the Surat session of the INC in 1907, when against the wishes of the Extremists, who preferred Lala Lajpat Rai, Ras Behari Ghosh was chosen as President. The issues on which the split came were the resolutions on self-government, boycott and National Education. The Surat session ended in pandemonium and the Moderates, who constituted the majority of the delegates, gained complete control over the Congress organisation. The Moderates eventually decided to have no truck with the Extremists, who seceded from the INC.

REVOLUTIONARY MOVEMENT IN INDIA AND ABROAD

The First Phase of Revolutionary Movement : Disillusioned with the constitutional methods of the Moderates and inspired by the extremist ideology, many young Indians chose the path of revolutionary activities. The decided to follow the footsteps of the Irish terrorists and the Russian Nihilists, to strike terror in the hearts of the British rulers and drive them out of India. Tilak's slogan of 'Militancy and not Mendicancy' inspired many young men to take to the path of militant nationalism, which was mainly centred in Maharashtra, Bengal and Punjab. The methods of these revolutionaries included forming secret societies, raising national volunteer forces, taking up social work during famines and epidemics, imparting physical and moral training, disseminating the ***Swadeshi*** and boycott message and killing tyrannical British officials. The revolutionaries assassinated oppressive officials and informers and committed dacoities, known as ***Swadeshi*** dacoities, to raise funds for arms and other financial needs.

One of the earliest terrorist deeds was done in Poona in 1897 by two young Chapekar brothers, Damodar and Balkrishna, when they murdered two notorious British officials, Rand and Amherst. They were later arrested and sentenced to death. The Chapekar brothers were associated with the revolutionary society ***Hindu Dharma Sangha***. The ***Arya Bandhav Samaj*** was another society formed under the inspiration of Tilak.

Foremost among the revolutionary associations in Maharashtra was the ***Abhinava Bharat Society*** founded by ***Vinayak Damodar Savarkar in* 1904.** The educational institutions provided a fertile breeding ground for the revolutionary ideas and activities of the society, which established branches in various towns of Maharashtra and Central Provinces. ***Anant Lakshman Karkare***, a leading member of this Society, ***murdered Jackson***, the District Magistrate of Nasik. This led to the arrest and trial of the revolutionaries of this Society in the Nasik Conspiracy case and 27 of them were found guilty and punished. V.D. Savarkar's brother Ganesh was transported for life for seditious writings and inciting war against the British Government.

In the Madras Province, ***Nilkantha Brahmachari and Vanchi Aiyar founded a secret Bharatha Matha Association***. Aiyar killed Ashe, the District Magistrate of Tiruneveli in 1911 and later on committed suicide.

In the Punjab, revolutionary terrorism had some links with recurring famines and increase in the land revenue and irrigation taxes. As early as in 1904, one J.M. Chaterji, whose family had settled in Saharanpur, founded the ***Bharat Mata Society***. Later he was joined by Lala Hardayal, Ajit Singh and Sufi Amba Prasad. The deportation of Lala Lajpat Rai and Sardar Ajit Singh provided further stimulus to the revolutionary feelings in the Punjab. After the foundation of the Ghadar Party in the USA, the Punjab became the centre of activities of the Ghadarites. Many revolutionaries from the Punjab, like Lala Hardayal and Bhai Parmanand joined the Ghadar Party movement in the USA.

Bengal was in the forefront of revolutionary terrorist activities. The revolutionary movement in Bengal derived its inspiration from the works of Bankim Chandra Chatterji and exhortations of Swami Vivekananda and Aurobindo Ghosh. One of the earliest and best known revolutionary societies in Bengal was the ***Anushilan Samiti***. Satish Chandra Bose and Pramathanath Mitra played a leading role in founding this society; Aurobindo Ghosh and Sister Nivedita, the Irish discipline of Swami Vivekananda, greatly encouraged and supported it. Another Anushilan Samiti was founded in Dacca (now Dhaka). The ***Dacca Anushilan Samiti*** was led by Pulin Behari Das and had about 500 branches in East Bengal. ***Atmonnati Samiti***, founded by Bipin Behari Ganguly, was another revolutionary society of Bengal. Sakharam Ganesh Deuskar, a Marathi scholar who was proficient in Bengali, provided a link between the revolutionaries of Bengal and Maharashtra.

Militant nationalism gained a powerful impetus after the partition of Bengal (1905) and a number of secret revolutionary societies, such as the ***Suhrid Samiti*** and the ***Sadhana Samiti*** of Mymensingh, the ***Swadesh Bandhav Samiti*** of Barisal and the ***Brati Samiti*** of Farridpur were founded, all of them being declared illegal. During the post-partition years of Bengal, a number of revolutionary papers and journals, such as the ***Sandhya*** edited by Brahmabandhab Upadhyay, the ***Bandemataram*** edited by Aurobindo Ghosh, the ***Yugantar*** edited by Bhupendra Datta and others, were published. The last named journal spawned a revolutionary society calling itself ***Yugantar***, with branches in various parts of Bengal. The Yugantar group led by Barindra Ghosh "breathed revolution in everything and pointed out how revolution was to be effected". The group manufactured bombs and made attempts on the lives of unpopular officials. Attempts were made on the lives of the Lieutenant Governors of East Bengal and Bengal, but they proved abortive. Prafulla Chaki and Khudiram Bose assassinated a vindictive Judge, Kingsford, at Muzaffarpur (Bihar). Prafulla Chaki committed suicide and Khudiram Bose was arrested and hanged. Shortly afterwards, 34 revolutionaries of the Yugantar group, including Barindra and Aurobindo Ghosh, were arrested and tried in the Alipur Conspiracy case. While the trial was in progress, the approver, the Public Prosecutor and a Deputy Superintendent of Police were assassinated. Most of the accused in the Alipur Conspiracy case were sentenced to long terms of imprisonment. Barindra was transported for life, but Aurobindo Ghosh was acquitted.

For revolutionaries striving for immediate and complete independence, the outbreak of the First World War seemed a heaven sent opportunity. In Bengal, political dacoities and assassinations reached the highest point in 1915-16. Most of the revolutionary groups rallied under Jatindranath Mukherji, popularly known as Bagha (Tiger) Jatin, who on being surrounded and outnumbered by the police in Balasore (Orissa) on September 9, 1915 put up a most heroic resistance before courting death.

Another great revolutionary of this period was Ras Behari Bose, who was a link between the revolutionaries of Bengal and the Punjab. He was the brain behind the attempted assassination of Viceroy Hardinge, when he was making state entry into Delhi. He also planned for armed mutiny of the Indian soldiers in the British army. The conspiracy was, however, exposed and Ras Behari Bose escaped to Japan, where he continued his revolutionary activities. During the Second World War he organised the Indian Independence League and the Indian National Army (I.N.A.).

Such forms of revolutionary activities, without a common plan of action and central leadership, were bound to peter out, as they had no mass base. They further faced great repression and were openly disowned by the Moderates, and even the Extremists were not quite comfortable about their methods. Also, the use of Hindu religious metaphors by them tended to alienate non-Hindu masses. All the same, their sheer bravery and selfless martyrdom added a halo to their names and the damage they inflicted on the British empire gained them an enormous reputation.

Revolutionary Movements Outside India: During this period, revolutionary activities and propaganda were conducted by Indians settled abroad, especially in the United Kingdom, the USA, France, Afghanistan and Germany. The India Home Rule Society, one of the earliest revolutionary societies outside India, was founded by Shyamji Krishna Varma who had settled in London in 1897. He gathered a group of Indian revolutionaries around him, the most prominent among whom where V.D. Savarkar, Hardayal and Madan Lal Dhingra. Shyamji Krishna Varma founded the Indian Home Rule Society with the object of securing Home Rule for India. For this purpose he started a paper, ***Indian Sociologist*** and founded the Indian House in London. The growing revolutionary approach of Shyamji and his associates drew the attention of the British Government and ***The Times*** and other newspapers in London criticised Shyamji and his associates. Shyamji thereupon left London and settled Paris and the political leadership of India House came to be vested on V.D. Savarkar. Savarkar's colleague Madan Lal Dhingra shot dead Curzon Wyllie on July 1, 1909 in London. Madan Lal Dhingra was arrested the hanged. Later on, Savarkar was arrested and sent to India to undergo trial in the Nasik Conspiracy case and other charges.

Bhikaiji Cama's Movement: Madam Bhikaiji Rustam K.R. Cama, an associate of Shyamji Krishna Varma, left India in 1902 and was engaged in making revolutionary propaganda against the British rule, both in Europe and America. She and Sardar Singh Rana lived in Paris and attended the International Socialist Congress at Stuttgart (Germany) in August 1907, as representatives of India. Madam Cama made a fiery speech exposing the disastrous results of the British rule in India and at the conclusion of the conference unfurled the National Flag of India—a tricolour in green, yellow and red.

The Ghadar Party Movement: At the turn of the century, a large number of Indians had settled down in the USA and Canada. About 1906, these Indians started nationalistic activities in the USA and began to publish material against the British rule in India. Taraknath Das, one of the leading Indians in the USA, formed the ***Indian Independence League*** in California in 1907 and the next year he began to publish the paper ***Free Hindustan***. Its object was to spread revolutionary ideas among Indians living in the USA. The result of all this activity was the emergence of several political organisations at different times and under different leaders. In November 1913 the ***Hind Association of America*** was founded by Sohan Singh Bhakana. It decided to publish a weekly paper **Ghadar** or ***Hindustan Ghadar***, in commemoration of the Revolt of 1857, in English, Urdu, Marathi and Gurumukhi, which gave the association its hallowed name the ***Ghadar Party***. Lala Hardayal was the guiding spirit of the ***Ghadar*** Party movement. The organisation began to function from the Yugantar Ashram in San Francisco, the place being named after the well-known revolutionary journal published in Calcutta. Almost every issue of the ***Ghadar*** contained poems urging upon Indians, among other things, to take up arms, rise in insurrection and kill the British. The Ghadar Party became very popular, particularly among the Indians living abroad. The ***Ghadar*** became the source for facts and ideas for other papers and thus the ***Ghadar*** became the source of world-wide revolutionary propaganda, on behalf of India. Lala Hardayal, Bhai Parmanand and Ram Chandra were the leading figures of the Ghadar Party movement. During the First World War, the Ghadar Party established contacts with the revolutionaries in India and planned a revolt against the British, but the plan fizzled out, the Ghadar Party itself having declined towards the end of the First World War.

Among other notable revolutionaries outside India were Raja Mahendra Pratap and Barkatullah who, with the support of Germany and Russia, set up the Provisional Government of India in Kabul.

THE SECOND PHASE OF THE REVOLUTIONARY MOVEMENT

The suspension of Non-Cooperation and the lack of any political activity in the country after 1922, disillusioned many spirited nationalist young men, who were further dissatisfied with Gandhiji's leadership and his strategy of non-violent struggle. They sought to overthrow the British rule through violent means, inspired by the revolutionary movements and uprisings elsewhere in Russia, China, Ireland, Turkey, Egypt, etc. The old revolutionary societies like ***Yugantar*** and ***Anushilan Samitis remerged***. A few new revolutionary and terrorist organisations were also founded by the new revolutionary terrorist leaders who emerged from the ranks of the enthusiastic and disillusioned non-cooperators. The Punjab, Delhi, United Provinces and Bengal became the focal points of the reborn revolutionary movement.

Revolutionary Movement in Northern India : Among the revolutionary organisations in northern India, the most noteworthy were the Hindustan Republican Association (H.R.A.) and its successor organisation, the Hindustan Socialist Republic Association (or Army). The H.R.A. was founded at Kanpur in October 1924, by Sachindranath Sanyal, Jogesh Chandra Chatterjee, Ramprasad Bismil and Chandra Shekhar Azad. Its declared objectives were : (*i*) to establish a Federal Republic of United States of India through an organised and armed revolution; (*ii*) to concentrate on political crimes, including political dacoities, to collect money and arms for the movement and (*iii*) to have various departments of the H.R.A. Ram Prasad Bismil introduced a novelty that the object of the political dacoities must be to secure money belonging to the Government.

It was accordingly decided to commit a train dacoity in a running train at Kakori on the Lucknow-Saharanpur section of the Northern Railway. The plot was successfully carried out: about ten H.R.A. revolutionaries plundered the Railway cash chest. The Government, however, unearthed the whole plot. Of the 29 arrested and tried in Kakori Conspiracy case, four revolutionaries—Ram Prasad Bismil, Asfaqullah Khan, Roshan Lal and Rajendra Lahiri—were sentenced to death.

The imprisonment of most of the H.R.A. leaders in the Kakori Conspiracy case and the ensuing police repression nearly finished off the H.R.A. as a revolutionary organisation. After some time, a fresh wave of revolutionaries, led by Chandra Shekhar Azad, the sole remaining absconder of the Kakori Conspiracy case, met at Ferozeshah Kotla ground in Delhi on September 9-10, 1928 and established the Hindustan Socialist Republican Association (H.S.R.A.) with the objective of establishing a Socialist Republican State in India. It was a democratic organisation in which majority decisions were to be binding upon all.

The first revolutionary act of the H.S.R.A. was the murder of Saunders, the Assistant Superintendent of police, Lahore, who had lathi-charged and mortally wounded Lala Lajpat Rai, during the anti-Simon Commission protest march at Lahore on October 28, 1928. Saunders was killed at the Lahore railway station on October 30, 1928 by Bhagat Singh, Chandra Shekhar Azad and Rajguru.

The next action of the HSRA was not only more daring but of outstanding heroism. After Saunders' murder, the revolutionaries had gone underground, but the police were terrorising innocent people. Unable to stand the sight of innocent people being made scapegoats and to draw the Government's wrath to themselves, the HSRA decided to send two of its members to commit a crime and court arrest. Accordingly, Bhagat Singh and Batukeshwar Dutta threw two crude bombs and some leaflets in the Central Legislative Assembly on April 8, 1929, when the Assembly was discussing the Public Safety Bill and the Trade Disputes Bill. Bhagat Singh and Dutt were arrested and tried in the Central Assembly Bomb case.

The arrest of Bhagat Singh and Batukeshwar Dutt, however, led to the arrest of most of the HSRA activists, who were tried together in the Lahore Conspiracy case. When in prison, the undertrials launched a hunger-strike to secure for themselves the status of political prisoners, instead of ordinary criminals. One of these hunger strikers, Jatin Das, died on the 64th day of his fast on September 12, 1929. Most of the HSRA revolutionaries were convicted in the Lahore Conspiracy case and three of them—Bhagat Singh, Sukh Dev and Rajguru—were hanged on March 23, 1931. The news of their hanging engulfed the entire nation in a death-like gloom.

. Chandra Shekhar Azad, who had been declared an absconder in the Kakori Conspiracy case, was declared an absconder in the Lahore Conspiracy case as well. Azad once again began organising underground activities. He organised a series of plots and revolutionary activities commencing in 1920, including a plot to murder the Viceroy by way of revenge for the Lahore Conspiracy case. But on February 27, 1931, Azad was surrounded by the police at Alfred Park, Allahabad and met a heroic death in the police encounter. With his death the curtain was rung down on the HSRA movement in northern India.

The Revolutionary Movement in Bengal: During this period, Bengal re-emerged as a great breeding-ground of revolutionary terrorism. The old revolutionary societies such as the ***Anushilan*** and ***Yugantar*** again became quite active. A number of new societies were also founded, such as ***Bengal Volunteers*** or "B.V. Party" by Hema Chandra Ghose and Lila Nag and ***Sri Sangha*** by Anil Roy.

Outstanding among the new revolutionary organisations in Bengal was the ***Indian Republican Army*** (IRA) founded by Surya Sen. Sen had actively participated in the Non-Cooperation movement. Later on, he became a teacher in one of the National Schools and was therefore popularly known as Master Da.

Surya Sen with his band of revolutionaries made regular military preparations, after which he issued a manifesto in the name of the Indian Republican Army, declaring war against the British, on April 19, 1930. Thereafter, members of the Indian Republican Army led by Surya Sen attacked the Police Armoury at Chittagong and ransacked the armoury, taking away the arms. Shortly thereafter, a provisional independent Government of India was set up with Surya Sen as its president.

After the Chittagong Armoury raid, revolutionary terrorist activities in Bengal witnessed a sudden spurt. Two revolutionaries shot dead the Inspector General of Prisons of Bengal in his office. In December 1931, two young girls shot dead the District Magistrate of Comilla. In February 1932, Bina Das shot at the Governor of Bengal while receiving her degree at the Convocation of the University of Calcutta. On September 22, 1932, a young woman revolutionary, Pritilata Waddedar, along with a group of revolutionaries raided the Railway Institute at Pahartali in Chittagong. During the raid, Pritilata was seriously wounded and to evade arrest, she committed suicide. Participation of such a large number of daring and bold women revolutionaries was the unique feature of the revolutionary movement in Bengal.

For three years after the Chittagong Armoury raid, the group of revolutionaries under Surya Sen carried on their activities in spite of numerous arrests and amid a veritable reign of terror let loose by the Government. In February 1933, however, Surya Sen was arrested after betrayal by a companion and was later on hanged. Surya Sen's death virtually brought to an end the revolutionary activities in Bengal. Most of the revolutionaries, who had strong leanings to socialism, after completing their long prison terms, joined the Communist party, the Congress Socialist Party, the Revolutionary Socialist Party and other Left parties and groups.

GANDHIAN MASS MOVEMENT

Mahatma Gandhi returned to India from South Africa in January 1915. In his book ***Hind Swarajya***, written in 1909, he interpreted ***Swaraj*** (self-rule) in a broad sense. His constructive work began with the foundation of the Sabarmati Ashram at Ahmedabad in May 1915. It was through involvement in two agrarian disputes, Champaran (in North Bihar) and Kaira (in Gujarat) and a labour dispute in Ahmedabad in 1917-18, that Gandhi emerged as an influential political leader. At all the three places Gandhiji used his technique of Satyagraha or passive resistance. His role in the Champaran and Kaira Satyagrahas has already been discussed in connection with the peasant movements. In Ahmedabad Gandhiji organised a movement in 1918 for increase in the wages of the mill workers. He brought about a settlement between the mill owners and the workers through arbitration. During the last two years of the First World War (1917-18), he maintained close contacts with the Congress and the Home Rule League and also with the Muslim leaders. But it was the repressive policy of the British Government which dragged him away from the shell of political isolation and made him launch the anti-Rowlatt Bills Satyagraha.

Anti-Rowlatt Satyagraha (1919): In view of the growing revolutionary terrorism and the on-going First World War, the Governor-General Chelmsford had appointed a Committee (the Sedition or Rowlatt Committee) under the Presidentship of Sydney Rowlatt, a Judge of the King's bench in London, to investigate the nature and extent of revolutionary activities and to suggest legislation, if necessary, to deal effectively with them. The Rowlatt Committee, which submitted its Report in April 1918, made a comprehensive review of the activities of militant nationalists and recommended special legislation, both punitive and preventive in character.

Two Bills based on the Rowlatt Committee's recommendations were placed before the Imperial Legislative Council. One was dropped; the other—the Anarchical and Revolutionary Crimes Act—was passed in March 1919. It provided for speedy trial of offences by a Special Court consisting of three High Court Judges. There was no appeal from this Court and it could accept evidence not admissible under the Indian Evidence Act. Besides, this Provincial Governments were given wide powers to search a place and arrest a suspected person without warrant.

As soon as the Government introduced the two Bills (February 6, 1919), Gandhiji decided to organise a ***Satyagraha*** campaign. He criticised the so-called Rowlatt Acts as "unjust, subversive of the principles of liberty and destructive of elementary rights of the individual". A ***Satyagraha Sabha*** was established, with Gandhiji as its president, to organise the campaign.

In the first stage of the anti-Rowlatt ***Satyagraha***, volunteers courted arrest through formal defiance of the law. The second stage w as to launch a countrywide ***hartal*** or strike on April 6, 1919. This was followed by mass protest and mob violence in Bombay, Ahmedabad and several other towns. But after the Jallianwala Bagh massacre on April 13, 1919, the anti-Rowlatt ***Satyagraha*** lost momentum.

The anti-Rowlatt Act ***Satyagraha*** transformed the Congress into a national body, with a new ideology and a new strategy under a new leader.

The Jallianwala Bagh Massacre: The anti-Rowlatt Act agitation was particularly severe in the Punjab which was suffering from the after-effects of wartime repression, forcible recruitment and the influence of the revolutionaries. The movement provoked a ***hartal*** in many parts of the Punjab and violent disturbances took place. Within a week of the ***hartal*** of April 6, a considerable part of the Punjab was aflame and the authorities put down the rebellion through such measures as "no civilised Government in modern times has ever been known to take against its own subjects." The Lieutenant Governor, Gen. Michal O'Dwyer, had already earned notoriety as an oppressive administrator. On April 9, 1919, he ordered the arrest of two local Congress leaders, Dr. Satyapal and Dr. Kitchlew, who were associated with the Reception Committee for the annual session of the I.N.C. to be held in December 1919.

To protest against their arrest and the British repression, a public meeting was held at Jallianwala Bagh in Amritsar on April 13, 1919, where O'Dwyer arrived with armoured cars and troops and fired on an unarmed peaceful crowd without warning, killing nearly 1,000 people and scores of others. The massacre of Jallianwala Bagh was followed by martial law and a veritable reign of terror prevailed in the Punjab.

To protest against the Jallianwala Bagh tragedy Rabindranath Tagore surrendered the knighthood conferred on him by the British Government and Sir Sankaran Nair, a former president of the I.N.C., resigned his membership of the Viceroy's Executive Council.

The Jallianwala Bagh tragedy introduced a dramatic change in the Indian political situation, which became further surcharged with the initiation of the Khilafat movement. The Amritsar session of the INC, held in December 1919, reflected the new aggressive mood of the people.

THE KHILAFAT MOVEMENT (1920-22)

The Jallianwala Bagh massacre took place at a time when the Indian Muslims were extremely agitated over the pan-Islamic Khilafat issue, which originated as a result of Turkey's entry into the First World War as an ally of Germany against Britain. The Sultan of Turkey, ruler of the vast Ottoman empire, was the Caliph (or Khalifa) of the Islamic world. In the First World War Turkey was defeated, the Ottoman Empire was dismembered and the Sultan of Turkey was deprived of all real authority even in the remaining dominions, as he was placed completely under the control of a High Commission appointed by the Allied powers.

The Muslims of India regarded the treatment of Turkey as a great betrayal on the part of Britain and other Allies and early in 1920 the Indian Muslims started a vigorous agitation to bring pressure on Britain to change its policy towards Turkey. This Khilafat Movement grew in strength on account of the sympathy and support which the Muslims received from Mahatma Gandhi, who was elected President of the All India Khilafat Conference in November 1919. The Amritsar session of the INC, held in December 1919, gave a great fillip to the Khilafat agitation.

Hitherto, the Congress had scrupulously avoided involvement in religious matters. Gandhiji felt that the movement provided an opportunity to unite Hindus and Muslims that might not come again for a hundred years. He wrote that the Congress plea for Hindu-Muslim unity "would be an empty phrase if the Hindus hold aloof from the Muslims when their vital interests are at stake".

Meanwhile, the Khilafatists formulated a three-point programme: (*i*) the Ottoman Caliph (the Sultan of Turkey) should retain his empire with sufficient temporal power to defend Islam; (*ii*) the Arab lands should remain under Muslim rule and (*iii*) the Sultan of Turkey should be the warden of the places sacred to the Muslims. "Khilafat Day" was observed on October 17, 1919 on an all-India scale and in an impressive manner.

At the special session of the I.N.C. held in Calcutta in September 1920 a resolution was passed, at Mahatma Gandhi's instance, to launch the Non-cooperation movement for two wrongs: (*i*) the British Government's attitude towards the Khilafat issue and (*ii*) its failure to protect the innocent people of the Punjab and punish the officers guilty of barbarous behaviour towards them.

THE NON-COOPERATION MOVEMENT (1920-22)

The Non-Cooperation movement, which was the first mass movement launched under the leadership of Mahatma Gandhi, was launched to press three main demands: (*i*) the Khilafat issue; (*ii*) the redressal of the Punjab wrongs and (*iii*) the attainment of ***Swaraj***.

The programme of the movement had two main aspects: Destructive and Constructive. Under the first category came: (*i*) surrender of titles and honorary offices and resignation from nominated seats in local bodies; (*ii*) refusal to attend official and non-official functions; (*iii*) gradual withdrawal of children from officially controlled schools and colleges; (*iv*) boycott of British courts by lawyers and litigants; (*v*) refusal on the part of the military, clerical and labour classes to offer themselves as recruits for service in Mesopotamia; (*vi*) boycott of elections to the Legislative Councils by candidates and voters and (*vii*) boycott of foreign goods.

The constructive programme of the Non-Cooperation movement comprised: (*i*) setting up of arbitration boards to take the place of courts; (*ii*) founding of national schools and colleges, where students leaving government schools and colleges might continue their education; (*iii*) promotion of ***Swadeshi***; (*iv*) popularisation of ***Charkha***, and ***Khadi***; (*v*) raising a Volunteer Corps. The AICC meeting at Vijayawada on March 31, 1921, outlined two more programmes; (*vi*) to collect one crore rupees for the Tilak Memorial ***Swarajya*** Fund; and (*vii*) to introduce 20 lakh ***charkhas*** into Indian households.

Progress of the Movement: The Non-Cooperation movement was initiated by Mahatma Gandhi on August 1, 1920 on his own authority before the matter was placed before the Calcutta Congress a month later. The movement started on a poignant note, with Bal Gangadhar Tilak passing away in Bombay on the day the movement was launched.

The Non-Cooperation movement evoked an unprecedented response throughout the country, particularly in western India, Bengal and North India. Bonfires of foreign cloth were made in various parts of the country. During this struggle, the principal weapon used against the Government was boycott of the legislatures, law courts and educational institutions. Teachers and students sacrificed their prospects by leaving government colleges and schools. New educational institutions such as the Jamia Millia Islamia and thc Kashi Vidhyapith were founded to provide education on national lines. As part of the boycott of the law courts, many members of the legal profession, such as Motilal Nehru and C.R. Das, gave up their lucrative practice. When the Prince of Wales landed in Bombay on November 17, 1921, he was welcomed with a nation-wide *hartal.*

The Government declared the Congress and Khilafat Volunteer organisations illegal. Nearly 30,000 persons courted arrest within a year of the launching of the movement. After the annual session of the INC at Ahmedabad in December 1921, Mahatma Gandhi sent a written ultimatum to the Viceroy threatening "Mass Civil Disobedience" if the Viceroy did not decide to reverse the Government's repressive policies within seven days.

Before the week elapsed, at Chauri Chaura, a small town in Gorakhpur district, U.P., twenty-two policemen were killed after they had fired on a political procession. The Chauri Chaura incident convinced Mahatma Gandhi that the country was not yet ready for the mass civil disobedience. He prevailed upon the Congress Working Committee, which met at Bardoli on February 12, 1922, to call off the movement.

The country was shocked at Mahatma Gandhi sounding "the order of retreat just when public enthusiasm was reaching the boiling point". The British Government, realising that Mahatma Gandhi's position had been weakened on account of his suddenly calling off the movement, arrested him in March 1922 and he was sentenced to six years of imprisonment.

An Appraisal of the Movement: The sudden suspension of the Non-Cooperation movement also led to the demise of the Khilafat issue and breakdown of the precariously balanced Hindu-Muslim harmony. Shortly after the movement was called off communalism became rampant all over the country and serious riots broke out. In Kerala, an anti-Zamindar bloodletting was witnessed, when Muslim Moplah peasants turned on Hindu landlords and money-lenders. The communal situation became far worse during the years 1921-27 than it had been ever before.

Mahatma Gandhi's promise to achieve ***Swaraj*** within a year of launching the movement was not fulfilled. The Punjab wrongs were also not redressed. Thus the Non-Cooperation movement failed to achieve any of its declared objectives. But its ultimate gain outweighed the immediate losses. The Congress had become a force to reckon with and thereafter it went from strength to strength. It generated a desire for freedom and inspired the people to challenge the colonial rule.

THE SWARAJYA PARTY

After the suspension of the Non-Cooperation movement the Congress was left without any political programme. Some congress leaders, such as C. Rajagopalachari and Dr. Rajendra Prasad, busied themselves with the constructive programme: handspinning on ***charkha***, uplift of the ***Harijans***, popularisation of temperance, etc. But a group of Congressmen, led by Motilal Nehru and Chitta Ranjan Das, wished to contest the elections in 1923 organised under the Government of India Act, 1919 and thus gain entry into the legislatures. Opinion within the Congress was thus divided between two schools of thought: the 'no-changers', who were opposed to Council entry and the 'pro-changers', who wanted to contest the elections. At the Gaya session of the Congress, held in December 1922, the 'no-changers', led by C. Rajagopalachari, defeated the 'pro-changers'. Thereupon, Chitta Ranjan Das, himself a pro-changer who had presided over the Gaya session, resigned from the Presidentship of the Congress. With Motilal Nehru and other 'pro-changers' he formed the Congress-Khilafat-Swarajaya Party, commonly known as the ***Swarajya Party***. Through successful propaganda, the new party rapidly gained in strength.

The ***Swarajya Party*** claimed to be an integral part of the Congress and professed its adherence to non-violent non-cooperation. It gained further strength at the special session of the Congress held in September 1923, which resolved that Congressmen could contest the elections. This gave the 'pro-changers' freedom to pursue their programme. A formal split in the Congress was also thus avoided.

The ***Swarajya Party*** set up a separate organisation with C.R. Das as its president and Motilal Nehru as secretary. The party pledged itself to a policy of "uniform, continuous and consistent obstruction with a view to make government through the (central) Assembly and (Provincial) Councils impossible." It had the active support of Congressmen like Vittalbhai Patel, Madan Mohan Malviya and M.R. Jayakar.

The elections to the legislatures were held in November 1923. Even though the ***Swarajists*** had only a few weeks to prepare and the electorate was only about 6.2 million or less than 3 per cent of the population, they won 42 out of the 101 elective seats in the Central Legislature Assembly, besides securing the support of independents led by Jinnah and the liberals. In the Provincial legislatures, too, they did quite well, securing a clear majority in the Central Provinces and becoming the largest party in Bengal. In Bombay and the United Provinces, too, they did quite well though not in Madras and the Punjab where strong casteist and communal forces in the form of the Justice and Unionist Parties, respectively, held sway.

The ***Swarajists*** did valuable work in the Central and Provincial Legislatures. In the Central Legislature they forced the appointment of Alexander Muddiman Committee to inquire into the defects of the Act of 1919. They fought for the repeal of repressive laws. They secured a number of economic benefits, such as the abolition of cotton excise duty, reduction of duty on salt, improvement in the condition of labour, protection of trade unions, etc. In the Central Provinces, where they commanded absolute majority in the Council, the ***Swarajists*** forced the ministers to resign and made dyarchy unworkable. In Bengal they voted out the Ministry and fought for the withdrawal of repressive laws. It was through ***Swarajist*** politics that the nationalist Indians got their first taste as parliamentarians.

But soon the ***Swarajya Party*** faced a host of problems and internal divisions which insinuated themselves on account of the party's proximity to prestige and powers of office. A trend grew within the party towards 'responsive cooperation' with the Government. The group advocating cooperation with the Government came to be known as 'Responsivists' and those opposed to it were known as 'Non-responsivists'. Religion also played a role in this discord. Communal-minded Muslims isolated themselves, while the so-called Respon-sivists' in their desire to safeguard Hindu interests began to cooperate with the Government. Inevitably, the discord had its impact on the fabric of the party. In the 1926 elections, though the ***Swarajya Party*** won 40 seats in the Central Legislature and half of the seats in Madras, in other Provinces it suffered badly. The ***Swarajists*** finally walked out of the Legislature in 1930. By early 1930 the Swarajist sun had set.

THE CIVIL DISOBEDIENCE MOVEMENT

First Phase of Civil Disobedience Movement and the Dandi March (1930-1931)

The Congress Working Committee had authorised Mahatma Gandhi to determine the time, place and the issue on which the Civil Disobedience movement was to be launched.

Gandhiji decided to inaugurate the movement by violating the Salt Laws on the sea-coast at Dandi: Salt was made an issue, because the Government controlled the sale of this indispensable commodity and imposed a tax on it which was felt most keenly by the poor. Mahatma Gandhi launched the Salt Satyagraha on March 12, 1930, when he marched from his Sabarmati Ashram (Ahmedabad) with some eighty hand-picked followers. After a 24-day long march he symbolically broke the Salt laws at Dandi on April 5, 1930. The breaking of the Salt Laws formally inaugurated the Civil Disobedience movement.

Programme of the Civil Disobedience Movement: Among the programmes outlined for the Civil Disobedience movement were the following :

(*i*) The violation of the Salt Law and other laws;

(*ii*) Non-payment of land-revenue, rent or other taxes;

(*iii*) Boycott of law courts, legislatures, elections, Government functions, Government schools and colleges;

(*iv*) Boycott of foreign goods and cloth and burning of foreign cloth;

(*v*) Peaceful picketing of shops selling liquor and other intoxicants;

(*vi*) Organising mass strikes and demonstrations;

(*vii*) Resigning Government jobs and not joining the civil, military or police services.

Progress of the Movement: In all provinces, people pursued the above programmes with great enthusiasm. In United Provinces and Gujarat, no-tax campaign was launched. Thousands of women, even from orthodox and aristocratic families, came out of their homes and offered themselves for arrest and imprisonment. In the North-West Frontier Province (NWFP), Khan Abdul Ghaffar Khan, popularly known as Frontier Gandhi, under the banner of his "Khudai Khidmatgar" (Servants of God) organisation, most actively participated in the movement with the his volunteers, who dressed up in red shirts. From their uniform they came to be known as Red Shirts. More than 60,000 persons were arrested in course of the movement in less than a year. In the North-East, the Manipuris joined the movement and the young Rani Gaidinliu with her Naga followers actively supported the movement.

The British Government, as usual, retaliated with repression. In June 1930, the Congress and its affiliate organisations were declared illegal and Mahatma Gandhi and all other Congress leaders were arrested. The Press was gagged and newspapers could not report on the dozens of police firings that took place. Scores of people died in these incidents. The private properties and lands of thousands of people were confiscated for non-payment of taxes.

Amidst these heroic deeds and official repression, when the movement was at its peak the Viceroy took the initiative of releasing the Congress leaders and invited Mahatma Gandhi for talks, which led to the Gandhi-Irwin Pact and the suspension of the Civil Disobedience movement.

GANDHI-IRWIN PACT—MARCH 5, 1931

During the course of the Civil Disobedience movement the Simon Commission Report had been published and to consider its recommendations the First Round Table Conference was summoned in London, in November 1930. The Congress boycotted the Conference, but other parties such as the Liberals, the Muslim League, the Hindu Mahasabha and the Princely States attended it. The absence of the Congress, however, rendered the conference pointless. Some of the Liberal leaders like Tej Bahadur Sapru, V.S. Sastri and M.R. Jayakar, on their return from the Conference appealed to Mahatma Gandhi to seek an interview with the Viceroy. To create appropriate conditions for talks between the Viceroy and the Congress leaders, other Congress leaders were released and Viceroy Lord Irwin invited the Congress for talks. The Congress authorised Gandhiji to negotiate a settlement with the Viceroy. After prolonged Gandhi-Irwin talks an agreement, known as the Gandhi-Irwin Pact, was signed between the two on March 5, 1931.

The highlights of this agreement were :

(*i*) On behalf of the Congress, Gandhiji agreed to discontinue the Civil Disobedience movement.

(*ii*) The Congress agreed to join the Second Round Table Conference for drafting the constitutional reforms on the basis of: (*a*) Federation, (*b*) Responsibility and (*c*) Safeguards or reservations in the interest of India for such matters as defence, external affairs, minorities and the financial credit of India.

(*iii*) The Viceroy agreed to withdraw ordinances promulgated in connection with the Civil Disobedience movement.

(*iv*) The Government agreed to release the agitators arrested in connection with the movement and to return properties confiscated on account of the movement.

(*v*) The Government agreed to permit the people living within a certain distance of the seashore to collect or manufacture sea salt free of duty.

(*vi*) The Government agreed to permit peaceful picketing of liquor and opium shops.

SECOND PHASE OF THE CIVIL DISOBEDIENCE MOVEMENT—(1932-1934)

Meanwhile Lord Willingdon had succeeded Irwin as the Viceroy and he flouted many provisions of the Gandhi-Irwin Pact. On his return to India, Mahatma Gandhi witnessed Government repression in full swing. Most of the important Congress leaders were also arrested. The Congress Working Committee, which met on January 1, 1932, therefore decided to resume the Civil Disobedience Movement if the Government did not make some positive gestures. The Government continuing with its repressive measures, the movement was resumed in early 1932.

The Government declared the Congress as an illegal body, and arrested most of the leading Congress leaders, including Jawaharlal Nehru and Khan Abdul

Ghaffar Khan. Nearly 90,000 men, women and children were arrested for participating in the movement. The movement was gaining strength when it was suddenly side-tracked, with the announcement by the British Prime Minister Ramsay Macdonald of his infamous Communal Award on August 16, 1932.

COMMUNAL AWARD AND POONA PACT

The Second Round Table Conference having failed to resolve the questions of electoral representation to different religious communities and the depressed classes, authorised the British Prime Minister to resolve it. Accordingly, Prime Minister Ramsay Macdonald announced his 'Communal Award' on August 16, 1932. According to this Award the Muslim, European and Sikh voters would elect their candidates by voting in separate communal electorates. There was also provision for separate electorate for the Depressed Classes, officially described as Scheduled Castes, as a separate community. Macdonald, however, promised to accept any alternative scheme mutually agreed upon by the Hindus and the Depressed Classes.

Gandhi's Fast unto Death and Poona Pact—September 25, 1932: At the Round Table Conference, Mahatma Gandhi had strenuously opposed the idea of a separate electorate for Depressed Classes and had declared that he would resist it with his life. True to his resolve Gandhiji wrote to the British Prime Minister on August 18, 1932 that he would commence the fast on September 20 in the Yervada prison, where he was lodged and it would cease only if the scheme was reviewed and the common electorate restored.

Poona Pact: Gandhiji's fast caused great alarm and anxiety all over the country and Pandit Madan Mohan Malaviya summoned a conference of various castes and political parties, including Dr. B.R. Ambedkar, the leader of the Depressed Classes League. The conference finally arrived at an agreement in Poona on September 25, 1932, the sixth day of Gandhiji's fast. A common electorate of all the Hindus was agreed upon, subject to two conditions: First, 148 seats in different Provincial Legislatures were reserved for the Depressed Classes in place of 71 as provided in the Communal Award, Secondly, 18 per cent of the seats in the Central Legislature were reserved for the Depressed Classes.

THE END OF THE CIVIL DISOBEDIENCE MOVEMENT

In the background of the Communal Award and Gandhi's fast unto death, the Civil Disobedience movement lost its momentum. After the Poona Pact Mahatma Gandhi lost interest in the movement and was fully engrossed in the anti-untouchability movement, which led to the foundation of the ***Harijan Sevak Sangh***.

The Congressmen, however, continued the movement under increasing British repression. The Delhi Congress session (April 1932) and the Calcutta Congress session (March 1933) were held while the official ban on the Congress was still in force. On May 8, 1933 Mahatma Gandhi announced a self-purification fast for 21 days for purification of himself and his associates "for greater vigilance and watchfulness in connection with the Harijan cause". The Government, keeping in view the nature and object of his fast, released him from prison. Immediately after his release Mahatma Gandhi recommended to the President of the Congress suspension of the movement for a month or six weeks. Accordingly the movement was suspended for about twelve weeks.

During these twelve weeks the mass Civil Disobedience movement virtually died out. In its place Mahatma Gandhi launched Individual Civil Disobedience on August 1, 1933. After a brief, listless progress, this movement, too, died down and by early 1934 was no longer in effect. In January 1934, the great earthquake in Bihar drew everyday's attention away from the political movements. In October 1934, Gandhiji decided to withdraw himself from active politics to devote all his time to the cause of Harijans.

THE QUIT INDIA MOVEMENT—AUGUST 1942

The failure of the Cripps Mission and the growing threat of Japanese aggression brought about a radical change in Mahatma Gandhi's attitude towards the British Government. The people's discontent with rising prices and wartime shortages was reaching an explosive stage. Japan won a series of dramatic victories in the Western Pacific. Malaya and Singapore were overrun and the retreating British troops surrendered

Rangoon in early March 1942. Soon the Japanese were at India's eastern frontier and brought India within the range of actual hostilities. Mahatma Gandhi came to believe that "the presence of the British in India is an invitation to Japan to invade India and their withdrawal removes the bait". He therefore asked the British "to leave India in God's hands or in modern parlance to anarchy".

The Quit India Resolution: The Congress Working Committee, which met at Wardha on July 14, 1942, passed a long resolution, generally called the 'Quit India' resolution. It renewed the demand that "British rule in India must end immediately" and reiterated the view that the freedom of India was "not only in the interest of India, but also that of Britain and of the cause of freedom to which the United Nations proclaim their adherence". The resolution finally proclaimed that "should this appeal fail the Congress will then be reluctantly compelled to utilise all the non-violent strength it might have gathered since 1920".

The All-India Congress Committee, which met in Bombay on August 7, 1942, ratified the Wardha Resolution with overwhelming majority. It sanctioned the non-violent mass struggle under the leadership of Gandhiji, but provided also for the contingency of his arrest. "When this happens, every man and woman who is participating in the movement must function for himself or herself within the four corners of the general instructions issued. Every Indian who desires freedom and strives for it must be his own guide urging him or her on a long hard road where there is no resting place and which leads ultimately to the independence and deliverance of India". Mahatma Gandhi, in his speech after the passage of the Quit India resolution, said: "Every one of you should from this moment onwards consider yourself a free man or woman and act as if you are free... I am not going to be satisfied with anything short of freedom. We shall do or die. We shall either free India or die in the attempt." The place where the AICC met and ratified the Quit India Resolution is now known as the August Kranti Maidan.

Progress of the Movement: The British Government was closely monitoring the situation and had made elaborate preparations to crush the proposed rebellion. The AICC meeting ended at around midnight on August 8, 1942. During that very night the police arrested Mahatma Gandhi, Maulana Abul Kalam Azad and all eminent Congress leaders. Within a week almost everyone who mattered in the Congress organisation was arrested.

The movement thereafter passed through three phases. During the first phase from August 9-13, there were wide-scale disturbances in Bombay, Ahmedabad, Poona, Delhi, etc. From August 11, the situation began to deteriorate rapidly. There were ***hartals***, concerted outbreaks of mob violence and sabotage directed either against communications of all kinds or against the Army and police. There was widespread destruction of the property of the railways and post and telegraphs. The events of these four days in August 1942 are known as "the great August uprising".

With the close of the first phase of the movement, three new trends became apparent: (*i*) orthodox non-violent Civil Disobedience movement; (*ii*) rise of serious crimes and (*iii*) drift towards revolutionary terrorism, leading to arson, sabotage and murderous assaults on public servants. The movement now entered the second phase, when the focus shifted to the countryside, with militant students fanning out from the cities to lead peasant rebellions. This phase saw the mushrooming of a large number of national governments lasting for a few days in many parts of United Provinces and Bihar.

After September 1942, on account of increasing British repression, the movement went underground. It now took the shape of revolutionary terrorist activities directed against blowing up of communication networks and attacks on police personnel. There was even an underground radio station, which functioned for some time. The movement during this last phase was supported by middle-level Congressmen and Congress Socialists like Achyut Patwardhan, Ram Manohar Lohia, Jayaprakash Narayan and Aruna Asaf Ali. Jayaprakash Narayan was the prominent leader of the movement, which continued till the end of 1943.

The British put down the movement with ruthless brutality. The Congress organisations were banned. There were lathi-charges, floggings, imprisonments, torture, machine-gun firing, bombing from airplanes and other such atrocities. The period marked the end of India's struggle for freedom. Independence was now placed on the immediate agenda of the national movement. There could be no retreat and future negotiations could only be on the manner of the transfer of power.

OTHER POLITICAL PARTIES AND MOVEMENTS

The year 1922-27 witnessed the emergence of other political forces besides the ***Swarajya Party***. The Moderates who had walked out of the INC in 1918, constituted themselves into the ***National Liberal League***, later known as the All-India Liberal Federation and cooperated with the Government. The complete rout of the Liberal League in the election of 1923 marked its end as an organised body. Nevertheless the party counted among its members some eminent persons who still exercised great influence on the political activities in the country, such as Srinivas Sastri, Tej Bahadur Sapru, B.C. Pal, etc.

The ***All-India Khilafat Committee*** also ceased to function after the abolition of Khilafat in Turkey by Mustafa Kamal Pasha in 1924. This led to the revival of the **All-India Muslim League** with M.A. Jinnah emerging as its leader in 1924. The ***Hindu Mahasabha***, a communal organisation of the Hindus founded in December 1918, also gained strength, when Madan Mohan Malaviya was elected as its President at the Belgaum session of the Sabha in December 1924. Another party which prospered during the period was the casteist ***Justice Party*** in Madras. On other fronts, too, the anti-Brahmin sentiments in the South gained strength in the 1920s. The different non-Brahmin organisations of South India were merged into a single all-India body and an ***All-India Non-Brahmin Conference*** was held at Belgaum on December 28, 1924, with A. Ramaswami Mudaliar as the Chairman. The Conference advocated communal representation to non-Brahmins both in elective bodies and in Government services.

In the Punjab, a ***Unionist Party*** was formed to protect the interests of the landed class. It later on formed a coalition Government with the Muslim League in the Punjab, where a number of movements were launched during the Post-Non-Cooperation years. The most important of these was the ***Akali movement*** for freeing the Sikh gurdwaras from the corrupt and pro-British hereditary Mahants. When the Akali movement took serious proportions, the British Government, apprehending that the Akali agitation might cause disaffection amongst the Sikh soldiers in the British army and the Sikh peasantry, passed a Bill in July 1925, which gave the Sikh community the right to elect their functionaries to manage their gurdwaras. The outcome of this Bill was the installation of the Shiromani Gurdwara Prabhandak Committee (SGPC) to manage the affairs of the gurdwaras.

Among the other important movements launched in various parts of the country in the intervening period were the ***Nagpur Flag Satyagraha***, the ***Borsad agitation***, and the ***Vaikom Satyagraha***. The Nagpur Flag ***satyagraha*** took place in mid-1923 against a local order banning the use of the Congress flag. Strong contingents were sent from Gujarat, forcing the Government to compromise. At Borsad in Khera district (Gujarat) there was a successful Gandhian ***satyagraha*** against the imposition of a poll tax on every adult to pay for police reinforcements required to suppress a wave of dacoities. In January 1923, on account of popular pressure, this tax was cancelled. The Vaikom ***Satyagraha*** in Travancore was led by the Ezhava Congress leader T.K. Madhavan in 1924-25, demanding temple entry for the untouchables. Other castes like the Nairs also participated but the movement ended in compromise after 20 months of struggle in March 1925, when the Government constructed diversionary roads for the untouchables.

THE LEFT MOVEMENT

The Leftist movement in India grew as a result of the development of modern industries, the acute economic distress between the two World Wars and the success of the Bolshevik Revolution in Russia. Some Indian intellectuals working within and outside India, decided to establish the Communist Party of India. Manabendra Nath Roy (actual name Narendranath Bhattacharya) visited Russia and came in contact with the Russian Communist Party. He also attended the Second Communist International held in Moscow in July-August 1920 and shortly after he founded the Communist Party of India in Tashkent in October 1920. Between 1921 and 1925, various formal Communist groups were established in many parts of the country and finally in December 1925, Satyabhakta organised an All-India Conference of the Communists at Kanpur. This Conference met under the Presidency of Singaravelu Chettiar, a Communist leader from Madras. The convening of this Conference is regarded as the formal beginning of the Communist Party of India in 1925.

The 1920s also witnessed the growth of peasant workers and other left organisations. In the first half of 1920 there were some 200 major labour strikes in the country. The All-India Trade Union Congress also held its first session in Bombay in October 1920, under the presidentship of Lala Lajpat Rai. Soon the Left influence was also felt on the INC. Jawaharlal Nehru and Subhas Bose laid the greatest emphasis on the socialist ideas. The growing socialist influence on the INC later on divided the Congress into "Leftist" and "Rightist" camps. In the early 1930s Socialist groups were formed by the Leftist Congressmen in provinces like Bihar, United Provinces, Bombay and Punjab. The second phase of revolutionary terrorism, which also progressed between 1922 and 1928, had very strong socialist leanings.

THE HOME RULE MOVEMENT

The outbreak of the First World War and release of Tilak in 1914 after the completion of his prison term, accelerated the launching of the Home Rule Movement by Tilak and Mrs. Annie Besant, both of whom decided to work in close cooperation to launch the movement.

The idea of starting a Home Rule League originated with Mrs. Besant. Realising that no real progress could be achieved without securing self-government, she plunged herself into political struggle. She was equally convinced that the Moderates, who at that time controlled the Congress, were too weak to work for Self-Government. The definite campaign for Home Rule began with the publication of a weekly review, ***The Commonwealth***, on January 2, 1914. The paper adopted as its cardinal programme, "religious liberty, national education, social reform and political reform" aiming at self-government for India within the British Commonwealth.

Two Home Rule Leagues were founded to pursue this programme, both Leagues being supportive of each other. Tilak founded the ***Indian Home Rule League*** in April 1916 and five months later in September 1916 Mr. Annie Besant started the ***Home Rule League***. There was an informal understanding between the two Leagues that Mrs. Besant's field of work would cover the whole of India, except Maharashtra and Central Provinces, where Tilak's League would carry on the work. Both launched a propaganda in favour of Home Rule through their respective papers—Mrs. Besant's ***Commonwealth*** and ***New India*** and Tilak's ***Mahratta*** and ***Kesari***. Both of them undertook an extensive lecture tour to instruct the masses on Home Rule. To suppress this movement which was growing in popularity, the British Government in July 1916, instituted a case against Tilak for certain speeches he had delivered at the Home Rule meetings; Mrs. Besant too was interned in 1917. These repressive measures, however, did not weaken the Home Rule movement. After Montagu's Declaration (August 1917) Mrs. Besant dropped her League, but Tilak continued his movement.

The Home Rule movement had two far-reaching political consequences. First, it infused the INC with new strength and vigour. The Home Rule movement had virtually eclipsed the Moderates from the political field, which they had dominated till the return of Tilak. On account of its widespread success, the Extremists were admitted to the Congress and Mrs. Besant was elected as President of the Congress in 1917, when she declared: "India is no longer on her knees for boons: she is on her feet for rights". Her election to the post marked a new era in the history of the Congress. Secondly, the Home Rule movement hastened the formulation of a new policy by the British Government which was defined in Montagu's Declaration (August Declaration).

MONTAGU DECLARATION (AUGUST, 1917)

The First World War, the rapid growth of the revolutionary activities and the popularity of the Home Rule movement had their combined impact on the British Government, which decided to effect a change in its policies and adopt a conciliatory attitude towards the demands of the Indian nationalists. On July 12, 1917 Edwin Montagu, during a debate in the House of Commons, made a scathing indictment of the whole system by which India was governed. He further supported the Indian claim for a greater say in managing their government.

Shortly thereafter, Montagu was appointed the Secretary of State of India. On August 20, 1917, Montagu made a historic Declaration in the House of Commons defining the goal of British policies in India. He defined this goal as the "increasing association of Indians in every branch of administration and the gradual development of self-governing institutions with a view to the progressive realisation of Responsible Government in India as an integral part of the British Empire".

The key expression in Montagu's announcement was "Responsible Government", in which the rulers are answerable to people's elected representatives. To follow up on his Declaration, Montagu visited India in November 1917, to ascertain the views of "all shades of political opinion" in India. On the basis of these discussions a detailed Report on Indian Constitutional Reforms was prepared, which was published in July 1918. This report in turn formed the basis of the Montagu-Chelmsford Reforms or the Government of India Act, 1919.

THE STRUGGLE IN THE PRINCELY STATES

THE PRAJA MANDAL MOVEMENT

There were about 600 big, small and tiny Princely States, which the British termed as the Native States, in which roughly one-third of India's population lived. Their rulers were feudal in outlook and autocratic and acted as the "Subordinate allies" of the British, being virtually their puppets.

During and after the Non-Cooperation movement, ***Praja Mandals*** or State People's Conferences were founded in various Princely States by the subjects of these States seeking the liberalisation and demonstration of the administration in their States. The movement spread and gradually began to coordinate its activities. In December 1927, Balwantrai Mehta and Mani Lal Kothari (from Gujarat) and G.R. Abhyankar of Bombay convened the ***All-India States' People's Conference***, which facilitated a great awakening among the people of the Princely States.

The Congress also supported this struggle. At the Lahore session of the Congress in 1929 Jawaharlal Nehru, outlining the policy of the Congress to the Princely States said: 'The India (Princely) States can not live apart from the rest of India and the only people of who have a right to determine the future of the States must be the people of those States."

In the 1930s the people of several Princely States, encouraged by the Civil Disobedience movement, launched movements for the acceptance of the principle of popular representation and self-government by election. Individual Congressmen also took part in these movements in various States. Gandhiji himself undertook a fast in support of such movement in the State of Rajkot. At the Haripura session of the Congress in 1938, one of the main issues discussed was the problem of the Princely States. In 1939, Jawaharlal Nehru became the President of the All-India States' People's Conference. Soon the Praja Mandal movement became inseparably linked with those of the rest of India.

THE RISE OF EXTREME COMMISSION

After the suspension of the Non-Cooperation movement, the Hindu-Muslim unity witnessed during the Khilafat days evaporated, giving way to communal violence and the Congress and the Muslim League parting ways. When the Simon Commission visited India, the Congress boycotted it; but the Muslim League led by Jinnah cooperated with it to promote the Muslim interests. Jinnah repudiated the Nehru Report and presented his own 'Fourteen Points'.

In 1930, the great poet Sir Mohammad Iqbal, while addressing the Allahabad session of the Muslim League declared that "the formation of a consolidated North-West India into a Muslim State appears to me to be the final destiny of Muslims". He thus initiated the idea of a separate Muslim State. Three years later, in 1933, a group of Muslim students studying in England, led by Rahamat Ali, proposed the creation of a separate Muslim State in North-West India, to be called Pakistan.

After the League's humiliating defeat in the elections of 1937, Jinnah turned to the Muslim masses and played the communal card. He launched a double-barrelled propaganda to whip up communalism; on the one hand, he accused Gandhiji of trying to establish "Hindu Raj"; on the other, he charged the Congress Governments with being ruthless to Muslims. Following from this, he propounded the two-nation theory, to the effect that Hindus and Muslims are not two communities but two separate nations.

Next, Jinnah began to pose the Muslim League as the sole representative organisation of the Indian Muslims. He threatened: "We will not let either the British or Mr. Gandhi to rule the Mussalamans. We want to be free." The stage now was set for the fatal demand. The Lahore session of the Muslim League, held on March 24, 1940, passed the Pakistan Resolution and rejected the Federal Scheme as envisaged in the Government India Act, 1935.

Meanwhile, the pressure was growing on the Government. The Congress was demanding complete independence after the War. The resignation of the Congress Ministries against the British war policies was also another cause of unease for the Government. In the circumstances, the British imperialists, as a part of their time-tested policy of divide and rule propped up and patronised the Muslim League as a counter balance to the Congress. Thus boosted, the Muslim League began to pose itself as the sole spokesman for all Muslims and to use its political power to veto any political settlement.

THE SECOND WORLD WAR AND THE NATIONAL MOVEMENT

On September 3, 1939, the Second World War broke out and the same day the Viceroy Linlithgow, without consulting the Indian people, declared India to be a belligerent and at war with Germany. Shortly afterwards, emergency legislations were rushed through the British Parliament and the Indian Legislative Assembly, curbing the autonomy of the Provincial Governments and restricting the civil liberties of the people. The Congress was not averse to the idea of offering support to the British war efforts, but in return demanded that "India must be declared an independent nation" and that during the war a genuine representative Government must be set up at the centre. Subhas Bose, as President of the Congress, opposed the policy of co-operation and believed that Britain's peril offered a rare opportunity to India to achieve freedom. Gandhiji's attitude, however, was still that India should not seek her independence out of Britain's ruin because that was not the way of non-violence. The Congress Working Committee, which met on September 8-15, 1939, stressed that "the issue of war and peace for India must be decided by the Indian people". When the British Government did not respond favourably, the Congress High Command directed the Congress Ministries in the Provinces to resign; they complied with the directive in October and November 1939. The British Government thereafter encouraged the Muslim League, which increasingly became an important part of the British war strategy.

The Second World War affected India in many ways. When Germany attacked the Soviet Union on June 22, 1941, the Indian Communists changed their anti-war and anti-British stand and came to support the British war efforts. Secondly, Japan's entry into the war and its speedy victories in South-east Asia, including the capture of Rangoon and Andamans, caused a near panic in India, leading to the launching of the Quit India movement. On the other hand Subhash Bose raised the Indian National Army with Japanese support.

THE INDIVIDUAL SATYAGRAHA—1940-41

Disillusioned with the August offer, the Congress decided to launch Individual Satyagraha, which was intended to preach openly against the War. It was launched on October 17, 1940 and as soon as an individual (or a small group was arrested), another took his place. One of the first Satyagrahis was Vinobha Bhave. But the movement created little enthusiasm and Mahatma Gandhi suspended it on December 17, 1940. On January 5, 1941, the campaign was started again. During the second phase of the movement, more than 20,000 Satyagrahis were arrested.

SUBHAS BOSE AND INDIAN NATIONAL ARMY (I.N.A.)

Meanwhile, another fight for independence was being waged beyond the eastern frontier of India by the

Indian National Army, led by Subhas Bose in cooperation with the Japanese.

Subhas Bose, after founding the Forward Bloc, in January 1941 escaped out of India and went to Berlin (Germany) via Moscow. He made anti-British propaganda from the Berlin radio station and raised "Free India" Units with the Indian prisoners of war in Germany.

The Indian National Army: In the meantime, Ras Behari Bose, an Indian revolutionary who had taken political refuge in Japan in 1915, organised the ***Indian Independence League*** with the support of Indian living in South-east Asia. In March 1942, Ras Behari convened a Conference in Tokyo at which it was decided to form the Indian National Army (INA) or Azad Hind Fauj. The nucleus of the INA was composed of the Indian soldiers who had surrendered to the Japanese troops after the fall of Singapore. The INA was initially organised by Captain Singh, an Indian officer of the British army in Malaya who had surrendered to the Japanese.

In June 1942, Ras Behari Bose convened another Conference of the Indian Independence League in Bangkok, which decided that INA would fight for India's independence. The Bangkok Conference also invited Subhas Bose to come to Japan. He reached Tokyo in June 1943. Shortly afterwards, Ras Behari Bose resigned the Chairmanship of the Indian Independence League of Subhas Bose, who was also named as the Supreme Commander of the INA.

The Japanese Government promised full support to the INA "to enable India to achieve full independence". On October 21, 1943, Subhas Bose set up a Provisional Government of Free India in Singapore. In March 1944, the INA commenced its military offensive and advanced towards Assam through Burma. The INA columns reached Kohima in Nagaland and laid siege of Imphal. But after a year the fortunes of war turned against Japan when the British troops recaptured Rangoon in May 1945 and the INA troops were forced to surrender and made prisoners. Three months later, Subhas Bose also died in air crash near Taiwan in August 1945. The last echo of the INA movement was heard when the INA prisoners were tried at the Red Fort in Delhi and were defended by a panel of lawyers who included Tej Bahadur Sapru, Bhulabhai Desai and Jawaharlal Nehru.

Partition of Bengal (1905): Lord Curzon's viceroyalty marked the high watermark of British imperialism in India. Curzon looked upon India as a "country where the Englishmen were to monopolise for all time all power and talk all the while of duty." He further believed that "the Indian's only business was to be governed and it was sacrilege on his part to have any other aspiration." Among Lord Curzon's administrative measures, the one that elicited the strongest opposition was the partition of Bengal in 1905, which was a concealed attack on Indian nationalism. The Presidency of Bengal was the most populous province of British India. It included not only West Bengal and the eastern part of the region (the present Bangladesh), but also Bihar and Orissa. Bengal was partitioned into two parts on the ostensible ground that it was too large to manage efficiently. The truncated new province of Bengal was to comprise Calcutta and 11 districts of West Bengal, the district of Darjeeling, as also the whole of Bihar and Orissa (including Sambalpur and the Oriya speaking areas), the majority of the population being Hindu. The part taken away was to be known as 'Eastern Bengal and Assam' comprising the Muslim-majority districts of Bengal, with its capital at Dacca. Explaining the political purpose behind this partition to his superiors in London, Curzon said he wanted to "split up and thereby to weaken a solid body of opponents" to the British rule. "Bengal united was power, which was to be broken by partition." Another objective behind the partition was to split up the Hindus and Muslims. The new province of Eastern Bengal and Assam was specially constituted so that Muslims would outnumber Hindus. This deliberate setting of one community against the other inevitably resulted in increased communal tension. The policy off rallying the Muslims against the Hindus was steadily pursued by the Government of Eastern Bengal and Assam during the years following the partition. Sir Bamfylde Fuller, the Lieutenant Governor of East Bengal, described the Muslims as his 'favourable wife'.

THE FOUNDATION OF ALL-INDIA MUSLIM LEAGUE

The partition of Bengal had created a communal divide. Shortly after the partition scheme was announced, a Muslim deputation, most of its members belonging to the aristocracy, led by the Agha Khan, the spiritual head of the Khoja Muslim community, met Lord Minto at Simla on October 1, 1906. The address presented by the deputation claimed a privileged position for Indian Muslims on the grounds of political importance, military service (i.e. enlistment in the Army) and the historical memories of their lost political glory. Minto gave a categorical assurance that the political rights and interests of the Muslims as a community would be safeguarded.

The Simla Deputation was followed in Eastern Bengal by Muslim meetings in support of the partition of Bengal. Demonstrations in support of official policies were encouraged by the Government as a counterstroke to the ***Swadeshi*** movement. Nawab Habibulla (or Salimullah) of Dacca, favoured by Lord Curzon, took the leadership of the pro-partition movement. In the wake of these developments, a meeting was held at *Dacca on December 30, 1906, where it was decided to form a political association, called the* ***All-India Muslim League****, with three objectives:* (1) to promote among Muslims loyalty to the British Government; (2) to protect and advance the political rights of the Muslims and (3) to prevent the rise among the Muslims of any feeling of hostility towards other communities without prejudice to other objects of the League. Incidentally, the League proposed "to controvert the growing influence of the INC". A comparison of the resolutions passed at the first meeting of the League and the Calcutta session of the Congress held the same month in 1906, shows just how well the League succeeded in doing this. The resolutions passed by the Congress demanded self-government, condemned the partition of Bengal and supported the boycott. League resolutions expressed loyalty to the British government, supported the partition and condemned the boycott. This opposition between the League and the Congress became more significant in the years to come and immeasurably weakened the Indian national movement.

During the years 1907-9, the main programme of the Muslim League was to fight for consolidation and extension of separate electorates. The Amritsar session of the League, held in 1908, demanded a separate electorate for the Muslims, which was conceded to them by the Morley-Minto reforms in 1909.

THE MORLEY-MINTO REFORMS OR THE INDIAN COUNCILS ACT, 1909

In 1905, Lord Minto succeeded Lord Curzon as the new Viceroy and shortly afterwards John Morley was appointed the Secretary of State for India in London. In view of the seething unrest and troubles in India, both of them decided to work out a scheme for the reform of the Legislative Councils. Passed by the British Parliament in 1911, the new statute, officially called the Indian Councils Act (1909), was popularly known as Minto-Morley Reforms. The main features of this Act were :

1. It increased the membership of non-officials in the Imperial and Provincial Legislative Councils.
2. The effective principle introduced by the Indian Councils Act, 1892, was further extended, so that in 1910 more than a hundred indirectly elected Indians took their seats in the Councils.
3. In the Provincial Legislature, the non-official members had the majority, but an official majority was retained at the Centre.
4. The Act provided for the appointment of an Indian to the Viceroy's Executive Council, as well as the Provincial Executive Councils.
5. The powers of the Legislature were also improved. The members could ask questions and even debate the budget, but could not vote on it. They could introduce legislative proposals, but could not enact laws.
6. The greatest evil of the Act of 1909 was the grant of separate electorate to the Muslims. The Muslim representatives to the Councils were elected not from the general electorate, but from a separate electorate consisting of Muslims alone. This meant in effect that the Muslim community was recognised as a completely separate section of the Indian nation.

The Minto-Morley Reforms satisfied neither the Moderates nor the Extremists. The Lahore session of the INC in 1909 expressed its strong disapproval of separate electorate formed on the basis of religion.

THE DELHI DURBAR AND THE ANNULMENT OF THE PARTITION OF BENGAL (DECEMBER 1911)

In early December 1911 King George V and the Queen Empress visited India. On December 12, 1911, a magnificent coronation Durbar was held in Delhi which was chosen as the seat of the imperial function, with the specific intention of impressing upon the oriental minds that the successors to the Mughals were not in anyway behind them in display of magnificence. The Delhi Durbar of 1911 was memorable for a number of historic announcements made by the Governor-General Lord Hardings on behalf of his sovereign.

1. It was decided to transfer the capital of British India from Calcutta to Delhi. Ostensibly the choice of Delhi as capital was "based on geographical, historical and political grounds." The 'geographical' factor was irrelevant, for Delhi was not situated in the heart of India. The historical factor meant a plan to mollify the Muslims by an apparent revival of the Mughal tradition. The actual factor for the transfer of the capital was 'political'. Calcutta, the storm-centre of anti-partition agitation, was to be reduced to the seat of a provincial capital a and Delhi, a city isolated from political currents, was to be the imperial seat. Soon after the Durbar, George V laid the foundation stone of the new capital of British India.
2. Another historic announcement was the annulment of the partition of Bengal, in the hope that it would stem the tide of rising nationalism and restore peace. In the wake to this annulment, a new province of Bengal, consisting of all Bengali-speaking districts except Sylhet, was created. Bihar and Orissa were separated from Bengal. Assam was created as a separate province, the status it had in 1874. The new province, however, included the Sylhet district as well.

The First World War (1914-1919) and India: The outbreak of the First World War in 1914 followed the formation of two blocks of great powers in Europe, viz. Triple ***Alliance*** (Germany-Austria, Italy and Turkey) and Triple ***Entente*** (France, Russia and England). The declaration of war by Great Britain against Germany on August 4, 1914, automatically made India a belligerent and dragged her into the great holocaust. The Indians, of course, had no voice in the decision.

India's manpower and resources were badly exploited during the war and Lord Hardings later on said in his autobiography that India had been "bled white" by the war. The Moderate leaders remained loyal and cooperative to the British war efforts in the hope that their demand for Self-Government would be fulfilled in return for their cooperation. But before and during the First World War there was a great wave of nationalism all over the world. The immediate impact of this nationalist wave in India was the launching of the Home Rule Movement by Mrs. Annie Besant and B.G. Tilak. To curb the revolutionary and terrorist activities, the Government introduced repressive laws, which included the Indian Criminal Law Amendment Act and the Defence of India Act, under which Special Tribunals were set up to try the revolutionary and terrorist cases. Under the Defence of India Act, hundreds of suspects were transported or interned without benefit of proper trial.

These repressive measures hit the revolutionaries very hard, but did not blunt their courage. They formulated plans for a general insurrection. An armed uprising in the Punjab was planned in 1915. The same year Indian troops in Singapore mutinied. Another unsuccessful wartime plot was the 'Silk Letters Conspiracy.' This was a plan for a general Muslim uprising against the British.

The Muslim League, which had been loyal to the British Government, was disenchanted on account of the declaration of war against Turkey, the premier Islamic State which had allied with Germany and Italy in the First World War. The repeated defeats of Turkey and talk of dismemberment of the Ottoman Empire after the First World War, further alienated the League from the Government and brought it closer to the Congress. The leaders of the ***Ehrar League***, such as Hakim Ajmal Khan, Mohammad Ali, Hasan Imam and others, very strongly proposed that Muslims should not remain subservient to the British Government, but should participate in the national movement. The events of the First World War and the prevalent sentiments was responsible for the Lucknow Pact and the Khilafat Movement.

THE LUCKNOW PACT (1916)

The Lucknow session of the I.N.C. in 1916 was a memorable event on account of two important developments. The first was the readmission of the Extremists, who had been expelled from the I.N.C. nine years earlier. Thus the Lucknow session was the first meeting of the united Congress. The second development was the bond of alliance between the Congress and the Muslim League. The League, which was disenchanted with the British Government on account of the reasons listed earlier, at its annual session in Bombay in 1915–which a number of Congress leaders also attended–appointed a Committee to draw up a scheme of political reforms in consultation with other communities. It was decided to hold the annual sessions of the League and Congress at the same place and during the same week.

During the simultaneous annual sessions of the League and the Congress held at Lucknow in December 1916, both passed resolutions separately for a joint scheme of constitutional reforms and reached an agreement to cooperate in the political field on the basis of a common programme. This aggrement is generally known as the *Lucknow Pact* or the *Congress-League Scheme.*

The Lucknow Pact exhorted the British Government to confer self-government on India at an early date, to expand the Provincial Legislative Councils and the Governor-General's Legislative Council and to provide for greater representation of the elected members on the expanded Councils. It further demanded that the powers of making appointments to the Indian Civil Service should vest in the Government of India and that the commissioned and non-commissioned ranks in the military and naval services should be thrown open to Indians. The Lucknow Pact also marked the formal acceptance of Separate Electorate for Muslims by the Congress, which was a positive gain for the Muslims because the Congress had so far opposed it.

It was but a temporary truce. The Muslim League still remained a separate entity, with a communal outlook, advocating for the Muslims political interests separate from those of the Hindus. The Congress and the League both worked together under the spirit of the Pact till the suspension of the Non-Cooperation movement after the **Chauri Chaura** incident in 1922. They parted ways and the League again became the sworn enemy of the Congress as well as the national movement. Dr. R.C. Mazumdar, who is very critical of the Lucknow Pact, is of the view: "For no one can doubt in the light of subsequent events, that the Congress action in 1916 well and truly laid the foundation on which Pakistan was built thirty years later." The Lucknow Pact opened the way to future resurgence of communalism in Indian politics.

MONTAGU-CHELMSFORD REFORMS OR THE GOVERNMENT OF INDIA ACT, 1919

Montagu described the Government of India Act, 1919, which was drawn up on the basis of the Montagu Declaration and Montagu-Chelmsford Report as "a bridge between the government by Parliament and government by the representatives of the people of India". It was a transitional stage in the development of self-government.

Features of Act: The principal features of the Act of 1919 were :

1. A provision was made for classification of central and provincial subjects.
2. The provincial subjects were divided into two groups: Reserved and Transferred. The Reserved subjects were with the Governor and Transferred subjects with the Indian Ministers. This division of subjects, known as 'Dyarchy' or dual government in the provinces, was the most important feature of the Act.
   The Reserved subjects included essential areas of law enforcement such as justice, police and revenue. The Transferred subjects included education, public health, public works, etc. The ministers in charge of them were to be responsible to provincial Legislative Councils.
3. Under the Act of 1919 the Central Legislature covered all central subjects, as also some matters falling within the scope of provincial subjects.
4. The Indian Executive comprised the Governor-General and his Executive Council.

5. No Bill of the Legislature could be deemed to have been passed unless assented to by the Governor-General. The latter could, however, enact a Bill without the assent of the Legislature.
6. The Governor-General's control over the Indian finances was also kept intact.
7. The Act provided for the establishment, for the first time, in India of a Public Service Commission.
8. Part V of the Act provided for a Statutory Commission to be set up, at the end of ten years after the Act was passed, to inquire into "the working of the system of government". The Simon Commission, appointed in 1927, was the outcome of this provision.

Appraisal: The changes introduced by the Act of 1919 were far short of self-government. The Act only provided for partial transfer of power to the electorate through the system of dyarchy. It prepared the ground for federalism through identity of provinces as administrative and financial units. But these measures were far too inadequate to satisfy the rapidly developing national aspirations.

Some neo-imperialist historians, popularly known as the Cambridge School, however, place the emphasis for the entry of the masses in the national movement, on the expansion of the electorate that resulted from the Act of 1919 and the more democratic style of functioning that it enforced on the politicians. While this may explain the functioning of certain politicians, the broadening of the electorate to five and a half million in the provinces and one and a half-million for the Imperial Legislature was certainly paltry to speak of. Many of the new electorates were illiterate peasants with little or no knowledge of these reforms. The other features of the Act were :

(*a*) Financial devolution.
(*b*) A bicameral legislature at the Centre.
(*c*) Dyarchy in the provinces which, unlike its dictionary meaning of two bodies being jointly vested with supreme power, transferred only certain departments like education, health, agriculture and local bodies with less political weight and little funds to ministers responsible to provincial legislature. Officials remained in control of the more vital departments like finance and law and order and provincial Governors too had veto powers. Revenue resources were divided between the provinces and the centre.
(*d*) The character of the central government remained unchanged except that a second Indian was included in the Governor-General's Executive Council.
(*e*) Separate electorates were further extended to Sikhs in the Punjab and non-Brahmins in Madras.

In respect of the twin requirements of financial devolution and need for a wider circle of collaborators, the Act greatly disappointed the Indians, apart from its other flaws like illogical division between Transferred and Reserved subjects and lack of basic trust between the two halves. Tilak described the Act as "extremely disappointing and unsatisfactory" and the Congress decided to boycott the elections which were to be held in November 1920.

ANTI-SIMON COMMISSION AGITATION–1928-29

The political atmosphere in the country at this time was thus marked by a ferment of revolutionary and terrorist activities. Communalism was also growing as a festering wound, which erupted sporadically in riots and bloodshed. Amidst this atmosphere came the sudden appointment of the Simon Commission in 1927. It was virtually a bombshell. According to a provision of the Government of India Act, 1919, a Statutory Commission was to be appointed ten years after the passage of the Act, that is in 1929, to inquire into the working of the Act and to propose further reforms, if needed. But the then Conservative Government in London pre-empted its appointment by two years, for fear that a Labour Government, which was seen to be likely to come to power in the forthcoming General Election, might appoint a Statutory Commission composed of members with liberal and pro-India views. The Commission was composed of seven British members of Parliament, with Sir John Simon as its Chairman. It had no Indian member.

Such composition of a Commission, intended to decide on the political future of India, was not acceptable to enlightened Indian political opinion. The INC, at its session held in Madras in December 1927, resolved to boycott the Commission "at every stage, everywhere and in every form". A complete ***hartal*** was observed in Bombay and other cities on February 3, 1928, the day the Simon Commission landed in Bombay. Wherever the Commission visited, complete ***hartal*** was observed and processions were taken out with the slogan, "Simon Go Back". At many places the police used brute force to crush the agitation. In Lahore Lala Lajpat Rai, while leading the anti-Simon Commission procession, was lathi-charged and mortally injured.

The Simon Commission paid two visits to India in 1928 and 1929. It submitted its Report in May 1930, which was later discussed at the Round Table Conference held in London. The anti-Simon Commission agitation was a turning point in India's struggle for freedom, because with this mass movement the Indian national movement entered a crucial phase.

NEHRU REPORT—1928

When the Congress gave a call to boycott the Simon Commission, Lord Birkenhead, the Secretary of State for India, threw a challenge to the Indian leaders to prepare a Constitution to which all parties would agree. The Indian leaders accepted the challenge and an All-Parties Conference was called between February and May 1928, which appointed a Committee under the Chairmanship of Motilal Nehru, to draft the proposed Constitution. The Nehru Committee submitted its Report on August 28, 1928, which was accepted by the All-Parties conference at Lucknow and passed with the only dissenting vote of M.A. Jinnah. Some important features of the Nehru Report were :

(*i*) India must be given Dominion status, which meant independence within the British Commonwealth.

(*ii*) India would be a Federation, having a bicameral Legislature at the Centre to which the Ministry would be responsible.

(*iii*) The Governor-General would be only the constitutional head with the same powers as the British Crown.

(*iv*) There was to be no separate electorate.

(*v*) Citizenship was also defined and fundamental rights enunciated.

The annual session of the INC held in Calcutta in December 1928, approved the Nehru Report by a majority vote and also served an ultimatum on the British Government to accept the Nehru Report on or before December 31, 1929, failing which the party would launch another mass movement. Since the British Government did not accept or spurn the Nehru Report, the Congress passed the Poorna Swarajya Resolution at its Lahore session (1929). With that, the Nehru Report itself became infructuous.

FOURTEEN POINTS OF JINNAH

M.A. Jinnah, the leader of the Muslim League, did not accept the Nehru Report on the ground that it discarded separate electorates for the minorities. The League wanted more safeguards for muslims. Jinnah thereafter drew up a list of demands, the so-called Fourteen Points, which represented the minimum demands of the Muslims. These included: (*i*) separate electorate for Muslims to be retained and supplemented by other concessions, such as one-third Muslim representation in the Central Cabinet and in all provincial Cabinets (although the Muslims constituted only one-fourth of the total population); (*ii*) creation of Muslim majority provinces and (*iii*) reservation of posts for Muslims in all services of the State, etc. The essence of Jinnah's Fourteen Points was to strike a profitable bargain with the Congress or to reject the Nehru Report.

THE GOVERNMENT OF INDIA ACT, 1935

Many years went into the framing of this Act. The appointment of the Simon Commission had been the first step. The Commission's Report, submitted in 1930, provided the basis for the discussions at the Round Table Conferences. In March 1933, the British Government published the main features of the constitutional reforms in a White Paper. A Bill based on the White Paper was introduced in the British Parliament on December 19, 1934. After months of protracted debates it was passed by the British Parliament and received the royal assent on August 2, 1935.

The Government of India Act, 1935, was unique in many respects. It was the longest piece of legislation ever passed by the British Parliament. It was the last constitutional measure introduced by the British in India and it survived for the longest period. It provided the groundwork for the negotiations that led to the final transfer of power into Indian hands.

The Government of India Act, 1935, had two main parts, dealing with the Federation of India and Provincial Autonomy. Some of its main features were :

1. It provided for the establishment of a 'Federation of India' consisting of Governor's Provinces and Princely States. The instrument of federation was to be an ***Instrument of Accession*** signed by the Princely States. While it was not necessary that all Princely States should join the Federation, the Federation could not be formed unless the acceding States sent not less than 104 members to the Council of States.
2. Dyarchy was withdrawn from the Provinces and implanted at the Centre. This meant that certain 'Reserved Subjects'—such as defence, tribal affairs, external affairs, etc. were to be administered exclusively by the Governor-General. In other federal subjects the Governor-General would be advised by his Council of Ministers. In other words, the new Act did not envisage a responsible Government at the Centre.
3. The proposed Federal Legislature was to be bicameral, with a Council of States with 250 members and a Federal Assembly of 375 members. The representatives of the Princely States in the Council of States and the Federal Assembly, numbering not more than 104 and 125 respectively, were to be nominated by their rulers, not elected by he people.
4. A threefold division of subjects was made—Federal, Provincial and concurrent.
5. Provision was made for the establishment of a Federal Court, with original, appellate and advisory jurisdiction. Appeals from its decisions lay to the Privy Council in London.
6. The most important feature of the Act was Provincial Autonomy. Dyarchy as introduced by the Act of 1919 was abolished. In every subject, Governors had to act on the advice of their ministers, who thus had effective control over the provincial administration. Ministers were appointed by the Governor but they were to be responsible to popularly elected legislative assemblies.

   The Act divided the British Indian provinces into two categories: 11 Governor's Provinces (Madras, Bombay, Bengal, United Provinces, Punjab, Bihar, Central Provinces and Berar, Assam, NWFP, Orissa and Sind) and 5 Chief Commissioner's Provinces. Provincial autonomy was to be introduced only in the Governor's Provinces.
7. The Act gave 'special powers' and 'responsibilities' to the Governors, which effectively crippled the powers of the ministers and undermined provincial autonomy. The Governors also held legislative powers of different kinds.

Political Reaction to the Act of 1935: The Federal scheme outlined in the Act was a non-starter because the Princely States did not join the proposed Federation, which would have meant the surrender of some of their autocratic powers. All the same, the Princely States were given representation to the Federal Legislature, because the British Government looked on the Princes as its natural allies. Their delegates were to be nominated by their rulers, not elected by the people. Commenting upon this state of affairs, Dr. Rajendra Prasad, the Congress President, said: "It will be a kind of Federation in which unabashed autocracy will sit entrenched in one-third of India and peep in now and then to strangle popular will in the remaining two-thirds."

Dyarchy, which had proved a total failure in the Provinces, was now going to be tried at the Centre. The elaborate system of 'safeguards' and special powers vested in the Governor-General and Governors, made a mockery of 'responsible government' and 'provincial autonomy'. Jawaharlal Nehru criticised the Act as " a charter of slavery". In his view the safeguard ridden Act was "a machine with strong brakes but no engine." A moderate leader like Madan Mohan Malviya said that the Act "has somewhat democratic appearance outwardly, but it is absolutely hollow from inside." ***Jinnah*** condemned the Federal scheme as "thoroughly rotten, fundamentally bad and totally unacceptable" because he felt that it would substantially increase the Hindu majority at the centre; but he was prepared to accept the provincial scheme, because it would ensure Muslim control of the four Muslim-majority Provinces.

As stated above, the Federal scheme was shelved, but elections to the Provincial Legislatures were held in January-February 1937, which caused radical changes in the Indian politics.

OTHER POLITICAL DEVELOPMENTS—1934-39

Among the other political developments between the fading out of the Civil Disobedience Movement and the outbreak of the Second Word War, the more notable ones were: (*a*) the emergence of the Congress Socialist Party; (*b*) the growth of the radical elements in the Congress led by Subhas Bose and (*c*) the rise of the popular movement in the Princely States, known as Praja Mandal movements.

The Congress Socialist Party: During this period the Left influence had become predominant in the Congress. In 1934 a significant section of Congressmen felt the need to form themselves into a group within the Congress to propagate the socialist ideas. In May that year, Acharya Narendra Dev, Jayprakash Narayan and Achyut Patwardhan, who were members of the Congress Working Committee, organised the Congress Socialist Party. The Congress Socialists, while being active in the peasants' and workers' movements, never lost sight of the fact that India's primary need was freedom. By 1935 the Congress Socialists accounted for about one-third of the Congress membership. The emergence of the Congress Socialist Party had a very important bearing on the Congress and the national movement in the coming years.

Emergence of the Radicals in the Congress: After the collapse of the Civil Disobedience movement two important changes were witnessed in the Congress—the first was the growing socialist influence on the Congress, with Subhas Bose and Jawaharlal Nehru emerging as its notable spokesmen. The second notable change was that the Congress got divided into two ideological groups—the conservative and the radical, led by Mahatma Gandhi and Subhas Bose respectively. During this period, Mahatma Gandhi had retired from active politics to devote himself to the cause of the Harijans.

Subhas Chandra Bose meanwhile began to emerge as a very powerful leader in the Congress, very critical of Gandhiji's ideology and policy of compromise. At its Haripura session (February 1938), where Subhas Bose was unanimously elected President, the Congress adopted two important resolutions. First, the people of Princely States were assured of moral support in their struggle against the rulers. Secondly, the Congress declared that India "could not be a party to an imperialist war" and "would not permit her manpower and resources to be exploited in the interest of British imperialism." The clouds of the Second World War had by then started hovering in the sky. Subhas Bose thought that war between Britain and Germany was inevitable. He also took the stand that "Britain's peril was India's opportunity" and wished to exploit it to secure freedom.

In this, however, he was opposed by Mahatma Gandhi and Jawaharlal Nehru, who were averse to the idea of taking advantage of Britain's peril. Gandhi, who was opposed to industrialisation, was further annoyed when Bose formed the National Planning Committee (forerunner of independent India's Planning Commission) for drawing up a comprehensive plan of economic development on the basis of industrialisation.

THE CRIPPS PROPOSALS—MARCH-APRIL 1942

Meanwhile the Second World War had taken an alarming turn. Germany had invaded the Soviet Union. After Japan attacked the U.S. naval base at Pearl Harbor (December 7, 1941), the U.S. had joined the Allied Powers in the war. It was under U.S. pressure after the fall of Rangoon to the Japanese forces that the British Government decided to send Sir Stafford Cripps, a member of the British Cabinet, to India, to find out a solution in consultation with the Indian leaders.

Sir Stafford Cripps spent three weeks in India (March-April 1942) and after discussions with the Indian leaders, announced his proposals in the form of a Draft Declaration, which may be summarised as under :

1. The British Government's object was the creation of a new Indian Union, which would have Dominion status.

2. A Constitution-making body, consisting of the elected representatives from the British Provinces and the Princely States was to be set up immediately after the war.
3. The Constitution framed by this body would be accepted and implemented subject to two conditions: (*a*) any Province of British India not prepared to accept this Constitution would retain its present constitutional position. With such non-acceding Provinces, the British Government might agree upon a new Constitution, giving them the same status as the Indian Union. (*b*) Every Princely State would be free to adhere to the Constitution or decline to do so.
4. During the War an Executive Council would be set up, composed of leaders of the principal sections of the Indian people. But the British Government would retain control of the defence of India as a part of their War effort. In exchange for these concessions, Britain asked for India's support in its war efforts.

Political Reaction to the Cripps Proposals: Both the Congress and the Muslim League found the Cripps proposals unacceptable. The Congress Working Committee, which met on April 11, 1942, while rejecting the Cripps proposals said that it would not be satisfied with mere promises for the future, "but with only realisation of freedom". The Working Committee had further objection to the composition of the Constitution making body in 'which the representatives from the Princely States would be nominated by their rulers, not elected by the people. The provision relating to the non-accession of provinces to the Union was a serious threat to Indian unity. Mahatma Gandhi rightly described it as "an invitation to the Muslim League to create Pakistan". The only operative part of the Cripps proposals was the formation of a Central Government to which all powers would be transferred, except defence which would be controlled by the British Government. Mahatma Gandhi called the proposals "a post-dated cheque on a failing bank".

The Muslim League rejected the Cripps proposals on two grounds: that it did not recognise separate electorate for the Constitution-making body and that the demand for the partition of India had not been conceded.

WAVELL PLAN AND SIMLA CONFERENCE—JUNE 25, 1945

The Second World War had ended in May 1945, but Japan had not yet surrendered. India was passing through an extremely uneasy phase. The memories of the serious disturbances during the Quit India movement were still raw; the defeat of the INA movement was a sad end to a heroic phase and the Muslim League had stepped up its demand for partition. To ease up the situation, the Viceroy Lord Wavell, who had succeeded Lord Linlithgow in October 1943, decided to take fresh measures. To begin with, the deadlock persisting since the resignation of the Congress Ministries in 1939 had to be broken. To create conditions conducive to a dialogue the members of the Congress Working Committee, arrested during the Quit India movement, were released.

On June 14, Wavell broadcast a plan, popularly known as the Wavell Plan. The essence of the plan was the formation of a new Executive Council at the Centre, in which all but the Viceroy and the Commander-in-Chief would be Indians. All portfolios except defence would also be held by the Indian members. The Executive Council was an interim arrangement, which was to govern the country until such time that "a new permanent constitution could be agreed upon and come to force". To consider these proposals and to progress towards the formation of the proposed Executive Council, a Conference of 21 Indian political leaders was invited to the summer capital of Simla in June 1945. The leaders included Maulana Abul Kalam Azad, the then President of the Congress, M.A. Jinnah, the leader of the Muslim League, the leaders of the Nationalist Party, Scheduled Castes, Sikhs, etc.

Jinnah, however, sabotaged the Simla Conference. He objected to the inclusion of any non-League Muslims in the Executive Council, with the claim that the Muslim League was the sole representative of Indian Muslims; the Congress therefore had no right to nominate Muslim members to the Executive Council. Jinnah also demanded, the addition to the retention of the Viceroy's veto, some other safeguards for the Muslim members, such as a provision requiring a clear two-thirds majority in case of proposals objected to the Muslim members. The Congress objected to these demands as unreasonable. As it was, Wavell had given the Muslims, who constituted only about 25 per cent of the total population of India, 6 representatives in an Executive Council of 14. Since the League would not relent on its demands, Wavell dropped the plan. At the Simla Conference, the Muslim League acquired the weapon of veto, which it threatened to use or actually used in the coming years, till India was partitioned. For this point onwards the communal question stood like a monster in the way of attainment of freedom.

Abul Kalam Azad, who represented the Congress at the Simla Conference, is of the view that the failure of Simla Conference marked a watershed in India's political history. It immensely strengthened the clout of the Muslim League. It was now quite clear that the Muslim League could make or mar the fortunes of the Muslims, as the British had presented it with the power to veto any constitutional proposal which was not to its liking.

GENERAL ELECTIONS IN INDIA—DECEMBER 1945

The Second World War came to an end with the surrender of Japan on August 15, 1945. A month before, in the general elections held in Britain, the Conservative Party of Winston Churchill was defeated and the Labour Party headed by Clement Attlee came to power with a resounding victory. Sir Pethick Lawrence was appointed the new Secretary of State for India in the new Labour Government.

The first step taken by the Attlee Government was to hold general elections in India, which had been held last in 1936. In the election results announced in December 1945, the Congress made its presence felt in the Central Legislative Assembly as also the Provincial Legislatures. In the Central Assembly, the Congress secured 91.3 per cent votes in the General Constituencies; the Muslim League won every Muslim seat. In the Provincial Legislature, the Congress won absolute majority in Bombay, Madras, United Provinces, Bihar, Orissa and Central Provinces. In the NWFP the Congress won 30 seats (including 19 Muslim) while the Muslim League got only 17. In the Punjab a Coalition Government of the Congress, Akalis and the Unionists was formed. The Muslim League could secure majority only in Bengal and Sind.

Ratings Mutiny—February 1946

About this time, on February 18, 1946, a section of Indians serving in the Royal Indian Navy, known as ratings (non-commissioned officers and sailors) mutinied in Bombay. They went on a hunger strike in protest against untold hardships regarding pay and food and the most outrageous racial discrimination, in particular derogatory references to their national character. The ratings took possession of some ships, mounted the guns and prepared to open fire on the military guards. It was largely due to the efforts of Vallabhbhai Patel that on February 23, 1946, the ratings surrendered; but not before ***hartals*** and strikes and even violent outbreaks that had broken out in Bombay and elsewhere claimed a death toll of more than 300 persons.

On February 19, 1946, the day after the Ratings Mutiny began, the British Government announced the sending of a Cabinet Mission to India.

GENESIS OF PAKISTAN, INDIA TOWARD INDEPENDENCE AND PARTITION

THE CABINET MISSION—MARCH-MAY 1946

The Cabinet Mission, composed of three British Cabinet Ministers—Sir Pethick Lawrence, the Secretary of State for India, Sir Stafford Cripps, President of the Board of Trade and A.V. Alexander, First Lord of the Admiralty—arrived in New Delhi on March 24, 1946. Sir Pethick Lawrence, while announcing the appointment of the Mission had made it clear that its objective was to set up quickly a machinery for drawing up the Constitution for independent India and to make necessary arrangements for an Interim Government. Thus the appointment of the Cabinet Mission was a virtual declaration of India's independence. Its most important task was to devise the mode or -methods for the transfer of power, to suggest measures for the formation of a Constitution-making machinery and also to set up an Interim Government.

The Cabinet Mission spent the first three weeks in discussions with the leaders of various political parties, members of the Viceroy's Executive Council, the rulers of Princely States, etc. After all these discussions, when it could not arrive at any agreed solution, the Cabinet Mission announced its own recommendations on May 16, 1946. Its main recommendations were as under :

1. The unity of India had to be retained.
2. The demand for Pakistan, as demanded by the Muslim League, was rejected on the ground that it would not solve the communal minority problem. In addition, partition would create many serious problems in defence, communi-cations and other areas.
3. There was to be a Union of India, consisting of the British Provinces and the Princely States. The Union Government and its Legislature were to have limited powers, dealing with only defence, foreign affairs and communications. The Union would have the powers necessary to raise the finances to manage these subjects.
4. All subjects other than the Union subjects and all residuary powers would vest in the Provinces.
5. The Princely States would retain all subjects and all residuary powers other than those ceded to the Union.
6. The Constitution-making body or the Constituent Assembly would be formed of representatives of Provincial Assemblies and the Princely States. Each Province was to be allotted a total number of seats in proportion to its population, roughly in the ratio of one representative to a million population. The Constituent Assembly was to consist of 293 members from the British Provinces and 93 members from the Princely States.
7. The Provinces were grouped into three categories—A, B and C. Group A was to consist of Madras, United Provinces, Bihar, Central Provinces and Orissa; Group B was to comprise (the Muslim-majority areas) of the Punjab, Sind, NWFP and Baluchistan; Group C was to include Bengal and Assam (where the Muslims had small majority over the rest). This measure of the Cabinet Mission was unique and also the most controversial. The grouping of Provinces was devised to satisfy the Muslim League, so as to give it a "substance of Pakistan" to exercise almost complete autonomy in the Muslim-majority provinces.

The Congress agreed to the proposals relating to the Constituent Assembly, but rejected the proposal regarding the formation of an Interim Government, because the Muslim League had been given disproportionate representation. The Muslim League at first accepted the Cabinet Mission plan on June 6, 1946, but on July 29 withdrew its acceptance and called upon Muslims "to resort to Direct Action to achieve Pakistan".

DIRECT ACTION DAY—AUGUST 16, 1946

The Muslim League now took a course of action which had no parallel in the recorded history of India. The Direction Action Day, fixed for August 16, was an invitation to the worst communal holocaust. On August 16 and the days following it bands of Muslim rowdies went on rampage of in-discriminate killings, arson, rape and looting. The events in Calcutta, on account of their sheer horrendousness, have been known as the "Great Calcutta killing". The Muslim League Government in Bengal encouraged and directly took part in organising attacks against the Hindus. A British report of the events records: "Between dawn on the morning of August 16, 1946 and dusk three days later, the people of Calcutta hacked, battered, burned, stabbed or shot 6,000 of each other to death and raped and maimed another 20,000."

This communal madness soon spread to other parts of North India, particularly East Bengal and Bihar. What followed Direct Action Day was a virtual civil war between the Hindus and Muslims. When the insensitive Government finally realised that the butchery, pillage and arson were no longer a one-way traffic, it cried halt and peace was restored after about a week.

Amidst this insanity and unreason, the lone symbol of sanity, courage and dignity was the seventy-seven year old Mahatma Gandhi, who went to Noakhali to restore peace.

THE INTERIM GOVERNMENT—SEPTEMBER 2, 1946

Four days before the great communal inferno was ignited, the Viceroy Lord Wavell invited Jawaharlal

Nehru, the leader of the largest party in India, to form an Interim Government, which was sworn in on September 2, 1946. It was composed of 12 members (including 3 Muslims) nominated by the Congress with Jawaharlal Nehru as its Vice- President. It was the first time since the coming of the British that the Government of Indian was in Indian hands.

The Muslim League at first refused to join the Interim Government, but was persuaded to change its stand. On October 13 five Congress appointees resigned to make way for the League's nominees. It became clear, however, that the Muslim League joined the Interim Government not to work sincerely and cooperate with the Congress, but to paralyse the functioning of the new Government. Liaqat Ali, who was given the Finance portfolio, used his position to bring this about. The tactics of the League effectively brought the business of the Government to a virtual standstill.

THE CONSTITUENT ASSEMBLY—DECEMBER 6, 1946

In the meantime elections to the Constituent Assembly were held between July and December 1946 and the Constituent Assembly met for the first time on December 6, 1946 with Dr. Rajendra Prasad as its President. The Muslim League, adhering to its resolution rejecting the Cabinet Mission Plan, refused to join the Constituent Assembly and began to press its demand for Pakistan. In view of the continued boycott of the Constituent Assembly by the League, the British Government finally ruled that the decisions of the Constituent Assembly would not be applicable to the Muslim majority areas. This decision further strengthened the hands of the League and crippled the working of the Constituent Assembly.

ATTLEE'S DECLARATION—FEBRUARY 20, 1947

While the country was passing through these uncertainties, Prime Minister Attlee announced on February 20, 1947, in the House of Commons, that the British would quit India after transfering power "into responsible hands not later than June 1948". Attlee apparently believed the announcement of the terminal date for the British withdrawal from India would bring pressure on the Indian people to settle their differences before then.

Attlee also announced the appointment of Lord Mountbatten as Viceroy in place of Lord Wavell. Lord Mountbatten, the 34th and the last British Governor-General and Viceroy, arrived in India on March 22, 1947 and immediately began to take measures for the transfer of power.

Renewed Communal Violence: Shortly after Attlee's declaration the Muslim League escalated the communal violence. By whipping up communal passions, it brought about the downfall of the non-League Coalition Ministry in the Punjab and again called for 'Direct Action'. In the renewed communal violence all the communities—the Hindus, the Muslims and the Sikhs—"vied with each other in the worst orgies of violence". The conflagration soon spread from the Punjab to the North-West Frontier Provinces and other parts of North India.

Mountbatten was meanwhile holding discussions with the Indian political leaders, but found that the leaders of the League were adamant about breaking up the country along communal lines. Mahatma Gandhi was vehemently opposed to the idea and had declared: "If the Congress wishes to accept partition it will be over my dead body. So long as I am alive, I will never agree to the partition of India". Another staunch opponent of the proposed partition was Abul Kalam Azad.

Mountbatten, after nearly two months of discussions, had come to the conclusion that partition was the only choice. The Congress leaders, too, were brought around to this view in the prevailing circumstances. Sardar Patel and Jawaharlal Nehru had first-hand experience of working with the Muslim League in the Interim Government, with its undiluted capacity to stall the functioning of administration. The Congress leaders had also to consider the widespread communal violence and bloodshed that was ravaging the country, Jinnah's uncompromising attitude on the issue of partition and the British decision to transfer power as soon as possible.

After the reluctant consent of the Congress for the partition of India, Lord Mountbatten held final discussions with the Congress, the League and the Sikh leaders, to seek their agreement on his partition plan. On June 3, 1947, Prime Minister Attlee announced the Partition Plan or the June 3rd Plan in the House of Commons.

THE JUNE THIRD PLAN

The June third Plan was essentially a plan for the partition of India. The plan dealt with "the method by which power will be transferred from British to Indian hands, in particular the methods by which the Muslim-majority provinces would choose whether they would remain in India or opt for the new entity", i.e. Pakistan. The plan laid down the following procedure :

1. The Provincial Legislative Assemblies of Bengal and the Punjab would meet in two parts separately, one representing the Muslim-majority districts and the other representing the remaining districts, to decide by vote for the partition of the provinces.
2. In case of Sind and Baluchistan a straight forward decision was to be taken by their respective Provincial Legislatures.
3. In the case of the North-West Frontier Province, the choice was to be made by the people through a referendum. A similar referendum was to be held in the Muslim-majority district of Sylhet in Assam.
4. Paramountcy in the Princely States would not be transferred to either of the successor States. In theory this meant that the Princely States would not become sovereign entities when the British left India.

The Implementation of June Third Plan: The Congress Working Committee, which met on June 3, 1947, approved of the partition plan; the All India Congress Committee, which met in New Delhi on June 14-15, ratified the approval. Pandit Govind Vallabh Pant, who moved the resolution for ratification, said that "this was the only way to achieve freedom and liberty for the country. It would assure an Indian Union with a strong centre. ....The choice today is between accepting the statement of June 3 or committing suicide." Not all approved of the plan, however. The Frontier Gandhi regarded the partition as treachery on the part of the Congress and felt that "the Khudai Khidmatgars were being thrown to the wolves". The Hindu Mahasabha also bitterly criticised the plan.

The Partition Plan was implemented with unprecedented speed and within ten weeks of the announcement of the plan partition became a reality. The Provincial Assemblies of East Bengal, West Punjab and Sind voted for Pakistan. In Baluchistan the decision to join Pakistan was made by a meeting of the Shah Jirga and the non-official members of Quetta Municipality. In the North West Frontier Province, Khan Abdul Ghaffar Khan and his followers boycotted the referendum; as a result, only 50.49 per cent of the voters took part in it, the majority of them voting in favour of joining Pakistan. In another referendum held in the Muslim-majority district of Sylhet, the majority voted for joining the Muslim-majority province of East Bengal.

The non Muslim-majority areas in the Punjab and in Bengal, as also the entire province of Assam (except a part of Sylhet) remained within the boundaries of India.

THE INDIAN INDEPENDENCE ACT-JULY 1947

Soon after partition was decided upon, the Indian Independence Bill was drafted, which was passed by the British Parliament in July 1947. Its main provisions were as follows :

1. The Act provided for setting up two independent Dominions, to be known as India and Pakistan, from August 15, 1947.
2. The territories of the Dominion of India would include the whole of British India exclusive of the territories constituting Pakistan, i.e. West Punjab, Baluchistan, NWFP, Sind and East Bengal. The exact boundaries of the two Dominions would be determined by a Boundary Commission.
3. The Legislature of each Dominion would have full power to make laws for that Dominion. No Act of the British Parliament passed after August 15, 1947, would have validity in either Dominion. In short, the jurisdiction of the British Parliament over India would cease from that date.

4. With effect from August 15, 1947, the British Government would cease to have any responsibility for the Government of British India and all Treaties and Agreements between His Majesty's Government and the rulers of Indian (Princely) States or any authority in tribal areas would lapse.
5. The two Dominions, as also the Provinces would be governed 'as nearly as may be' in accordance with the Act of 1935 unless and until the Constituent Assembly concerned made other provision.
6. Provision was made for the division of the Armed Forces and the Civil Services between the new Dominions. Each Dominion would exercise authority over its armed forces and civil services.

The Integration of Princely States: Under the Indian Independence Act, British paramountcy over the Princely States was to lapse on August 15, 1947. In theory this meant that the States would become sovereign entities when the British left India. The Congress, however, did not recognise the right of any state in India to declare its independence and to live in isolation from the rest of India. With less than a month remaining before independence, the problem of the Princely States was posing another serious concern. It was to the credit of Vallabhbhai Patel and V.P. Menon who successfully brought about the integration of Princely States. Sardar Patel, who was both stern and statesman like, persuaded the Princes that it was in their own interest to join the Indian Union. After protracted negotiations a settlement was arrived at, and rulers of all States geographically contiguous to India, with the exception of Hyderabad, Junagarh and Kashmir, signed the Instrument of Accession and Stand-still Agreement with India before August 15, 1947.

The Nawab of Junagarh wanted to accede to Pakistan, but a popular uprising against him forced him to flee to Pakistan. The Maharaja of Kashmir acceded to India in October 1947 when irregular Pakistani troops invaded his state. The Nizam of Hyderabad was forced to accede to the Indian Union under the pressure of internal anarchy and military action against him.

THE DIVIDED FREEDOM

On August 7, 1947, M.A. Jinnah left India for Karachi. The Constituent Assembly of Pakistan, which met on August 11, elected him first as President; three days later he was sworn in as Governor-General of Pakistan.

The Constituent Assembly of the Indian Union met on the night of August 14, 1947. In a stirring speech to the members of the Constituent Assembly on the eve of independence Jawaharlal Nehru said: "At the stroke of midnight hour, when the world sleeps, India will awake to life and freedom. A moment comes, which comes but rarely in history, when we step out from the old to the new, when an age ends, when the soul of a nation, long suppressed, finds utterance. It is fitting that at this moment we take the pledge of dedication to the service of India and her people and to the still larger cause of humanity."

The Constituent Assembly then appointed Lord Mountbatten the First Governor-General of the Dominion. On the morning of August 15, the new Cabinet headed by Jawaharlal Nehru was sworn in. The independence we achieved was only a divided freedom which was accompanied by a great human tragedy in the form of communal hatred and cruelty of which was there is no parallel in the recorded history of India. It will suffice to say that India had to pay a very heavy price for her freedom.

16. THE CONSTITUTIONAL DEVELOPMENTS (1773-1950)

S.No.	Year	Act/Legislation	Main Features
1.	1773, 3rd May	**The Regulating Act**	The affairs of the East India Company began to attract attention in England following its acquisition, in 1765, of the Diwani Rights over the Provinces of Bengal, Bihar and Orissa. The anomally of a commercial combine exercising political control, the resultant administrative anarchy, the accumulation of ill-gotten wealth by the servants of the Company, etc., were sharply questioned in the British Parliament. Lord North's Government in England set up a secret and Select Committee to prove into the affairs of the Company. The reports of the two Committees paved the way for thc Act of Parliament called the Regulating Act to enforce governmental control to enforce and regulate the affairs of the Company. (i) The Regulating Act made the Presidency of Bengal supreme over those of Bombay and Madras. The Governor of Bengal was made the Governor-General of the three territories. The "Governor-General in Council" was given the power of superintendence, direction and control over the remaining two presidencies. (ii) The Governor-General was to be assisted by four Councillors. Their tenure of office was fixed as 5 years. The Governor-General and his Council were required to work on the principle of a collegiate executive. (iii) The Governor-General-in-Council were required to obey the orders of the Directors and keep them constantly informed about all matters relating to the interests of the Company. (iv) The Governor-General-in-Council were empowered to make rules, ordinances and regulations for the better government of the Company's entire territories. This may be described as the beginning of the law making power of the Government in India. (v) The Supreme Court of Judicature was established at Calcutta, consisting of a Chief Justice and three other Judges.
2.	1781	**Bengal Judicature Act**	The object of the Act was to remove ambiguities about the powers and jurisdiction of the Supreme Court and

			define precisely its relations with the Governor-General-in-Council and the Company Courts, and to lay down, what laws the Supreme Court was to administer. It was laid down that the Supreme Court had no jurisdiction in matters concerning revenue and collection thereof. The rules and forms of the Supreme Court were to respect the religion and usages of the people of India.
3.	**1784**	**Pitt's India Act**	In the title of the Act, the Company's territories were called "the British possessions in India", which was the first clear assertion of the British Crown's claim of ownership over the Indian territories acquired by the Company. It established a Board of Control, which was to be appointed by the Crown. The Board was given the power to superintend, direct and control all civil, military and revenue affairs of the Company. The Act also created a separate department of the British Government in England, whose only function was to exercise control over the Directors of the Company and the Indian administration. The Pitt's India Act, thus, established for the first time, regular instrument of British India to control the affairs of the East India.
4.	**1793**	**Charter Act**	The Act extended the privileges of the Company for another 20 years. Subsequent, to the Regulating Act, Charter Acts were passed after every twenty years, i.e., 1793, 1833 and 1853.
5.	**1813**	**Charter Act**	Under the Charter Act of 1813, tradc with India was opened to all British citizens, except the tea trade and trade with China. A Church establishment was created at the expense of the Company in India.
6.	**1833**	**Charter Act**	It was an elaborate Act and was intended to improve the administrative system of India. The Governor General of Bengal was named as the Governor-General of India and was given full authority to superintend, direct and control Government of the remaining parts of India in all matters, relating to the civil, military and revenue administration. A duty was laid on the Governor-General-in-Council to pass legislation for improving the condition of Indians without injuring their sentiments. The Indian Slavery Act and many other progressive legislations were the result of this policy. A Law Member, for purely legislative purposes, was added to the Governor-General' Council.
7.	**1853**	**Charter Act**	The Board of Control was authorised to make rules and regulations governing appointments to the services in India. As a result, the Indian Civil Service Examination

			was thrown open to the public and entry to that service was made possible through an open competition. The most striking provision of the Act of 1853 was the extension of the Executive Council of the Governor-General for legislative purpose. The Council assumed the function of a petty Parliament or an Anglo-Indian House of Commons.
8.	**1858**	**The Act for the Better Government of India or Government of India Act**	This Act was passed by the British Parliament after the supression of the Revolt of 1857. The Act, in the first instance, transferred the Government of India from the Company to the Crown. India was henceforth, to be governed directly in the name of the Crown. The East India Company was abolished. All the powers which were, hitherto, exercised by the Court of Directors and Board of Control were transferred to the Secretary of State for India, who was to be one of the Cabinet Ministers. The salary of the Secretary of State and of his establishment was to be paid from the Indian revenues. The various changes introduced by the Act were formally announced in India by a Proclamation of Queen Victoria on November 1, 1858.
9.	**1861**	**Indian Councils Act**	The Indian Council Act of 1861, is an important landmark in the Constitutional History of India. Under this Act, Indians were nominated, for the first time, to the Supreme Legislative Council for the purpose of legislation. These members were to be not less than six and not more than twelve. They were to be nominated by the Governor-General for the two years terms. Not less than one-half of these members were required to be non-officials. The Act also provided for local legislatures in Madras and Bombay and empowered the Governor-General-in-Council to set-up similar bodies in Bengal and other provinces at his discretion.
10.	**1892**	**Indian Councils Act**	The Act of 1892, expanded the Executive Council of the Governor-General for purposes of legislation. A system of indirect election for the non-official members to the Councils was evolved. The functions of these Councils were enlarged, which were in the nature of executive functions. The right of putting questions to Executive Councillors and the right of discussing Budget were conceded for the first time. However, the official majorities were maintained in the Supreme Legislative Council as well as in the Provincial Councils.
11.	**1909**	**Indian Councils Act or Minto-Morley Reforms**	Officially known as the Indian Councils Act or the (Govenrment of India Act, 1909, the Minto-Morley Reforms is named after their official sponsors, Minto the then Viceroy and

			Governor-General of India and John Morley (1838-1923), the Secretary of State for India. The chief merit of Act, lay in its provisions to further enlarge the Legislative Councils and at the same time make them more representative and effective. This was sought to be done under two main heads-Constitutional and functional. The number of the additional members was considerably raised in the Imperial as well as the Provincial Councils. In the Imperial Council, a majority of the official members was maintained; whereas in the Provincial Councils, there were majorities of non-official members, though not elected members, except in Bengal, where there was a small majority of elected members. The Act provided for the appointment of an Indian to the Viceroy's Executive Council, as well as the Provincial Executive Councils. The powers of the Councils were also enlarged. The members could ask questions and even debate the budget but could not vote on it. The greatest evil of the Act was the grant of separate electorate to Muslims.
12.	**1919**	**The Government of India Act or Montagu-Chelmsford Reforms**	The Montagu-Chelmsford Reforms, named after their principal co-sponsors, E.S. Montagu (1879-1924), the then Secretary of State for India and Lord Chelmsford, the then Viceroy and Governor General of India, were logical sequel to the historic Montagu Declaration of August 20, 1917, which defined the goal of British policies in India as the "increasing association of Indians in every branch of administration and the gradual development of self-governing institutions with a view to the progressive realisation of Responsible Government." In terms of the August Declaration, there was to be gradual transfer of authority to Indian hands. As a step towards it, the dyarchy or dual government was introduced in the provinces, which was the most important feature of the Act. Under it, ministers responsible to their respective legislatures held charge of the 'Transferred' subjects, while the provincial Governor and his Councillors were to be incharge of the 'Reserved' subjects. A bicameral legislature was set-up at the centre and a second Indian member was included in the Governor-General's Executive Council. The Act provided for the establishment, for the first time in India, of a Public Service Commission. The Communal or Separate Electorate, injected into the body politic of India under the Morley-Minto Reforms of 1909, was further extended to the Sikhs, Europeans, Anglo-Indians and Christians in Provinces where the influence (of these Communities could be weighty.

| 13. | 1935 | The Government of India Act | The Act was the outcome of the Simon Commission Report, deliberationts at the Round Table Conferences and the White Paper introduced in the British Parliament on December 19, 1934. It is the longest and the last constitutional measure introduced by the British in India. It provided for the establishment of a Federation of India consisting of Governor's Provinces and the Princely States. However, the Federal scheme was a non-strater, because the Princely States did not join the proposed Federation, which would have meant the surrender of their autonomy and autocratic powers. The Dyarchy introduced in the Provinces by the Act of 1919, was abolished and in its place the Provincial Autonomy was introduced, which was the most important feature of the Act.
All subjects of the provincial administration were placed in the hands of Ministers who belonged to the elected legislature. The Act gave 'Special Powers' and 'Responsibilities' to the Governors, which effectively curbed the powers of the minisners and undermined the provincial autonomy. The Act divided British Indian provinces into two categories :
11 Governor's Provinces and 5 Chief Commissioner Provinces. Provincial autonomy was introduced only in Governor's Provinces. The Act of 1935 enlarged the legislature in the provinces. Six provinces (Assam, Bengal, Bihar, Bombay, Madras and the United Provinces) were to have the bicameral legislature or two houses, known as the Legislative Council and the Legislative Assembly. The rest of the provinces had only the unicameral legislature, namely the Legislative Assembly.
Dyarchy which was abolished from the provinces was implanted at the Centre. This meant that certain 'Federal Subjects', such as defence, external affairs, tribal affairs, etc., were 'Reserved Subjects', which were to be exclusively administered by the Viceroy and Governor-General. In the administration of other 'Federal Subjects', the Governor-General was to be aided and advised by a Council of Ministers whose number was not to exceed 10. The Federal Ministry was to be formed on the usual Cabinet lines except that it was to include the representatives of important minorities.
The Federal Legislature was to be bicameral consisting of the Federal Assembly and the Council of State, which was |

			to be the permanent body with one-third of its members retiring every three years. In both Houses, the Princely States were given their quota of representation. The Act of 1935 separated Burma from India. Sind and North West Frontier Province were given the status of provinces.
14.	**1947**	**Indian Independence Act**	The object of the Act, which was passed by the House of Commons on July 15, 1947 and the House of Lords on the following day, was to give legal effect to June 3rd Plan of Lord Mountbatten. - This Act provided for the partition of India and the establishment of two new dominions—India and Pakistan-on August 15, 1947. - The absence of a legally constituted Parliament in either of the proposed Dominions was overcome by giving the Constituent Assemblies of both the Dominions the dual status and functions of the Legislature and the Constitution making body. - All laws enforced in British India on August 15, 1947, would remain applicable, until amended by the Dominion Legislature. - Pending the framing of a new Constitution, each of the Dominions and all Provinces were to be governed in accordance with the Government India Act, 1935. - The Act provided for termination of the suzerainty of the British Crown over the Princely States. All treaties, agreements and functions exercised by His Majesty with regard to the Princely States and their rulers were to lapse from August 15, 1947.
15.	**January 26, 1950**	**The Constitution of India**	After the transfer of power was effected, the Constituent Assembly of India, with Dr. Rajendra Prasad as its President, prepared the Draft of the new Constitution of India in February 1948. The Constitution was finally adopted by the Constituent Assembly on November 26, 1949 and came into force on January 26, 1950, when the Republic of India was born.

17. HISTORY OF THE WORLD

THE RENAISSANCE: ITS MEANING

Renaissance is a comprehensive term which includes all the intellectual changes that were in evidence at the end of the Middle Ages. It marked the achieving of the Modern times. The intellectual revival was stimulated by the crusades and explorations. It was evident in the interest in the past and a desire for understanding the present. One of its attributes was the development of that inquisitiveness which is necessary for intellectual progress. Interest in what the earlier civilizations had contributed was great and the classics were revived. The spirit of the Renaissance was different than in Medieval times. The Medievals attitude towards the classics was utilitarian. Now, the classical culture appealed not merely because it supplied useful information but also because of a genuine interest and enjoyment that the adviser found in it.

The Renaissance included much that was not found in art and literature. In economic life, the simple agricultural ways of the warrior were altered by commerce and industry. In social relationship, the warrior, the noble man's castle and the bishop's palace gave way to the crowded and busy towns.

There was a new political consciousness evident in the decline of the papacy and the empire. Astronomy, physiology and medicine were investigated with sound scientific procedure, instead by the old method of the church and inroads of science on theological scholasticism paved the way for the Reformation. Man was in the process of making a fundamental change in his attitude towards himself and the world in which he lived. This point of view is commonly called Humanism. The Humanists were interested primarily in classical literature, but the effect of this interest focused more attention on things of this world—an exaltation of human nature. The natural, the human, and the sensual were given preference over the esthetical, the supernatural and the theological.

HOW RENAISSANCE STARTED?

It is difficult to determine the forces that actually started the Renaissance. It is more evident in some places than in other places and even where it was most manifest, it represented the thoughts and actions of only a small percentage of the people. Certain leaders stands out in retrospect. Roger Bacon, Alhertun Magnus, Thomas Aquinas, St. Francis of Assisi, Cimabu and Dante—moving spirit of the new era––lived in the 13th century. The scientific spirit, a religious enlightenment a new technique in art and architecture, and a new type of literature served as a background for the Renaissance. Petrarch (1304-1374) was an enthusiastic student of Latin because of its style and form. He had a heart intellectual influence, not only in Florence, his home, but also throughout Europe. He enjoyed the patronage of Pope Clement-VI, Emperor Charles-IV, the king of Neples, and many others. Petrarch found copies of some of Cicero's orations that had been lost. Scholars, through their teachings, spread interest in the classics.

Wealthy and influential individuals became patrons of the new movement. King Francis-I of France invited Italian classical scholars to his country to train Frenchmen in the "new learnings". Henry-VIII of England, Charles-V of Spain, Sigismund-I of Poland, and Christian-II of Denmark encouraged scholars to come to their courts. The Medici family in Florence, the dogs of Venice, and some of the Popes of the Roman catholic offered protection and money to struggling students and artists. The Medici spent large sums of money for old manuscripts and established in Florence an academy devoted to the study of platonic philosophy. Nicholas-V (1497) began the new famous collection of manuscripts in the Vatican and Lured Vallr (1407-1457), a famous scholar, who exposed many false claims of the church. Leo-X, who died in 1521, was a patron of art, music and classical literature. The printing press was of inestimable value in encouraging learning and the invention of movable type for printing (1450) was one of the most significant factors in the preservation. The supply of books was increased greatly; in one year (of the 16th century) more than 24,000 copies of one of Eranmus's books were printed. Besides, printing was more accurate than copying by hand and as consequence, books were more dependable.

THE SPREAD OF RENAISSANCE

As the preceding paragraph indicates, the Renaissance began in Italy. Italy, because of its location, was the logical place. The trade and commerce of Italian merchants had concentrated there most of the wealth of Western Europe. Ideas soon spread to other countries and national cultures, which were closely associated with political developments, arose. The golden age of the Italian Renaissance ended in the first quarter of the 16th century, with the death of Pope Leo-X. The spark of culture that was the spirit of Humanism had crossed the Alps into Germany into France and into England. By the second half of the 15th century, cultured activities were slowly gaining ground in Germany. Renchin (1415-1522) was the great German scholar of the classic. In Germany, as subsequent history reveals, the revival of learning was unproductive in art and literature. The Germans attempted to connect Humanism and Theology and to instill the spirit of reform into classical learning. This had its consummation in Luther's conflict with the papacy.

The intellectual revival began to manifest itself in France at the beginning of the 16th century. Charles-VIII led a French army into Nepales, where he made contracts with the learning of Italy. Several important scholars, including Eranmus, were attracted to Paris, where they taught at the university. Chancer was a leader in the cultural revival in England. Oxford and Cambridge universities, especially Oxford were centres of the cultural activity. John Colet (1466-1517), a religious, enthusiast, sought the regeneration of religion from the allergical interpretation of medieval theology. At St. Paul's, he established a grammar school, which was put under secular management. Numerous schools of this kind were founded until, by the beginning of the 17th century.

THE RENAISSANCE IN ARTS

Throughout the Middle Ages and well into the Renaissance, Art was dominated very largely by the Christian church. Christian art in the early period was tender and human. However, organised theology had a devastating effect on art, which became a vehicle of dogma. The church patronized art on condition that be symbolic of moral virtues and mysteries of the faith. The aim was not to express an ideal or to portray a science but to make the work appear to the something sacred in itself. There was tendency on the part of the churchmen to wider the beach between art and life, to recoil in horror from realism, the human body, and the whole external world. Under such restrictions, art tended to become hard, conventional and grotesque. The spirit of Humanism sought a simpler and more restrained art than what had been typical of the Middle Ages.

The artistic revival in Italy began with a reaction against the domination of the Byzantine tradition. Cimabue (1240-1302) and Giotto (1276-1337) paved the way for the establishment of a new school. Giotto, in particular had a sense of humour, a love for the realistic, and a knack for combining homely incidents with religious themes.

He took a long step from the formalized technique of previous painting towards a purer form of naturalism. Painting was less influenced by classical works than were architecture and sculpture. Paintings of ancient Greece and Rome were scare and the artists of Renaissance had an opportunity to the original. The spirit of Humanism prevailed in painting, but the subject matter was distinctly Cheistian.

RENAISSANCE IN SCULPTURE AND ARCHITECTURE

SCULPTURE

Painting and sculpture were the most important aspect of Renaissance art. Many of the observations which apply to sculpture as well. In technique, the sculptor could rely more closely on classical traditions than could the painter, because sculpture was more highly developed in classical time and the work was in a state of better preservation. Ghiberti (1378-

1455) produced his magnificent doors for the Baptistery at Florence, which Michelangelo cleared "worthy of being placed at the entrance to paradise." Donatello (1386-1466) whose early period of intense realism gave way to a more modified style under the influence of Classic art, exerted in turn, a far reaching influence over the sculpture of later times. The statue of St. George, in Florence, is probably his best-known work. Another is great equestrian "Gattamelta" for Padna. This decorative reliefs for the singing gallery of the cathedral at Florence present groups of "Young Angels", or dancing children with wings, expressing the joyous rhythm of music. They are clothed in garments that reveal rather than conceal the form of the body. Luca Della Robbia (1399-1482) and other gifted members of his family worked in glazed terracotta and produced decorations noted for purity and simplicity. Michelangelo, known for his sculpture and architecture as well as for his painting, was more revolutionary as a sculptor than as a painter. He considered himself essentially a sculptor. Some of his best works in sculpture was done for the Medici family in Florence, the most noted being figures for tombs in the Medici Chapel. The gigantic statue of David in Florence is a masterpiece of anatomical study and suggests, in the massive head, intellectual superiority. The colossal "Moses", made for the touch of Pope Julius II, has been described as "half prize-fighter, half-Jupiter." The 'Pieta' one of his early sculptures, shows the virgin uncleared form of the crucified Christ. In this group, deep emotion is expressed with stirring realism.

ARCHITECTURE

There was a decided travel towards classicism in Renaissance architecture. The Gothic style, which was essentially Christian in origin, was discarded for the arch, the dance and columns characterizing the Greek and Roman models. In Italy, the Gothic had never really taken root and Rome was the centre for the early development of Renaissance architecture. Interest in the remains of Roman structures was aroused by Brunelleschi (1377-1466) who pointed out the virtues of those buildings, which were rapidly disappearing. Raphael, in 1518, made a personal appeal to the Pope to protect what remained of the architecture of ancient Rome. These and other forces concentrated interest on the revival, of classical designs. It should be noted that while the classic element was basic in Renaissance architecture, there was in the later on emphasis upon design and ornamentation that is not found in the classic style. In the later period, the tendency became so predominant that it degenerated into what is called the **baroque**—a style extremely ornate.

One of the most familiar examples of Renaissance architecture is St. Peter's church in Rome. The ground plan is that of a Latin cross and the structure is approached by a noble piazza with curving double cannonades. The crowning feature of the building is a huge and majestic dome of beautiful proportions, planned by Michelangelo. In the interior, all the available space is adorned with coloured marble and stucco reliefs. Many good examples of Renaissance architecture are found in palaces and secular buildings. This emphasizes the tendency noted in paintings and sculpture, a shifting from the medieval absorbing interest in further life to a universal emphasis on the individual and his earthly existence.

THE RENAISSANCE IN MUSIC

Renaissance music, more than any of the other arts of the time was free from classical influence. The music of the Middle Ages was mostly religious upheaval of the 16th century. Martin Luther ran the advantage of the popularized use of music in his church. In contrast to the medieval Roman Catholic method, he wished the people to take an active part in congregational singing, just as he desired them to read the Bible for themselves. Latin chants, hymns, and Moravian religious songs to which he added some of his own composition publishing them in 1524. This was the first popular religious hymnbook in history. John Calvin had the psalms set to music. He was, however, too insistent upon closely following the Bible phraseology to allow much originality.

The Roman Catholic Church was not to the outdone in their movement. In 1564, a commission of cardinals was appointed to study the possibilities of changes in music for the church. They selected Polestrina (1524-1594) to provide a musical setting for the man. He wrote the "Man of Pope Marcellus" and man hymns, which rank him as one of the earliest of the great modern composers.

One of his compositions, "Improperia" (Reproaches) has been sung in the Sistine Chapel on every Good Friday, since 1560. His influence in the musical world reached beyond the limits of the Roman Catholic Church. Phillip Neri, in the middle of the 16th century, founded the order of Oratorians in Rome. Bibical stores were presented, set to the music of choruses and musical instruments. This served as a forerunner of the modem opera.

Several fundamental changes were made in music in the 16th century. The use of "major" and "minor" was submitted for earlier "modes". Particular attention was given to harmony rhythm and symmetry. The comparing of different melodies and polyphong—the combining of several independent voice parts—were introduced. Musical instruments were improved. The simple rabic was changed into a violin and the spinet and the harpsichord were developed from the clavichord.

THE RENAISSANCE IN LITERATURE

In the development of Renaissance literature, there was much development. While Italy was the home of many of the most famous literary figures of the Renaissance, a literature typical of that period can be found in France, England, Germany and Spain. The evolution of literature from a type dictated by churchmen and scholastics to one embodying secularism and individualism is similar to what took place in art, therefore, the process need not be repeated in detail, at this point. Renaissance literature has a strong impress of idiosyncracy and specific experience, a widening consent between the writer and everything connected with man. Interest in the scientific study of language and in the principles and rules of compositions of the Greek and Latin languages, but the same spirit was carried over into the study of the new languages on a scientific basis. Scientific dictionaries for Netherlands, Italian, German, French and Spanish were prepared in the 16th century. 'Von Gesner' published (1553) in Latin, an analysis of more than 100 spoken languages, which was the first step towards comparative philosophy. Literary criticism had begun by the middle of the 16th century. A group in France with Ronsard at their head, organised a society to reform the French language. That a similar movement was under way in England is shown in a famous work by Sir Phillip Sidney. While most of these works were efforts to revive the classical spirit, if not the classical language, it is evident that all over Europe, vernacular prose was, gradually being raised to a position of literary dignity.

RENAISSANCE LITERATURE AND RELIGION

Protestantism had a great influence on the development of literature. The desire to reach the common man and the possibilities that religious propaganda were of great impetus to literary expression. Luther's translation of the Bible into German helped to develop that language for general use. Crammer's Book of Common Prayer and Tyndale's translation of the New Testament into English were important factors in shaping the English language. Calvin's **Institutes of the Christian Religion** and the **Spiritual Exercises** of Loyala not only were important in the realm of religion, but also became enduring examples in the national literature of France and Spain. The protestant Reformation and the Catholic Counter Reformation were attended by the publication of a vast amount of controversial literature in the language of the common people.

To conclude, it may be said that the Renaissance literature was characterized by a revived interest in classical literature. Literary activity, however, was not confused to the classical style. There was a tendency to break away from Latin and Greek and to seek expression in the vernacular languages—Italian, French, English, Spanish and German. This was a significant step, not only in bringing about the development of national political institutions. The religious controversies of the 16th century led to an effort on the part of leaders to reach the masses with propaganda. That type of literature was read by many people who would not have taken time or trouble to read novels, poetry or scientific works.

THE RENAISSANCE IN SCIENCE

Science had made some progress in the Middle Ages, but the spirit of modern science was born with the Renaissance. Science in the Middle Ages struggled against restrictions, and there were many falters to be destroyed before it could continue unhampered. The church was opposed to what it branded the Leatherish practice of scientists. Superstitions were common and to the masses were much more acceptable than were scientific explanations. Physicians, in general disrepute, often were looked upon as athoists in those earlier times. The Renaissance, however, brought about an interest in all things pertaining to man and the thirst for new achievements led to a critical observation of natural phenomena. The spirit of learning was manifested in science as much as in any other field of endeavour, if not more.

THE REFORMATION

The concept of unity in the Middle Ages was attacked by Humanism and by the spirit of individualism. The Renaissance rebelled against intellectual unity and centralized control. The rise of the national state shattered the medieval concept of a universal state. The final assault was the Reformation, which attacked the monopolistic power of the universal church, one of the greatest of all medieval institutions. This great religious upheaval not only was the evidence of a great religious change, but also proclaimed the dawn of a new era.

LINK BETWEEN THE RENAISSANCE AND THE REFORMATION

While both the Renaissance and the Reformation aided in the breakdown of the old order and each contributed to the establishment of the new, they operated individually and in some cases, were opposed to each other. Some Protestant Humanist utilized classical studies in religious controversies but Humanism stimulated pagan learning, which austere protestant condemned. It rebelled against the other worldliness of scholastic Christianity, while leading Protestants revived supernaturalism even witchcraft. Many of the early Humanists were loyal Roman Catholics, critical of ecclesiastical excesses, but interested primarily in merely reforming the established church. Some Protestants were in fact, bitter critics of the cult of humanity and of beauty expressed in the Renaissance.

THE POSITION OF THE CHURCH BEFORE THE REFORMATION

The Roman Catholic Church held a very powerful position in the Middle Ages. Its authority was accepted as final in religion and as a necessity in an orderly civilized society. It was crowned with the sanctity of having been founded by Jesus Christ and was considered a perfect order, whose officials were above any coercion. They had control of the means of salvation, no one outside the church could possibly be saved. The masses accepted these conditions as a matter of course. The apparent security of the church and the predominance of its power were challenged quite unexpected in the 16th century.

VULNERABILITY OF THE CHURCH

The Roman Catholic Church was typical institution of the Middle Ages. It was monopolistic, absolute and uncompromising. The inquiring spirit of the Renaissance revolted against this monopoly. Many of the Humanists were critical of the practices of the church in the Middle Ages. The scholarly training that many of them received in the classical studies made them religious controversialists. The clergy often were so poorly informed that they could not hold their own against the more cultivated Humanist laymen. Heavy ecclesiastical taxation antagonized the growing capitalistic class, the peasantry, the bourgeoise and the aristocracy. Certain Protestant sects encouraged economic individualism. They demanded the removal of the stigma of personal wealth gained through commercial occupations and were willing to pursuit of monetary profits for the businessman. In reality, there were four main forces that attacked the authority of the medieval church :

1. The growing power of the nation-states.
2. Members of the clergy who opposed the centralized authority of the Pope.
3. Reformers who condemned evil practices in the church, and
4. The middle class.

THE DECLINE OF THE CHURCH

The general decline of the church began long before the time of the Renaissance. In fact, evidence of decline followed closely on the time of greatest ascendancy, under Innocent III in the 13th century. The great accomplishment of Innocent III set a pace that his less capable successors found it difficult to follow.

The accumulation of wealth and worldly power offered a temptation for the clergy to neglect their spiritual duties and become engrossed in worldly pursuits. Abuses in the church were not a fundamental cause for the decline, but they did provide weapons for opponents to use. Some of the Popes did violate energy, Christian ideal and exposed themselves and the church to justified criticism.

THE CHURCH AND POLITICS

When the church assumed the duties of a state and when it sought to interfere in the political affairs of other states, it assumed a role that was quite foreign to religion itself. The administration of the Papa1 States was not so troublesome, but when the supervision of the Holy Roman Empire was assume and interference in the political affairs of national states began, the church became involved in countless difficulties. The investitatine struggle should have been a warming, but it went unheeded. As early as the 13th century, conflicts between the king of England and the king of France on the one hand and Pope Boniface VIII on the other, developed over the right to tax church property. The Pope, incensed by the obstinacy of state officials, issued the bull. **Clericis Laicos** (1296), which declared the taxation of church property by the state unlawful, under penalty of excommunication. These high-sounding statements had little effect on a strong nation-state. Papacy and kingship came to grasps and the papacy lost. In 1303, Boniface died, humiliated and disgraced.

From 1305 to 1378, another disaster befell the papacy, with the election of Clement V, it fell into the hands of the French and the seat of the church was moved from Rome to Avignon. The church lost none of its outward pomp and ceremony while at Avignon, but it did suffer from being dominated by the French. The English government did not like the idea of being under a French pope or to give money to the later to live in luxury. National governments in other Places, besides England passed laws to limit or in some cases to prevent papal intervention in the affairs of the state altogether. In most cases, the government in their opposition to the church were supported by the rising middle class.

THE GREAT DIVIDE

After Clement V, when the time came to elect another pope, they were confronted with other difficulties. In the confusion that followed the change, two popes were elected, one representing French interests and the other representing Italian interests. The Great Western Schism or Divide (1378-1415), the name given to this period of confusion, resulted in conflicts that were carried even to the battle field. Scholars wrote books supporting one side or the other and temporal rulers took the attar in hand-mostly of course, to further their own selfish interests. For the test of its material power but also a scandal. The Church was supposedly a single organization established by Christ, with a Pope as his successors on earth. How can a man serve two masters?

People lost respect for the institution and turned to heresies? The Great Schism was healed but the power of the papacy was never completely restored. The reorganization of the church was completed and the bishop of Rome again became the recognized head of the church but weakened in prestige and authority. Heresies grew in number and became increasingly threatening to the universal authority of the church.

REUCHLIN AND ERASMUS

Reuchlin (1455-1522) and Erasmus (1466-1536) were the chief players in the prologue to the drama of the Reformation. Reuchlin was a philologist who point out the inconsistencies of the interpretations of scholastic theologians, made on the basis of a literal use of the text of the Bible. Erasmus was by far the more influential of the two. He is the most prominent scholar and apostle of learning of the Renaissance. Erasmus was not a theologian and he did not question the basic principles of the Roman Catholic Church. In his book, **In Praise of Folly**, (1509) he bitterly denounced the worldliness, the greed, the dirt and the vulgarity of churchmen as well as laymen.

He ridiculed superstition which he believed disgraced the creed of Christendom. He opposed to more ceremonial observances such as indulgences. He criticised the church but never did he advocate an open revolt. He hated fanaticism, which he saw manifested in Luther's work. He was opposed to strife, he believed in reasonableness and culture and did his best to encourage moderation for both sides in the controversy. But the tempo of the struggle prevented both sides from listening to his reason. Erasmus in his last important work condemned Luther for excesses which, he believed were throwing Europe into a state of anarchy.

THE EARLY REFORMERS

In the years preceding the Reformation, there were numerous attack made on the church by many leaders. Some of these leader's attack were mild in their criticisms but were branded as heretics by the church. Savonaroda (1452-1498) in Florence, advocated liberty of thought and attacked the abuses of the methods of government in the church. He was burned at the stake. John Wycliffe (1330-1384) rebelled in England. He was against the arbitrary power of the pope, preached against transubtantiation and translated the Bible into English. He was forbidden to lecture at the university of Oxford and after he died, the Council ordered his body taken from conservated ground and thrown upon a dunghill. John Hun (1369-1415), a Bohemian, struggled for church reform hand recommended a return to the teachings of the Bible. He was condemned by the Council of Constance and burned at the stake. The Albigenses, a religious seed in southern France, opposed subordination to dogma and were slaughtered by crusaders sent by the People. A similar society, the Waldenses, led by Peter Waldo were persecuted because they preferred to follow the teachings of the Bible rather than the dictates of the clergy. The leaders of these heretical sects were destroyed, but their ideas lived on and bore fruits in a later generation.

COMPUTION IN THE CHURCH

The Reformation, was hastened because of scandals commonly associated with the clergy. Pope Alexander-VI (1492-1503) was a moral degenerate. Leo-X (1513-1521) extracted money from the people in order to build the basilica of St. Peter's church in Rome. He created church offices and sold them; he pawned palace furniture, pontifical jewels and the statues of the apostles. Conditions were equally bad among the lower clergy. They neglected their religious duties and lived lives of luxury similar to those of the noblemen of the time. Much of the church money was collected from the middle class. The member of this group, which was becoming more powerful, welcomed the opportunity to oppose the church for financial reasons, if for no other. The concurrence of a number of forces culminated in the revolt itself. The church organization was weakened and it overstepped its authority at a time when caution would have been better. Intellectual progress had destroyed many of the practices that had been a source of strength for the church. Finally, the church found a formidable opponent in the national state.

REFORMATION IN GERMANY: LUTHERANISM

Quite logically, the Reformation began in Germany. Many Germans were not good Roman Catholics, either by temperament or by training. They were far enough removed from Rome to make contacts difficult. There was no strongly centralised government in Germany to aid the church in carrying out its decrees. Also it was home of Martin Luther, a fearless and dynamic critic of the church. Luther (1483-1546) was a well educated man, much concerned about the problem of eternal salvation. He contested the Catholic idea of good works as a means of salvation and insisted that only through faith, could the soul be saved. He was a reformer at first but he came to a breaking point with the church over the sale of indulgences and through the admission that he questioned papal infallibility.

There was much misunderstanding and abuse concerning indulgences. An indulgence was a promise of remission in part or in entirely of the penalty after death on account of sin. However, the sinner had to repent and do some form of penance. A part of the penance might be in the form of donating money for worthy ecclesiastical purposes. One of the papal agents, Tetzel practice by accepting money under very questionable circumstances. Luther condemned the procedure and questioned the whole system of indulgences.

Many of the German princes wanted civil war and they saw in the work of Luther, an excuse for war. If all the parties had wanted peace, the theological issues might have been adjusted. Nobles and peasants for greatly divergent reasons, came to the support of Luther. He had no sympathy with the peasants' revolt and sided with the nobles against them. Warfare broke out between Catholic and Protestant states. Order of Augsburg (1555). According to the agreement, each prince might dictate the religion he wished his subjects to have, provided that it was either Lutheranism or Roman Catholicism. Lutheranism thus was recognised and its rights were defined.

The revolt did not stop here. Luther's influence reached beyond the territorial limits of Germany. He assailed abuses prevailed in all countries; he appealed to individualism in religion and the spirit of individualism appealing doctrine in his "justification by faith". Lutheranism spread into other countries especially to the Scandinavian states, where it was more generally accepted than in the Germany. The precedent for protest had been set.

CALVINISM

Protestantism, by its very nature, was conducive to the development of many sects. Besides the Lutherans, two other large groups developed, the Calvinists and the Anglicans. Calvinism, unlike Lutheranism was not the work of one man, as the name might suggest. The pioneer work for the establishment of Calvinism was performed by Zwingli (1484-1531). His opposition to the church was primarily political in nature, but he preached against fasting, the celebracy of the clergy and the veneration of the saints. He insisted more strongly on the Bible and diverged radically from the form of service in the Catholic Church. He broke from the church in 1523.

Zwingli was killed in 1531, but in 1536, his work was renewed by Calvin (1509-1564) with more aggressiveness than he himself had shown. Calvin believed that he had been divinely called to forsake Catholicism and establish a purer Christianity. His **Institutes of the Christian Religion** (1536) was the first scholarly statement of the Protestant cause comparable to what medieval church fathers had done for Catholic theology. Calvin believed in a strict interpretations of the Bible and in a rigid rule of etiquette. He demanded that there be no more festivals, no more jovial ruinous and no work theatres. He was very uncompromising in his views. He wished adultery to be punished by death and he was responsible for servants being burned for a disagreement over the mystery of the Trinity. Calvinism soon spread into France, the Netherlands, Germany, Hungary, Poland, Scotland and England.

ANGLICANISM

Anglicanism was the changed form adopted by the third large group of the Protestant sects. It became the faith and order of the established church of England and the Protestant Episcopal Church in the Unites States and from it originated the Methodist Church. In many respects, Anglicanism was more conservative and evolutionary than either Lutheranism or Calvinism. It was highly nationalistic. At first, Anglicans recognised the supremacy of the bishop of Rome by the 16th century. A great deal of independence in the interpretation of doctrine had been introduced.

With the succession of the Tudor family in 1485 English nationalism began to take definite form. Henry-VII (1485-1509) had the support of the middle class, which was opposed to the policies of the church, but it was not until the reign of Henry- VIII (1509-1547) that a definite break came and then on seemingly insignificant question of his marital relationship. The church supported the unfortunate queen and Henry-VIII gained the support of the opponents of the church. Parliament empowered him to stop payments of anatase to the Pope and to appoint bishops without the sanction of the papacy. Parliament in 1534, declared the king the "only supreme head on earth of the Church of England" and inflicted the penalty of treason on anyone who should deny the king's ecclesiastical supremacy. Parliament enacted the church creed into "the Six Articles (1539) which resembled the Roman Catholic doctrine." The chief difference was the substitution of the king of England for the pope at Rome as the official head of the church.

The Church of England became really protestant in the reign of Edward-VI (1547-1553). The service books were translated into English and the Book of Common Prayer (1552) omitted the Mars and substituted the word **table** for **altor**. There was a Catholic reaction in the rule of Mary (1553-1558) but Elizabeth (1558-1603) supported the Anglican Church.

She assumed the title **Supreme Governor**. The **Book of Common Prayer** was revived and Parliament defined the Anglican doctrine more fully in the "Thirty-nine Articles". They recommended appeal to the scriptures as the source of religious faith, repudiated the Catholic Mars, and insisted on justification by faith alone.

CHANGES IN RELIGION

The various Protestant sects introduced a great number of divergent ideas into religion. The changes however, were not so complete as one might think. Both Catholics and orthodox protestant accepted both the Old and the New Testament without question. Salvation remained the most important function of all the churches and skeptics and dissenters were not tolerated even by the protesters. In general, the protestant condemned the sale of indulgences, emphasised a more direct form of worship than was in the practice in the Roman Catholic Church and modified the Catholic doctrine of transubstantiation.

COUNTER REFORMATION

One of the important results of the Protestants Revolt was the impetus to reform without the Roman Catholic Church. There were many loyal Catholics who were not willing to break from the fundamental ideas of the church but who saw the urgent need for reform without disturbing the organisation of the church of questioning the validity of the dogma. The Council of Trent (1545-1563) laboriously undertook to remove some of the most glaring abuses and to restore unity in the church. The representatives confirmed the main points in Catholic theology, but condemned the sale of church offices and demanded that the clergy adhere more strictly to their duties. The practice of the sale of indulgences was abolished. Other changes were made, following the Council of Trent. The Papal Index, a yearly list of dangerous and heretical books that Catholics should not read, was issued and the medieval Ecclesiastical Court of Inquisition was revived.

Several orders were formed. The Society of Jesus, founded by Ignatius Loyala (1491-1556) was one among the most important. Strict and unquestioning obedience, was required. Members of the society sought to augment the power of the Roman Catholic Church through the establishment of schools and through missionary work. Many of the members lectured in universities were accomplished diplomats or became confessors of princes. Their influence spread as far as the America's and the Orient.

The Count Reformation removed many of the abuses in the church. If it had come earlier, the strength of the Protestant cause would have been lessened. The success of the Counter Reformation can be measured to a degree by the fact that the rapid spread of Protestantism was halted. Southern Germany, France, Poland, some of the Swiss cautions and savoy were brought back to the Catholic faith, while Protestantism was driven out of Italy and Spain. The Roman Catholic Church is still one of the great religious organisations in the world.

EFFECTS IN OTHER FIELDS

The results of the religious upheavals of the 16th century carry over into other fields of activity. There was a tendency for both Catholics and Protestants to take their religion seriously to prove by their conduct that religion represented a high moral standard. Puritanism, with its strict moral code and intolerance arose and flourished.

Books were censored, blasphemy was condemned and observance of the Sabbath was demanded. Protestants rebelled against the use of art for church decoration and against handsome church buildings as degrading to religion. Educational progress was hindered. Universities were attacked as strong-holds of the hated scholastic theology. People were encouraged to read the Bible and ponder to religion rather than to spend their time on science and literature. Nationalism was encouraged through the revolts. Protestant sects were in many respects a manifestation of nationalism. The medieval restrictions on business were removed. Usually was recognised as a legitimate business and property in contrast to the Old Testament idea, was regarded as a sign of God's blessing.

REPRESENTATIVE GOVERNMENT IN PRACTICE: ORIGIN OF PARLIAMENT

No other European country illustrates the evolution of a government from absolutism to democracy any better than does England. In the early period, the government was absolute and was based upon distinctly feudalistic practices. The English parliamentary system can be traced to Magna Charta (1215), one of the most famous documents in English history. King John, was forced to sign the document. The rights granted were not intended for the common people but for the barons and the clergy. Its most important service has been to stand as a constant reminder that the people had once risen to defend their rights against a despotic king. There is mention of a Great Council, whose function was to contest to the levy of taxes. Simon-de-Montfort summoned a parliament (1265) and invited two burgesses from each of 21 towns to sit with the barons to safeguard their liberties from upsusption by the king. In 1295, Edward-I called an assemblage that was similar to the later parliaments, in that two groups were found comparable to the House of Lords and the House of Commons.

GROWTH IN AUTHORITY

Originally, parliament seems to have been regarded as a body to advise and to grant requests of the king for subsidies. For a long time (in theory it is still true), the right to make laws was considered a royal prerogative. Not until the middle of the 17th century did parliament became a really aggressive force in the English government. By the end of the 17th century, members of parliament enjoyed freedom of speech, had power to levy taxes, controlled the appointment and removal of judges, controlled the army through appropriations and gradually assumed supreme authority over the nation. It was a long struggle, first between the noblemen and the king and then between the commoners and the noblemen, before England ahead a democratic form of government.

STRUGGLE BETWEEN CROWN AND PARLIAMENT

A crisis in the struggle between king and parliament came in the Stuart period. James-I (1603-1625) decided to ignore parliament, which incensed at the king' actions, answer was a dissolution of the legislative body. Charles-I (1625-1649) in a quarrel over religion, decided to do away with parliament altogether. Financial difficulties soon forced him to call a meeting. Members of parliament were in a angry word when they convened.

They abolished the courts and commissions that the king had used, they impeached and imprisoned some of his most trusted ministers and they passed a resolution to the effect that parliament must meet at least once every three years. Charles led an army against his unusual opponents, who were under the leadership of Oliver Cromwell. The Royalists were defeated and Charles was led to the Scaffold (1649).

The establishment of the commonwealth and immediately following, the protectorate marks a unique period in English history. It is the only break in the monarchy—the only time the English ever had a real dictator and the only time they ever had a written constitution (The Instrument of Government). The protectorate was not to the liking of the English people and when Cromwell, the dictator, died, there was little trouble in restoring the Stuarts in the person of Charles-II (1660-1685). Neither he nor James-II (1685-1688) profited from the unfortunate experiences of the former Stuarts. They insisted on reestablishing Roman Catholicism and disregarding parliament. James lost the support of the people and when faced with an invading army led by William of Orange, he fled to France. The Glorious Revolution deposed the Stuarts and made way for the accession of William and Mary.

THE GLORIOUS REVOLUTION

A significant step in establishing the prestige of the English Parliament was accomplished in the Glorious Revolution. The members of parliament drew up a definite set of instructions to protect its rights and restrict the power of the crown (The Bill of Rights, 1689). This act and succeeding acts (The Act of Settlement, 1701) provided that, thenceforth, the king had to belong to the Anglican Church, he was denied the right "to suspend" laws and was compelled to guarantee free speech and proceedings for members of parliament. This marked the end of absolute monarchy and the entrenchment of parliament in power in England.

The Bill of Rights was distinctly a middle-class victory. It established firmly the idea of representative government and became a charter of liberty for England. In addition, it provided an inspiration for the American and French revolutionists in the 18th century.

RISE OF NAZISM IN GERMANY

Rise of Nazi Party in Germany: German public did not respect the Weimer Republic, and her prestige downed due to financial crisis in democracy and international cooperation. They lost their trust in government ways and policies. German people worked for a leader who could end their crisis. They got a leader in form of Adolf Hitler who sounded the bigule of Germany once again. Hitler became all in all to his militarized Nazi group.

Early Life of Hitler: Hitler was born on 20th April, 1889 at Brono in Austria to a ordinary serviceman. He tried to be a great artist in his early youth but useless. When he did not get admission in Imperial Art Academy of Vienna, he started to earn his livings by work of painting in houses. Then his thoughts became mature. The feeling of hatred towards communists and jews emerged in him. He became the worshipper of greatness of German nationality and German caste and he had no faith in parliamentary government.

Hitler preferred the life of courage and bravery to peaceful life. So, when first world war started, he joined German army and got the rank of 'Iron cross' due to his ability and bravery.

At the defeat of Germany in the world war, Hitler became angry. He considered the cause of defeat of Germany the politicians, so he decided to enter in politics. He established a political group called National Socialist "German Labour Party" or Nazi Party.

CAUSES OF RISE OF HITLER AND HIS NAZI PARTY

(*i*) Insult of Versailles: The insulting conditions of Versailles hurt the feelings of German National feelings which made him more rude towards the Winner whereas the old Germans became discouraged and sad, the young Germans and soldiers became eager to develop their fatherland. They considered the Treaty of Versailles as bad mark of their forehead and they were anxious to regain their ancient dignity. They looked for a leader who could give them old dignity. By taking the advantage of their revengeful feelings, Hitler gave the slogan of regaining national dignity and made youths, soldiers and middle class people in his favour. The aggressive programme of Nazi Party and their slogan, End of Versailles treaty were liked by the German people very much.

(*ii*) Caste System and Character: German caste was of militarian attitude by nature. They had the feeling of discipline and bravery worship. They got Hitler who could be their Father.

(*iii*) Disbelief and Dis-Interest in parliamentary government: German people did not like the democratic parliamentary government. German people had great dissatisfaction towards republican government's policies and methods. German people were perplexed to see that government did only promises. So, German people wanted a strong personality who could improve their condition. Hitler and his Nazi party took advantage of this mental state of people.

(*iv*) Financial crisis of 1930: Hitler and Nazi party got a great success due to financial crisis in 1930. The financial crisis was more horrible than other countries. Hitler introduced his political leadership at such a time. He declared again and again that the government who had surrendered before imperialistic countries was responsible for that bad condition. If Germany wants to progress or to spend a prestigious life, this idle government should have to be rooted out. Not only this, but Hitler also got the co-operation of middle class and lower middle class people by rising the anti-capitalistic feeling. Hitler said that capitalists and Nazi of Germany were responsible for financial crisis. In June 1931, the peasants were in debt of 3 Arab dollar. Hitler revolted to abolish these debts. So farmers became in favour of Nazi party and many industrialists also supported Hitler being afraid of communism.

In fact, this financial crisis gave the basis to Nazi party. Hitler left an image on German people that only Nazi party or Hitler could get the people rid of financial crisis very soon.

(*v*) Personality of Hitler: Hitler's own character helped him to come to power. Church was deprived to the control of its finances. He was a great orator, who could control and influence audience of millions of people. According to G. Hardy, "He had supreme power, whether it was devil in place of divine." "According to F. Lee Benns, "Hitler was a wise psychologist, a clever leader and a good actor. He was a resourceful revolutionist, a perplexed workman and an able organiser."

His technique of propaganda helped him to carry the audience with him. He thundered. He asked for blood. He infused politics with a religious fervour. He was a fanatic in his views and was able to hypnotise all those who came to hear his speeches. The result was that his followers began to swell and ultimately he was led to power.

(*vi*) Attractive Programme: Hitler's attractive programme was also a main cause of his rise. His programme was according to wishes, traditions and views of German people. Whatever the people had been thinking for a long time, Hitler said them openly and promised to fulfil them. As Hitler was an image of German's ambition, he got support of people. Germans considered the Treaty of Versailles as insulting treaty. Hitler promised to break it. The people were worshippers of brakmen as Fredrick. Great Bismarck and Koser etc., believed in army power, and supporter of monarchy and dictatorship. Hitler increased this feeling of Germans and called democracy, "A system of starved, and cowards." He showed this belief in principle of "power is right." Nazi Party adopted those principles of German thinkers which were popular among people as militarism of Fredrick. Principle of supremacy of state by Hegal, Brave worship of Fichte and 'Power is Right' of Novelis. Jew opposition of Mavits demand of its extra states for expansion of Germany and supremacy of Aryans or Germans by Hosten Ster but Chamberlain.

Hitler's programme of extreme nationalism soon became popular among German people. Germany accepted Hitler as a reforming leader of their country and considered it good to follow him blindly like Bismarck and Kesar.

(*vii*) Fear of Communism: The fear of communism was also a main cause of rise of Hitler and Nazi party. German communist party was progressing day by day. Hitler considered it the biggest thorn of his way. So, he threatened people more against communism. He encouraged the capitalists and public to fight against communism. The capitalists considered communism as their biggest enemy. So they gave their money to Nazi Party to fight against communism. The public had also been afraid of communism due to Hitler's reasonable and impressive propaganda. So, the public also supported Nazi Party.

(*viii*) Support of German Youths, Soldiers and Bureaucracy: One important reason of success of Nazi Party was that German Youth, Soldiers and state workers supported the Nazis.

(*ix*) Jews Opposition: Hitler's Jews opposition also was one reason of his success. The Jews were minor but rich. Big capitalists were Jews. Public hated them considering them an exploiter. Hitler took advantage of this condition and said that the defeat of Germany in 1918 was due to only district of the Jews. So the Jews should be rooted out. The public became much influenced by him. Due to these causes Hitler became successful and became supreme in Germany.

Expansion of Europe: Imperialism stands for, according to longer, "urge or striving for rule or control, political or economic, direct or indirect of one state, nation or people or other similar groups."

One of the remarkable features of the nineteenth century was the feverish attempt of the European powers to extend their control over the non-European-world. It was a century during which the white races seized other regions of the earth which still remained un-appropriated or were too weak to pressure themselves inviolated. Increasingly, large areas of South America by France, England, Australia etc., because they were incapable of opposing any effecting resistance to the deadly weapons of modern civilization. They were brought under European Control, and ever lands of ancient civilizations were not fully immune from the grasping tentacles of European imperialism. Consequently, India, Indonesia and Indo-China and central Asia came under England, French, Russia and Dutch rule. The out cry for colonies and spheres of influence is strikingly illustrated by the scramble for African and the attempted portion of China. It has transferred the rivalry of the European nations from Europe to other parts of the world, but mainly to South-North America but these continents became mostly free. Attention was directed to Africa and Asia. Europe is no longer the stage of history.

World Politics: Foreign policy tends more and more to become world policy and the whole world is now the field of active diplomacy. Concerns of remote lands have become matter of supreme momat to the colonial European Powers. The era of world politics has dawned and the world was in the process of being

Europeanised upto 1945. After second world war, Europe lost supremacy and most of the countries gradually became free.

Colonial Empire: The expansion of Europe is, however not a novelty. From the fifteenth century, Europe had turned her eyes upon the non-European world and in the course of the next two centuries, Spain, Portugal, Holland, England and France laid the foundation of their colonial empire in Australia, America and other Islands. Much of the history of Europe during this period is taken up with the rivalries of European nations for colonial and commercial expansion. But, in the early part of the 19th century the colonial movement seemed to have lost much of its former vitality. This was due to the fact that the colonial empires built up by European nations were crumbling to pieces on all sides. Between 1763 and 1825, there was not an empire which did not suffer, serious loss, all others fell into ruin. Great Britain had lost her thirteenth American colonies in 1783. Early in the 19th century, the Spanish colonies in America likewise revolted and became free and Brazil established its independence from Portugal in 1822. These colonial disasters confirmed the growing conviction in the minds of European statesmen that empire-building was hardly, worth the trouble and money expended upon it. Disraeli, the Prime Minister, of England echoed the prevailing mood of apathy and discouragement when he said, "These wretched colonies will be independent in a few years and are like a mill-store round our necks".

Mercantile Theory's decline: Lastly, the mercantile theory that colonies where beneficial and necessary to the mother country was gradually losing its appeal on account of the sharp criticisms directed against it by economist like Toogot and Adam Smith who stood for the new economic theory of laissez-faire. With the growth of the Free Trade movement, the very foundation and utility of the old colonial policy based on mercantilism, was undermined. People began to lose faith in the value of colonies. But as the century progressed, several focuses were found at work, which created a new impetus for colonial expansion. This revival of imperialism (the new Imperialism as it is called) was largely the result of the new economic Conditions produced by the Industrial Revolution.

Impact of Science: The brilliant triumphs of modem science and engineering immensely improved transport communication. The result was that the conquest and occupation of distant land became infinitely more feasible. The requirements of modern industries led to enormously increased demands for raw tropical products and thereby enhanced the value of colonies as sources of suppose.

Industrial Change: The Industrial Revolution caused large-scale production which demanded new and wider markets. But the new market for manufactured goods in the last quarter of the 19th century, instead of expanding was in the process of rapid shrinkage owing to the adoption of protective tariffs by the leading industrial nations except great Britain.

Impact of adoption of Protection policy: The ideal of the protectionist creed was national self-sufficiency. But this was impossible for industrialised Europe without controlling those undeveloped tropical fertile regions which produce some of the indispensable and rare raw materials. Hence the economic policy of protection gave a mighty stimulus to imperialism. It is note worthy that the last quarter of the nineteenth century which saw the adoption of high protecting tariffs by most of the European nations, was the very period of rapid colonial expansion.

Increase in Population: Need for colonies was also felt as outlets for expanding population. Economic distress and periodical recurrence of unemployment forced people to find new homes and careers abroad. To the ardent nationalists, this loss of nation's manhood was highly deplorable.

Surplus Capital: Lastly like surplus population, surplus capital sought investment in newly opened up countries where greater returns could be had. This sort of economic penetration was often the forerunner of political control as in the case of Egypt and Morocco etc.

Political Factor: Lenin said, "Imperialism is highest stage of capitalism" but the economic factor, although the most powerful and fundamental was not the sole cause of modern imperialism." There were also political motives which supplied powerful incentives as in case of annexation of Siberia by Russia which at that time was annexed due to must for imperial expansion. Nations which have already acquired a far-flung empire, felt the urgent necessity of having naval bases and cooling stations as in case of Aden and Singapore. Secondly, as the temper of the age grew more militaristic, the nations of Europe came to realise that the colonies might have also a military value. During the 19th century, thousands of emigrants left Europe for Argentina, America, Brazil and other countries. This meant the passing away of so many citizens under an alien flag and the consequent loss of the military manhood of a nation. Hence to conserve the man power of a nation it was found necessary to have colonies where the emigrants might remain under the allegiance of the mother country. This was the argument which appealed most strongly to Germany and in a less degree to Italy, as both of them were losing by emigration, millions of their own subjects. In the second place, conquered subjects of comparatively backward races might be turned into an efficient military force available for the use of the conquering power. This motive appealed very strongly to France whose stable and stationary population contrasted unfavourably with the rapid increase of population in Germany.

National Honour and Prestige: Lastly, the spirit of national pride and hunger for pomp show and prestige supplied a very strong incentive to colonial expansion. This spirit was specially strong in the two new states of Italy and Germany. In the exuberance of patriotic pride which duly followed the achievements of their national unity, they wanted to establish their status as world power. The huge colonial empire of Britain had set a standard and the idea was rapidly growing that the possession of colonies was part of the prestige and proper equipment of a great power. Otherwise, they would appear like dwarfs before giants. With the entry of these two states, the competition for overseas possessions became antagonistic and keener. Everywhere, nationalism became aggressive and staunch patriotism "developed from love of country into love of more country". In the beginning, Spain boasted "Sun never sets in her empire" but when Spain lost Empire, Britishers proudly said "Sun never sets in British Empire".

Golden Jubilee of Queen Victoria and Silver Jubilee of George V made all world jealous of her power.

Role of Christian Missionaries: Along with the economic and political motives of imperialism there were also religious and humanitarian considerations. The desire to spread Christianity has always been a striking characteristic of the Christian church in all ages. Foreign Christian missions of Spain and Portugal were followed by American Christian missions which become, in many cases, the forerunners of official. Finally, of Government penetration, and the need of the official protection was often requested by the missionaries themselves and for new converts. In Africa and in the Islands of the South Sea, the missionaries often led the way for the merchants and then for the military penetration and occupation. In many cases, there was undoubtedly a serious desire to raise the civilisation of backward people and to teach them new scientific outlook and principles of health and Sanitation. But unfortunately, the civilising propaganda of the missionaries had very often been neutralised by the shameless immorality and heartless cruelty exhibited by European officials and merchants in their dealing with the subject people. Christian missionary propaganda have done much to further the cause of imperialism.

New Areas of Expansion: Asia and Africa in 19th century lagged behind in developing new destructive weapons, therefore they came under the sway of imperialist powers. The two regions of the world which have been subjected most to European exploitation are Asia and Africa. The latter has been completely partitioned among European powers so that probably with the exception of Liberia, a small republic state was created for the settlement of liberated Negroes, there was no independent country in Africa. The ancient empire of Abyssinia or Ethiopia maintained its independence till 1935, but it had to succumb to the capacity of Fascist imperialism. In the Asia, the impact of the Europe was also very great in that direction. In north, Russia built up a great empire extending from the Urals to the pacific, while the South Britain extended her possessions in India, and Burma, and France sliced off Indo-China. China was forcibly opened up by the European powers, with the united states co-operation. But the tide of hostile European intervention was checked by the rise of Japan who by her victory over Russia became the leading Asiatic state and stirred up the feeling of the self rule and the forces of nationalist feeling in Asia with results which are still being worked out. Iran and central Asia became European spheres of influence.

IMPERIALISM IN ASIA

Russian Expansion in Asia: By far the greatest expansion of the European countries into Asia was that made by Russia. She grabbed largest territory of Asia incorporating whole of northern Asia. She possessed 7 times land to whole of India, three times to U.S.A. and much more than whole Western Europe. She had long been seeking in Europe Viz. contact with the ocean. Baffled in her attempts to secure this in Europe, she paid her serious attention to Asia in order to secure the long wished outlet to an icefree sea.

Russian Expansion in South Asia: From the middle of the 19th century, she began to advance in two directions southward in the direction of Persia and Afghanistan and eastward into Mongolia and China etc. In the course of her southwards advance, she conquered the Trans-Caspian region and came within striking distance of India. This aroused the keenest apprehension in Great Britain and made Anglo-Russian relations very critical and various Afghan wars took place between British India and Afghanistan during the last three decades of the nineteenth century.

Russian Expansion in Central Asia: In central Asia, the main stages of the Russian progress were marked by the occupations of Tashkand (1864), Samarkand (1866) and Khiva (1873). At the time of the Treaty of Berlin in 1878, the Frontier of Afghanistan had been reached. This expansion caused difficulties between Britain and Afghanistan with the result that an Anglo-Afghan war followed (1871-79). It had the effect of checking Russian advance in the direction of India by placing on the throne of Afghanistan on Amir i.e. ruler friendly to Britain and heavily subsidised by the Indian Government-checked in this region. Russia moved in on other, she completed the conquest of Turkistan in 1881, occupied Mery in 1884 and seized Punjdeh, a border district of Afghanistan. This brought her within a chance of war with Britain, but the crisis passed away. Russia tried to penetrate in Persia, Tibet and Afghanistan etc. but Anglo-Russian convention of a 1907 checked the Russian expansion in central Asia and eased to be a cause of friction between the two powers. Russia recently had occupied Afghanistan and this was modern cause of antagonism between Russia and U.S.A., China and Pakistan.

In the east, Russia pushed her way towards the pacific with comparative ease. In the fifties China was weak and in the grips of serious troubles. She was convulged by a civil war known as the 'Tai Ping Rebellion, and was at the same time engaged in hostilities with France and Great Britain etc. Russia took advantage of China's embarrassment, weakness and forced her to conclude the Treaty of Aigum in 1858, by which she acquired very large and considerable territory down to the Amur river. Two years later, she secured more territory farther south along the Pacific coast, and at its Southern extremity built a strong port which served as a naval base and which was renamed Vladivostok or "dominator of the East." Thus, acquisition brought Russian boundary into touch with Korea and went half-way towards encircling Man-Churia. But as Vladivostok remains mostly ice-bound during some months of year, Russia sought an ice-free port farther south. This meant further penetration into Manchuria, and in this attempt she cashed with Japan. In 1905, Russia was defeated by the rising power of Japan. Thus Russia became one of the greatest imperialist power whose empire is still expanding and is the most important factor in the growing far Eastern Question. Recently Russia had occupied Afghanistan, cultivated friendship with India and Vietnam but is daggers drawn with China, Pakistan and Japan and U.S.A. etc.

The French in Indo-China i.e. Vietnam, Laos and Cambodia: While Russia was encroaching upon the northern territories of China, France and Great Britain were making similar in roads upon the fringe of states in the South, which recognised only nominal Chinese overlordships. French imperialism in Asia became very active in the time of Napoleon III and by 1868, the whole of Cochin-China was annexed. The next object of French ambition was Annam and Tonkin, and a protectorate was established over them after a short war with China in (1885). In 1868, Kwangcho Wan was acquired. Thus, France acquired a large territory in Asia, larger than France itself.

The British Empire in Asia: Great Britain on the southwest completed the circle of foreign aggressors upon Chinese soil. Step by step the British had conquered whole India and then began to look for further expansion in the east and north. In 1885, they deposed the Burmese king and annexed Burma which was nominal and traditional tributary state of China. They acquired Malaysia, Singapore, Ceylon, Hongkong and many other Islands and places.

It should be noted that the Chinese Empire was weak and largely divided into China, proper and nominal tributaries which afforded the most tempting field for European exploitation. It was vast but loosely Knit together and the Govt. was inefficient. Besides, China was very rich in mineral and natural resources.

All these circumstances made China, the most important state in Asia in the game of imperialism and for the East became the scene of the keenest competition due to rivalry among imperialist powers. China escaped from direct thralldom. Now she is most populated and a powerful country of the world.

Middle and Near East: Iran in the Middle East and Asiatic Turkey in the Near East increasingly felt the pressure of European imperialism. The Southward expansion of Russia brought her to the nearest border of Persia and early in the twentieth century northern Persia came under Russian influence. But in Asia, Russia was Britain's greatest rival. Russian influence in Persia alarmed the British Government very much. In particular, Britain was vitally interested in preventing the Persian Gulf from falling under the control of a hostile Russian power, as that would menace her hold upon India. So she resented and became active in Southern Persia and brought it under her influence. Frictions continued, but in 1907 they were ended due to the fear of German imperialism by the Anglo-Russian convention. But the northern half of Persia was assigned as Russia's sphere of influence, while the British interests were declared predominant in the South eastern corner of the country, specially in the Persian Gulf between the two spheres lay a neutral zone running across the centre of the country. This economic partition was arbitrarily made without consulting Persia, and that unfortunate country found itself placed between two milestones of rapacious imperialism. Persia has, indeed, tried to revitalise herself. In 1906, there was nationalist upheaval and Shah was compelled to grant a Majlis or Parliament.

This was followed, two years later, by a revolution which dethroned the Shah and set up his youthful son in place on throne. The work of reform was resumed earnestly with vigour, but the Selfish policy of Russia and Britain probably made it difficult to achieve any considerable success.

In the Near East, economic imperialism was in full swing in Asiatic Turkey. Commercial treaties, known as "capitulations" insured to the foreigners extra-territorial rights and financial control. Russian aggression at the expense of Turkey was traditional and in the course of expansion in the Causcasion region, Russia, rounded off the eastern end of the Black sea and lot of territory and thought of controlling all Balkan States. France's interests were mainly financial, and were confined mostly to Syria. Britain was keenly interested in the control of Ottoman Empire as her communication with India lay across it. To these, interested powers was added towards the close of the 19th century. Germany who by posing as the political protector of Turkey, obtained very valuable commercial concessions. But her grand project was the Baghdad Railway, which, had it been materialised, would have opened Turkey to German exploitation both economically and politically. The project caused great uneasiness in the diplomatic circles of Europe and the Eastern Question seemed to regain its old importance. But the Great War came and changed the situation in Asiatic Turkey. Defeat of Turkey brought into existence Iraq, Syria, Israel, Jordan, Lebnan and South Arabia etc. into world stage.

SOCIALISM

Origin: Middle class rule superceded the domination of the aristocracy of the old regime. The middle class demanded written constitutions, in order that political arbitrary interference by absolute monarchs and against the aspirations of the lower class. When the new governments were established, legislation restricting business enterprises was abolished and little if anything was done to improve conditions of the workers. Socialism was the proletariat's answer to the restrictions imposed upon them by middle class rule. The socialist idea of political organization has many variations ranging from legislative reform without disturbing the political structure of the state to a general overthrow of existing governments and the establishment of a political order controlled by the workers.

The root of socialism can be traced to the French Revolution, when all sorts of ideas for the reconstruction of society were born. Babeuf, the "Father of Socialism", advocated compulsory nationalization of wealth, social equality and abolition of property. He observed:

"When I see the poor without the clothing and shoes which they themselves are engaged in making and contemplate the small minority who don't work and yet want for nothing, I am convinced that government is still the old conspiracy of the few against the many, only it takes a new form."

Babeuf popularized his ideas through his own newspaper and through many popular songs that he sponsored. Charged with causing an uprising, he was arrested and executed in 1797.

Utopian Socialism: A group of idealists, including Saint-Simon, Omen, and Fourier, sponsored what has been called Utopian socialism named after Sir Thomas More's social groups into large, family like organizations in order that the unit could live together. Own's experiments at New Lanark in England to which we have referred and at New Harmony in Indians are examples. Saint-Simon (1760-1825), one of the many Frenchmen who fought in the American Revolution under Washington, spent a fortune on an unsuccessful social experiment. He advocated common ownership of all land and capital, to be managed scientifically by the state. His slogan was "From each according to his capacity and to each according to his need".

Fourier (1772-1837) believed that people should be divided into industrial communities consisting of about 1800 persons each. The earnings should be divided, after each citizen was given a stated sum, giving labour five parts, capital four and talent three parts of the remainder. Several attempts were made to carry out his plans. Book Form Colony in Massachusetts was such an experiment made in America. Greeley Hawthorne and Dana were prominent Americans interested in the scheme. The Christian socialist may be classed as Utopian socialists. They believed that the ideal society could be reached through the application of the principles of Christianity. The Utopian socialists had only a small following even among the working class. Their ideas were too theoretical and idealistic to be carried out but they did attract the attention of reformers to the need for change and thus indirectly accomplished great deal.

Decline: The Socialist movement had made little headway in England and in the European countries by the middle of the 19th century. Most of the experiments before that time had failed miserably. The leaders were theorists who dissatisfied with the existing conditions in society found satisfaction in planning idea Utopia in which property was held in the possible exception of own the socialists writers before Marx paid no attention to either of the questions as to how their experiment could be realised or how it could be made practicable. Most of them believed that mankind when informed of the virtues of their scheme, would flock to its support. In this, they were disappointed and because of that, their Plans, were discredited.

Karl Marx: Marx (1818-1883) was the founder of Scientific Socialism. He formulated his theory and then proceeded to sketch the kind of society that he desired. He provided the workingmen's organization with a social philosophy and a program for social reform. Marx had a varied career. After the collapse of the revolution in 1848, he was expelled from France and settled in London. He spent his life in writing and organizing workers throughout Europe.

Communist Manifesto and Das Kapital: The communist Manifesto, one of the most famous documents in the history of socialism was written by Marx and his co-worker, Frederick Engles (1820-1895) during the Paris Revolution of 1848. This was an impassioned appeal to the workers of Europe to write and throw off their chanis. Das Kapital was a much more detailed and scholarly work on the Socialist theory. Modern Scientific Socialism involved in the theory of value and the materialistic conception of history.

Surplus Value: Marx's Theory of value contends that labour is the source of value and that all wealth is produced by it. Labourers under the capitalistic system do not receive the total product. In fact they receive just enough for themselves and their families to live on, "a living wage". The "Surplus" wealth, which the capitalist receives is the difference between what labourers produce and what they receive. The appropriation of surplus value constitutes what Marx called the fundamental injustice of the modern industrial system. This, he believed was little short of a slave society. The workman works under a free contract that he voluntarily enters but as he is unprovided with the means of production he has no alternative except to sell his labour to the capitalist who pockets the proceeds after a meagre wage is paid.

Materialistic Conception of History: In his materialistic conception of history Marx explained the rise of the small privileged class. First he showed that the most determining factor in history is the interplay of economic forces. He believed in the, inevitability of a class war. In fact he contended that class war has existed in every period of history but that it became especially pronounced in the 18th and 19th centuries with the introduction of the factory system, where money, machines and industries are the chief sources of wealth. The capitalists drove the nobles from power and established a government dominated by bourgeois capitalists. Marx predicted that this capitalistic stage would pass and that the proletariat would rise to power and obtain the means of production. The victory of the proletariat would cause the complete alteration of the social structure and the abolition of all class distinction.

Importance of Marx's Influence: The influence of Marx would be difficult to over-estimate. The Russian Communist state was based upon his fundamental concepts and since its origin it has been a great influence on the proletariat. It predicts ultimate victory for the working class. Workers have a definite program and a definite assurance that in spite of temporary setbacks they will succeed. Almost every form of socialism leans heavily on the works of Marx for a program.

Fabian Socialism: Marxian Socialism as has been noted was distinctly revolutionary. It preached the inevitability of class war. Not all social-minded people were willing to go that far. An influential group which sponsored what is called evolutionary socialism was the Fabian Society in England. It was organized in 1884 with an aim for "the reorganization of society by the emancipation of land and industrial capital from individual and class ownership and vesting them in the community for the common benefit." The members were mainly journalists, artists, literary men and women, social workers and teachers. They took their name from the Roman general Quints Fabius whose tactics they copied in endeavoring to conquer by delay. They spread their propaganda through the publication of pamphlets, three quarters of a million were circulated within less than 10 years.

The Fabians, unlike Marx do not attack capital as being stolen funds of labour but admit that the capitalist has a useful part to play in society. The capitalists deserved a reward for the organization of industry but ultimately they should be superseded by paid employers. The Fabians believed that there were many values created wholly by the community which should be used not for private profit but for the benefit of the whole community. The instruments of production—railways, mines, roads and canals-should be utilized for the general welfare, instead of being exploited for the enrichment of a few.

Syndicalism: Another form of social control that attracts considerable attention is syndicalism. It is based on trade union organization which is considered to be the foundation of the new society and the means whereby it can be brought into existence. It accepts the Marxian theory of an inevitable struggle between capital and labour and proposes the abolition of private ownership of the means of production. This provides for a producer's control giving the workers charge of the economic and political affairs of the state. Syndicalism claims to be more the product of the workers than any other form of socialism and consequently is much more in conformity with their needs. Its efficiency is also emphasized. If workers own and control the industry in which they work, they will have a greater personal interest in the conduct of the plant and enjoy a greater amount of freedom than that offered by the capitalistic system.

Guild Socialism: Guild Socialism, which is closely associated with syndicalism, aimed at "the abolition of the wage system and the establishment of self-government in industry by the workers, through a democratic system of national guilds, working in conjunction with other democratic functional organizations in the community". The administration was not intended to be so democratic as the other forms of socialism. Power and responsibility in the importance of the work that the individuals perform. Guild Socialists believed that industry should be supervised by technical experts and not by unskilled workmen. Furthermore, the interests of the consumer were to be taken into consideration. Thus, they proposed to guarantee through consumer's councils, which, acting in cooperation with producers guilds would fix prices and control the distribution of goods.

Anarchism: The most radical form of socialism is anarchism. Originally, the anarchists were affiliated with the communists, but they were expelled in 1869 at the fourth congress of the First International. Under the leadership of Bakunin (1814-1876) and Kropatkin (1842-1921), a separate organization was formed. They preached the destruction of existing governments.

MULTIPLE CHOICE QUESTIONS

1. The Indus Valley Civilisation is
   (a) About ten thousand years old
   (b) Seven thousand years old
   (c) Five thousand years old
   (d) Three thousand years old
2. The biggest building at Mohenjo-daro was the:
   (a) Assembly Hall
   (b) Great Bath
   (c) Rectangular Building
   (d) Great Granary
3. Name the city which had houses with entrances on the main street.
   (a) Kalibangan (b) Lothal
   (c) Mohenjo-daro (d) Chanhu-daro
4. Find out the most acceptable cause that made the Harappans move away from their urban settlements.
   (a) Ecological changes
   (b) Foreign invasion
   (c) Demographic changes
   (d) Hydrological changes
5. (A): In comparison to the Egyptians and Sumerians, Indus people made limited use of their script and languages.
   (R): The 'pictographic' script of the Indus people is derived partly from the 'Cuneiform' writing of the Sumerians and partly from the 'Hieroglyphics' of the Egyptians.
   (a) Both (A) and (R) are correct and (R) explains (A).
   (b) Both (A) and (R) are correct but (R) does not explain (A).
   (c) (A) is correct but (R) is not.
   (d) (A) is wrong but (R) is not.
6. Harappan people had a common burial system which is proved by:
   (a) The earth burials with head of the dead normally laid towards the north.
   (b) The burial of commonly used items with the dead.
   (c) Both (a) and (b) above.
   (d) The burial of the dead body in the sitting posture.
7. Pair the Harappan settlements with the banks of rivers on which they were located:

	Sites		Banks of Rivers
A.	Lothal	I.	Indus
B.	Kalibangan	II.	Sutlej
C.	Ropar	III.	Ravi
D.	Harappa	IV.	Ghaggar
E.	Mohenjo-daro	V.	Bhogava

	A	B	C	D	E
(a)	V	IV	II	III	I
(b)	II	V	I	IV	III
(c)	IV	V	II	III	I
(d)	V	IV	III	II	I

8. Four largest Harappan settlements in the Indo-Pak subcontinent are
   (i) Harappa (ii) Mohenjo-daro
   (iii) Ganeriwala (iv) Dholavira
   (v) Kalibangan
   (a) (i), (ii), (iv) and (v)
   (b) (i), (ii), (iii) and (iv)
   (c) (ii), (iii), (iv) and (v)
   (d) (i), (iii), (iv) and (v)
9. Which of the following birds was worshipped by the Harappan people?
   (a) Crow (b) Peacock
   (c) Pigeon (d) Eagle
10. Match the following ancient sites with their respective archaeological findings:

	Sites		Findings
A.	Lothal	1	Ploughed field
B.	Kalibangan	2.	Dockyard
C.	Dholvira	3.	Terracotta replica of a plough

D. Banwali 4. An inscription comprising ten large sized signs of the Harappan script.

	A	B	C	D
(a)	1	2	3	4
(b)	2	1	4	3
(c)	1	2	4	3
(d)	2	1	3	4

11. Which of the following was the most important industry of the Harappans at Lothal and Chanhudaro?
(a) Ship building (b) Bead making
(c) Weaving (d) Metallurgy

12. The Indus Valley people used lime and expensive burnt bricks instead of sun dried bricks, because of
(a) Advanced technology
(b) Better planning
(c) A moist climate on account of the close proximity of the civilisation to the river valleys.
(d) Their knowledge of the manufacture of lime.

13. The Indus Valley Civilisation specialised in
(a) Town Planning (b) Architecture
(c) Craftsmanship (d) All of these

14. The Indus religion did not include the worship of
(a) Forces of Nature.
(b) Mother Goddess.
(c) Certain animal chimeras and their anthropic figures.
(d) Trees and their spirits.

15. How many granaries are there in Harappa?
(a) Six (b) Four
(c) Eight (d) Seven

16. The largest number of Harappan sites in post-independence India have been discovered in
(a) Rajasthan
(b) Punjab and Haryana
(c) N.W. Uttar Pradesh
(d) Gujarat

17. Which of the following was not the likely purpose of the Great Bath in the citadel at Mohenjo-daro?
(a) Swimming exercises and water sports.
(b) Some elaborate ritual of vital importance, including a corporate social life.
(c) Storage of water to be used during drought or emergency.
(d) Community bathing.

18. In most of the Indus seals, there is representation of:
(a) Tiger
(b) Elephant
(c) Humped bull
(d) Humpless bull or unicorn bull

19. No trace of ______ has been found in the Indus Valley Civilisation.
(a) Sugarcane (h) Mustard
(c) Sesamum (d) Barley

20. The number of seals which constitute the primary source of knowing the Civilization of the Indus Valley people is about:
(a) 1,000 (b) 2,000
(c) 3,000 (d) 4,000

21. The three prominent characteristics of the Indus Valley sites are :
(a) I. Baked bricks and pottery
II. Highly organised drainage and sewage system
III. Town planning
(b) I. Sun dried bricks
II. Artificial irrigation
III. Elaborate sewage system
(c) I. Burial sites
II. Furniture and pottery
III. Remains of houses and other buildings
(d) I. Script
II. Ceramic evidence
III. Town planning

22. In the Bronze Age Civilizations, which of the civilization covered the largest area?
(a) Indus Valley (b) Sumerian
(c) Minoan (d) Crete

23. The expansion of archaeological research has recovered within the century, over a dozen buried civilizations. Which among of the following were the contemporaries of the Indus Civilization yet distinctive from each other

(a) Greek, Sumerian and Minoan
(b) Sumerian, Egypt and Mesopotamia
(c) Mohanjodaro, Sutkagendor
(d) Chanhudaro and Amri

24. Which of the following does not relate to Carnelian beads?
(a) According to available information they were not made anywhere in the contemporary world.
(b) Lothal and Chanhudaro were the main production centres.
(c) It helps to chronologically point out the middle Bronze Age.
(d) It was found in Mesopotamia and Susa.

25. On what basis has the time span of the Harappan Civilization now been fixed between 2300 B.C. and 1750 B.C.?
(a) Radio-carbon dating (C-14)
(b) Details of links between the Harappan Civilization and the ancient civilizations of West Asia and Harappan Civilization.
(c) Latest findings in Rajasthan, Gujarat, Chandigarh, Haryana, Madhya Pradesh etc.
(d) Common pottery designs and other antiques.

26. What is the distinguishing feature of the Harappan Civilization from other contemporary civilizations of the World?
(a) Development of science and technology.
(b) Uniform weights and measures and commercial contacts.
(c) Religious beliefs and social life.
(d) Town planing, drainage and sanitation.

27. A Yogi of the Harappan seals wearing a three horned cap and surrounded by animals has been identified with:
(a) Rudra (b) Murugan
(c) Mahayogeshwar (d) Pasupati Shiva

28. Which of the following Vedas was the earliest composition?
(a) Rigveda (b) Samaveda
(c) Yajurveda (d) Atharvaveda

29. The Veda which is partly a prose work is:
(a) Atharvaveda (b) Samaveda
(c) Yajurveda (d) Rigveda

30. In the Vedic period, the people called *Panis*. were:
(a) Those who controlled trade
(b) Cattle-breeders
(c) Cowherds
(d) Ploughmen

31. What did the term *niyoga* stand for in the Vedic society?
(a) The performance of Vedic sacrifices by a woman independently
(b) The vow of celibacy taken by a woman of aristocratic society
(c) Cohabitation of a childless widow with her husband's brother until the birth of a son
(d) Symbolic self-immolation of a widow at the death of her husband

32. Match the following Vedic gods with their actual status or functions :
A. Pushan B. Savitri
C. Aditi D. Dyaus
I. God of heaven and father of Surya
II. Mother of Surya
III. God of light
IV. God of marriages

	A	B	C	D
(a)	(IV)	(III)	(II)	(I)
(b)	(IV)	(II)	(III)	(I)
(c)	(II)	(III)	(IV)	(I)
(d)	(I)	(II)	(III)	(IV)

33. The famous Vedic saying, "War begins in the minds of men", is stated in the
(a) Rigveda
(b) Samaveda
(c) Atharvaveda
(d) Mundaka Upanishad

34. Which of the following was not one of the reasons for the gradual weakening of the tribal assemblies in the later Vedic period?
(a) Increase in the royal power.
(b) In large territorial states ordinary people could not travel long distances to attend their meetings.
(c) The assemblies acquired an aristocratic character which took away most of their effectiveness.
(d) They also surrendered some of their activities to the new officials called *ratnins*.

35. Among the various units of the tribal kingdom (rashtra) of the Vedic society, which one of the following was the basic unit?
(a) *Vish* (b) *Jana*
(c) *Kula* (d) *Grama*

36. Which of the following statements about the system of taxation and revenue administration in the Later Vedic period is *NOT* correct?
(a) Settled life and stable agriculture led to the production of surplus which could be collected by the king in the form of taxes.
(b) The king received regular contributions from the people in the shape of *bali* and *shulka*
(c) One-sixth of the produce of the land was payable to the king
(d) An official called *bhagadugha* collected the royal share of the produce.

37. In the Vedic Age
(a) polygamy was unknown
(b) child marriage became prominent
(c) widows could remarry
(d) hypergamy was allowed

38. Which of the following is/are matched correctly?
I. *Samaveda*—melody.
II. *Athrvaveda*—mainly magical spells.
III. *Aranyakas*—forest books.
IV. *Srauta Sutra*—ceremonies of domestic life.
(a) I and III (b) II and III
(c) I, II and III (d) I, III and IV

39. Name the Rig Vedic god who is believed to be the upholder of the "*Rita*" or Cosmic order.
(a) Agni (b) Soma
(c) Indra (d) Varuna

40. 'Sruti' literature does not include the
(a) *Vedangas* (b) *Brahmanas*
(c) *Upanishads* (d) *Aranyakas*

41. Where do we find the mention of the Eastern and the Western Seas for the first time?
(a) *Aithareya Brahmana*
(b) *Kausitaki Brahmana*
(c) *Taittiriya Brahmana*
(d) *Satapatha Brahmana*

42. Which varna comprised mainly the common mass in the Vedic period?
(a) Brahmins (b) Kshatriyas
(c) Shudras (d) Vaishyas

43. The earliest tribal assembly was
(a) *Gana* (b) *Vidhata*
(c) *Samiti* (d) *Sabha*

44. Where does the term *Gotra* occur for the first time?
(a) Sama Veda (b) Rig Veda
(c) Atharva Veda (d) Yajur Veda

45. Which part of the Vedic literature narrates about the passage of human soul from life to life?
(a) *Brahmanas* (b) *Samhitas*
(c) *Upanishads* (d) *Aranyakas*

46. Social rituals and *Samaskaras* from conception to cremation have been mentioned in the
(a) *Grihya Sutras* (b) *Upanishads*
(c) *Dharma Sutras* (d) *Strauta-Sutras*

47. Name the sage who is believed to have Aryanised South India.
(a) Vashishtha (b) Agastya
(c) Yagyavalkya (d) Vishwamitra

48. The four-fold division of society is expressly mentioned in
(a) *Satapatha Brahmana*
(b) *Purusa-sukta of Rigveda*
(c) *Yajurveda*
(d) *Hiranyagarbha-sukta*

49. Which is the most accepted date of the composition of the Rig veda?
(a) 1500 BC (b) 1500 B.C. to 1000 BC
(c) 1000 BC (d) About 4500 BC

50. Which of the following was NOT a result of the Aryan invasion?
(a) Emergence of predominantly agrarian economy.
(b) Emergence of caste system based on specialisation in particular crafts or branch of knowledge.
(c) Opening of new geographic areas.
(d) Discovery of the rich iron deposits in Magadha leading to great improvement in technology.

51. Identify the wrong statement about the concept of kingship in the later Vedic period.
(a) The king was to be a Kshatriya
(b) A glamour was created around the king and in the ritualism he was sometimes also represented as a god
(c) Kingship became hereditary
(d) A class alliance developed between the priests and the warriors

52. Which of the following descriptions of the Later Vedic officials is NOT correct?
(a) *Kshattri*-Chamberlain.
(b) *Sangrahitri*-Treasurer.
(c) *Bhagadugha*-Collection of taxes.
(d) *Rajanya*-Clerks.

53. To whom is the Gayatri Mantra dedicated?
(a) Savitri (A solar deity)
(b) Surya (Sun)
(c) Soma (God of the intoxicating juice)
(d) Maruts (Storm Gods)

54. The Rig veda Samhita devotes one fourth of its hymns to:
(a) Indra (b) Maruts
(c) Rudra (d) Agni

55. Match the following

Terms	Meaning
A. *Vapta*	1. Milker of the cow, referring to daughter.
B. *Goghna*	2. Cow-killer, referring to guest.
C. *Suta*	3. Not to be killed, referring to cow.
D. *Aghanva*	4. Barber
E. *Duhitri*	5. Charioteer

(a) A-4, B-2, C-5, D-3, E-l
(b) A-5, B-1, C-3, D-2, E-4
(c) A-1, B-5, C-2, D-4, E-3
(d) A-3, B-4, C-I, D-5, E-2

56. Match the following:

1. *Yoga*	A. Patanjali
2. *Nyaya*	B. Gautama
3. *Sankhya*	C. Kapila
4. *Uttara Mimansa or Vedanta*	D. Badarayana
5. *Vaisesika*	E. Kanda
6. *Purva Mimansa*	F. Jamini

(a) 1-E, 2-F, 3-A, 4-D, 5-B, 6-C
(b) 1-B, 2-A, 3-F, 4-E, 5-C, 6-D
(c) 1-F, 2-D, 3-E, 4-C, 5-B, 6-A
(d) 1-A, 2-B, 3-C, 4-D, 5-E, 6-F

Instructions : In questions 57 and 58, (A) stands for Assertion and (R) stands for Reason. Write (a) if only (A) is correct; (b) if only (R) is correct (c) if both (A) and (R) are correct and (R) explains (A); and (d) if both (A) and (R) are correct but (R) does not explain (A).

57. Assertion (A) : The pivotal theme of *Upanishads* is "Tat-Tvam-Asi" i.e. Brahman is 'Atman' and 'Atman' is Brahman.
Reason (R) : *Upanishads* express a strong reaction against cults, rituals and priestly domination of later Vedic age.

58. Assertion (A) : Aryans were literate people even before they came to India.
Reason (R) : Probably, since 700 BC, Aryans started using a script.

59. *Upanishads* are books on
(a) religion (b) philosophy
(c) yoga (d) law

60. The tribal nature of the Rig Vedic society is evident from frequent occurrence of various terms which stand for kin-based units such as·
(a) *Jana, vis, grama, kula, sardha*
(b) *Rathakara, taksan*
(c) *Gomat, gavesana, gopati*
(d) *Mahajanapada*

61. Match the following

Terms		Meaning
A. *Girha*	I	Early Vedic tribes
B. *Gramin*	II	Important member of royal entourage
C. *Vis*	III	Pivot of Rig Vedic society
D. *Druhyas*	IV	Kin-based units of Rig Vedic Society

	A	B	C	D
(a)	III	II	IV	I
(b)	I	II	III	IV
(c)	II	III	IV	I
(d)	IV	III	II	I

62. Which of the following *Vedangas* contains the *Srauta, Grahya* and *Dharma Sutras*?

(a) Shiksha (b) Kalpa
(c) Nirukta (d) Chhanda

63. Which of the following *mahajanapadas* is/are NOT mentioned in the *Anguttara Nikaya* ?

I. Sibi II. Basarna
III. Gandhara IV. Kamboja
(a) I and II (b) I and III
(c) II only (d) I only

64. Match the following lists of *Mahajanapadas* and their locations:

List I (Mahajanapadas)	**List II (Location)**
A. Vajji	1. Vaishali
B. Vatsa	2. Bundelkhand
C. Chedi	3. Kosam
D. Anga	4. Bhagalpur

(a) A-1, B-2, C-3, D-4
(b) A-1, B-3, C-2, D-4
(c) A2, B-1, C-4, D-2
(d) A-3, B-2, C-4, D-1

65. Which of the following *janapadas* was known for cotton textile/es and a horse market?

(a) Magadha (b) Anga
(c) Kashi (d) Kosala

66. Who of the following kings was a friend of Gautam Buddha?

(a) Prasenajita (b) Bimbisar
(c) Sisupal (d) Ajatsatru

67. Which amongst the following *mahajanpadas* is referred to as *Ganasanga* in contemporary literary works ?

(a) Vajjis (b) Avanti
(c) Surasena (d) Asmaka

68. In which of the following years did Alexander invade India ?

(a) 317 BC (b) 326 BC
(c) 321 BC (d) 320 BC

69. Match the following lists of *mahajanapadas* and their capitals:

List I (Mahajanapadas)	**List II (Capitals)**
A. Gandhara	1. Taxila
B. Kamboja	2. Rajpur
C. Asmaka	3. Potana
D. Saurasena	4. Mathura

(a) A-1, B-2, C-3, D-4
(b) A-2, B-1, C-3, D-4
(c) A-1, B-2, C-4, D-3
(d) A-2, B-3, C-1, D-4

70. Matsya *mahajanapada* covered

(a) Alwar, Bharatpur and Jaipur in Rajasthan
(b) Munger and Bhagalpur in Bihar
(c) Faizabad, Gonda and Bahraich in Uttar Pradesh
(d) Rohilkhand and part of Central Doab in Uttar Pradesh

71. Which of the following is NOT true about republics in the sixth century BC?

(a) Every tribal oligarch claimed a share in revenues from peasants
(b) Every tribal oligarch was free to maintain his own little army
(c) Rublics functioned under the leadership of the oligarchic assemblies
(d) Brahmanas had a considerable influence in the republics.

72. Bimbisara, under whom Magadh emerged as a major territorial power in the sixth century BC, belonged to

(a) Maurya dynasty
(b) Haryanka dynasty
(c) Sisunaga dynasty
(d) Nanda dynasty

73. Consider the following points :

I. Advantageous geographical location
II. Availability of natural resources
III. Use of elephants on a large scale in wars
IV. Unorthodox character of the society

Which of the above were the factors that led to prominence of the Magadha empire in the sixth century BC?

(a) I, II and III (b) I and II
(c) I, II and IV (d) I, II, III and IV

74. Who of the following were the first non-kshatriya rulers?

(a) Haryankas (b) Sisunagas
(c) Nandas (d) Mauryas

75. Who amongst the following Iranian rulers was the first to invade India in 518 BC ?

(a) Darius (b) Kadphises I
(c) Kadphises II (d) Gondophernes

76. Which of the following were the effects of Persian invasion on India ?
(a) Introduction of Aramic form of writing
(b) Opening of a new sea route
(c) Promotion to Indo-Iranian trade
(d) All of the above

77. Which of the following was NOT an outcome of Alexander's invasion in 326 BC?
(a) Establishment of direct contact between India and Greece in different fields
(b) Promotion to expansion of the Mauryan empire in north-west India
(c) Opening up of four distinct routes between India and Greece.
(d) Development of Kharoshthi script.

78. Match the following :

	Buddhist Council	**Places**
A.	First	1. Pataliputra
B.	Second	2. Vaisali
C.	Third	3. Rajagriha
D.	Fourth	4. Kashmir

(a) A-3, B-2, C-l, D-4
(b) A-2, B-3, D-4, C-1
(c) A-2, B-1, C-3, D-4
(d) A-4, B-3, C-2, D-1

79. Identify the place which is said to be the birth place of Buddhism.
(a) Rajagriha (b) Kusinagara
(c) Lumbini (d) Sarnath

80. Who were the first teachers of the Buddha, after his great renunciation?
(a) Alar and Udraka
(b) Ananda and Ashvaghosh
(c) Sariputra and Maudagalyayana
(d) Alara and Kalam

81. Which of the following is not a biography of Lord Buddha?
(a) *Lalitavistara* (b) *Mahavastu*
(c) *Nidankatha* (d) *Mahavamsa*

82. Which of the following was added to the Buddhist cannonical texts by the Fourth Buddhist Council?
(a) *Dhammapada*
(b) *Jatakas*
(c) Vibhashas or commentaries
(d) *Kathavatthu Prakarana*

83. During the reign of which of the following kings did Mahayanism formally come into existence?
(a) Ajatashatru (b) Dharmpala
(c) Ashoka (d) Kanishka

84. Zen Buddhism, introduced in the twelfth century AD, found its adherents mainly among the warriors and influenced Japanese culture considerably. The key to enlightenment, according to Zen Buddhism, is:
(a) Recollection (b) Virtuous life
(c) Meditation (d) Piety

85. Which of the following statements correctly describes the difference between a *chaitya* and a *stupa*?
(a) *Chaitya* is a religious term, while *stupa* is an architectural term for a mound containing a relic of the Buddha and later on of leading Buddhist saints
(b) *Chaitya* is a place of prayer/worship, while stupa is a funeral monument
(c) *Chaityas* were constructed by the monasteries while stupas were constructed by the king and the rich merchants
(d) *Chaityas* represent Mahayanism while stupas represent Hinayanism.

86. Find out the number of stories included in the Jatakas?
(a) 750 (b) 320
(c) 860 (d) 500

87. Which of the following is known as the Turning of the Wheel of Law (*Dharmachakrapravartana*)?
(a) The practice of setting the wheel in motion everyday in the morning in the *Sanghas*.
(b) The first sermon preached by the Buddha at the Deer Park at Sarnath.
(c) The continuous existence of human beings like the wheel of causes and effects.
(d) The extinction of *Karma* leading to the achievement of nirvana.

88. Match the following :

	List I	**List II**
1.	Rahul	A. Buddha's father
2.	Alara Kalam	B. Buddha's cousin
3.	Suddhodhana	C. Buddha's son

4.	Devadatta	D.	The sage who taught meditation to Buddha.
5.	Siddharta	E.	Buddha's original name.

(a) 1-A, 2-E, 3-D, 4-B, 5-C
(b) 1-C, 2-D, 3-A, 4-B, 5-E
(c) 1-E, 2-D, 3-B, 4-A, 5-C
(d) 1-B, 2-A, 3-E, 4-D, 5-C

89. Which of the following was NOT one of the "Three Jewels" of Buddhism.
(a) Buddha (b) Ahimsa
(c) Dhamma (d) Sangha

90. Bring out the correct statement regarding the first Buddhist Council.
(i) Ananda and Upali laid down the *Sutta Pitaka* and *Vinaya Pitaka* respectively.
(ii) Its proceedings were conducted in Sanskrit.
(iii) It was held during the lifetime of Buddha.
(iv) Its main purpose was to maintain the purity of Buddha's teachings.
(a) i and iv (b) All of them
(c) i and ii (d) ii, iii, iv

91. The first Buddhist nun was
(a) Gautami (b) Mahamaya
(c) Yasodhara (d) Sujata

92. The first *Tirthankara*, according to Jaina tradition, was
(a) Hemchandra (b) Rishabha
(c) Sthulabahu (d) Augisara

93. Which of the following is NOT among the 'three ratnas' or gems of Jainism?
(a) Full knowledge (b) Action
(c) Liberation (d) Belief in God

94. What was the name of the Jaina monk under whose leadership a large Jain community migrated from Magadha (South Bihar) to Shravanabelagola in Karnataka in the fourth century BC?
(a) Nagarjuna (b) Samghadasa
(c) Haribhadra (d) Bhadrabahu

95. Which of the following were NOT one of the royal patrons of Jainism?
(a) Satvahanas
(b) Gangas
(c) Chalukyas of Gujarat
(d) Rashtrakutas

96. Which of the following issues led to the split of Jainism into two sects, namely, *Digambaras* and *Shvetambaras*?
(a) Interpretation of certain philosophical canons
(b) Compilation of the teachings of Mahavira
(c) Whether or not the monks should wear clothes
(d) Idol worship

97. Which of the following pairs of Jain religious texts and their contents is NOT correctly matched?
(a) *Angas*-explain the Jain doctrines through big ends.
(b) Chheda sutras-explain the rules of discipline of the monastic order.
(c) *Mulasutras*-deal with the basic doctrines of Jainism.
(d) *Prakimas*-deal with monastic order of the nuns.

98. At which of the following places did Mahavira's death take place?
(a) Kusinagara (b) Vaishali
(c) Rajagriha (d) Pava

99. Find out the point which was not a similarity between Buddhism and Jainism.
(a) Both had equal faith in *ahimsa*.
(b) Both believed in the Law of Doctrine or Karma.
(c) Both accepted followers without any caste distinction.
(d) Both were agnostic and rejected the Vedic thoughts.

100. The real founder of Jainism was:
(a) Vardhaman Mahavira
(b) Neminath
(c) Parsvanath
(d) Rishabhanath

101. Match the following

List I	List II
1. Gosala	A. Leader of the *Digambaras* Maskariputra
2. Bhadrabahu	B. A Jaina monk for whom a huge statue was installed at Shravanabelagola
3. Bahubali	C. Chairman of the second (Gomateswara) Jaina Council

4. Devardhi	D. Leader of the *Svetambaras* (Kshamasraman)
5. Sthulabahu	E. Colleague of Mahavira for six years during his wandering.

(a) I -E, 2-A, 3-B, 4-C, 5-D
(b) I-A, 2-C, 3-D, 4-E, 5-B
(c) I-A, 2-B, 3-C, 4-D, 5-E
(d) I-B, 2-C, 3-A, 4-D, 5-E

102. Arrange in chronological order the following Incarnations:
(i) Vamana or Dwarf
(ii) Kurma or Tortoise
(iii) Varaha or Boar
(iv) Narasimha or Man-Lion
(v) Matsya or Fish
(a) i, ii, v, iii, iv (b) iii, v, i, iv, ii
(c) ii, i, iv, iii, v (d) v, ii, iii, iv, i

103. Name the earliest known follower of Bhagavatism.
(a) Demetrius (b) Antialkidas
(c) Megasthenese (d) Heliodorus

104. The traces of the Bhagavata cult is not found in the:
(a) *Upanishads* (b) *Brahmanas*
(c) *Puranas* (d) *Epics*

105. Arrange the Avatars in the chronological order.
(i) Rama (ii) Kelkin
(iii) Krishna (iv) Buddha
(v) Parasurama
(a) v, i, iii, iv, ii (b) ii, iv, i, iii, v
(c) v, iv, ii, iii, i (d) i, ii, iii, v, iv

106. What was the other name for "Tevaram"?
(a) Dravida Veda (b) Pattapattu
(c) Prabhandhas (d) Ettatogai

107. Where did Buddha attain enlightenment?
(a) Lumbini (b) Sarnath
(c) Bodh Gaya (d) Kusinagara

108. The sacred books of Jains are called:
(a) *Agama-Sidhanta*
(b) *Angas*
(c) *Parvas*
(d) *Upangas*

109. Who wrote *Milanda-panho*?
(a) Buddhadutta (b) Nagasena
(c) Buddaghosha (d) Kautilya

110. Among the 12 *Angas*, which was the most important?
(a) Second (b) Fifth
(c) Sixth (d) First

111. The Jainas have an extensive poetic literature called *Charitras* and *Prabandhas*. What aspect does the *Charitras* deal with?
(a) The stories of Tirthankarar and mystical sages.
(b) The story of Jaina monks and laymen who flourished at that time.
(c) The characteristics that all monks should necessarily acquire.
(d) It contains Jaina doctrines.

112. Who was responsible for the revival of Brahmanical Hinduism?
(a) Kautilya (b) Harshavardhana
(c) Bijjala (d) Shankaracharya

113. Which is the source material that has the first reference to Sage Krishna, son of Devaki, as a disciple of Rishi Ghora?
(a) *Chandogya Upanishad*
(b) *Purana*
(c) *Bhagvad Gita*
(d) *Angas*

114. Match the following terms :

List I	**List II**
A. *Nivritti*	I. Prescribing perfection of all duties
B. *Pravritti*	II. Withdrawal from all actions
C. *Samnyasa*	III. Self purification
D. *Atma-siddhi*	IV. Detachment in action

	A	B	C	D
(a)	I	II	III	IV
(b)	II	I	IV	III
(c)	III	IV	II	I
(d)	IV	III	I	II

115. Identify correctly the following terms :

List I	**List II**
A. Upasaka	I. Monk
B. Bhikshu	II. Lay disciple
C. Samgha	III. Eight-fold Path
D. Ashtangika-marga	IV. Community of Buddhist monks

	A	B	C	D
(a)	I	II	III	IV
(b)	II	I	IV	III
(c)	IV	III	II	I
(d)	III	IV	II	I

116. 'The torch that would dispel the gloom of misery and ignorance was lighted at Gaya under the Holy tree'. Whom is the author referring to?
(a) Buddha (b) Mahavira
(c) Asoka (d) Krishna

117. Which of the following is true with regard to common points in Buddhism and Jainism?
(a) Hinayanism accepted the fundamental doctrines of the old school. The Mahayanism introduced the concept of image worship as also the deification of Buddha.
(b) *Hinayanists* regarded salvation of individuals as the goal; whereas *Mehayanists* emphasised on the salvation of all beings.
(c) The school of *Hinayanism* stated that the path to salvation was through observance of the prescribed moral precepts. The Mahayanism school differed and laid stress on worship of Buddha and Bodhisattvas.
(d) High and lower castes were allowed as devotees.

118. Buddhist literary texts attach importance to a Buddhist overseas mission. To which place was the mission sent?
(a) Java (b) Sumatra
(c) Malaysia (d) Sri Lanka

119. Jaina is a derivative from
(a) Jina 'the conqueror' which refers to Mahavira.
(b) From the want to live.
(c) It is taken from the name of the last Tirthankar.
(d) It is a term that was freshly coined by Mahavira.

120. Vardhamana was said to have attained Nirvana under the
(a) Sal tree (b) Pipal tree
(c) Neem tree (d) Banyan tree

121. During his lifetime, Mahavira's teachings were confined to the Ganga Valley. But in later centuries, they spread to many regions. Which of the following was not such region?
(a) Gujarat (b) Rajasthan
(c) Karnataka (d) West Bengal

122. There is evidence to show that Vishnu cult spread overseas in the early centuries of the Christian era. Which was the place that this cult spread to?
(a) Greece (b) Cambodia
(c) Thailand (d) China

123. In all how many Buddhist Councils were held?
(a) Four (b) Three
(c) Two (d) One

124. One of the edicts discovered in 1915, which gave the name of its author as King Ashoka, Priyadarsi, is:
(a) Mansehra Edict (b) Girnar Edict
(c) Maski Edict (d) Sarnath Inscription

125. When and by whom were the Ashokan inscription and their Brahmi script deciphered for the first time?
(a) 1787-John Tower
(b) 1810-Harry Smith
(c) 1825-Charles Metcalfe
(d) 1837-James Prinsep

126. The Ashoka Major Rock Edicts which tell us about the Sangam Kingdom include rock edict
(a) I and X (b) I and XI
(c) II and XIII (d) II and XIV

127. Which of the following statements about the guilds of the artisans of the Mauryan period are true?
(i) They came into existence for the first time during the Mauryan period.
(ii) Their members enjoyed certain rights and performed certain duties as well.
(iii) Wages of their members were determined according to both the quality and the quantity of work.
(iv) Fines and penalties were given for inferior or fraudulent work.

Select the correct answers from codes given below:
(a) i, ii and iii (b) ii, iii and iv
(c) i, iii and iv (d) All of them

128. During the Mauryan period, the state did not have the monopoly of:
(a) Mines and forests
(b) Pearl fisheries
(c) Ferries and bridges
(d) Slaughter houses and gambling houses

Instructions: For answering the questions from 129 to 131, read the following instructions carefully:
Mark (a) if both "Assertion" (A) and "Reason" (R) are correct, and if 'R' is the correct explanation or justification for 'A'
Mark (b) if both 'A' and 'R' are correct, but 'R' is not the correct explanation or justification for 'A';
Mark (c) if only 'A' is correct; and
Mark (d) if only 'R' is correct.

129. Assertion (A) : Under Bindusara, the Mauryan empire came to consist of even the southernmost parts of India.
Reason (R) : The early Tamil texts mention the Mauryan invasion of the far south, including Tamil Nadu and Kerala.

130. Assertion (A) : During the Mauryan period, even the kings faced great amount of insecurity.
Reason (R) : According to Megasthenese, Chandragupta Maurya did not sleep for two nights successively in the same bed room.

131. Assertion (A) : Ashoka made repeated references to the concept of "Svarga" and styled himself as the "Devanampriya".
Reason (R) : Ashoka's *Dhamma* was nothing but reformed Brahmanism.

132. In which of the following Major Rock Edicts does Asoka introduce the institution of *dhamma-mahamatta* for the first time?
(a) Rock Edict II (b) Rock Edict III
(c) Rock Edict IV (d) Rock Edict V

133. Unfortunately; the original document of Megasthenese's Indica has not survived and what remains are only quotations from it in various classical texts. Which of the following was not one of the later Greek writers to quote from Megasthenese?
(a) Pliny (b) Strabo
(c) Diodorus (d) Arrian

134. Who credited Bindusara with conquering the "land between the two seas"?
(a) Kautilya (b) Megasthenese
(c) Visakhadatta (d) Taranath

135. Name the Ceylonese ruler who is believed to have modelled himself on the lines of Ashoka?
(a) Tissa (b) Ranasinghe
(c) Veerasinghe (d) Mahabali

136. Name the class which is conspicuous by its absence from the list of seven classes given by Megasthenese.
(a) Artisans (b) Cultivators
(c) Traders (d) Philosophers

137. Name the Major Rock Edict of Ashoka that explains and summarises the "Dhamma".
(a) Fifth (b) Eleventh
(c) Twelfth (d) Thirteenth

138. There are______spokes in the "Dhamma Chakra".
(a) Twenty (b) Twenty two
(c) Twenty-four (d) Thirty

139. Name the Buddhist stupa which is believed to have been originally built in brick by Ashoka.
(a) Barhut Stupa (b) Nalanda Stupa
(c) Sanchi Stupa (d) Amravati Stupa

140. Find out the incorrect statements about Megasthenese's *Indica.*
(i) It divided Mauryan society into seven classes.
(ii) The original form of Indica has come down to us.
(iii) It has given information about the prevalence of slavery and usury in India during the Mauryan period.
(iv) The details of the military administration of Mauryas and the account of the urban life has been narrated by Megasthenese.
(a) ii and iii (b) i and iii
(c) ii and iv (d) i and iv

141. Name the animals represented on the abacus of the capital of the Sarnath Pillar of Ashoka.
(i) Horse (ii) Bull
(iii) Lion (iv) Elephant
(v) Tiger
(a) i, ii, iii, iv (b) i, ii, iii, iv, v
(c) iii, iv, vi (d) ii, iv, v, iv

142. The Mauryan silver coin was called
(a) Nishka (b) Pana
(b) Shatamana (d) Kakini

143. Identify the conspicuous difference in the message of the Pillar Edicts as compared to the Rock Edicts.
(a) There is a hint of fanaticism about dhamma and of megalomania in the Pillar Edicts.
(b) Rock Edicts are addressed to common people and Pillar Edicts to the Buddhist order.
(c) The main stress in the Pillar Edicts is on social welfare measures
(d) The Pillar Edicts are mainly devoted to the moral aspects of *dhamma* and Ahsoka's attachment to Buddhism.

144. Identify the Mauryan king, who in his old age abdicated the throne and followed the Jain Saint Bhadrabahu to the South:
(a) Bindusara
(b) Samprati
(c) Chandragupta Maurya
(d) Dasharatha

145. The Rock Edicts of Ashoka were discovered in
(a) 13th century (b) 18th century
(c) 19th Century (d) 20th Century

146. Name the city which served as a meeting point for trade routes from east to west and from north to south.
(a) Ujjain (b) Kausambi
(c) Paithan (d) Mathura

147. Name the port which has been called as "Padouke" by the author of the *Periplus of the Erythrean Sea.*
(a) Paithan (b) Sopara
(c) Barbaricum (d) Arikamedu

148. Which of the following rulers did not belong to the Sunga dynasty?
(a) Bhagvata (b) Vasudeva
(c) Devabhuthi (d) Agnimitra

149. Find out the port where the largest Roman settlement and a Roman Factory have been discovered.
(a) Tamralipti (b) Muziris
(c) Arikamedu (d) Bharukachchha

150. Who was the court physician of Kanishka?
(a) Nagasena (b) Susruta
(c) Charaka (d) Asvagosha

151. Who was the founder of Sunga Dynasty?
(a) Pushyamitra (b) Agnimitra
(c) Devabhuthi (d) Kirtivarman

152. Several foreign kingdoms were carved out in the post Mauryan period. Which one of the following has been wrongly listed as a foreign kingdom?
(a) Bactrian-Greeks (b) Parthians
(c) Sakas (d) Vakatakas

153. According to the most commonly accepted view, Kanishka ascended the throne in
(a) 78 AD (b) 58 AD
(c) 125 AD (d) 248 AD

154. Who is the author of *Buddhacharita*?
(a) Banabhatta (b) Ashvagosha
(c) Parshava (d) Vasumitra

155. Which Satavahana ruler is credited with having increased the naval power of the empire which provided a fillip to trade with foreign countries?
(a) Hala
(b) Gautamiputra Satakarni
(d) Apilaka
(c) Vasishtiputra Sri Pulamayi

156. During the rule of the Satavahanas, India
(a) had trade relations with countries of South East Asia.
(b) had trade relations with western countries of Asia and with Europe.
(c) had trade relations only with Afghanistan and China
(d) did not have overseas trade.

157. Patanjali, the famous grammarian, was a contemporary of
(a) Agnimitra Sunga
(b) Pushyamitra Sunga
(c) Vasudev Kanva
(d) Gautamiputra Satakarni.

158. The founder of the Satavahana Dynasty is
(a) Simukha (b) Yajnasri Satakarni
(c) Pulamayi I (d) Sri Satakarni

159. Who were the first foreign rulers of North-Western India in the post-Mauryan period?
(a) Bacterian-Greeks (b) Sakas
(c) Kushanas (d) Parthians

160. The most famous Saka ruler in India was
(a) Nahapana (b) Rudradaman I
(c) Ushavadata (d) Ghamatika

161. Which of the following pair is wrongly matched?
(a) Sungas—Vidisha
(b) Satvahanas—Pratisthana
(c) Kanvas—Kausambi
(d) Kushanas—Purushapura

162. Which of the following is/are true about the Indo-Greeks?
I. They were the first rulers to issue gold coins in India.
II. They were the first to issue coins that can be definitely associated with particular dynasty.
III. They enabled fusion of Indian and Greek cultures in Gandhara in north-west which gave rise to new Graeco-Buddhist art or the Gandhara School of Art.
IV. A great schism took place within Buddhism during Indo-Greek period.
(a) All are true (b) I, II and IV
(c) I & II (d) I, II & III

163. Match the following:

List I (Kings)	**List II (Events)**
A. Gondophernes	1. Started Saka Era in 78 AD
B. Kanishka	2. Started Vikram Era in 58 BC, after his victory over Sakas.
C. Vikramaditya	3. Married Rudradaman's daughter, but was defeated by him twice.
D. Gautamiputra	4. St. Thomas came to India to Yajnasri propagate Christianity during his reign.

(a) A-4, B-1, C-2, D-3
(b) A-3, B-1, C-2, D-4
(c) A-3, B-4, C-2, D-1
(d) A-3, B-2, C-4, D-1

164. Arrange the following dynasties chronologically:
(I) Pallavas (II) Satavahanas
(III) Kanvas (IV) Sungas
(a) IV, III, I, II (b) IV, III, II, I
(c) III, IV, II, I (d) III, I, IV, II

165. What is a "Prasasti"?
(a) Private Endowment
(b) Eulogy of a King
(c) Royal Charter
(d) Copper Plate

166. Identify the famous woman ruler of the Gupta period.
(a) Kumaradevi (b) Rajyashri
(c) Kuber-Naga (d) Prabhavati-Gupta

167. Who started the Gupta Era and when?
(a) Ghatatkacha in 300 AD.
(b) Srigupta in 309-10 A.D.
(c) Chandragupta-I in 319-20 AD.
(d) Samudragupta in 324 AD.

168. Identify the wrong statement regarding Gupta polity:
(I) They took up exalted social titles like Rajadhiraja, Maharajadhiraja etc.
(II) A council of ministers, called Mantriparishad or Mantrimandalam assisted the King.
(III) Gupta kings claimed divine origin and supernatural powers for themselves.
(IV) They did not possess the authority to make their own laws nor modify or interpret the existing laws.
(a) III only (b) I & IV
(c) I & III (d) IV only

169. Identify the Gupta ruler who is believed to have got converted to Buddhism and also founded the Nalanda University
(a) Purugupta (b) Kumaragupta -I
(c) Buddhagupta (d) Skandagupta

170. Which of the following book is considered as the Guptan equivalent to Kautilya's *Arthasastra* of the Mauryas?
(a) Kamandaka's *Nitisara*
(b) Kaliyugaraja *Vrithantha*
(c) *Narada Smriti*
(d) *Brihaspati Smriti*

171. Which of the following Chinese pilgrims to India gives us some information about the first Gupta ruler?
(a) Hiuen Tsang (b) Fahien
(c) Hsing (d) Wang Hiuen Tse

172. Who is the author of the famous *Allahabad Prasasti*?
(a) Kalidasa (b) Sudraka
(c) Harisena (d) Ravikirti

173. Which one of the following Gupta rulers is said to have agreed to surrender his wife to a Saka ruler to protect the interests of his people?
(a) Srigupta (b) Ghatotkacha
(c) Ramagupta (d) Kumaragupta

174. Which of the following non-Gupta inscriptions give us information about the Guptas?
(i) Inscriptions of Kadambas
(ii) Those of Varman Dynasty
(iii) Those of the Rashtrakutas
(iv) Those of the Chalukyas
Choose the correct answer from the codes below:
(a) All of them (b) i and ii only
(c) i, ii, iii (d) ii, iii, iv.

175. Arrange the following Gupta emperors in the chronological order.
(i) Samudragupta
(ii) Kumaragupta-I
(iii) Chandragupta-I
(iv) Skandagupta
(v) Ghatotkachagupta
(vi) Chandragupta-II
Select the answer from the codes below.
(a) v, iii, i, vi, ii and iv
(b) iii, iv, i, ii, vi, and v
(c) iv, ii, v, i, vi, and iii
(d) ii, i, iv, vi, v and iii

176. The first Indian scholar who treated Mathematics as a distinct subject was
(a) Aryabhatta (b) Vijayanandul
(c) Varahamihira (d) Brahma Gupta

177. Match the following:

List I (Types of Gupta Temples)	List II (Examples)
1. Flat-roofed square temple.	A. Deogarh and Bhitargaon temples.
2. Square temple with a storey or *Vimana*.	B. Maniyar Math.
3. Square temple with a *Shikhara* or tower.	C. Temple Number XVII at Sanchi.
4. Rectangular temple.	D. Parvati and Siva temples at Nachna Kuthara and Bhumara respectively.
5. Circular temple.	E. Kapoleswara Temple at Aihole.

(a) I-D, 2-A, 3-E, 4-C, 5-B
(b) I-C, 2-D, 3-A, 4-E, 5-B
(c) I-A, 2-E, 3-A, 4-C, 5-D
(d) I-B, 2-C. 3-D, 4-A, 5-E

Directions : For answering questions from 178 to 181, read the following instructions carefully:
Mark (a) if both "Assertion" and "Reason" are correct and if 'R' justifies or explains 'A'
Mark (b) if both 'A' and 'R' are correct but 'R' does not explain or justify 'A'
Mark (c) if only 'A' is correct,
Mark (d) if only 'R' is correct.

178. **Assertion (A) :** Land grants made by Gupta Emperors undoubtedly indicate that the king had the supreme ownership of land.
Reason (R) : In these land grants, the Gupta Emperors, particularly later Guptas, transferred comprehensive right to the donees.

179. **Assertion (A) :** Under the Guptas, Nivi Dharma kinds of trusteeship of land was prevalent in many parts of North India.
Reason (R) : Nivi Dharma kind of land tenure was the only type prevalent in Eastern India also.

180. **Assertion (A) :** The Nalanda and Gaya copper plate grants of Samudragupta are the earliest records of the Gupta period that throw light on the 'Agrahara' grants.
Reason (R) : The above grants give not only financial powers but also administrative rights to the recipients.

181. **Assertion (A) :** The Gupta period is rightly called the "Golden Age" of the Sanskrit grammar and literature.

Reason (R) : The Sakas and Kushanas and even the Mahayana Buddhists patronised Sanskrit much before the Imperial Guptas.

182. Identify the false statement with regard to Chandragupta?
(a) He was known as Lichchavidauhita.
(b) He was the son of Ghatotkacha.
(c) He married the Lichchavi princess Kumaradevi.
(d) He had adopted the title of *Maharajadhiraja*.

183. Which of the following titles was not adopted by Chandragupta II?
(a) *Vikramaditya* (b) *Narendrachandra*
(c) *Simhachandra* (d) *Devaputra*

184. Who among the following rulers was called Kaviraja?
(a) Kumaragupta-I
(b) Chandragupta-I
(c) Chandragupta Vikramaditya
(d) Samudragupta

185. Match the following:

List I (Book)	List II (Subject)
A. *Ritusamhara*	1. Political play dealing with the plot of Chanakya to overthrow the last of Nanda rulers
B. *Mrichchhakatika*	2. Lyrical Poems
C. *Mudra Rakshasa*	3. About the astronomy
D. *Panchasidhantika*	4. Love story of Charulata and Vasantsena

(a) A-4, B-1, C-4, D-2
(b) A-2, B-4, C-1, D-3
(c) A-2, B-4, C-3, D-1
(d) A-4, B-2, C-1, D-3

186. Which of the following Gupta inscriptions gives the most decisive argument in favour of the exclusive state ownership of land?
(a) Paharpur Copper Plate
(b) Mehrauli Iron Pillar
(c) Eran Stone Pillar
(d) Nalanda Copper Plate

187. Identify the title taken up by Harsha after his accession to the throne.
(a) Gunaraja (b) Avanisimha
(c) Maharaja (d) Siladitya

188. Bring out the correct statement/statements.
(i) Harsha is reported to have brought a tooth relic of the Buddha from Kashmir.
(ii) Harsha issued a very large number of gold and silver coins.
(iii) Kashmir was annexed by Harsha in one of his military campaigns.
(iv) The feudal practice of rewarding and paying officers with grants of revenue bearing lands on a large scale had begun under Harsha.
(a) i, ii, iv (b) ii and iii
(c) i and iv (d) i and ii

189. Banabhatta was the author of
(i) *Kadambini*
(ii) *Panchatantra*
(iii) *Parvathy Parinay*
(iv) *Ratnamalika*
(v) *Harshacharita*
(a) ii, iii, iv (b) ii and iv
(c) i, ii, v (d) i, iii, v

190. Which of the following inscriptions gives us information about the conquest of Valabhi by Harshavardhana?
(a) Aihole Pillar Inscription
(b) Junagarh Rock Inscription
(c) Damodarpur Copper Plate
(d) Nausasi Copper Plate

191. Harsha is said to have held two great religious assemblies. Which of the following places were the venues for these assemblies?
(i) Thaneswar (ii) Kanauj
(iii) Vallabhi (iv) Prayag
Choose the correct codes given below:
(a) i and ii (b) ii and iii
(c) iii and iv (d) ii and iv

192. Match List I with List II and choose the answer using the codes given below the lists:

List-I	List-II
1. Prabhakaravardhana	A. Harsha's mother
2. Rajyavardhana	B. Harsha's sister
3. Rajyashri	C. Harsha's brother-in-law

4. Yashoda D. Harsha's father
5. Grahavarman E. Harsha's brother
(a) 1-C, 2-D, 3-A, 4-B, 5-E
(b) l-E, 2-D, 3-B, 4-A, 5-C
(c) 1-D, 2-E, 3-B, 4-A, 5-C
(d) I -D, 2-B, 3-E, 4-C, 5-A

Directions : For answering questions 193 and 194 read the following instructions carefully:-

Mark (a) if only Assertion 'A' is true.
Mark (b) if only Reason 'R' is true.
Mark (c) if both 'A' and 'R' are true and if 'R' is the correct explanation or justification of 'A'.
Mark (d) if both 'A' and 'R' are true, but if 'R' is not the correct explanation or justification for 'R'.

193. **Assertion (A) :** The practice of *Sati* was quite widespread among the higher classes during Harsha's period
Reason (R) : Bana has recorded that Harsha's mother committed *Sati* after the death of her husband

194. **Assertion (A) :** Harsha issued a very large number of gold and silver coins.
Reason (R) : The feudal practice of rewarding and paying officer with grants of revenue-bearing lands on a large scale had begun under Harsha.

195. Hieun Tsang, a Chinese pilgrim, visited India during the reign of Harsha:
I. To study at Buddhist University of Nalanda.
II. To collect Buddhist texts from India.
III. To study the life of Indian people.
IV. As a Chinese Ambassador to India.
(a) I & II
(b) II, & III
(c) III & IV
(d) All the above are true

196. Which of the following books was not authored by Harsha?
(a) *Priyadarshika* (b) *Ratnavali*
(c) *Nagananda* (d) *Parvathy Parinay*

197. Name the founder of the Chalukyas of Badami?
(a) Vijayaditya (b) Kirtivarman-I
(c) Vikramaditya-I (d) Kirtivarman-II

198. The temples found in Aihole are.
(i) Melagitti Sivalaya
(ii) Ladhkhan Temple
(iii) Jain Temple of Meguti
(iv) Durga Temple
(v) Hucimalligudi
(a) i, ii, v (b) ii, iii, iv, v
(c) i, ii and iv (d) ii, iii and v

199. In the post-Gupta period royal deeds of lands were known as *Sasanas* and private persons deeds were called :
(a) Lankikalekha
(b) Karyalekha
(c) Both (a) and (b) above
(d) Adhikarlekha

200. Which of the following literary sources is NOT relevant for the agrarian condition of the post-Gupta period ?
(a) Kalhana's *Rajatarangini.*
(b) Jimutavahan's *Dayabhaga*
(c) Medathiti's commentary on *Manusmiriti*
(d) Bana's *Harshacharita*

201. Which of the following Chalukyan king assumed the title of Vatapikonda?
(a) Narsimhavarman I
(b) Pulakesin II
(c) Vikramaditya II
(d) Mahendravarman I

202. The Pallavas and the Chalukyas were constantly involved in a conflict for establishing supremacy over which of the following area?
(a) Madurai (b) Tanjore
(c) Vengi (d) Guntur

203. The finest specimens of Pallava architecture are
(a) Temples of Madurai
(b) Temples of Tanjore
(c) Rock-cut Rath temple at Mahabalipuram
(d) Kailashnath temple of Ellora

204. Which of the following are true about Shankaracharya?
I. He adopted the Buddhist practice of sangha.
II. He taught that knowledge alone led to salvation
III. His philosophy is called the Advaita-Vedanta or non-dualist vedanta

IV. He accepted the Brahmanical organisation of social life on caste basis as representing the collective experience and wisdom of the race

(a) II, III, & IV (b) II & III
(c) I, II & III (d) All are true

205. Mark the Pallava ruler who was the worshipper of Vishnu, the rest being devotees of Siva.
(i) Nandivarman-II (ii) Mahendravarman-I
(iii) Simhavishnu (iv) Narasimhavarman-II
(a) i and iii (b) ii-and iv
(c) iii only (d) iv only

206. Match the following lists :

List I (Pallava Temples)	List II (Examples)
1. Nandia Group	A. Mukteshwara Temple at Kanchi.
2. Mahendra Group	B. Rock-cut Temples at Bhairavakonda.
3. Rajasimha Group	C. Monolithic Temples at Mahabalipuram.
4. Narasimha Group	D. Kailashnath Temple at Kanchi.

(a) I-C, 2-A, 3-B, 4-D
(b) I-A, 2-B, 3-D, 4-C
(c) I-C, 2-A, 3-B, 4-D
(d) I-D, 2-B, 3-A, 4-C

207. Which Pala ruler founded the famous Vikramasila University for the Buddhists?
(a) Mahipala (b) Devapala
(c) Gopala (d) Dharmapala

208. Which Prathihara ruler had the famous poet, Rajasekhara, at his court?
(a) Vatsaraja (b) Mahipala
(c) Nagabhatta-II (d) Mihira Bhoja

209. Which of the following is wrongly matched?
(a) Sena dynasty—Founded by Vijaya Sena.
(b) Pala dynasty—Founded by Gopala.
(c) Prathihara dynasty—Founded by Bhoja.
(d) Rastrakuta dynasty—Founded by Amogavarsha.

210. Name the Pala ruler who was the first to plunge into the tripartite struggle.
(a) Devapala (b) Mahipala
(c) Dharmapala (d) Gopala

211. The first invasion of India by Sultan Mahmud Ghazni was in:
(a) 1004. AD (b) 1001 AD
(c) 1000 AD (d) 999 AD

212. Muhammad Ghori was defeated by Prithviraj Chauhan in the battle of
(a) Tarain (b) Panipat
(c) Thaneswar (d) Chandawar

213. The Arab merchant, Suleiman, came to India in 9th century in the kingdom of
(a) Vijaysena of Sena dynasty
(b) Mihira Bhoja of Prathihara dynasty
(c) Gopala of the Pala dynasty
(d) Dantidurga of Rashtrakuta dynasty

214. Match the following lists :

List I (Dynasties)	List II (Capital)
A. Chalukyas	1. Kanchipuram
B. Yadavas	2. Dvarasamudra
C. Kakatiyas	3. Kalyani
D. Hoysalas	4. Devagiri
E. Cholas	5. Warangal

(a) A-5, B-2, C-3, D-4, E-1
(b) A-3, B-4, C-5, D-2, E-1
(c) A-4, B-3, C-2, D-1, E-5
(d) A-3, B-4, C-2, D-5, E-1

215. The city of Dhillika (Delhi) was founded by the
(a) Chauhans (b) Tomars
(c) Pawars (d) Pariharas

216. Which of the following are the four *Agnikula* class of Rajputs?
(a) Tomars, Pariharas, Chauhans, Pawars
(b) Chandellas, Tomars, Solankis, Chauhans
(c) Chandellas, Pariharas, Chauhans, Pawars
(d) Pariharas, Chauhans, Pawars, Solankis

217. **Assertion (A) :** Among the numerous Rajput clans which rose into prominence in the 10th century AD, four claimed a special status and started calling themselves the '*Agnikula*'.
Reason (R) : The four *Agnikula* clans which dominated early Rajput politics claimed descent from a mythical figure who rose out of a sacrificial fire pit near Mt. Abu.
(a) A is correct, but R is wrong.
(b) A is wrong, but R is correct.

(c) Both 'A' and 'R' are correct, and 'R' is the correct explanation or justification for 'A'.
(d) Both 'A' and 'R' are correct, and, 'R' is not the correct explanation or justification for 'A'.

218. Firdausi, the author of *Shahnamah*, was the poet-laureate at the court of:
(a) Prithviraj Chauhan
(b) Muhammad Ghori
(c) Mahmud of Ghazni
(d) Qutb-ud-din-Aibak

219. Who wrote *Kathasaritsagara*?
(a) Kalhana (b) Jayadeva
(c) Somadeva (d) Firdausi

220. Which sect was greatly influenced by Tantricism?
(a) Vrajayana (b) Mahayana
(c) Hinayana (d) Digambars

221. Name the temple built in *Nagara* style and located at Khajuraho.
(i) Devi Jagadamba
(ii) Nilakanteswara
(iii) Parsvnath
(iv) Kandariya Mahaveda
(v) Duladeo
(a) i, ii, iii, iv (b) i, iii, iv, v
(c) ii, iv, v (d) i, iii, v

222. The parties involved in the tripartite struggle over the control of Kannauj during the period 750-1000 AD were
(a) Chandellas, Chalukyas and Rastrakutas
(b) Chandellas, Chalukyas and Palas
(c) Palas, Prathiharas and Rastrakutas
(d) Palas, Pariharas and Rastrakutas

223. Halebid is associated with
(a) Cholas (b) Kakatiyas
(c) Hoysalas (d) Chalukyas

224. Pampa, Panna and Ranna are regarded as the three gems of
(a) Kannada poetry (b) Tamil poetry
(c) Telugu poetry (d) Malayalam poetry

225. Who founded the *Lingayat* Movement?
(a) Basvaraja (b) Ramanuja
(c) Sankaracharya (d) Kamban

226. Which Chola King conquered the Sri Vijaya empire of the Sailendra rulers by sending a naval expedition?
(a) Rajendra-I (b) Parantaka-II
(c) Rajaraja-I (d) Virarajendra

227. Name the Chola ruler whose original name was Arumolivarman.
(a) Rajendra-I (b) Rajaraja-I
(c) Vikramachola (d) Virarajendra

228. "Uttaramerur Inscription" gives us information about
(a) Diplomatic relations between the Cholas and the Sailendras
(b) Autonomous village administration of the Cholas
(c) Origin of the Cholas
(d) Military achievements of Rajaraja-I

229. Which is the tallest of all medieval Indian Temples?
(a) Kailasa Temple at Ellora
(b) Sun Temple at Konark
(c) Nilakanteswara Temple at Udaypur
(d) Brihadeswara Temple at Tanjore

230. Name the Chola ruler who sent an embassy of 72 merchants to China in 1077 AD.
(a) Kulottunga-I (b) Rajaraja-II
(c) Kulottunga-II (d) Rajendra-I

231. Arrange the following Chola emperors in the correct sequence.
(i) Rajaraja-I (ii) Parantaka
(iii) Rajendra-I (iv) Adityachola
(v) Vijayala (vi) Uttamachola
Select the answer from the codes below
(a) iv, ii, i, v, iii and vi
(b) ii, iii, i, vi, iv and v
(c) v, iv, ii, vi, i and iii
(d) iii, i, ii, v, iv and vi

232. What is the ascending order of the following units of administration in the Chola period?
(i) *Valanadus* (ii) *Nadus*
(iii) *Mandalams* (iv) *Kurrams*
Select the correct answer from the codes given below:
(a) iii, ii, i and iv (b) i, ii, iii and iv
(c) iv, i, ii and iii (d) iv, ii, i and iii

233. Match list-I with list II and select the answer using the codes given below the lists.

List-I	List II
1. *Ur*	A. General assembly of an urban centre
2. *Sabha*	B. Tank land
3. *Nagaram*	C. General assembly of an ordinary village
4. *Eripatti*	D. General assembly of Brahmins
	E. Pasture land

Codes

(a) l-D, 2-C, 3-A, 4-E
(b) l-E, 2-D, 3-B, 4-A
(c) l-C, 2-D, 3-A, 4-B
(d) l-A, 2-B, 3-C, 4-D

234. *Ramayana*—a classic in Tamil Literature, was written by:
(a) Kamban (b) Ottakuttan
(c) Pulagendi (d) Pampa

235. The central feature of Indian Society during AD 750-1200 was
(a) Feudalism (b) Liberalism
(c) Egalitarianism (d) Brotherhood

236. The style of temple architecture that was prevalent under Chola dynasty was:
(a) *Nagara* style (b) *Dravida* style
(c) *Gopuram* style (d) *Solanki* style

Instructions: In questions 237 and 238 two statements each—assertion and reason—are given. You have to mark (a) if assertion is true, but reason is wrong; (b) if assertion is wrong but reason is true; (c) if both assertion and reason are true and later is the correct explanation of the former; and (d) if both assertion and reason are true but later is not the correct explanation of the former.

237. **Assertion (A):** Taxes were collected by the *Ur* or *Sabha* in the Chola villages.
Reason (R): The feudatories of *Cholas* were not allowed to collect the taxes directly from the tax-payer.

238. **Assertion (A):** Lokmahadevi, the queen of Rajaraja-l, performed "Hiranya-garbha" ceremony, i.e., passing one's body through a golden cow.
Reason (R): The Chola region is significant for laying greater stress on 'Yajna' or sacrifice than on 'Dana' or gift.

239. Who was the first Muslim ruler of Delhi?
(a) Iltutmish
(b) Allauddin Khalji
(c) Qutbuddin Aibek
(d) Mahmud of Ghazni

240. Who was the first among the Delhi Sultans who requested and obtained letters of investiture from the Caliph?
(a) Balban (b) Iltutmish
(c) Jalaluddin Khalji (d) Firuz Tughluq

241. The Lodhi rulers were:
(a) Pure Afghans
(b) Pure Turks
(c) Timurid Turks
(d) Turks settled in Afghanistan

242. A Persian historian of the Sultanate period who accompanied Alauddin Khalji on his expedition to Chittor was:
(a) Shams-i-Siraj Afif
(b) Ziauddin Barani
(c) Amir Khusrau
(d) Minhaj-us-Siraj

243. What was *Abwab*?
(a) Toll tax
(b) Religions taxes such as Zakat
(c) Taxes on merchandise and custom duties
(d) Miscellaneous kinds of taxes like the house taxes, grazing tax, irrigation tax etc.

244. Qutbuddin Aibak cannot be called the sovereign ruler of the Sultanate because:
(a) He did not assume the title of Sultan
(b) He did not issue the coins nor the *Khutba* was read in his name
(c) Both (a) and (b)
(d) Instead of Delhi, he mostly stayed in Lahore

245. The Sultans of the so-called Slave Dynasty are also sometimes known as 'Ilbari Turks' because they belonged to the tribe of Ilbari in Turkestan. Which of the following rulers did not belong to Ilbari tribe?
(a) Qutbuddin Aibak
(b) Iltutmish
(c) Nasiruddin Mahmud
(d) Ghiyasuddin Balban

246. The *Diwan-i-Wizarat* had under it other minor departments, each under a distinct officer of its own. Which of the following heads of departments did not help the wazir in the management of state finances?
(a) *Mushrif-i-mumalik* or Accountant General
(b) *Mustawfi-i-mumalik* or Auditor-General
(c) *Diwan-i-mustakharaj* or the officer incharge to realise the arrears of revenue collectors.
(d) *Diwan-i-riyasat* or Department in charge of public grievances, weights and measures, markets, etc.

247. Which of the contemporary historians was appointed as the chief Qazi of Delhi by Sultan Muhammad-bin Tughlaq?
(a) Ibn Batutah
(b) Zia-ud-din Barani
(c) Shams-i-Siraj Afif
(d) None of these

248. Which of the following gives the administrative divisions of the empire in the correct descending order?
(a) Provinces, shiqs, parganas and villages
(b) Parganas, shiqs, villages
(c) Shiqs, parganas, qasbahs
(d) Iqtas, parganas, shiqs and villages

249. The term used for measurement of land in the Sultanate period was:
(a) *Kismat-i-ghalla* (b) *Ghalla-bakshi*
(c) *Masahat* (d) *Ghazi*

250. Muhammad-bin-Tughluq introduced a token currency in lieu of the prevalent silver tanka. Identify the metal used for making the token currency.
(a) Bronze (b) Brass
(c) Copper (d) Nickel

251. The land revenue-yielding territories of the Sultanate were divided into Khalisa or Crown lands and _____ lands.
(a) Inam (b) Barren
(c) Iqta (d) Waqf

252. Bring out the correct statements about Raziya Sultana.
(i) She was murdered by some bandits at Kaithal after being deposed by the nobbles
(ii) Iltutmish nominated her as his successor
(iii) She was successful in coming to the throne immediately after her father's death
(iv) She was the only daughter to be preferred to sons by any ruler of India
(v) Her fondness for the Abyssinian slave Yaqub turned the nobbles against her
(a) i, ii, iv, v (b) ii, iii, iv
(c) iii, iv, v (d) i, ii, iii

253. "*Chahalga*" or "*Chalisa*" came into existence during the reign of:
(a) Balban
(b) Raziya Sultana
(c) Iltutmish
(d) Nasiruddin Muhammad

254. In pursuit of Jalaluddin, the fugitive Khwarizmi prince, Chengiz Khan, the famous Mongol warrior, came to India's border in the reign of:
(a) Balban (b) Iltutmish
(c) Alauddin Khilji (d) Muhammad-bin-Tughlaq

255. The reign of eight Delhi Sultans was witnessed by
(a) Amir Khusrau
(b) Ziauddin Barani
(c) Shams-i-Siraj Afif
(d) Minhaj-us-Siraj

256. What is the correct chronological sequence of the Delhi Sultans of *Mameluk* dynasty?
(i) Raziya
(ii) Nasiruddin Muhammad
(iii) Balban
(iv) Kaiqubad
(v) Qutbuddin Aibak
(vi) Iltutmish
(a) v, i, iii, vi, ii, iv (b) ii, i, iii, vi, iv, v
(c) v, vi, i, ii, iii, iv (d) i, ii, iii, iv, v, vi

257. Arrange in proper chronological order of the experiments of Muhammad-bin-Tughlaq,
(i) Introduction of token currency
(ii) Transfer of capital from Delhi to Daulatabad
(iii) Enhancement of land revenue to 50% in the doab area
(iv) Establishment of a separate department of agriculture
(v) Appointment of a new set of revenue officers
(a) ii, i, iii, iv, v (b) iv, v, ii, iii, i
(c) ii, iv, i, iii, v (d) v, iii, ii, i, iv

258. Who was the founder of the city of Agra?
(a) Firuz Tughlaq
(b) Muhammad-bin-Tughlaq
(c) Alauddin Khilji
(d) Sikander Lodi

259. What is the descending order of the ranks of nobility under Delhi Sultanate?
(i) Khan (ii) Malik
(iii) Amir (iv) Sar-i-Khail
(a) i, ii, iv, iii (b) ii, i, iv, iii
(c) i, ii, iii, iv (d) iii, ii, iv, i

260. Name the Delhi Sultans born of Hindu mothers:
(i) Firuz Tughlaq
(ii) Sikander Lodi
(iii) Nasiruddin Khusrau
(iv) Balban
(v) Alauddin Khilji
(vi) Ghiyasuddin Tughlaq
(a) ii, iv, v (b) i, ii, iv
(c) iii, iv, v, vi (d) i, ii, iii, vi

261. Name the two historians of Delhi Sultanate period, whose works had the same title, *Tarikh-i-Firuzshahi*.
(a) Ziauddin Barani and Amir Khusrau
(b) Minhaj-us-Siraj and Amir Khusrau
(c) Shams-i-Siraj Afif and Ziauddin Barani
(d) Amir Khusrau and Shams-i-Siraj Afif

262. Match the following:

1. *Diwan-i-Risalat*	A. Department of slaves
2. *Diwan-i-Kohi*	B. Military Department
3. *Diwan-i-Arz*	C. Department of Records and Correspondence
4. *Diwan-i-Bandagani*	D. Agricultural Department
5. *Diwan-i-Wazarat*.	E. Finance Department
6. *Diwan-i-Insha*	F. Department of Ecclesiastical Affairs, Public Charities and Foreign' Affairs.

(a) 1-B, 2-B, 3-A, 4-F, 5-C, 6-E
(b) l-E, 2-F, 3-B, 4-A, 5-C, 6-D
(c) 1-F, 2-D, 3-B, 4-A. 5-E, 6-C
(d) 1-A, 2-C, 3-D, 4-B, 5-F, 6-E

263. Identify the motifs used by the Delhi Sultans in their constructions which were borrowed from the Hindus.
(i) Bell
(ii) Lotus
(iii) Geometrical and floral designs
(iv) Swastika
(a) ii, iii, iv (b) i and iii
(c) iii and iv, (d) i, ii, iv

Instructions for Questions 264-267 : (A) stands for Assertion and (R) stands for Reason. Write (a) if only (A) is correct; (b) if only (R) is correct; (c) if both (A) and (R) are correct and (R) is the correct explanation of (A); and (d) if both (A) and (R) are correct but (R) is not the proper explanation of (A).

264. Assertion (A) : Slave Sultans are also called Ilbari Turks.
Reason (R) : Ilbari in Arabic language means 'the owned'.

265. Assertion (A) : The nobility under Muhammad-bin-Tughlaq was a highly homogeneons one.
Reason (R) : Royal intervention in the lqta system was at its peak under Muhammad-bin-Tughlaq.

266. Assertion (A) : During the Delhi Sultanate period, there originated the differentiation between the Hindustani and the Carnatic schools of music.
Reason (R) : The Turks brought with them a number of new musical instruments as well as several new modes, airs and scales.

267. Assertion (A) : Muhammad-bin-Tughlaq's policy of introducing to-ken currency was not a completely miscalculated idea.
Reason (R) : Prior to Muhammad, the token currency was also successfully experimented by Ghai Khatu of Iran and Qublai Khan of China.

268. The first French settlement in India was :
(*a*) Pondicherry (*b*) Goa
(*c*) Hooghly (*d*) Chander nagar

269. Match List I with List II

List I (States)	List II (Founders)
A. Hyderabad	1. Saadat Khan
B. Qudh	2. Nizamul Mulk
C. Bengal	3. Saadat Ullah Khan
D. Arcot	4. Mursid Quli Khan

Code :

	A	B	C	D
(a)	1	2	3	4
(b)	2	1	4	3
(c)	1	3	2	4
(d)	3	1	4	2

270. Which of the following is wrongly matched ?
(a) Qutab Minar - Aibak & Iltutmish
(b) Dhai Din Ka Jhonpara - Ibrahim Lodi
(c) Alai Darwaza - Alauddin Khilji
(d) Red Palace - Balban

271. Who of the following may be rightly called the first Turkish empire builder in India?
(a) Aibak
(b) Alauddin Khilji
(c) Muhammad bin Tughlaq
(d) Sikander Lodi

272. The Ministers during the Sultanate period were appointed and dismissed by:
(a) Ulema (b) the Caliph
(c) the Sultan (d) Wazir

273. Which among the following is incorrect?
I. Kharaj was a land tax
II. Zakat was a tax on land held by Muslims
III. Jizya was a religious tax levied on non-Muslims
IV. Ushr was a religious tax levied on Muslims
(a) II & IV (b) II only
(c) IV only (d) None of the above

274. Match the following:

A. Muhammad bin Tughlaq	1. Land revenue assessment based on actual measure-ment.
B. Firuz Tughlaq	2. Restoration of the prestige of the Crown
C. Balban	3. Creation of the department of agriculture
D. Alauddin KhIlji	4. Creation of the Employment Bureau

(a) A-3, B-4, C-2, D-1
(b) A-4, B-3, C-2, D-1
(c) A-4, B-3, C-1, D-2
(d) A-1, B-4, C-2, D-3

275. Who built the fort city of Siri?
(a) Muhammad bin Tughlaq
(b) Iltutmish
(c) Jalaluddin Khilji
(d) Alauddin Khilji

276. Which of the following is wrongly matched?
(a) Namdeva-Maharashtra
(b) Chaitanya-Bengal
(c) Narsinha Mehta-Gujarat
(d) Vallabhacharya-Gujarat

277. Who among the following gurus introduced the Gurmukhi script for the spoken language of the Punjabis?
(a) Guru Nanak (b) Guru Angad
(c) Guru Amardas (d) Guru Ramdas

278. The monism preached by which of the following leaders of the Bhakti movement is known as suddha-advaita or 'Pure Non-Duality?
(a) Ramanuja (b) Vallabhacharya
(c) Ramananda (d) Chaitanya

279. The historical reason for Sufi saints isolating themselves from society was that:
(a) Their mystical doctrine of union with God through love was regarded as heretical and attacked by orthodox Islam.
(b) They preached escapism and worldly detachment.
(c) They found a congenial atmosphere for nurturing their ideas in India, away from social surroundings.
(d) Their views were unacceptable to the general masses.

280. What was the term used by the *Sufis* for the successor nominated by the teacher of a particular order or *silsilah*?
(a) Pir (b) Murid
(c) Wali (d) Khanqah

281. The *Sufi* order, which was popularised in India by the first Mughal emperor Babur, was:
(a) Naqshbandiya (b) Qadiriya
(c) Suhrawardi (d) Chishtiya

282. The earliest Vaishnava Bhakti saints from the South were:
(a) Alvars (b) Nayanars
(c) Bhagavatas (d) Virashaivites

283. Who of the following leaders of the Bhakti movement was greatly influenced by Islam?
(a) Ramanuja (b) Namdeva
(c) Chaitanya (d) Ramananda.

284. The Bhakti saint, who was not a worshipper of Krishna, was:
(a) Vallabhacharya (b) Mirabai
(c) Surdas (d) Ramananda

285. Who said, "If by worshipping stones, one can find God, I shall worship a mountain" :
(a) Kabir (b) Nanak
(c) Tuka Ram (d) Chaitanya.

286. In which region of India was the *Firdausi* order popular?
(a) In and around Delhi (b) Sind
(c) Bihar (d) The Deccan

287. Which of the following is incorrect with regard to *Chishti* order of *Sufis*?
(a) It was founded in India by Khwaja Moinuddin Chishti.
(b) The most famous of the *Chishti* saints were Nizamuddin Auliya and Nasiruddin Chirag-i-Delhi.
(c) The Chishti saints led an austere, simple life and conversed with people in their dialect, Hindawi or Hindi.
(d) They accepted the service of state and some of them held important posts in the ecclesiastical department.

288. In which building do Arches constructed on the true scientific principles (True arches) appear for the first time ?
(a) Tomb of Iltutmish
(b) tomb of Balban
(c) Sultan Garhi
(d) Alai Darwaza

289. Horse shoe arch is a distinctive feature of one of the following buildings. Identify it.
(a) Alai Drwaza (b) Tomb of Iltutmish
(c) Sultan Garhi (d) Tomb of Balban

290. Islamic architecture is basically characterised by :
(a) arcuate form (b) trabeculate form
(c) floral designs (d) secular form

291. Give the original construction on which the Quwwat-ul-Islam mosque was built ?
(a) A Jain temple
(b) A tenth-century Chauhan temple dedicated to Vishnu
(c) A Hindu temple dedicated to Shiva
(d) None of the above

292. Who was the author of the famous Hindi classic *Padmavat*?
(a) Malik Muhammad Jaisi
(b) Padmanabha Patta
(c) Vachaspati
(d) Vidyapati Upadhyaya

293. Which famous poet was given the name of Sadi?
(a) Hasan-i-Dehlwi
(b) Shaikh Jamali Kambo
(c) Aziz-ud-din Khalid
(d) Yahya-bin-Ahmad Sirhindi

294. Lilavati a work written by Bhaskara. It deals with
(a) Astronomy (b) Mathematics
(c) Chemistry (d) Metallurgy

295. Match the works with their authors

	Works		**Authors**
A.	*Tarikh-i-Firoz Shahi*	I.	Firoz Shah Tughlaq
B.	*Futuhat-i-Firoz Shahi*	II.	Yahya-bin-Sirhindi
C.	*Tarikh-i-Alai*	III.	Zia-ud-din Barani
D.	*Tarikh-i-Mubarak Shahi*	IV.	Khusrau

	A	B	C	D
(a)	III	I	IV	II
(b)	III	IV	I	II
(c)	II	I	IV	III
(d)	IV	I	III	II

296. The Sangama brothers—Harihara and Bukka—the founders of the Vijayanagara empire, returned to the fold of Hinduism from Islam, at the initiative of :
(a) Sayana (b) Vallabhacharya
(c) Madhavacharya (D) Vidyaranya

297. Name the area that was not a bone of contention between the Bahamanis and the Vijayanagara rulers.
(a) Konkan
(b) Tungabhadra Doab
(c) Kaveri Delta
(d) Krishna-Godavari Delta

298. Name the Vijayanagara ruler who was defeated by Firuz Bahmani and forced to pay a huge war indemnity as well as offer his daughter in marriage.
(a) Bukka-I (b) Deva Raya-I
(c) Deva Raya II (d) Harihara

299. Name the Portugese Governor in India who concluded a friendship treaty with Krishnadeva Raya around 1511 AD.
(a) Nino da Cunha (b) Vasco da Gama
(c) D' Almeida (d) Albuquerque

300. Which Bahmani Sultan shifted the capital from Gulbarga to Bidar?
(a) Ahmed Shah Wali
(b) Tajuddin Firuzshah
(c) Muhammad Shah-I
(d) Muhammad Shah-II

301. The Gol Gumbaj at Bijapur, the world's second largest dome and famous for the so-called 'whispering gallery, was built by:
(a) Ismail Adilshah
(b) Muhammad Adilshah
(c) Yusuf Adilshah
(d) Muhammad Gawan

302. Name the temples built by Krishnadeva Raya at Hampi,Vijayanagara.
(i) Varadaraja Temple
(ii) Parvathi Temple
(iii) Krishnaswamy Temple
(iv) Vitthalswamy Temple
(v) Hazara Ramaswamy Temple
(vi) Ekambaranatha Temple
(a) ii, iv, v (b) i, iii, vi
(c) iii, iv, v (d) i, ii, iii, v

303. Arrange the units of administration of Vijayanagara Empire in the descending order.
(i) *Valanadus* (ii) *Gramas*
(iii) *Mandaams* (iv) *Nadus*
(v) *Sthalas* (vi) *Kurrams*
(a) iv, vi, ii, v, i, iii (b) ii, iv, iii, i, v, vi
(c) i, ii, iii, iv, v, vi (d) iii, i, vi, iv, v, ii

304. Match the following.

1.	Uthaman	A.	*Ramacharitamanas*
2.	Tulsidas	B.	*Sur Sagar*
3.	Surdas	C.	*Padmavat*
4.	Nur Muhammad	D.	*Chitravati*
5.	Jayasi	E.	*Indravati*

(a) 1-A, 2-B, 3-C, 4-D, 5-E
(b) 1-D, 2-A, 3-B, 4-E, 5-C
(c) 1-B, 2-C, 3-E, 4-A, 5-D
(d) 1-E, 2-D, 3-C, 4-B, 5-A

305. Who were the worst enemy of the Vijayanagar empire in the long run?
(a) The incompetence of the rulers of the Aravidu dynasty
(b) The Hindu feudatories (*paraigars*) of the Vijayanagar empire
(c) The Deccani Sultanates
(d) The haughtiness of the later rulers of the Vijayanagar empire

306. Identify the musical instrument that acquired a prominent place in the Vijayanagar empire.
(a) *Vina* (b) *Nadaswaram*
(c) *Cymbals* (d) *Mridangam*

307. Krishnadeva Raya belonged to the:
(a) Sangama dynasty
(b) Saluva dynasty
(c) Tuluva dynasty
(d) Aravidu dynasty

308. The President of the Imperial Council of the Empire of Vijayanagar was:
(a) Prime Minister (b) Sabhanayaka
(c) King (d) Mahadandanayaka

309. The *nayakas* in the empire of Vijayanagar were:
(a) Feudal chiefs
(b) Hereditary military governors
(c) Military commanders
(d) High civil and military officers

310. Custom/toll official of which place is mentioned in Sangam texts ?
(a) Thenmadurai (b) Uraiyur
(c) Puhar (d) Tanjore

311. The king of Vijayanagar, who appointed Muslims in his army, granted lands to them, built a mosque and kept a copy of the *Koran* before his throne, so that the Muslims could pay respect to it, was:
(a) Harihara (b) Devaraya I
(c) Devaraya II (d) Krishnadeva Raya

312. The rajaguru or the great royal teacher of Krishnadeva Raya was:
(a) Vyasaraja (b) Vidyaranya
(c) Lakshmidhara (d) Vamana Bhata

313. As per the latest researches, the so-called battle of Talikota, fought between the Deccani Muslim states and Vijayanagar, was actually fought at:
(a) Bannihatti
(b) Between villages Rakkasi-Tangadi
(c) Talikota town
(d) Raichur Doab

314. Who were *Kaikkolas*?
(a) Temple priests
(b) A community of acrobats
(c) An influential community of weavers living around temple precincts
(d) An anti-religious group which entertained the people by caricaturing the various godheads.

315. The most famous state festival of the empire of Vijayanagar was:
(a) Spring (Vasant festival)
(b) Mahanavami
(c) Brahmotsavam
(d) Ramanavami

316. Identify the South Indian dance traditions that appeared for the first time in the Vijayanagar period -
(a) Krishnattam (b) Yakshagana
(c) Vyomalata (d) Mohini Attam

317. Identify the Vijayanagar coin which were in circulation and were the most widely recognised currency all over the world.
(a) Dinar (b) Huna
(c) Panam (d) Varaha or Pagoda

318. Name the river on whose bank was the city of Vijayanagar located.
(a) Kaveri (b) Krishna
(b) Wainganga (d) Tungabhadra

319. During the rule of which of the following kings did Orissa face aggression from Krishnadev Raya of Vijayanagar as well as from Qutb Shahi kingdom of Golconda?
(a) Kapilendra (b) Purushottama
(c) Prataprudra (d) Govinda

320. Before the coming of the Muslim rulers, Kashmir was known to be a centre of:
(a) Buddhism (b) Jainism
(c) Vaishnavism (d) Shaivism

321. The ruler of Kashmir who has been described as the Akbar of Kashmir was:
(a) Alauddin Shah
(b) Shihabuddin Shah
(c) Shahi Khan (Zainul Abidin)
(d) Haider Shah

322. The Muslim kingdom of Golconda grew up on the ruins of the old Hindu kingdom of:
(a) Devagiri (b) Dwarasamudra
(c) Warangal (d) Kanchi

323. Bring out the incorrect statement about Alauddin Husain Shah of Bengal.
(a) He liberally conferred high posts upon the Hindu subjects
(b) He was a famous poet of Bengali literature
(c) The Bengali literature made a remarkable progress during his time
(d) The creative genius of the people of medieval Bengal reached its peak point

324. From the tribe of Ahoms was formed a section of the ________ tribe.
(a) Bhuiya (b) Kachari
(c) Bodo (d) Shan

325. The famous '*Kirtistambha*' at Chittor was built by:
(a) Rana Sangram Singh
(b) Rana Hamir
(c) Rana Ratan Singh
(d) Rana Kumbha

326. Name the founder of the city of Ahmedabad.
(a) Muzaffar Shah-II (b) Ahmed Shah-I
(c) Muzaffar Shah-I (d) Bahadur Shah

327. Find out the occasion for the construction of the 'Tower of Victory' at Chittor by Rana Kumbha.
(a) His victory against the Khan of Nagaur
(b) His victory against Rao Jodha of Marwar
(c) His victory over Ahmad Shah of Gujarat
(d) His victory over Mahmud Khilji of Malwa

328. Why did Mahmud Begarha attack Dwarka?
(a) To check the rising power of Portuguese in the Indian seas
(b) To loot the wealth of the temples
(c) To destroy the temples
(d) To suppress the pirates who preyed on the pilgrim traffic to Mecca

329. Identify the significance of Malwa's geographical situation.
(a) It was surrounded on two sides by inaccessible hill ranges and by the rivers Narmada and Tapti on the remaining two sides

(b) For the Delhi rulers, it was the route to the Arabian sea
(c) It commanded the trunk routes from North India to Gujarat as well as South India
(d) It was surrounded by the warring kindgoms of Gujarat, Khandesh and Mewar

330. Who founded the fortress city Mandu, the capital of Malwa?
(a) Ahmad Shah (b) Hushang Shah
(c) Muzaffar Shah (d) None of the above

331. In the second Battle of Panipat, Hemu, the Hindu general, who led the Afghan forces against the Mughals, was the general of:
(a) Sher Shah
(b) Muhammad Adil Shah
(c) Islam Shah
(d) Sikander Shah

332. Name the person whose outrageous behaviour is believed to be chiefly responsible for the revolt of Bairam Khan against Akbar.
(a) Pir Mohammad (b) Todar Mal
(c) Man Singh (d) Birbal

333. Name the Rajput dynasties which voluntarily submitted itself to Akbar.
(a) Sisodias (b) Kachchawas
(c) Rathors (d) Hadas

334. In the battle of Haldighati in 1576, the Rajput force of Maharana Pratap Singh was defeated by
(a) Raja Man Singh (b) Pir Muhammad
(c) Prince Salim (d) Akbar

335. The Mughal 'Jagir' was equivalent to Delhi Sultanate's
(a) Inam (b) Waqf
(c) Iqta (d) Khalisa

336. Taj Mahal was designed by
(a) Ustad Mansur (b) Ustad Isa
(c) Ustad Rohini (d) Ustad Shamsher

337. Náme the person who wrote the history of Aurangzeb in total secrecy. What was the name of the work?
(a) Aquil Khan Razi's *Zafar Namah-i-Alamgiri*
(b) Khafi Khan's *Muntakhab-ul-Lubab*
(c) Mirza Muhammad Kazim's *Alamgir Namah*
(d) Muhammad Saqi's *Masir-i-Alamgiri*

338. Which of the following Mughal buildings is said to possess the unique feature of being exactly equal in length and breadth?
(a) Red Fort (b) Taj Mahal
(c) Buland Darwaja (d) Agra Fort

339. Who amongst the following Frenchmen visited India six times during regime of Shahjahan and Aurangzeb and wrote his accounts of India in his work '*Six Voyages*' ?
(a) Tavernier (b) Manucci
(c) Thevenot (d) Bernier

340. Name the person/persons who invited Babur to invade India.
(i) Daulat Khan Lodi
(ii) Mahmud Lodi
(iii) Bhara Mal of Amber
(iv) Rana Sanga of Mewar.
(v) Alam Khan Lodi
(a) i, ii, iii (b) ii, iii, iv
(c) i, iv, v (d) iii, iv, v

341. Which of the four sons of Shah Jahan fought for the throne between 1656-1658?
(i) Shuja (ii) Murad
(iii) Khusrau (iv) Dawar Bakhs
(v) Aurangzeb (vi) Dara Shikoh
(a) ii, iv, v, vi (b) i, iii, iv
(c) iv, v, vi (d) i, ii, v, vi

342. Name the Persian version of the *Mahabharat*, translated during Akbar's reign.
(a) Akbar Namah (b) Iqbal Namah
(c) Sakinat-ul-Auliya (d) Razmnamah

343. Whose reign has been called the 'Golden Age of the Mughals'?
(a) Shah Jahan (b) Akbar
(c) Jahangir (d) Aurangzeb

344. Match the following:

1.	Patta	A. Revenue acceptance deed
2.	Qabuliyat	B. Market town
3.	Mohur	C. Mughal silver coin
4.	Qasbah	D. Revenue title deed
5.	Shahrukh	E. Mughal gold coin

(a) 1-C, 2-A, 3-B, 4-D, 5-E
(b) 1-A, 2-B, 3-C, 4-D, 5-E
(c) l-D, 2-A, 3-E, 4-B, 5-C
(d) 1-B. 2-A, 3-D, 4-C, 5-E

345. Which one of the following Mughal emperors is credited with the composition of many Hindi songs ?
(a) Humayun (b) Babur
(c) Akbar (d) Jehangir

346. Identify the contemporary work of the Mughal period which is useful for obtaining information on the agrarian conditions.
(a) *Tawarikh-i-Alfi*
(b) *Akbarnama*
(c) *Muntakhab-ul-Lubab*
(d) *Ain-i-Akbari*

347. Name the branch of Mughal army where foreigners like Ottomans and Portuguese were employed.
(a) Matchlockmen (b) War-boat operators
(c) Navy (d) Artillery

348. Name the Mughal queen whose name was written on all the Mughal farmans and inscribed on the coins.
(a) Nur Jahan (b) Mariam Makani
(c) Maham Anaga (d) Mumtaz Mahal

349. Which among the following titles was/were not assumed by the Mughal Emperor, Akbar ?
1. Caliph 2. Ghazi
3. Imam 4. Mujahid.
(a) 1,2,3 (b) 2,3
(c) Only 1 (d) Only 2

350. Akbar did not construct:
(a) Purana Qila (b) Agra Fort
(c) Allahabad Fort (d) Lahore Fort

351. Which among the following statements about Nadir Shah's invasion is/are true ?
1. Nicknamed 'Iran's Napoleon, Nadir Shah invaded India during the reign of Muhammad Shah, a later Mughal Emperor.
2. In order to take on Nadir Shah in the battle field, the Mughal Emperor sent an army under Nizam-ul-Mulk, Qamiruddin and Khan-e-Dauran.
3. After defeating Mughals in the Battle of Karnal in February 1739, Nadir Shah was ready to go back to Iran with a sum of Rs. 50 lakh. But Khan-e-Dauran instigated him to enter Delhi and rob the imperial exchequer.
4. Nadir Shah entered the Mughal capital city of Delhi on March 20, 1739, his soldiers put to death around 20,000 inhabitants and plundered Delhi.
(a) 1,2,3 (b) 1,4
(c) 1,2,4 (d) 1,2,3,4

352. What was the original name of Tansen?
(a) Makaranda Pande
(b) Baz Bahadur
(c) Lal Kalwant
(d) Ramtanu Pande

353. One of the rebellious upsurge in Aurangzeb's reign had a peasant-agrarian background—identify it.
(a) Sikhs
(b) Marathas
(c) Jats and Satnamis
(d) Rajputs

354. What was/were the cause(s) of war of succession between the sons of Shah Jahan?
(a) Removal of Mir Jumla, a confident of Aurangzeb, from the office of wazir.
(b) Unfounded rumour of Shah Jahan's death and succession of Dara Shikoh to the throne.
(c) Shah Jahan's special affection for Dara Shikoh, leading to rivalry between and Aurangzeb.
(d) Both (b) and (c).

355. In which language did Babur write his memoirs, called Tuzuk-i-Baburi?
(a) Persian (b) Arabic
(c) Mongol (d) Turkish

356. Which revenue system among the following is also known as the 'Bandobast' system?
(a) Zabti (b) Dahsala
(c) Nasaq (d) Kankut

357. Which great Mughal is credited with prohibiting 'Sati' unless the widow herself, of her own free will, persistently desired it?
(a) Akbar (b) Babur
(c) Humayun (d) Jahangir

358. Match the following Lists of mughal emperors and places of their tombs:

List I (Mughal Kings)	**List II (Places of their Tombs)**
1. Babur	A. Kabul
2. Humayun	B. Delhi
3. Akbar	C. Sikandra
4. Jahangir	D. Lahore
5. Shahjahan	E. Agra
6. Aurangzeb	F. Aurangabad

(a) 1-A, 2-C, 3-B, 4-E, 5-F, 6-D
(b) 1-A, 2-B, 3-C, 4-D, 5-E, 6-F
(c) 1-B, 2-C, 3-D, 4-E, 5-F, 6-A
(d) 1-B, 2-D, 3-C, 4-A, 5-E, 6-F

359. What was a '*tanab*' in the Mughal period?
(a) A revenue circle of the smallest size.
(b) A uniform medium size unit of measurement.
(c) A measuring instrument made of bamboo sticks joined by iron rings.
(d) A register containing information about cultivators, their lands and assessed revenue.

360. Arrange the following events of Jehangir's reign in the chronological order:
(i) Captain Hawkin's visit to Jahangir's court.
(ii) Sir Thomas Roe's arrival at Jahangir's court.
(iii) Mahabat Khan's revolt and capture of Jahangir.
(iv) Prince Khurram's revolt against his father.
(v) Jahangir's marriage with Nur Jahan.
(vi) Issue of 12 famous ordinances.
Choose the correct answer from the codes below:
(a) i, ii, v, vi, iii and iv
(b) vi, v, i, ii, iv and iii
(c) ii, iv, iii, v, vi and i
(d) vi, i, v, ii, iv and iii

361. The world famous 'Peacock Throne' was kept in which of the following Mughal buildings?
(a) Diwan-i-Khas at Fatehpur Sikri
(b) New Agra Fort
(c) The Rang Mahal of the Red Fort at Delhi
(d) The Diwan-i-Aram of the Red Fort at Delhi

362. Match the following lists of the Mughal agrarian terms and their meaning

List-I (Terms)	**List-II (Meaning)**
1. *Jama*	A. Assessed or stipulated revenue from a unit of land.
2. *Hasil*	B. Final and permanent assessed revenue from a unit of land.
3. *Dastur*	C. Revenue actually collected or realised from a unit of land.
4. *Bahi*	D. A particular unit of land.
5. *Bigha*	E. A revenue register kept at the village level.

(a) 1-A, 2-C, 3-B, 4-E, 5-D
(b) 1-A, 2-B, 3-C, 4-D, 5-E
(c) 1-B, 2-C, 3-D, 4-A, 5-E
(d) 1-C, 2-A, 3-B, 4-E, 5-D

363. Match List I with List II and select the answer from the codes given below the lists:-

List-I	**List-II**
1. Battle of Samel	A. Defeat of Afghans under Ibrahim Lodhi by Babur.
2. Battle of Bilgram	B. Defeat of Rajputs under Rana Sanga by Babur.
3. Battle of Ghagara	C. Defeat of Afghans under Mahmud Lodi by Babur.
4. Battle of Khanwa	D. Final defeat of Humayun by Sher Shah.
5. First Battle of Panipat	E. Defeat of Rajputs under Maldeo of Marwar by Sher Shah.

(a) 1-E, 2-D, 3-C, 4-B, 5-A
(b) 1-D, 2-C, 3-B, 4-A, 5-E
(c) 1-C, 2-E, 3-D, 4-B, 5-A
(d) 1-B, 2-A, 3-E, 4-C, 5-D

364. Which of the following buildings are found at Fatehpur Sikri?
(i) Tomb of Salim Chisti
(ii) Buland Darwaza
(iii) Palaces of Mariam and Sultana
(iv) Humayun's Tomb

(v) Panch Mahal
(vi) Rang Mahal
Select the answer from the codes below:-
(a) All of them (b) i, ii, iii and iv
(c) i, ii, iii and v (d) ii, iii, iv and vi

Directions for Questions 365-367 : For attempting questions 365 to 367 please read the following instructions carefully

Mark (a) if 'Assertion' (A) is correct and 'Reason, (R) is wrong; Mark (b) if 'A' is wrong and 'R' is correct;
Mark (c) if both 'A' and 'R' are correct, and if 'R' is the correct explanation or justification for 'A';
Mark (d) if both 'A' and 'R' are correct and if 'R' is not the correct explanation or justification for 'A'.

365. **Assertion (A) :** Both Shahajahan and Aurangazeb expanded the Khalisa lands considerably at the expense of the Jagir lands
Reason (R) : The number of mansabdars of the Mughal empire increased from around 2000 in 1605 to almost 12,000 by 1675

366. **Assertion (A) :** Among the several rebellions to rock the Mughal empire during the time of Aurangazeb, that of the Rathors of Jodhpur is an important and serious one.
Reason (R) : The Rathors were goaded into rebellion by Aurangazeb's refusal to recognize Ajit Singh, the posthumous son of Jaswant Singh, as the legal heir.

367. **Assertion (A) :** The European traders were instrumental in introducing and developing the institution of 'Hundis' in Mughal India.
Reason (R) : The merchant class of Mughal period was highly stratified class economically as well as socially.

368. Find out the correct statements regarding Bahadur Shah.
(i) He ruled from 1700 to 1712.
(ii) He took the title of Shah Alam I after becoming the Emperor.
(iii) He fought a war of succession with his brothers before he became the Emperor.
(iv) His reign witnessed the outbreak of the Maratha Civil War between Sahu and Tara Bai.
(a) ii & iv (b) ii, iii, iv
(c) i, iii, iv (d) i & ii

369. What is the correct chronological sequence for the following Mughal Emperors?
(i) Akbar-II (ii) Alamgir-II
(iii) Bahadur Shah-II (iv) Shah Alam-II
(a) iii, i, iv, ii (b) ii, iii, i, iv
(c) ii, iv, i, iii (d) iv, iii, ii, i

370. Give the correct chronological sequence:
(i) Nadir Shah's invasion of India.
(ii) First invasion of Ahmad Shah Abdali in India.
(iii) Banda Bahadur led the revolt of the Sikhs.
(iv) British captured Delhi.
(a) iii, i, ii, iv (b) i, ii, iii, iv
(c) iv, i, iii, ii (d) i, iv, ii, iii

371. The tendency towards carving out autonomous states first became prominent and started to gain momentum since the period of:
(a) Muhammad Shah
(b) Bahadur Shah I
(c) Ahmad Shah
(d) Farrukhsiyar

372. Murshid Quli Khan, the Mughal governor of Bengal, basically was:
(a) An Afghan
(b) A Persian
(c) A South Indian Brahmin
(d) An Iraqi

373. Who among the following was defeated by Ahmad Shah Abdali in the Third Battle of Panipat?
(a) Sikhs (b) Marathas
(c) Jats (d) Rajputs

374. Who among the following 18th century Indian rulers has been called 'Plato of his tribe'?
(a) Sawai Jai Singh (b) Badam Singh
(c) Suraj Mal (d) Guru Gobind Singh

375. After the Third Battle of Panipat, Ahmad Shah Abdali invaded India thrice to punish:
(a) The Jats (b) The Sikhs
(c) The Satnamis (d) The Marathas

376. Who was responsible for the transformation of the Sikh from a devotional religious sect into a militant anti-Muslim brotherhood in the 17th century?
(a) Guru Teg Bahadur
(b) Guru Amar Singh
(c) Guru Arjan Das
(d) Guru Hargobind

377. Ranjit Singh was the chief of:
(a) Nihang Misl
(b) Ramgarhia Misl
(c) Sukerchakia Misl
(d) Dalewalia Misl

378. The institution of Guruship ended with the demise of Guru Gobind Singh and the spiritual authority passed to:
(a) Granth Sahib
(b) The Almighty
(c) The sayings of the earlier Gurus
(d) The initiation ceremony

379. Identify the distinguished Rajput ruler of the 18th century who was a great law maker, astronomer, town-planner and scientist.
(a) Dalel Singh of Bundi
(b) Rana Jagat Singh of Mewar
(c) Sawai Jai Singh of Amber
(d) Abhai Singh of Marwar

380. The world famous diamond, the Koh-i-noor, came to Ranjit Singh from:
(a) Dost Muhammad
(b) Nadir Shah
(c) Zaman Shah
(d) Shah Shuja

381. The founder of the autonomous kingdom of Awadh was:
(a) Asaf-ud-Daula (b) Safdarjung
(c) Saadat Khan (d) Shiya-ud-Daula

382. The state of Hyderabad was founded by:
(a) Chin Qalich Khan
(b) Nasir Jang
(c) Muzaffar Jang
(d) Zulfiqar Khan

383. Who amongst the following Sultans of Bengal shifted his capital from Murshidabad to Monghyr?
(a) Mir Qasim (b) Mir Jafar
(c) Shiraj-ud-daulah (d) Shuja-ud-din

384. Hyder Ali established his authority over Mysore by overthrowing
(a) Devraj (b) Nanjaraj
(c) Kaviraja (d) Krishna Raj

385. Who amongst the following was the most important Rajput ruler in the early eighteenth century?
(a) Uday Singh (b) Sawai Madho Singh
(c) Sawai Jai Singh (d) Ajit Singh

386. Match the following list:

	List I (Officials)		List II (Functions)
A.	*Pandit Rao*	1.	In-charge of charity
B.	*Samant*	2.	Finance Minister
C.	*Sachiva*	3.	In-charge of correspondence and provincial accounts
D.	*Amatya*	4.	Foreign Minister
E.	*Danadhyaksha*	5.	Court recorder
		6.	Royal Chaplain

(a) A-6, B-4, C-3, D-2, E-l
(b) A-4, B-l, C-6, D-5, E-2
(c) A-4, B-6, C-3, D-5, E-2
(d) A-6, B-4, C-3, D-l, E-2

387. Who was regarded as the "Nana Saheb"?
(a) Balaji Viswanath
(b) Balaji Baji Rao
(c) Sawai Madhav Rao
(d) Baji Rao-I

388. Put in correct chronological sequence, the successors of Shivaji.
(i) Sahu (ii) Shivaji II
(iii) Rajaram (iv) Sambhaji
(v) Ram Raja
(a) iv, iii, ii, i, v (b) ii, i, v, iii, iv
(c) v, iv, ii,i, iii (d) i, ii, iii, v, iv

389. Identify the correct statements about the Third Battle of Panipat in 1761:
(i) Full utilisation of the guerilla tactics of warfare was made by Marathas.
(ii) Ahmad Shah Abdali led the Afghan forces and Balaji Baji Rao led the Maratha forces.
(iii) Sadasiva Rao Bhan and Viswas Rao along with the other leaders were killed in the battle.

(iv) In spite of all possible help from the Rajput chiefs, the Marathas were defeated by the Afghans.

(a) iii only (b) i, ii, iv
(c) ii, iii, iv (d) iii and iv

390. Match the following lists:

List I (Maratha Confederacis)	List II (Headquarters)
1. Holkar	A. Nagpur
2. Scindhia	B. Poona
3. Peshwa	C. Indore
4. Gaekwad	D. Baroda
5. Bhonsle	E. Gwalior

(a) 1-B, 2-E, 3-A, 4-C, 5-D
(b) 1-C, 2-E, 3-B, 4-D, 5-A
(c) 1-A, 2-B, 3-C, 4-D, 5-E
(d) 1-D, 2-A, 3-E, 4-C, 5-B

391. What was '*Saranjam*' of the Marathas?
(a) Tribute paid by the Maratha chiefs to the ruler.
(b) Revenue system in which measurement of land was the basis of assessment of land revenue.
(c) In lieu of salaries, the military commanders and the big officials were assigned lands.
(d) Tax collected from traders and merchants.

392. Next to Shivaji, who was the greatest exponent of *guerilla* warfare?
(a) Balaji Viswanath (b) Tarabai
(c) Baji Rao-I (d) Rajaram

393. Shivaji was born in
(a) Poona in the year 1615.
(b) Raigarh in the year 1622.
(c) Purandhar in the year 1607.
(d) Shivner in the year 1627.

394. In 1637, Shivaji inherited a Jagir from his father for the maintenance of his mother as well as himself. Identify the Jagir:
(a) Javli (b) Poona
(c) Toma (d) Kolhapur

395. Shivaji signed the Treaty of Purandhar in which year and with whom?
(a) 1650—Afzal Khan
(b) 1660—Raja Jaswant Singh
(c) 1665—Raja Jai Singh
(d) 1645—Shaista Khan

396. Identify the two Maratha states that always remained hostile to each other.
(a) Holkar-Gaikwads
(b) Gaikwad-Bhonsle
(c) Scindhia-Bhonsle
(d) Holkar-Scindhia

397. After the Third Battle of Panipat, the lost glory of the Marathas was regained by:
(a) Madhav Rao I (b) Balaji II
(c) Raghunath Rao (d) Balaji Baji Rao

398. The Peshwas originally were:
(a) Successors of Yadavas of Devagiri
(b) Bhonsle Marathas
(c) Chitpawan Brahmins
(d) Malaviya Brahmins

399. From whom did the Marathas in all probability secure training in the art of *guerilla* warfare?
(a) Mir Jumla of Golconda
(b) Malik Amber, the Abyssinian minister of Ahmednagar
(c) Malik Kafur
(d) Mir Jaffar

400. Who was Dadaji Kondadeva?
(a) Shivaji's father
(b) Shivaji's maternal uncle
(c) Shivaji's guardian tutor
(d) Peshwas of Poona

401. Jai Singh besieged the fort of Purandhar, because it was
(a) Shivaji's place of refuge.
(b) Reported to be the weakest fort.
(c) Surrounded by Mughal territory.
(d) Located at the heart of Shivaji's territories and he had lodged his family and treasures there.

402. Shivaji's system of administration was largely borrowed from the administrative practices of:
(a) The Mughal empire
(b) The Deccani states
(c) The Empire of Vijayanagar
(d) Both (b) and (c)

403. After the fall of Raigarh to the Mughals, the next capital of the Maratha government was:
(a) Satara (b) Kolhapur
(c) Pune (d) Supa

404. Which of the following successors of Shivaji approached the British government on many occasions to help them against the Peshwa?
(a) Ramaraja (b) Sahu II
(c) Pratap Singh (d) Shahji Appasaheb

405. Match the following lists of Maratha ministers and their responsibilities:

	List I	List II
A.	*Sumant or Dabir*	1. Personal safety of king
B.	*Sar-i-Naubat*	2. Charitable work
C.	*Waqia Navis*	3. Foreign affairs
D.	*Pundit Rao*	4. Recruitment and training of army

Code:
(a) A-1, B-2, C-3, D-4
(b) A-2, B-1, C-3, D-4
(c) A-4, B-3, C-1, D-2
(d) A-3, B-4, C-1, D-2

406. Match the following lists of army classes under the Marathas and their Attributes.

	List I (Class of Army	List II (Attributes)
A.	Foot soldiers	1. Expert in guerilla warfare
B.	Bargis	2. Part of Cavalry, recruited with fixed pay and horses
C.	Silahdars	3. Part of cavalry who got a share in war booty but not a regular pay.

(a) A-1, B-2, C-3 (b) A-1, B-3, C-2
(c) A-2, B-3, C-1 (d) A-3, B-2, C-1

407. Which of the following is correct about ***Chauth*** and ***Sardeshmukhi***?
(a) The *Chauth* amounted to one-fourth of the standard revenue assessment of the place
(b) Sardeshmukhi was an additional levy of 10 per cent
(c) *Chauth* and *Sardeshmukh* were levied as a safeguard against Maratha forces
(d) All of the above

408. Who among the following were the first Europeans to set up trading settlements in India?
(a) Dutch (b) Portuguese
(c) French (d) Spanish

409. Who captured Goa for the Portuguese in 1510?
(a) Albuquerque (b) Vasco-da-Gama
(c) Sir Thomas Roe (d) Duplex

410. Which two Europeans were involved in the Battle of Wandiwash in 1760?
(a) Portuguese and Spanish
(b) Dutch and British
(c) French and British
(d) Portuguese and British

411. Which were the two headquarters of the French East India Company on the eastern coast of India?
(a) Fort William and Arcot
(b) Arcot and Karikal
(c) Chandernagore and Masulipatnam
(d) Chandernagore and Pondicherry

412. Vasco da Gama found out a new route to India and in 1498 reached?
(a) Pulicat (b) Karikal
(c) Goa (d) Calicut

413. What was the occasion for the Portuguese to hand over Bombay to the British?
(a) Growth of peaceful relations between the English and the Portuguese as a result of Portugal's independence from the control of Spain.
(b) The marriage of Charles II with the Portuguese princess Catherine of Braganza.
(c) The defeat of Spanish Armada by the British in 1588.
(d) The Treaty of Madrid concluded in 1630.

414. Identify the positive effects of the beginning of European Commerce in India.
(i) Money economy grew up.
(ii) International market relations were set-up.
(iii) Increased quantity of India's export.
(iv) Price hike was fast.
(v) Indian agriculture was further commercialised.
(a) i, iv, v (b) ii, iii, iv
(c) i, ii, iii, v (d) i, ii, iii

415. Name the Europeans whose missionary activities were more important than trade and commerce.
(a) Dutch (b) Portuguese
(c) Danes (d) Swedish

416. Who were first to be allowed to make war, conclude treaties, acquire territories and build fortresses?
(a) The Netherlanders
(b) French
(c) British
(d) Portuguese

417. What was the commercial aim of the Portuguese in India?
(a) Oust Arabs and Persians from India's maritime trade.
(b) Capture pepper and other superior spices trade.
(c) Capture textiles and spice trades.
(d) Capture territories on the Western coast.

418. The English East India Company's first 'Presidency' in India was
(a) Madras (b) Masulipatnam
(c) Surat (d) Hughli

419. Who were the interlopers ?
(a) Indian brokers through whom the Europeans bought commodities from India.
(b) Portuguese pirates in the Indian Ocean.
(c) Mughal revenue officials.
(d) English merchants who, in spite of the company's monopoly, traded independently.

420. When did the Danes arrive in India and formed an East India Company?
(a) 1615 (b) 1614
(c) 1616 (d) 1617

421. Identify Fort St. George and Fort William with their respective settlement.
(a) Madras and Calcutta
(b) Bombay and Calcutta
(c) Calcutta and Madras
(d) Madras and Bombay

422. Bring out the correct statements about British expansion in Madras
(i) In 1658, all the English settlements on the Coromandal and in Eastern India were placed under the control of Fort St. George.
(ii) In 1801, Lord Wellesley created the Madras presidency as it existed till Indian Independence.
(iii) In 1640, the British obtained the site of Madras from the Raja of Valikondapuram.
(iv) The British built a fortfied factory, viz. Fort St George, at Madras.
(a) i, ii, iii (b) i & iii
(c) i, ii, iv (d) ii, iii, iv

423. When and by whom were the Portuguese driven out of Hughli in Bengal?
(a) 1631-Qasim Khan
(b) 1666-Prince Shuja
(c) 1625-Shaista Khan
(d) 1650-Prince Murad

424. Match the following lists of years and remarkable developments in the East India Company:

List I (Development in East India Company)	**List II (Year)**
A. Establishment of factory of Masulipatnam	1. 1651
B. Jehangir's firman to establish a factory at Surat	2. 1667
C. Receipt of the right from the Nawab of Bengal to carry trade on payment of a fixed duty	3. 1616
D. Receipt of Aurangzeb's firman to trade in Bengal	4. 1609

(a) A-1, B-2, C-3, D-4
(b) A-3, B-4, C-1, D-2
(c) A-3, B-4, C-2, D-1
(d) A-4, B-3, C-1, D-2

425. The Dutch set up its first factory of Masulipatam in
(a) 1605 (b) 1610
(c) 1616 (d) 1641

426. Match the following lists of Portuguese's penetration into India and the year:

List I (Portuguese Penetration)	List II (Year)
A. Establishment of a factory at Cochin	1. 1510
B. Defeat hands of Gujarat at the bends of Almeida	2. 1661
C. Capture of Goa from Bijapur	3. 1509
D. Gifting of Bombay to Prince Charles of England as dowry	4. 1502

(a) A-1, B-2, C-3, D-4
(b) A-2, B-1, C-3, D-4
(c) A-4, B-3. C-1, D-2
(d) A-3, B-4, C-1, D-2

427. In which of the following years was the Dutch East India Company formed?
(a) 1599 (b) 1600
(c) 1602 (d) 1607

428. The Battle of Plassey was fought between
(a) Mir Qasim, Shuja-ud-Daulah and East India Company
(b) Siraj-ud-Daulah and East India Company
(c) Haider Ali and East India Company
(d) Tipu Sultan and East India Company

429. Who among the following was twice made the Nawab of Bengal by the East India Company?
(a) Mir Jafar (b) Mir Qasim
(c) Siraj-ud-Daulah (d) Shah Alam-II

430. The British paramountcy in India was completed in 1856 with
(a) Annexation of Punjab
(b) Annexation of Sind
(c) Annexation of Carnatic
(d) Annexation of Awadh

431. Match the following :

A. Treaty of Seringapatam	1. 1792
B. Death of Haider	2. 1782
C. Treaty of Mangalore	3. 1784
D. Death of Tipu	4. 1799

(a) A-1, B-2, C-3, D-4
(b) A-2, B-l, C-4, D-3
(c) A-4, B-3, C-1, D-2
(d) A-3, B-4, C-2, D-1

432. Identify the signatories to the Tripartite Treaty.
(i) Ranjit Singh (ii) Lord Auckland
(iii) Shah Shuja (iv) Zaman Shah
(v) William Bentick
(A) i, ii, iii (b) ii, iv, v
(c) i, iv, v (d) i, iii, iv

433. By which Governor General and when was the Carnatic state annexed?
(a) Lord Minto-1808
(b) Lord Wellesly-1801
(c) Sir John Shore-1797
(d) Lord Cornwallis-1792

434. Identify the Englishman, who gave all the information about the "Black-Hole Episode", though in a single-sided way.
(a) Stephenson (b) Minchin
(c) John Surman (d) Holwell

435. Match the following :
A. Hector Munro B. Nazm-ud-daula
C. Robert Clive D. Shuja-ud-din
1. The first Nawab of Bengal, Bihar and Orissa.
2. Battle of Plassey
3. Battle of Buxar
4. The last Nawab of Bengal, Bihar and Orissa.
(a) A-4, B-2, C-l, D-3
(b) A-l, B-3, C-4, D-2
(c) A-3, B-4, C-2, D-1
(d) A-2, B-l, C-3, D-4

436. The Treaty of Seringapatam signed by Tipu and Cornwallis, contained:
(i) Payment of a war indemnity of about Rs. 3 crores by Tipu.
(ii) Giving two sons of Tipu as hostages to the British camp.
(iii) Surrender of almost half of Tipu's territories, which were to be shared among the English, the Nizam and the Marathas.
(iv) Stationing of a British Resident at Seringapatam.
(a) ii, iii, iv (b) iii & iv
(c) i, ii, iii, iv (d) i, ii, iii

437. How many wars were fought between the Marathas and the East India Company?
(a) 4 (b) 3
(c) 2 (d) 1

438. The Subsidiary Alliance System was used by
(a) Warren Hastings
(b) Dalhousie
(c) Cornwallis
(d) Wellesley

439. The annexation of which of the following states by the British was not done by using Doctrine of Lapse?
(a) Jhansi (b) Nagpur
(c) Awadh (d) Satara

Instructions: In questions 440 & 441, (A) stands for Assertion; (R) stands for Reason. Write (a) if only (A) is correct; Write (b) if only (R) is correct; Write (c) if both (A) and (R) are correct and (R) explains (A); and Write (d) if both (A) and (R) are correct but (R) does not explain (A).

440. Assertion (A): Battle of Buxar was less important than the Battle of Plassey, from the military point of view.
Reason (R): Due to superior military techniques, the British won the Battle of Buxar.

441. Assertion (A): The Dual system of Government was an adroit measure of Clive to mask the real position of the Company in Bengal.
Reason (R): The serious defects inherent in the Dual Government

442. Ranjit Singh died in 1839 and this led to anarchy and confusion within his dominion. But finally a ruler was placed on the throne under the regency of mother Rani Jhindan. Who was he ?
(a) Kharak Singh (b) Gulab Singh
(c) Dalip Singh (d) Dhian Singh

443. What was the most important reason for the First Anglo-Sikh War (1845-46) ?
(a) The attempts of the English Company to interefere with the internal matters of the Lahore state.
(b) The agreement entered between the Dogra Chief, Gulab Singh, and the English to sell Kashmir to the former
(c) To divert the energies of ungovernable Khalsa army
(d) The war-like peparations of the English across the Sutlej

444. Awadh was annexed by Lord Dalhousie in 1856. Which one of the following statements about Nawab Wajid Ali Shah, the last Nawab of Awadh, is NOT correct ?
(a) He was a great patron of Indian music and dance
(b) He had good command over Persian and Urdu languages and wrote several books
(c) He is regarded as the father of modern Urdu langauge
(d) The prolonged period of peace and prosperity during his rule resulted in the growth of a distinct Lucknow culture around the Oudh court

445. Which amongst the following was NOT annexed to the British empire under Subsidiary Alliance?
(a) Hyderabad (b) Mysore
(c) Jodhpur (d) Jhansi

446. Consider the following points:
I. Naval superiority
II. Home government's complete approval to policies and programmes
III. Control over Bengal
IV. Comparatively secure geographical position of England

Which of the above were the causes of the English success in India against the French?
(a) I, II, III and IV
(b) I, II and III
(c) I, III and IV
(d) I and III

447. Which of the following is wrongly matched?
(a) Treaty of Surat: 1775
(b) Treaty of Salbai: 1782
(c) Treaty of Deogaon: 1803
(d) Treaty of Bassein: 1805

448. Consider the following points:
I. Right to the English to free trade in Avadh
II. Approval to stationing of a British army in Avadh at the cost of the Nawab
III. Granting of Kora and Allahabad districts to the Mughal emperor Shah Alam II
IV. Diwani of Bengal, Bihar and Orissa to the British.

Which amongst the above were the highlights of the Treaty of Allahabad (1765) between the Mughal emperor, Nawab of Avadh and the English?

(a) I, II, III and IV (b) I, III and IV
(c) I and IV (d) III and IV

449. The Marathas were defeated in the Anglo-Maratha wars due to
(a) lack of capable leadership
(b) military weaknesses
(c) failure in estimating correctly the strength of the British
(d) all of the above

450. Which of the following is NOT true about Tipu Sultan?
(a) Attempt to establish a Navy on modern lines
(b) Setting up of a Board of Admiralty
(c) Opposition to French soldiers' setting up a Jacobin Club in Serinagpatnan
(d) Plantation of the Tree of Liberty at Serinagpatnam

451. Which of the following is true about the Treaty of Lahore (1846) between the English and the Sikhs ?
(a) The territories lying to the south of river Sutlej were given to the English
(b) Sir Henry Lawrence was appointed as Brithish Resident of Lahore
(c) The English got control over Kashmir region
(d) All of the above

452. Who of the following were the British officers who expelled the Pindaris from Malwa and Chambal regions in 1817?
(a) Thomas Hislop
(b) John Malcom
(c) Both (a) and (b)
(d) Neither (a) nor (b)

453. Consider the following:
I. End of dual system of government
II. Setting up of the Calcutta Madrasa in 1781
III. Impeachment on charges of murder and bribery
IV. Permanent Settlement of Bengal

Warren Hastings was associated with which of the following?
(a) I, II and III (b) II, III and IV
(c) I, III and IV (d) I and II

454. Which of the following were the highlights of Cornwallis' regime?
I. Permanent Settlement of Bengal
II. Reorganization of revenue courts
III. Compilation of 'Cornwallis Code'
IV. Establishment of the ***thanas***
(a) I and III (b) I and II
(c) I, III and IV (d) I, II, III and IV

455. Who of the following Governor-Generals is associated with Subsidiary Alliance System?
(a) Lord Cornwallis (b) Lord Wellesley
(c) Lord Mayo (d) Lord Dalhousie

456. Which of the following did **NOT** occur during the Governor-Generalship of William Bentinck?
(a) Abolition of **sati**
(b) Macaulay's Reforms
(c) Establishment of a Medical College at Calcutta
(d) Annexation of Sindh to the British empire

457. Who was the first Governor-General of India?
(a) Warren Hastings
(b) Willian Bentinck
(c) Lord Dalhousie
(d) Lord Canning

458. Who was the first Viceroy of India?
(a) Lord Dalhousie
(b) Lord Canning
(c) Warren Hastings
(d) Robert Clive

459. Match the following lists of Viceroys and events:

List I (Viceroys)	**List II (Events)**
A. Lord Canning	1. Kuka movement
B. John Lawrence	2. Setting up of Department of Agriculture
C. Lord Mayo	3. Famine Commission under Campbell
D. Lord Northbrooke	4. Transfor of the government from the Company to the British crown

(a) A-4, B-3, C-2, D-1
(b) A-3, B-4, C-2, D-1
(c) A-1, B-2, C-3, D-4
(d) A-2, B-1, C-4, D-3

Who was the Viceroy of India when the Indian National Congress was formed?
(a) Lord Ripon (b) Lord Northbrooke
(c) Lord Dufferin (d) Lord Lansdowne

Lord Ripon was associated with
(a) removal of Vernacular Press Act
(b) resolution for institution of local-self government
(c) enactment of the First Factory Act
(d) all of the above

Match the following columns of Viceroys and Events;

List I (Viceroys)	List II (Events)
A. Lord Ripon	1. Introduction of the Ilbert Bill
B. Lord Lytton	2. Appointment of a Famine Commission under Strachey
C. Lord Dufferin	3. Annexation of Upper Burma
D. Lord Hardinge II	4. A coronation Durbar at Delhi

(a) A-1, B-2, C-3, D-4
(b) A-2, B-1, C-3, D-4
(c) A-3, B-4, C-1, D-2
(d) A-4, B-2, C-3, D-1

Who amongst the following Viceroys ruled for the longest period?
(a) Lord Curzon (b) Lord Hardinge II
(c) Lord Willingdon (d) Lord Linlithgow

Consider the following :
I. Enactment of Cooperative Credit Societies Act
II. Establishment of Agricultural Research Institute at Pusa
III. Establishment of an Archaeological Department
IV. Constitution of a Police Commission under Andrew Frazer

Which of the above events occurred during Curzon?
(a) I, II, III and IV (b) I, II and III
(c) II, III and IV (d) III and IV

465. Lord Linlithgow's Viceroylty is remarkable for
(a) arrival of the Cripps Mission
(b) beginning of the Quit India Movement
(c) both (a) and (b)
(d) Neither (a) nor (b)

466. The Indo-Afghan border or the **Durand Line** was demarcated during the viceroyalty of
(a) Lord Elgin I (b) Lord Lansdowne
(c) Lord Chelmsford (d) Lord Reading

467. Who was the Viceroy of India when the Muslim League launched the heinous 'Direct Action Day'?
(a) Lord Linlithgow
(b) Lord Wavell
(c) Lord Mountbatten
(d) C. Rajagopalachari

468. Which of the following is/are wrongly matched?
I. Lytton : Lee Commission
II. Mayo : Scholarship scheme
III. Ripon: Repeal of Vernacular Press Act
IV. Canning : Queen Victoria's Proclamation
(a) II, III and IV (b) I and II
(c) II and IV (d) IV only

469. Railways were introduced in India when the Governor-General was
(a) Curzon (b) Dalhousie
(c) Hardinge (d) Ripon

470. "White Mutiny" by the European soldiers was staged during the period of
(a) Canning (b) Ripon
(c) Dalhousie (d) Mayo

471. Lord Dalhousie introduced the first railways in 1853 which ran between:
(a) Calcutta and Bombay
(b) Agra and Madras
(c) Bombay and Thane
(d) Calcutta and Agra

472. Who was the Viceroy of India when the Jallianwala Incident took place.?
(a) Lord Hardinge II
(b) Lord Chelmsford
(c) Lord Reading
(d) None of the above

473. The title of 'Viceroy' was added to the centre office of the Govenror-General of India for the first-time in
(a) 1848 A.D. (b) 1858 A.D.
(c) 1862 A.D. (d) 1856 A.D.

474 Which of the following is wrongly matched?
(a) The Pitt's India Act (1784)—Board of Control to guide and control Company's affairs.
(b) Charter Act of 1813—Company's monopoly of trade with India ended.
(c) Charter Act of 1833—Company's debt taken over by the Government of India.
(d) Charter Act of 1853—To regulate Company's affairs.

475. Who abolished the system of Dual Government in Bengal?
(a) Clive (b) Cornwallis
(c) Warren Hastings (d) William Bentinck

476. The credit of creation of the Covenanted Civil Service of India, which came to be regarded as the Indian Civil Service from 1861 onwards, goes to
(a) Warren Hastings (b) William Bentinck
(c) Wellesley (d) Cornwallis

477. Which one of the following Acts of British India strengthened the Viceroy's authority over his executive council by substituting "portfolio" or departmental system for corporate functioning ?
(a) Indian Council's Act, 1892
(b) Government of India Act, 1858
(c) Indian Councils Act, 1861
(d) Indian Councils Act, 1909

478. Match the following list of charter Acts and their provision:

	List I (Charter Act)	**List II (Provision)**
A.	Charter Act, 1793	1. Company's monopoly of trade with India
B.	Charter Act, 1813	2. Company's monopoly of trade with China and in tea
C.	Charter Act, 1833	3. Company's trade monopoly ended
D.	Charter Act, 1853	4. Separation of legislative and executive councils

(a) A-1, B-2, C-3, D-4
(b) A-2, B-1, C-3, D-4
(c) A-4, B-3, C-2, D-1
(d) A-3, B-2, C-4, D-1

479. Lord Wellesley founded the Fort William College for training of the civil servants at Calcutta in
(a) 1800 (b) 1802
(c) 1805 (d) 1807

480. Which of the following Acts provided that all recruitments to the coveted Civil Services were to be through competitive examination?
(a) Charter Act of 1813
(b) Charter Act of 1833
(c) Charter Act of 1853
(d) Indian Councils Act, 1909

481. Which of the following Commissions dealt with the Civil Services?
(a) Charles Aitchison Commission, 1886
(b) Lord Lee Commission, 1923
(c) Both (a) and (b)
(d) Neither (a) nor (b)

482. Which of the following Commissions recommended the establishment of a Public Service Commission?
(a) Aitchison Commission
(b) Lee Commission
(c) Hunter Commission
(d) None of the above

483. High Courts were established at Calcutta, Madras and Bombay in
(a) 1853 (b) 1858
(c) 1865 (d) 1870

484. The first Law Commission to codify Indian rules and regulations was constituted under
(a) Metcafe (b) Macaulay
(c) Aitchison (d) None of the above

485. Which of the following is NOT correct about the development of local-self government during the British rule?
(a) The Indian Council Act of 1861 inaugurated the policy of legislative devolution

(b) In 1870 came Mayo's Resolution on financial decentralisation
(c) In 1908, the Royal Commission on Decentralisation reviewed the entire subject of self-government
(d) Under the Government of India Act 1919, local self-government became a reserved subject.

486. Which of the following Acts delegated the power of framing laws to the Governor-General-in-Council?
(a) Charter Act of 1833
(b) Charter Act of 1853
(c) The Government of India Act of 1919
(d) The Government of India Act of 1935

487. Which of the following Acts provided for the establishment of a Federal Public Service Commission and Provincial Public Service Commission?
(a) The Government of India Act, 1909
(b) The Government of India Act, 1919
(c) The Government of India Act, 1935
(d) The Independence of India Act, 1947

488. The Charter Act of 1833 accepted educational qualifications for the ICS appointment under its
(a) Clause 86 (b) Clause 76
(c) Clause 87 (d) Clause 82

489. **Assertion (A) :** The British introduced a uniform civil code for all Indians irrespective of their religion.
Reason (R) : A Law Commission headed by Lord Macaulay codified all the available Indian laws.
(a) Both (A) and (R) are correct and (R) explains (A)
(b) Both (A) and (R) are correct but (R) does not explain (A)
(c) Only (A) is correct
(d) Only (R) is correct

490. Who was the founder of 'Drain Theory' which, among others, exposed the constant drain of wealth from India to England?
(a) S.N. Bannerjee
(b) Gopal Krishna Gokhale
(c) Dadabhai Naoroji
(d) M.K. Gandhi

491. Why did British resort to the 'Downward Filtration Theory' till 1854 ?
(a) To justify their social policy in India
(b) To justify their education policy in India
(c) To justify their industrial policy in India
(d) To justify their commercial policy in India

492. Match the following :

A. Permanent Settlement	1. Parts of Madras and Bombay Presidencies
B. Ryotwari Settlement	2. Gangetic Valley, North-West Provinces, Punjab.
C. Mahalwari Settlement	3. Bengal and Bihar

(a) A-3, B-l, C-2 (b) A- 1, B-2, C-3
(c) A-3, B-2, C-l (d) A-2, B-l, C-3

493. How was India converted into "a classic colony" in the 19th century?
(a) By converting her into an importer and absorber of British machine made goods.
(b) By turning her into a fertile ground for British capital investment.
(c) By converting her into a producer of raw materials to feed British industries.
(d) Both (a) and (c).

494. With whom was the Permanent Settlement made?
(a) With the peasant, cultivators.
(b) With the muqaddams
(c) With the zamindars
(d) With the village communities.

Instructions: In question 495, (A) stands for Assertion. (R) stands for Reason. Write (a) if only (A) is correct; (b) if only (R) is correct; (c) if (A) and (R) are both, correct and (R) is the proper explanation of (A); and (d) if (A) and (R) are both correct but (R) does not explain (A).

495. **Assertion (A):** In the Mercantile stage of British colonialism in India, large scale ekport of British goods to India was absent
Reason (R): In the first stage of colonialism, the British did not introduce any basic change in India's economy, society and culture.

496. Heavy industries could not develop in India during the 19th century primarily due to :
(a) Inadequate production of coal
(b) The lack of capital
(c) The lack of raw material
(d) The lack of skilled labour

497. Which was NOT a genuine hurdle in the growth of Indian industries under the British?
(a) Capital sources
(b) Competition from industries of Europe
(c) Policy of free-trade
(d) Absence of state protection to infant industries

498. Regarding British industrial capitalism which of the following is NOT correct ?
(a) When the Industrial Revolution of Britain picked up, three was opposition to the Company Rule in India
(b) Limiting the trade of the East India Company to the export of opium to China was in the interest of British manufacturers
(c) The whole British policy was deliberately planned to make India an agricultural appendage to British imperial interests
(d) With the end of the Company rule, British Industrialists and merchants were able to establish their capitalist hold

499. What made the British invest their capital in India ?
(a) The British rule was characterised by benevolent despotism. Hence they believed in the welfare of the people
(b) The British wanted India to become an Industrial country
(c) British capitalism was confronted with the problem of surplus capital
(d) The British wanted to improve trade with India

500. Identify one of the following which was NOT one of the reasons for the conditions of trade going against India and the decline of her purchasing power ?
(a) Destruction of its principal foreign exchange earning industry, namely, cotton-weaving
(b) The price of Indian cotton was higher and its quality was poorer than that of the American cotton
(c) The demand for pepper, sugar and cinnamon had also fallen off considerably
(d) Short falls in the production of bullion in the country

501. The British invested large capital in Inc various enterprises. Which one of the fo ing industry did NOT attract British cap
(a) Cotton textile (b) Shipping
(c) Insurance (d) Tea plantation

502. Which of the following was NOT one c reasons why railways constituted a drai India?
(a) Interest on foreign investments remitted outside India
(b) The stock was purchased in Englar
(c) They were financially losing concer
(d) Excessive salaries were paid to European employees who sent savings to England

503. The British contributed to the poverty o Indian peasants by :
(a) Crating an aristocratic class of zamir
(b) Encouraging fragmentation of lands
(c) Imposing high revenue charges
(d) Bestowing proprietary rights in lan peasants

504. Which was NOT a feature of the new system under the British ?
(a) The individual land-holder was dir linked with the centralised state
(b) The village panchayats retained the pc to settle all land disputes
(c) The bonds which originally tied the vi peasant to the village collectively b down
(d) The peasant paid rack-rent

505. Which was NOT a ruinous feature of In agriculture under the British ?
(a) Extreme sub-division of land and fragmentation
(b) Land holdings became more and more economic
(c) Commercialisation of agriculture
(d) Increase in the number and powe zamindars

506. Which of the following was/were the dem of the Permanent Settlement ?
(I) It proved harmful for the zamindars could not realise dues from cultiva and wee forced to surrender their la

(II) It led to rise of absentee landism, with landlords neglecting the lands
(III) It made the condition of tillers miserable by making them completely dependent on the zamindars
(IV) It divided the society into two hostile classes, viz., zamindars and tenants
(a) I, II and III only (b) I only
(c) II and IV only (d) I, II, III and IV

507. Indicate one of the following systems which helped develop the closest ties between the people and the government ?
(a) Ryotwari system
(b) Zamindari system
(c) Mahalwari system
(d) Mootadari system

508. The British introduced 'Mahalwari System' in :
(a) The Gangetic valley, the North-West Province, part of Central India, and the Punjab
(b) Bengal, Bihar, Orissa, Northern districts of Madras and districts of Varanasi, coastal districts of Andhra
(c) In parts of Madras and Bombay Presidencies
(d) In Central India and Awadh

509. The spread of landlordism was marked by the growth of :
(a) Aristocracy (b) Capitalism
(c) Sub-infeudation (d) Cultivation

510. Commercialisation of agriculture had manifold impact. Which one of the following has been wrong listed ?
(a) It resulted in steady increase in food production which considerably brought down prices of agricultural products
(b) It gave a serious setback to the self-sufficient character of village community in India
(c) It resulted in the rise of a powerful class of money-lenders in the villages
(d) It resulted in more land being brought under cultivation

511. Which of the measures taken by Britain was the most revealing in the context of economic exploitation of India by the British?
(a) Two laws of the British Parliament in 18th Century forbade the use of cotton and silk goods imported from India
(b) At one time the Court of Directors stopped the import of printed calico be cause of pressure from Manchester merchants
(c) Daniel Defoe in his novel 'Robinson Crusoe' complained that the cloth from India had crept into their houses, closets and bedchambers
(d) Laws were passed forbidding the use of printed or dyed cotton cloth and in 1760 a lady was fined £ 200 for possessing an imported handkerchief

512. Which period of Modern India was the most disgraceful in the brazen exploitation of the country ?
(a) The Diwani era from 1765 to 1765
(b) The period from 1757 to 1765
(c) The period from 1813 to 1858
(d) The period from 1853 to 1919

513. Which was the main difference between the previous conquerors of India and the British?
(a) The previous conquerors had come as conquerors while the British came as traders
(b) The previous conquerors had gradually become a part of Indian life but the British conquerors never became an integral part of Indian life
(c) The previous conquerors had come through land routes, the British came via sea and established naval supremacy
(d) The previous conquerors belonged to Central Asia, but the British being Europeans were ethnically and culturally different

514. A striking characteristic of Indian cultural Renaissance was:
(a) Growth of new schools of philosophy.
(b) Birth of new regional languages.
(c) Research oriented study of the past history and antiquities of India.
(d) Growth of novel at the expense of other forms of writing.

515. What was the objective of the Vaikom Satyagraha launched in Kerala?
(a) Remove untouchability.
(b) Force the temple authorities to appoint non-brahmins as priests.
(c) Ban the institution of Devadasis for temple service.
(d) Open the temples for the entry of the lower castes avarnas.

516. Find out the aspect of the caste system which was condemned by all social reformers.
(a) Ashram System (b) Jati system
(c) Untouchability (d) Varna System

517. Who said "If it was proved to me that it (untouchability) is an essential part of Hinduism I for one would declare myself an open rebel against Hinduism itself"?
(a) B.R. Ambedkar (b) M.K. Gandhi
(c) B.G. Tilak (d) Jyotiba Phule

518. The earliest movement which took up the cause of lower caste against Brahmana domination was
(a) Nair Service Society
(b) Satya Shodak Society
(c) Mahajan Sangam
(d) Vokkaliga Sangha

519. Which of the following is false regarding Prarthana Samaj.
(a) It was founded by MG. Ranade.
(b) It was an off-shoot of Brahmo Samaj.
(c) It was a reform movement within Hinduism and concentrated on social reforms.
(d) It was founded in 1867 in Bombay.

520. Who founded the 'Bhil Seva Mandal' in 1922 to elevate the condition of the Bhils and other aboriginals in India?
(a) C.F. Andrews
(b) Amritlal Vithaldas Thakkar
(c) Gurusadave Damle
(d) Krishnaji Keshav Datta

521. There was growth of communalism in India due to the Arya Samaj's programme of:
(a) Eradication of untouchability
(b) The *Shuddhi* movement
(c) Spread of Education among women
(d) Propagation of western education and teaching of science.

522. Swami Dayanand
(i) Attacked the spread of western sciences.
(ii) Organised social services during natural calamities, like floods, droughts, epidemics etc.
(iii) Encouraged inter-caste marriages and widow remarraige.
(iv) Opposed child marriages and polygamy.
(a) ii and iii (b) all of the above
(c) i, ii, iv (d) ii, iii, iv

523. Identify the institution which was turned into Benaras Hindu University by Madan Mohan Malaviya.
(a) Bethune college for women started in 1849 by Ishwar Chandra Vidyasagar.
(b) Hindu college founded in 1817 by David Hare.
(c) Vedanta college founded in 1825 by Rammohan Roy.
(d) Central Hindu school established by Mrs. Annie Besant.

524. "Patriotism is religion and religion is love for India"-whose utterance is this?
(a) Raj Narain Bose
(b) Swami Vivekananda
(c) Bal Gangadhar Tilak
(d) Bankim Chandra Chatterjee

525. Identify the prominent members of the "Servants of India Society".
(i) N.M. Joshi (ii) N.H. Kunzru
(iii) Shri Ram Bajpai (iv) Jyotiba Phule
(v) Gopal Ganesh Agarkar
(a) i, iv, v (b) ii, iii, iv
(c) i, ii, iii (d) iii, iv, v

526. Where did Vivekananda attend the World's Parliament of Religion in 1893?
(a) Chicago (b) New York
(c) Washington (d) Alaska

527. Raja Ram Mohan Roy founded a new religious society, the Brahmo Samaj. Its purpose was to purify Hinduism and to preach theism (worship of a single God). This society was founded in
(a) 1823 (b) 1826
(c) 1828 (d) 1829

528. Identify the social reformer of Maharashtra who adopted the pen name of "Lokahitawadi"?
(a) Atmaram Panduranga
(b) Bal Gangadhar Tilak
(c) Gopal Hari Deshmukh
(d) Krishna Shastri Chaplunkar

529. The Arya Samajists struck deep roots among the
(a) Landless labourers
(b) Harijans
(c) Bureaucracy
(d) Trading Community

530. In 1888, Sir Syed Ahmed founded the
(a) Patriotic Association
(b) Upper Indian Mohammadan Association
(c) National Conference
(d) Muslim League

531. Who was called the Saint of Dakshineswar?
(a) Sant Jnaneshwar
(b) Ramakrishna Paramhansa
(c) Chaitanya Mahaprabhu
(d) Vivekananda

532. In the beginning of the 19th century, Indian Society was suffering from many social and religious ills. What exposed the weakness and decay of Indian Society ?
(a) Impact of Western Culture
(b) Traditional Indian ideas and institutions
(c) The economic exploitation of India
(d) All of the above

533. The main factor(s) which promoted several socio-religious movements in India during the nineteenth century was/were
(a) The spirit of rationalism which impelled Indians to think of all-round development of the country along modern lines
(b) Efforts of Sir William Jones, H.E. Wilson and other Orientalist scholars who encouraged Indians to discover the glories of India's past
(c) Growing activities of Christian Missionaries which made Indian think of putting their own house in order to check possible conversion of Indians to Christianity
(d) All of the above

534. Which of the following are true with regard to Brahmo Samaj?
(I) It laid emphasis on human dignity
(II) It opposed ideal worship
(III) It criticised social evils like Sati
(IV) It incorporated the teachings of other religious
(a) I, II, III and IV (b) I, II and III only
(c) I, II and III only (d) I and IV only

535. Which statement on Keshab Chandra Sen's Brahmo Samaj is incorrect?
(a) It put women's education in the forefront
(b) It discarded image worship
(c) It opposed polygamy, caste, child marriage, purdah system, but favoured widow re-marriage
(d) It believed in the divinity and infallibility of the Vedas

536. Paramahans Mandali, a movement against idolatory and caste system in Maharashtra, was founded by
(a) Jyotiba Phule
(b) M.G. Ranade
(c) Dr. Atmaram Pandurang
(d) Gopal Hari Deshmukh

537. Name one of the following which was NOT the point in the programme of social reform of the Prarthana Samaj.
(a) Intermarriage among different castes
(b) Interdining among different castes
(c) Remarriage of widows
(d) Preaching of unity of God

538. Which one of the following followers of Dayanand rendered great service to the cause of western education by establishing DAV schools and colleges ?
(a) Pandit Guru Dutt
(b) Swami Sharadanand
(c) Mahatma Hans Raj
(d) Lala Lajpat Raj

539. English was made the medium of instruction in India in
(a) 1844 (b) 1835
(c) 1833 (d) 1813

540. Which of the following considered the Magna Carta of English education in India?
(a) Wood's Dispatch
(b) Raleigh Commission
(c) Saddler Commission
(d) Hunter Commission

541. Where did Jonathan Duncan start a Sanskrit College in 1791 to promote the study of Hindu law and philosophy?
(a) Bombay (b) Pune
(c) Calcutta (d) Banaras.

542. In 1823, the Government formed a committee to guide it on educational matters. What was the name of the committee?
(a) General Committee on Public Instruction
(b) British Committee on Public Instruction
(c) Prinsep Committee on Oriental Education.
(d) Adams Committee on Oriental Education.

543. Which of the following Acts provided for one lakh rupees per annum for educational activities in India?
(a) Charter Act of 1813
(b) Charter Act of 1833
(c) Charter Act of 1853
(d) None of the above

544. Who of the following brought forward the 'Infiltration Theory' of education?
(a) Charles Wood (b) Lord Macaulay
(c) Charles Metcalfe (d) W.W. Hunter

545. Which of the following recommended the establishment of one university each in Calcutta, Mumbai and Madras?
(a) Wood's Despatch
(b) Hunter Committee
(c) The Indian Universities Act
(d) Saddler Committee

546. Match the following list of committees/Act and the years in which their recommendations come:

List I (Committee/Acts)	List II (Year of Recommendations)
A. Hunter Committee	1. 1929
B. Indian Universities Act	2. 1882-83
C. Saddler Committee	3. 1904
D. Hartog Committee	4. 1917-19

(a) A-1, B-2, C-3, D-4
(b) A-2, B-3, C-1, D-4
(c) A-2, B-3, C-4, D-1
(d) A-3, B-2, C-4, D-1

547. Which of the following was NOT a feat the Indian Universities Act of 1904?
(a) The Governor-General-in-Counci empowered to define the territorial of a university.
(b) The Governor-General-in-Council empowered to decide the affiliati universities.
(c) The Government's control ove universities was decreased
(d) The Government was to appoint Fe in a university.

548. Which of the following universities was set up on the recommendations of the Sa Committee?
(a) Madras University
(b) Aligarh University
(c) Patna University
(d) Dacca University

549. Which of the following were the recomm tions of the Saddler committer?
I. A 12-year school course upto interme
II. A 3-year degree course
III. A 7-year course through the m tongue of the students
IV. Introduction of universal free compulsory education for children bet 6 and 11 years
(a) I, II, III and IV (b) I, II and IV
(c) I and II (d) III and IV

550. The Sargeant Plan of Education came in
(a) 1944 (b) 1945
(c) 1948 (d) 1950

551. A committee was set up in 1937 to work the details of the Wardha Education Sch of Gandhiji. Who was the head of the com tee?
(a) Govind Ballabha Pant
(b) Rajendra Prasad
(c) Zakir Hussain
(d) Vallabhbhai Patel

552. Which of the following was the first newspaper published in India?
(a) *The Digadarshan*
(b) *The Calcutta Gazette*
(c) *The Bengal Gazette*
(d) *The Indian Gazette*

553. Which of the following was the first weekly whose publication ceased following the Licensing Regulations of 1823?
(a) *Mirat-ul-Akhbar*
(b) *Sambad Kaumudi*
(c) *Banga-Duta*
(d) *Bombay Samachar*

554. Who amongst the following is called the 'Liberator of the Indian Press'?
(a) Macaulay (b) Metcalfe
(c) Rippon (d) Irwin

555. Consider the following statements with respect to the Vernacular Press Act, 1878 :
I. It was passed during the Viceroylty of Lord Ripon
II. District magistrates were authorised to enter the premises of any vernacular publication for inspection
III. District magistrates were authorised to get assurance from the publisher of not publishing anything which might excite the public disaffection
IV. The Act was repealed by Dufferin after the formation of the Indian National Congress.

Which of the above are correct?
(a) I, II, III and IV (b) I, II and III
(c) II and III (d) I and III

556. Which of the following legislations empowered the magistrates to confiscate the press which published any material exciting the public to resort to violence?
(a) Censorship Act, 1799
(b) Licensing Regulations, 1823
(c) Press and Registration of Books Act, 1867
(d) Newspaper Act, 1908

557. Which of the following is NOT true about the Sapru Committee?
(a) The Sapru Committee was set up in 1912.
(b) The Committee recommended to repeal the Newspaper Act of 1908
(c) The Committee recommended to repeal the Indian Press Act of 1910
(d) The Committee's chairman, Tej Bahadur Sapru, was the Law Member of the Viceroy's Executive Council.

558. *East Indian* was founded by
(a) R. Williams (b) Robet Knight
(c) Thomas Bennett (d) Henry Vivian Derozio

559. Match the following list of newspapers/magazines and their founders/editors:

List I (Newspaper/Magazines)	List II (Founders/Editors)
A. *Bengali*	1. Virendranath Chattopadhyaya
B. *Som Prakash*	2. Taraknath Das
C. *Talvar*	3. Ishwar Chandra Vidyasagar
D. *Free Hindustan*	4. Surendranath Banerjee

(a) A-4, B-3, C-1, D-2
(b) A-3, B-4, C-1, D-2
(c) A-4, B-3, C-2, D-1
(d) A-1, B-2, C-3, D-4

560. Who was the founder of *Darpan*?
(a) Ishwar Chandra Vidyasagar
(b) Sachindranath Sanyal
(c) Bal Shastri Jambekar
(d) Jyotiba Phule

561. Match the following list of newspaper/magazines and their founders/editors:

List I (Newspaper/Magazine)	List II (Founder/Editor)
A. *Bahishkrit Barat*	1. Sachindranath Sanyal
B. *Kudi Arasu*	2. Gopal Hari Deshmukh
C. *Bandi Jivan*	3. B.R. Ambedkar
D. *Satpatra Series*	4. E.V. Ramaswamy Naicker

(a) A-4, B-3, C-1, D-2
(b) A-3, B-4, C-1, D-2
(c) A-4, B-3, C-2, D-1
(d) A-1, B-2, C-3, D-4

562. Which of the following is wrongly matched?
(a) *Rast Goftar* : Dadabhai Naroaji
(b) *Hindu Patriot* : Girishchandra Ghosh
(c) *Indian Mirror* : Devendranath Tagore
(d) *Bombay Chronicle* : Robert Knight

563. Which of the following was termed as "Gagging Act"?
(a) Censorship Act, 1799
(b) Licensing Act, 1857
(c) Vernacular Press Act, 1878
(d) Newspaper Act, 1908

564. Who amongst the following founded *The National Herald* in 1938?
(a) Subhas Chandra Bose
(b) Jawaharlal Nehru
(c) Mahatma Gandhi
(d) Vallabhbhai Patel

565. Which of the following is wrongly matched?
(a) *Amrit Bazar Patrika* : Sisir Kumar Ghosh
(b) *The Hindu* : G.S. Aiyar
(c) *Tribune* : Dayal Singh Majeetia
(d) *Swadshmitran* : Shyamji Krishnavarma

566. Who founded *Leader*?
(a) Madan Mohan Malaviya
(b) Lala Lajpt Rai
(c) C.R. Das
(d) Motilal Nehru

567. Which thought is directly associated with western democracy?
(a) Marxism (b) Fascism
(c) Liberalism (d) None of these

568. What are the main thoughts or concepts of the world fabianism?
(a) Marxism, Liberalism, Fascism
(b) Marxism, Nationalism, Gandhism
(c) Liberalism, Marxism, Fascism
(d) Liberalism, Gandhism, Individualism

569. The main theme of Liberalism was?
(a) State (b) Rights
(c) Liberty (d) Society

570. Who is the founder of Liberalism
(a) Plato (b) Locke
(c) Hobbes (d) Rousseau

571. The basic theory of Liberalism is—
(a) Individual liberty (b) Social justice
(c) Equality (d) Nationalism

572. What is the another name of Scientific socialism?
(a) Marxism
(b) Communism
(c) Socialism
(d) Democratic socialism

573. 'Imperialism is the last stage of capitalism' is the theory of—
(a) Individualist (b) Utopianism
(c) Fascism (d) Marxism

574. Religion is the opium to the public. This is the statement of—
(a) Marx (b) Benthem
(c) Lenin (d) Green

575. Who was the supporter of materialism?
(a) Hegal (b) Gandhi
(c) Marx (d) Green

576. Before Plato who gave the thought of socialism?
(a) Socrates (b) Emos
(c) Pythagoras (d) Karl Marx

577. Who were the great apologists of the Henry of Liberation?
1. John Stuart Mill
2. John Milton
3. John
(a) 1 and 2 (b) 2 and 3
(c) 1 and 3 (d) 1, 2 and 3

578. What was the begining period of Nicolas-V in respect of collect of manuscript?
(a) 1497 A.D. (b) 1507 A.D.
(c) 1515 A.D. (d) 1527 A.D.

579. Leo-X was mainly associated with—
(a) Diplomacy
(b) Architecture
(c) Music and literature
(d) Sculpture

580. Renchin belong to—
(a) England (b) America
(c) China (d) Germany

581. What was the Governing period of John Colet?
(a) 1455 to 1500 A.D.
(b) 1466 to 1517 A.D.
(c) 1505 to 1535 A.D.
(d) 1440 to 1490 A.D.

582. The artistic revival in Italy was a reaction against
(a) Bysontime tradition
(b) Catholic tradition
(c) Imperialism
(d) Humanism

583. Leonardo-da-Vinci was associated with
(a) Writing (b) Sculpture
(c) Art (d) Diplomacy

584. Which one of the following is not related to Leonardo-da-Vinci
(a) Monalisa
(b) The Last Supper
(c) Virginia Wolf
(d) The Virgin of Rocks

585. Which one of the following is not associated with Renaissance period?
(a) Michelanelo
(b) Raphael
(c) Leonardo-da-Vinci
(d) M.F. Hussain

586. The Venetian school is an excellent example of—
(a) Secularization of Renaissance Art
(b) Creation of political thought
(c) Collection of historical remains
(d) Training center for the literature

587. Ghiberti was associated with a—
(a) painting (b) architecture
(c) literature (d) music and dance

588. John Calvin is associated with—
(a) painting (b) architecture
(c) music (d) literature

589. Who founded the order of Ortorians in Rome?
(a) Phillip Neri (b) Chapel
(c) John Calvin (d) John Paul

590. Fransis Becon has contributed with his—
(a) Poems (b) Essays
(c) Dramas (d) Novels

591. Copernicus gave the idea that—
(a) heavenly Bodies Revolve
(b) heavenly Bodies do not Revolve
(c) they sometimes revolve and some time do not revolve
(d) All of these

592. Who formulated the mathematical laws in support of Copernicus?
(a) Newton (b) Kepler
(c) Vasco-de-Gama (d) Colombus

593. Who discovered that blood circulated from the heart to the Arteries?
(a) William Harvey (b) Halley
(c) Galen (d) Paradus

594. Who invented logarithms and made practical use of decimal points?
(a) Stevin (b) Descarts
(c) Desarges (d) Napier

595. Who wrote the book "In Praise of Folly"?
(a) Fransis Becon (b) Alexander Pope
(c) Erasmus (d) John Milton

596. Who wrote the famous political book "The Prince"?
(a) Locke (b) Hobbes
(c) Machiavelli (d) J.S. Mill

597. If you have to study and collect data about a group of tribals living in a remote area. Which technique would you use?
(a) Interview (b) Questionnaire
(c) Observation (d) Case of study

598. If a researcher deliberately includes some of the sampling units in a sample it is known as
(a) Random (b) Qouta
(c) Purposive (d) Stratified

599. Which of the following aspects of a research investigation the research design is asso-ciated?
(a) Plan
(b) Structure
(c) Strategy
(d) All of the above

600. The ultimate aim of scientific research according to F.A. Kerlinger is to develop
(a) Concepts (b) Theories
(c) Hypothesis (d) Models

601. Which of the following type of research is concerned with testing cause and effect relationship?
(a) Pure (b) Exploratory
(c) Explanatory (d) Applied

Directions (602-652) : The following questions consist of two statements, one labelled as 'Assertion A' and other labelled as 'Reason R'. You are to examine the two statements, carefully and decide if the 'Assertion A' and the 'Reason R' are individually true and if so, whether the Reason is a correct explanation of the Assertion. Select your answer to these item using the codes given below.
(a) Both 'A' and 'R' true and 'R' is the correct explanation of 'A'.
(b) Both 'A' and 'R' are true, but 'R' is not a correct explanation of 'A'.
(c) 'A' is true but 'R' is false.
(d) 'A' is false but 'R' is true.

602. **A :** Itsing refers to the donation of some villages to Chinese Buddhists at Nalanda Monastery by Sri Gupta, the founder of the Gupta dynasty.
R : He visited India during the second half of the seventh century A.D.

603. **A :** Aryan culture of Rigvedic times overlays the Indus culture.
R : The geographical extent of the Rigvedic culture coincides with that of the Harappan culture.

604. **A :** The Harappan civilization can be described as dynamic, changing and progressive in its arts, crafts and techniques.
R : The Harappan people were keen to learn from outsiders.

605. **A :** The gotra of the Kshatriya or Vaisya was not based on the claim to descent from an ancient age.
R : For a gotra of a Kshatriya or a Vaisya followed that of his Brahman Purohita.

606. **A :** Greek invaded India after Ashoka's death.
R : Mauryan Empire had started declining.

607. **A :** Mauryan kings after Ashoka issued debased coinage.
R : There was scarcity of precious metals in India.

608. **A :** Ashoka preached Dharma.
R : Ashoka became a convert to Buddhism.

609. **A :** Mauryan Empire declined after Ashoka.
R : He had sapped the martial spirit of the ruling classes.

610. **A :** During Mauryan period foreigners were welcomed at Patliputra.
R : The municipality in the city had a special committee to look after the welfare of foreigners.

611. **A :** Kautilya shared the popular superstitions of his time.
R : Kautilya advised the king to avert eight specific kinds of providential visitation, viz. fire, flood, pestilences, famine, rats, snakes, tigers and demons.

612. **A :** The city of Taxila revolted twice during the Mauryan period.
R : The Mauryan emperors were despots.

613. **A :** Jainism did not secure a mass following.
R : Ajatsatru was a great patron of Jainism.

614. **A :** An important feature of the Buddhist architecture is the column.
R : Columns existed in many ancient Buddhist monasteries.

615. **A :** Manimegalai is a Buddhist supplement to Silappudigatram.
R : Budhism was the predominant religion of the Sangam age.

616. **A :** Martial arts were given a backseat by the Sangam people.
R : To the warrior a peaceful death in bed was looked upon as a disgrace.

617. **A :** The birth of a daughter was not wished during the Rig Vedic period.
R : The position of woman was pathetic in the Rig Vedic age.

618. **A :** Sama Veda is invaluable to the historians.
R : But for 75 hymns, the Sama Veda mostly contains the hymns from the Rig Veda.

619. **A :** Aryans were literate people even before their arrival in India.
R : Aryans probably started using a script only from 700 BC onward.

620. **A :** The Bhagavata religion spread to western India and northern Deccan.

R : The Yadaya–Satvata–Vrishni people of Mathura migrated to different regions.

A : The later Vedic people came to know more and more about physiological structure of animals.

R : The Aranyakas give us details of the flora and fauna of the forest.

A : Tantrism was acquired by Shaktism from Vajnayanism.

R : Most of the surviving literature on the tantric form of Shakti worship were composed in medieval times.

A : The pre-Gupta period was marked by the political fragmentation of the Indian subcontinent.

R : Guilds of Merchants and artisans flourished during this period.

A : Yogachara school produced many important philosophers and logicians.

R : Yogachara School is a more popular and influential than Madhyamika school.

A : Indus people were known for their plasticity of mind.

R : Excavations at Harappa, Mohenjodaro and other sites reveal that the Indus people imitated some cosmetics used by the Sumerians.

A : The Indus people believed in ghosts and evil spirits.

R : Excavations at several Indus sites reveal that Indus people used amulets.

A : The Kushanas carried on sea trade through the Persian Gulf and the Red Sea.

R : They maintained a well–organized navy.

A : Harrapan had trade relation with Sumerians.

R : Sumerians provided food grains to Harappans.

A : In South India, Agriculture was the principal occupation of the Megalithic people.

R : They introduced tank irrigation.

A : Rigveda was never a popular text.

R : It was a ritual text.

A : The Jainas follow the practice of worshipping image of Tirthankaras.

R : They denied the existence of a Supreme being.

632 **A :** Bhagavatism became popular in the Gupta Period.

R : Gupta rulers were great devotees of Krishna.

633. **A :** Asoka reduced the land revenue of Lumbani by $1/8^{th}$.

R : Buddha was born at Lumbani.

634. **A :** Jain as are atheist.

R : They reject the Vedas.

635. **A :** Indus valley people were primarily the worshippers of male God.

R : A seal resembling Shiva has been found.

636. **A :** Bhaga and Bali did not feature in post Gupta period.

R : They were replaced by new taxes.

637. **A :** Harappans were not aware of the true arch.

R : Harappans used carbelled arch for covering drains.

638. **A :** The Vaishyas and Sudras welcomed the new hetrodox religions.

R : Hetrodox religions attacked the caste system and stood for its abolition.

639. **A :** Adultery was among the lesser sins and if an adulterous wife underwent penance, she regained her status.

R : Adultery was very common in ancient India.

640. **A :** A wealthy person in Rig Vedic period was known as "Gomat".

R : Cattle were considered to be synonymous with wealth.

641. **A :** The position of women had declined in the later Vedic period.

R : In that period we have reference to widow remarriage being permitted under certain circumstances.

642. **A :** Harsha seems to have subjugated Kalinga.

R : Kalinga region used the Harsha era (AD 606) to record different events.

643. **A :** Buddhists accept the precept to refrain from harming living being.

R : Buddhism precludes Buddhists from eating meat.

644. **A :** Some human skeletons, including one in which the skull bears cut marks, were discovered at Mohenjodaro.
R : The Aryans destroyed many of the Harappan sites.

645. **A :** The actual collection of that taxes in Chola villages was the concern of the Ur or the Sabha.
R : The Chola officials were not allowed to collect the taxes directly from the taxpayer.

646. **A :** Some Pallava kings prohibited the entry of royal officers in the granted village.
R : The granted villages were directly administered by the kings.

647. **A :** Anuloma marriages were in vogue during the Gupta period.
R : The Gupta monarchs wanted to absorb the foreigners into the Hindu fold.

648. **A :** The Kushanas issued a large number of gold coins.
R : The period was marked by flourishing trade.

649. **A :** The post–Gupta period witnessed the expansion of the Kayastha caste in North India.
R : The number of land grants substantially increased.

650. **A :** The Arthashastra of Kautilya provided for the office of the superintendent of trade.
R : The state engaged in extensive trade.

651. **A :** Some Gurjara-Pratihara kings of the early medieval period were initiated Saktas.
R : They are described in the inscriptions as Parama Bhagavata bhakta.

652. **A :** Bindusara ruled a vast empire.
R : The Deccan was conquered by him.

653. Match the List I with List II and select the correct answer using the code given below the lists

List I		**List II**
(A) Paleolithic age	1.	Pallavaram
(B) Mesolithic age	2.	Bagore
(C) Neolithic age	3.	Burzhome
(D) Chalcolithic age	4.	Alamgirpur

Codes :

	A	B	C	D
(a)	1	2	4	3
(b)	1	2	3	4
(c)	4	3	2	1
(d)	4	3	2	1

654.

List I (Places)	**List II (Years of the Excavation)**
(A) Mohenjodaro	1. 1921
(B) Harappa	2. 1924–61
(C) Lothal	3. 1954–58
(D) Kalibangan	4. 1953

Codes :

	A	B	C	D
(a)	2	1	3	4
(b)	2	1	4	3
(c)	1	2	4	3
(d)	1	2	3	4

655.

List I (Places)	**List II (Rivers)**
(A) Chanhudaro	1. Ghaggar
(B) Harappa	2. Saraswati
(C) Banwali	3. Ravi
(D) Kalibangan	4. Indus

Codes :

	A	B	C	D
(a)	1	2	3	4
(b)	4	3	2	1
(c)	4	3	1	2
(d)	2	3	4	1

656.

List I	**List II**
(A) Impression of cloth on Sealing	1. Alamgirpur
(B) Impression of cloth on a trough	2. Mohenjodaro
(C) Fragment of a woven cloth	3. Lothal
(D) Remnants of fire altars	4. Kalibangan

Codes :

	A	B	C	D
(a)	3	1	2	4
(b)	2	3	4	1
(c)	4	2	1	3
(d)	3	4	2	1

657. List I (Harappan sites) | **List II (Burial customs)**

(A) Harappa — 1. Brick chamber or cist
(B) Lothal — 2. Coffin burial
(C) Kalibangan — 3. Pot burial
(D) Surkotada — 4. Double burial

Codes :

	A	B	C	D
(a)	2	4	1	3
(b)	4	2	1	3
(c)	2	4	3	1
(d)	4	2	3	1

658. List I (Authors) | **List II (Their works)**

(A) Sir John Marshall — 1. Mohenjodaro and Indian civilization
(B) G.L. Possehl — 2. Lothar and Indus civilization
(C) S.R. Rao — 3. The Indus civilization
(D) Mortimer Wheeler — 4. Ancient cities of the Indus

Codes :

	A	B	C	D
(a)	4	1	2	3
(b)	1	4	3	2
(c)	4	1	3	2
(d)	1	4	2	3

659. List I | **List II**

(A) Brahmin — 1. Arms
(B) Kshatriya — 2. Face
(C) Vaishya — 3. Feet
(D) Sudra — 4. Thighs

Codes :

	A	B	C	D
(a)	1	2	3	4
(b)	2	1	4	3
(c)	1	2	4	3
(d)	2	1	3	4

660. List I | **List II**

(A) Bal Gangadhar Tilak — 1. Central Asia
(B) Dayanand Saraswati — 2. Arctic Region
(C) Max Mueller — 3. Germany
(D) Mc Donell — 4. Austro Hungary Region
(E) Penka — 5. Tibet

Codes :

	A	B	C	D	E
(a)	2	5	1	4	3
(b)	5	2	4	1	3
(c)	2	4	5	1	3
(d)	5	2	3	1	4

661. List I | **List II**

(A) Ali Murad — 1. Sind
(B) Daimabad — 2. Haryana
(C) Rakhigarhi — 3. Gujarat
(D) Rojdi — 4. Maharashtra

Codes :

	A	B	C	D
(a)	1	4	2	3
(b)	1	2	3	4
(c)	3	2	4	1
(d)	3	4	2	1

662. List I (Sites) | **List II (Discoveries)**

(A) Lothal — 1. Pasupati Mahadev Seal
(B) Chanhudaro — 2. Bronze sticks inccribed
(C) Mohenjodaro — 3. Bronze Models of bullock–carts and ikkas
(D) Harappa — 4. Stone Symbal of female sex organs

Codes :

	A	B	C	D
(a)	3	2	1	4
(b)	2	3	1	4
(C)	2	3	4	1
(d)	3	2	4	1

663. List I | **List II**

(A) Kalibangan — 1. here the lower town was fortified
(B) Chanhudaro — 2. bead makers' shop was unearthed
(C) Harappa — 3. The only place which yields the evidence of coffin burial
(D) Mohenjodaro — 4. associated with the discovery of a beared man carved in steatite and bronze dancing girl

Codes :

	A	B	C	D
(a)	4	3	2	1
(b)	1	2	3	4
(c)	3	2	1	4
(d)	4	2	3	1

664. **List I** | **List II**

List I	List II
(A) "The enemy of the Harappans was nature"	1. Dales
(B) "Indra therefore stands completely exonerated"	2. K.M. Srivastava
(C) "On circumstantial evidence Indira stands accused"	3. M. Wheeler
(D) "The civilization perished as result of internal decay accelerated by the shock of barbarian raids"	4. O. Childe

Codes :

	A	B	C	D
(a)	1	2	3	4
(b)	4	3	2	1
(c)	1	2	4	3
(d)	4	3	1	2

665.

List I	List II
(A) Copper rhinoceros	1. Chanhudaro
(B) Serpent Goddess	2. Lothal and Kalibangan
(C) Medical beliefs and surgical skills	3. Gumla
(D) Bronze model of bullock carts and ikkas	4. Daimabad

Codes :

	A	B	C	D
(a)	1	2	3	4
(b)	4	3	1	2
(c)	1	2	4	3
(d)	4	3	2	1

666.

List I	List II
(A) Harappa	1. Discovered by R.D. Banerjee
(B) Chanhudaro	2. Discovery of rice husk
(C) Mohenjodaro	3. The first Indus site to be discovered
(D) Rangpur	4. The only Indus city without a citadel

Codes :

	A	B	C	D
(a)	4	3	1	2
(b)	3	4	1	2
(c)	3	4	2	1
(d)	4	3	2	1

667.

List I	List II
(A) Manda	1. Easternmost Site
(B) Bhagatrav	2. Southernmost Site
(C) Alamgirpur	3. Northernmost Site
(D) Sutkagendor	4. Westernmost Site

Codes :

	A	B	C	D
(a)	2	3	4	1
(b)	2	3	1	4
(c)	3	2	1	4
(d)	3	2	4	1

668.

List I	List II
(A) Harappa	1. Temple like structure
(B) Lothal	2. Horse remains
(C) Sarkotada	3. Dockyard
(D) Mohenjodaro	4. "H" cemetery

Codes :

	A	B	C	D
(a)	1	2	3	4
(b)	4	3	2	1
(c)	4	3	1	2
(d)	1	2	4	3

669.

List I	List II
(A) Copper	1. Rajasthan
(B) Tin	2. Bihar
(C) Lapis-Lazuli	3. Afghanistan
(D) Jade	4. Central Asia

Codes :

	A	B	C	D
(a)	1	2	3	4
(b)	2	1	3	4
(c)	2	1	4	3
(d)	1	2	4	3

670.

List I	List II
(A) M. Wheeler	1. 2700 – 2500 B.C.
(B) Ernest Mackey	2. 2800 – 2500 B.C.
(C) John Marshall	3. 3250 – 2750 B.C.
(D) Vatsa	4. 2500 – 1500 B.C

Codes :

	A	B	C	D
(a)	2	4	3	1
(b)	4	3	1	2
(c)	4	2	3	1
(d)	2	3	4	1

671.

List I	List II
(A) Early Palaeolithic	1. Microliths
(B) Middlle Palaeolithic	2. Scraper flakes
(C) Upper Palaeolithic	3. Hand axes and cleaver
(D) Mesolithic	4. Blade and Burins

Codes :

	A	B	C	D
(a)	2	3	1	4
(b)	3	2	4	1
(c)	3	2	1	4
(d)	2	3	4	1

672.

List I	List II
(A) Red sandstone male torso	1. Harappa
(B) Terracotta Carts	2. Mohenjodaro
(C) Polychrome goblet	3. Mehargarh
(D) Copper buffalo	4. Daimabad

Codes :

	A	B	C	D
(a)	1	2	3	4
(b)	4	3	2	1
(c)	1	3	2	4
(d)	4	2	3	1

673. Match List I with List II and select the correct answer from the code given below.

List I (Site)	List II (Cultures)
(A) Sarai–Nahar–Rai	1. Upper Paleolithic
(B) Patne	2. OCP
(C) Saipal	3. Megalithic
(D) Mahurjhari	4. Mesolithic

Codes :

	A	B	C	D
(a)	4	1	2	3
(b)	1	2	3	4
(c)	4	3	2	1
(d)	1	4	2	3

674. Match the modern names of river with their old names

List I (Modern Names)	List II (Old Names)
(A) Jhelum	1. Vitasta
(B) Chenab	2. Asikni
(c) Ravi	3. Parushni
(D) Byas	4. Vitasha

Codes :

	A	B	C	D
(a)	1	2	3	4
(b)	2	1	4	3
(c)	1	3	2	4
(d)	4	2	1	3

675. Match the Brahmana books with the Vedas

List I (Vedas)	List II (Brahmanas)
(A) Rig Veda	1. Aitreya and Kaushitaki
(B) Sama Veda	2. Jaminiya and Tanya maha Brahman
(C) Yajur Veda	3. Shatapatha
(D) Atharva Veda	4. Gopatha

Codes :

	A	B	C	D
(a)	2	1	4	3
(b)	1	2	3	4
(c)	3	1	4	2
(d)	4	3	2	1

676.

List I	List II
(A) Gramni	1. Treasurer
(B) Sangrihitra	2. Chief of sects
(C) Ganas	3. Revenue Collector
(D) Bhagduta	4. Tribal Republic

Codes :

	A	B	C	D
(a)	4	1	2	3
(b)	2	1	4	3
(c)	1	4	3	2
(d)	2	3	1	4

677.

List I	List II
(A) Maruts	1. Protector of cattle
(B) Ushas	2. Gods of storm
(c) Pushan	3. Goddess of Eternity
(D) Aditi	4. Goddess of Dawn

Codes :

	A	B	C	D
(a)	2	1	4	3
(b)	4	2	3	1
(c)	2	4	1	3
(d)	4	2	3	1

678. Match the Sutra literature with the science or subject they deal with

List I	List II
(A) Kalp	I. etymology
(B) Shiksha	II. phonetics
(C) Nirukta	III. ritual
(D) Chanda	IV. metre

Codes :

	A	B	C	D
(A)	II	I	IV	III
(B)	II	III	I	IV
(C)	III	IV	II	I
(D)	IV	III	I	II

679. Match the three Sangam with number of Pandyan kings who patronized them.

List I	List II
(A) First Sangam	1. 49
(B) Second Sangam	2. 59
(C) Third Sangam	3. 89

Codes :

	A	B	C
(a)	3	2	1
(b)	1	2	3
(c)	2	3	1
(d)	1	3	2

680. Match List I with List II and select the answer from the codes given below

List I	List II
(A) Kurunji	1. Raiding expedition
(B) Palai	2. Siege
(C) Mullai	3. Pitched battles
(D) Marudam	4. Cattle raiding
(E) Neydal	5. Turning the country side into waste lands

Codes :

	A	B	C	D	E
(a)	4	5	1	3	2
(b)	5	4	3	2	1
(c)	4	5	1	2	3
(d)	2	1	3	5	4

681.

List – I (Chief Priest)	List – II (Functions)
(A) Hota	1. Supervising the entire sacrificial act.
(B) Udgatri	2. Singing chants at various stages
(C) Adhvarya	3. Invoking the deities.
(D) Brahmin	4. Making offerings in the fire.

Codes :

	A	B	C	D
(a)	3	4	1	2
(b)	2	3	4	1
(c)	3	2	4	1
(d)	1	4	3	2

682. Match the items of List I with List II.

List – I	List – II
(A) Kadaisiar	1. Tax Collection
(B) Pulaiyans	2. Village assembly
(C) Variyar	3. Agriculture labourers
(D) Manram	4. Rope–makers

Codes :

	A	B	C	D
(a)	4	2	3	1
(b)	1	3	2	4
(c)	3	4	1	2
(d)	2	1	4	3

683. Match the following

List I	List II
(A) Ajivika	1. deterministic ascetics
(B) Charvakas	2. denied the authority of the Vedas and the soul
(C) Bhagavatism	3. symbolized the spirit of the creative

Codes :

	A	B	C
(a)	1	2	3
(b)	3	2	1
(c)	2	1	3
(d)	3	1	2

684.

List I (Personalities)	List II (Relationship with Mahavira)
(A) Chetaka, the Lichchhavi	1. Father ruler of Vaishali

(B) Sidhartha, the head of the Jnatrika clan — 2. Mother
(C) Chellana the Lichchhavi princess — 3. Maternal uncle
(D) Trishala, another Lichchhavi princess — 4. Niece

Codes :

	A	B	C	D
(a)	1	3	2	4
(b)	3	1	4	2
(c)	2	1	4	3
(d)	1	3	2	4

685. Match List I with List II and select the answer from the given codes below:

List I	List II
A. Angas	1. Four
B. Prakiranka	2. Six
C. Chedsutra	3. Ten
D. Mulasutra	4. Twelve

Codes :

	A	B	C	D
(a)	4	1	2	3
(b)	4	2	3	1
(c)	4	3	2	1
(d)	4	1	3	2

686. Match the officers with their respective function.

List I	List II
A. Samaharta	1 Chief collector
B. Sannidhata	2. Chief treasurer
C. Uparika	3. Governor
D. Rajjuka	4. Land surveyor of revenue officer

Codes :

	A	B	C	D
(a)	1	2	4	3
(b)	2	1	3	4
(c)	1	3	4	2
(d)	1	2	3	4

687.

List I	List II
A. Dronomukha	1. 80 villages
B. Kharavatika	2. 400 villages
C. Sangrahana	3. 200 villages
D. Sthaniya	4. 10 villages

Codes :

	A	B	C	D
(a)	4	3	1	2
(b)	3	1	4	2
(c)	1	3	4	2
(d)	2	3	4	1

688. Which one of the following pairs not correctly matched?

a. Fourteen Major Rock Edicts - various principles of Dhamma
b. Seven Pillar Rock Edicts - Appendix to Rock Edicts
c. Bhabru Inscription - New Administration by Ashoka
d. Barabar cave inscription - Ashoka's Tolerance

(a) c & d (b) a & c
(c) only b (d) only c.

689.

List I (Gupta emperors)	List II (Inscription)
A. Samudragupta	1. Baigram Copper Plate
B. Kumaragupta I	2. Paharpur Copper Plate
C. Chandragupta III	3. Eran Stone Pillar
D. Buddhagupta	4. Unagarh Rock
E. Skandagupta	5. Udayagiri Caves

Codes :

	A	B	C	D	E
(a)	4	2	3	1	5
(b)	3	1	5	2	4
(c)	3	5	4	1	2
(d)	2	3	1	4	5

690.

List I (Periods)	List II (Pottery)
A. Chalcolithic	1. Red ware
B. Vedic	2. Black and Red ware
C. Pre-Mauryan	3. Painted Grey ware
D. Pre-Gupta and Gupta	4. Northern Black Polished ware

Codes :

	A	B	C	D
(a)	3	2	1	4
(b)	2	3	4	1
(c)	1	2	3	4
(d)	2	1	4	3

691. Match the kings with their dates of accession and death

List I	List II
A. Bindusar	1. 298 – 273 B.C.
B. Chandragupta I	2. 319 – 335 A. D.
C. Samudragupta	3. 335 – 375 A.D.
D. Ashoka	4. 273 – 232 B.C.

Codes :

	A	B	C	D
(a)	1	2	3	4
(b)	2	1	4	3
(c)	2	4	1	3
(d)	3	1	2	4

692.

List I (Inscriptions)	List II (Gods)
A. Udayagiri cave	1. Vishnu
B. Junagarh	2. Shiva
C. Indore Copper Plate	3. Swami Mahasena
D. Bilsad pillar	4. Sun God

Codes :

	A	B	C	D
(a)	3	1	4	2
(b)	4	1	2	3
(c)	2	1	4	3
(d)	4	3	2	1

693. Match each era with the year it began

List I	List II
A. Kalachuri Era	1. 606 A.D.
B. Harsina Era	2. 58 B.C.
C. Vikrama Era	3. 78 A.D.
D. Shaka Era	4. 248 A.D

Codes :

	A	B	C	D
(a)	4	1	2	3
(b)	1	4	3	2
(c)	3	2	4	1
(d)	2	3	1	4

694. Which one of the following pairs is not correctly matched?

List I		List II
A. Ravi	-	Parushni
B. Jhelum	-	Vitasta
C. Chenab	-	Iravadi
D. Byas	-	Vipasha

(a) A (b) C
(c) D (e) A & C both.

695. Match List I with List II and select the answer from the codes given below.

List I	List II
A. Nigam	1. Gardener
B. Sarthawaha	2. Fisherman
C. Malakara	3. Merchant guild
D. Dasaka	4. Head of caravan traders

Codes :

	A	B	C	D
(a)	4	3	2	1
(b)	1	2	3	4
(c)	3	4	1	2
(d)	3	4	2	1

696. Which among the following pairs is correctly matched?

List I		List II
A. Khadyotipatika	-	Head of the army
B. Mahadandanayaka	-	Chief of the revenue
C. Baladhikrita	-	Superintendent of the royal kitchan
D. Ranabhandadhikrita	-	Incharge of military exchequer

(a) a & b (b) a & c
(c) only c (d) only d

697. Which one of the following pairs is NOT correctly matched?

List I		List II
(a) Udiyanjerai	:	Chera king
(b) Nedunjeliyan	:	Pandya king
(c) Senganan	:	Chola king
(d) Pari	:	Pallava king

(a) b (b) c
(c) a (d) d

698. Match the Tamil works with their authors.

List I (Books)	List II (Authors)
A. Shilapadikaram	1. Tiruvalluvar
B. Manimekalai	2. Ilango Adigal
C. Tiru–Kural	3. Agastya
D. Akkaliyam	4. Sittalai–Sattanar

Codes :

	A	B	C	D
(a)	2	4	1	3
(b)	4	2	3	1
(c)	2	3	1	4
(d)	1	2	3	4

699. Which of the following pairs is not correctly matched?

	List I		List II
A.	Major Rock Edict II	-	Measures of social welfare
B.	Major Rock Edict III	-	Respect to Brahmins
C.	Major Rock Edict IV	-	System of Dhammayatras
D.	Major Rock Edict VI	-	Need for efficient organization of administration.

(a) A (b) C
(c) D (d) B

700. Which is NOT a correct pair?

A. Rajanya - Kshatriya
B. Anuloma - marriage of a higher varna man with lower varna woman
C. Praliloma - marriage of a lower varan man with higher varna woman
D. Niyoga - Separation of a woman from her lover or husband.

(a) C (b) D
(c) A (d) B

701. **List I** **List II**

A. Udranga 1. State official
B. Uparika 2. A type of land tax
C. Vishti 3. Territorial division
D. Vithi 4. Forced labour
5. Administrative department

Codes :

	A	B	C	D
(a)	4	5	2	3
(b)	2	1	4	3
(c)	2	4	3	5
(d)	3	4	1	2

702. **List I** **List II**

A. Barbarism 1. Port on the western sea–coast
B. Barygaza 2. Roman Settlement
C. Poduke 3. Port on the Indus delta
D. Paithan 4. Mart on the Godavari
5. City of Kamarupa

Codes :

	A	B	C	D
(a)	3	1	2	4
(b)	2	1	4	3
(c)	1	4	3	5
(d)	2	3	5	4

703. **List I** **List II**

A. Panchsindhantika 1. Varahamihra
B. Nyayabhasya 2. Vatsayana
C. Tale of Ten Princes 3. Dandin
D. Indica 4. Megasthenes

Codes :

	A	B	C	D
(a)	1	2	3	4
(b)	2	1	3	4
(c)	2	1	4	3
(d)	1	2	4	3

704. Which is NOT correct pair?

A. Paithan - Pratisthan
B. Peshawar - Puruspur
C. Pataliputra - Kusumdhwaj
D. Tamluk - Barbaricum

(a) B (b) C
(c) A (d) D

705. Match the dynasties or kings with their capitals

	List I		List II
A.	Mauryas and Kanvas	1.	Partisthana
B.	Gurjara Partiharas	2.	Partisthana
C.	Rashtrakutas	3.	Kanauj
D.	Satavahanas	4.	Pataliputra

Codes :

	A	B	C	D
(a)	1	2	3	4
(b)	4	3	2	1
(c)	1	3	2	4
(d)	3	1	4	2

Directions (Q. 706 to 755) : The following questions consist of two statements, one labelled as 'Assertion A' and other labelled as 'Reason R'. You are to examine the two statements, carefully and decide if the 'Assertion A' and the 'Reason R' are individually true and if so, whether the Reason is a correct explanation of the Assertion. Select your answer to these item using the codes given below.

(a) Both 'A' and 'R' true and 'R' is the correct explanation of 'A'.
(b) Both 'A' and 'R' are true, but 'R' is not a correct explanation of 'A'.
(c) 'A' is true but 'R' is false.
(d) 'A' is false but 'R' is true.

706. **A :** North India between AD 750 and 1200 witnessed the emergence and full growth of a new political-socio-economic structure.
R : There is total unanimity among historians to describe this new structure as a "feudalism."

707. **A :** The position of the Chola feudatories remained subservient to the Chola kings unlike the feudatories of the Rashtrikutas.
R : The Chola villages enjoyed autonomy and the feudatories simply passed king's share of revenue.

708. **A :** The Rajput rulers of north India during the early medieval period were essentially hereditary leaders of feudal communities.
R : They were neither benevolent despots nor could they be autocratic despots.

709. **A :** Dharmapala assumed the title of "Uttarapathaswamin".
R : At a durbar held in Kanauj, the rulers of Bhoja, Matsya, Madnasa, Kuru, Yavana, Avanti and Yadu bowed down respectfully before Dharampala.

710. **A :** In the early medieval period most of the craftsmen and artisans were classified as untouchables.
R : The Smriti writers of this period regard handicrafts as unclean professions.

711. **A :** North Indian temples were the main targets of muslim invasions in the 11th century A.D.
R : The best contribution of Rajput rulers lies in their promotion of art and architecture.

712. **A :** The traditional Varna division was gradually losing its former significance.
R : Man's social status was to be increasingly decided by his property.

713. **A :** Slave sultans are also called *Ilbari* Turks.
R : *Ilbari* in Arabic language means 'the owned'.

714. **A :** Muhammad Tughluq was the first Sultan who focused on agriculture and created a new department of agriculture namely "Amir–E–Kohi".
R : He wanted to promote the export of crops.

715. **A :** Polygamy was more commonly practiced by the lower castes than the upper castes in ancient India.
R : The upper castes had a larger share in the social surplus than the lower castes during the period.

716. **A :** Chola ascendancy declined in 12th century A.D.
R : Their resources were exhausted by frequent wars.

717. **A :** Tampralipti ceased to be a port in Pre–Gupta period.
R : Indians traded with Roman countries.

718. **A :** The government of Afghan dynasties was based on the spirit of biradari (obligation of the clan).
R : Afghan Sultanate could not expect much support either from the Turks of the Indian convert Islam.

719. **A :** Akbar claim or divinity for himself.
R : He thought that in country of many beliefs such as India, the sovereign should not be associated with any one particular religion.

720. **A :** The invasion of Krishna Deva Rai into the territories of Praprudra were inconclusive.
R : Krishna Dev Rai invaded the territories of Gajapati not for the latter's extinction but only for the recovery of lost territories.

721. **A :** Jai Singh succeeded in persuading Shivaji to come to Aurangjeb's Court and enter imperial service.
R : Shivaji was dissatisfied with the terms offered.

722. **A :** The nayaka system of the Vijayanagar period increased the control of the king over the provinces and local units of administration.

R : Under this system nayakas or palegars were granted amaram in lieu of salaries in return for their services to the state.

723. A : According to Domingo Paes, Devadasis held a highly respectable position in the Vijayanagar society.

R : The Devadasi system or the practice of appointing dancing girls to temples came into existence in south India for the first time under Vijayanagar rulers.

724. A : Kabir preached the brotherhood of man and pleaded for Hindu-Muslim unity.

R : He made a sharp criticism of the caste and religious distinctions prevalent in his period.

725. A : Guru Nanak laid great stress on the need of a guru for spiritual guidance.

R : He permitted his followers to form a new religious sect, called Sikhism, during his life time.

726. A : Ramdas Samarth, the spiritual guide of Shivaji, was a varakari.

R : His work, Dasatodha, gives advice to people on all aspects of worldly life.

727. A : The enormous increase in the member of samantas in the early medieval kingdoms created serious problems for their rulers.

R : Contemporary texts describe the samantas as potential enemies of the king and their contingents as the weakest link in the king's defence.

728. A : The post of malik naib was generally filled only when a ruler was weak or a minor.

R : Ala-ud-din Khalji gave this high post to Malik Kafur as a mark of special favour.

729. A : Firoz Tughluq reversed the whole trend of the centralization of the 'iqta' system by the previous rulers.

R : He fixed the estimated revenues of the iqtas for allowing the muqtis to appropriate all increase of revenue.

730. A : Ala-ud-din prohibited the sale and use of liquor in Delhi.

R : He wanted to uphold religious and moral standards.

731. A : With the introduction of sericulture in India by the Turks, the Indian silk industry received a boost.

R : The Indians started exporting raw silk to Persia and Afghanistan from the time of Delhi Sultans.

732. A : Alauddin Khalji imposed price control in Delhi.

R : He wanted to pay lower wages to artisans building his palaces in Delhi.

733. A : The subsistence level agrarian production of early Medieval India arose out to the practical economics of the situation.

R : The peasantry of this period did not go for any significant surplus production in the fear of the impending demand for large share from the feudal lord.

734. A : Al-Baruni notes the absence of any significant difference between the Vaishyas and Sudras.

R : The rise of the various strata of landed gentry led to the decline of Vaishyas and advance of Sudras.

735. A : The Chishti Silsilah was the most prominent and popular one among all Sufi orders of the period of the Delhi Sultanate.

R : The Chisti Silsilah had, as its spheres of influence, UP, Bihar, Bengal, Orissa and Deccan.

736. A : Aurangzeb banned music at the Mughal court.

R : He had no time for amusement.

737. A : Shahjahan's Deccan Policy after 1636 A.D. was successful.

R : Shahjahan had spent a lot of time in Deccan and has personal experience and knowledge of the Deccan.

738. A : All Mansabdars were jagirdars, but all jagirdars were not Mansabdars.

R : A few Mansabdars were paid in cash and not through the assignment of Jagirs.

739. A : The Mughal emperors had complete sovereignty not only internally but also externally.

R : They refused to recognize any external authority like the Caliph as their superior.

740. A : A major characteristic feature of Mughal India was the slow increase or near stagnation in agricultural production.

R : There is sufficient evidence to show a gradual expansion in the total area under cultivation during the Mughal period.

741. **A :** The European traders were instrumental in introducing and developing the institution of Hundis in Mughal period.

R : The Merchant class of the Mughal period was a highly stratified class economically as well as socially.

742. **A :** Azam Shah requested Shahu to take charge of Narmada region during his absence from Maharashtra.

R : It was felt that Shahu's presence in the region would weaken Tarabai and safeguard Mughal possessions during Azam's absence

743. **A :** In 1666 the king of Portugal sold Bombay to Charls II of England.

R : Charles II married Catherine of Braganza, sister of Portuguese king.

744. **A :** The British used the rebellion of Shobha Singh, a Zamindar of Burdwan district, as an excuse to fortify their settlement at Sutanati in 1696.

R : The British were driven out of their settlement at Sutanati by the Mughal governor of Bengal in 1687.

745. **A :** The attitudes of Indian traders was on the whole friendly towards the Europeans.

R : European commerce caused a substantial rise in the revenue of Indian rulers.

746. **A :** Increasing European trade resulted in inflation in India.

R : The beginning of European commerce was accompanied by an increase in the inflow of bullion, both gold and silver, into India.

747. **A :** Jahangir executed Guru Arjun Deva.

R : The Sikh Guru had supported rebellions Khusro.

748. **A :** There was no spirit of nationalism among the people of the Mughal Empire.

R : Mughal India lacked the elements which promote nationalism.

749. **A :** Wazir-ul Mulk left Mughal Empire Muhammad Shah to realize his own ambition of founding the state of Hyderabad.

R : Muhammad Shah, instead of supporting his able Wazir, intrigued against him.

750. **A :** The culture of the Mughal period is generally termed as the Mughal court culture.

R : The Mughal court culture was an antithesis of Indian culture.

751. **A :** Akbar dispensed with the practice of keeping revenue records in the local languages, in addition to Persian.

R : In Mughal India, Persian language and literature was well developed and widely in use.

752. **A :** The Maratha Army under Shivaji was quite swift in mobility.

R : It avoided pitched battle.

753. **A :** Drastic Change in the superstructure of monument built in medieval India became feasible.

R : Variety of building materials, designs and techniques were available.

754. **A :** The Bhakti saint Vallabhacharya professed Suddhavaitva philosophy.

R : He completely identified the individual soul with Brahman and did not subscribe to the distinction between two.

755. **A :** The Agrarian crisis began in the later part of 17th century.

R : The oppressed peasantry joint the local rebel leaders and zamindars.

756. Match the following

	List I		List II
A.	Harsha's accession	1.	647 A.D
B.	Mohd. Bin Kasim's invasion	2.	671 A.D.
C.	I-tsing visited India	3.	712 A.D
D.	Harsha's death	4.	606 A.D.

Codes :

	A	B	C	D
(a)	1	2	3	4
(b)	2	1	4	3
(c)	4	3	2	1
(d)	1	4	3	2

757. Match the temples with the cities they are associated with.

	List I		List II
A.	Meenakshi temple	1.	Madurai
B.	Nataraja temple	2.	Chidambaram
C.	Vithal and Hazara temples	3.	Hampi
D.	Ladh Khan temple	4.	Aihole

Codes :

	A	B	C	D
(a)	1	2	3	4
(b)	2	1	3	4
(c)	2	1	4	3
(d)	1	2	4	3

758. **List I (Authors)** | **List II (Books)**

A. Al-Beruni — 1. Khazain-ul-Futuh
B. Hasan Nizami — 2. Tabaqat-Nasiri
C. Minhaj-us-Siraj — 3. Taj-ul-Maathir
D. Amir Khusru — 4. Kitab-fi-Tahqiq

Codes :

	A	B	C	D
(a)	1	2	3	4
(b)	4	3	2	1
(c)	1	3	2	4
(d)	4	2	3	1

759. Who among the following Delhi Sultan were born to Hindu mothers?

List I | **List II**

(i) Ala-ud-din Khalji (ii) Nasirud-din Khusrau
(iii) Balban (iv) Firoz Tughlaq
(v) Sikandar Lodi

(a) All the them (b) ii and iv only
(c) ii, iv and v only (d) i, ii, iii, and v

760. Which is/are not correctly matched ?

List I | **List II**

A. Iltutmish - The first Delhi Sultan to acquire a Mansur
B. Mohd.-bin Tughluq - Remove the name of the Caliph from the Sikka and Khutba
C. Raziya - The first woman Ruler of Delhi Sultanate
D. Balban - The only Delhi Sultan to acquire two Mansur.

(a) A only (b) A & B only
(c) D only (d) none of them

761. **List I** | **List II**

A. Sikka — 1. Letter of investiture
B. Khutba — 2. Infidel or Unbeliever
C. Mansur — 3. Coin
D. Kaafir — 4. Friday Prayer

Codes :

	A	B	C	D
(a)	3	4	2	1
(b)	4	3	1	2
(c)	4	3	2	1
(d)	3	4	1	2

762. **List I** | **List II**

A. Dagh — 1. Kissing the Sultan's feet
B. Sijda — 2. Branding of horses
C. Paibos — 3. Prostration in front of the Sultan
D. Nauroz — 4. Persian New year

Codes :

	A	B	C	D
(a)	2	3	1	4
(b)	3	2	1	4
(c)	3	2	4	1
(d)	1	2	4	3

763. Which one of the following is correctly matched.

(a) Battle of Waihind - Defeat of the Hindustani ruler Muhammad of Ghur
(b) Battle of Tarain I - Defeat of Prithviraj Chauhan
(c) Battle of Tarain II - Defeat of Muhammad of Ghur by Prithviraj Chauhan
(d) Battle of Chandawar - Defeat of Jaya Chandra of Kanauj by Muhammad of Ghur

764. Which Sultan wanted to find a new religion, but was advised against it by the ulema?

(a) Balban
(b) Alu-ud-din Khalji
(c) Muhammad Tughluq
(d) Iltutmish.

765. Match the following

List I | **List II**

A. Barbak — 1. In charge of the royal household
B. Amir–i–Hajeb — 2. In charge of the royal court

C. Sar–i–Jandar 3. In charge of scrutiny of visitors to the court
D. Vakil–i–Dar 4. In charge of the security of the Sultan

Codes :

	A	B	C	D
(a)	2	3	4	1
(b)	3	2	1	4
(c)	3	1	2	4
(d)	1	3	4	2

766. Following are the foreign travellers who visited India during medieval period. Who is not correctly matched with his year of arrival?
(a) Ibn-i-Batuta — 1333–34
(b) Nicolo de Conti — 1420
(c) Abdur Razzak — 1443
(d) Domingo Paes — 1535

767. Match the following

	List I		List II
A.	Qutub Minar	1.	Iltutmish
B.	Tughluqabad	2.	Alauddin Khalji
C.	Siri Fort	3.	Firoz Tughluq
D.	Hauz Khas	4.	Muhammad Tughluq

Codes :

	A	B	C	D
(a)	1	4	2	3
(b)	3	2	4	1
(c)	1	2	3	4
(d)	2	1	4	3

768. Which one of the following pairs is wrong?
(a) Nizam Shahi - Ahmadnagar
(b) Adil Shahi - Bijapur
(c) Barid Shahi - Berar
(d) Qutub Shahi - Golconda

769.

	List I		**List II**
A.	Qutubuddin Aibak	1.	Ghulam Dynasty
B.	Jalaluddin Khalzi	2.	Tughluq Dynasty
C.	Khizra Khan	3.	Khalzi Dynasty
D.	Gayasuddin	4.	Sayyed Dynasty

Codes :

	A	B	C	D
(a)	1	3	4	2
(b)	3	1	2	4
(c)	4	3	2	1
(d)	1	2	3	4

770. What is the correct chronology of dynasties that ruled Vijayanagar?
(a) Sangam, Tuluva, Saluva, Aravidu
(b) Sangam, Saluva, Tuluva, Aravidu
(c) Aravidu, Sangam, Tuluva, Saluva
(d) Tuluva, Sangam, Saluva, Aravidu

771. Match List I with List II

	List I		**List II**
A.	Raja Karan	1.	Gujarat
B.	Hamir Deva	2.	Ranthambhor
C.	Ratan Singh	3.	Chittor

Codes :

	A	B	C
(a)	3	2	1
(b)	2	1	3
(c)	1	2	3
(d)	3	1	2

772. Which of the following is correctly paired?
(a) Diwan-i-Mustakhraj - Balban
(b) Diwan-i-Kohi - Allauddin Khalji
(c) Diwan-i-Arz - Muhammad Tughluq
(d) Diwan-i-Bandagan - Firoz Tughluq

773.

	List I	**List II**
A.	Mushrit-i-Mumalik	1. Accountant General
B.	Mustauf-i-Mumalik	2. Auditor General
C.	Barid-i-Mumalik	3. Head of Intelligence Dept.
D.	Amir Munshi	4. Head of Records Dept.

Codes :

	A	B	C	D
(a)	1	2	4	3
(b)	1	2	3	4
(c)	2	1	3	4
(d)	3	2	1	4

774.

	List I	**List II**
A.	Barid	1. Intelligence Agent
B.	Qazi	2. Market Superintendent
C.	Shahna	3. Civil Judge
D.	Ahl-i-Saif	4. Warrior Class

Codes :

	A	B	C	D
(a)	1	2	3	4
(b)	4	3	2	1
(c)	1	3	2	4
(d)	4	2	3	1

775. Match the following

	Kings		**Region**
A.	Harananda	1.	Devagiri
B.	Ramachandra	2.	Malva
C.	Prataprudra Deva	3.	Warangal

Codes :

	A	B	C
(a)	2	1	3
(b)	3	1	2
(c)	1	2	3
(d)	2	3	1

776. Which of the following correctly matched?

(a) Hauz Khas - Firoz Tughluq
(b) Siri fort - Iltutmish
(c) Qutubminar - Muhammad Tughluq
(d) Tughluqabad - Alauddin Khalji

777.

	List I (King)		**List II (Dynasty)**
A.	Bhoja of Malva	1.	Chandela
B.	Jayachandra	2.	Gahadaval
C.	Mihira Bhoj	3.	Paramara
D.	Paramardideva	4.	Pratihara

Codes :

	A	B	C	D
(a)	3	1	4	2
(b)	4	2	3	1
(c)	3	2	4	1
(d)	4	1	3	2

778.

	List I (Books)		**List II (Authors)**
A.	Futuh-us-Salatin	1.	Firoz Shah Tughluq
B.	Futuhat-e-Firozshahi	2.	Isami
C.	Tarikhi-e-Firozshahi	3.	Amir Khusru
D.	Kharainul–fuluh	4.	Barani

Codes :

	A	B	C	D
(a)	2	1	4	3
(b)	1	2	3	4
(c)	2	1	3	4
(d)	4	2	1	3

779. Of the following pairs of the various departments begun by the respective Sultans, which one is incorrect?

(a) Diwan-e-Mustakkharaj - Alauddin Khilji
(b) Diwan-e-Amir Kohi - Mohammad Tughluq
(c) Diwan-e-Khairat - Firoz Tughluq
(d) Diwan-e-Riyasat - Balban

780.

	List I (Foreign traveller)		**List II (Country)**
A.	Abdur Razzak.	1.	Morocco
B.	Nicolo Conti	2.	Persia
C.	Fernao Nuniz	3.	Italy
D.	Ibn Batuta	4.	Portugal

Codes :

	A	B	C	D
(a)	1	2	3	4
(b)	2	3	4	1
(c)	3	4	1	2
(d)	2	3	1	4

781. The Hindu Goddess 'Lakshsmi' has been depicted on the coins of the Muslim ruler:

(a) Iltutmish
(b) Firoz Tughluq
(c) Mahmud Ghaznavi
(d) Mohammad Ghori

782. What is the chronological sequence of the Bhakti saints

A. Chaitanya B. Kabir
C. Guru Nanak D. Mirabai

(a) A B C D
(b) D B A C
(c) B A C D
(d) C D A B

783. Arrange the following saints of Maharashtra dharma in the correct sequence

1. Eknatha 2. Namdeva
3. Ramdas 4. Tukaram
5. Jnanadeva

(a) 4 2 1 5 3
(b) 3 4 2 1 5
(c) 5 3 4 2 1
(d) 1 5 3 4 2

784.

	List I		**List II**
A.	Haq	1.	Creator
B.	Khalq	2.	Created
C.	Pir	3.	Teacher
D.	Murid	4.	Disciple

Codes :

	A	B	C	D
(a)	2	1	3	4
(b)	4	2	1	3
(c)	3	4	2	1
(d)	1	2	3	4

785. **List I** **(Authors)** / **List II** **(Books)**

List I (Authors)	List II (Books)
A. Gulbadan Begam	1. Tarikh-i-Mubarakshahi
B. Ishwar Das Nagar	2. Tarikh-i-Shershahi
C. Yahya bin Ahmad	3. Humayun Namah
D. Abbas Khan Sarwani	4. Futuhat-i-Alamgiri

Codes :

	A	B	C	D
(a)	1	2	3	4
(b)	4	3	2	1
(c)	3	4	1	2
(d)	3	1	4	2

786. Who among the following completed the Shalimar Garden in Lahore?
(a) Akbar (b) Jahangir
(c) Shahjahan (d) Aurangzeb

787. With which Mughal general did Shivaji sign the 'Treaty of Purandhar'?
(a) Jaswant Singh (b) Jai Singh
(c) Shaista Khan (d) Diler Khan

788. Which one of the following correctly matched?
(a) Tulsidas – Sur Sagar
(b) Surdas – Padmavat
(c) Jayasi – Ramcharit Manas
(d) Nur Muhammad – Indravati

789. During the reign of which later Mughal did Nadir Shah invade India?
(a) Ahmad Shah
(b) Muhammad Shah
(c) Shah Alam
(d) Alamgir II

790. Which one of the following painters committed suicide due to mental imbalance.
(a) Abdul Samad (b) Daswant
(c) Basawan (d) Mahesh

791. Nur Jahan's junta, apart from herself, consisted of:
(i) Mohd khan (ii) Asaf khan
(iii) Prince Khurram (iv) Sher Afghan
(a) only i, ii, and iv (b) only ii, iii and iv
(c) i, ii, iii, and iv only (d) all of them

792. Who among the following Englishmen was given title of "Khan" by Jahangir?
(a) Thomas Roe (b) Ralph Fitch
(c) Hawkins (d) Newbery

793. Arrange the following battles of the Mughal Period in the chronological order:
(i) Battle of Ghagara
(ii) Battle of Panipat I
(iii) Battle of Chunar
(iv) Battle of Khanwa
(a) iii, ii, i, iv (b) ii, i, iv, iii
(c) iii, i, iv, ii (d) ii, iv, i iii,

794. Pick out the correct code giving the chronology of the following events of Aurangzeb's reign.
(i) Conquest of Bijapur and Golconda
(ii) Rebellion of the Jats under Gokla
(iii) Reimposition of the Jiziya
(iv) Shivajis visit to the Mughal court
(a) iv, iii, i, ii (b) iv, ii, iii, i
(c) ii, iv, i, iii (d) ii, iii, iv, i

795.

List I	List II
A. Babur	1. Lahore
B. Humayun	2. Sikandrabad
C. Akbar	3. Delhi
D. Jahangir	4. Kabul

Codes :

	A	B	C	D
(a)	1	2	3	4
(b)	4	3	2	1
(c)	4	2	3	1
(d)	1	3	2	4

796. Which of the following is incorrectly matched?
(a) Muhtasibs - Censors of public morals
(b) Waqia Navis - News Reporters
(c) Khufia Navis - Secret letter writers
(d) Harkaras - Judicial inspectors

797. Match the following with given code:

List I	List II
A. Qazi-ul-Quzat	1. Revenue and finance
B. Muhtasib	2. Army organization
C. Diwan-i-Kul	3. Custodian of public morals
D. Mir Bakshi	4. Administration of Justice

Codes :

	A	B	C	D
(a)	3	4	2	1
(b)	4	3	1	2
(c)	3	2	4	1
(d)	2	3	1	4

798. Which among the following is not correct
(a) Goa - Albuquerque
(b) Madras - Francis Day
(c) Pondicherry - Francis Martin
(d) Calcutta - Gerald Aungier

799. When and where did the French establish their first factory in India?
(a) 1660 - Masulipattanam
(b) 1664 - Chandernagar
(c) 1665 - Mahe
(d) 1668 - Surat

800. **List I (Painters)** **List II (Style of Painting)**

List I (Painters)	List II (Style of Painting)
A. Basawan	1. Persian
B. Mansur	2. Flora and Fauna
C. Mir Syed Ali	3. Caricature
D. Miskin	4. European

Codes :

	A	B	C	D
(a)	2	4	1	3
(b)	4	2	3	1
(c)	1	2	3	4
(d)	2	1	4	3

801. **List I** **List II**

List I	List II
A. Poona	1. Peshwa
B. Gwalior	2. Sindhia
C. Nagpur	3. Gayekwad
D. Baroda	4. Bhonsle

Codes :

	A	B	C	D
(a)	1	2	3	4
(b)	4	2	3	1
(c)	1	2	4	3
(d)	3	2	4	1

802. Read the following events of Akbar's reign and find their correct chronological order from the code given bellow:
1. formation of provinces
2. branding of horses
3. introduction of Mansabdari
4. abolition of Jezia

Codes :
(a) 1,2,3,4 (b) 2,1,4,3
(c) 3,4,1,2 (d) 4,2,1,3

803. Match List I with List II

List I	List II
A. Jama	1. Assessed revenue
B. Hasil	2. Collected revenue
C. Dastur	3. Final and Permanent assessment
D. Bigha	4. Unit of land

Codes :

	A	B	C	D
(a)	2	3	4	1
(b)	1	2	3	4
(c)	4	1	2	3
(d)	3	4	1	2

804. Muhammad Gawan was the wazir and vakil of
(a) Muhammad Shah I
(b) Ahmad Shah Wali
(c) Taj-ud-din Firoj Shah
(d) Muhammad Shah III

Directions (Q. 805 to 854) : The following questions consist of two statements, one labelled as 'Assertion A' and other labelled as 'Reason R'. You are to examine the two statements, carefully and decide if the 'Assertion A' and the 'Reason R' are individually true and if so, whether the Reason is a correct explanation of the Assertion. Select your answer to these item using the codes given below.
(a) Both 'A' and 'R' true and 'R' is the correct explanation of 'A'.
(b) Both 'A' and 'R' are true, but 'R' is not a correct explanation of 'A'.
(c) 'A' is true but 'R' is false.
(d) 'A' is false but 'R' is true.

805. **A :** The Buland Darwaza at Fatehpur Sikri was built by Akbar in 1602.
R : He wanted to commemorate his conquest of Gujarat.

806. **A :** The Mughal Farman of 1717 to the British has been described as the "Magna Carta of the company".
R : It revoked the privileges granted to the British by the Farman of 1691.

807. **A :** Sirajud–daula seized the English Factory at Chandranagar in June 1756.
R : The British gave protection to the enemies of Siraj-ud-daula and refused to surrender them to the Nawab.

808. **A :** The British won the battle of Plassey without any real fighting.

R : The battle of Plassey gave the British a political foothold in Bengal.

809. **A :** From the military point of view, the Battle of Buxar was much less important than the battle of Plassey.

R : The British won the battle of Buxar due to their superior military techniques.

810. **A :** Akbar founded " Din-i-Ilahi"

R : He disliked Islam.

811. **A :** The social reform movement was a middle class movement.

R : Middle class was educated.

812. **A:** Early National movement was a grand failure.

R : It did not reach the masses.

813. **A :** The Mahalwari system was modified version of Ryotwari system.

R: The Mahalwari system enabled the British to revise the revenue demand periodically.

814. **A :** Duplex was defeated by Clive in the second Carnatic war.

R : British had superior arms and superior techniques of warfare.

815. **A:** The Month-scale, introduced by Shahjahan in the mansab system, was a device to express the ratio between the assessed revenue and the actually realized amount.

R : It required the Mansabdars to maintain the contingents only for a limited number of month that for the whole year.

816. **A :** Jyotirao Phule established the Satyashadak Samaj in 1873.

R : He wanted to bring together the people of different religions.

817. **A :** In 1761 Haider Ali became the *de facto* ruler of Mysore.

R : Haider Ali continued to recognize Chikka Krishna Raja I as the lawful ruler of Mysore.

818. **A :** After 1748 the Nawab of Awadh came to be called the "Nawab-wazirs".

R: Since 1748 the Nawabs of Awadh held both the Nawabship of Awadh and wazirship of the Mughal Empire simultaneously.

819. **A :** The treaty of Allahabad was concluded by the British with the Mughal Emperor Shah Alam II.

R : The Mughal emperor granted the diwani of Bengal, the Bihar and Orissa to the East India Company in 1765.

820. **A :** In the war of succession Aurangzeb killed Dara Shikoh.

R : Dara was a heretic.

821. **A :** The English introduced western education in India.

R : They wanted to make Indian aware of scientific and rational advancement.

822. **A :** The Caste movements in British India were failure.

R : Caste Hindus were opposed to it.

823. **A :** Wood's Dispatch of 1854 is generally known as the "Magna Carta of English Education in India".

R : It outlined a comprehensive plan for the future development of education system in India.

824. **A :** Lord Dalhousie was the first real governor-general of India.

R : He was the first governor–general of India without any additional charge.

825. **A :** The Indian council and advisory body to the Secretary of state for India, consisted of 15 members.

R : Half of its members were Indian.

826. **A :** The first split in the All India Trade Union Congress took place in 1929.

R : The Great Economic Depression resulted in differences of opinion among the AITUC leaders.

827. **A :** The Moplah rebellion was antizamindas as well as anti–British in nature.

R : Most of the local zamindar were Christians.

828. **A :** In the first phase of trade union movement in India, covering 1875 to 1919, two Factory Act were passed.

R : This phase was marked by the absence of trade unions in India.

829. **A :** The Cabinet Mission rejected the Muslim League's demand for a separate state of Pakistan.

R : The Cabinet Mission felt that a separate State of Pakistan would contain a large proportion of non–Muslim population, and a sizeable population of Muslims would be left in India.

830. A : Jawaharlal Nehru aimed at the achievement of Democratic socialism.

R : He wanted socialism for the poor and democracy to keep the elite class in good humour.

831. A : Arya Samajis were responsible for the rise of extremism in the Indian National Congress.

R : Many of them in a forefront of the National Movement.

832. A : Swami Dayanand was the first to recommend Swadeshi.

R : He was the first to use the word Swaraj.

833. A : British residents in India vehemently protested against Ilbert Bill.

R : The bill proposed to establish social equality in the administration of justice.

834. A : Raja Ram Mohan Ray was one of the first Indian leaders to start an agitation for political reforms.

R : He founded the Landholders Society at Calcutta in 1838.

835. A : Dadabhai Naoroji organized the East India Association in London.

R : He wanted to influence the British public opinion.

836. A : Dwarakanath Tagore was one of the founder–member of the Landholders Society of Calcutta.

R : The society was the first example of an organized constitutional agitation of redress of grievances.

837. A : The Bombay Association founded in 1852 was the first political association in the Bombay Presidency.

R : The Madras Native Association was at first a branch of the British Indian Association of Calcutta but later became an independent organization.

838. A : Indian Association of Calcutta was the most important of all the pre-Congress nationalist organizations.

R : It was the only pre-Congress organization which seriously tried to become an all India body through convening two all-India conferences.

839. A : Gandhi's technique of Satyagrah is holding on to truth.

R : Civil disobedience, in Gandhi's opinion, could be more dangerous and powerful than armed rebellion.

840. A : The Indian nationalist movement for the first time in its history acquired a real mass base during the Non–Cooperation Movement.

R : A large number of peasants and workers participated in the Non–Cooperation Movement.

841. A : The Federation of Indian Chambers of Commerce and Industry (FICCI) opposed the Civil Disobedience Movement.

R : G.D. Birla donated between one to five lakh rupees to the Civil Disobedience Movement.

842. A : C. Rajagopalachari and Bhulabhai Desai resigned from the Congress in July 1942.

R : They had differences with Gandhi on the question of starting a mass movement during the course of the war.

843. A : The Revolt of 1942 or the August Rebellion attained its maximum popular intensity in Eastern Uttar Pradesh and western and northern Bihar.

R : Uttar Pradesh and Bihar had the maximum concentration of British troops before the outbreak of the Revolt.

844. A : Subhash Chandra Bose defeated Pattabhi Sitaramayya in his re-election as president of the Congress at the Tripura session in 1939.

R : Sitaramayya's candidature in this election was supported by Gandhi.

845. A : In 1916 Maulana Mohammad Ali and Abul Kalam Azad resigned from the Legislative Council.

R: The Rowlatt Act was passed by the Government in spite of being opposed by all Indian members of the Legislative Council.

846. A : Till the fag end of the 19th century, Tilak did not advocate "passive resistance".

R : Till his death, his idea of self-government, meaning to him complete autonomy, did not change.

847. A : During the time of Akbar, for every ten cavalrymen, the mansabdars had to maintain twenty horses.

R : horses had to be rested while on march and replacements were necessary in times of war.

848. A : Gokhale claimed self–government not as a matter of right but as a reward by the display of wisdom, experience and moderation.

R : He was greatly influenced by British ideas of moderation and peaceful evolution.

849. A : Bipin Chandra Pal was a moderate till 1904.

R : Bipin Chandra Pal along with Ajit Singh, was deported by the British in 1907 for his extremist views.

850. A : The Chittagong armoury was seized by Surya Sen and his group.

R : Surya Sen escaped to Japan along with his followers.

851. A : Rash Bihari Bose was captured and executed by the British.

R : He along with Sachin Sanyal, planned to organize a coordinated revolt in February 1915.

852. A : In the early stage of revolutionary terrorism in India, Muslim kept aloof or remained hostile.

R : Most of the early secret societies were marked by intense religiousity.

853. A : Shah Alam II spent the initial years as an Emperor far away from his capital.

R : There was always a lurking danger of foreign invasion from the northwest frontier.

854. A : By 1927 some of the Mahars started burning the Manu Smriti.

R : It demonstrated the sharp break of the Mahars with Hindus.

855. What is the correct chronology of the following latter Mughals?

(I) Farukh Siyar (II) Jahandar Shah
(III) Ahmad Shah (IV) Shah Alam I
(V) Muhammad Shah

(a) V, II, I, IV and III
(b) IV, II, I, V and III
(c) II, V, I, IV, and III
(d) II, IV, I, V and III

856. When and by whom were the Portuguese driven out of Hugli in Bengal?

(a) 1625 - Shaista Khan
(b) 1631 - Qasim Khan
(c) 1656 - Prince Murad
(d) 1666 - Prince Shuja

857. **List I** / **List II**

List I	List II
A. 1498	1. Arrival of Carbal
B. 1500	2. Arrival of Vasco de Gama
C. 1503	3. Arrival of Almeida
D. 1505	4. Arrival of Albuquerque

Codes :

	A	B	C	D
(a)	1	2	4	3
(b)	2	3	1	4
(c)	2	1	3	4
(d)	2	1	4	3

858. Which one of the following is not correctly paired?

(a) Alfanso de Albuquerque - Second Governor
(b) Nino do Cunha - Transferred headquarters from Kochin to Goa.
(c) Martin Alfonso - Accompanied by Jesuit saint Francisco Xavier to India
(d) Francisco de Almeida - Lost Ormuz to the British

859. At which of the following places on the west coast did the English have their factories?

(i) Ahmedabad (ii) Salsette
(iii) Baroda (iv) Broach

(a) all of them (b) i, ii and iii only
(c) i, iii and iv only (d) i, ii and iv only

860. Which of the following items were not imported by Europeans from India?

(i) Sugar (ii) Porcelain
(iii) Raw silk (iv) Pepper
(v) Bullion

(a) ii and iii (b) ii, iii and iv
(c) ii, and v (d) all of them

861. With Whom did Sivaji sign the treaty of Purandhar and when?

(a) 1645 - Shaista Khan
(b) 1656 - Afzal Khan
(c) 1660 - Raja Jaswant singh
(d) 1665 - Raja Jai Singh

862. **List I** **(Marathas)** / **List II** **(Sivaji's relation)**

A. Shaliji Bhosle — 1. Daughter-in-law
B. Jija Bai — 2. Mother
C. Tarabai — 3. Father

Codes :

	A	B	C
(a)	1	2	3
(b)	3	2	1
(c)	1	3	2
(d)	3	1	2

863. **List I** / **List II**

A. Majumdar — 1. In charge of royal correspondence
B. Waqenavis — 2. In charge of Intelligence, post and household affairs
C. Chitins — 3. In charge of ecclesiastical affairs and charities
D. Dabir — 4. Initially accountant general, later finance minister

	A	B	C	D
(a)	1	2	3	4
(b)	2	1	3	4
(c)	2	1	4	3
(d)	1	2	4	3

864. Which of the following is correctly matched?
(a) Prant – Kama Vistar
(c) Grama – Karkun
(b) Pargana – Patel
(d) Taraf – Mamlatdar

865. Which of the following is correctly matched?
(a) Treaty of Durai Sarai (1665) - Sivaji and Jai Singh
(b) Treaty of Porandhar (1719) - Balaji Wishwanath and Hussain Ali
(c) Treaty of Warna (1731) - Shahu and Siuaji II
(d) Treaty of Rampur (1737) - Baji Rao I and Nizam-ul-Mulk

866. **List I** / **List II**

A. First Anglo–Mysore — 1. Sir Eyre Coote
B. Second Anglo–Mysore — 2. General Stuart
C. Third Anglo–Mysore War — 3. General Smith
D. Fourth Anglo–Mysore War — 4. Major General Meadows

Code:

	A	B	C	D
(a)	3	1	4	2
(b)	3	1	2	4
(c)	1	2	4	3
(d)	1	3	2	4

867. Arrange the following successors of Ranjit Singh in the Chronological order:
(i) Sher Singh (ii) Kharak Singh
(iii) Dalip Singh (iv) Nihal Singh
(a) ii, i, iii, and iv (b) iii, ii, iv and i
(c) i, ii, iv and iii (d) Ii, iv, i, and iii

868. **List I** / **List II**

A. Treaty of Faizabad — 1. 1765
B. Treaty of Allahabad — 2. 1773
C. Subsidiary Treaty — 3. 1775
D. Treaty of Benara — 4. 1801

Codes :

	A	B	C	D
(a)	1	3	2	4
(b)	3	1	4	2
(c)	3	4	1	2
(d)	1	2	3	4

869. When and by which governor general was the Carnatic state annexed?
(a) 1792 – Lord Cornwallis
(b) 1797 – Sir John Shore
(c) 1801 – Lord Wellesely
(d) 1808 – Lord Minto

870. When and whom did sir Charles Napier replace as the British resident in Sind?
(a) 1840 – Alexander Burnes
(b) 1841 – Sir John Keane
(c) 1843 – Sir Eyre Coote
(d) 1842 – Major James Outram

871. **List I** / **List II**

A. Robert Clive — 1. Battle of Buxer
B. Hector Munro — 2. Battle of Plassey
C. Shuja-ud-din — 3. The last Nawab of Bengal, Bihar and Orissa
D. Najm-um-daula — 4. The first Nawab of Bengal, Bihar and Orissa

Codes :

	A	B	C	D
(a)	2	1	4	3
(b)	1	2	4	3
(c)	2	1	3	4
(d)	1	2	3	4

872. Arrange the following Viceroys in chronological order

(1) Harding II (2) Reading
(3) Chelmsford (4) Curzon
(5) Minto II

Select the answer from the codes given below:

(a) 4, 5, 1, 3, 2, (b) 2, 3, 1, 5, 4
(c) 4, 5, 1, 2, 3 (d) 5, 4, 1, 3, 2

873. What is the chronological order of the following revenue systems in British India ?

1. Auctioning system
2. Permanent settlement
3. Ryotwari system
4. Mahalwari system

Choose the answer from the codes given below :

(a) 1, 2, 4, 3 (b) 2, 1, 4, 3
(c) 1, 2, 3, 4, (d) 2, 1, 3, 4

874. Arrange the correct chronological sequence in which the following Governor Generals ruled in India?

1. Lard Mayo
2. Lord Lytton
3. Sir John Lawrence
4. Lord Northbrook

(a) 4, 1, 3, 2 (b) 1, 3, 2, 4
(c) 3, 1, 4, 2 (d) 2, 4, 3, 1

875. Match List I with List II

List I	List II
A. Jonatham Duncan	1. Permanent Settlement
B. Thomas Munrol	2. The Ryotwari Settement
C. Cornwallis	3. Permanent Settlement of Bengal
D. Holt Mackenzie	4. Mahalwari settlement

Codes :

	A	B	C	D
(a)	1	3	2	4
(b)	3	1	4	2
(c)	1	2	3	4
(d)	2	1	4	3

876. Which of the following books is not correctly matched with the author ?

	List I (Author)	List II (Book)
(a)	Dada Bhai Naoraji	Poverty and un-British Rule in India
(b)	R.C. Dutt	Economic History of India
(c)	William Digby	Prosperous British India
(d)	D.R. Gadgil	Indian Industry, Today and Tomorrow.

877. By which Act did education officially come under Indian control for the first time?

(a) Indian councils Act of 1892
(b) Indian councils Act of 1909
(c) Government of India Act of 1919
(d) Government of India Act of 1935

878. Which act was responsible for the ultimate death of Presidency system?

(a) Regulating Act of 1773
(b) Pitt's India Act of 1784
(c) Charter Act of 1813
(d) Charter Act of 1833

879. Match List I with List II.

List I	List II
A. First Governor General of Fort William	1. Warren Hastings
B. First Chief justice of Supreme Court	2. Elijah Impey
C. First law member of the governor general's council Macaulay	3. Lord
D. First viceroy as well	4. Lord Canning governor general of India

Codes :

	A	B	C	D
(a)	2	1	3	4
(b)	4	3	2	1
(c)	1	2	3	4
(d)	2	1	4	3

880. When did the practice of holding ICS examinations simultaneously in England as well in India begin?
(a) 1912 (b) 1922
(c) 1932 (d) 1935

881. Arrange the following in chronological order:
(i) Second Round Table conference
(ii) Gandhi-Irwin Pact
(iii) Communal Award
(iv) Poona Pact
(a) i, ii, iii, iv (b) ii, i, iii, iv
(c) i, ii, iv, iii (d) iv, iii, ii, i

882. During the British rule the only British king to visit India and hold his magnificent Durbar, was:
(a) Edward VII (b) George V
(c) James II (d) Edward VI

883.

List I (Name of the organization)	List II (Places of Foundation)
A. Brahma Samaj	1. Bombay
B. Seva Samiti	2. Allahabad
C. Arya Samaj	3. Kolkata
D. Deccan Education Society	4. Poona

Codes :

	A	B	C	D
(a)	1	2	3	4
(b)	2	1	4	3
(c)	3	2	1	4
(d)	2	3	1	4

884. The Nehru Report of 1928 recommended as India's political objective.
(a) loose federation
(b) complete independence
(c) dominion status
(d) none of these

885.

List I (Places)	List II (Britishers who recaptured them)
A. Delhi	1. General John Nicholson
B. Luckhow	2. Sir Colin Campbell
C. Allahabad	3. Major General Havelock
D. Kanpur	4. Brigadier General Neil

Codes :

	A	B	C	D
(a)	1	2	3	4
(b)	1	2	4	3
(c)	2	1	3	4
(d)	3	2	1	4

886.

List I	List II
A. Servants of India society	1. Madras
B. Women's Indian Association	2. Bombay
C. Indian Reform Association	3. Kolkata

Codes :

	A	B	C
(a)	1	2	3
(b)	2	1	3
(c)	1	3	2
(d)	3	2	1

887. The first Anglo–Maratha war was fought between
(a) 1775 – 1782 (b) 1770 – 1775
(c) 1773 – 1774 (d) 1780 – 1784

888.

List I	List II
A. Rahnumai Mazdyas nan Sabha	1. Deoband
B. Dar-ul-Ulum	2. Bombay
C. Nadwah-ul-Ulama	3. Aligarh
D. Muhammadan Educational Conference	4. Lucknow

Codes :

	A	B	C	D
(a)	1	2	3	4
(b)	2	1	4	3
(c)	1	4	3	2
(d)	4	1	2	3

889. Which of the following persons were the prominent members of the Aligarh movement?
1. Altaf Husain Hali
2. Dr. Nazir Ahmad
3. Abdul Kalam Azad
4. Nawab Mushin-ul Mulk
5. Chirag Ali
6. Badruddin Tyabji
(a) 1, 2, 4, 5 (b) 1, 2, 4, 6
(c) 1, 2, 5, (d) Only 1 & 2

890. Which of the following is correctly matched?
(a) Atmiya Sabha – Radhakant Deva
(b) Dharma Sabha – Debendranath tagore
(c) Tattvabodhini Sabha – Rammohan Roy
(d) Prarthana Samaj – Dr. Atmaram Pandurang

891. Which of the following are known as the Bombay Triumvirate?
(a) B.G. Tilak, G.K. Gokhale and M.B. Joshi
(b) Ferozshah Mehta, K.T. Telang and Badruddin Tyabji
(c) B.G. Tilak, G.G. Agarkar and G.H. Deshmukh
(d) Dadabhai Naoroji, K.T. Telang and R.G. Bhandarker

892. Which of the following persons were the prominent members of the Ahrar Movement?
1. Hakim Ajmal Khan
2. Syed Nazir Hussain
3. Hasan Imam
4. Maulana Zafar Ali Khan
5. Chiragh Ali
6. Mazhar-ul-Huq.

(a) 1, 2, 3 & 4 (b) 2, 3, 4 & 5
(c) 1, 3, 4 & 6 (d) All of them

893. Which of the following were the objectives of the Nadwah-ul-Ulama, founded by Shibli Nomani in 1894?
1. Recasting the Muslim education system
2. Developing religious sciences
3. Reforming Muslim morals
4. Putting an end to theological controversies within Islam

Choose the answer from the codes given below:
(a) 1, 2, & 3 (b) 2, 3 & 4
(c) 1, 2, & 4 (d) All of them

894.

List I (Movements)	**List II (Regions)**
(A) Self-respect Movement	1. Mahavashtna
(B) Nair Movement	2. Tamilnadu
(C) Mahar Movement	3. Travancore state
(D) Mahishya Movement	4. Bengal

Codes :

	A	B	C	D
(a)	2	3	1	4
(b)	3	2	1	4
(c)	3	2	4	1
(d)	2	3	4	1

895. When and where was the All-India Kisan Sabha formed
(a) 1935 - Bombay (b) 1938 - Calcutta
(c) 1936 - Lucknow (d) 1942 – Kanpur

896.

List I (Paper/Journal)	**List II (Founder)**
A. Bengal Gazette	1. J.M. Hicky
B. Mirat-ul-Akhbar	2. Raja Rammohan Roy
C. Rast Goftar	3. Dadabhai Naoroji
D. Kesari	4. B.G. Tilak

Codes :

	A	B	C	D
(a)	4	3	2	1
(b)	1	2	3	4
(c)	1	3	2	4
(d)	4	2	3	1

897.

List I (Organization)	**List II (Founders)**
A. Land holders society Association	1. Dadabhai Naoroji
B. British India Society	2. Devendra Nath Tagore
C. Brithish India Association	3. William Adam
D. East India	4. Dwaraknath Tagore

Codes :

	A	B	C	D
(a)	1	2	3	4
(b)	4	3	2	1
(c)	1	3	2	4
(d)	4	2	3	1

898. Which of the following revolutionary organization is not correctly matched with its founder?
(a) Bengal volunteer - Hemchandra Ghosh
(b) Sri Sangha - Anil Roy
(c) Indian Republic Army - Surya Sen
(d) Yogantar Samiti - Lila Nag

899. Which of the following commission is generally known as Hunter Commission?
(a) Wood's Dispatch 1854
(b) Indian Education Commission 1882
(c) Religion Commission 1902
(d) Saddler Commission (1917-19)

900. What is the chronological order of the following Governor Generals

1. Minto I
2. John Shore
3. Lord Cornawallis
4. Lord Warren Hastings
5. Wellesley

Select the answer from the codes given below :

(a) 4, 3, 2, 5, & 1, (b) 4, 2,3, 1, & 5
(c) 4, 3, 2, 5, & 1 (d) 4, 3, 4, 1 & 5

ANSWERS

1	2	3	4	5	6	7	8	9	10
(c)	(d)	(b)	(d)	(a)	(c)	(a)	(a)	(c)	(b)
11	**12**	**13**	**14**	**15**	**16**	**17**	**18**	**19**	**20**
(b)	(c)	(d)	(a)	(a)	(d)	(c)	(d)	(a)	(b)
21	**22**	**23**	**24**	**25**	**26**	**27**	**28**	**29**	**30**
(a)	(a)	(b)	(b)	(a)	(d)	(d)	(a)	(c)	(a)
31	**32**	**33**	**34**	**35**	**36**	**37**	**38**	**39**	**40**
(c)	(a)	(c)	(a)	(c)	(c)	(c)	(c)	(d)	(a)
41	**42**	**43**	**44**	**45**	**46**	**47**	**48**	**49**	**50**
(d)	(d)	(b)	(c)	(c)	(a)	(b)	(b)	(b)	(b)
51	**52**	**53**	**54**	**55**	**56**	**57**	**58**	**59**	**60**
(a)	(d)	(a)	(a)	(a)	(d)	(d)	(b)	(b)	(a)
61	**62**	**63**	**64**	**65**	**66**	**67**	**68**	**69**	**70**
(a)	(b)	(a)	(b)	(c)	(a)	(a)	(b)	(a)	(a)
71	**72**	**73**	**74**	**75**	**76**	**77**	**78**	**79**	**80**
(d)	(b)	(d)	(c)	(a)	(d)	(d)	(a)	(d)	(a)
81	**82**	**83**	**84**	**85**	**86**	**87**	**88**	**89**	**90**
(b)	(c)	(d)	(c)	(a)	(d)	(b)	(b)	(b)	(a)
91	**92**	**93**	**94**	**95**	**96**	**97**	**98**	**99**	**100**
(a)	(b)	(d)	(d)	(a)	(c)	(c)	(d)	(a)	(a)
101	**102**	**103**	**104**	**105**	**106**	**107**	**108**	**109**	**110**
(a)	(d)	(d)	(b)	(a)	(a)	(c)	(a)	(b)	(b)
111	**112**	**113**	**114**	**115**	**116**	**117**	**118**	**119**	**120**
(a)	(d)	(a)	(b)	(b)	(a)	(d)	(d)	(a)	(a)
121	**122**	**123**	**124**	**125**	**126**	**127**	**128**	**129**	**130**
(d)	(b)	(a)	(c)	(d)	(c)	(b)	(d)	(c)	(a)
131	**132**	**133**	**134**	**135**	**136**	**137**	**138**	**139**	**140**
(c)	(d)	(a)	(d)	(a)	(c)	(b)	(c)	(c)	(a)
141	**142**	**143**	**144**	**145**	**146**	**147**	**148**	**149**	**150**
(a)	(c)	(a)	(c)	(c)	(a)	(d)	(b)	(c)	(c)

151	152	153	154	155	156	157	158	159	160
(a)	(d)	(a)	(b)	(c)	(b)	(b)	(a)	(a)	(b)
161	**162**	**163**	**164**	**165**	**166**	**167**	**168**	**169**	**170**
(c)	(d)	(a)	(b)	(b)	(d)	(c)	(a)	(b)	(a)
171	**172**	**173**	**174**	**175**	**176**	**177**	**178**	**179**	**180**
(b)	(c)	(c)	(c)	(a)	(a)	(b)	(a)	(c)	(c)
181	**182**	**183**	**184**	**185**	**186**	**187**	**188**	**189**	**190**
(b)	(a)	(d)	(d)	(b)	(a)	(d)	(c)	(d)	(d)
191	**192**	**193**	**194**	**195**	**196**	**197**	**198**	**199**	**200**
(d)	(c)	(c)	(b)	(a)	(d)	(d)	(b)	(c)	(d)
201	**202**	**203**	**204**	**205**	**206**	**207**	**208**	**209**	**210**
(a)	(c)	(c)	(d)	(a)	(b)	(d)	(b)	(d)	(d)
211	**212**	**213**	**214**	**215**	**216**	**217**	**218**	**219**	**220**
(c)	(a)	(b)	(b)	(b)	(d)	(c)	(c)	(c)	(a)
221	**222**	**223**	**224**	**225**	**226**	**227**	**228**	**229**	**230**
(b)	(c)	(c)	(a)	(a)	(a)	(b)	(b)	(d)	(a)
231	**232**	**233**	**234**	**235**	**236**	**237**	**238**	**239**	**240**
(c)	(d)	(c)	(a)	(a)	(b)	(d)	(a)	(c)	(b)
241	**242**	**243**	**244**	**245**	**246**	**247**	**248**	**249**	**250**
(a)	(c)	(d)	(c)	(a)	(d)	(a)	(a)	(c)	(a)
251	**252**	**253**	**254**	**255**	**256**	**257**	**258**	**259**	**260**
(c)	(a)	(c)	(b)	(a)	(c)	(a)	(d)	(c)	(d)
261	**262**	**263**	**264**	**265**	**266**	**267**	**268**	**269**	**270**
(c)	(c)	(d)	(a)	(b)	(c)	(c)	(a)	(b)	(b)
271	**272**	**273**	**274**	**275**	**276**	**277**	**278**	**279**	**280**
(b)	(c)	(a)	(a)	(d)	(d)	(b)	(b)	(a)	(c)
281	**282**	**283**	**284**	**285**	**286**	**287**	**288**	**289**	**290**
(a)	(a)	(b)	(d)	(a)	(c)	(d)	(b)	(a)	(a)
291	**292**	**293**	**294**	**295**	**296**	**297**	**298**	**299**	**300**
(a)	(a)	(a)	(b)	(a)	(d)	(c)	(b)	(d)	(a)
301	**302**	**303**	**304**	**305**	**306**	**307**	**308**	**309**	**310**
(b)	(c)	(d)	(b)	(b)	(a)	(c)	(a)	(b)	(c)
311	**312**	**313**	**314**	**315**	**316**	**317**	**318**	**319**	**320**
(c)	(a)	(b)	(c)	(b)	(b)	(d)	(d)	(c)	(d)
321	**322**	**323**	**324**	**325**	**326**	**327**	**328**	**329**	**330**
(c)	(c)	(b)	(d)	(d)	(b)	(d)	(d)	(c)	(b)

331	332	333	334	335	336	337	338	339	340
(b)	(a)	(b)	(a)	(c)	(b)	(b)	(b)	(a)	(c)
341	342	343	344	345	346	347	348	349	350
(d)	(d)	(a)	(c)	(d)	(d)	(d)	(a)	(d)	(a)
351	352	353	354	355	356	357	358	359	360
(c)	(d)	(c)	(d)	(d)	(a)	(a)	(b)	(c)	(d)
361	362	363	364	365	366	367	368	369	370
(d)	(a)	(a)	(c)	(d)	(c)	(b)	(b)	(c)	(a)
371	372	373	374	375	376	377	378	379	380
(a)	(c)	(b)	(c)	(d)	(d)	(c)	(a)	(c)	(d)
381	382	383	384	385	386	387	388	389	390
(c)	(a)	(a)	(b)	(c)	(a)	(b)	(a)	(a)	(b)
391	392	393	394	395	396	397	398	399	400
(c)	(c)	(d)	(b)	(c)	(d)	(a)	(c)	(b)	(c)
401	402	403	404	405	406	407	408	409	410
(d)	(d)	(a)	(c)	(d)	(a)	(d)	(b)	(a)	(c)
411	412	413	414	415	416	417	418	419	420
(d)	(d)	(b)	(c)	(c)	(a)	(b)	(c)	(d)	(c)
421	422	423	424	425	426	427	428	429	430
(a)	(a)	(a)	(b)	(a)	(c)	(c)	(a)	(b)	(d)
431	432	433	434	435	436	437	438	439	440
(a)	(a)	(b)	(d)	(c)	(d)	(a)	(d)	(c)	(b)
441	442	443	444	445	446	447	448	449	450
(d)	(c)	(c)	(d)	(d)	(a)	(d)	(a)	(d)	(c)
451	452	453	454	455	456	457	458	459	460
(d)	(c)	(a)	(d)	(b)	(d)	(b)	(b)	(a)	(c)
461	462	463	464	465	466	467	468	469	470
(d)	(a)	(d)	(a)	(c)	(b)	(b)	(b)	(b)	(a)
471	472	473	474	475	476	477	478	479	480
(c)	(b)	(b)	(d)	(c)	(d)	(c)	(a)	(a)	(c)
481	482	483	484	485	486	487	488	489	490
(c)	(b)	(c)	(b)	(d)	(a)	(c)	(c)	(a)	(c)
491	492	493	494	495	496	497	498	499	500
(b)	(a)	(d)	(c)	(a)	(a)	(a)	(c)	(c)	(d)
501	502	503	504	505	506	507	508	509	510
(b)	(c)	(c)	(b)	(c)	(d)	(a)	(a)	(c)	(a)

511	512	513	514	515	516	517	518	519	520
(c)	(a)	(b)	(c)	(d)	(c)	(b)	(b)	(a)	(b)
521	**522**	**523**	**524**	**525**	**526**	**527**	**528**	**529**	**530**
(b)	(d)	(d)	(d)	(c)	(a)	(c)	(c)	(d)	(a)
531	**532**	**533**	**534**	**535**	**536**	**537**	**538**	**539**	**540**
(b)	(d)	(d)	(a)	(d)	(d)	(d)	(c)	(b)	(a)
541	**542**	**543**	**544**	**545**	**546**	**547**	**548**	**549**	**550**
(d)	(a)	(a)	(b)	(a)	(c)	(c)	(a)	(c)	(a)
551	**552**	**553**	**554**	**555**	**556**	**557**	**558**	**559**	**560**
(c)	(c)	(a)	(b)	(c)	(d)	(a)	(d)	(a)	(c)
561	**562**	**563**	**564**	**565**	**566**	**567**	**568**	**569**	**570**
(b)	(d)	(c)	(b)	(d)	(a)	(c)	(c)	(c)	(b)
571	**572**	**573**	**574**	**575**	**576**	**577**	**578**	**579**	**580**
(a)	(a)	(d)	(a)	(d)	(a)	(a)	(a)	(c)	(d)
581	**582**	**583**	**584**	**585**	**586**	**587**	**588**	**589**	**590**
(b)	(a)	(c)	(c)	(d)	(a)	(b)	(c)	(a)	(b)
591	**592**	**593**	**594**	**595**	**596**	**597**	**598**	**599**	**600**
(b)	(b)	(a)	(d)	(c)	(c)	(c)	(c)	(d)	(b)
601	**602**	**603**	**604**	**605**	**606**	**607**	**608**	**609**	**610**
(c)	(b)	(d)	(d)	(a)	(a)	(c)	(b)	(c)	(a)
611	**612**	**613**	**614**	**615**	**616**	**617**	**618**	**619**	**620**
(a)	(b)	(b)	(a)	(c)	(d)	(c)	(d)	(d)	(a)
621	**622**	**623**	**624**	**625**	**626**	**627**	**628**	**629**	**630**
(c)	(d)	(b)	(c)	(d)	(a)	(c)	(c)	(a)	(c)
631	**632**	**633**	**634**	**635**	**636**	**637**	**638**	**639**	**640**
(b)	(c)	(a)	(b)	(d)	(a)	(b)	(c)	(c)	(a)
641	**642**	**643**	**644**	**645**	**646**	**647**	**648**	**649**	**650**
(b)	(a)	(c)	(b)	(b)	(c)	(c)	(a)	(a)	(c)
651	**652**	**653**	**654**	**655**	**656**	**657**	**658**	**659**	**660**
(a)	(a)	(c)	(a)	(b)	(a)	(a)	(d)	(b)	(a)
661	**662**	**663**	**664**	**665**	**666**	**667**	**668**	**669**	**670**
(a)	(b)	(b)	(a)	(d)	(b)	(c)	(b)	(a)	(c)
671	**672**	**673**	**674**	**675**	**676**	**677**	**678**	**679**	**680**
(b)	(a)	(a)	(a)	(a)	(b)	(c)	(b)	(b)	(c)
681	**682**	**683**	**684**	**685**	**686**	**687**	**688**	**689**	**690**
(c)	(c)	(a)	(b)	(c)	(d)	(d)	(d)	(b)	(d)

691	692	693	694	695	696	697	698	699	700
(a)	(c)	(a)	(b)	(c)	(d)	(d)	(a)	(b)	(b)
701	**702**	**703**	**704**	**705**	**706**	**707**	**708**	**709**	**710**
(b)	(a)	(a)	(d)	(b)	(c)	(b)	(a)	(a)	(a)
711	**712**	**713**	**714**	**715**	**716**	**717**	**718**	**719**	**720**
(b)	(d)	(c)	(c)	(c)	(a)	(d)	(a)	(b)	(d)
721	**722**	**723**	**724**	**725**	**726**	**727**	**728**	**729**	**730**
(b)	(d)	(c)	(a)	(c)	(d)	(a)	(a)	(a)	(c)
731	**732**	**733**	**734**	**735**	**736**	**737**	**738**	**739**	**740**
(c)	(c)	(a)	(a)	(a)	(c)	(a)	(d)	(a)	(b)
741	**742**	**743**	**744**	**745**	**746**	**747**	**748**	**749**	**750**
(d)	(a)	(d)	(c)	(b)	(d)	(a)	(c)	(a)	(c)
751	**752**	**753**	**754**	**755**	**756**	**757**	**758**	**759**	**760**
(a)	(b)	(c)	(a)	(b)	(c)	(a)	(b)	(c)	(c)
761	**762**	**763**	**764**	**765**	**766**	**767**	**768**	**769**	**770**
(d)	(a)	(d)	(b)	(a)	(d)	(a)	(c)	(a)	(b)
771	**772**	**773**	**774**	**775**	**776**	**777**	**778**	**779**	**780**
(c)	(a)	(b)	(c)	(a)	(a)	(c)	(a)	(d)	(b)
781	**782**	**783**	**784**	**785**	**786**	**787**	**788**	**789**	**790**
(d)	(c)	(a)	(d)	(c)	(c)	(b)	(d)	(b)	(b)
791	**792**	**793**	**794**	**795**	**796**	**797**	**798**	**799**	**800**
(b)	(c)	(d)	(b)	(b)	(d)	(b)	(d)	(d)	(a)
801	**802**	**803**	**804**	**805**	**806**	**807**	**808**	**809**	**810**
(c)	(d)	(b)	(d)	(d)	(c)	(d)	(b)	(d)	(c)
811	**812**	**813**	**814**	**815**	**816**	**817**	**818**	**819**	**820**
(a)	(d)	(d)	(c)	(c)	(c)	(a)	(a)	(d)	(c)
821	**822**	**823**	**824**	**825**	**826**	**827**	**828**	**829**	**830**
(b)	(d)	(a)	(a)	(d)	(c)	(d)	(b)	(a)	(a)
831	**832**	**833**	**834**	**835**	**836**	**837**	**838**	**839**	**840**
(a)	(d)	(a)	(c)	(a)	(b)	(b)	(a)	(b)	(a)
841	**842**	**843**	**844**	**845**	**846**	**847**	**848**	**849**	**850**
(d)	(a)	(c)	(b)	(d)	(c)	(d)	(a)	(c)	(c)
851	**852**	**853**	**854**	**855**	**856**	**857**	**858**	**859**	**860**
(d)	(a)	(c)	(a)	(b)	(b)	(d)	(d)	(c)	(c)
861	**862**	**863**	**864**	**865**	**866**	**867**	**868**	**869**	**870**
(d)	(b)	(a)	(d)	(c)	(a)	(d)	(b)	(c)	(d)

871	872	873	874	875	876	877	878	879	880
(a)	(a)	(c)	(c)	(c)	(d)	(c)	(d)	(c)	(b)
881	**882**	**883**	**884**	**885**	**886**	**887**	**888**	**889**	**890**
(b)	(b)	(c)	(c)	(b)	(b)	(b)	(b)	(a)	(d)
891	**892**	**893**	**894**	**895**	**896**	**897**	**898**	**899**	**900**
(b)	(c)	(d)	(a)	(c)	(b)	(b)	(c)	(b)	(a)